Peterson's
Culinary
SCHOOLS

10th Edition

PETERSON'S

A **nelnet.** COMPANY

PETERSON'S

A **nelnet.** COMPANY

About Peterson's, a Nelnet company

Peterson's (www.petersons.com) is a leading provider of education information and advice, with books and online resources focusing on education search, test preparation, and financial aid. Its Web site offers searchable databases and interactive tools for contacting educational institutions, online practice tests and instruction, and planning tools for securing financial aid. Peterson's serves 110 million education consumers annually.

For more information, contact Peterson's, 2000 Lenox Drive, Lawrenceville, NJ 08648; 800-338-3282; or find us on the World Wide Web at www.petersons.com/about.

Editor: Linda Seghers; Production Editor: Mark D. Snider; Research Project Manager: Steve Sauermelch; Programmer: Alex Lin; Manufacturing Manager: Ivona Skibicki; Composition Manager: Linda M. Williams; Client Relations Representatives: Danielle Vreeland, Mimi Kaufman, Karen D. Mount, Eric Wallace

ISBN-13: 978-0-7689-2177-9
ISBN-10: 0-7689-2177-5

Printed in Canada

10 9 8 7 6 5 4 3 2 1   09 08 07

Tenth Edition

CONTENTS

A NOTE FROM THE PETERSON'S EDITORS

For ten years, Peterson's has given students and parents the most comprehensive, up-to-date information on culinary institutions in the United States and abroad. *Peterson's Culinary Schools* features advice and tips on the culinary school search and selection process, such as how to choose and pay for a cooking school and how to then make the most of your culinary career.

Opportunities abound for culinary students, and this guide can help you find what you want in a number of ways:

- For advice and guidance in the culinary school search and selection process, just turn the page to our **So You Want a Career in the Culinary Arts** section. Providing insight into how to know which school is right for you and why, "Choosing a Cooking School" explains the increasingly important role a cooking school education has in a cooking career. Wondering how you'll pay? "Paying for Your Culinary Education" has all the tips and answers so that you'll wonder no more! "Charting a Successful Culinary Career" answers that burning question: What else can I do with a cooking degree besides open a restaurant? Finally, "Culinary Apprenticeships" outlines the benefits of this three-year training option.

- You'll then want to read through "How to Use This Guide," which explains the infor-

mation presented in the individual culinary school profiles, lists culinary degree and certificate acronyms, and defines how we collect our data.

- Up next is the **Quick-Reference Chart**, where programs are listed geographically, and you can see at a glance the areas of spcialization (culinary arts, baking and pastry, management) and credentials they offer.

- Following that are the **Profiles of Professional Programs** and **Profiles of Apprenticeship Programs.** Here you'll find our unparalleled culinary program descriptions, arranged alphabetically by state and by country. They provide a complete picture of need-to-know information about culinary schools and apprenticeship programs, including program affiliation, areas of study, facilities, student and faculty profiles, expenses, and financial aid and housing availability. All the information you need to apply is placed together at the conclusion of each profile.

- If you already have specifics in mind, turn to the **Indexes.** Here you can search for a culinary school based on the certificate, diploma, or degree programs they offer. If you already have schools in mind that pique your interest, you can use the **Alphabetical Listing of Schools and Programs** to search for these schools.

Peterson's publishes a full line of resources to help guide you and your family through the culinary school admissions process. Peterson's publications can be found at your local bookstore, library, and high school guidance office—or visit us on the Web at www.petersons.com.

We welcome any comments or suggestions you may have about this publication and invite you to complete our online survey at www.petersons.com/booksurvey.

Your feedback will help us to provide personalized solutions for your educational advancement.

Schools will be pleased to know that Peterson's helped you in your selection. Admissions staff members are more than happy to answer questions, address specific problems, and help in any way they can. The editors at Peterson's wish you great success in your culinary school search!

So You Want a Career in the Culinary Arts

CHOOSING A COOKING SCHOOL

Andrew Dornenburg and
Karen Page

*N*o matter how strong a chef's inspirations, they are not enough to give rise to greatness. They must be carefully honed and refined through directed effort. The palate, which allowed a chef to first learn what he or she found most enjoyable, must be trained to discern subtleties in flavors and flavor combinations and to critique as well as taste.

Similarly, basic cooking techniques must be mastered, with speed and efficiency developed over repeated efforts, in order to be able to create desired effects. This is what leads chefs into professional kitchens and, increasingly, into professional cooking schools.

Cooking is a profession that places extraordinary emphasis on continuous learning, and today a chef's first formal education often takes place in a cooking school classroom. There are hundreds of cooking schools both in the United States and abroad, offering opportunities to learn about specialties ranging from vegetarian to confectionery to microwave cooking.

While many of the country's leading chefs reached the top of the profession without the benefit of a cooking school degree, an overwhelming majority of chefs recommend cooking school as the most expeditious start for an aspiring chef today. Cooking school offers an opportunity to gain exposure in a concentrated period of time to an immense amount of information, from cooking techniques (knife skills, sauté, grill) to theory (nutrition, sanitation) to international/regional cuisines (French, Italian, Asian).

A cooking school diploma can also be an important credential in opening doors and demonstrating commitment to the field. "I only hire cooking school graduates," says Patrick O'Connell, who himself doesn't hold a cooking school degree. "If I had to do it again at this point in history, I would probably go to culinary school." Alfred Portale is even more adamant. "I think that if you can go to cooking school, you should. I feel very strongly about it," he says. "It immediately legitimizes you as a professional and exposes you to a broad base of information, even though not much of it is practical. It certainly puts you at a greater advantage than someone who's self-taught or learns going up through the ranks."

While attending cooking school full-time represents a certain trade-off in terms of the opportunity versus the cost of foregoing a full-time income while at school, the vast majority of chefs interviewed see it as an investment well made. In fact, the cooking school naysayers have little criticism for the cooking schools themselves; they reserve it for the popular misconception that merely attending cooking school can create a chef, which they believe often misleads people without a real passion for food and cooking into the profession. "Cooking schools do an important job," says Anne Rosenzweig, "but the final results depend a lot on the students." Victor Gielisse concurs: "Cooking school gives aspiring chefs a tremendous foundation. But school alone cannot give you a passion for food. It's impossible. Not even the best teacher can do that."

Given the abundance of reputable cooking schools and programs, there is likely to be an option to suit everyone's specific budget, time frame, and other needs. From four-year bachelor's degree programs to certificate programs that can be completed in a few brief months to one-session cooking demonstrations by culinary experts, there are numerous opportunities to learn about cooking in a classroom. With the hundreds of cooking schools available, it is up to the prospective students to research various options to determine which offers the best fit.

CHOOSING THE *RIGHT* COOKING SCHOOL

The decision as to whether and where to attend is highly personal and dependent on many factors: What program length best suits your needs? Is location a factor for you? What is your budget for school? Are you looking to attend full-time or part-time? During the day or in the evening? While it is not our intention to recommend specific schools, we hope that the following tips on evaluating cooking schools will help guide your eventual decision.

- Consider taking the time to ask some chefs at restaurants in your area to recommend cooking schools to you.
- Read all of the literature available from each of the schools you're considering. This alone should address some of your most basic concerns, such as the range of course offerings and whether the program costs are within your reach.
- Plan to spend a day at each of the schools you're seriously considering.
- Ask a lot of questions of administrators, instructors, and even students.

Find out whether they offer (or require) an externship program or an international study program. Ask what kind of placement assistance they provide to graduating students and alumni. Find out where some of their recent graduates are working and what the breadth of the school's network is. Who are some of their most successful alumni? Are typical alumni working in the kinds of places you'd like to work in someday? Spend time talking with other students, and decide if they're the type of people with whom you'd enjoy learning and spending time. You'll be happiest at a school that offers a "good fit."

Certain schools attract a national (and even international) student body. Other schools tend to attract a greater proportion of their students from their regions, and local chef alumni may show some preference to graduates of their alma maters over graduates of other programs. Still other schools tend to draw more closely from their immediate vicinities.

Schools also differ in their orientation to particular types of cuisine—everything from the haute cuisine of France to low-fat vegetarian cooking.

Programs vary in length and emphasis. Four-year programs often offer courses in management, marketing, communications, nutrition, and financial management in addition to hands-on cooking. Two-year programs augment course work with intensive kitchen experience.

For those unable or unwilling to dedicate two to four years to their culinary education, another option is a short-term program. Upon completing a course and passing practical and written examinations demonstrating mastery of that course, a diploma is awarded. Students can extend their training by participating in an extern program, which places students in the professional area of their choice for an additional period.

Don't think that if you can't attend school full-time you can't receive a fine education. "If you don't have enough money, you can still attend part-time," emphasizes Dieter Schorner. Schorner, an experienced chef, has taught classes in the evening at New York City Technical College. "I found some of the most dedicated teachers at this little college," he says.

Courtesy The French Culinary Institute/Matthew Septhimus

ADMISSIONS REQUIREMENTS AND PROCESSES

If you're aiming for a competitive program, getting in presents the next hurdle. Some of the top schools aren't able to admit everyone who applies. At other, less competitive programs, merely submitting an application and application fee is all it takes. Given the increasing demand for trained cooks and chefs, many cooking schools have been expanding their programs to be able to accommodate more students.

The admissions process, depending on the school, may be simple and straightforward or more involved. The Culinary Institute of America, for example, requires a completed application form, an application fee, and a high school transcript, as well as transcripts from any postsecondary studies and at least two letters of reference from employers, food service instructors, or Culinary Institute alumni. The application form itself asks whether applicants have traveled extensively in or outside the United States, attended seminars/lectures on the food industry, and read books and/or magazines about the food service industry. In addition, applicants must submit an essay explaining why they wish to enter the food service field, what research on the industry they have done, details of their food service background, and why they're interested in attending The Culinary Institute of America.

The New England Culinary Institute requires applicants to submit a written personal statement on their background and experiences, why they have decided to seek a career in the culinary arts, and their reasons for applying to the New England Culinary Institute. Also required are three letters of recommendation; copies of high school, vocational school, or college transcripts; and the application form and an application fee.

While some local cooking schools will have less rigorous application processes, most schools will require you to apply well in advance of your desired date of attendance, so plan ahead.

BEFORE ATTENDING COOKING SCHOOL

Some schools see prior work experience as a plus but not a prerequisite. Many cooking schools, however, require work experience in a kitchen as a condition of admission.

Indeed, getting some real-world exposure to a kitchen is a good idea whether the school admissions process requires it or not. Not everyone who's attracted by the perceived "glamour" of the profession finds that the reality of the work is a good fit. Is cooking something you could come to love as a profession? It's best for all concerned that a reality check be taken sooner rather than later.

Larry Forgione says, "I think people really ought to think about whether this is what they really want to do before they jump into it with both feet. I might suggest stepping in with one foot—working weekends at a place, hanging out at a restaurant to understand what the restaurant business is all about." While the glamorous image of restaurant business might help to attract people to the profession, only those who have actually worked in a kitchen know the intense effort involved.

In addition to practical experience, other preparation can provide an edge at cooking school. If you can't work full-time in a kitchen, consider getting some part-time experience working for a caterer or gourmet store or as a waiter or waitress. Spend as much time as you can reading about food and cooking, if you don't already. In addition, restaurant experience before cooking school offers an opportunity to determine what area a student might want to specialize in—for example, cooking on the line or pastry.

You may, in addition, have prior academic or work experience in a field unrelated to cooking. Prior experience can be a great help in preparing you for the rigors of a tough cooking school program and difficult first jobs. You are likely to have already developed study habits and writing skills. Also, food is so basic that few fields don't offer some degree of overlap—from art to science to history. Alfred Portale's work in jewelry design certainly hasn't hurt his reputation for artistic presentation, and Barbara

Tropp's academic training has helped her to succeed as both a chef and an author. If you have already invested time and energy in another field, you are likely to ask good questions and have a clear idea of what you are looking to get out of your education.

AT COOKING SCHOOL

While at cooking school, it's important to make the most of your opportunity. Use classroom time to ask questions and learn as much as possible. Take advantage of extracurricular learning. Volunteer to assist professors and visiting chefs with special events, and make an effort to get to know them. Aside from the knowledge they can pass along, these interactions get you noticed and may spawn leads on future jobs.

Some chefs found that the most important lessons they learned came outside the classroom. "I spent a lot of time in the library," says Gary Danko.

Danko advises, "Be serious when you go to cooking school. Make sure you have some books to draw from, and that you spend some time and really pick the instructors' brains. Ask them every question you can. Spend extra time cooking with instructors. Volunteer for things—because that's where the real learning comes from, putting in the extra time."

Many chefs emphasize how much their in-class learning was complemented by their outside work in a kitchen while attending school and suggest that students maximize their learning by working while attending school. Allen Susser says, "I think you need to see the real side of the ideal things you're cooking in the school kitchen." Mary Sue Milliken goes so far as to recommend that

Courtesy The French Culinary Institute/Matthew Septhimus

students work full-time while they attend cooking school: "If the schedule is too rigorous, this is probably not a good career choice."

Working while attending school can serve many purposes. It can reinforce what you are learning in the classroom and point out what you are not. Jasper White advises working during cooking school "because then you can start applying things every day and retain a lot more." It can give you the extra practice on your knife and other skills and allow you to pursue other interests in food, such as ethnic cuisine or catering, that may not be covered. White loved his work at the Waccabuc Country Club in Westchester County, NY: "We did buffets on Sundays; I got to use a lot from school that I wouldn't have had a chance to use otherwise."

Any experience is what you make of it—you don't have to work at a four-star restaurant in order to learn. Susan Feniger worked at a fish market in Poughkeepsie, NY, while attending The Culinary Institute of America. A former coworker of mine worked at the sandwich counter at a wine and cheese store while attending cooking school, in order to educate himself about cheeses. I know another cooking school student who chose to work in catering instead of a restaurant because of the flexibility in scheduling, which allowed her to learn and practice her culinary skills without the intense pressure of daily service at a restaurant. She was also able to see a wide variety of food at the catering company—from 200 wontons to an entire theme dinner centered around the early settlers in Boston. There is a price to pay for all of this—less sleep, not to mention less energy and time for other school activities. While the burden of such a workload might give pause to some, leading chefs seemed to be in agreement with Nietzsche's principle: "That which does not kill me makes me stronger."

EXTERNSHIPS

An externship is a period of time spent working in a restaurant for the purpose of gaining practical on-the-job experience and may be paid or nonpaid. Some schools mandate serving an externship as a requirement for graduation, while others offer it as an option to students. Certain schools even offer a chance to work abroad or at leading resorts. It's important to research the options available through the school you're interested in and, if there's a particular restaurant you'd like to serve an externship with, to take an active role in doing all you can to pursue it. Find out which faculty or administration members have the strongest ties to the restaurant and speak with them, write a letter to the chef, or possibly offer to

work for free until the time your official externship commences.

Every experience is different. Some restaurants have students cook on the line, while others allow externs to do only basic prep work. André Soltner requires that The Culinary Institute of America students he takes into his kitchen at Lutèce (NYC) commit to a minimum one-year externship, which maximizes both the student's learning and his restaurant's ability to benefit from it. If an externship is offered or required, make the most of it. Work in the best kitchen into which you can get hired. If you make a good impression, you may find yourself with an offer for permanent employment; at worst, you'll end up with a good reference for future jobs. At the New England Culinary Institute, 70 percent of second-year internships turn into first jobs.

One extern I know was passed over for a permanent pastry position due to his inexperience, yet kept coming in on his own time to keep his skills sharp while looking for a job at another restaurant. When the pastry chef left unexpectedly, he was hired into the position. Another extern received an offer to join a restaurant as garde-manger because of her excellent work habits and attitude (including coming in early, staying late, working fast, and taking direction well). While she had no experience, her work habits spoke volumes about her potential and she was given a chance to prove herself.

AFTER GRADUATION

Chefs emphasize the importance of viewing graduation from cooking school as merely a starting point in one's education. André Soltner puts it this way: "I think cooking schools give students the basics they need.

But they are not accomplished chefs. They are just coming out of school. A doctor, after his four years, goes to a hospital not as the chief surgeon but as an intern. We have to look at cooking school graduates as what they are." Schools and parents were attributed with feeding students' expectations. "Parents send their kids for two years at The Culinary Institute of America and then think they are André Soltner or Paul Bocuse," Soltner notes. "But they are not."

Cooking school graduates might find themselves tempted with offers to become full-fledged chefs upon graduation—welcomed by students, at least in part, due to the sometimes substantial debt incurred through financing cooking school. However, leading chefs speak discouragingly of the notion of accepting a job as a chef too soon. In her speech to a graduating class at The Culinary Institute of America, Debra Ponzek used the opportunity not to pump up graduates' hopes and expectations but to implore them: "Don't take a chef's job!" She explained, "It's hard to go back, once you realize there are things you didn't learn. Many people want to make the jump [to a chef's position] too quickly." Patrick Clark agrees. "Don't look for glory right away. When you get there, it's harder."

Some chefs advise that after graduation you should work with your "idols," in order to continue your education. Upon graduating from The Culinary Institute of America, Alfred Portale answered an ad and was selected to work at the food shop that Michel Guérard was opening at Bloomingdale's. He recalls: "Here I'm just out of school, and I'm standing in a kitchen with Michel Guérard, the Troisgros brothers—all these huge French guys, all my idols. It was thrilling. I learned all the butchering and the charcuterie, the poaching and the smoking, and the stuffing and the sausage making, and all that kind of stuff that young cooks dream about. After putting in a year with these guys, they invited me to France. So I spent a year working first at Troisgros and then with Guérard. I had a car and toured France, spending the last six weeks in Paris, going out every day and every night, going to every bookstore, every cooking store, just learning and submerging myself in everything."

After graduating from The Culinary Institute of America, Gary Danko began a dogged cross-country pursuit to track down Madeleine Kamman, to persuade her to let him study with her. While Danko says she expressed reservations about working with a newly minted culinary school graduate, he set out to change her mind. "I pulled up in my car the first day of class with all these local products that I'd been working with—goat cheese, guinea hens, ducks, geese, lamb, you name it. She saw that I was very serious about cooking and she sort of took me under her arm."

CONTINUING EDUCATION

Just because you graduate from cooking school doesn't mean the learning process ends. In this profession, it should never end.

Allen Susser says, "Going to school is only one of the first steps to growth and development in understanding what to do in a kitchen and what to do with cuisine."

While I was cooking during the lunch shift at Biba, I made it a point to attend Boston University's Seminars in the Culinary Arts in the evening, where I was able to take classes with local chefs, such as Jody Adams and Gordon Hamersley, and visiting luminaries like Julia Child, Lorenzo de'Medici,

Julie Sahni, and Anne Willan. The Boston Public Library sponsored a Cooks in Print series, which, in lecture format, offered wonderful opportunities to learn about food from leading chefs like Jasper White. The Schlesinger Library at Radcliffe College also offers panels of leading culinary experts on various issues, from food safety to customer service, which are open to the public. To find similar kinds of programs in your local areas, check with adult education and continuing education programs, with your local library, or with local chapters of national associations, such as the International Association of Wine and Food.

Many cooking schools also sponsor continuing education programs for working chefs, where one can spend anywhere from a day to a month learning more about cooking.

Nancy Silverton took a break from her career to attend Lenôtre (the namesake school of noted French pastry chef, Gaston Lenôtre), in France, to study pastry. "I was working at Michael's, which at the time was considered one of the top restaurants in Los Angeles, and my desserts were very well regarded. I went to Lenôtre and thought I might end up teaching them a few things." Silverton was surprised and humbled to find herself in classes with pastry chefs, some of whom owned their own pastry shops and who had been working in the field for 30 to 40 years. Silverton admits, "That's when I first came to realize that you never learn it all."

If you do decide to pursue cooking school, as recommended by the majority of chefs we interviewed, the most important point to keep in mind is to stay focused on what you're hoping to get out of it. Work for at least a year, in order to confirm your interest, before making such an important investment in your career. This will give you a more realistic view of the profession and also make you more focused once you're at school. If an externship is offered, take advantage of it. Work at the best restaurant you can get into, and learn and absorb everything you can. And, once you graduate, beware the paradox of "commencement": you're not a master chef yet—you've just taken the first important step in beginning to acquire an important base of knowledge on which to build. As Jimmy Schmidt says, "Remember: A building is only as strong as its foundation. If you don't have a strong foundation, you can never erect a skyscraper."

Andrew Dornenburg and Karen Page are coauthors of the James Beard Award–winning book Becoming a Chef: With Recipes and Reflections from America's Leading Chefs *(New York: John Wiley and Sons, Inc., 2003, © by the authors), from which this article is excerpted with permission. Their other books include* Culinary Artistry, Dining Out, Chef's Night Out, The New American Chef, *and* What to Drink With What You Eat. *Their Web site is www.becomingachef.com, at which free subscriptions are available to their award-winning monthly e-Newsletter.*

PAYING FOR YOUR CULINARY EDUCATION

Madge Griswold

Madge Griswold

Finding and Applying for Scholarships

*C*ulinary training can be expensive—nearly as expensive as attending a private university and sometimes more expensive than attending a public university. Few prospective students can simply pay the bills from their own savings. Some depend on their parents' generosity to fund their studies. Fortunately, help is available through loans and other financial aid programs and also in the form of scholarships.

Once you have decided which schools are most appealing to you, contact the financial aid office at each to determine exactly what kind of assistance is available. Some schools even have work-study arrangements that allow students to work part-time and study as well.

Financial aid offices at culinary schools administer financial aid programs of various kinds and also provide basic advice about securing educational loans. You should consider this advice to be an integral part of your overall career planning. Financing your degree should be viewed as a long-term investment in your professional career. You should understand how this complex system works to be sure you are getting the best deal possible.

You may be eligible for grant assistance if financial need is proved. A grant is an outright award of money, whereas a loan must be paid back. Financial aid officers are more than happy to counsel you about such options.

Scholarship awards are usually based on talent and potential. Financial need may or

Financial Assistance at a Glance

Grants—*outright awards based on financial need. Ask the financial aid advisers at the schools you are interested in for details.*

Scholarships—*awards for culinary study based on talent or potential for excellence in the culinary field. Scholarships are awarded by both schools and organizations related to the culinary field. If you are interested in applying for culinary scholarships, ask about them when discussing options with the financial aid office.*

Loans—*available to persons who qualify for them. Loans, unlike grants and scholarships, must be paid back once you graduate. Ask the financial aid advisers at the schools you are interested in for details or ask about student loans at your local bank. Many schools have a list of "preferred lenders" that may offer better borrowing terms and conditions for students attending their institution.*

Work-Study Programs—*programs that allow students to work while studying. Ask the financial aid advisers at the schools you are interested in whether such programs exist at the institution and how you can be considered for these worthwhile programs.*

avenues. Additional information is provided later in this article, but you should also do your own research using the Web. A good place to start is at Peterson's (www. petersons.com) or the FinAid! page at www. finaid.org.

When you plan for your culinary education, you'll want to find the best mix of grants, scholarships, loans, and work-study opportunities. In many cases, loans for education can be used to support a student's whole educational experience, including tuition, room and board, books, tools, and transportation. The financial aid office will put together the best aid "package" to meet your needs. If you feel this aid "package" is not sufficient, you should meet with the aid office either to reexamine your current situation or investigate other alternatives.

Many local community colleges have established fine culinary programs that are considerably cheaper than traditional programs at private institutions. You may want to consider programs at some of the community schools described in this guide. Many schools have excellent reputations locally and offer generous financial aid packages and scholarship assistance. And remember, culinary education is only part of preparing for a career in the culinary field. The rest is *you*—your knowledge, your talents, your creativity, and your overall work experience.

may not be considered when a scholarship is awarded. Requirements for scholarship candidates are established by the donors of specific scholarships. Scholarships are awarded by culinary schools themselves and also by a number of professional culinary associations. A serious applicant in need of substantial financial assistance should explore all of these

APPLYING FOR SCHOLARSHIPS

Almost all culinary schools award scholarships to truly promising students, so remember to ask for information about each school's requirements. In addition, many organizations associated with the culinary field award scholarships. You will want to begin addressing the scholarship application process even before you send in your admission application because the scholarship process can take longer than the admission process.

Each organization that provides scholarship aid has its own criteria for making awards, its own application process, and its own time frame. Many of these organizations evaluate applications only once a year. Some do it two or three times a year. Some organizations offer scholarships only for specialized kinds of study or to students with specific talents and characteristics. Others administer a broad range of scholarships.

Scholarships awarded by organizations (other than schools) are of two kinds:

- **Awards for specific schools.** These awards are usually for tuition credit, although occasionally some aid is given for room and board, books, uniforms, or tools.
- **Awards of a specific cash value that can be used at a variety of institutions.** Awards like these are usually designated by the donors to be applied only against tuition. They cannot be used to help pay for room and board, books, tools, uniforms, or getting to and from school. Cash-value awards generally are paid by the awarding organization directly to the chosen institution. Rarely, if ever, is money paid directly to a student to use as he or she wishes.

Since decisions about scholarship aid are based on the promise of achievement in the culinary field and not just financial need, it's a good idea to think through what kind of impression you want to make on the person or committee who will be evaluating your application. Here are some pointers from an experienced scholarship committee judge:

- Fill out the application neatly; neatness makes a good impression. Remember, you will be asked to perform your culinary work neatly. A neatly prepared application gives an indication that you can do that.
- Check your spelling carefully. If you are unsure of how to spell a word, look it up in a dictionary. Spelling errors detract from the message you are trying to communicate.
- Fill in all the information and submit all materials requested. You could be disqualified for not following directions.
- Be sure that all materials requested to be sent separately *are* sent separately. Frequently, letters of recommendation are requested separately to give some privacy to the referees and to ensure that they actually are the authors of the letters.
- List all work experience in the culinary field. Culinary work often demands long hours and considerable physical and mental effort. The fact that you have worked in the culinary field and understand the demands of your chosen career is important to judges. If you have done volunteer work in the culinary field, be sure to list that as well.
- Throughout the evaluation process, be prepared to explain your goals in life and your plans for the next few years. Lofty ambitions may be lauded but unrealistic plans are not.
- If you are asked to write an essay, write it yourself. This should be obvious; it's cheating if someone else writes your essay. A reviewer who suspects that you have not written your own essay may disqualify your entire application. Don't try to impress reviewers with flowery language or French culinary terms unless you actually have worked in a French kitchen and need to describe a station or task in French because

of it. Don't list impossible or outrageous goals. If you are 18, it's unlikely that in five years you will be the executive chef in a prominent hotel or own your own restaurant. Remember that the readers of your application are food professionals who are well aware of how long it takes to achieve a position in the field and how much it costs to start a restaurant. If you are having difficulty setting time frames, get advice from a teacher or mentor.

- When you write an essay, be original. If you have had unique experiences that have influenced you to become involved in the culinary profession, by all means include them, but don't say that ever since you were a little child you have wanted to go into the culinary field. It may be true, but it's trite. Tell the reader what is unique and special about you, why you deserve the scholarship, and what it will enable you to do with your life.

THE SCHOLARSHIP INTERVIEW

These interviews can be fun because you may find that you and your interviewer have many experiences and ideas in common. Your interviewer will probably put you at ease quickly. Your interviewer is interested in learning how well you speak and how well you present yourself. Conversation with you will convey to the interviewer how committed you are to your culinary goals and something about yourself other than your culinary side. You might be asked "what do you do when you are not cooking?" Your interviewer will also try to make sure you really understand just what the scholarship can and cannot do for you. Often interviewers act as advisers to candidates, pointing out opportunities they may have overlooked. An interview can be an excellent opportunity for you to present what is unique about you and why you deserve to be given a specific award. Look forward to this opportunity.

WHERE TO FIND SCHOLARSHIPS

In addition to the schools themselves, a number of organizations award scholarships for culinary education. Read this list carefully before requesting information. Some organizations give scholarships only for very specific purposes. Others give scholarships only for management training or for graduate work.

American Culinary Federation (ACF)

This long-established association of professional cooks has a membership of nearly 20,000 and more than 240 chapters in many cities. In addition to its apprenticeship program, which provides an excellent alternate approach to culinary training, the ACF awards some scholarships on the national level. Contacts at the local level will be able to provide information about any scholarships awarded by a local chapter. For information about a local chapter, contact the ACF at 800-624-9458. Information about scholarships at the national level may be obtained by calling this number or by writing to:

American Culinary Federation
180 Center Place Way
St. Augustine, FL 32095
Phone: 904-824-4468 or
    800-624-9458 (toll-free)
Fax: 904-825-4758
E-mail: memberservices@acfchefs.net
www.acfchefs.org

American Dietetic Association (ADA)

This organization is made up of nearly 65,000 members, 75 percent of whom are registered dietitians. It only awards scholarships for registered dietitians working toward master's degrees. If you think you are eligible, contact them at:

American Dietetic Association
120 South Riverside Plaza, Suite 2000
Chicago, IL 60606-6995
Phone: 800-877-1600 (toll-free)
www.eatright.org

American Institute of Wine & Food (AIWF)

A nonprofit organization created to promote appreciation of wine and food and encourage scholarly education in gastronomy, this nearly 6,000-member organization has twenty-nine chapters in U.S. cities. Only certain chapters of the AIWF give scholarships for culinary education. Some are administered by the individual chapters; others are administered through the facilities of the International Association of Culinary Professionals (IACP) Foundation scholarship committee. You can reach AIWF at:

The American Institute of Wine & Food
213–37 39th Avenue
Box 216
Bayside, NY 11361
Phone: 800-274-2493 (toll-free)
Fax: 718-279-2324
www.aiwf.org

Careers through Culinary Arts Program, Inc. (C-CAP)

A school-to-work program, established in a number of major metropolitan areas, C-CAP integrates culinary training at the high school level with work and business experience. C-CAP provides awards and scholarships ranging from $1000 to full tuition and assists students in making college and career choices. If you are a high school student, ask your

guidance counselor if there is a C-CAP program in your area and how you might participate.

Careers through Culinary Arts
Program, Inc.
250 West 57th Street, Suite 2015
New York, NY 10107
Phone: 212-974-7111
Fax: 212-974-7117
E-mail: info@ccapinc.org
www.ccapinc.org

Confrérie de la Chaîne des Rôtisseurs

A long-established organization for promoting appreciation of fine food and wine, this society has members in more than seventy countries and has granted $215,000 scholarships to thirteen qualifying schools since 1996. Scholarships are established directly with culinary schools. Interested candidates should ask financial aid officers at specific schools about these awards.

Confrérie de la Chaîne des Rôtisseurs
Chaîne House at Fairleigh Dickinson
University
285 Madison Avenue
Madison, NJ 07940-1099
Phone: 973-360-9200
Fax: 973-360-9330
E-mail: chaine@chaineus.org
www.chaineus.org

International Association of Culinary Professionals (IACP) Foundation

This charitable and educational affiliate of the International Association of Culinary Professionals has, as one of its functions, the administration of scholarships that provide either tuition-credit assistance at specific institutions or financial assistance that can be applied to a variety of institutions. The IACP Foundation scholarship committee awards scholarships on an annual cycle, with an application deadline of December 15 for scholarships beginning the following July 1. Interested applicants should consult the IACP Foundation office, since deadlines sometimes change. Contact them at:

IACP Foundation
304 West Liberty Street, Suite 201
Louisville, KY 40202
Phone: 502-581-9786
Fax: 502-589-3602
E-mail: iacp@hqtrs.com
www.iacp.com

International Foodservice Editorial Council (IFEC)

Dedicated to the improvement of media communications quality in the food field, this small organization of food service magazine editors and public relations executives awards between four and six scholarships annually to persons seeking careers that combine food service and communications.

IFEC
P.O. Box 491
Hyde Park, NY 12538-0491
Phone: 845-229-6973
Fax: 845-229-6993
E-mail: ifec@aol.com
www.ifec-is-us.com

International Food Service Executives Association (IFSEA)

A long-established educational and community service association, this group provides some scholarships of its own and also provides information about scholarships offered by other organizations.

IFSEA
304 West Liberty Street, Suite 201
Louisville, KY 40202
Phone: 502-583-3783
Fax: 502-589-3602
E-mail: ghobby@hqtrs.com
www.ifsea.com

James Beard Foundation

This prominent organization of food professionals, devoted to the ideals and principles of legendary American cook and writer James Beard, awards a number of substantial scholarships each year. The application deadline is usually in May.

The James Beard Foundation
Scholarship Program
6 West 18th Street, 10th Floor
New York, NY 10011
Phone: 212-627-1128
Fax: 212-627-1064
E-mail: scholarships@jamesbeard.org
www.jamesbeard.org

Les Dames d'Escoffier (LDEI)

This association has chapters in many major cities. One of its major purposes is the creation and awarding of scholarships to assist women with culinary training. These scholarships are awarded directly by the chapters. Women who are interested in applying for such scholarships should contact LDEI's executive director, Greg Jewell, at gjewell@aecmanagement.com, or visit their Web site at www.ldei.org.

National Restaurant Association Educational Foundation

An educational organization that produces a variety of courses, video training sessions, seminars, and other educational opportunities for persons in the hospitality industry, this group also offers scholarships.

National Restaurant Association
    Educational Foundation
175 West Jackson Boulevard, Suite 1500
Chicago, IL 60604-2702
Phone: 312-715-1010 (Chicagoland) or
    800-765-2122 (toll-free)
E-mail: info@nraef.org
www.nraef.org

Women Chefs and Restaurateurs (WCR)

An association specifically designed to promote the education and advancement of women in the culinary profession and to promote the industry overall, the WCR awarded forty-five internships and scholarships for women in 2005. For further information, contact them at:

WCR
304 West Liberty Street, Suite 201
Louisville, KY 40202
Phone: 502-581-0300 or 877-927-7787
Fax: 502-589-3602
www.womenchefs.org

Madge Griswold, CCP, is an author and culinary historian, past Chairman of the Board of Trustees of the International Association of Culinary Professionals Foundation, founding Chairman of the American Institute of Wine & Food's Baja Arizona chapter, and a member of the James Beard Foundation. Among her most recent publications are two sections of Culinaria: The United States, A Culinary Discovery, Cologne: Könemann. *She is a member of the editorial advisory board of the journal* Gastronomica.

CHARTING A SUCCESSFUL CULINARY CAREER

Barbara Sims-Bell

What Else Can You Do with a Cooking Degree (besides open a restaurant)?

You love to cook; garlic essence smells better to you than an expensive French perfume; your friends and family say you should have a restaurant (well, maybe not your family); and right now you're seriously studying the choice of the best culinary training you can afford to allow you to live your dream. But it is never too early to contemplate the future, to think about opportunities that will come along after culinary training.

Chef, caterer, pastry cook, and restaurant cook are merely the most familiar four; there are hundreds of jobs in the food industry. You may want to consider preparing for positions in management as executive chef, or sales as catering director, or administration in food and beverage management. Maybe you'll want to explore developing specialty products—a line of sauces, dressings, or convenience foods, for example—for retail or wholesale markets. There are also teaching opportunities in professional cooking schools (possibly even the one you choose to attend). Others set out to become a restaurant consultant to entrepreneurs who want to start a restaurant or improve the one they own. Still another option is food writing and editing for magazines and books devoted to food and cooking.

For any of these career directions, you'll find the best and the broadest preparation in an accredited school program. You will come out with a certificate or a degree, and forever after when you are asked, "Where did you get your training?" you can refer to an accepted and respected credential in professional cooking. This training provides you with a lifelong basis for understanding quality raw ingredients, creating balance and pleasure in combined flavors, and presenting a beautiful plate to the diner.

Yes, you keep learning, but culinary school gives you a base of knowledge to test and compare to new trends, new ingredients, and your own creativity.

WHERE CAN I GO FROM HERE?

When most culinary students start their training, they believe they have found the work they want to do for the rest of their lives—and many are right. But some are surprised when they find so much routine and boredom and repetitive tasks. You haven't seen appetizers until you've assembled 3,000 identical stuffed puffs for a hotel reception. House salad? You'll clean and prep cases of the same greens and garnishes day after day. And the signature white chocolate mousse and meringue dacquoise layers you always wanted to perfect? You'll be preparing untold orders for it every evening. You have to love it.

If managerial positions are more to your liking, you'll need skills in addition to cooking. Managers create the working environment for the staff, often developing a sixth sense to recognize problems before they rupture. They are the motivational force that drives the staff. They must understand finance and business reports and their implications. They must have highly sensitive character judgment and the ability to manage people from hiring to mentoring to firing.

If your interests take you into catering and sales, think about these skills: You'll need to be able to research a product and explore your market. You'll need to really enjoy being with people. You'll need to draw on strong self-esteem to take "no" and not take it personally. You'll need internal discipline to keep the work flowing. You'll need communication skills to persuade people that your product is best. And you'll need to be strongly motivated to make a sale.

WHERE DO I FIT?

To choose a career path that seems right for you, you'll need to define your own personality profile, whether it gives you the skills you need if you want to move higher or take a detour and move sideways. Or do you need to add some skills that you haven't yet developed?

One approach is to see a qualified career counselor for an evaluation of your strengths and weaknesses. Even if you reject or overrule the findings, you may gain an understanding of yourself that you didn't have before. Career testing extracts from us an inventory of our preferences.

Professional career counselors have the training, experience, and credentials to help you explore some of the possible choices that tempt you. They use finely tuned tests, such as Myers-Briggs, Holland, and Strong Interest. Then they interpret the test reports to give you additional guidance, either to follow your obvious bent or to stretch yourself into other areas with training and exploration. As in everything, there are quacks and there are bona fide wizards. The best course is to check the credentials of anyone you're considering.

Whether or not you seek outside career guidance, you should do some soul-searching on your own. Take stock of who you are. What are your best skills? Break them down into culinary, service, finance, research, communication, and management. Some of the categories will be longer than others; that tells you where you've placed your learning emphasis and where you'll have to work a bit harder. Think about your lifestyle and workplace values. Is independence something you seek, or do routine and stability matter more? Are you aiming for wealth or is leisure time now more important? Another significant list is what leisure activities you enjoy the most, then rating them by cost, whether they are solitary or social activities, and whether you've been able to fit them into your life lately. Are you a risk taker or do you proceed with caution? Even the most cautious of us can be successful entrepreneurs, but your own slant between these two types is important for you to know.

GETTING THE WHOLE CULINARY PICTURE

An easy and enjoyable way to learn about the spectrum of food-related jobs is by joining one or more professional organizations. Among the largest are the American Culinary Federation (ACF) and the International Association of Culinary Professionals (IACP). There are regional culinary groups—guilds, societies, alliances—in many large urban areas, and if the school you choose doesn't have the information, someone at IACP headquarters will be able to give you a current name and address near you to contact. Even if you are not yet a bona fide culinarian, as soon as you are enrolled in a professional program, you can usually join in the student-member category—at a lower annual dues rate. Most organizations allow guests to come to their meetings and pro-

grams—a good way to get connected and see if you feel comfortable in the group before joining.

Among the rewards of joining a local culinary group are friendships; meeting potential mentors; learning from varied guest speakers; job leads; customer referrals when another member is too booked to take the work; learning unrelated skills when you volunteer to work on program, membership, and communication committees; contributing to the community when you volunteer to work on a food-related benefit; and the lifelong asset of connections.

Take an inventory of "Whom do I know who I can call about this?" Culinary groups provide a wealth of leads and good food and wine to enjoy. Get the name and phone number, call to find out when and where the next meeting will be, and ask if they welcome guests. When you get there tell the greeter "I'm new here; who can I talk to about (baking, catering kitchens, ethnic ingredient stores, this organization, volunteering)"—pick a topic and start listening. Bring your business cards (not having them is unforgivable), give them out, and be sure to take cards from members you meet. Write the date of the meeting and what you talked about on the back before you go to sleep that night. Thus begins the building of a personal network, the invaluable channel to your peers.

The first time I met a friend of mine she was working as a waitress at a sort-of-Italian café where our Roundtable for Women in Foodservice chapter was having a program titled "Networking." I was moderating the panel, and the waitress was mesmerized by the dynamic group of professional women who were the au-

Stephanie Hersh

Stephanie Hersh defined her career goal of being a pastry chef at the age of 6 with the gift of a Betty Crocker Easy-Bake Oven. It was simplistic cause and effect: She produced the sweet offerings from batters, and everyone fluttered around telling her she was "terrific." She figured this could last her whole lifetime if she just kept on making cake. Her granny lived nearby and regularly let the diminutive yet determined youngster bake alongside her, making family desserts and good, sweet stuff.

Her parents were a harder nut to crack, insisting on scholastic accomplishment, first in her private high school, then in a four-year college. Looking back, she thinks it was the best for her because "I needed to grow up before going to culinary school." She worked part-time in restaurants, both front of the house and back, making some headway in the cooking hierarchy as she became more experienced. The work was everything she dreamed: It gave her pleasure, satisfaction, self-esteem, self-confidence. Her personality drove her to "always be the best," and she knew that to be best she had to have professional training. The restaurant business was changing at that time, and she knew it would no longer be possible to work up in kitchens from dishwasher to executive chef. Restaurant owners were hiring the applicant with the best culinary education. In 1985, Stephanie graduated from The Culinary Institute of America in Hyde Park, New York.

Her first professional job as a hotel pastry chef in Boston was a rude awakening. For the first time, pastries became work to do and get done, and it wasn't fun. She still had her pastry shop dream, and to feed her savings faster she devised a dual plan, based on her new goals—"I just wanted to cook and enjoy it and make money." Stephanie took a job as a private chef, live-in, for a small family with two professional working parents and 2 children. With her daytimes freed up, she enrolled at Katharine Gibbs School, figuring she could still be a private chef and work days as a secretary, with almost no living expenses. Then something happened.

Julia Child phoned the school asking if they had a graduate to recommend, commenting that it would be nice if the person knew something about cooking. When they described Stephanie's culinary background, she turned her down, saying that she really wanted a secretary, not a chef. Stephanie was in the school office when it happened and asked permission to call Julia back so she could press her case for herself. There was serious persuasion involved on Stephanie's part, but the statement was repeated: "I just want a secretary; I don't need anyone to work in my kitchen." Stephanie agreed that she just wanted to be a secretary. The next morning, minutes after arriving at the Cambridge house, Stephanie was in the kitchen prepping three recipes for demonstration stages and cooking aromatic fish stew for serving. Julia had forgotten she had agreed to a television taping/interview and greeted Stephanie with a fistful of recipe copies and almost no instruction except "just wiggle a finger at me when you've got it all ready," while she went back to the camera crew.

Suddenly Stephanie Hersh was an administrator, a facilitator, an essential sidekick, and accepted—smack, dab, in the center of the high-profile food industry. She loved her job. Her schooling continued, and, with Julia's encouragement, Stephanie was the first graduate in Boston University's master's program in gastronomy. She later ran her own business, Chef Steph, through which she sold cakes and pastries and organized cooking parties for children. An active member of IACP, Hersh lives and works in New Zealand.

dience. I noticed her enthusiasm, talked to her a bit, and encouraged her to join our chapter. With a university degree in soils science, she was working as a server "because that is what I like to do more than anything else"—and her people skills were what I continued to notice as she joined the chapter, came to meetings, and changed jobs a few times. Within a year, she

Courtesy The French Culinary Institute/Matthew Septhimus

was hired by the oldest established winery in our region as Tasting Room Manager and now is its local Sales Manager. Her education in soils and geology gave her a head start in understanding wine production for her job. "Who you know" only opens the door, but "what you know" gets you the job.

TRAVEL STAGES FOR A CAREER

If you have already identified some role models in the food industry and have learned a little about their lives and careers, you know that a long stretch of steady, hard work is the story of their success. We can divide that stretch into sections, though, and understand ways that your own success can be a realistic goal.

Beginner

Focus on a career plan for yourself as early as you can. You will make changes, take detours, and acquire unrelated skills that you want to use, but having a predetermined route tells you whether you're lost or just on a scenic loop. Use the professional network you are gathering right away. At first that may be primarily your fellow students and your teachers, but they are an important network for you to maintain. How do you use them? As questions arise in your mind, ask "Whom do I know who might answer this?" Make contact with the person, ask your questions, strengthen your bond. Ask your teachers and your mentors about industry conferences and trade shows you can attend, and make an effort to go. The more you know what is going on in the food industry, the better you can steer yourself to success. Donate your time and skills to publicized events—does your school or your restaurant put on fund-raisers for community projects? Volunteer to assist, to cook, to serve, or to do whatever is needed and talk to your peers at the event. Remember, always take your business cards and give them out as you are collecting new ones. Write on the backs! As soon as you become a "head chef"—whether in your own restaurant or as an employee—create some public appearance opportunities for yourself. Participate in community benefits that feature a group of local chefs providing the food. If you are developing a product through the restaurant or on your own, find opportunities to have guests taste it at local events. If you author a cookbook, offer to do book signings at local bookstores. Work closely with your culinary peers, participate in public events as much as possible, and barter your services for product. Keep your name out there, and it will become your billboard.

Intermediate

This is the stage to position yourself for publicity. The first step is to run your business (whether self-owned or profit-sharing status) so well you can be absent on tour. Go to Beard House dinners in New York City, and talk to them about scheduling you to cook one. Contact the nearest chapter of the American Institute of Wine & Food and ask if it will set up a program using you as a guest chef. Develop your public speaking skills; if you need help with public speaking, contact your local adult education program for workshops and local coaches. The better you can hold your audience's attention while you speak (and this includes table side in your restaurant), the more you will promote your success. As soon as you are confident speaking to medium-size groups (50 to 200 people) and have something to talk about, offer to be a speaker at professional conferences: the American Culinary Federation, the International Association of Culinary Professionals, and regional culinary organizations. After a few more experiences, and when word of your entertainment value gets around, you will be paid travel and lodging expenses to be a speaker (and in time you'll be paid an honorarium, as well). At this midcareer stage, you can search out ways to market your name, and offers will come to you unsolicited: consider allowing your name to be used on aprons or chef's clothing labels (this can be either your own merchandise line or the use of your name). Newcomers to the restaurant business looking for help and advice may turn to you, and you can decide whether to give it freely or charge as a consultant (probably a little of both, depending on the circumstances). By now, you recognize the need for a support network to help you manage some of these outside activities: a lawyer, an accountant, a marketing assistant, and possibly a booking agent. Don't sit back thinking that when you need them they will be there. As with everything, you have to look ahead and look out for yourself.

Advanced

If you're doing it right, now is the stage to get paid for having fun. If you still want to cook, you'll be doing it, probably with one or two trained cooks behind you so you can take care of the peripheral business you've created. Here are some ways you'll find to stimulate your creative juices and make money at the same time: You'll be paid an honorarium and expenses as a speaker. You'll be recruited to head business development teams for other culinary start-ups. You'll be paid for product and service endorsements. You may spin off your name or your label on merchandise for royalties. You'll attract potential investors and/or buyers for expansion or retirement from your own restaurant or company. If this is fun for you, you'll find the time to do it.

Graduate

This is the time to be a mentor and a philanthropist within your culinary community. When you were a beginner in professional training, your school probably brought in the best local chefs to inspire you. You may have received a culinary scholarship from one of the professional organizations. Now it's your turn to be on the giving side. You'll still get requests to speak and be paid well for most of the gigs, but consider giving some time to smaller groups of the next generation of chefs. The appearances you'll get paid for will be keynoter, industry spokesperson, and expert; consider being on a panel or a roundtable to answer questions one-on-one. You will be offered an investment position in food companies solely as an adviser. The fee you get for endorsements will be higher than ever. To truly be a graduate in this career field, you will consciously find, promote, and mentor promising individuals who can advance the industry in the future. Well done!

KEEPING YOUR OPTIONS OPEN

The future of any career, say, ten or twenty years ahead, is excruciatingly difficult to find in focus. Whether you look through a camera's viewer or through eyeglasses customized to your needs, you make physical adjustments to bring a faraway object into focus.

Once you have chosen a culinary school for your training and started instruction, it's already time to start asking about future opportunities. Bombard your chefs at school with questions about what you need to know for jobs that sound enticing to you. You may not act on that information for several years, but you've started to adjust your focus whenever you gather more knowledge about future opportunities.

The speck on the horizon that is your future career is barely visible now, but as you move toward it or look for it through a magnifier, you will develop your own vision, and it will become excitingly clear to you. Good luck to every one of you.

_____

Barbara Sims-Bell was the founder of and primary instructor at the Santa Barbara Cooking School from 1979 to 1985. She is the author of two books about careers and jobs in the culinary field, Career Opportunities in the Food and Beverage Industry, *New York: Facts on File, 1995, and* FoodWork—Jobs in the Food Industry and How to Get Them, *Santa Barbara, Calif.: Advocacy Press, 1994.*

CULINARY APPRENTICESHIPS

American Culinary Federation

A Three-Year Commitment

*C*ulinary apprenticeships are three-year on-the-job training programs reinforced by related instruction from educational institutions. Many successful apprenticeship programs offer an associate degree. Apprentices receive three years of documented work experience while receiving an education that is specific to the industry, and apprentice graduates can confidently accept a job based on the experience received during their apprenticeship program. These graduates also receive Certified Cook status through the American Culinary Federation (ACF) National Certification Program. The ultimate designation of Chef comes through additional experience and education.

Upon graduation, apprentices can earn between $25,000 and $32,000. An apprenticeship is a three-year commitment to work full-time (6,000 hours) under a qualified supervising chef while attending school part-time (minimum of 192 hours per year). Apprentices can expect competitive pay during the three years of training. The average cost for school is between $1000 and $4000 per year during a three-year period—a dynamic "earn-while-you-learn" program.

The success of apprenticeship comes from the commitment made by the industry chef and management, the education institution, and the American Culinary Federation (local and national). Each of these entities is responsible for maintaining high-quality standards.

Employers of apprentices enjoy the benefit of committed and loyal culinarians who enhance the enthusiasm and positive attitudes of the entire staff. Apprentices enter a kitchen starting at the beginning, giving the supervising chef the unique opportunity to develop a mentorship relationship with the apprentice. The *Training Log* cultivates this relationship by requiring a weekly entry by the apprentice. The supervising chef periodically reviews these entries.

The ACF Apprenticeship Program offers a unique connection between industry and education. The standard curriculum and competencies are delivered by the supervising chef in tandem with the educational institution. An apprenticeship can strengthen many ACF chapters by providing chefs with a purpose: to share their culinary knowledge and expertise.

The ACF Apprenticeship Program began in 1976 with a grant from the United States government. Today, it is one of two programs remaining from that training initiative and is the seventh-largest apprenticeship program in the United States.

_____

Reprinted with the permission of the American Culinary Federation.

How to use this guide

Peterson's Culinary Schools is a comprehensive guide to culinary schools in the United States and abroad. The guide provides detailed descriptions of more than 500 professional degree and apprenticeship programs.

QUICK-REFERENCE CHART

The **Quick-Reference Chart** lists programs by state and country, indicates what degrees or awards are offered, and notes if the program offers degree specializations in the areas of culinary arts, baking and pastry, or management. Please be aware that there are other degree specializations, and you will have to refer to individual profiles to discover what an individual program may offer beyond these popular ones.

PROFILES OF PROFESSIONAL PROGRAMS

Peterson's Culinary Schools profiles are organized into two main sections, each arranged alphabetically by state within the United States and by country. The first section includes profiles of professional programs and the second, profiles of apprenticeship programs.

Professional programs offer formalized instruction in a class setting. A diploma, degree, or certificate is awarded to the student at the end of successful completion of a predetermined curriculum of courses and a minimum number of credit hours. Workplace training in the form of an externship or work-study program may be an option but is not usually required. An apprenticeship is essentially an on-the-job training program. Typical apprenticeship programs entail completion of a specific term (typically, three years or 6,000 hours) of full-time employment for wages in a food service kitchen under a qualified chef. Classroom culinary instruction is usually required in addition to the scheduled work, and a certificate may be awarded.

General Information. Indicates private or public institution, coeducational or single-sex, type of institution, and the campus

29

setting. The founding year of the institution is also listed, as is institutional accreditation information.

Program Information. Indicates the year the program started offering classes, program accreditation, the program calendar (semester, quarter, etc.), the type of degrees and awards offered, degree and award specializations, and the length of time needed to complete the degree or award.

Program Affiliation. Lists those organizations to which the school or program belongs.

Areas of Study. Includes the courses available.

Facilities. Lists the number and types of facilities available to students.

Student Profile. Provides the total number of students enrolled in the program and the number who are full-time and part-time and the age range of students.

Faculty. Provides the total number of faculty members, the number who are full-time and part-time, and the number who are culinary accredited, industry professionals, master bakers, or master chefs. The names of prominent faculty members and their degree or certificate level are listed if provided. The faculty-student ratio is also listed.

Special Programs. Notes special educational opportunities offered by the program.

Typical Expenses. Includes information on full-time, part-time, in-state, and out-of-state tuition costs; special program-related fees; and application fees. Dollar signs without further notation refer to U.S. currency.

Financial Aid. Provides information on the number and amount of program-specific loans and scholarships awarded during the 2004–05 or 2005–06 academic year and unique financial aid opportunities available to students. (This section covers only culinary-related financial aid and does not include types of financial aid that are open to all students, such as Pell Grants and Stafford Loans.)

Housing. Indicates the type of on-campus housing available, as well as the typical cost of off-campus housing in the area.

Application Information. Provides information on application deadlines, the number of students who applied for admission to the program and the number of students accepted to the program for the 2004–05, 2005–06, or 2006–07 academic year, and application materials that are required.

Contact. Includes the name, address, telephone and fax numbers, and e-mail address (if provided) of the contact person for the program and the Web address of the program or institution.

PROFILES OF APPRENTICESHIP PROGRAMS

Program Information. Indicates if the apprenticeship program is directly sponsored by a college, university, or culinary institute; if the program is approved by the American Culinary Federation; if an apprentice is eligible to receive a degree from a college or university upon successful completion of the program; and if any special apprenticeships are available.

Placement Information. Provides the number and types of locations where apprentices may be placed and lists the most popular placement locations of participants.

Apprentice Profile. Indicates the number of participants, the age range of participants, and the application materials a prospective apprentice must submit.

Typical Expenses. Provides information on the basic costs of participating in the program as well as the application fee and special program-related fees.

Entry-Level Compensation. Indicates the typical salary for an apprentice at the beginning of the apprenticeship program.

Contact. Includes the name, address, telephone and fax numbers, and e-mail address (if provided) of the contact person for the apprenticeship program.

INDEXES

Two indexes are available at the end of the book. The first, **Certificate, Diploma, and Degree Programs**, lists programs by whether they offer a certificate or diploma or a degree (associate, bachelor's, master's, or doctoral). The second index, **Alphabetical Listing of Schools and Programs**, is an alphabetical list by name of the program or institution.

CULINARY DEGREES AND CERTIFICATES

Below is a list of degrees and certificates common to the culinary and hospitality industries. You'll often see these acronyms following the names of faculty members to indicate their level of education and certification.

AA	Associate of Arts
AAC	American Academy of Chefs
AAS	Associate of Applied Science
BA	Bachelor of Arts
BS	Bachelor of Science
CAGS	Certificate of Advanced Graduate Study
CC	Certified Culinarian
CCC	Certified Chef de Cuisine
CCE	Certified Culinary Educator
CCM	Certified Club Manager
CCP	Certified Culinary Professional
CDM	Certified Dietary Manager
CDN	Certified Dietetics Nutritionist
CEC	Certified Executive Chef
CEPC	Certified Executive Pastry Chef
CFBE	Certified Food and Beverage Executive
CFBM	Certified Food and Beverage Manager
CFE	Certified Food Executive
CFSC	Certified Food Service Consultant
CFSM	Certified Food Service Manager
CHA	Certified Hotel Administrator
CHAE	Certified Hospitality Accounting Executive
CHE	Certified Hospitality Educator
CHM	Certified Hospitality Manager
CMB	Certified Master Baker
CMC	Certified Master Chef
CMPC	Certified Master Pastry Chef
CPC	Certified Pastry Culinarian
CPCE	Certified Professional Catering Executive
CRDE	Certified Rooms Division Executive
CSC	Certified Sous Chef
CWC	Certified Working Chef
CWPC	Certified Working Pastry Chef
DFS	Doctor of Food Service
DTR	Dietetic Technician, Registered
EdD	Doctor of Education
EPC	Executive Pastry Chef
FADA	Fellow of the American Dietetic Association
FMP	Food Service Management Professional
FCSI	Foodservice Consultants Society International
HRTA	Hotel, Restaurant, and Travel Administration
LD	Licensed Dietitian
LRD	Licensed Registered Dietician
MA	Master of Arts
MBA	Master of Business Administration
MEd	Master of Education

MHRIM	Master of Hotel, Restaurant, and Institutional Management
MOF	Meilleur Ouvrier de France
MPC	Master Pastry Chef
MPH	Master of Public Health
MPS	Master of Professional Studies
MS	Master of Science
MSA	Master of Science in Administration
MSEd	Master of Science in Education
PhD	Doctor of Philosophy
RD	Registered Dietitian
REHS	Registered Environmental Health Sanitarian

DATA COLLECTION PROCEDURES

Information in this book was collected in both summer/fall 2005 and fall 2006 using questionnaires. Changes may occur after publication, so be sure to contact the institutions directly for the most current information on their programs.

QUICK-REFERENCE CHART

CULINARY PROGRAMS AT-A-GLANCE—U.S.

State/School	Credentials Offered	Culinary Arts	Baking and Pastry	Management
Alabama				
ACF Greater Montgomery Chapter				
Alabama Agricultural and Mechanical University	B, M			■
Bishop State Community College	C, A			■
CULINARD–The Culinary Institute of Virginia College	D, A, B	■	■	■
The Gulf Coast Culinary Institute	C, A	■	■	■
Jefferson State Community College	C, A	■		■
Lawson State Community College	C			
Tuskegee University	B			■
The University of Alabama	B			■
Wallace State Community College	D			
Alaska				
Alaska Vocational Technical Center	C	■	■	
University of Alaska Anchorage	C, A, B	■		■
University of Alaska Fairbanks	C, A	■	■	
Arizona				
Arizona Culinary Institute	D	■	■	■
Arizona Western College	C, A	■		■
The Art Institute of Phoenix	D, A, B	■	■	
Central Arizona College	C, A	■		■
Chefs Association of Southern Arizona, Tucson				
Cochise College	C, A	■		

*Credentials: **C** = Certificate; **D** = Diploma; **A** = Associate Degree; **B** = Bachelor's Degree; **M** = Master's Degree; **Ph.D.** = Doctorate*
No credential or program information appears for apprenticeship programs.

35

State/School	Credentials Offered	Culinary Arts	Baking and Pastry	Management
Arizona *(continued)*				
Maricopa Skill Center	C			
Northern Arizona University	C, B	■		■
Pima Community College	C, A	■		
Scottsdale Community College	C, A	■		■
Scottsdale Culinary Institute	C, A	■	■	
Arkansas				
Arkansas Culinary School, Inc.	C, A	■	■	
Arkansas Tech University	B			■
University of Arkansas at Pine Bluff	B			■
California				
American River College	C, A	■	■	■
The Art Institute of California–Los Angeles	A, B	■		■
The Art Institute of California–Orange County	A	■		
The Art Institute of California–San Diego	A, B	■		■
Bauman College: Hollstic Nutrition & Culinary Arts	C			
Cabrillo College	C, A	■		
California Culinary Academy	C, A	■	■	■
California School of Culinary Arts	D, A	■	■	■
California State Polytechnic University, Pomona	B			■
Chef Eric's Culinary Classroom	C	■	■	
City College of San Francisco	A	■		■
College of the Canyons	A			■
College of the Sequoias	C			■
Contra Costa College	C, A	■	■	
The Culinary Institute of America	C	■	■	

Credentials: **C** = Certificate; **D** = Diploma; **A** = Associate Degree; **B** = Bachelor's Degree; **M** = Master's Degree; **Ph.D.** = Doctorate
No credential or program information appears for apprenticeship programs.

State/School	Credentials Offered	Culinary Arts	Baking and Pastry	Management
Cypress College	C, A	■		■
Diablo Valley College	C	■	■	■
Epicurean School of Culinary Arts	C		■	
Glendale Community College	C	■		■
Kitchen Academy	D	■		
Lake Tahoe Community College	C, A	■		
Long Beach City College	C, A	■	■	■
Los Angeles Mission College	C, A	■		■
Merced College	C, A			■
MiraCosta College	C, A			■
Mission College	C, A			■
Modesto Junior College	C, A	■		
Monterey Peninsula College	C, A		■	■
Mt. San Antonio College	C, A			■
Napa Valley College	C	■		
National Culinary and Bakery School	C	■	■	
The New School of Cooking	D	■	■	
Opportunities Industrialization Center–West	C	■		
Orange Coast College	C, A	■		■
Orange Empire Chefs Association				
Oxnard College	C, A	■		■
Quality College of Culinary Careers	C, A	■	■	
Richardson Researches, Inc.	D			
Riverside Community College	C, A	■		
Saddleback College	C, A	■		
San Diego Mesa College	C, A			■
San Francisco Culinary/Pastry Program				

State/School	Credentials Offered	Culinary Arts	Baking and Pastry	Management
California (*continued*)				
San Joaquin Delta College	C, A	■	■	
Santa Barbara City College	C, A	■		■
Santa Rosa Junior College	C	■	■	■
University of San Francisco	B			■
Victor Valley College	C, A			■
Westlake Culinary Institute	C	■	■	
West Valley Occupational Center	C		■	
Yuba College	C, A			■
Colorado				
ACF Colorado Chefs Association				
The Art Institute of Colorado	D, A, B	■		■
Colorado Mountain College	A	■		
Colorado State University	B, M, Ph.D.			■
Cook Street School of Fine Cooking	D	■		
Culinary School of the Rockies	D	■	■	
Front Range Community College	C, A	■		■
Johnson & Wales University	C, A, B	■	■	■
Mesa State College	C, A	■		
Metropolitan State College of Denver	C, B	■		■
Pikes Peak Community College	C, A	■	■	■
Pueblo Community College	C, A		■	■
School of Natural Cookery	C			
University of Denver	B			■
Connecticut				
Briarwood College	A			■
Center for Culinary Arts	D	■		

*Credentials: **C** = Certificate; **D** = Diploma; **A** = Associate Degree; **B** = Bachelor's Degree; **M** = Master's Degree; **Ph.D.** = Doctorate*
No credential or program information appears for apprenticeship programs.

Peterson's Culinary Schools

State/School	Credentials Offered	Culinary Arts	Baking and Pastry	Management
Center for Culinary Arts, Shelton	D	■		
Connecticut Culinary Institute	D	■	■	
Gateway Community College	C, A	■		■
Manchester Community College	C, A	■		■
Naugatuck Valley Community College	C, A	■		■
Norwalk Community College	C, A	■		■
University of New Haven	A, B, M			■
Delaware				
Delaware Technical and Community College	D, A	■		■
University of Delaware	B, M			■
District of Columbia				
Howard University	B			■
Florida				
ACF Central Florida Chapter				
ACF Greater Ft. Lauderdale Chapter				
ACF Palm Beach County Chefs Association				
ACF Treasure Coast Chapter				
The Art Institute of Fort Lauderdale	D, A, B	■		■
The Art Institute of Tampa	A	■		
Atlantic Technical Center	C	■		
Bethune-Cookman College	B			■
Broward Community College	A			■
Capital Culinary Institute of Keiser College	A	■	■	
Charlotte Technical Center	C	■		
Daytona Beach Community College	A	■		■

State/School	Credentials Offered	Culinary Arts	Baking and Pastry	Management
Florida (*continued*)				
Florida Community College at Jacksonville	C, A	■		■
Florida Culinary Institute	D, A, B	■	■	■
Florida State University	B			■
Gulf Coast Community College	A	■		■
Hillsborough Community College	C, A	■		■
Indian River Community College	A	■		■
Johnson & Wales University	A, B	■	■	■
Lindsey Hopkins Technical Education Center	C	■		
Lorenzo Walker Institute of Technology	C	■		
McFatter Technical Center	C	■		
Miami Lakes Education Center	C			
Northwood University, Florida Campus	A, B			■
Notter School of Pastry Arts	C			
Palm Beach Community College	A			■
Pensacola Junior College	A	■		■
Pinellas Technical Education Center–Clearwater Campus	C	■		
St. Thomas University	B, M			■
Sheridan Technical Center	C	■		
The Southeast Institute of the Culinary Arts	C, D	■	■	■
South Florida Community College	C, A			■
Tampa Bay Culinary Association				
Technical Education Center–Osceola				
University of Central Florida	B, M			■

Credentials: *C* = Certificate; *D* = Diploma; *A* = Associate Degree; *B* = Bachelor's Degree; *M* = Master's Degree; **Ph.D.** = Doctorate
No credential or program information appears for apprenticeship programs.

State/School	Credentials Offered	Culinary Arts	Baking and Pastry	Management
Valencia Community College	C, A	■	■	■
Webber International University	A, B			■
Georgia				
ACF Golden Isles of Georgia, Culinary Association				
The Art Institute of Atlanta	D, A, B	■	■	■
Atlanta Technical College	D	■		
Augusta Technical College	C, D	■		■
Chattahoochee Technical College	D, A	■		
Coastal Georgia Community College	C	■		
Georgia Southern University	B			■
Georgia State University	C, B, M			■
North Georgia Technical College	C, D, A	■	■	■
Savannah Technical College	D, A	■		
West Georgia Technical College	D	■		
Hawaii				
Leeward Community College	C, A		■	■
Maui Community College	C, A	■	■	■
University of Hawaii–Kapiolani Community College	C, A	■	■	
Idaho				
Boise State University	C, A	■		
Brigham Young University–Idaho	A, B	■		■
College of Southern Idaho	C, A	■	■	
Idaho State University	C, A	■		■
Illinois				
College of DuPage	C, A	■	■	■
College of Lake County	C, A	■		■

State/School	Credentials Offered	Culinary Arts	Baking and Pastry	Management
Illinois (*continued*)				
The Cooking and Hospitality Institute of Chicago	A	■	■	
Elgin Community College	C, A	■	■	■
The Illinois Institute of Art–Chicago	C, A, B	■	■	■
Joliet Junior College	C, A	■	■	■
Kendall College	C, A, B	■	■	■
Lexington College	A, B			■
Lincoln Land Community College	C, A	■	■	■
Northwestern Business College	A			■
Parkland College	C, A			■
Rend Lake College	C, A	■		■
Robert Morris College	A, B	■		■
Southwestern Illinois College	C, A	■		■
Triton College	C, A	■	■	■
University of Illinois at Urbana–Champaign	B			■
Washburne Culinary Institute	C, A	■	■	
William Rainey Harper College	C, A	■	■	■
Wilton School of Cake Decorating and Confectionery Arts	C			
Indiana				
Ball State University	A, B			■
Indiana University–Purdue University Fort Wayne	A, B			■
Ivy Tech Community College–Central Indiana	C, A	■	■	■
Ivy Tech Community College–Northeast	A	■	■	
Ivy Tech Community College–Northwest	C, A	■	■	■

Credentials: **C** = *Certificate;* **D** = *Diploma;* **A** = *Associate Degree;* **B** = *Bachelor's Degree;* **M** = *Master's Degree;* **Ph.D.** = *Doctorate*
No credential or program information appears for apprenticeship programs.

State/School	Credentials Offered	Culinary Arts	Baking and Pastry	Management
Iowa				
Des Moines Area Community College	A	■		■
Iowa Lakes Community College	D, A			■
Iowa State University of Science and Technology	B, M, Ph.D.			■
Kirkwood Community College	C, D, A	■	■	■
Kansas				
American Institute of Baking	C		■	
Johnson County Community College	A			■
Johnson County Community College				
Johnson County Community College	A			■
Kansas City Kansas Area Technical School	C			■
Kansas State University	B, M, Ph.D.			■
Wichita Area Technical College	D, A			■
Kentucky				
Elizabethtown Community and Technical College	C, D	■		■
Jefferson Community and Technical College	C, A	■		■
Sullivan University	D, A, B	■	■	■
Western Kentucky University	B			■
Louisiana				
Culinary Institute of New Orleans	C, D, A	■	■	■
Delgado Community College				
Delgado Community College				
Delgado Community College	C, D, A	■	■	■
Elaine P. Nunez Community College	C, A	■		

State/School	Credentials Offered	Culinary Arts	Baking and Pastry	Management
Louisiana (*continued*)				
Louisiana Culinary Institute, LLC	A	■		
Louisiana Technical College–Baton Rouge Campus	C, D	■		
Louisiana Technical College–Jefferson Campus	D	■		
Louisiana Technical College–Lafayette Campus	D	■		
Louisiana Technical College–Sidney N. Collier Campus	C, D	■		
Louisiana Technical College–Sowela Campus	D	■		
Nicholls State University	A, B	■		
Sclafani Cooking School, Inc.	C	■	■	
Southern University at Shreveport	C, A			■
University of Louisiana at Lafayette	B			■
Maine				
Eastern Maine Community College	C, A	■		■
Southern Maine Community College	A	■		
York County Community College	C, A	■		■
Maryland				
Allegany College of Maryland	A	■	■	
Anne Arundel Community College	A		■	
Anne Arundel Community College				
Anne Arundel Community College	C, A	■	■	■
Baltimore International College	C, A, B	■	■	■
L'Academie de Cuisine	C	■	■	

*Credentials: **C** = Certificate; **D** = Diploma; **A** = Associate Degree; **B** = Bachelor's Degree; **M** = Master's Degree; **Ph.D.** = Doctorate*
No credential or program information appears for apprenticeship programs.

State/School	Credentials Offered	Culinary Arts	Baking and Pastry	Management
University of Maryland Eastern Shore	B			■
Wor-Wic Community College	C, A			■
Massachusetts				
Boston University	C, D, M	■		
Bristol Community College	A	■	■	
Bunker Hill Community College	C, A	■		
The Cambridge School of Culinary Arts	C, D	■		
Cape Cod Community College	C, A	■		■
Endicott College	B			■
International Institute of Culinary Arts	C, D	■	■	■
Massachusetts Culinary Association				
Massasoit Community College	C, A	■		
Middlesex Community College	C, A	■		■
Newbury College	C, A, B	■	■	■
North Shore Community College	C, A	■		
Michigan				
ACF Blue Water Chefs Association				
ACF Michigan Chefs de Cuisine Association				
Baker College of Muskegon	C, A, B	■	■	■
Central Michigan University	B			■
Ferris State University	C, A, B			■
Grand Rapids Community College	C, A	■	■	■
Henry Ford Community College	C, A	■	■	■
Macomb Community College	C, A	■	■	■
Michigan State University	B, M			■

State/School	Credentials Offered	Culinary Arts	Baking and Pastry	Management
Michigan (*continued*)				
Mott Community College	C, A	■	■	■
Northern Michigan University	A, B			■
Northwestern Michigan College	A	■		
Northwood University	A, B			■
Oakland Community College	C, A	■	■	■
Schoolcraft College	C, A	■	■	
Minnesota				
The Art Institutes International Minnesota	C, A, B	■	■	■
Hennepin Technical College	C, D, A	■		
Hibbing Community College	D, A	■		■
Le Cordon Bleu Minneapolis/St. Paul	A	■	■	
Normandale Community College	A			■
St. Cloud Technical College	D	■		
Saint Paul College–A Community & Technical College	C, D, A	■	■	
South Central College	D, A	■		■
University of Minnesota, Crookston	A, B			■
Mississippi				
Copiah-Lincoln Community College	C, A			■
East Mississippi Community College	A			■
Hinds Community College	A	■		■
Meridian Community College	A			■
Mississippi Gulf Coast Community College	D			■
Mississippi University for Women	C, B	■		

Credentials: C = Certificate; D = Diploma; A = Associate Degree; B = Bachelor's Degree; M = Master's Degree; Ph.D. = Doctorate
No credential or program information appears for apprenticeship programs.

State/School	Credentials Offered	Culinary Arts	Baking and Pastry	Management
Northeast Mississippi Community College	A			■
Missouri				
Chefs de Cuisine of St. Louis Association				
College of the Ozarks	B			■
Columbia Missouri Chapter ACF				
East Central College	C, A	■		
Missouri State University	B			■
Ozarks Technical Community College	A	■		■
Penn Valley Community College	A			
St. Louis Community College at Forest Park	C, A	■	■	■
Saint Louis University	B, M	■		
University of Central Missouri	B			■
University of Missouri– Columbia	B, M			■
Montana				
Flathead Valley Community College	C, A	■		■
The University of Montana– Missoula	C, A, B	■		■
Nebraska				
ACF Professional Chefs and Culinarians of the Heartland				
Central Community College– Hastings Campus	D, A	■		■
Metropolitan Community College	A	■	■	■
Southeast Community College, Lincoln Campus	A	■		■

State/School	Credentials Offered	Culinary Arts	Baking and Pastry	Management
Nevada				
The Art Institute of Las Vegas	D, A	■		
Community College of Southern Nevada	C, A	■	■	■
The Fraternity of Executive Chefs of Las Vegas				
High Sierra Chefs Association				
Truckee Meadows Community College	C, A	■	■	
University of Nevada, Las Vegas	B	■		■
New Hampshire				
ACF Greater North New Hampshire Chapter				
Atlantic Culinary Academy at McIntosh College	A	■		
New Hampshire Community Technical College	C, D, A	■		
Southern New Hampshire University	C, A, B, M	■	■	■
University of New Hampshire	A			■
New Jersey				
Atlantic Cape Community College	C, A	■	■	■
Bergen Community College	C, A	■		■
Brookdale Community College	C, A	■	■	
Burlington County College	C, A	■	■	■
County College of Morris	C, A	■		■
Culinary Education Center of Monmouth County	C, A	■	■	
Hudson County Community College	C, A	■	■	■
Middlesex County College	C, A	■		■
Morris County School of Technology	C	■		

*Credentials: **C** = Certificate; **D** = Diploma; **A** = Associate Degree; **B** = Bachelor's Degree; **M** = Master's Degree; **Ph.D.** = Doctorate*
No credential or program information appears for apprenticeship programs.

State/School	Credentials Offered	Culinary Arts	Baking and Pastry	Management
Technical Institute of Camden County	D	■		
Thomas Edison State College	A, B			■
Union County College	A			■
New Mexico				
Central New Mexico Community College	C, A	■	■	■
Culinary Business Academy	C			
Institute for Culinary Awakening	C	■		
New Mexico State University	B			■
Santa Fe Community College	C, A	■	■	■
Southwestern Indian Polytechnic Institute	C, A	■		■
New York				
The Art Institute of New York City	C, A	■	■	■
Broome Community College	C, A			■
Buffalo State College, State University of New York	C, B			■
Culinary Academy of Long Island	C	■	■	■
The Culinary Institute of America	A, B	■	■	■
Erie Community College, City Campus	C, A	■	■	
Erie Community College, North Campus	A	■		■
The French Culinary Institute at the International Culinary Center	C, D	■	■	
Fulton-Montgomery Community College	A			■
Genesee Community College	A			■

State/School	Credentials Offered	Culinary Arts	Baking and Pastry	Management
New York *(continued)*				
The Institute of Culinary Education	D	■	■	■
Julie Sahni's School of Indian Cooking	D	■		
Katharine Gibbs School	A			■
Keuka College	B			■
Mid–Hudson Culinary Association				
Mohawk Valley Community College	C, A	■		■
Monroe College	A, B	■		■
Monroe Community College	C, A			■
Nassau Community College	C, A			■
New York Institute of Technology	C, A, B	■	■	■
New York University	B, M, Ph.D.			■
Niagara County Community College	C, A	■	■	■
Niagara University	B			■
Onondaga Community College	C, A	■		■
Paul Smith's College of Arts and Sciences	C, A, B	■	■	■
Plattsburgh State University of New York	B			■
Rochester Institute of Technology	B, M			■
St. John's University	B			■
Schenectady County Community College	C, A	■		■
State University of New York College at Cobleskill	C, A, B	■		■
State University of New York College at Oneonta	B			■

*Credentials: **C** = Certificate; **D** = Diploma; **A** = Associate Degree; **B** = Bachelor's Degree; **M** = Master's Degree; **Ph.D.** = Doctorate*
No credential or program information appears for apprenticeship programs.

State/School	Credentials Offered	Culinary Arts	Baking and Pastry	Management
State University of New York College of Agriculture and Technology at Morrisville	A, B			■
State University of New York College of Technology at Alfred	A	■	■	■
State University of New York College of Technology at Delhi	A, B	■		■
Suffolk County Community College	A	■		
Sullivan County Community College	C, A	■		■
Syracuse University	B			■
Tompkins Cortland Community College	A			■
Westchester Community College	A			■
North Carolina				
ACF Sandhills/Cross Creek Chefs Association				
ACF Triad Chapter NC				
Alamance Community College	C, D, A	■		
The Art Institute of Charlotte	A, B	■		
Asheville-Buncombe Technical Community College	A	■	■	■
Central Piedmont Community College	C, D, A	■	■	■
East Carolina University	B, M			■
Guilford Technical Community College	C, D, A	■		
Johnson & Wales University	A, B	■	■	■
Sandhills Community College	A	■		■
Southwestern Community College	C, A	■		

State/School	Credentials Offered	Culinary Arts	Baking and Pastry	Management
North Carolina *(continued)*				
The University of North Carolina at Greensboro	B, M, Ph.D.			■
Wake Technical Community College	A	■		■
Wilkes Community College	C, A	■	■	
North Dakota				
Bismarck State College	C, A			■
North Dakota State College of Science	D, A			■
North Dakota State University	B			■
Ohio				
ACF Cleveland Chapter				
ACF Columbus Chapter				
The Art Institute of Ohio–Cincinnati	A	■		
Ashland University	B			■
Cincinnati State Technical and Community College	C, A	■		■
Columbus State Community College	C, A			■
Cuyahoga Community College, Metropolitan Campus	C, A	■		■
Hocking College	A	■		■
The Loretta Paganini School of Cooking	C, D	■	■	
Owens Community College	C, A	■		■
Sinclair Community College	C, A	■		■
The University of Akron	C, A	■		■
Zane State College	C, A	■		
Oklahoma				
Carl Albert State College	C, A			■
Great Plains Area Vocational Technical Center	C			

*Credentials: **C** = Certificate; **D** = Diploma; **A** = Associate Degree; **B** = Bachelor's Degree; **M** = Master's Degree; **Ph.D.** = Doctorate*
No credential or program information appears for apprenticeship programs.

State/School	Credentials Offered	Culinary Arts	Baking and Pastry	Management
Meridian Technology Center	C	■		
Metro Area Vocational Technical School District 22	C			■
Oklahoma State University, Okmulgee	A	■		
Oregon				
Central Oregon Community College	C, A	■		■
Chemeketa Community College	C, A			■
Lane Community College	C, A	■		■
Linn-Benton Community College	A			■
Oregon Coast Culinary Institute	A	■	■	■
Oregon Culinary Institute	D, A	■		
Southern Oregon University	B			■
Western Culinary Institute	D, A	■	■	■
Pennsylvania				
ACF Laurel Highlands Chapter				
The Art Institute of Philadelphia	D, A	■	■	
The Art Institute of Pittsburgh	D, A, B	■		■
The Art Institute Online	B	■		■
Bucks County Community College	C, A			■
Bucks County Community College				
Bucks County Community College	C, A	■	■	■
Central Pennsylvania College	A			■
Commonwealth Technical Institute	D, A	■		
Delaware County Community College	A			■
Drexel University	B	■		■

State/School	Credentials Offered	Culinary Arts	Baking and Pastry	Management
Pennsylvania *(continued)*				
Harrisburg Area Community College	C, D, A	■		■
Indiana University of Pennsylvania	C, B	■	■	■
JNA Institute of Culinary Arts	D, A	■		■
Keystone College	C, A	■		■
Lehigh Carbon Community College	C, A	■		■
Luzerne County Community College	C, D, A		■	■
Marywood University	C, B, M			■
Mercyhurst College	A, B	■		■
Northampton County Area Community College	D, A	■		■
Penn Foster Career School	A			■
Pennsylvania College of Technology	A, B	■	■	■
Pennsylvania Culinary Institute	A	■	■	■
The Restaurant School at Walnut Hill College	A, B	■	■	■
Seton Hill University	B			■
Westmoreland County Community College	C, A	■	■	■
Widener University	B, M			■
Winner Institute of Arts & Sciences Culinary Education	D	■		
Yorktowne Business Institute	C, D, A	■	■	■
YTI Career Institute	D, A	■	■	■
Rhode Island				
Johnson & Wales University	A, B, M	■	■	■
South Carolina				
The Culinary Institute of Charleston	C, D, A	■	■	■

*Credentials: **C** = Certificate; **D** = Diploma; **A** = Associate Degree; **B** = Bachelor's Degree; **M** = Master's Degree; **Ph.D.** = Doctorate*
No credential or program information appears for apprenticeship programs.

State/School	Credentials Offered	Culinary Arts	Baking and Pastry	Management
Greenville Technical College	C, A	■	■	■
Horry-Georgetown Technical College	C, A	■	■	
University of South Carolina	B, M			■
South Dakota				
Mitchell Technical Institute	D	■		
South Dakota State University	B, M, Ph.D.			■
Tennessee				
The Art Institute of Tennessee–Nashville	D, A, B	■	■	■
Gaylord Opryland Culinary Institute				
Nashville State Technical Community College	C, A	■		
Walters State Community College	C, A	■		■
Texas				
The Art Institute of Dallas	C, A	■		■
The Art Institute of Houston	D, A, B	■		■
Austin Community College	C, A	■		■
Central Texas College	C, A	■		■
Collin County Community College District	C, A	■		■
Culinary Academy of Austin, Inc.	C, D	■	■	
Culinary Institute Alain and Marie LeNôtre	D, A	■	■	
Del Mar College	C, A	■	■	■
El Paso Community College	C, A	■		■
Galveston College	C, A	■		■
Lamar University	C, B, M	■		■
Northwood University, Texas Campus	A, B			■
Odessa College	C, A	■		

State/School	Credentials Offered	Culinary Arts	Baking and Pastry	Management
Texas *(continued)*				
St. Philip's College	C, A	▪	▪	▪
San Jacinto College–Central Campus	C, A	▪		▪
South Texas College	C, A	▪		▪
Stephen F. Austin State University	B, M			▪
Texas A&M University–Kingsville	B			
Texas Culinary Academy	A	▪		
Texas State Technical College–Waco Campus	C, D, A	▪		▪
University of Houston	C, B, M			▪
University of North Texas	B, M			▪
Utah				
Salt Lake Community College	C, A			▪
Utah Valley State College	A	▪		
Vermont				
Champlain College	C, A, B			▪
Johnson State College	B			▪
New England Culinary Institute	C, A, B	▪	▪	▪
Virginia				
The Art Institute of Washington	A	▪		
James Madison University	B			▪
J. Sargeant Reynolds Community College	A	▪		▪
Norfolk State University	B			▪
Northern Virginia Community College	C, A	▪		▪
Stratford University	D, A, B	▪	▪	▪
Tidewater Community College	C, A	▪		▪
Virginia Intermont College	A, B	▪	▪	▪
Virginia State University	B			▪

*Credentials: **C** = Certificate; **D** = Diploma; **A** = Associate Degree; **B** = Bachelor's Degree; **M** = Master's Degree; **Ph.D.** = Doctorate*
No credential or program information appears for apprenticeship programs.

State/School	Credentials Offered	Culinary Arts	Baking and Pastry	Management
Washington				
The Art Institute of Seattle	D, A	■	■	
Bates Technical College	A	■		
Bellingham Technical College	C, A	■	■	
Clark College	C, A	■	■	■
Highline Community College	C, A			■
Lake Washington Technical College	C, A	■	■	
North Seattle Community College	C, A	■		■
Olympic College	C, A	■		
Seattle Central Community College	C, A	■		
South Puget Sound Community College	C, A		■	■
South Seattle Community College	C, A		■	■
Spokane Community College	C, A	■	■	■
Washington State University	B			■
West Virginia				
Mountain State University	A, B	■		
Shepherd University	C, A	■		
West Virginia Northern Community College	C, A	■		
Wisconsin				
ACF Chefs of Milwaukee, Inc.				
Blackhawk Technical College	C, A	■	■	
Fox Valley Technical College	C, A	■	■	■
Gateway Technical College	C, A	■		■
Madison Area Technical College	D, A	■	■	■
Milwaukee Area Technical College	D, A	■	■	■
Moraine Park Technical College	C, D, A	■	■	■

State/School	Credentials Offered	Culinary Arts	Baking and Pastry	Management
Wisconsin *(continued)* Nicolet Area Technical College	C, D, A	■	■	■
University of Wisconsin–Stout	B, M			■
Waukesha County Technical College	C, D, A	■	■	■
Wyoming				
Sheridan College	C, A	■		■

Credentials: ***C*** *= Certificate;* ***D*** *= Diploma;* ***A*** *= Associate Degree;* ***B*** *= Bachelor's Degree;* ***M*** *= Master's Degree;* ***Ph.D.*** *= Doctorate*
No credential or program information appears for apprenticeship programs.

CULINARY PROGRAMS AT-A-GLANCE—CANADA

School	Credentials Offered	Culinary Arts	Baking and Pastry	Management
The Art Institute of Vancouver	C, D	■	■	■
Canadore College of Applied Arts & Technology	C, D	■		■
Culinary Institute of Canada	C, D	■	■	
Dubrulle International Culinary & Hotel Institute of Canada	C, D, A	■	■	■
Humber College of Applied Arts & Technology	C, D	■		
Le Cordon Bleu Paris, Ottawa Culinary Arts Institute	C, D	■	■	
Liaison College	D			■
Malaspina University–College	C	■		
Mount Saint Vincent University	C, D, B			■
Niagara College Canada	C, D, B	■		■
Northern Alberta Institute of Technology	C, D	■	■	■
Northwest Culinary Academy of Vancouver	C, D	■	■	
Okanagan University College	C, D	■		
Pacific Institute of Culinary Arts	D	■	■	
St. Clair College of Applied Arts and Technology	C, D	■		■
Southern Alberta Institute of Technology	C			
Southern Alberta Institute of Technology				
Southern Alberta Institute of Technology	C, D	■	■	
Stratford Chefs School	D	■		
University of Guelph	B, M			■

*Credentials: **C** = Certificate; **D** = Diploma; **A** = Associate Degree; **B** = Bachelor's Degree; **M** = Master's Degree; **Ph.D.** = Doctorate*
No credential or program information appears for apprenticeship programs.

■ CULINARY PROGRAMS AT-A-GLANCE—INTERNATIONAL ■

Country/School	Credentials Offered	Culinary Arts	Baking and Pastry	Management
Australia				
Canberra Institute of Technology	C, D	■		■
Le Cordon Bleu Australia	C, D, B, M	■	■	■
Le Cordon Bleu Sydney Culinary Arts Institute	D	■	■	■
Finland				
Haaga Institute Polytechnic	B			■
France				
Ecole des Arts Culinaires et de l'Hôtellerie de Lyon	C, D, B, M	■		■
Ecole Supérieure de Cuisine Française Groupe Ferrandi	C	■	■	
Le Cordon Bleu	C, D	■	■	
Greece				
Alpine Center for Hotel & Tourism Management	C	■		■
Ireland				
Ballymaloe Cookery School	C	■		
Italy				
APICIUS–The Culinary Institute of Florence	C	■	■	■
The International Cooking School of Italian Food and Wine	C	■		
Italian Culinary Institute for Foreigners–USA	C, D	■		
Italian Food Artisans	C	■		
Italian Institute for Advanced Culinary and Pastry Arts	C	■		
Scoula di Arte Culinaria "Cordon Bleu"	C	■	■	

Credentials: *C* = Certificate; *D* = Diploma; *A* = Associate Degree; *B* = Bachelor's Degree; *M* = Master's Degree; **Ph.D.** = Doctorate
No credential or program information appears for apprenticeship programs.

Country/School	Credentials Offered	Culinary Arts	Baking and Pastry	Management
Japan				
Le Cordon Bleu Japan	C	■	■	
New Zealand				
The New Zealand School of Food and Wine	C	■		■
Peru				
Le Cordon Bleu Peru	D	■	■	■
Philippines				
Center for Culinary Arts, Manila	C, D	■	■	■
Republic of Korea				
Le Cordon Bleu Korea	C, D	■		
South Africa				
Christina Martin School of Food and Wine	C, D	■	■	
Switzerland				
DCT Hotel and Culinary Arts School, Switzerland	C, D	■	■	■
United Kingdom				
Cookery at the Grange	C	■		
Le Cordon Bleu–London Culinary Institute	C, D	■	■	
Leith's School of Food and Wine	C, D	■		
Rosie Davies	C	■		
Tante Marie School of Cookery	C, D	■		
Virgin Islands (British)				
New England Culinary Institute at H. Lavity Stoutt Community College	A	■		
Virgin Islands (U.S.)				
University of the Virgin Islands	A			■

PROFILES OF PROFESSIONAL PROGRAMS

ALABAMA

ALABAMA AGRICULTURAL AND MECHANICAL UNIVERSITY

Nutrition and Hospitality Management

Normal, Alabama

GENERAL INFORMATION
Public, coeducational, university. Urban campus. Founded in 1875. Accredited by Southern Association of Colleges and Schools.

PROGRAM INFORMATION
Offered since 1985. Accredited by American Dietetic Association. Program calendar is divided into semesters. 2-year master's degree in nutrition and hospitality management. 4-year bachelor's degree in hospitality management. 4-year bachelor's degree in general dietetics.

PROGRAM AFFILIATION
American Dietetic Association.

AREAS OF STUDY
Hospitality management; nutrition.

FACILITIES
Catering service; 2 laboratories; 2 lecture rooms; student lounge; teaching kitchen; delicatessen; kiosk breakfast.

STUDENT PROFILE
46 total: 43 full-time; 3 part-time.

FACULTY
5 total: 3 full-time; 2 part-time. 1 is a master baker; 1 is a culinary-certified teacher. Prominent faculty: Mrs. Ann Warren, MS, RD, LD; Dr. Johnson Kamalu; Nahid Sistani, PhD, RD, LD; Dr. Ola Goode Sanders. Faculty-student ratio: 1:12.

TYPICAL EXPENSES
Application fee: $10. In-state tuition: $118 per credit hour part-time. Out-of-state tuition: $236 per credit hour part-time. Program-related fee includes $20 for lab fees per course.

FINANCIAL AID
In 2004, 1 scholarship was awarded (award was $750). Employment placement assistance is available. Employment opportunities within the program are available.

HOUSING
Apartment-style and single-sex housing available. Average off-campus housing cost per month: $400–$665.

APPLICATION INFORMATION
Students may begin participation in January, June, and August. Application deadline for fall is July 15. Application deadline for spring is December 1. Application deadline for summer is May 15. In 2004, 5 applied; 5 were accepted. Applicants must have high school diploma.

CONTACT
Ann D. Warren, Coordinator, Nutrition and Hospitality Management, PO Box 232, Normal, AL 35762. Telephone: 256-858-4103. Fax: 256-858-5433. E-mail: ann.warren@ email.aamu.edu. World Wide Web: http://www.aamu.edu.

BISHOP STATE COMMUNITY COLLEGE

Commercial Food Service

Mobile, Alabama

GENERAL INFORMATION
Public, coeducational, two-year college. Suburban campus. Founded in 1965. Accredited by Southern Association of Colleges and Schools.

PROGRAM INFORMATION
Offered since 1965. Accredited by American Culinary Federation Accrediting Commission. Program calendar is divided into semesters. 18-month certificate in commercial food service. 2-year associate degree in commercial food service.

PROGRAM AFFILIATION
American Culinary Federation.

AREAS OF STUDY
Baking; beverage management; buffet catering; controlling costs in food service; convenience cookery; culinary French; culinary skill development; food preparation; food purchasing; food service communication; food service math; garde-manger; international cuisine; introduction to food service; kitchen management; management and human resources; meal planning; meat cutting; meat fabrication; menu and facilities design; nutrition; patisserie; restaurant opportunities; sanitation; saucier; seafood processing; soup, stock, sauce, and starch production; wines and spirits.

FACILITIES
Bake shop; cafeteria; catering service; classroom; computer laboratory; demonstration laboratory; food production kitchen; laboratory; learning resource center; lecture room; library.

Bishop State Community College *(continued)*

TYPICAL STUDENT PROFILE
63 full-time.

FINANCIAL AID
Employment placement assistance is available.

APPLICATION INFORMATION
Students may begin participation in January, May, and August. Applications are accepted continuously. Applicants must have a high school diploma or GED.

CONTACT
Director of Admissions, Commercial Food Service, 414 Stanton Street, Mobile, AL 36617. Telephone: 251-662-5372. Fax: 251-471-5961. World Wide Web: http://www.bishop.edu/techcarv.htm.

CULINARD–THE CULINARY INSTITUTE OF VIRGINIA COLLEGE

Culinary Arts

Birmingham, Alabama

GENERAL INFORMATION
Private, coeducational, four-year college. Urban campus. Founded in 1989. Accredited by Accrediting Council for Independent Colleges and Schools.

PROGRAM INFORMATION
Offered since 2000. Accredited by American Culinary Federation Accrediting Commission. Program calendar is divided into quarters. 18-month diploma in culinary arts (weekend program). 21-month occupational associate in culinary arts. 24-month occupational associate in pastry, baking, and confectionary arts. 4-year bachelor's degree in culinary arts management. 50-week diploma in pastry, baking, and confectionary arts.

PROGRAM AFFILIATION
American Culinary Federation; American Institute of Baking; American Institute of Wine & Food; Chefs Collaborative 2000; Confrerie de la Chaine des Rotisseurs; Council on Hotel, Restaurant, and Institutional Education; International Association of Culinary Professionals; International Food Service Executives Association; James Beard Foundation, Inc.; National Restaurant Association; National Restaurant Association Educational Foundation; Research Chefs Association; Retailer's Bakery Association; Southern Foodways Alliance; The Bread Bakers Guild of America; U.S. Pastry Alliance; Women Chefs and Restaurateurs; Women's Foodservice Forum.

AREAS OF STUDY
Baking; beverage management; buffet catering; confectionary show pieces; controlling costs in food service; convenience cookery; culinary French; culinary skill development; food preparation; food purchasing; food service communication; food service math; garde-manger; international cuisine; kitchen management; management and human resources; meal planning; meat cutting; meat fabrication; menu and facilities design; nutrition; nutrition and food service; patisserie; restaurant opportunities; sanitation; saucier; seafood processing; soup, stock, sauce, and starch production; wines and spirits.

FACILITIES
Bake shop; bakery; catering service; 10 classrooms; 5 computer laboratories; demonstration laboratory; food production kitchen; garden; gourmet dining room; learning resource center; 10 lecture rooms; library; public restaurant; student lounge; 5 teaching kitchens.

STUDENT PROFILE
400 full-time. 160 are under 25 years old; 197 are between 25 and 44 years old; 43 are over 44 years old.

FACULTY
18 total: 15 full-time; 3 part-time. 17 are industry professionals; 1 is a culinary-certified teacher; 1 is a certified sanitarian; 1 registered dietitian. Prominent faculty: Antony Osborne; Melinda Rice, BS; Jerome Queyriaux; John Wilson. Faculty-student ratio: 1:16.

SPECIAL PROGRAMS
Student hot food competitions, student Knowledge Bowl competitions, student externships.

TYPICAL EXPENSES
Application fee: $100. Tuition: $34,450 per culinary arts degree; $38,450 per pastry, baking, and confectionary arts degree full-time, $325 per credit hour part-time. Program-related fees include $995 for cutlery tool kit and uniforms; $130 for supplement fee for baking program tools.

FINANCIAL AID
In 2005, 5 scholarships were awarded (average award was $1000). Employment placement assistance is available. Employment opportunities within the program are available.

HOUSING
Average off-campus housing cost per month: $450.

APPLICATION INFORMATION
Students may begin participation in January, February, April, May, July, August, October, and November. Applications are accepted continuously. Applicants must interview; submit a formal application, letters of reference, and an essay.

CONTACT
Mr. Joe Rogalski, Director of Admissions, Culinary Arts, 65 Bagby Drive, Birmingham, AL 35209. Telephone: 205-802-1200. Fax: 205-802-7045. E-mail: jrogalski@vc.edu, admissions@vc.edu. World Wide Web: http://www.culinard.com.

See color display following page 92.

THE GULF COAST CULINARY INSTITUTE

James H. Faulkner State Community College
Hospitality Management Services

Gulf Shores, Alabama

GENERAL INFORMATION
Public, coeducational, two-year college. Urban campus. Founded in 1965. Accredited by Southern Association of Colleges and Schools.

PROGRAM INFORMATION
Offered since 1994. Accredited by American Culinary Federation Accrediting Commission, Council on Hotel, Restaurant and Institutional Education. Program calendar is divided into semesters. 1-year certificate in dietary management. 1-year certificate in pastry/baking. 1-year certificate in condominium/resort management. 1-year certificate in hotel/restaurant management. 1-year certificate in culinary arts. 2-year associate degree in dietary management. 2-year associate degree in pastry/baking. 2-year associate degree in condominium/resort management. 2-year associate degree in hotel/restaurant management. 2-year associate degree in food service management. 2-year associate degree in culinary arts. 3-year associate degree in pastry/baking apprenticeship. 3-year associate degree in culinary arts apprenticeship.

PROGRAM AFFILIATION
American Culinary Federation; American Institute of Baking; American Wine Society; Confrerie de la Chaine des Rotisseurs; Council on Hotel, Restaurant, and Institutional Education; National Restaurant Association; National Restaurant Association Educational Foundation; Retailer's Bakery Association; Society of Wine Educators.

AREAS OF STUDY
Baking; beverage management; cake decorating; confectionery show pieces; controlling costs in food service; culinary French; culinary skill development; food preparation; food purchasing; food service math; garde-manger; international cuisine; introduction to food service; management and human resources; meal planning; meat cutting; meat fabrication; menu and facilities design; nutrition; patisserie; sanitation; saucier; seafood processing; soup, stock, sauce, and starch production; spices and aromatics; wines and spirits.

FACILITIES
Bakery; 4 classrooms; computer laboratory; 2 demonstration laboratories; food production kitchen; garden; gourmet dining room; 2 laboratories; learning resource center; 2 lecture rooms; library; 2 student lounges; teaching kitchen.

Enjoy the pristine beaches of the Gulf of Mexico as you study to be a chef with a program accredited by the American Culinary Federation and the Council on Hotel/Restaurant and Institutional Education. State-of-the-art facilities, outstanding faculty, and required, paid internships all at a fraction of the cost of most culinary schools.

www.gulfcoastculinaryinstitute.com

The Gulf Coast Culinary Institute *(continued)*

STUDENT PROFILE

155 total: 120 full-time; 35 part-time. 60 are under 25 years old; 44 are between 25 and 44 years old; 16 are over 44 years old.

FACULTY

12 total: 3 full-time; 9 part-time. 7 are industry professionals; 5 are culinary-certified teachers. Prominent faculty: Ron Koetter, CEC, CCE, AAC; Jim Hurtubise, CWPC; Edward Bushaw, CHA, CFBE. Faculty-student ratio: 1:15.

SPECIAL PROGRAMS

Culinary competitions, 2-year paid internship.

TYPICAL EXPENSES

In-state tuition: $93 per semester hour. Out-of-state tuition: $186 per semester hour. Program-related fees include $200 for cutlery; $80 for uniform.

FINANCIAL AID

In 2005, 6 scholarships were awarded (average award was $1000). Program-specific awards include American Culinary Federation scholarship $5000, Alabama Hospitality Association $5000. Employment placement assistance is available. Employment opportunities within the program are available.

HOUSING

Coed housing available. Average on-campus housing cost per month: $380. Average off-campus housing cost per month: $400.

APPLICATION INFORMATION

Students may begin participation in January, May, and August. Applications are accepted continuously. In 2005, 75 applied; 75 were accepted. Applicants must submit a formal application.

CONTACT

Edward Bushaw, Director, James H. Faulkner State Community College Hospitality Management Services, 3301 Gulf Shores Parkway, Gulf Shores, AL 36542. Telephone: 251-968-3103. Fax: 251-968-3120. E-mail: ebushaw@ faulknerstate.edu. World Wide Web: http://www. gulfcoastculinaryinstitute.com.

JEFFERSON STATE COMMUNITY COLLEGE

Hospitality Management Division

Birmingham, Alabama

GENERAL INFORMATION

Public, coeducational, two-year college. Suburban campus. Founded in 1965. Accredited by Southern Association of Colleges and Schools.

PROGRAM INFORMATION

Offered since 1988. Accredited by American Culinary Federation Accrediting Commission. Program calendar is divided into semesters. 1-year certificate in food service management. 2-year associate degree in hotel/motel management. 2-year associate degree in culinary arts. 2-year associate degree in food service management.

PROGRAM AFFILIATION

American Culinary Federation; Confrerie de la Chaine des Rotisseurs.

AREAS OF STUDY

Baking; beverage management; buffet catering; confectionery show pieces; controlling costs in food service; convenience cookery; culinary French; culinary skill development; food preparation; food purchasing; food service communication; food service math; garde-manger; introduction to food service; kitchen management; management and human resources; meal planning; meat cutting; meat fabrication; nutrition; patisserie; sanitation; saucier; seafood processing; soup, stock, sauce, and starch production; wines and spirits.

FACILITIES

Bake shop; classroom; computer laboratory; demonstration laboratory; 2 food production kitchens; gourmet dining room; laboratory; learning resource center; library; snack shop; student lounge.

TYPICAL STUDENT PROFILE

60 total: 35 full-time; 25 part-time. 33 are under 25 years old; 20 are between 25 and 44 years old; 7 are over 44 years old.

SPECIAL PROGRAMS

3-year culinary apprenticeship leading to certification with American Culinary Federation.

FINANCIAL AID

Employment placement assistance is available. Employment opportunities within the program are available.

APPLICATION INFORMATION

Students may begin participation in January and August. Applications are accepted continuously. Applicants must submit a formal application, an essay, and letters of reference.

CONTACT

Director of Admissions, Hospitality Management Division, 2601 Carson Road, Birmingham, AL 35215-3098. Telephone: 205-856-7898. Fax: 205-815-8499. World Wide Web: http://www.jscc.cc.al.us/.

LAWSON STATE COMMUNITY COLLEGE

Commercial Food Services/Culinary Arts

Birmingham, Alabama

GENERAL INFORMATION
Public, coeducational, two-year college. Small-town setting. Founded in 1949. Accredited by Southern Association of Colleges and Schools.

PROGRAM INFORMATION
Program calendar is divided into semesters. 2-semester certificate in commercial foods.

AREAS OF STUDY
Baking; buffet catering; controlling costs in food service; culinary skill development; food preparation; food purchasing; food service communication; introduction to food service; kitchen management; meal planning; meat fabrication; menu and facilities design; nutrition; sanitation; soup, stock, sauce, and starch production.

FACILITIES
Classroom; computer laboratory; demonstration laboratory; learning resource center; lecture room; library; public restaurant; snack shop; student lounge; teaching kitchen.

TYPICAL STUDENT PROFILE
25 total: 19 full-time; 6 part-time.

SPECIAL PROGRAMS
Culinary competitions.

FINANCIAL AID
Employment placement assistance is available. Employment opportunities within the program are available.

APPLICATION INFORMATION
Students may begin participation in January, June, and August. Application deadline for fall is August 27. Application deadline for spring is January 1. Applicants must submit a formal application.

CONTACT
Director of Admissions, Commercial Food Services/ Culinary Arts, 3060 Wilson Road, SW, Birmingham, AL 35221-1798. Telephone: 205-929-6378. Fax: 205-929-6362. World Wide Web: http://www.ls.cc.al.us.

TUSKEGEE UNIVERSITY

Tuskegee, Alabama

GENERAL INFORMATION
Private, coeducational, comprehensive institution. Small-town setting. Founded in 1881. Accredited by Southern Association of Colleges and Schools.

PROGRAM INFORMATION
Accredited by American Dietetic Association. Program calendar is divided into semesters. 4-year bachelor's degree in hospitality management.

PROGRAM AFFILIATION
American Dietetic Association.

AREAS OF STUDY
Nutrition.

FACILITIES
Bake shop; bakery; cafeteria; catering service; classroom; coffee shop; computer laboratory; demonstration laboratory; food production kitchen; garden; gourmet dining room; laboratory; learning resource center; lecture room; library; public restaurant; snack shop; student lounge; teaching kitchen; vineyard.

STUDENT PROFILE
13 total: 11 full-time; 2 part-time. 10 are under 25 years old; 3 are between 25 and 44 years old.

FACULTY
2 total: 2 full-time. 2 are culinary-certified teachers. Faculty-student ratio: 1:7.

TYPICAL EXPENSES
Tuition: $5845 per semester full-time, $480 per per credit hour part-time. Program-related fee includes $100 for technology (per semester).

FINANCIAL AID
Employment placement assistance is available.

HOUSING
Apartment-style and single-sex housing available. Average on-campus housing cost per month: $400.

APPLICATION INFORMATION
Students may begin participation in January, June, and August. Applications are accepted continuously. Applicants must interview; submit a formal application and an essay.

CONTACT
Robert L. Laney, Vice President/Director of Admissions and Enrollment Management, Old Administration Building, Suite 101, Tuskegee, AL 36088-1920. Telephone: 334-727-8500. Fax: 334-727-4402. E-mail: moore@tuskegee.edu. World Wide Web: http://www.tuskegee.edu.

THE UNIVERSITY OF ALABAMA

Restaurant and Hospitality Management

Tuscaloosa, Alabama

GENERAL INFORMATION
Public, coeducational, university. Suburban campus. Founded in 1831. Accredited by Southern Association of Colleges and Schools.

The University of Alabama *(continued)*

PROGRAM INFORMATION
Offered since 1986. Accredited by American Association of Family and Consumer Sciences. Program calendar is divided into semesters. 4-year bachelor's degree in restaurant and hospitality management.

PROGRAM AFFILIATION
American Dietetic Association; American Hotel and Lodging Association; Council on Hotel, Restaurant, and Institutional Education; National Restaurant Association; National Restaurant Association Educational Foundation.

AREAS OF STUDY
Baking; beverage management; buffet catering; controlling costs in food service; convenience cookery; food preparation; food purchasing; food service communication; food service math; introduction to food service; kitchen management; management and human resources; meal planning; menu and facilities design; nutrition and food service; restaurant opportunities; sanitation; soup, stock, sauce, and starch production; wines and spirits.

FACILITIES
2 classrooms; 2 computer laboratories; food production kitchen; learning resource center; library; public restaurant; food science laboratory; 2 multimedia rooms.

TYPICAL STUDENT PROFILE
114 full-time. 110 are under 25 years old; 4 are between 25 and 44 years old.

SPECIAL PROGRAMS
Practicum in hospitality management (1000 hours) or internship in hospitality management (400–600 hours).

HOUSING
Coed, apartment-style, and single-sex housing available.

APPLICATION INFORMATION
Students may begin participation in January and August. Applications are accepted continuously.

CONTACT
Director of Admissions, Restaurant and Hospitality Management, Box 870158, Tuscaloosa, AL 35487. Telephone: 205-348-9147. Fax: 205-348-3789. World Wide Web: http://www.ches.ua.edu/RHM/.

WALLACE STATE COMMUNITY COLLEGE

Commercial Foods and Nutrition

Hanceville, Alabama

GENERAL INFORMATION
Public, coeducational, two-year college. Rural campus. Founded in 1966. Accredited by Southern Association of Colleges and Schools.

PROGRAM INFORMATION
Offered since 1973. Program calendar is divided into semesters. 18-month diploma in commercial foods and nutrition.

AREAS OF STUDY
Baking; buffet catering; controlling costs in food service; convenience cookery; food preparation; food purchasing; food service communication; food service math; introduction to food service; kitchen management; meal planning; nutrition and food service; sanitation.

FACILITIES
Cafeteria; catering service; 2 classrooms; 3 computer laboratories; demonstration laboratory; food production kitchen; 3 gourmet dining rooms; laboratory; learning resource center; lecture room; library; public restaurant; snack shop; 3 student lounges; teaching kitchen.

TYPICAL STUDENT PROFILE
18 full-time.

FINANCIAL AID
Employment placement assistance is available. Employment opportunities within the program are available.

HOUSING
Apartment-style and single-sex housing available.

APPLICATION INFORMATION
Students may begin participation in January, June, and September. Applications are accepted continuously. Applicants must submit a formal application.

CONTACT
Director of Admissions, Commercial Foods and Nutrition, PO Box 2000, Hanceville, AL 35077-2000. Telephone: 256-352-8227. Fax: 256-352-8228.

ALASKA

ALASKA VOCATIONAL TECHNICAL CENTER

Culinary Arts and Sciences Department

Seward, Alaska

GENERAL INFORMATION
Public, coeducational institution. Rural campus. Founded in 1969. Accredited by Council on Occupational Education.

PROGRAM INFORMATION
Offered since 1972. Accredited by American Culinary Federation Accrediting Commission. 302-training day certificate in professional cooking and baking.

PROGRAM AFFILIATION
American Culinary Federation; National Restaurant Association; National Restaurant Association Educational Foundation.

AREAS OF STUDY
Baking; beverage management; buffet catering; confectionery show pieces; controlling costs in food service; culinary skill development; food preparation; food purchasing; food service math; garde-manger; international cuisine; introduction to food service; kitchen management; management and human resources; meal planning; meat cutting; meat fabrication; menu and facilities design; nutrition; nutrition and food service; patisserie; sanitation; saucier; soup, stock, sauce, and starch production; wines and spirits.

FACILITIES
Bakery; cafeteria; classroom; computer laboratory; food production kitchen; learning resource center; library; public restaurant; teaching kitchen.

TYPICAL STUDENT PROFILE
70 total: 20 full-time; 50 part-time.

FINANCIAL AID
Employment placement assistance is available. Employment opportunities within the program are available.

HOUSING
Coed and apartment-style housing available.

APPLICATION INFORMATION
Students may begin participation in August and October. Applications are accepted continuously. Applicants must have high school diploma or GED, be 18 years of age, and meet physical requirements for program.

CONTACT
Director of Admissions, Culinary Arts and Sciences Department, PO Box 889, 809 2nd Avenue, Seward, AK 99664. Telephone: 800-478-5389. Fax: 907-224-4143. World Wide Web: http://www.avtec.alaska.edu.

UNIVERSITY OF ALASKA ANCHORAGE

Division of Culinary Arts and Hospitality

Anchorage, Alaska

GENERAL INFORMATION
Public, coeducational, comprehensive institution. Suburban campus. Founded in 1954. Accredited by Northwest Association of Schools and Colleges.

PROGRAM INFORMATION
Offered since 1972. Accredited by American Dietetic Association. Program calendar is divided into semesters. 1-year certificate in culinary arts. 2-semester certificate in dietary management. 2-year associate degree in culinary arts. 4-year bachelor's degree in hospitality and restaurant management.

PROGRAM AFFILIATION
American Culinary Federation; American Dietetic Association; Council on Hotel, Restaurant, and Institutional Education; Dietary Managers Association; Institute of Food Technologists; International Association of Culinary Professionals; National Association of Catering Executives; National Restaurant Association; National Restaurant Association Educational Foundation.

AREAS OF STUDY
Baking; beverage management; buffet catering; controlling costs in food service; culinary French; culinary skill development; food preparation; food purchasing; food service math; garde-manger; kitchen management; management and human resources; meal planning; meat cutting; meat fabrication; menu and facilities design; nutrition; patisserie; restaurant opportunities; sanitation; saucier; seafood processing; soup, stock, sauce, and starch production; wines and spirits.

FACILITIES
Bake shop; 3 classrooms; computer laboratory; demonstration laboratory; 2 food production kitchens; garden; gourmet dining room; learning resource center; lecture room; library; public restaurant; 3 teaching kitchens.

STUDENT PROFILE
455 total: 390 full-time; 65 part-time. 25 are under 25 years old; 50 are between 25 and 44 years old; 25 are over 44 years old.

FACULTY
11 total: 6 full-time; 5 part-time. 4 are industry professionals; 1 is a culinary-certified teacher; 5 are registered dietitians. Prominent faculty: Timothy Doebler, CCE, MS; Dr. Anne Bridges, RD, MS, Ed; Carrie Benton, RD, LD, MS. Faculty-student ratio: 1:20.

SPECIAL PROGRAMS
2 semesters of study at either University of Nevada, Las Vegas or Northern Arizona University for students in bachelor's program (required), 1800-hour internship (required for registered dietitians).

University of Alaska Anchorage *(continued)*

TYPICAL EXPENSES
Application fee: $40. In-state tuition: $84 per credit. Out-of-state tuition: $256 per credit. Program-related fees include $350 for cutlery, uniforms; $50 for lab fee; $50 for meat fabrication course; $90 for grocery items.

FINANCIAL AID
In 2004, 7 scholarships were awarded (average award was $3000). Program-specific awards include In house scholarship opportunities. Employment placement assistance is available. Employment opportunities within the program are available.

HOUSING
Coed, apartment-style, and single-sex housing available. Average off-campus housing cost per month: $700.

APPLICATION INFORMATION
Students may begin participation in January and August. Application deadline for fall is June 1. Application deadline for spring is September 1. In 2004, 68 applied. Applicants must submit a formal application and have high school diploma or GED; minimum age 18.

CONTACT
Timothy Doebler, Director, Division of Culinary Arts and Hospitality, 3211 Providence Drive, Cuddy Hall, Anchorage, AK 99508. Telephone: 907-786-4728. Fax: 907-786-1402. E-mail: aftwd@uaa.alaska.edu. World Wide Web: http://www.uaa.alaska.edu.

UNIVERSITY OF ALASKA FAIRBANKS

Culinary Arts

Fairbanks, Alaska

GENERAL INFORMATION
Public, coeducational, university. Suburban campus. Founded in 1917. Accredited by Northwest Association of Schools and Colleges.

PROGRAM INFORMATION
Offered since 1986. Program calendar is divided into semesters. 1-year certificate in culinary arts. 1-year certificate in cooking. 1-year certificate in baking. 2-year associate degree in culinary arts.

PROGRAM AFFILIATION
American Culinary Federation; International Association of Culinary Professionals; International Food Service Executives Association; National Restaurant Association; National Restaurant Association Educational Foundation.

AREAS OF STUDY
Baking; buffet catering; confectionery show pieces; controlling costs in food service; convenience cookery; culinary French; culinary skill development; food preparation; food purchasing; food service math; garde-

manger; international cuisine; introduction to food service; kitchen management; meal planning; meat cutting; meat fabrication; nutrition; patisserie; sanitation; saucier; seafood processing; soup, stock, sauce, and starch production; wines and spirits.

FACILITIES
Cafeteria; 2 classrooms; food production kitchen; student lounge; teaching kitchen.

TYPICAL STUDENT PROFILE
185 total: 45 full-time; 140 part-time.

FINANCIAL AID
Employment placement assistance is available. Employment opportunities within the program are available.

HOUSING
Coed housing available.

APPLICATION INFORMATION
Students may begin participation in January and September. Applications are accepted continuously. Applicants must submit a formal application.

CONTACT
Director of Admissions, Culinary Arts, 604 Barnette Street, Fairbanks, AK 99701. Telephone: 907-455-2800. Fax: 907-455-2828. World Wide Web: http://www.tvc.uaf.edu.

ARIZONA

ARIZONA CULINARY INSTITUTE

Scottsdale, Arizona

GENERAL INFORMATION
Private, coeducational, culinary institute. Suburban campus. Founded in 2001.

PROGRAM INFORMATION
Offered since 2001. Program calendar is continuous. 9-month diploma in culinary arts, baking, and restaurant management.

PROGRAM AFFILIATION
American Culinary Federation; American Institute of Wine & Food; International Association of Culinary Professionals; National Association of Catering Executives; National Restaurant Association; National Restaurant Association Educational Foundation; Society of Wine Educators.

AREAS OF STUDY
Baking; beverage management; confectionery show pieces; controlling costs in food service; culinary French; culinary skill development; food preparation; food purchasing; food service math; garde-manger; international cuisine; introduction to food service; kitchen management; management and human resources; meat cutting; meat

PROFESSIONAL **CHEF** TRAINING

- A complete and well-balanced nine-month diploma program

- Small classes average 10-16 students per kitchen

- Founded and operated by experienced culinary educators

- New facility with five kitchens and student run restaurant

- Job placement

- Financial Aid *if qualified*

Arizona Culinary Institute

Scottsdale, Arizona

Call Toll Free
866-294-2433
www.azculinary.com

10585 North 114th Street
Suite 401
Scottsdale, Arizona 85259
480-603-1066

Arizona Culinary Institute *(continued)*

fabrication; menu and facilities design; nutrition; patisserie; restaurant opportunities; sanitation; saucier; soup, stock, sauce, and starch production; wines and spirits.

FACILITIES
2 bakeries; 3 classrooms; computer laboratory; 3 food production kitchens; gourmet dining room; learning resource center; 2 lecture rooms; library; public restaurant; student lounge; 5 teaching kitchens.

STUDENT PROFILE
210 full-time. 95 are under 25 years old; 86 are between 25 and 44 years old; 29 are over 44 years old.

FACULTY
12 total: 11 full-time; 1 part-time. 10 are industry professionals; 2 are culinary-certified teachers. Prominent faculty: Jennifer Sedig; Glenn Humphrey, CEC, CCE; Michael Dudley; Jason Warden. Faculty-student ratio: 1:8.

SPECIAL PROGRAMS
3-month paid internship.

TYPICAL EXPENSES
Application fee: $25. Tuition: $21,810 per diploma. Program-related fee includes $1605 for knives, books, uniforms, supplies.

FINANCIAL AID
In 2004, 15 scholarships were awarded (average award was $500); 140 loans were granted (average loan was $20,000). Employment placement assistance is available. Employment opportunities within the program are available.

HOUSING
Average off-campus housing cost per month: $400–$700.

APPLICATION INFORMATION
Students may begin participation in January, February, April, May, July, August, September, and November. Applications are accepted continuously. In 2004, 310 applied; 210 were accepted. Applicants must submit a formal application, an essay, high school diploma/GED.

CONTACT
Admissions Director, 10585 North 114th Street, Suite 401, Scottsdale, AZ 85259. Telephone: 480-603-1066. Fax: 480-603-1067. E-mail: info@azculinary.com. World Wide Web: http://www.azculinary.com.

See display on page 73.

ARIZONA WESTERN COLLEGE

Culinary Arts/Hospitality and Dietary Management Program

Yuma, Arizona

GENERAL INFORMATION
Public, coeducational, two-year college. Rural campus. Founded in 1962. Accredited by North Central Association of Colleges and Schools.

PROGRAM INFORMATION
Offered since 1996. Accredited by Dietary Manager Program accredited by Dietary Managers Association. Program calendar is divided into semesters. 2-semester certificate in dietary manager. 2-semester certificate in culinary arts. 2-year associate degree in hotel/restaurant management.

PROGRAM AFFILIATION
American Dietetic Association; Dietary Managers Association.

AREAS OF STUDY
Baking; food preparation; food purchasing; garde-manger; international cuisine; management and human resources; meal planning; nutrition; restaurant opportunities; sanitation; soup, stock, sauce, and starch production.

FACILITIES
Classroom; computer laboratory; food production kitchen; gourmet dining room; learning resource center; lecture room; library.

STUDENT PROFILE
15 total: 10 full-time; 5 part-time. 10 are under 25 years old; 3 are between 25 and 44 years old; 2 are over 44 years old.

FACULTY
4 total: 1 full-time; 3 part-time. 3 are industry professionals; 1 is a registered dietitian. Prominent faculty: Nancy L. Meister, RD, MPH; Ross Smith; Bill Pike; Valerie Cook, CDM. Faculty-student ratio: 1:15.

SPECIAL PROGRAMS
Placement in local restaurants for field experience, placement in local extended-care facilities for institutional food experience.

TYPICAL EXPENSES
In-state tuition: $456 per semester full-time (in district), $38 per credit hour part-time. Out-of-state tuition: $2736 per semester full-time, $44 per credit hour (under 6 hours) part-time. Program-related fees include $340 for lab food fees; $600 for books; $40 for uniforms.

FINANCIAL AID
Employment placement assistance is available.

HOUSING

Coed housing available. Average off-campus housing cost per month: $450.

APPLICATION INFORMATION

Students may begin participation in January and August. Application deadline for spring is January 15. Application deadline for fall is August 15. In 2004, 15 applied; 15 were accepted. Applicants must submit a formal application and an essay.

CONTACT

Nancy L. Meister, Coordinator, Culinary Arts/Hospitality and Dietary Management Program, PO Box 929, Yuma, AZ 85366. Telephone: 928-344-7779. Fax: 928-317-6119. E-mail: nancy.meister@azwestern.edu. World Wide Web: http://www.azwestern.edu.

THE ART INSTITUTE OF PHOENIX

Phoenix, Arizona

GENERAL INFORMATION

Private, coeducational, four-year college. Urban campus. Founded in 1995. Accredited by Accrediting Council for Independent Colleges and Schools.

PROGRAM INFORMATION

Offered since 1996. Accredited by Associate Degree Program is ACF accredited (American Culinary Federation). Program calendar is divided into quarters. 12-quarter bachelor's degree in culinary arts. 3-quarter diploma in baking and pastry. 3-quarter diploma in art of cooking. 6-8-quarter associate degree in culinary arts.

PROGRAM AFFILIATION

American Culinary Federation; Arizona Women in Food and Wine; Confrerie de la Chaine des Rotisseurs; International Association of Culinary Professionals; National Restaurant Association; National Restaurant Association Educational Foundation; Society of Wine Educators; Women Chefs and Restaurateurs.

AREAS OF STUDY

Baking; beverage management; buffet catering; confectionery show pieces; controlling costs in food service; convenience cookery; culinary French; culinary skill development; food preparation; food purchasing; food service communication; food service math; garde-manger; international cuisine; introduction to food service; kitchen management; management and human resources; meal planning; meat cutting; meat fabrication; menu and facilities design; nutrition; nutrition and food service; patisserie; restaurant opportunities; sanitation; saucier; seafood processing; soup, stock, sauce, and starch production; wines and spirits.

FACILITIES

Bakery; 11 computer laboratories; 2 food production kitchens; learning resource center; 24 lecture rooms; library; public restaurant; student lounge; 3 teaching kitchens.

STUDENT PROFILE

124 total: 25 full-time; 99 part-time.

FACULTY

12 total: 9 full-time; 3 part-time. 12 are industry professionals; 2 are master chefs; 9 are culinary-certified teachers. Prominent faculty: Walter Leible, CMC; Bill Sy, MBA, CEC, CMC-China; Joseph La Villa, PhD, CEC, Certified Sommelier. Faculty-student ratio: 1:20.

SPECIAL PROGRAMS

Culinary competitions, ACF sanitation, nutrition, and management certification training, C-cap teacher and consumer workshops.

TYPICAL EXPENSES

Application fee: $150. Tuition: $387 per per credit hour full-time, $387 per per credit hour part-time. Program-related fees include $890 for supply kit (associate degree); $880 for supply kit (diploma program); $890 for supply kit (bachelor program).

FINANCIAL AID

In 2005, 20 scholarships were awarded. Employment placement assistance is available. Employment opportunities within the program are available.

HOUSING

Apartment-style housing available.

APPLICATION INFORMATION

Students may begin participation in January, April, July, and October. Applications are accepted continuously. In 2005, 189 applied; 117 were accepted. Applicants must interview; submit a formal application and an essay.

CONTACT

Jerry Driskill, Director of Admissions, 2233 West Dunlap Avenue, Phoenix, AZ 85021. Telephone: 800-474-2479. Fax: 602-331-5301. E-mail: aipxadm@aii.edu. World Wide Web: http://www.aipx.edu.

See color display following page 380.

CENTRAL ARIZONA COLLEGE

Hotel and Restaurant Management/Culinary Arts/Nutrition and Dietetics

Coolidge, Arizona

GENERAL INFORMATION

Public, coeducational, two-year college. Rural campus. Founded in 1970. Accredited by North Central Association of Colleges and Schools.

Central Arizona College *(continued)*

PROGRAM INFORMATION
Offered since 1990. Accredited by American Culinary Federation Accrediting Commission, Council on Hotel, Restaurant and Institutional Education. Program calendar is divided into semesters. 1-year certificate in dietary manager. 17-credit certificate in restaurant management. 17- to 19-credit certificate in cook's level I. 18-credit certificate in hotel/lodging management. 2-year associate degree in hotel and restaurant management. 2-year associate degree in dietetic technician. 2-year associate degree in cook level 2-culinary apprenticeship.

PROGRAM AFFILIATION
American Culinary Federation; American Dietetic Association; Council on Hotel, Restaurant, and Institutional Education; National Restaurant Association; National Restaurant Association Educational Foundation.

AREAS OF STUDY
Baking; beverage management; controlling costs in food service; culinary skill development; food preparation; food purchasing; food service math; garde-manger; hotel management; introduction to food service; management and human resources; nutrition; nutrition and food service; restaurant management; sanitation.

FACILITIES
Classroom; coffee shop; demonstration laboratory; snack shop.

STUDENT PROFILE
60 total: 40 full-time; 20 part-time. 40 are under 25 years old; 20 are between 25 and 44 years old.

FACULTY
4 total: 2 full-time; 2 part-time. 1 is a culinary-certified teacher; 2 are registered dietetic technicians; several registered dietitians. Prominent faculty: Gayle K. Haro, CCE, ACF, MEd, CHE; Glenna McCollum, MPH, RD; Janice Pratt, CHA, CHE, MBA, MEd. Faculty-student ratio: 1:10.

SPECIAL PROGRAMS
Apprenticeship Program (ACF Resort and Country Club Chefs).

TYPICAL EXPENSES
In-state tuition: $55 per credit full-time (in district), $55 per credit part-time. Out-of-state tuition: $80 per credit full-time, $80 per credit part-time. Program-related fee includes $50 for uniform.

FINANCIAL AID
Employment opportunities within the program are available.

HOUSING
Coed housing available.

APPLICATION INFORMATION
Students may begin participation in January and August. Applications are accepted continuously. Applicants must submit a formal application, letters of reference, and an essay.

CONTACT
Gayle Haro, Culinary Arts Instructor, Hotel and Restaurant Management/Culinary Arts/Nutrition and Dietetics, 8470 North Overfield Road, Coolidge, AZ 85228. Telephone: 520-426-4403. Fax: 520-426-4259. E-mail: gayle_haro@centralaz.edu. World Wide Web: http://www.centralaz.edu.

COCHISE COLLEGE

Culinary Arts

Ft. Huachuca, Arizona

GENERAL INFORMATION
Public, coeducational, two-year college. Rural campus. Founded in 1962. Accredited by North Central Association of Colleges and Schools.

PROGRAM INFORMATION
Program calendar is divided into semesters. 1-year certificate in sous-chef. 2-year associate degree in culinary arts. 6-month certificate in chef garde-manger. 6-month certificate in chef de cuisine/food preparation. 6-month certificate in chef patissier.

PROGRAM AFFILIATION
American Culinary Federation; Council on Hotel, Restaurant, and Institutional Education; National Restaurant Association; National Restaurant Association Educational Foundation; United States Personal Chef Association.

AREAS OF STUDY
Baking; beverage management; confectionery show pieces; controlling costs in food service; culinary French; culinary skill development; food preparation; food purchasing; food service math; garde-manger; international cuisine; introduction to food service; kitchen management; management and human resources; meal planning; meat cutting; menu and facilities design; nutrition; nutrition and food service; patisserie; sanitation; saucier; soup, stock, sauce, and starch production; wines and spirits.

FACILITIES
Cafeteria; classroom; food production kitchen.

SPECIAL PROGRAMS
Culinary competitions.

FINANCIAL AID
Employment placement assistance is available.

APPLICATION INFORMATION
Students may begin participation in January, March, June, August, and October. Applications are accepted continuously. Applicants must submit a formal application.

CONTACT
Director of Admissions, Culinary Arts, 901 North Colombo, Sierra Vista, AZ 85635. Telephone: 520-515-5336. Fax: 520-515-5452. World Wide Web: http://www.cochise.org/hospitality/default.htm.

MARICOPA SKILL CENTER

Food Preparation Program

Phoenix, Arizona

GENERAL INFORMATION
Public, coeducational, adult vocational school. Urban campus. Founded in 1962. Accredited by North Central Association of Colleges and Schools.

PROGRAM INFORMATION
Offered since 1977. Program calendar is year-round, year-round. 14-week certificate in pantry goods maker (salad maker). 18-week certificate in baker's helper. 18-week certificate in kitchen helper. 27-week certificate in cook's apprentice.

PROGRAM AFFILIATION
National Restaurant Association; National Restaurant Association Educational Foundation.

AREAS OF STUDY
Baking; food preparation; food service math; introduction to food service; meat cutting; restaurant opportunities; soup, stock, sauce, and starch production.

FACILITIES
Cafeteria; catering service; classroom; demonstration laboratory; food production kitchen; learning resource center; lecture room; public restaurant; student lounge; teaching kitchen.

STUDENT PROFILE
40 full-time.

FACULTY
1 total: 1 full-time. 1 is a culinary-certified teacher; 1 is a certified food service manager. Prominent faculty: Bill Collins. Faculty-student ratio: 1:10.

TYPICAL EXPENSES
Tuition: $143.50 per 35-hour week. Program-related fees include $685 for lab fees (materials used in class); $5 for registration; $5 for graduation; $70 for book fees.

FINANCIAL AID
In 2004, 1 scholarship was awarded (award was $500). Employment placement assistance is available.

HOUSING
Average off-campus housing cost per month: $300–$500.

APPLICATION INFORMATION
Students may begin participation year-round. Applications are accepted continuously. In 2004, 40 applied; 40 were accepted. Applicants must submit student information form and make financial arrangements, complete TABE assessment.

CONTACT
Michelle Sandoval, Recruiter, Food Preparation Program, 1245 East Buckeye Road, Phoenix, AZ 85034. Telephone: 602-238-4331. Fax: 602-238-4307. E-mail: michelle. sandoval@gwmail.maricopa.edu. World Wide Web: http://www.maricopaskillcenter.com.

NORTHERN ARIZONA UNIVERSITY

School of Hotel and Restaurant Management

Flagstaff, Arizona

GENERAL INFORMATION
Public, coeducational, university. Small-town setting. Founded in 1899. Accredited by North Central Association of Colleges and Schools.

PROGRAM INFORMATION
Offered since 1987. Accredited by Council on Hotel, Restaurant and Institutional Education, Accreditation Commission for Programs in Hospitality Administration. Program calendar is divided into semesters. Certificate in managing customer service. 15-credit hour certificate in international tourism management. 15-credit hour certificate in restaurant management. 15-week certificate in culinary arts for management. 4-year bachelor's degree in international hospitality management. 4-year bachelor's degree in hotel and restaurant management.

PROGRAM AFFILIATION
Council on Hotel, Restaurant, and Institutional Education; International Food Service Executives Association; National Restaurant Association; National Restaurant Association Educational Foundation.

AREAS OF STUDY
Beverage management; controlling costs in food service; food preparation; food purchasing; introduction to food service; management and human resources; restaurant opportunities; sanitation; wines and spirits.

FACILITIES
Classroom; coffee shop; computer laboratory; demonstration laboratory; food production kitchen; gourmet dining room; learning resource center; lecture room; public restaurant; student lounge; teaching kitchen.

Northern Arizona University *(continued)*

STUDENT PROFILE

850 total: 800 full-time; 50 part-time. 640 are under 25 years old; 120 are between 25 and 44 years old; 40 are over 44 years old.

FACULTY

23 total: 16 full-time; 7 part-time. 21 are industry professionals; 1 is a master chef; 1 is a master baker; 2 are culinary-certified teachers; 8 are CHE, 3 CHA. Prominent faculty: Dr. Matt Casado; Dr. Gary Vallen; Dr. Claudia Jurowski; Allen Z. Reich, PhD. Faculty-student ratio: 1:20.

SPECIAL PROGRAMS

Paid internships, summer program in Europe, International Student Exchange program.

TYPICAL EXPENSES

Application fee: $25. In-state tuition: $2197 per semester full-time, 1-6 credits $221 per credit per semester, 7 hours $2112 per credit per semester part-time. Out-of-state tuition: $6511 per semester full-time, semester part-time. Program-related fees include $20 for computer supplies; $40 for food production materials and supplies; $40 for bar and beverage; $20 for hospitality leadership; $10 for introduction to property management.

FINANCIAL AID

In 2004, 110 scholarships were awarded (average award was $700). Employment placement assistance is available. Employment opportunities within the program are available.

HOUSING

Coed, apartment-style, and single-sex housing available. Average on-campus housing cost per month: $363. Average off-campus housing cost per month: $500.

APPLICATION INFORMATION

Students may begin participation in January, May, and August. Application deadline for fall is March 1. Application deadline for spring is December 1. In 2004, 900 applied. Applicants must submit a formal application and ACT or SAT scores, high school diploma.

CONTACT

Kim Knowles, Coordinator of Advisement, School of Hotel and Restaurant Management, NAU Box 5638, Building 33A, Flagstaff, AZ 86011-5638. Telephone: 928-523-9050. Fax: 928-523-1711. E-mail: kim.knowles@nau.edu. World Wide Web: http://www.hrm.nau.edu.

PIMA COMMUNITY COLLEGE

Culinary Arts Program

Tucson, Arizona

GENERAL INFORMATION

Public, coeducational, two-year college. Urban campus. Founded in 1966. Accredited by North Central Association of Colleges and Schools.

PROGRAM INFORMATION

Offered since 1970. Program calendar is divided into semesters. 1-year certificate in culinary arts. 2-year associate degree in culinary arts.

PROGRAM AFFILIATION

Chefs Association of Southern Arizona; Slow Food International.

AREAS OF STUDY

Baking; beverage management; controlling costs in food service; culinary skill development; food preparation; food service math; garde-manger; international cuisine; management and human resources; meal planning; meat cutting; meat fabrication; menu and facilities design; nutrition; nutrition and food service; sanitation; saucier; seafood processing; soup, stock, sauce, and starch production; wines and spirits.

FACILITIES

Cafeteria; catering service; 4 classrooms; computer laboratory; demonstration laboratory; food production kitchen; learning resource center; library; public restaurant; teaching kitchen.

STUDENT PROFILE

72 full-time. 15 are under 25 years old; 45 are between 25 and 44 years old; 12 are over 44 years old.

FACULTY

9 total: 1 full-time; 8 part-time. 5 are industry professionals; 1 is a master baker; 1 is a culinary-certified teacher. Prominent faculty: Barry Infuso, CEC, CCE, AAC; Alan Zeman, CEC, AAC; Jan Osipowitcz, CEC; Rohan Warishani, CPC. Faculty-student ratio: 1:12.

SPECIAL PROGRAMS

Culinary Club, culinary team, apprenticeship (3 years).

TYPICAL EXPENSES

In-state tuition: $39 per credit hour. Out-of-state tuition: $67 per credit hour. Program-related fees include $250 for textbooks/notebooks; $150 for knives/supplies; $100 for uniforms.

FINANCIAL AID

Program-specific awards include Culinary Club Scholarship, Chef's Association Scholarship. Employment placement assistance is available. Employment opportunities within the program are available.

HOUSING

Average off-campus housing cost per month: $300.

APPLICATION INFORMATION

Students may begin participation in January and August. Applications are accepted continuously. In 2004, 220 applied; 72 were accepted. Applicants must interview, and application, placement test scores, or academic transcripts.

CONTACT

Barry Infuso, Director, Culinary Arts Program, 5901 South Calle Santa Cruz, Tucson, AZ 85709-6080. Telephone: 520-206-5164. Fax: 520-206-5143. E-mail: barry.infuso@pima.edu. World Wide Web: http://www.pima.edu.

SCOTTSDALE COMMUNITY COLLEGE

Culinary Arts Program

Scottsdale, Arizona

GENERAL INFORMATION

Public, coeducational, two-year college. Suburban campus. Founded in 1969. Accredited by North Central Association of Colleges and Schools.

PROGRAM INFORMATION

Offered since 1984. Program calendar is divided into semesters. 2-semester certificate in professional culinary arts. 2-semester certificate in culinary arts. 2-year associate degree in professional culinary arts. 2-year associate degree in culinary arts. 2-year associate degree in hospitality management.

PROGRAM AFFILIATION

National Restaurant Association; Women Chefs and Restaurateurs.

AREAS OF STUDY

Baking; beverage management; buffet catering; controlling costs in food service; culinary skill development; dining room service; food preparation; food purchasing; food service communication; food service math; garde-manger; international cuisine; introduction to food service; kitchen management; management and human resources; meal planning; meat cutting; meat fabrication; menu and facilities design; nutrition; nutrition and food service; patisserie; restaurant opportunities; sanitation; saucier; seafood processing; soup, stock, sauce, and starch production; soup, stock, sauce, and starch production.

FACILITIES

Bake shop; 3 classrooms; demonstration laboratory; 2 food production kitchens; gourmet dining room; learning resource center; lecture room; library; 2 public restaurants; student lounge; teaching kitchen.

STUDENT PROFILE

72 full-time. 29 are under 25 years old; 36 are between 25 and 44 years old; 7 are over 44 years old.

FACULTY

12 total: 4 full-time; 8 part-time. 8 are industry professionals; 4 are culinary-certified teachers. Prominent faculty: Dominic O'Neill, AAS; Karen Chalmers, BA; Tom Greenwalt, AAS, CCE, CEPC; Michael Wheelan, BA. Faculty-student ratio: 1:12.

SPECIAL PROGRAMS

Culinary competitions.

TYPICAL EXPENSES

In-state tuition: $4200 per certificate; $6060 per degree. Out-of-state tuition: $8400 per certificate; $10,200 per degree. Program-related fees include $425 for lab fee (per semester); $350 for uniforms; $525 for knives/bakery supplies.

FINANCIAL AID

In 2004, 5 scholarships were awarded (average award was $1000); 25 loans were granted (average loan was $2000). Employment placement assistance is available.

APPLICATION INFORMATION

Students may begin participation in January and August. Applications are accepted continuously. In 2004, 600 applied; 72 were accepted. Applicants must interview, and interview; submit a formal application, an essay, and placement scores in English, reading and math.

CONTACT

Karen Chalmers, Program Director, Culinary Arts Program, 9000 East Chaparral Road, Scottsdale, AZ 85256. Telephone: 480-423-6241. Fax: 480-423-6091. E-mail: karen.chalmers@sccmail.maricopa.edu. World Wide Web: http://www.sc.maricopa.edu/culinary.

SCOTTSDALE CULINARY INSTITUTE

Le Cordon Bleu

Scottsdale, Arizona

GENERAL INFORMATION

Private, coeducational, culinary institute. Suburban campus. Founded in 1986. Accredited by Accrediting Commission of Career Schools and Colleges of Technology.

PROGRAM INFORMATION

Offered since 1986. Accredited by American Culinary Federation Accrediting Commission. Program calendar is divided into six-week cycles, six-week cycles. 15-month associate degree in Le Cordon Bleu Culinary Arts. 9-month certificate in Le Cordon Bleu Patisserie and Baking.

PROGRAM AFFILIATION

American Culinary Federation; American Institute of Wine & Food; Council on Hotel, Restaurant, and Institutional Education; International Association of Culinary Professionals; International Wine & Food Society; James Beard Foundation, Inc.; National Restaurant Association; Phoenix Restaurant Association; Women Chefs and Restaurateurs.

Scottsdale Culinary Institute *(continued)*

AREAS OF STUDY

Baking; beverage management; buffet catering; confectionery show pieces; controlling costs in food service; culinary skill development; food preparation; food purchasing; food service communication; food service math; garde-manger; international cuisine; introduction to food service; management and human resources; meal planning; meat cutting; meat fabrication; menu and facilities design; nutrition; nutrition and food service; patisserie; restaurant opportunities; sanitation; saucier; seafood processing; soup, stock, sauce, and starch production; wines and spirits.

FACILITIES

2 bake shops; 2 catering services; 5 classrooms; demonstration laboratory; 2 food production kitchens; garden; 2 gourmet dining rooms; learning resource center; 3 lecture rooms; library; 2 public restaurants; student lounge; 10 teaching kitchens; meatroom/butcher shop.

SPECIAL PROGRAMS

Paid externships, culinary competitions, participation in community and resort events.

FINANCIAL AID

Employment placement assistance is available. Employment opportunities within the program are available.

APPLICATION INFORMATION

Students may begin participation in January, February, April, May, July, August, October, and November. Applications are accepted continuously. Applicants must submit a formal application, essay, academic transcripts, and have a high school diploma or GED.

CONTACT

Director of Admissions, Le Cordon Bleu, 8100 East Camelback Road, Suite 1001, Scottsdale, AZ 85251. Telephone: 800-848-2433. Fax: 480-990-0351. World Wide Web: http://www.chefs.com.

ARKANSAS

ARKANSAS CULINARY SCHOOL, INC.

Pulaski Technical College Arkansas Culinary School, Inc.

Little Rock, Arkansas

GENERAL INFORMATION

Private, coeducational, culinary institute. Urban campus. Founded in 1995.

PROGRAM INFORMATION

Offered since 1995. Accredited by Arkansas State Department of Higher Education. Program calendar is divided into semesters. 1-year certificate in culinary arts. 1-year certificate in Baking and Pastry Arts. 2-year associate degree in Culinary Arts.

PROGRAM AFFILIATION

American Culinary Federation; National Restaurant Association; National Restaurant Association Educational Foundation.

AREAS OF STUDY

Baking; beverage management; buffet catering; confectionery show pieces; controlling costs in food service; convenience cookery; culinary French; culinary skill development; food preparation; food purchasing; food service communication; food service math; garde-manger; international cuisine; introduction to food service; kitchen management; management and human resources; meal planning; meat cutting; meat fabrication; menu and facilities design; nutrition; nutrition and food service; patisserie; restaurant opportunities; sanitation; saucier; seafood processing; soup, stock, sauce, and starch production; wines and spirits.

FACILITIES

Bakery; 4 classrooms; computer laboratory; demonstration laboratory; food production kitchen; laboratory; learning resource center; library; student lounge; teaching kitchen.

STUDENT PROFILE

65 total: 60 full-time; 5 part-time. 20 are under 25 years old; 40 are between 25 and 44 years old.

FACULTY

11 total: 4 full-time; 7 part-time. 7 are industry professionals; 5 are culinary-certified teachers. Prominent faculty: Allison Shaskan, BA, MA; Todd Gold, CEC, CCA; Jamie McAfee, CEC; Katie Tomlinson, MS, RD. Faculty-student ratio: 1:12.

SPECIAL PROGRAMS

Culinary competitions, culinary anthropology; summer credit in Italy.

TYPICAL EXPENSES

Application fee: $30. Tuition: $80 per credit hour (plus $500-$740 lab fees) part-time. Tuition: $2500 per semester (average).

FINANCIAL AID

In 2005, 20 scholarships were awarded (average award was $1500-$2000).

HOUSING

Average off-campus housing cost per month: $400–$600.

APPLICATION INFORMATION

Students may begin participation in January, June, and August. Applications are accepted continuously. In 2005, 100 applied; 85 were accepted. Applicants must interview; submit a formal application, letters of reference, an essay, transcripts, GRE/high school diploma.

CONTACT

Ms Allison Shaskan, Executive Director, Pulaski Technical College Arkansas Culinary School, Inc., 4901 Asher Avenue, Little Rock, AR 72204. Telephone: 866-804-CHEF(2433). E-mail: info@arkansaschef.com. World Wide Web: http://www.arkansaschef.com/.

ARKANSAS TECH UNIVERSITY

Hospitality Administration

Russellville, Arkansas

GENERAL INFORMATION

Public, coeducatinal, comprehensive institution. Small-town setting. Founded in 1909. Accredited by North Central Association of Colleges and Schools.

PROGRAM INFORMATION

Offered since 1983. Program calendar is divided into semesters. 4-year bachelor's degree in hospitality administration.

PROGRAM AFFILIATION

Council on Hotel, Restaurant, and Institutional Education.

FACILITIES

2 classrooms; computer laboratory; 2 food production kitchens; gourmet dining room; learning resource center; 2 lecture rooms; student lounge; teaching kitchen.

TYPICAL STUDENT PROFILE

51 full-time. 30 are under 25 years old; 21 are between 25 and 44 years old.

SPECIAL PROGRAMS

400-600 hour internship with 6 hours college credit, 80 hours of work experience, workshops in special problems and topics.

FINANCIAL AID

Employment placement assistance is available.

HOUSING

Coed and apartment-style housing available.

APPLICATION INFORMATION

Students may begin participation in January, June, July, and August. Applications are accepted continuously. Applicants must submit a formal application and high school and/or college transcripts, ACT or SAT scores for entering freshmen.

CONTACT

Director of Admissions, Hospitality Administration, Department of Parks, Recreation and Hospitality Administration, Russellville, AR 72801. Telephone: 479-968-0386. Fax: 479-968-0600. World Wide Web: http://www.atu.edu.

UNIVERSITY OF ARKANSAS AT PINE BLUFF

Food Service Restaurant Management

Pine Bluff, Arkansas

GENERAL INFORMATION

Public, coeducational, comprehensive institution. Urban campus. Founded in 1873. Accredited by North Central Association of Colleges and Schools.

PROGRAM INFORMATION

Offered since 1957. Accredited by American Dietetic Association. Program calendar is divided into semesters. 4-year bachelor's degree in food service and restaurant management. 4-year bachelor's degree in dietetics and nutrition.

PROGRAM AFFILIATION

American Dietetic Association; Council on Hotel, Restaurant, and Institutional Education.

AREAS OF STUDY

Food service management; nutrition; nutrition and food service; restaurant management.

FACILITIES

Cafeteria; 2 computer laboratories; food production kitchen; 3 laboratories; learning resource center; 2 lecture rooms; 3 libraries; student lounge; teaching kitchen.

TYPICAL STUDENT PROFILE

39 full-time.

FINANCIAL AID

Employment placement assistance is available.

HOUSING

Single-sex housing available.

APPLICATION INFORMATION

Students may begin participation in January and August. Applications are accepted continuously. Applicants must submit a formal application.

CONTACT

Director of Admissions, Food Service Restaurant Management, PO Box 4971, 1200 North University Drive, Pine Bluff, AR 71611. Telephone: 870-575-8813. Fax: 870-543-8823. World Wide Web: http://www.uapb.edu.

CALIFORNIA

AMERICAN RIVER COLLEGE

Hospitality Management Program

Sacramento, California

GENERAL INFORMATION
Public, coeducational, two-year college. Suburban campus. Founded in 1955. Accredited by Western Association of Schools and Colleges.

PROGRAM INFORMATION
Offered since 1975. Program calendar is divided into semesters. 1-year certificate in introductory baking. 1.5-year certificate in restaurant management. 1.5-year certificate in culinary arts. 2-year associate degree in culinary arts.

PROGRAM AFFILIATION
American Culinary Federation; National Restaurant Association.

AREAS OF STUDY
Baking; dining room management; food preparation; kitchen management; restaurant management.

FACILITIES
Bake shop; classroom; gourmet dining room; laboratory; lecture room.

TYPICAL STUDENT PROFILE
200 total: 120 full-time; 80 part-time. 60 are under 25 years old; 110 are between 25 and 44 years old; 30 are over 44 years old.

SPECIAL PROGRAMS
Culinary competitions, student-run fine dining restaurant open to public.

APPLICATION INFORMATION
Students may begin participation in January, June, and August. Applications are accepted continuously.

CONTACT
Director of Admissions, Hospitality Management Program, 4700 College Oak Drive, Sacramento, CA 95841-4286. Telephone: 916-484-8656. Fax: 916-484-8880. World Wide Web: http://www.arc.losrios.edu/chef.

THE ART INSTITUTE OF CALIFORNIA–LOS ANGELES

School of Culinary Arts

Santa Monica, California

GENERAL INFORMATION
Private, coeducational, four-year college. Urban campus. Founded in 1997. Accredited by Accrediting Commission of Career Schools and Colleges of Technology.

PROGRAM INFORMATION
Offered since 1998. Program calendar is divided into quarters. 21-month associate degree in culinary arts. 36-month bachelor's degree in culinary management.

PROGRAM AFFILIATION
American Culinary Federation; National Restaurant Association.

AREAS OF STUDY
Baking; beverage management; buffet catering; confectionery show pieces; controlling costs in food service; convenience cookery; culinary French; culinary skill development; food preparation; food purchasing; food service communication; food service math; garde-manger; international cuisine; introduction to food service; kitchen management; management and human resources; meal planning; meat cutting; meat fabrication; menu and facilities design; nutrition; patisserie; restaurant opportunities; sanitation; saucier; seafood processing; soup, stock, sauce, and starch production; wines and spirits.

FACILITIES
Bake shop; 4 classrooms; computer laboratory; gourmet dining room; learning resource center; library; 4 teaching kitchens.

TYPICAL STUDENT PROFILE
350 full-time.

FINANCIAL AID
Employment placement assistance is available. Employment opportunities within the program are available.

HOUSING
Apartment-style housing available.

APPLICATION INFORMATION
Students may begin participation in January, April, July, and October. Applications are accepted continuously. Applicants must interview; submit a formal application, an essay, and have a high school diploma or GED.

CONTACT
Director of Admissions, School of Culinary Arts, 2900 31st Street, Santa Monica, CA 90405-3035. Telephone: 310-752-4700 Ext. 122. Fax: 310-450-1262. World Wide Web: http://www.aicala.artinstitutes.edu/.

See color display following page 380.

THE ART INSTITUTE OF CALIFORNIA–ORANGE COUNTY

Culinary Arts

Santa Ana, California

GENERAL INFORMATION
Private, coeducational, two-year college. Suburban campus. Founded in 2000. Accredited by Accrediting Council for Independent Colleges and Schools.

PROGRAM INFORMATION
Offered since 2001. Accredited by American Culinary Federation Accrediting Commission. Program calendar is divided into quarters. 1.5-year associate degree in culinary arts.

PROGRAM AFFILIATION
American Culinary Federation; National Restaurant Association.

AREAS OF STUDY
Baking; beverage management; confectionery show pieces; controlling costs in food service; culinary French; culinary skill development; food preparation; food purchasing; food service communication; food service math; garde-manger; international cuisine; introduction to food service; kitchen management; management and human resources; nutrition; nutrition and food service; patisserie; restaurant opportunities; sanitation; soup, stock, sauce, and starch production.

FACILITIES
4 classrooms; 4 computer laboratories; food production kitchen; learning resource center; 8 lecture rooms; library; 2 public restaurants; snack shop; student lounge; 3 teaching kitchens; baking and pastry kitchen.

SPECIAL PROGRAMS
Art Institute Culinary Cook-off Competition.

FINANCIAL AID
Employment placement assistance is available. Employment opportunities within the program are available.

HOUSING
Apartment-style housing available.

APPLICATION INFORMATION
Students may begin participation in January, April, July, and October. Applications are accepted continuously. Applicants must interview; submit a formal application, an essay, have high school diploma or GED.

CONTACT
Director of Admissions, Culinary Arts, 3601 Sunflower Avenue, Santa Ana, CA 92704. Telephone: 888-549-3055. Fax: 714-556-1923. World Wide Web: http://www.aicaoc. artinstitutes.edu.
See color display following page 380.

THE ART INSTITUTE OF CALIFORNIA–SAN DIEGO

San Diego, California

GENERAL INFORMATION
Private, coeducational, four-year college. Suburban campus. Founded in 1981. Accredited by Accrediting Commission of Career Schools and Colleges of Technology.

PROGRAM INFORMATION
Offered since 2002. Program calendar is divided into quarters. 21-month associate degree in culinary arts. 36-month bachelor's degree in culinary management.

PROGRAM AFFILIATION
International Association of Culinary Professionals; National Restaurant Association; National Restaurant Association Educational Foundation; Women Chefs and Restaurateurs.

AREAS OF STUDY
Baking; beverage management; buffet catering; confectionery show pieces; controlling costs in food service; convenience cookery; culinary French; culinary skill development; food preparation; food purchasing; food service communication; food service math; garde-manger; international cuisine; introduction to food service; kitchen management; management and human resources; meal planning; meat cutting; meat fabrication; menu and facilities design; nutrition; nutrition and food service; patisserie; restaurant opportunities; sanitation; saucier; seafood processing; soup, stock, sauce, and starch production; wines and spirits.

FACILITIES
Bake shop; cafeteria; 2 classrooms; 8 computer laboratories; demonstration laboratory; food production kitchen; gourmet dining room; learning resource center; lecture room; library; public restaurant; snack shop; student lounge; 3 teaching kitchens.

TYPICAL STUDENT PROFILE
165 full-time. 115 are under 25 years old; 50 are between 25 and 44 years old.

FINANCIAL AID
Employment placement assistance is available. Employment opportunities within the program are available.

HOUSING
Apartment-style housing available.

APPLICATION INFORMATION
Students may begin participation in January, April, July, and October. Applications are accepted continuously. Applicants must interview; submit a formal application and an essay.

The Art Institute of California–San Diego *(continued)*

CONTACT
Director of Admissions, 7650 Mission Valley Road, San Diego, CA 92108. Telephone: 858-598-1208. Fax: 619-291-3206. World Wide Web: http://www.aicasd.artinstitutes.edu.
See color display following page 380.

BAUMAN COLLEGE: HOLLSTIC NUTRITION & CULINARY ARTS

Natural Chef Training Program

Berkley, California

GENERAL INFORMATION
Private, coeducational, culinary institute. Urban campus. Founded in 1984.

PROGRAM INFORMATION
Offered since 1997. Program calendar is divided into semesters. 5-month certificate in natural chef.

PROGRAM AFFILIATION
Sonoma County Culinary Guild; World Association of Chefs and Cooks.

AREAS OF STUDY
Buffet catering; controlling costs in food service; culinary skill development; ethnic cuisine; food preparation; food purchasing; food service math; healthy professional cooking; international cuisine; kitchen management; meal planning; menu and facilities design; nutrition; nutrition and food service; organic gardening; sanitation; saucier; soup, stock, sauce, and starch production; vegetarian cooking.

FACILITIES
Classroom; computer laboratory; demonstration laboratory; food production kitchen; learning resource center; lecture room; library; teaching kitchen.

STUDENT PROFILE
96 full-time. 35 are under 25 years old; 50 are between 25 and 44 years old; 11 are over 44 years old.

FACULTY
13 total: 5 full-time; 8 part-time. 5 are master bakers; 13 are culinary-certified teachers; 1 is a gardening teacher. Prominent faculty: Ed Bauman, PhD, NC; Sascha Weiss; Catherine McConkie, NC; Kathy Cummins, Natural Chef Instructor. Faculty-student ratio: 1:12.

SPECIAL PROGRAMS
French intensive organic gardening, classes in herbal remedies and cooking for a variety of health problems, personal chef focus.

TYPICAL EXPENSES
Tuition: $7450 per 5 months. Program-related fees include $367.95 for class materials (including books, chef's coat, apron, and knives), software, thermometer; $100 for registration; $20 for STRF fee.

FINANCIAL AID
Employment placement assistance is available. Employment opportunities within the program are available.

HOUSING
Average off-campus housing cost per month: $500.

APPLICATION INFORMATION
Students may begin participation in March and September. Applications are accepted continuously. In 2004, 96 applied; 96 were accepted. Applicants must interview; submit a formal application, letters of reference, an essay, resume, photo.

CONTACT
Marlina Eckel, Enrollment Coordinator, Natural Chef Training Program, PO Box 940, Penngrove, CA 94951. Telephone: 800-987-7530. Fax: 707-795-3375. E-mail: inquiry@baumancollege.org. World Wide Web: http://www.iet.org/cai.html.

CABRILLO COLLEGE

Culinary Arts and Hospitality Management

Aptos, California

GENERAL INFORMATION
Public, coeducational, two-year college. Suburban campus. Founded in 1959. Accredited by Western Association of Schools and Colleges.

PROGRAM INFORMATION
Accredited by American Culinary Federation Accrediting Commission. Program calendar is divided into semesters. 2-year associate degree in culinary arts. 34-unit certificate in culinary arts.

PROGRAM AFFILIATION
American Culinary Federation; National Restaurant Association; Santa Cruz Area Restaurant Association.

AREAS OF STUDY
Baking; beverage management; buffet catering; controlling costs in food service; culinary skill development; ethnic cuisine; food preparation; food purchasing; food service management; food service math; introduction to food service; kitchen management; management and human resources; meal planning; meat cutting; meat fabrication; menu and facilities design; nutrition; nutrition and food service; patisserie; restaurant opportunities; sanitation; saucier; seafood processing; soup, stock, sauce, and starch production; wines and spirits.

FACILITIES

Bakery; cafeteria; 2 catering services; 3 classrooms; 3 computer laboratories; demonstration laboratory; 2 food production kitchens; garden; gourmet dining room; 3 laboratories; learning resource center; lecture room; library; public restaurant; snack shop; student lounge; teaching kitchen.

TYPICAL STUDENT PROFILE

260 total: 60 full-time; 200 part-time.

FINANCIAL AID

Employment placement assistance is available. Employment opportunities within the program are available.

APPLICATION INFORMATION

Students may begin participation in February, June, and September. Applications are accepted continuously. Applicants must submit a formal application and academic transcripts.

CONTACT

Director of Admissions, Culinary Arts and Hospitality Management, 6500 Soquel Drive, Aptos, CA 95003-3194. Telephone: 831-479-5749. Fax: 831-479-5743. World Wide Web: http://www.cabrillo.edu.

CALIFORNIA CULINARY ACADEMY

San Francisco, California

GENERAL INFORMATION

Private, coeducational, culinary institute. Urban campus. Founded in 1977. Accredited by Accrediting Commission of Career Schools and Colleges of Technology.

PROGRAM INFORMATION

Offered since 1977. Accredited by American Culinary Federation Accrediting Commission. Program calendar is continuous. 30-week certificate in baking and pastry arts. 45-week associate degree in hospitality and restaurant management. 60-week associate degree in culinary arts.

PROGRAM AFFILIATION

American Culinary Federation; American Institute of Wine & Food; International Association of Culinary Professionals; James Beard Foundation, Inc.; National Restaurant Association; National Restaurant Association Educational Foundation; The Bread Bakers Guild of America; Women Chefs and Restaurateurs.

AREAS OF STUDY

Baking; beverage management; buffet catering; casino and gaming; confectionery show pieces; controlling costs in food service; culinary French; culinary skill development; food preparation; food purchasing; food service math; garde-manger; global cuisine; international cuisine; introduction to food service; kitchen management; management and human resources; meat cutting; meat fabrication; menu and facilities design; nutrition; nutrition and food service; patisserie; restaurant opportunities;

sanitation; saucier; seafood processing; soup, stock, sauce, and starch production; wines and spirits.

FACILITIES

Bake shop; 6 bakeries; cafeteria; 10 classrooms; coffee shop; computer laboratory; 6 demonstration laboratories; 8 food production kitchens; gourmet dining room; 5 laboratories; library; 2 public restaurants; snack shop; student lounge; 3 teaching kitchens; retail shop; mixology laboratory; casino.

TYPICAL STUDENT PROFILE

2000 full-time.

SPECIAL PROGRAMS

3-month externship, culinary competitions, dining club.

FINANCIAL AID

Employment placement assistance is available. Employment opportunities within the program are available.

HOUSING

Coed housing available.

APPLICATION INFORMATION

Students may begin participation year-round. Applications are accepted continuously. Applicants must interview; submit a formal application and have proof of high school graduation or GED.

CONTACT

Director of Admissions, 625 Polk Street, San Francisco, CA 94102. Telephone: 800-229-2433. Fax: 415-771-2194. World Wide Web: http://www.baychef.com.

CALIFORNIA SCHOOL OF CULINARY ARTS

Le Cordon Bleu Programs

Pasadena, California

GENERAL INFORMATION

Private, coeducational, culinary institute. Urban campus. Founded in 1994. Accredited by Accrediting Council for Independent Colleges and Schools.

PROGRAM INFORMATION

Offered since 1994. Accredited by ACF Educational Assurance (Patisserie and Baking). Program calendar is clock-hour. 30-week diploma in Le Cordon Bleu Patisserie and Banking. 42-week diploma in Le Cordon Blue Patisserie and Banking. 51-week diploma in Le Cordon Bleu Hospitality and Restaurant Management. 60-week associate degree in Le Cordon Bleu Culinary Arts.

PROGRAM AFFILIATION

American Culinary Federation; California Restaurant Association; International Association of Culinary

California School of Culinary Arts *(continued)*

Professionals; National Restaurant Association; National Restaurant Association Educational Foundation; Women Chefs and Restaurateurs.

AREAS OF STUDY
Baking; beverage management; buffet catering; confectionery show pieces; controlling costs in food service; convenience cookery; culinary French; culinary skill development; food preparation; food purchasing; food service communication; food service math; garde-manger; international cuisine; introduction to food service; kitchen management; management and human resources; meal planning; meat cutting; meat fabrication; menu and facilities design; nutrition; nutrition and food service; patisserie; restaurant opportunities; sanitation; saucier; seafood processing; soup, stock, sauce, and starch production; wines and spirits.

FACILITIES
Bake shop; bakery; catering service; classroom; computer laboratory; demonstration laboratory; food production kitchen; gourmet dining room; learning resource center; 13 lecture rooms; library; public restaurant; student lounge; 15 teaching kitchens; café.

STUDENT PROFILE
1693 full-time.

FACULTY
98 total: 83 full-time; 15 part-time. 76 are industry professionals; 7 are (academic instructors). Prominent faculty: Donald R. Andrews, Jr., PhD; Angela Goodman, Executive Chef; Joshua Orlando, CWPC, CCE; Alyson Cook, CEC; David Edens, CCC. Faculty-student ratio: 1:16 (Lab Courses).

SPECIAL PROGRAMS
ACF culinary competitions, Epicurean Club (gourmet dining club), Confiserie Bleu (baking club).

TYPICAL EXPENSES
Application fee: $75. Tuition: $24950–$43,950 per 30–60 weeks. Program-related fees include $2102 for uniforms, books, and tool kit (associate degree); $1919 for uniform books, and tool kit (P&B diploma); $4301 for uniforms, books, tool kit, and computer (Hospitality and Restaurant Management diploma).

FINANCIAL AID
Employment placement assistance is available. Employment opportunities within the program are available.

HOUSING
Average off-campus housing cost per month: $700.

APPLICATION INFORMATION
Students may begin participation in January, February, April, May, July, August, October, and November. Applications are accepted continuously. Applicants must interview; submit a formal application and pre-enrollment exam, high school diploma or equivalent.

CONTACT
Edwin Colon, Vice President, Admissions, Le Cordon Bleu Programs, 521 East Green Street, Pasadena, CA 90026. Telephone: 888-900-CHEF. Fax: 626-403-8494. E-mail: ecolon@scsca.com. World Wide Web: http://www.csca.edu. **See color display following page 92.**

CALIFORNIA STATE POLYTECHNIC UNIVERSITY, POMONA

The Collins School of Hospitality Management

Pomona, California

GENERAL INFORMATION
Public, coeducational, comprehensive institution. Suburban campus. Founded in 1938. Accredited by Western Association of Schools and Colleges.

PROGRAM INFORMATION
Offered since 1973. Accredited by Council on Hotel, Restaurant and Institutional Education. Program calendar is divided into quarters. 4-year bachelor's degree in hotel and restaurant management.

PROGRAM AFFILIATION
American Culinary Federation; Council on Hotel, Restaurant, and Institutional Education; International Association of Culinary Professionals; National Restaurant Association; National Restaurant Association Educational Foundation; Society of Wine Educators.

AREAS OF STUDY
Beverage management; beverage marketing; club management; controlling costs in food service; culinary product development; food preparation; food purchasing; food service math; hotel management; introduction to food service; kitchen management; management and human resources; meal planning; menu and facilities design; restaurant management; restaurant opportunities; sanitation; soup, stock, sauce, and starch production; wines and spirits.

FACILITIES
10 classrooms; computer laboratory; food production kitchen; gourmet dining room; laboratory; 5 lecture rooms; library; public restaurant; student lounge; 2 demonstration auditoriums.

SPECIAL PROGRAMS
Participation at national trade shows.

HOUSING
Coed housing available.

APPLICATION INFORMATION
Students may begin participation in January, March, and September. Application deadline for spring is November 15. Application deadline for summer is

March 1. Application deadline for fall is April 1. Application deadline for winter is September 1. Applicants must submit a formal application.

CONTACT
Director of Admissions, The Collins School of Hospitality Management, 3801 West Temple Avenue, Pomona, CA 91768-2557. Telephone: 909-869-2275. Fax: 909-869-4805. World Wide Web: http://www.csupomona.edu/~cshm/.

CHEF ERIC'S CULINARY CLASSROOM

Professional and Recreational Cooking School

Los Angeles, California

GENERAL INFORMATION
Private, coeducational, culinary institute. Urban campus. Founded in 2003.

PROGRAM INFORMATION
Offered since 2003. Program calendar is continuous. 10-week certificate in baking program. 10-week certificate in advanced meal preparation/presentation. 10-week certificate in International cuisines of the world. 20-week certificate in comprehensive culinary arts program.

AREAS OF STUDY
Baking; buffet catering; controlling costs in food service; convenience cookery; culinary French; culinary skill development; food preparation; food purchasing; food service communication; food service math; garde-manger; international cuisine; introduction to food service; meal planning; meat cutting; meat fabrication; nutrition; nutrition and food service; plating and presentation; restaurant opportunities; sanitation; seafood processing; soup, stock, sauce, and starch production; special events management.

FACILITIES
Classroom; demonstration laboratory; food production kitchen; gourmet dining room; lecture room; library; student lounge; teaching kitchen; special event room.

STUDENT PROFILE
750 total: 150 full-time; 600 part-time. 100 are under 25 years old; 400 are between 25 and 44 years old; 250 are over 44 years old.

FACULTY
6 total: 2 full-time; 4 part-time. 4 are industry professionals; 2 are culinary-certified teachers; specialty guest instructors. Prominent faculty: Chef Eric J. Crowley, Professional Programs/Recreational Class; Wendy Jacobs-Riche, Baking Instructor. Faculty-student ratio: 1:6.

SPECIAL PROGRAMS
Over 40 special recreational classes-3 hours long/summers only, Children's Culinary Academy I & II, 4-week introduction to culinary arts program-beginning and advanced.

TYPICAL EXPENSES
Tuition: $900–$1000 per 10 week programs; $2000 for 20 week program (includes jacket, apron and CIA text book) full-time, $75 per recreational individual classes part-time.

FINANCIAL AID
In 2004, 1 scholarship was awarded (award was $2000). Program-specific awards include Culinary Chef I $2000-payment plans available, Culinary Chef 2/3-$1000 each-can make 2 payments, Culinary Baking I $900-can make 2 payments. Employment placement assistance is available.

APPLICATION INFORMATION
Students may begin participation year-round. Applications are accepted continuously.

CONTACT
Chef Eric J. Crowley, President, Professional and Recreational Cooking School, 2366 Pelham Avenue, Los Angeles, CA 90064. Telephone: 310-470-2640. Fax: 310-470-2642. E-mail: cheferic@culinaryclassroom.com. World Wide Web: http://www.culinaryclassroom.com.

CITY COLLEGE OF SAN FRANCISCO

Culinary Arts and Hospitality Studies Department

San Francisco, California

GENERAL INFORMATION
Public, coeducational, two-year college. Urban campus. Founded in 1935. Accredited by Western Association of Schools and Colleges.

PROGRAM INFORMATION
Offered since 1936. Accredited by American Culinary Federation Accrediting Commission. Program calendar is divided into semesters. 4-semester associate degree in hotel management. 4-semester associate degree in food service management. 4-semester associate degree in culinary arts.

PROGRAM AFFILIATION
American Culinary Federation; American Institute of Wine & Food; California Hotel and Motel Association; California Restaurant Association; Council on Hotel, Restaurant, and Institutional Education; Gastronomic Club; Women Chefs and Restaurateurs.

AREAS OF STUDY
Baking; beverage management; buffet catering; confectionery show pieces; controlling costs in food service; culinary French; culinary skill development; food preparation; food purchasing; food service communication; food service math; garde-manger; hospitality accounting; hospitality law; hospitality marketing; international cuisine; introduction to food service; kitchen management; management and human resources; meat cutting; meat fabrication; menu and facilities design; nutrition; nutrition and food service; orientation to hospitality; patisserie;

City College of San Francisco *(continued)*

restaurant opportunities; sanitation; saucier; seafood processing; soup, stock, sauce, and starch production; wines and spirits.

FACILITIES
Bake shop; cafeteria; catering service; 3 classrooms; computer laboratory; demonstration laboratory; food production kitchen; gourmet dining room; 3 lecture rooms; library; public restaurant; snack shop; 5 teaching kitchens.

TYPICAL STUDENT PROFILE
250 total: 220 full-time; 30 part-time. 50 are under 25 years old; 150 are between 25 and 44 years old; 50 are over 44 years old.

SPECIAL PROGRAMS
240-hour internship at one of 100 hotels/restaurants in Bay area.

FINANCIAL AID
Program-specific awards include Hotel and Restaurant Foundation scholarships. Employment placement assistance is available. Employment opportunities within the program are available.

APPLICATION INFORMATION
Students may begin participation in January and August. Application deadline for spring is November 13. Application deadline for fall is April 10. Applicants must submit a formal application, an essay, international students must submit TOEFL scores (minimum 475).

CONTACT
Director of Admissions, Culinary Arts and Hospitality Studies Department, 50 Phelan Avenue, SW156, San Francisco, CA 94112-1821. Telephone: 415-239-3152. Fax: 415-239-3913. World Wide Web: http://www.ccsf.edu/hotelandrestaurant.

COLLEGE OF THE CANYONS

Hotel and Restaurant Management

Santa Clarita, California

GENERAL INFORMATION
Public, coeducational, two-year college. Suburban campus. Founded in 1969. Accredited by Western Association of Schools and Colleges.

PROGRAM INFORMATION
Offered since 1990. Program calendar is divided into semesters. 2-year associate degree in hotel management. 2-year associate degree in restaurant management. 2-year associate degree in combined hotel and restaurant management.

AREAS OF STUDY

Beverage management; controlling costs in food service; hospitality law; hotel operations; kitchen management; management and human resources; nutrition and food service; restaurant opportunities; sales/marketing; sanitation.

FACILITIES

Classroom; computer laboratory; learning resource center; library.

TYPICAL STUDENT PROFILE

100 full-time.

SPECIAL PROGRAMS

Internships, wine tasting appreciation class.

FINANCIAL AID

Employment placement assistance is available.

APPLICATION INFORMATION

Students may begin participation in January, June, and August. Applications are accepted continuously. Applicants must submit a formal application.

CONTACT

Director of Admissions, Hotel and Restaurant Management, 26455 Rockwell Canyon Road, Santa Clarita, CA 91355. Telephone: 661-362-3712. Fax: 661-259-8302. World Wide Web: http://www.coc.cc.ca.us/.

COLLEGE OF THE SEQUOIAS

Consumer Family Studies

Visalia, California

GENERAL INFORMATION

Public, coeducational, two-year college. Rural campus. Founded in 1925. Accredited by Western Association of Schools and Colleges.

PROGRAM INFORMATION

Offered since 1992. Program calendar is divided into semesters. 13-unit certificate in basic food service. 28-unit certificate in food service management.

AREAS OF STUDY

Baking; buffet catering; confectionery show pieces; controlling costs in food service; culinary skill development; food preparation; food service math; introduction to food service; kitchen management; management and human resources; meal planning; menu and facilities design; nutrition; nutrition and food service; sanitation; saucier; soup, stock, sauce, and starch production.

FACILITIES

Classroom; computer laboratory; demonstration laboratory; food production kitchen; learning resource center; lecture room; library.

TYPICAL STUDENT PROFILE

42 total: 12 full-time; 30 part-time. 10 are under 25 years old; 25 are between 25 and 44 years old; 7 are over 44 years old.

APPLICATION INFORMATION

Students may begin participation in January and August. Applications are accepted continuously. Applicants must submit a formal application.

CONTACT

Director of Admissions, Consumer Family Studies, 915 South Mooney Boulevard, Visalia, CA 93277-2234. Telephone: 559-730-3700. World Wide Web: http://www.cos.edu.

CONTRA COSTA COLLEGE

Culinary Arts

San Pablo, California

GENERAL INFORMATION

Public, coeducational, two-year college. Urban campus. Founded in 1948. Accredited by Western Association of Schools and Colleges.

PROGRAM INFORMATION

Offered since 1964. Program calendar is divided into semesters. 2-year certificate in cooking. 2-year certificate in baking. 3-year associate degree in culinary arts.

PROGRAM AFFILIATION

National Restaurant Association.

AREAS OF STUDY

Baking; buffet catering; confectionery show pieces; controlling costs in food service; culinary French; culinary skill development; food preparation; food purchasing; food service communication; food service math; garde-manger; international cuisine; introduction to food service; kitchen management; management and human resources; meal planning; meat cutting; meat fabrication; menu and facilities design; nutrition; patisserie; sanitation; saucier; seafood processing; soup, stock, sauce, and starch production; wines and spirits.

FACILITIES

Bakery; cafeteria; 2 classrooms; 4 computer laboratories; gourmet dining room; 2 laboratories; library; public restaurant; 2 teaching kitchens.

TYPICAL STUDENT PROFILE

140 total: 100 full-time; 40 part-time.

SPECIAL PROGRAMS

Related internships, culinary competitions.

Contra Costa College *(continued)*

FINANCIAL AID
Program-specific awards include California Restaurant Association scholarships. Employment placement assistance is available. Employment opportunities within the program are available.

APPLICATION INFORMATION
Students may begin participation in January and August. Applications are accepted continuously. Applicants must submit a formal application.

CONTACT
Director of Admissions, Culinary Arts, 2600 Mission Bell Drive, San Pablo, CA 94806-3195. Telephone: 510-235-7800 Ext. 4409. Fax: 510-236-6768. World Wide Web: http://www.contracosta.cc.ca.us.

THE CULINARY INSTITUTE OF AMERICA

The Culinary Institute of America at Greystone

St. Helena, California

GENERAL INFORMATION
Private, coeducational, culinary institute. Rural campus. Founded in 1946. Accredited by Accrediting Commission of Career Schools and Colleges of Technology.

PROGRAM INFORMATION
Offered since 1946. Program calendar is divided into semesters. 30-week certificate in accelerated culinary arts. 30-week certificate in baking and pastry arts.

PROGRAM AFFILIATION
American Culinary Federation; American Dietetic Association; American Institute of Baking; American Institute of Wine & Food; Confrerie de la Chaine des Rotisseurs; Council on Hotel, Restaurant, and Institutional Education; International Association of Culinary Professionals; International Foodservice Editorial Council; James Beard Foundation, Inc.; Napa Valley Wine Library Association; National Association for the Specialty Food Trade, Inc.; National Restaurant Association; Oldways Preservation and Exchange Trust; Society of Wine Educators; Sommelier Society of America; The Bread Bakers Guild of America; Women Chefs and Restaurateurs.

AREAS OF STUDY
Baking; confectionery show pieces; culinary skill development; food preparation; food service math; garde-manger; international cuisine; nutrition; patisserie; sanitation; saucier; soup, stock, sauce, and starch production; wines and spirits.

FACILITIES
2 bake shops; cafeteria; 7 classrooms; computer laboratory; 2 demonstration laboratories; garden; library; 6 teaching kitchens; amphitheater.

STUDENT PROFILE
86 full-time. 68 are under 25 years old; 18 are between 25 and 44 years old.

FACULTY
11 total: 8 full-time; 3 part-time. 12 are industry professionals; 1 is a master chef; 1 is a master baker; 5 are culinary-certified teachers. Prominent faculty: Robert Jörin, CEPC, CCE, CHE, CMB; Adam Busby, CHE, CMC. Faculty-student ratio: 1:18.

TYPICAL EXPENSES
Application fee: $30. Tuition: $9590 per semester. Program-related fees include $325 for general fee; $845 for books and supplies; $1085 for board (mandatory).

FINANCIAL AID
Program-specific awards include ACAP Dean's Scholarship ($2000), Classic Residences by Hyatt Scholarship ($5,000). Employment placement assistance is available. Employment opportunities within the program are available.

HOUSING
Coed housing available. Average on-campus housing cost per month: $750. Average off-campus housing cost per month: $750.

APPLICATION INFORMATION
Students may begin participation in January, March, July, September, and October. Applications are accepted continuously. In 2004, 100 applied. Applicants must interview; submit a formal application, letters of reference, an essay, academic transcripts, and pass math entrance exam (for baking and pastry program) only.

CONTACT
Catherine Reble, Program Coordinator, The Culinary Institute of America at Greystone, 2555 Main Street, St. Helena, CA 94574. Telephone: 707-967-2402. Fax: 707-967-2410. E-mail: c_reble@culinary.edu. World Wide Web: http://www.prochef.com.

See display on page 251. See display on page 251.

CYPRESS COLLEGE

Hotel/Restaurant and Culinary Arts

Anaheim, California

GENERAL INFORMATION
Public, coeducational, two-year college. Suburban campus. Founded in 1966. Accredited by Western Association of Schools and Colleges.

PROGRAM INFORMATION

Offered since 1971. Program calendar is divided into semesters. 2-year associate degree in food service management. 2-year certificate in food service management. 2-year certificate in culinary arts. 2-year certificate in hotel operations. 2.5-year associate degree in culinary arts. 2.5-year associate degree in hotel operations.

PROGRAM AFFILIATION

American Culinary Federation; Council on Hotel, Restaurant, and Institutional Education; Foodservice Educators Network International; International Food Service Executives Association; National Restaurant Association; National Restaurant Association Educational Foundation.

AREAS OF STUDY

Baking; buffet catering; controlling costs in food service; culinary skill development; food preparation; food purchasing; garde-manger; international cuisine; introduction to food service; kitchen management; management and human resources; menu and facilities design; nutrition; restaurant opportunities; sanitation; soup, stock, sauce, and starch production; wines and spirits.

FACILITIES

Bake shop; bakery; cafeteria; catering service; 4 classrooms; coffee shop; computer laboratory; demonstration laboratory; food production kitchen; garden; gourmet dining room; laboratory; learning resource center; 2 lecture rooms; library; public restaurant; snack shop; student lounge; teaching kitchen.

TYPICAL STUDENT PROFILE

425 total: 300 full-time; 125 part-time.

SPECIAL PROGRAMS

Internships, culinary competitions.

FINANCIAL AID

Employment placement assistance is available. Employment opportunities within the program are available.

APPLICATION INFORMATION

Students may begin participation in January, June, and August. Application deadline for spring is January 10. Application deadline for summer is May 1. Application deadline for fall is August 10. Applicants must submit a formal application.

CONTACT

Director of Admissions, Hotel/Restaurant and Culinary Arts, 1830 West Romneya Drive, Anaheim, CA 92801. Telephone: 714-808-4640. Fax: 714-808-4550. World Wide Web: http://www.cypresscollege.org.

DIABLO VALLEY COLLEGE

Hotel and Restaurant Management Program

Pleasant Hill, California

GENERAL INFORMATION

Public, coeducational, two-year college. Suburban campus. Founded in 1949. Accredited by Western Association of Schools and Colleges.

PROGRAM INFORMATION

Offered since 1971. Accredited by American Culinary Federation Accrediting Commission. Program calendar is divided into semesters. 18-month certificate of achievement in hotel administration. 2-year certificate of achievement in restaurant management. 2-year certificate of achievement in culinary arts. 2-year certificate of achievement in baking and pastry.

PROGRAM AFFILIATION

American Culinary Federation; National Restaurant Association.

AREAS OF STUDY

Baking; beverage management; controlling costs in food service; culinary skill development; food preparation; food purchasing; food service math; garde-manger; international cuisine; management and human resources; meat cutting; meat fabrication; menu and facilities design; nutrition; nutrition and food service; patisserie; restaurant opportunities; sanitation; soup, stock, sauce, and starch production; wines and spirits.

FACILITIES

Bake shop; catering service; 6 classrooms; coffee shop; computer laboratory; demonstration laboratory; 2 food production kitchens; gourmet dining room; learning resource center; 6 lecture rooms; library; public restaurant; snack shop; 2 teaching kitchens.

TYPICAL STUDENT PROFILE

200 total: 150 full-time; 50 part-time.

SPECIAL PROGRAMS

3-week exchange program with France.

FINANCIAL AID

Employment placement assistance is available.

APPLICATION INFORMATION

Students may begin participation in January, June, and August. Applications are accepted continuously. Applicants must submit a formal application.

CONTACT

Director of Admissions, Hotel and Restaurant Management Program, 321 Golf Club Road, Pleasant Hill, CA 94523-1544. Telephone: 925-685-1230 Ext. 2555. World Wide Web: http://www.dvc.edu.

EPICUREAN SCHOOL OF CULINARY ARTS

Los Angeles, California

GENERAL INFORMATION
Private, coeducational, culinary institute. Urban campus. Founded in 1985.

PROGRAM INFORMATION
Offered since 1985. Program calendar is continuous. 10-week certificate in baking II. 12-week certificate in baking I. 12-week certificate in professional chef II. 25-week certificate in professional chef I.

AREAS OF STUDY
Baking; culinary skill development; international cuisine; meal planning; nutrition; seafood processing; soup, stock, sauce, and starch production.

FACILITIES
Classroom.

STUDENT PROFILE
250 part-time. 25 are under 25 years old; 163 are between 25 and 44 years old; 62 are over 44 years old.

FACULTY
5 total: 5 part-time. 3 are industry professionals; 2 are master bakers; 3 are culinary-certified teachers. Prominent faculty: Eric Crowley; Teri Appleton; Suzanne Griswold; Roxannn Jullatot. Faculty-student ratio: 1:12.

TYPICAL EXPENSES
Tuition: $65 per class part-time.

FINANCIAL AID
Employment placement assistance is available.

APPLICATION INFORMATION
Students may begin participation year-round. Applications are accepted continuously. Applicants must submit an informal application.

CONTACT
Shelley Janson, Director, 8500 Melrose Avenue, Los Angeles, CA 90069. Telephone: 310-659-5990. Fax: 310-659-0302. E-mail: epicurean5@aol.com. World Wide Web: http://EpicureanSchool.com.

GLENDALE COMMUNITY COLLEGE

Food and Nutrition Culinary Arts Department

Glendale, California

GENERAL INFORMATION
Public, coeducational, two-year college. Suburban campus. Founded in 1927. Accredited by Western Association of Schools and Colleges.

PROGRAM INFORMATION
Offered since 1974. 1- to 2-year certificate in dietary services supervisor. 1- to 2-year certificate in hotel/restaurant management. 2-year certificate in restaurant management/culinary arts.

PROGRAM AFFILIATION
American Culinary Federation; National Restaurant Association.

AREAS OF STUDY
Baking; beverage management; buffet catering; controlling costs in food service; convenience cookery; culinary skill development; food preparation; food purchasing; food service math; garde-manger; international cuisine; introduction to food service; management and human resources; meal planning; menu and facilities design; nutrition; nutrition and food service; patisserie; restaurant opportunities; sanitation; saucier; soup, stock, sauce, and starch production; wines and spirits.

FACILITIES
Bake shop; catering service; classroom; computer laboratory; demonstration laboratory; food production kitchen; garden; gourmet dining room; laboratory; learning resource center; library; teaching kitchen.

SPECIAL PROGRAMS
Short seminars in wine tasting and ServSafe Certification, co-op work experience and internships in hotels, culinary competition.

FINANCIAL AID
Employment placement assistance is available. Employment opportunities within the program are available.

APPLICATION INFORMATION
Students may begin participation in January, June, July, and September. Applications are accepted continuously. Applicants must submit a formal application and be a high school graduate.

CONTACT
Director of Admissions, Food and Nutrition Culinary Arts Department, 1500 North Verdugo Road, Glendale, CA 91208-2894. Telephone: 818-240-1000 Ext. 5597. Fax: 818-551-5255.

KITCHEN ACADEMY

Hollywood, California

GENERAL INFORMATION
Public, coeducational, culinary institute. Urban campus. Founded in 2005. Accredited by Accrediting Council for Independent Colleges and Schools.

PROGRAM INFORMATION
Offered since 2005. 30-week diploma in professional culinary arts.

CULINARD. WHERE BREAD IS BROKEN AND CAREERS ARE BUILT.

Food, good food, does not stand alone. It is a part of culture, encompassing history, geography and tradition, and Culinard's program reflects this awareness. At Culinard, we teach the knowledge and skills needed to prepare distinctive dishes. We also teach the cultural sensitivity and global awareness that makes the preparation of food something that satisfies both the body and soul. Our instructors are among the best in their fields.

Like you, they have a passion for food, a taste for success, and they have worked together to develop a comprehensive curriculum that will engage and inspire you. They will walk you carefully through the necessary steps to becoming a chef. Our curriculum will introduce you to the techniques you need to prepare excellent food and the knowledge you need to turn your passion for food into a rewarding career.

The Culinary Institute of Virginia College

65 Bagby Drive / Birmingham, AL 35209
205.802.1200 / 1-877-CULINARD / www.culinard.com

(FINANCIAL AID IS AVAILABLE FOR THOSE WHO QUALIFY.)

AREAS OF STUDY

Baking; culinary skill development; food preparation; meat fabrication; patisserie; saucier; soup, stock, sauce, and starch production.

FACILITIES

Coffee shop; computer laboratory; demonstration laboratory; 4 food production kitchens; gourmet dining room; 4 laboratories; library; 4 teaching kitchens.

STUDENT PROFILE

175 full-time. 100 are under 25 years old; 75 are between 25 and 44 years old.

FACULTY

10 total: 10 full-time. 10 are industry professionals; 10 are culinary-certified teachers. Prominent faculty: Jennifer Farris, Campus Director; Alexx Guevara, Instructor; Dan Mattern; Eric Greenspan. Faculty-student ratio: 1:16.

SPECIAL PROGRAMS

Event Tie-in Through Hollywood Entertainment.

TYPICAL EXPENSES

Application fee: $100. Tuition: $18,000 per 30 week program. Program-related fees include $45 for STRF fee; $500 for books and supplies.

FINANCIAL AID

Program-specific awards include Federal aid programs available. Employment placement assistance is available. Employment opportunities within the program are available.

APPLICATION INFORMATION

Students may begin participation in January, February, April, May, July, August, October, and November. Applications are accepted continuously. Applicants must interview; submit a formal application and Wonderlic Exam.

CONTACT

Pam Ramirez, Director of Admissions, 6370 West Sunset Boulevard, Hollywood, CA 90028. Telephone: 866-548-2223. Fax: 323-460-4198. E-mail: tehrhardt@careered.com. World Wide Web: http://www.kitchenacademy.com.

LAKE TAHOE COMMUNITY COLLEGE

Culinary Arts Department

South Lake Tahoe, California

GENERAL INFORMATION

Public, coeducational, two-year college. Small-town setting. Founded in 1975. Accredited by Western Association of Schools and Colleges.

PROGRAM INFORMATION

Offered since 2000. Program calendar is divided into quarters. 1-year certificate of achievement in culinary arts.

1- to 2-year advanced certificate in culinary arts. 2- to 3-year associate degree in culinary arts.

PROGRAM AFFILIATION

American Center for Wine, Food and the Arts; American Culinary Federation; Chefs Collaborative 2000; Copia; National Restaurant Association Educational Foundation; Oldways Preservation and Exchange Trust.

AREAS OF STUDY

Baking; beverage management; buffet catering; controlling costs in food service; culinary skill development; food preparation; food purchasing; food service math; garde-manger; history of food and cooking; ice carving; international cuisine; introduction to food service; kitchen management; management and human resources; nutrition; patisserie; restaurant opportunities; sanitation; soup, stock, sauce, and starch production; wines and spirits.

FACILITIES

Bake shop; cafeteria; catering service; classroom; computer laboratory; demonstration laboratory; food production kitchen; garden; gourmet dining room; lecture room; public restaurant; teaching kitchen.

TYPICAL STUDENT PROFILE

140 total: 65 full-time; 75 part-time.

SPECIAL PROGRAMS

Field trips and classes in Napa Valley and San Francisco Bay area, paid externships in Lake Tahoe and regional restaurants and resorts, membership in Tahoe Epicurean Club.

FINANCIAL AID

Program-specific awards include Foundation Scholarship for advanced classes at CIA Greystone. Employment placement assistance is available. Employment opportunities within the program are available.

APPLICATION INFORMATION

Students may begin participation in January, April, July, and September. Applications are accepted continuously.

CONTACT

Director of Admissions, Culinary Arts Department, One College Drive, South Lake Tahoe, CA 96150. Telephone: 530-541-4660 Ext. 334. Fax: 530-541-7852. World Wide Web: http://www.ltcc.cc.ca.us.

LONG BEACH CITY COLLEGE

Culinary Arts

Long Beach, California

GENERAL INFORMATION

Public, coeducational, two-year college. Urban campus. Founded in 1927. Accredited by Western Association of Schools and Colleges.

Long Beach City College *(continued)*

PROGRAM INFORMATION
Offered since 1949. Accredited by American Dietetic Association. Program calendar is divided into semesters. 0.5-year certificate in food handlers certification. 1-year certificate in dietetic service supervisor. 1.5-year associate degree in restaurant management. 1.5-year associate degree in catering management. 1.5-year associate degree in commercial baking and pastry. 1.5-year associate degree in hotel/restaurant management. 1.5-year certificate in dietetic technician. 1.5-year certificate in restaurant management. 1.5-year certificate in catering management. 1.5-year certificate in commercial baking and pastry. 1.5-year certificate in culinary arts. 2-year associate degree in dietetic technician. 2-year associate degree in dietetic service supervisor. 2-year associate degree in culinary arts.

PROGRAM AFFILIATION
Academic Culinaire Paris; American Culinary Federation; American Dietetic Association; American Institute of Baking; Confrerie de la Chaine des Rotisseurs; French Chefs Association of California; National Restaurant Association; National Restaurant Association Educational Foundation; Société Culinaire Philanthropique; The Bread Bakers Guild of America; Toques Blanches.

AREAS OF STUDY
Baking; beverage management; buffet catering; controlling costs in food service; culinary French; culinary skill development; food preparation; food purchasing; food service communication; food service math; garde-manger; international cuisine; introduction to food service; kitchen management; meal planning; meat cutting; meat fabrication; menu and facilities design; nutrition; nutrition and food service; patisserie; restaurant opportunities; sanitation; saucier; seafood processing; soup, stock, sauce, and starch production; wines and spirits.

FACILITIES
2 bake shops; 2 cafeterias; 2 catering services; 4 classrooms; coffee shop; 2 computer laboratories; 4 demonstration laboratories; 4 food production kitchens; garden; gourmet dining room; 2 learning resource centers; 4 lecture rooms; 2 libraries; 2 public restaurants; 2 snack shops; 2 student lounges; 3 teaching kitchens.

STUDENT PROFILE
155 total: 37 full-time; 118 part-time. 63 are under 25 years old; 64 are between 25 and 44 years old; 28 are over 44 years old.

FACULTY
20 total: 4 full-time; 16 part-time. 18 are industry professionals; 3 are culinary-certified teachers. Prominent faculty: Romain E. Bertein, CCE, CEC; Frank Madrigal, CWC. Faculty-student ratio: 1:30.

SPECIAL PROGRAMS
Culinary set competitions, food expositions and field trips (produce, meat, and seafood processing companies).

TYPICAL EXPENSES
Application fee: $350. Tuition: $26 per unit full-time (in district), $26 per unit part-time. Program-related fees include $200 for books; $100 for uniforms; $150 for cutlery.

FINANCIAL AID
In 2004, 16 scholarships were awarded (average award was $200–$300). Program-specific awards include home economics and dietetics scholarships.

HOUSING
Average off-campus housing cost per month: $450.

APPLICATION INFORMATION
Students may begin participation in January, June, and August. Applications are accepted continuously. In 2004, 155 applied; 155 were accepted. Applicants must submit a formal application.

CONTACT
Romain E. Bertein, Department Chair (culinary), or Linda Huy, Program Director (dietetics), Culinary Arts, 4901 East Carson Stree, Long Beach, CA 90808. Telephone: 562-938-4502. Fax: 562-938-4334. E-mail: rbertein@lbcc.edu or lhyu@lbcc.cc.ca.us. World Wide Web: http://www.lbcc.edu.

LOS ANGELES MISSION COLLEGE

Sylmar, California

GENERAL INFORMATION
Public, coeducational, two-year college. Suburban campus. Founded in 1974. Accredited by Western Association of Schools and Colleges.

PROGRAM INFORMATION
Offered since 1975. Program calendar is divided into semesters. 17-unit certificate in culinary arts. 2-year associate degree in food management production. 34-unit certificate in food service management.

PROGRAM AFFILIATION
American Culinary Federation; American Dietetic Association; International Food Service Executives Association; National Restaurant Association; National Restaurant Association Educational Foundation.

AREAS OF STUDY
Baking; buffet catering; controlling costs in food service; culinary skill development; food preparation; food purchasing; food service communication; international cuisine; introduction to food service; kitchen management; meal planning; menu and facilities design; nutrition; nutrition and food service; restaurant opportunities; sanitation; seafood processing; soup, stock, sauce, and starch production.

FACILITIES
Cafeteria; catering service; coffee shop; 2 demonstration laboratories; 2 food production kitchens; gourmet dining room; learning resource center; library; 2 teaching kitchens.

TYPICAL STUDENT PROFILE
318 total: 64 full-time; 254 part-time. 233 are under 25 years old; 61 are between 25 and 44 years old; 24 are over 44 years old.

SPECIAL PROGRAMS
Culinary competitions, 108-hour internship program (paid or non-paid), Skill Awards in restaurant management and baking.

APPLICATION INFORMATION
Students may begin participation in February and September. Application deadline for spring is February 15. Application deadline for fall is September 15. Applicants must submit a formal application.

CONTACT
Director of Admissions, 13356 Eldridge Avenue, Sylmar, CA 91342-3200. Telephone: 818-364-2696. Fax: 818-833-3307. World Wide Web: http://lamission.edu.

MERCED COLLEGE

Merced, California

GENERAL INFORMATION
Public, coeducational, two-year college. Small-town setting. Founded in 1962. Accredited by Western Association of Schools and Colleges.

PROGRAM INFORMATION
Offered since 1980. Program calendar is divided into semesters. 2-year associate degree in food service technician. 36-hour certificate in National Restaurant Association ServSafe Program.

AREAS OF STUDY
Food preparation; food purchasing; introduction to food service; meal planning; menu and facilities design; nutrition; nutrition and food service; sanitation.

FACILITIES
Classroom; computer laboratory; demonstration laboratory; teaching kitchen.

TYPICAL STUDENT PROFILE
9 total: 6 full-time; 3 part-time. 6 are under 25 years old; 3 are between 25 and 44 years old.

APPLICATION INFORMATION
Students may begin participation in January and August. Applications are accepted continuously. Applicants must submit a formal application.

CONTACT
Director of Admissions, 3600 M Street, Merced, CA 95348-2898. Telephone: 209-384-6056. Fax: 209-384-6122. World Wide Web: http://www.merced.cc.ca.us.

MIRACOSTA COLLEGE

Hospitality, Restaurant, and Tourism Management

Oceanside, California

GENERAL INFORMATION
Public, coeducational, two-year college. Suburban campus. Founded in 1934. Accredited by Western Association of Schools and Colleges.

PROGRAM INFORMATION
Offered since 1985. Accredited by Council on Hotel, Restaurant and Institutional Education. Program calendar is divided into semesters. 1-semester certificate in dining room operations. 1-year certificate in catering operations. 1-year certificate in travel and tourism management. 1-year certificate in food service operations. 2-year associate degree in travel and tourism management. 2-year certificate in hospitality management. 2-year certificate in restaurant management. 3-year associate degree in hospitality management. 3-year associate degree in restaurant management.

PROGRAM AFFILIATION
Council on Hotel, Restaurant, and Institutional Education; International Food Service Executives Association; National Restaurant Association Educational Foundation.

AREAS OF STUDY
Controlling costs in food service; food purchasing; introduction to food service; management and human resources; nutrition; restaurant opportunities; sanitation; wines and spirits.

FACILITIES
Cafeteria; computer laboratory; learning resource center; 2 lecture rooms; library; vineyard.

TYPICAL STUDENT PROFILE
105 total: 45 full-time; 60 part-time. 30 are under 25 years old; 45 are between 25 and 44 years old; 30 are over 44 years old.

FINANCIAL AID
Employment placement assistance is available. Employment opportunities within the program are available.

APPLICATION INFORMATION
Students may begin participation in January, June, and August. Applications are accepted continuously. Applicants must submit a formal application.

CONTACT
Director of Admissions, Hospitality, Restaurant, and Tourism Management, One Barnard Drive, Oceanside, CA

MiraCosta College *(continued)*

92056. Telephone: 760-757-2121 Ext. 6404. Fax: 760-795-6804. World Wide Web: http://www.miracosta.edu.

MISSION COLLEGE

Hospitality Management Program

Santa Clara, California

GENERAL INFORMATION
Public, coeducational, two-year college. Urban campus. Founded in 1967. Accredited by Western Association of Schools and Colleges.

PROGRAM INFORMATION
Offered since 1967. Accredited by American Culinary Federation Accrediting Commission, Council on Hotel, Restaurant and Institutional Education. Program calendar is divided into semesters. 2-semester certificate in food service fundamentals. 3-semester certificate in food service. 4-semester associate degree in food service management.

PROGRAM AFFILIATION
American Culinary Federation; Council on Hotel, Restaurant, and Institutional Education; Hospitality Sales and Marketing Association International; National Association of Catering Executives; National Association of College and University Food Service; National Restaurant Association; National Restaurant Association Educational Foundation.

AREAS OF STUDY
Baking; beverage management; buffet catering; controlling costs in food service; culinary skill development; food preparation; food purchasing; international cuisine; introduction to food service; kitchen management; management and human resources; meal planning; meat cutting; meat fabrication; menu and facilities design; nutrition; nutrition and food service; restaurant operation; restaurant opportunities; sanitation; saucier; seafood processing; soup, stock, sauce, and starch production; wines and spirits.

FACILITIES
Bake shop; catering service; 4 classrooms; computer laboratory; demonstration laboratory; food production kitchen; gourmet dining room; 2 lecture rooms; 2 public restaurants; teaching kitchen.

TYPICAL STUDENT PROFILE
400 total: 250 full-time; 150 part-time.

SPECIAL PROGRAMS
Attendance at national conferences and NRA show, culinary competitions.

FINANCIAL AID
Program-specific awards include industry-sponsored awards. Employment placement assistance is available. Employment opportunities within the program are available.

APPLICATION INFORMATION
Students may begin participation in January, May, and August. Application deadline for fall is September 4. Application deadline for spring is February 4. Application deadline for summer is June 7. Applicants must submit a formal application and have high school diploma or GED.

CONTACT
Director of Admissions, Hospitality Management Program, 3000 Mission College Boulevard, Santa Clara, CA 95054-1897. Telephone: 408-855-5252. Fax: 408-855-5452. World Wide Web: http://www.wvmccd.cc.ca.us/mc.

MODESTO JUNIOR COLLEGE

Culinary Arts

Modesto, California

GENERAL INFORMATION
Public, coeducational, two-year college. Urban campus. Founded in 1921. Accredited by Western Association of Schools and Colleges.

PROGRAM INFORMATION
Offered since 1998. Program calendar is divided into semesters. 1-year certificate in culinary arts. 2-year associate degree in culinary arts.

AREAS OF STUDY
Baking; beverage management; buffet catering; controlling costs in food service; culinary French; culinary skill development; food preparation; food purchasing; food service communication; food service math; garde-manger; international cuisine; introduction to food service; kitchen management; management and human resources; meal planning; meat cutting; meat fabrication; menu and facilities design; nutrition; nutrition and food service; patisserie; restaurant opportunities; sanitation; saucier; soup, stock, sauce, and starch production; wines and spirits.

FACILITIES
Bake shop; catering service; classroom; 3 computer laboratories; demonstration laboratory; food production kitchen; 2 learning resource centers; lecture room; library.

STUDENT PROFILE
30 full-time.

FACULTY
6 total: 1 full-time; 5 part-time. 4 are industry professionals; 1 is a culinary-certified teacher. Faculty-student ratio: 1:30.

TYPICAL EXPENSES
Tuition: $364 per semester full-time (in district), $26 per unit part-time. Program-related fee includes $125 for lab fee.

FINANCIAL AID
In 2004, 8 scholarships were awarded (average award was $125). Employment placement assistance is available. Employment opportunities within the program are available.

APPLICATION INFORMATION
Students may begin participation in August. Applications are accepted continuously. In 2004, 30 were accepted. Applicants must regular community college application/registration process.

CONTACT
Bob Glatt, Instructor, Culinary Arts, 435 College Avenue, Modesto, CA 95350-5800. Telephone: 209-575-6975. Fax: 209-575-6989. E-mail: glattb@yosemite.cc.ca.us. World Wide Web: http://mjc.yosemite.cc.ca.us/.

MONTEREY PENINSULA COLLEGE

Hospitality Program

Monterey, California

GENERAL INFORMATION
Public, coeducational, two-year college. Small-town setting. Founded in 1947. Accredited by Western Association of Schools and Colleges.

PROGRAM INFORMATION
Offered since 1975. Program calendar is divided into semesters. 1-year certificate in hospitality operations. 2-semester certificate of completion in baking and pastry arts. 2-semester certificate of completion in food service management. 2-semester certificate of completion in line cook. 2-year associate degree in restaurant management.

PROGRAM AFFILIATION
American Hotel and Lodging Association; Council on Hotel, Restaurant, and Institutional Education; Monterey County Hospitality Association.

AREAS OF STUDY
Baking; beverage management; culinary skill development; food purchasing; garde-manger; nutrition; sanitation; special events management.

FACILITIES
2 classrooms; laboratory; teaching kitchen.

STUDENT PROFILE
70 total: 40 full-time; 30 part-time. 25 are under 25 years old; 11 are between 25 and 44 years old; 4 are over 44 years old.

FACULTY
10 total: 1 full-time; 9 part-time. 3 are industry professionals; 3 are master chefs; 1 is a master baker. Prominent faculty: Paul Lee, CEC; Sylvia Langland, RD; Kay Covert, RD; André Adam. Faculty-student ratio: 1:15.

TYPICAL EXPENSES
In-state tuition: $11 per unit. Out-of-state tuition: $130 per unit.

FINANCIAL AID
Program-specific awards include local scholarships provided by Hospitality Association.

HOUSING
Average off-campus housing cost per month: $800.

APPLICATION INFORMATION
Students may begin participation in January and August. Applications are accepted continuously. Applicants must submit a formal application and application prior to start date.

CONTACT
Mary Nelson, Director, Hospitality Program, 980 Fremont Street, Monterey, CA 93940. Telephone: 831-646-4134. Fax: 831-759-9675. E-mail: mnelson@mpc.edu. World Wide Web: http://www.mpchospitalityprogram.com.

MT. SAN ANTONIO COLLEGE

Restaurant and Hospitality Management

Walnut, California

GENERAL INFORMATION
Public, coeducational, two-year college. Suburban campus. Founded in 1946. Accredited by Western Association of Schools and Colleges.

PROGRAM INFORMATION
Offered since 1946. Program calendar is divided into semesters. 1-year certificate in restaurant/food service management. 1-year certificate in hospitality management. 1-year certificate in food services. 1-year certificate in catering. 2-year associate degree in restaurant/hospitality management.

AREAS OF STUDY
Accounting; beverage management; food preparation; food purchasing; food service communication; food service math; introduction to food service; management and human resources; menu and facilities design; nutrition; nutrition and food service; restaurant opportunities; sanitation.

FACILITIES
Classroom; computer laboratory; demonstration laboratory; lecture room.

Mt. San Antonio College *(continued)*

SPECIAL PROGRAMS
Job internships (paid/unpaid).

FINANCIAL AID
Employment placement assistance is available. Employment opportunities within the program are available.

APPLICATION INFORMATION
Students may begin participation in January and August. Applications are accepted continuously. Applicants must submit a formal application.

CONTACT
Director of Admissions, Restaurant and Hospitality Management, 1100 North Grand Avenue, Walnut, CA 91789. Telephone: 909-594-5611 Ext. 4139. Fax: 909-468-3936. World Wide Web: http://www.mtsac.edu.

NAPA VALLEY COLLEGE

Napa Valley Cooking School

St. Helena, California

GENERAL INFORMATION
Public, coeducational, culinary institute. Suburban campus. Founded in 1996. Accredited by Western Association of Schools and Colleges.

PROGRAM INFORMATION
Offered since 1996. Program calendar is divided into semesters. 14-month certificate in culinary arts.

PROGRAM AFFILIATION
American Culinary Federation.

AREAS OF STUDY
Baking; buffet catering; controlling costs in food service; culinary French; culinary skill development; food preparation; food purchasing; food service math; garde-manger; international cuisine; introduction to food service; kitchen management; meat cutting; meat fabrication; menu and facilities design; nutrition; nutrition; nutrition and food service; patisserie; restaurant opportunities; sanitation; saucier; seafood processing; soup, stock, sauce, and starch production; vegetarian cookery; wine and food; wines and spirits.

FACILITIES
Classroom; computer laboratory; food production kitchen; garden; lecture room; library; student lounge; teaching kitchen; vineyard.

STUDENT PROFILE
18 full-time. 3 are under 25 years old; 14 are between 25 and 44 years old; 1 is over 44 years old.

FACULTY
17 total: 2 full-time; 15 part-time. 16 are industry professionals; 1 is a master chef; 1 is a culinary-certified teacher; 1 is a Master of Wine. Prominent faculty: Barbara Alexander, CEC; Krista Garcia; Kevin McKenzie; Dieter Doppelfeld, CMC. Faculty-student ratio: 1:9.

SPECIAL PROGRAMS
Tours of wineries and local farms, 5-month externship.

TYPICAL EXPENSES
Application fee: $25. Tuition: $15,500 per program (includes fees).

FINANCIAL AID
Program-specific awards include 2 Culinary Institute of America scholarships ($1000), various culinary association scholarships ($1000–$5000). Employment placement assistance is available.

APPLICATION INFORMATION
Students may begin participation in August. Applications are accepted continuously. In 2004, 30 applied; 18 were accepted. Applicants must interview; submit a formal application, letters of reference, high school diploma/GED, academic transcripts, and 200-word essay describing career interest.

CONTACT
Barbara Alexander, Director of Culinary Programs, Napa Valley Cooking School, 1088 College Avenue, St. Helena, CA 94574. Telephone: 707-967-2930. Fax: 707-967-2909. E-mail: balexander@campus.nvc.cc.ca.us. World Wide Web: http://www.napacommunityed.org/cookingschool.

NATIONAL CULINARY AND BAKERY SCHOOL

La Mesa, California

GENERAL INFORMATION
Private, coeducational, culinary institute. Suburban campus. Founded in 1993.

PROGRAM INFORMATION
Offered since 1993. Program calendar is continuous. 10-week certificate in bakery. 4-month certificate in culinary arts.

PROGRAM AFFILIATION
National Restaurant Association Educational Foundation.

AREAS OF STUDY
Baking; confectionery show pieces; controlling costs in food service; culinary French; culinary skill development; food preparation; food purchasing; food service math; garde-manger; international cuisine; introduction to food service; kitchen management; meal planning; meat cutting; meat fabrication; menu and facilities design; nutrition; patisserie;

restaurant opportunities; sanitation; saucier; seafood processing; soup, stock, sauce, and starch production.

FACILITIES
Bake shop; bakery; catering service; classroom; demonstration laboratory; food production kitchen; lecture room; library.

STUDENT PROFILE
75 full-time.

FACULTY
5 total: 5 full-time. 2 are industry professionals; 1 is a master baker; 3 are culinary-certified teachers. Prominent faculty: Dal Smith; Margaret Patt. Faculty-student ratio: 1:6.

SPECIAL PROGRAMS
Field trips to places of work, catering events for internships, organic mushroom farms.

TYPICAL EXPENSES
Application fee: $100. Tuition: $9800 for culinary; $6000 for bakery program. Program-related fee includes $250 for culinary knife set (optional).

FINANCIAL AID
Employment placement assistance is available.

HOUSING
Average off-campus housing cost per month: $400.

APPLICATION INFORMATION
Applications are accepted continuously. Application deadline for for each session: 2 weeks prior to start. In 2004, 75 applied; 75 were accepted. Applicants must interview, and demonstrated desire and passion to become professional chef.

CONTACT
Dal Smith or Margaret Pott, Owner, 8400 Center Drive, La Mesa, CA 91942. Telephone: 619-461-2800. Fax: 619-461-2881. E-mail: natlschools@nationalschools.com. World Wide Web: http://www.nationalschools.com.

THE NEW SCHOOL OF COOKING

Culver City, California

GENERAL INFORMATION
Private, coeducational institution. Urban campus. Founded in 1999.

PROGRAM INFORMATION
Offered since 1999. Program calendar is continuous. 10-week diploma in professional baking. 10-week diploma in culinary arts advanced. 20-week diploma in culinary arts.

PROGRAM AFFILIATION
American Culinary Federation; International Association of Culinary Professionals; James Beard Foundation, Inc.; Women Chefs and Restaurateurs.

AREAS OF STUDY
Baking; culinary French; culinary skill development; food preparation; patisserie; soup, stock, sauce, and starch production.

FACILITIES
Classroom; demonstration laboratory; food production kitchen; teaching kitchen.

STUDENT PROFILE
72 part-time. 5 are under 25 years old; 55 are between 25 and 44 years old; 12 are over 44 years old.

FACULTY
9 total: 3 full-time; 6 part-time. 4 are culinary-certified teachers. Prominent faculty: Carol Cotner Thompson; Amanda Cushman; May Parich; Jet Tila. Faculty-student ratio: 1:12.

TYPICAL EXPENSES
Tuition: $2400 for culinary arts; $1200 for culinary arts advanced; $1200 for professional baking.

FINANCIAL AID
Employment placement assistance is available.

APPLICATION INFORMATION
Students may begin participation year-round. Applications are accepted continuously.

CONTACT
Anne Smith, Owner, 8690 Washington Boulevard, Culver City, CA 90232. Telephone: 310-842-9702. E-mail: annesmith@newschoolofcooking.com. World Wide Web: http://www.newschoolofcooking.com.

OPPORTUNITIES INDUSTRIALIZATION CENTER–WEST

Culinary Arts Program

Redwood City, California

GENERAL INFORMATION
Private, coeducational, adult vocational school. Suburban campus. Founded in 1965. Accredited by Western Association of Schools and Colleges.

PROGRAM INFORMATION
Offered since 1965. Accredited by Western Association of Schools and Colleges. Program calendar is continuous, year-round. 3-month certificate in culinary arts.

PROGRAM AFFILIATION
National Restaurant Association; National Restaurant Association Educational Foundation.

AREAS OF STUDY
Baking; buffet catering; controlling costs in food service; culinary French; culinary skill development; food preparation; food purchasing; food service communication;

Opportunities Industrialization Center–West *(continued)*

food service math; garde-manger; international cuisine; introduction to food service; kitchen management; management and human resources; meal planning; meat cutting; menu and facilities design; nutrition; nutrition and food service; patisserie; restaurant opportunities; sanitation; saucier; seafood processing; soup, stock, sauce, and starch production; wines and spirits.

FACILITIES
Catering service; classroom; food production kitchen; learning resource center; lecture room; library; public restaurant.

STUDENT PROFILE
70 total: 45 full-time; 25 part-time. 10 are under 25 years old; 10 are between 25 and 44 years old; 10 are over 44 years old.

FACULTY
4 total: 3 full-time; 1 part-time. 4 are industry professionals; 1 is a culinary-certified teacher. Prominent faculty: L. Adam Weiner; Betty Basile, GM. Faculty-student ratio: 1:6.

SPECIAL PROGRAMS
Two-week externship (unpaid).

FINANCIAL AID
Program-specific awards include opportunity to work with caterers. Employment placement assistance is available. Employment opportunities within the program are available.

APPLICATION INFORMATION
Students may begin participation year-round. Applications are accepted continuously. In 2004, 50 applied; 45 were accepted. Applicants must submit a formal application.

CONTACT
Carlos Mercado, Counselor, Culinary Arts Program, 1200 O'Brien Drive, Menlo Park, CA 94025. Telephone: 650-330-6467. Fax: 650-324-3419. World Wide Web: http://www.oicw.org/culinary.html.

ORANGE COAST COLLEGE

Hospitality Department

Costa Mesa, California

GENERAL INFORMATION
Public, coeducational, two-year college. Suburban campus. Founded in 1947. Accredited by Western Association of Schools and Colleges.

PROGRAM INFORMATION
Offered since 1964. Accredited by American Culinary Federation Accrediting Commission. Program calendar is semester plus summer session. 1-year certificate in

institutional dietetic service supervisor. 1-year certificate in fast food service. 1-year certificate in culinary arts. 1-year certificate in child nutrition programs. 1-year certificate in catering. 2-year associate degree in hotel management. 2-year associate degree in culinary arts. 2-year associate degree in food service management. 2-year certificate in restaurant supervision. 2-year certificate in institutional dietetic technician. 3-year certificate in cook apprentice. 30-month certificate in institutional dietetic service manager.

PROGRAM AFFILIATION
American Culinary Federation; American Dietetic Association; California Restaurant Association; Confrerie de la Chaine des Rotisseurs; International Food Service Executives Association; National Association of College and University Food Service; Retailer's Bakery Association.

AREAS OF STUDY
Baking; beverage management; buffet catering; controlling costs in food service; convenience cookery; culinary skill development; dining room management; food preparation; food purchasing; food service communication; food service math; garde-manger; hotel and restaurant law; international cuisine; introduction to food service; kitchen management; management and human resources; meal planning; meat cutting; meat fabrication; menu and facilities design; nutrition; nutrition and food service; patisserie; restaurant opportunities; sanitation; saucier; seafood processing; soup, stock, sauce, and starch production.

FACILITIES
Bake shop; bakery; cafeteria; catering service; 4 classrooms; computer laboratory; 2 food production kitchens; gourmet dining room; lecture room; library; public restaurant; student lounge.

TYPICAL STUDENT PROFILE
400 total: 200 full-time; 200 part-time. 90 are under 25 years old; 250 are between 25 and 44 years old; 60 are over 44 years old.

SPECIAL PROGRAMS
Food show seminar (3 three-hour sessions), student hot food team.

FINANCIAL AID
Employment placement assistance is available. Employment opportunities within the program are available.

APPLICATION INFORMATION
Students may begin participation in January and August. Applications are accepted continuously. Applicants must submit a formal application.

CONTACT
Director of Admissions, Hospitality Department, 2701 Fairview Road, PO Box 5005, Costa Mesa, CA 92628-5005. Telephone: 714-432-5835. Fax: 714-432-5609. World Wide Web: http://www.orangecoastcollege.com.

Oxnard College

Hotel and Restaurant Management

Oxnard, California

GENERAL INFORMATION
Public, coeducational, two-year college. Suburban campus. Founded in 1975. Accredited by Western Association of Schools and Colleges.

PROGRAM INFORMATION
Offered since 1985. Program calendar is divided into semesters. 2-year associate degree in restaurant management. 2-year associate degree in culinary arts. 2-year associate degree in hotel management. 2-year certificate in restaurant management. 2-year certificate in hotel management. 2-year certificate in culinary arts.

PROGRAM AFFILIATION
American Culinary Federation; Council on Hotel, Restaurant, and Institutional Education; National Restaurant Association Educational Foundation.

AREAS OF STUDY
Baking; beverage management; buffet catering; controlling costs in food service; convenience cookery; culinary French; culinary skill development; food preparation; food purchasing; food service communication; food service math; garde-manger; international cuisine; introduction to food service; kitchen management; management and human resources; meal planning; menu and facilities design; nutrition; nutrition and food service; restaurant opportunities; sanitation; soup, stock, sauce, and starch production; wines and spirits.

FACILITIES
Bake shop; cafeteria; catering service; 2 classrooms; computer laboratory; demonstration laboratory; 2 food production kitchens; gourmet dining room; laboratory; learning resource center; lecture room; library; public restaurant; teaching kitchen.

TYPICAL STUDENT PROFILE
140 total: 70 full-time; 70 part-time.

SPECIAL PROGRAMS
153-hour hospitality internship, sanitation certification (ServSafe Education Foundation NRA).

FINANCIAL AID
Employment placement assistance is available. Employment opportunities within the program are available.

APPLICATION INFORMATION
Students may begin participation in January, June, and August. Application deadline for fall is August 18. Application deadline for spring is January 12. Application deadline for summer is June 15. Applicants must submit a formal application.

CONTACT
Director of Admissions, Hotel and Restaurant Management, 4000 South Rose Avenue, Oxnard, CA 93033-6699. Telephone: 805-986-5869. Fax: 805-986-5806. World Wide Web: http://www.oxnard.cc.ca.us/.

Quality College of Culinary Careers

Fresno, California

GENERAL INFORMATION
Private, coeducational, culinary institute. Urban campus. Founded in 1994. Accredited by Accrediting Commission of Career Schools and Colleges of Technology.

PROGRAM INFORMATION
Offered since 2000. Accredited by American Culinary Federation Foundation Accrediting Commission. Program calendar is continuous. 14-week certificate in culinary arts. 2-week certificate in bartending. 2-year associate degree in professional baking and pastry chef. 2-year associate degree in professional cooking and culinary arts. 30-week certificate in culinary chef. 40-week certificate in food and beverage manager.

PROGRAM AFFILIATION
American Culinary Federation; California Restaurant Association; National Restaurant Association.

AREAS OF STUDY
Baking; beverage management; buffet catering; controlling costs in food service; culinary skill development; food preparation; food purchasing; food service communication; food service math; garde-manger; ice carving; international cuisine; introduction to food service; kitchen management; meal planning; meat cutting; meat fabrication; menu and facilities design; nutrition; nutrition and food service; patisserie; restaurant opportunities; sanitation; saucier; seafood processing; soup, stock, sauce, and starch production; wines and spirits.

FACILITIES
Bake shop; bakery; catering service; 3 classrooms; coffee shop; computer laboratory; 2 food production kitchens; gourmet dining room; laboratory; learning resource center; lecture room; library; student lounge; teaching kitchen.

STUDENT PROFILE
40 full-time.

FACULTY
4 total: 4 full-time. 4 are industry professionals; 4 are culinary-certified teachers. Prominent faculty: John Moore, CEC, CCE. Faculty-student ratio: 1:7.

SPECIAL PROGRAMS
Culinary competitions.

Quality College of Culinary Careers *(continued)*

TYPICAL EXPENSES
Tuition: $5000-$36,000 per certificate.

FINANCIAL AID
Employment placement assistance is available. Employment opportunities within the program are available.

HOUSING
Average off-campus housing cost per month: $600.

APPLICATION INFORMATION
Students may begin participation year-round. Applications are accepted continuously. Applicants must interview; submit a formal application, letters of reference, and an essay.

CONTACT
Admissions Office, 1776 North Fine Avenue, Fresno, CA 93726. Telephone: 800-542-2225. Fax: 559-264-4454. E-mail: lonney.edwards@qualitycollege.edu. World Wide Web: http://www.qualityschool.com/food.htm.

RICHARDSON RESEARCHES, INC.

Oakland, California

GENERAL INFORMATION
Private, coeducational, confectionery food consultancy company. Urban campus. Founded in 1972.

PROGRAM INFORMATION
Offered since 1977. 1-week diploma in gourmet continental chocolates. 1-week diploma in chocolate technology. 1-week diploma in confectionery technology. 3-day diploma in chocolate compound coatings.

PROGRAM AFFILIATION
Institute of Food Technologists; National Confectioners Association of the US; Retail Confectioners International.

AREAS OF STUDY
Confectionery and chocolate technologies.

FACILITIES
Computer laboratory; demonstration laboratory; laboratory; lecture room.

TYPICAL STUDENT PROFILE
18 full-time.

APPLICATION INFORMATION
Students may begin participation in March, June, July, October, and November. Applications are accepted continuously. Applicants must submit a formal application.

CONTACT
Director of Admissions, 5545 Hilltop Crescent, Oakland, CA 94618. Telephone: 510-653-4385. World Wide Web: http://www.richres.com.

RIVERSIDE COMMUNITY COLLEGE

Culinary Academy

Riverside, California

GENERAL INFORMATION
Public, coeducational, two-year college. Suburban campus. Founded in 1916. Accredited by Western Association of Schools and Colleges.

PROGRAM INFORMATION
Offered since 1997. Program calendar is divided into semesters. 1-year certificate in culinary arts. 60-unit associate degree in culinary arts.

PROGRAM AFFILIATION
American Culinary Federation; California Restaurant Association.

AREAS OF STUDY
Baking; culinary skill development; food preparation; food purchasing; kitchen management; meal planning; restaurant opportunities; sanitation; saucier; soup, stock, sauce, and starch production.

FACILITIES
Bake shop; bakery; catering service; 2 classrooms; coffee shop; computer laboratory; 3 demonstration laboratories; food production kitchen; gourmet dining room; 3 laboratories; learning resource center; 2 lecture rooms; library; public restaurant; 3 teaching kitchens.

STUDENT PROFILE
123 total: 23 full-time; 100 part-time.

FACULTY
4 total: 4 full-time. 3 are industry professionals; 1 is a master baker; 3 are culinary-certified teachers; 1 is a technical assistant. Prominent faculty: Bobby Moghaddam; David Avalos; Martin Gilligan; Robert Baradan. Faculty-student ratio: 1:22.

SPECIAL PROGRAMS
Field trips, food competitions, Skills USA/VICA Club.

TYPICAL EXPENSES
In-state tuition: $260 per semester full-time (in district), $26 per unit part-time. Out-of-state tuition: $2030 per semester full-time, $203 per unit part-time. Tuition for international students: $2220 per semester full-time, $222 per unit part-time. Program-related fees include $228.21 for uniforms; $186.30 for tools (cutlery); $375 for books; $40 for hat fee.

FINANCIAL AID
In 2004, 3 scholarships were awarded. Employment placement assistance is available. Employment opportunities within the program are available.

APPLICATION INFORMATION
Students may begin participation in January, May, and October. Application deadline for winter is October 3. Application deadline for spring is January 30. Application

deadline for fall is May 22. In 2004, 300 applied; 100 were accepted. Applicants must interview; submit a formal application and take aptitude test.

CONTACT
Mr. Bobby Moghaddam, Director, Culinary and Hospitality Program, Culinary Academy, 2038 Iowa Avenue, Suite 100, Riverside, CA 92507. Telephone: 909-955-3311. Fax: 909-222-8095. E-mail: bobby.moghaddam@rcc.edu. World Wide Web: http://www.rcc.edu.

SADDLEBACK COLLEGE

Foods/Nutrition/Culinary/Family and Consumer Sciences

Mission Viejo, California

GENERAL INFORMATION
Public, coeducational, two-year college. Suburban campus. Founded in 1967. Accredited by Western Association of Schools and Colleges.

PROGRAM INFORMATION
Program calendar is divided into semesters. 1-year certificate in foods. 1-year certificate in catering. 1-year certificate in culinary arts. 1.5-year certificate in advanced culinary arts. 2-year associate degree in foods. 2-year associate degree in catering. 2-year associate degree in culinary arts. 2.5-year associate degree in advanced culinary arts.

AREAS OF STUDY
Baking; beverage management; buffet catering; culinary French; culinary skill development; food preparation; garde-manger; international cuisine; introduction to food service; meal planning; nutrition; nutrition and food service; restaurant opportunities; sanitation.

FACILITIES
Classroom; laboratory.

APPLICATION INFORMATION
Students may begin participation in January and August. Applicants must submit a formal application.

CONTACT
Director of Admissions, Foods/Nutrition/Culinary/Family and Consumer Sciences, 28000 Marguerite Parkway, Mission Viejo, CA 92692. Telephone: 949-582-4598. Fax: 949-582-4223. World Wide Web: http://www.saddleback.cc.ca.us/eat/col/cert19.html.

SAN DIEGO MESA COLLEGE

San Diego, California

GENERAL INFORMATION
Public, coeducational, two-year college. Urban campus. Founded in 1964. Accredited by Western Association of Schools and Colleges.

PROGRAM INFORMATION
Offered since 1964. Accredited by American Dietetic Association. Program calendar is divided into semesters. 2-year associate degree in food service occupations. 2-year certificate in dietetic supervision.

PROGRAM AFFILIATION
American Culinary Federation; American Dietetic Association.

AREAS OF STUDY
Baking; buffet catering; controlling costs in food service; culinary French; food preparation; food purchasing; garde-manger; kitchen management; meat cutting; meat fabrication; menu and facilities design; nutrition; sanitation; saucier; seafood processing; soup, stock, sauce, and starch production.

FACILITIES
Bake shop; bakery; cafeteria; catering service; classroom; 2 computer laboratories; 2 demonstration laboratories; food production kitchen; garden; gourmet dining room; laboratory; learning resource center; library; public restaurant; snack shop; student lounge; teaching kitchen.

TYPICAL STUDENT PROFILE
300 total: 200 full-time; 100 part-time. 180 are under 25 years old; 90 are between 25 and 44 years old; 30 are over 44 years old.

FINANCIAL AID
Employment opportunities within the program are available.

APPLICATION INFORMATION
Students may begin participation in January and September. Application deadline for fall is June 1. Application deadline for spring is February 1. Applicants must have a high school diploma.

CONTACT
Director of Admissions, 7250 Mesa College Drive, San Diego, CA 92111-4998. Telephone: 619-388-2370. World Wide Web: http://intergate.sdmesa.sdccd.cc.ca.us/hotel_motel/course_list.htm.

SAN JOAQUIN DELTA COLLEGE

Family, Consumer, and Health Sciences Division

Stockton, California

GENERAL INFORMATION
Public, coeducational, two-year college. Urban campus. Founded in 1935. Accredited by Western Association of Schools and Colleges.

PROGRAM INFORMATION
Offered since 1979. Accredited by American Culinary Federation Accrediting Commission. Program calendar is divided into semesters. 1-semester certificate in basic culinary arts. 3-semester certificate in baking and pastry. 3-semester certificate in advanced culinary arts. 4-semester associate degree in baking and pastry. 4-semester associate degree in culinary arts.

PROGRAM AFFILIATION
American Culinary Federation; California Restaurant Association; National Restaurant Association.

AREAS OF STUDY
Baking; beverage management; buffet catering; controlling costs in food service; culinary skill development; food preparation; food purchasing; food service math; garde-manger; introduction to food service; kitchen management; management and human resources; meal planning; menu and facilities design; nutrition; nutrition and food service; patisserie; restaurant opportunities; sanitation; saucier; soup, stock, sauce, and starch production.

FACILITIES
Bakery; cafeteria; 2 classrooms; food production kitchen; public restaurant.

TYPICAL STUDENT PROFILE
120 total: 80 full-time; 40 part-time.

SPECIAL PROGRAMS
Culinary Arts Skills Workshop, culinary competitions, field trips.

FINANCIAL AID
Employment placement assistance is available.

APPLICATION INFORMATION
Students may begin participation in January, June, and August. Applications are accepted continuously. Applicants must submit a formal application.

CONTACT
Director of Admissions, Family, Consumer, and Health Sciences Division, 5151 Pacific Avenue, Stockton, CA 95207-6370. Telephone: 209-954-5516. Fax: 209-954-5514. World Wide Web: http://www.deltacollege.edu.

SANTA BARBARA CITY COLLEGE

Hotel, Restaurant, and Culinary Program

Santa Barbara, California

GENERAL INFORMATION
Public, coeducational, two-year college. Suburban campus. Founded in 1908. Accredited by Western Association of Schools and Colleges.

PROGRAM INFORMATION
Offered since 1970. Accredited by American Culinary Federation Accrediting Commission. Program calendar is divided into semesters. 4-semester certificate in restaurant management. 4-semester certificate in hotel management. 4-semester certificate in culinary arts. 5-semester associate degree in restaurant management. 5-semester associate degree in hotel management. 5-semester associate degree in culinary arts.

PROGRAM AFFILIATION
American Culinary Federation; American Institute of Wine & Food; California Restaurant Association; Confrerie de la Chaine des Rotisseurs; Council on Hotel, Restaurant, and Institutional Education; International Association of Culinary Professionals; National Restaurant Association; National Restaurant Association Educational Foundation; The Bread Bakers Guild of America.

AREAS OF STUDY
Baking; bartending; beverage management; buffet catering; confectionery show pieces; controlling costs in food service; convenience cookery; culinary French; culinary skill development; food preparation; food purchasing; food service communication; food service math; garde-manger; international cuisine; introduction to food service; kitchen management; management and human resources; meal planning; meat cutting; meat fabrication; menu and facilities design; nutrition and food service; patisserie; restaurant opportunities; restaurant ownership; sanitation; saucier; seafood processing; soup, stock, sauce, and starch production; wines and spirits.

FACILITIES
Bake shop; cafeteria; catering service; 3 classrooms; coffee shop; computer laboratory; demonstration laboratory; 5 food production kitchens; garden; gourmet dining room; laboratory; learning resource center; lecture room; library; 2 public restaurants; 2 snack shops; student lounge; 3 teaching kitchens; 2 food preparation laboratories.

TYPICAL STUDENT PROFILE
165 total: 150 full-time; 15 part-time. 116 are under 25 years old; 41 are between 25 and 44 years old; 8 are over 44 years old.

SPECIAL PROGRAMS
Student-run food operation, culinary competitions.

FINANCIAL AID
Program-specific awards include scholarships from private sources. Employment placement assistance is available. Employment opportunities within the program are available.

APPLICATION INFORMATION
Students may begin participation in January and August. Application deadline for spring is November 1. Application deadline for fall is June 1. Applicants must interview; submit a formal application.

CONTACT
Director of Admissions, Hotel, Restaurant, and Culinary Program, 721 Cliff Drive, Santa Barbara, CA 93109-2394. Telephone: 805-965-0581 Ext. 2457. Fax: 805-962-0257. World Wide Web: http://www.sbcc.net/.

SANTA ROSA JUNIOR COLLEGE

Culinary Arts

Santa Rosa, California

GENERAL INFORMATION
Public, coeducational, two-year college. Urban campus. Founded in 1918. Accredited by Western Association of Schools and Colleges.

PROGRAM INFORMATION
Offered since 1985. Program calendar is divided into semesters. 1-semester certificate in front house operations. 1-semester certificate in culinary support services. 1-semester certificate in baking and pastry. 1-year certificate in culinary arts.

AREAS OF STUDY
Baking; buffet catering; controlling costs in food service; culinary French; culinary skill development; food preparation; food purchasing; food service communication; food service math; garde-manger; international cuisine; introduction to food service; kitchen management; meal planning; meat cutting; meat fabrication; nutrition; nutrition and food service; patisserie; restaurant opportunities; sanitation; saucier; seafood processing; soup, stock, sauce, and starch production; wines and spirits.

FACILITIES
Bake shop; 2 bakeries; catering service; 2 classrooms; coffee shop; demonstration laboratory; food production kitchen; garden; gourmet dining room; 2 lecture rooms; public restaurant; teaching kitchen; wine education classroom.

TYPICAL STUDENT PROFILE
900 total: 200 full-time; 700 part-time. 450 are under 25 years old; 360 are between 25 and 44 years old; 90 are over 44 years old.

SPECIAL PROGRAMS
Opportunities to work on special events with well-known chefs from Sonoma County.

FINANCIAL AID
Employment placement assistance is available. Employment opportunities within the program are available.

HOUSING
Coed housing available.

APPLICATION INFORMATION
Students may begin participation in January, March, June, August, and October. Applications are accepted continuously.

CONTACT
Director of Admissions, Culinary Arts, 1501 Mendocino Avenue, CFS Department, Santa Rosa, CA 95401-4395. Telephone: 707-527-4591. World Wide Web: http://www.santarosa.edu/.

UNIVERSITY OF SAN FRANCISCO

Hospitality Management Program

San Francisco, California

GENERAL INFORMATION
Private, coeducational, university. Urban campus. Founded in 1855. Accredited by Western Association of Schools and Colleges.

PROGRAM INFORMATION
Offered since 1982. Accredited by The Association to Advance Collegiate Schools of Business (AACSB). Program calendar is divided into 4-1-4. 4-year bachelor's degree in hospitality industry management.

PROGRAM AFFILIATION
American Hotel and Lodging Association; International Foodservice Editorial Council; National Restaurant Association Educational Foundation.

AREAS OF STUDY
Beverage management; controlling costs in food service; culinary skill development; events management; food preparation; food purchasing; food service communication; food service math; introduction to food service; kitchen management; management and human resources; meal planning; menu and facilities design; nutrition and food service; restaurant opportunities; sanitation; seafood processing; soup, stock, sauce, and starch production; wines and spirits.

FACILITIES
Demonstration laboratory; food production kitchen; gourmet dining room; lecture room; library; teaching kitchen.

STUDENT PROFILE
100 full-time. 97 are under 25 years old; 3 are between 25 and 44 years old.

University of San Francisco *(continued)*

FACULTY

6 total: 3 full-time; 3 part-time. 3 are industry professionals; 1 is a culinary-certified teacher. Prominent faculty: Thomas Costello, FSCI, MA; K. O. Odsather, CHA; Jean-Marc Fullsack; Jeff Scharosch. Faculty-student ratio: 1:33.

SPECIAL PROGRAMS

San Francisco Educational Symposium, Celebrity Chef Cruise.

TYPICAL EXPENSES

Application fee: $55. Tuition: $26,680 per year full-time, $955 per unit part-time.

FINANCIAL AID

In 2004, 3 scholarships were awarded (average award was $3000); 3 loans were granted (average loan was $6627). Program-specific awards include Joseph Drown Scholarship and Loan Fund, various endowed scholarships, partial tuition to full-tuition scholarships for transfer students. Employment placement assistance is available. Employment opportunities within the program are available.

HOUSING

Coed, apartment-style, and single-sex housing available. Average off-campus housing cost per month: $800–$1500.

APPLICATION INFORMATION

Students may begin participation in January and August. Application deadline for fall is February 1. Application deadline for spring is December 15. Application deadline for for fall early action is November 15. In 2004, 95 applied; 60 were accepted. Applicants must submit a formal application, letters of reference, an essay, SAT scores, high school and/or college transcripts.

CONTACT

Mike Hughes, Director, Undergraduate Admissions, Hospitality Management Program, 2130 Fulton Street, San Francicso, CA 94117-1046. Telephone: 415-422-6563. Fax: 415-422-2217. E-mail: admissions@usfca.edu. World Wide Web: http://www.usfca.edu/sobam/under/hosp/hospitality.html.

VICTOR VALLEY COLLEGE

Restaurant Management

Victorville, California

GENERAL INFORMATION

Public, coeducational, two-year college. Small-town setting. Founded in 1961. Accredited by Western Association of Schools and Colleges.

PROGRAM INFORMATION

Offered since 1966. Program calendar is divided into semesters. 2-year certificate in restaurant management. 3-year associate degree in restaurant management.

PROGRAM AFFILIATION

California Restaurant Association; Council on Hotel, Restaurant, and Institutional Education; National Association of College and University Food Service; National Restaurant Association; National Restaurant Association Educational Foundation.

AREAS OF STUDY

Buffet catering; food preparation; introduction to food service; kitchen management; nutrition; sanitation.

FACILITIES

Catering service; 3 classrooms; computer laboratory; 2 food production kitchens; learning resource center; library; teaching kitchen.

TYPICAL STUDENT PROFILE

145 total: 70 full-time; 75 part-time.

FINANCIAL AID

Employment placement assistance is available. Employment opportunities within the program are available.

APPLICATION INFORMATION

Students may begin participation in January and August. Applications are accepted continuously.

CONTACT

Director of Admissions, Restaurant Management, 18422 Bear Valley Road, Victorville, CA 92392-5849. Telephone: 760-245-4271 Ext. 2228. Fax: 760-956-1638. World Wide Web: http://www.vvc.edu.

WESTLAKE CULINARY INSTITUTE

Let's Get Cookin'

Westlake Village, California

GENERAL INFORMATION

Private, coeducational, culinary institute. Suburban campus. Founded in 1988.

PROGRAM INFORMATION

Offered since 1988. Program calendar is divided into semesters. 24-week (part-time) certificate in professional cooking. 3-week certificate in catering, beginning course. 5-session certificate in baking.

PROGRAM AFFILIATION

American Institute of Wine & Food; International Association of Culinary Professionals; James Beard Foundation, Inc.; National Association for the Specialty Food Trade, Inc.; Women Chefs and Restaurateurs.

AREAS OF STUDY
Baking; culinary French; culinary skill development; food preparation; international cuisine; meal planning; sanitation; saucier; seafood processing; soup, stock, sauce, and starch production; wines and spirits.

FACILITIES
Classroom; teaching kitchen.

TYPICAL STUDENT PROFILE
72 part-time.

SPECIAL PROGRAMS
Tours of produce market, special restaurant dinners, Basic Techniques for Creative Cooking (twice a year).

FINANCIAL AID
Employment placement assistance is available.

APPLICATION INFORMATION
Students may begin participation in March and September. Applications are accepted continuously. Applicants must submit a formal application.

CONTACT
Director of Admissions, Let's Get Cookin', 4643 Lakeview Canyon Road, Westlake Village, CA 91361. Telephone: 818-991-3940. Fax: 805-495-2554. World Wide Web: http://www.letsgetcookin.com.

WEST VALLEY OCCUPATIONAL CENTER

Culinary Arts

Woodland Hills, California

GENERAL INFORMATION
Public, coeducational, occupational education center. Urban campus. Founded in 1976. Accredited by Western Association of Schools and Colleges.

PROGRAM INFORMATION
Program calendar is divided into semesters. 20-week certificate in baking fundamentals. 20-week certificate in cake decorating. 20-week certificate in cook apprentice/catering.

PROGRAM AFFILIATION
Retailer's Bakery Association.

AREAS OF STUDY
Baking; buffet catering; commercial cake decoration; culinary skill development; food preparation; garde-manger; meal planning; sanitation; soup, stock, sauce, and starch production.

FACILITIES
Bake shop; bakery; catering service; 2 classrooms; food production kitchen; teaching kitchen.

TYPICAL STUDENT PROFILE
100 full-time. 25 are under 25 years old; 25 are between 25 and 44 years old; 50 are over 44 years old.

SPECIAL PROGRAMS
Internships (unpaid), articulation with community college.

FINANCIAL AID
Employment placement assistance is available. Employment opportunities within the program are available.

APPLICATION INFORMATION
Students may begin participation in February, July, and September. Applications are accepted continuously.

CONTACT
Director of Admissions, Culinary Arts, 6200 Winnetka Avenue, Woodland Hills, CA 91367. Telephone: 818-346-3540. World Wide Web: http://www.lausd.K12.ca.us/WVOC/index.html.

YUBA COLLEGE

Food Service Management

Marysville, California

GENERAL INFORMATION
Public, coeducational, two-year college. Suburban campus. Founded in 1927. Accredited by Western Association of Schools and Colleges.

PROGRAM INFORMATION
Offered since 1981. Accredited by American Culinary Federation Accrediting Commission. Program calendar is divided into semesters. 1-semester certificate in ServSafe (National Education Foundation). 1-year certificate in food service management. 2-year associate degree in food service management.

PROGRAM AFFILIATION
California Restaurant Association.

AREAS OF STUDY
Baking; beverage management; buffet catering; confectionery show pieces; controlling costs in food service; convenience cookery; culinary skill development; food preparation; food purchasing; food service communication; food service math; garde-manger; international cuisine; introduction to food service; kitchen management; meal planning; meat cutting; meat fabrication; menu and facilities design; nutrition and food service; patisserie; restaurant opportunities; sanitation; saucier; seafood processing; soup, stock, sauce, and starch production.

FACILITIES
Bake shop; bakery; catering service; 2 classrooms; coffee shop; 4 computer laboratories; demonstration laboratory; 3 food production kitchens; gourmet dining room; 3

Yuba College *(continued)*

laboratories; learning resource center; 2 lecture rooms; library; public restaurant; snack shop; student lounge; 3 teaching kitchens.

TYPICAL STUDENT PROFILE
32 total: 20 full-time; 12 part-time.

SPECIAL PROGRAMS
Culinary competitions (Skills USA).

FINANCIAL AID
Employment placement assistance is available. Employment opportunities within the program are available.

HOUSING
Coed housing available.

APPLICATION INFORMATION
Students may begin participation in January and August. Application deadline for fall is August 19. Application deadline for spring is January 30. Applicants must submit a formal application.

CONTACT
Director of Admissions, Food Service Management, 2088 North Beale Road, Marysville, CA 95901-7699. Telephone: 530-741-6720. Fax: 530-741-6872. World Wide Web: http://www.yuba.cc.ca.us.

COLORADO

THE ART INSTITUTE OF COLORADO

School of Culinary Arts

Denver, Colorado

GENERAL INFORMATION
Private, coeducational, four-year college. Urban campus. Founded in 1952. Accredited by Accrediting Council for Independent Colleges and Schools.

PROGRAM INFORMATION
Offered since 1994. Accredited by American Culinary Federation Accrediting Commission. Program calendar is divided into quarters. Associate degree in banquet and catering operations. 12-month diploma in the art of cooking. 21-month associate degree in culinary arts. 39-month bachelor's degree in culinary management.

PROGRAM AFFILIATION
American Culinary Federation; American Dietetic Association; American Institute of Wine & Food; Council on Hotel, Restaurant, and Institutional Education; Institute of Food Technologists; International Association of Culinary Professionals; International Food Service Executives Association; James Beard Foundation, Inc.; National Restaurant Association; National Restaurant

Association Educational Foundation; Society of Wine Educators; Sommelier Society of America; United States Personal Chef Association.

AREAS OF STUDY
Baking; beverage management; buffet catering; confectionery show pieces; controlling costs in food service; convenience cookery; culinary French; culinary skill development; food preparation; food purchasing; food service communication; food service math; garde-manger; hospitality law; international cuisine; introduction to food service; kitchen management; management and human resources; meat cutting; meat fabrication; menu and facilities design; nutrition; nutrition and food service; patisserie; restaurant opportunities; sanitation; saucier; seafood processing; soup, stock, sauce, and starch production; wines and spirits.

FACILITIES
Bakery; catering service; 3 classrooms; computer laboratory; 2 food production kitchens; garden; gourmet dining room; learning resource center; 4 lecture rooms; library; public restaurant; student lounge; 3 teaching kitchens.

TYPICAL STUDENT PROFILE
510 total: 450 full-time; 60 part-time. 125 are under 25 years old; 355 are between 25 and 44 years old; 30 are over 44 years old.

SPECIAL PROGRAMS
Field trips abroad in Italy and France (optional), ACF student team and individual competitions.

FINANCIAL AID
Program-specific awards include campus-based institutional grant program, scholarships to attend professional association conventions. Employment placement assistance is available. Employment opportunities within the program are available.

HOUSING
Coed and apartment-style housing available.

APPLICATION INFORMATION
Students may begin participation in January, April, July, and October. Applications are accepted continuously. Applicants must interview; submit a formal application and an essay.

CONTACT
Director of Admissions, School of Culinary Arts, 1200 Lincoln Street, Denver, CO 80203. Telephone: 303-837-0825. Fax: 303-860-8520. World Wide Web: http://www.aic.artinstitutes.edu.

See color display following page 380.

Colorado Mountain College

Culinary Institute

Keystone and Vail, Colorado

GENERAL INFORMATION
Public, coeducational, two-year college. Rural campus. Founded in 1967. Accredited by North Central Association of Colleges and Schools.

PROGRAM INFORMATION
Offered since 1993. Accredited by American Culinary Federation Accrediting Commission. Program calendar is divided into semesters. 3-year associate degree in culinary arts (with apprenticeship).

PROGRAM AFFILIATION
American Culinary Federation.

AREAS OF STUDY
Baking; beverage management; buffet catering; controlling costs in food service; convenience cookery; culinary French; culinary skill development; food preparation; food purchasing; food service communication; food service math; garde-manger; international cuisine; introduction to food service; kitchen management; management and human resources; meal planning; meat cutting; meat fabrication; menu and facilities design; nutrition; nutrition and food service; patisserie; restaurant opportunities; sanitation; saucier; seafood processing; soup, stock, sauce, and starch production.

FACILITIES
Bake shop; bakery; 6 cafeterias; 4 catering services; 10 classrooms; coffee shop; 2 computer laboratories; 4 demonstration laboratories; 12 food production kitchens; 5 gourmet dining rooms; learning resource center; 12 lecture rooms; library; 12 public restaurants; snack shop; teaching kitchen.

STUDENT PROFILE
75 full-time.

FACULTY
12 total: 2 full-time; 10 part-time. 8 are industry professionals; 2 are culinary-certified teachers. Prominent faculty: Kevin Clarke, CC, JD; Paul Serzacca, CEC; Todd Rymer, CEC. Faculty-student ratio: 1:15.

SPECIAL PROGRAMS
ACF apprenticeships at resorts in Keystone and Vail, culinary competitions.

TYPICAL EXPENSES
In-state tuition: $1032 per year full-time (in district), $43 per credit hour part-time (in district), $1728 per year full-time (out-of-district), $72 per credit hour part-time (out-of-district). Out-of-state tuition: $5544 per year

Colorado Mountain College *(continued)*

full-time, $231 per credit hour part-time. Program-related fee includes $850 for tools and texts.

FINANCIAL AID
In 2004, 6 scholarships were awarded (average award was $800). Employment placement assistance is available. Employment opportunities within the program are available.

HOUSING
Coed and apartment-style housing available. Average on-campus housing cost per month: $350–$450. Average off-campus housing cost per month: $1000.

APPLICATION INFORMATION
Students may begin participation in June and September. Application deadline for fall (Vail) is July 1. Application deadline for summer (Keystone) is January 15. In 2004, 100 applied; 30 were accepted. Applicants must interview; submit a formal application, letters of reference, an essay, academic transcripts, Accuplacer test scores, or ACT/SAT scores.

CONTACT
Central Admissions, Culinary Institute, 831 Grand Avenue, Glenwood Springs, CO 81601. Telephone: 800-621-8559. Fax: 970-947-8324. E-mail: joinus@coloradomtn.edu. World Wide Web: http://www.coloradomtn.edu.

COLORADO STATE UNIVERSITY

Department of Food Science and Human Nutrition

Fort Collins, Colorado

GENERAL INFORMATION
Public, coeducational, university. Urban campus. Founded in 1870. Accredited by North Central Association of Colleges and Schools.

PROGRAM INFORMATION
Offered since 1990. Program calendar is divided into semesters. 2-year master's degree in nutrition and food science. 4-year bachelor's degree in nutrition and food science. 4-year bachelor's degree in restaurant and resort management. 4-year doctoral degree in food science and nutrition.

PROGRAM AFFILIATION
Council on Hotel, Restaurant, and Institutional Education; National Restaurant Association; National Restaurant Association Educational Foundation.

AREAS OF STUDY
Beverage management; buffet catering; controlling costs in food service; food preparation; food purchasing; management and human resources; nutrition; nutrition and food service; sanitation; wines and spirits.

FACILITIES
Bakery; 6 classrooms; demonstration laboratory; teaching kitchen.

TYPICAL STUDENT PROFILE
395 full-time.

SPECIAL PROGRAMS
Summer school in Switzerland and Italy.

FINANCIAL AID
Employment placement assistance is available. Employment opportunities within the program are available.

HOUSING
Coed and apartment-style housing available.

APPLICATION INFORMATION
Students may begin participation in January and August. Application deadline for fall is July 1. Application deadline for spring is December 1. Applicants must submit a formal application.

CONTACT
Director of Admissions, Department of Food Science and Human Nutrition, 207 Gifford Building, Fort Collins, CO 80523-1571. Telephone: 970-491-5127. Fax: 970-491-7252. World Wide Web: http://www.colostate.edu.

COOK STREET SCHOOL OF FINE COOKING

Professional Food and Wine Career Program

Denver, Colorado

GENERAL INFORMATION
Private, coeducational, culinary institute. Urban campus. Founded in 1999. Accredited by Accrediting Council for Continuing Education and Training.

PROGRAM INFORMATION
Offered since 1999. Accredited by State of Colorado Department of Higher Education, Veterans Administration. Program calendar is divided into quarters. 18-week diploma in culinary arts.

PROGRAM AFFILIATION
American Culinary Federation; American Institute of Wine & Food; Confrerie de la Chaine des Rotisseurs; International Association of Culinary Professionals; James Beard Foundation, Inc.; National Restaurant Association; United States Personal Chef Association.

AREAS OF STUDY
Baking; controlling costs in food service; culinary French; culinary skill development; fish fabrication; food preparation; French regional cuisine; garde-manger; international cuisine; Italian regional cuisine; meal planning; meat cutting; meat fabrication; menu and facilities design; patisserie; restaurant opportunities;

sanitation; saucier; seafood processing; soup, stock, sauce, and starch production; wines and spirits.

FACILITIES
Bake shop; classroom; coffee shop; demonstration laboratory; food production kitchen; teaching kitchen.

STUDENT PROFILE
58 full-time. 14 are under 25 years old; 34 are between 25 and 44 years old; 10 are over 44 years old.

FACULTY
5 total: 4 full-time; 1 part-time. 1 is an industry professional; 4 are culinary-certified teachers. Prominent faculty: Michael Comstedt, CEC, CCE; Peter Ryan, CC; Lexie Justice; Dale Eiden, CEC. Faculty-student ratio: 1:8.

SPECIAL PROGRAMS
3-week culinary education tour in France and Italy.

TYPICAL EXPENSES
Application fee: $150. Tuition: $24,000 per full program with European culinary tour.

FINANCIAL AID
In 2005, 6 scholarships were awarded (average award was $3500); 35 loans were granted (average loan was $24,000). Employment placement assistance is available. Employment opportunities within the program are available.

HOUSING
Average off-campus housing cost per month: $650–$900.

APPLICATION INFORMATION
Students may begin participation in January, April, July, and October. Applications are accepted continuously. In 2005, 96 applied; 64 were accepted. Applicants must interview; submit a formal application, letters of reference, an essay, high school/college transcripts.

CONTACT
Alan Hill, Admissions Director, Professional Food and Wine Career Program, 1937 Market Street, Denver, CO 80202. Telephone: 303-308-9300. Fax: 303-308-9400. E-mail: admissions@cookstreet.com. World Wide Web: http://www.cookstreet.com.

CULINARY SCHOOL OF THE ROCKIES

Professional Culinary Arts Program

Boulder, Colorado

GENERAL INFORMATION
Private, coeducational, culinary institute. Urban campus. Founded in 1991. Accredited by Accrediting Council for Continuing Education and Training.

Classically French
Radically Different

Culinary School of the Rockies offers three intense, short-term Professional Programs:

Culinary Arts - full-time, six-month culinary program, featuring a four-week study in France.

Chef Track - part-time, 23-week evening program with top Colorado guest Chefs Instructors.

Pastry Arts - 23-day, full-time intensive course, covering the essentials of pastry and baking.

"Culinary Arts provided me a head start - I definitely recommend this course to anyone who is serious about a career in food and restaurants."

Owen Clark
Culinary Arts, January 2005
Cook, *WD50* Restaurant, New York
Voted one of the top 50 restaurants
in the world by *Restaurant* Magazine

303.494.7988 / www.culinaryschoolrockies.com

PROGRAM INFORMATION
Offered since 1996. Program calendar is divided into semesters. 1-month diploma in pastry arts. 23-week diploma in chef track. 6-month diploma in culinary arts.

PROGRAM AFFILIATION
American Institute of Wine & Food; Chefs Collaborative; Chefs Cooperative; International Association of Culinary Professionals; James Beard Foundation, Inc.; National Restaurant Association; Slow Food International; Women Chefs and Restaurateurs.

AREAS OF STUDY
Baking; controlling costs in food service; culinary French; culinary skill development; food preparation; food purchasing; fundamentals of sensory awareness; garde-manger; international cuisine; kitchen management; meal planning; meat cutting; meat fabrication; menu and facilities design; nutrition and food service; palate development and education; patisserie; restaurant opportunities; sanitation; saucier; seafood processing; soup, stock, sauce, and starch production; wines and spirits.

FACILITIES
Classroom; demonstration laboratory; food production kitchen; garden; learning resource center; lecture room; library; teaching kitchen.

STUDENT PROFILE
88 total: 56 full-time; 32 part-time.

FACULTY
4 total: 3 full-time; 1 part-time. 4 are culinary-certified teachers. Prominent faculty: David Olson; Andrew Floyd; Elizabeth Perreault; Deanna Scimio. Faculty-student ratio: 1:8.

SPECIAL PROGRAMS
1-month study in Avignon, France (includes work in a French restaurant).

TYPICAL EXPENSES
Application fee: $75. Tuition: $27,400 (6-month diploma); $11,550 (24-week diploma); $5860 (1-month diploma). Program-related fee includes $1400 for books, clothing, and knives.

FINANCIAL AID
In 2004, 1 scholarship was awarded (award was $8000); 75 loans were granted (average loan was $15,000). Program-specific awards include Sallie Mae Career Training Loans. Employment placement assistance is available. Employment opportunities within the program are available.

HOUSING
Average off-campus housing cost per month: $750.

APPLICATION INFORMATION
Students may begin participation in January, April, July, and October. Applications are accepted continuously. In 2004, 150 applied; 90 were accepted. Applicants must interview; submit a formal application, letters of reference, an essay, copy of most recent school transcript.

CONTACT
Karen Barela, Assistant Director, Professional Culinary Arts Program, 637 South Broadway, Suite H, Boulder, CO 80305. Telephone: 303-494-7988. Fax: 303-494-7999. E-mail: admissions@culinaryschoolrockies.com. World Wide Web: http://www.culinaryschoolrockies.com.
See display on page 112.

FRONT RANGE COMMUNITY COLLEGE

Hospitality/Food Management

Fort Collins, Colorado

GENERAL INFORMATION
Public, coeducational, two-year college. Suburban campus. Founded in 1968. Accredited by North Central Association of Colleges and Schools.

PROGRAM INFORMATION
Offered since 1998. Program calendar is divided into semesters. 10-credit certificate in beginning culinary arts. 2-year associate degree in hospitality/food management. 6-credit certificate in restaurant operations. 6-credit certificate in hotel operations. 8-credit certificate in advanced culinary arts. 9-credit certificate in hospitality supervision.

PROGRAM AFFILIATION
Colorado Restaurant Association; Council on Hotel, Restaurant, and Institutional Education; National Restaurant Association; National Restaurant Association Educational Foundation.

AREAS OF STUDY
Baking; controlling costs in food service; culinary skill development; food preparation; food purchasing; food service management; garde-manger; hospitality management; introduction to food service; kitchen management; management and human resources; menu and facilities design; nutrition; nutrition and food service; patisserie; restaurant opportunities; sanitation.

FACILITIES
Bake shop; classroom; computer laboratory; demonstration laboratory; food production kitchen; laboratory; learning resource center; lecture room; library.

TYPICAL STUDENT PROFILE
65 total: 40 full-time; 25 part-time.

SPECIAL PROGRAMS
Culinary exhibitions, summer Rocky Mountain Resorts internships, three experiential internships.

FINANCIAL AID
Employment placement assistance is available. Employment opportunities within the program are available.

Front Range Community College *(continued)*

APPLICATION INFORMATION
Students may begin participation in January and August. Applications are accepted continuously. Applicants must submit a formal application.

CONTACT
Director of Admissions, Hospitality/Food Management, 4616 South Shields Street, Fort Collins, CO 80526. Telephone: 970-204-8240. Fax: 970-204-0466. World Wide Web: http://frontrange.edu.

JOHNSON & WALES UNIVERSITY

College of Culinary Arts

Denver, Colorado

GENERAL INFORMATION
Private, coeducational, four-year college. Urban campus. Accredited by New England Association of Schools and Colleges.

PROGRAM INFORMATION
Accredited by American Dietetic Association. Program calendar is divided into quarters. Certificate in garnish your degree. 2-year associate degree in culinary arts. 2-year associate degree in baking and pastry arts garnish. 4-year bachelor's degree in food service management. 4-year bachelor's degree in culinary nutrition.

PROGRAM AFFILIATION
American Culinary Federation; American Dietetic Association; American Institute of Baking; American Institute of Wine & Food; Confrerie de la Chaine des Rotisseurs; Council on Hotel, Restaurant, and Institutional Education; Institute of Food Technologists; International Association of Culinary Professionals; International Food Service Executives Association; James Beard Foundation, Inc.; National Restaurant Association; National Restaurant Association Educational Foundation; The Bread Bakers Guild of America.

AREAS OF STUDY
Baking; beverage management; buffet catering; food purchasing; garde-manger; management and human resources; meat cutting; nutrition; patisserie; sanitation.

FACILITIES
3 bake shops; bakery; cafeteria; catering service; 21 classrooms; 2 coffee shops; 5 computer laboratories; demonstration laboratory; 2 gourmet dining rooms; 8 laboratories; learning resource center; 6 lecture rooms; library; 2 public restaurants; snack shop; 5 student lounges; 7 teaching kitchens; storeroom; wine & beverage lab; University events center; nutrition lab; culinary computer lab; soups, stocks & sauce kitchen.

STUDENT PROFILE
654 total: 643 full-time; 11 part-time. 569 are under 25 years old; 78 are between 25 and 44 years old; 7 are over 44 years old.

FACULTY
18 total: 15 full-time; 3 part-time. 4 are industry professionals; 2 are culinary-certified teachers. Prominent faculty: John Johnson, CCC, CCE, AAC; Peter Henkel, CEC; Jerry Comar, CEPC; Carrie Stebbins, Certified Sommelier. Faculty-student ratio: 1:18.

SPECIAL PROGRAMS
Every culinary student gets a real-life, career-building work experience through internship or co-op, international study, ACF-certification and 1-year membership for all completing associates degree.

TYPICAL EXPENSES
Tuition: $20,826 per year. Program-related fees include $951 for general fee; $250 for orientation fee; $300 for reservation deposit; $954 for weekend meal plan.

FINANCIAL AID
In 2005, 256 scholarships were awarded (average award was $5084); 385 loans were granted (average loan was $5476). Employment placement assistance is available.

HOUSING
Coed housing available. Average on-campus housing cost per month: $1000.

APPLICATION INFORMATION
Applications are accepted continuously. In 2005, 1047 applied; 1006 were accepted. Applicants must submit a formal application.

CONTACT
David McKlveen, Director of Admissions, College of Culinary Arts, 7150 Montview Boulevard, Denver, CO 80220. Telephone: 877-598-3368. Fax: 303-256-9333. E-mail: admissions.den@jwu.edu. World Wide Web: http://culinary.jwu.edu.

See color display following page 332.

MESA STATE COLLEGE

Colorado Culinary Academy

Grand Junction, Colorado

GENERAL INFORMATION
Public, coeducational, comprehensive institution. Urban campus. Founded in 1925. Accredited by North Central Association of Colleges and Schools.

PROGRAM INFORMATION
Offered since 1998. Program calendar is divided into semesters. 1-year certificate in culinary arts. 2-year associate degree in culinary arts.

PROGRAM AFFILIATION
American Culinary Federation; National Restaurant Association; National Restaurant Association Educational Foundation.

AREAS OF STUDY
Baking; beverage management; controlling costs in food service; culinary skill development; food preparation; food purchasing; food service math; food service supervision; garde-manger; introduction to food service; meat cutting; meat fabrication; menu and facilities design; nutrition; nutrition and food service; sanitation; saucier; seafood processing; soup, stock, sauce, and starch production; wines and spirits.

FACILITIES
Bake shop; cafeteria; 4 classrooms; coffee shop; 2 computer laboratories; 2 demonstration laboratories; food production kitchen; gourmet dining room; learning resource center; teaching kitchen; baking kitchen.

SPECIAL PROGRAMS
Culinary competitions.

FINANCIAL AID
Employment placement assistance is available. Employment opportunities within the program are available.

HOUSING
Coed housing available.

APPLICATION INFORMATION
Students may begin participation in January, June, and August. Application deadline for fall is August 23. Application deadline for spring is January 17. Applicants must interview; submit a formal application.

CONTACT
Director of Admissions, Colorado Culinary Academy, 2508 Blichmann Avenue, Grand Junction, CO 81505. Telephone: 970-255-2632. Fax: 970-255-2626. World Wide Web: http://www.mesastate.edu.

METROPOLITAN STATE COLLEGE OF DENVER

Hospitality, Meeting, and Travel Administration Department

Denver, Colorado

GENERAL INFORMATION
Public, coeducational, four-year college. Urban campus. Founded in 1963. Accredited by North Central Association of Colleges and Schools.

PROGRAM INFORMATION
Offered since 1963. Accredited by North Central Association of Colleges and Schools. Program calendar is divided into semesters. Certificate in Sommelier Diploma.

4-year bachelor's degree in hotel administration. 4-year bachelor's degree in culinary arts administration. 4-year bachelor's degree in restaurant administration.

PROGRAM AFFILIATION
American Culinary Federation; American Hotel and Lodging Association; Council on Hotel, Restaurant, and Institutional Education; International Food Service Executives Association; Les Amis d'Escoffier Society; National Restaurant Association; National Restaurant Association Educational Foundation; Slow Food International; Tasters Guild International.

AREAS OF STUDY
Beers; healthy professional cooking; kitchen management; nutrition; restaurant opportunities; wines and spirits.

FACILITIES
Bake shop; catering service; 4 classrooms; computer laboratory; demonstration laboratory; food production kitchen; gourmet dining room; learning resource center; 4 lecture rooms; library; public restaurant; 5 student lounges; teaching kitchen.

STUDENT PROFILE
475 total: 250 full-time; 225 part-time. 30 are under 25 years old; 40 are between 25 and 44 years old.

FACULTY
18 total: 7 full-time; 11 part-time. 5 are industry professionals; 3 are culinary-certified teachers; 1 is a Sommelier, 1 MCFE. Prominent faculty: Jackson Lamb, MS, CCE, CCC; John Dienhart, PhD; Michael Wray, MBA, Sommelier, MCFE; Rick Diaz, CEC. Faculty-student ratio: 1:12.

SPECIAL PROGRAMS
Swiss Hotel School exchange, international culinary and wine tours for college credit, Certified Cellar Manager Program, International Sommelier Guild Diploma, Tips Program, Bar-Code Certificate.

TYPICAL EXPENSES
Application fee: $25. In-state tuition: $3700 per year full-time (in district), $350 per credit hour part-time. Out-of-state tuition: $7400 per year full-time, $700 per credit hour part-time. Tuition for international students: $7400 per year full-time, $700 per credit hour part-time. Program-related fees include $200 for cutlery and uniforms; $9 for per credit hour program fee.

FINANCIAL AID
In 2004, 45 scholarships were awarded (average award was $750); 40 loans were granted (average loan was $2500). Program-specific awards include 2 Super Value Club Foods scholarships ($2000); 10 Southern Wine and Spirits Scholarship ($2000), Colorado Restaurant Association scholarship ($1000), International Sommelier Guild (10 at $75), 5 Culinary ProStart scholarships ($1000), Co Lodging Association 5 at $1000. Employment placement assistance is available. Employment opportunities within the program are available.

Metropolitan State College of Denver *(continued)*

HOUSING
Apartment-style housing available. Average on-campus housing cost per month: $550. Average off-campus housing cost per month: $650.

APPLICATION INFORMATION
Students may begin participation in January and August. Application deadline for fall is August 15. Application deadline for spring is January 15. In 2004, 110 applied; 90 were accepted. Applicants must submit a formal application.

CONTACT
Michael Wray, Professor, Restaurant and Culinary Administration, Hospitality, Meeting, and Travel Administration Department, Campus Box 60, PO Box 173362, Osner, CO 80217. Telephone: 303-556-3152. Fax: 303-556-8046. E-mail: wraym@mscd.edu. World Wide Web: http://www.mscd.edu.

PIKES PEAK COMMUNITY COLLEGE

Culinary Institute of Colorado Springs

Colorado Springs, Colorado

GENERAL INFORMATION
Public, coeducational, two-year college. Urban campus. Founded in 1968. Accredited by North Central Association of Colleges and Schools.

PROGRAM INFORMATION
Offered since 1986. Accredited by American Culinary Federation Accrediting Commission. Program calendar is divided into semesters. 1-year certificate in food service management. 1-year certificate in culinary arts. 1-year certificate in baking. 2-year associate degree in culinary arts.

PROGRAM AFFILIATION
American Culinary Federation; National Restaurant Association; National Restaurant Association Educational Foundation.

AREAS OF STUDY
Baking; beverage management; buffet catering; confectionery show pieces; controlling costs in food service; convenience cookery; culinary French; culinary skill development; food preparation; food purchasing; food service communication; food service math; garde-manger; international cuisine; introduction to food service; kitchen management; management and human resources; meal planning; meat cutting; meat fabrication; menu and facilities design; nutrition; nutrition and food service; patisserie; restaurant opportunities; sanitation; saucier; seafood processing; soup, stock, sauce, and starch production; wines and spirits.

FACILITIES
Bake shop; bakery; catering service; classroom; coffee shop; 2 computer laboratories; demonstration laboratory; food production kitchen; laboratory; learning resource center; lecture room; library; 2 snack shops; student lounge; teaching kitchen.

STUDENT PROFILE
350 total: 150 full-time; 200 part-time. 150 are under 25 years old; 150 are between 25 and 44 years old; 50 are over 44 years old.

FACULTY
11 total: 2 full-time; 9 part-time. 6 are industry professionals; 3 are master bakers; 2 are culinary-certified teachers. Prominent faculty: Robert Hudson, CEC, CCE; Richard Carpenter; Michael Paradiso; Darrin Bristol. Faculty-student ratio: 1:15 lab; 1:30 lecture.

SPECIAL PROGRAMS
Culinary competitions, two-semester paid internship, guest speakers for local organizations.

TYPICAL EXPENSES
In-state tuition: $831.30 per semester for degree; $831.30 per semester for certificate full-time, $100.60 per credit hour part-time. Out-of-state tuition: $355.95 per credit hour part-time. Program-related fee includes $100 for lab course.

FINANCIAL AID
In 2004, 15 scholarships were awarded (average award was $1500). Employment placement assistance is available. Employment opportunities within the program are available.

HOUSING
Average off-campus housing cost per month: $400–$800.

APPLICATION INFORMATION
Students may begin participation in January, June, and August. Applications are accepted continuously. In 2004, 150 applied. Applicants must interview; submit a formal application and take placement test.

CONTACT
Robert Hudson, Department Chair, Culinary Institute of Colorado Springs, 5675 South Academy Boulevard, Colorado Springs, CO 80906. Telephone: 719-540-7371. Fax: 719-540-7453. E-mail: rob.hudson@ppcc.edu. World Wide Web: http://www.ppcc.edu/.

PUEBLO COMMUNITY COLLEGE

Hospitality Studies

Pueblo, Colorado

GENERAL INFORMATION
Public, coeducational, two-year college. Urban campus. Founded in 1933. Accredited by North Central Association of Colleges and Schools.

PROGRAM INFORMATION
Offered since 1984. Accredited by American Culinary Federation Accrediting Commission. Program calendar is divided into semesters. 1-semester certificate in intermediate production. 1-semester certificate in dining service. 1-semester certificate in beginning production/baking. 2-year associate degree in hospitality studies.

PROGRAM AFFILIATION
American Culinary Federation; National Restaurant Association Educational Foundation.

AREAS OF STUDY
Baking; beverage management; controlling costs in food service; culinary skill development; food preparation; food purchasing; food service communication; garde-manger; legal aspects of food service management; management and human resources; meal planning; nutrition; nutrition and food service; sanitation; soup, stock, sauce, and starch production.

FACILITIES
Bake shop; bakery; 2 classrooms; computer laboratory; food production kitchen; gourmet dining room; learning resource center; 2 lecture rooms; library.

TYPICAL STUDENT PROFILE
95 total: 70 full-time; 25 part-time.

FINANCIAL AID
Employment placement assistance is available. Employment opportunities within the program are available.

APPLICATION INFORMATION
Students may begin participation in January, May, and September. Applications are accepted continuously. Applicants must submit a formal application and have high school diploma or GED.

CONTACT
Director of Admissions, Hospitality Studies, 900 West Orman Avenue, Pueblo, CO 81004-1499. Telephone: 719-549-3071. Fax: 719-543-7566. World Wide Web: http://www.pueblocc.edu.

SCHOOL OF NATURAL COOKERY

Professional Course, The Main Course

Boulder, Colorado

GENERAL INFORMATION
Private, coeducational, culinary institute. Small-town setting. Founded in 1983.

PROGRAM INFORMATION
Offered since 1983. Accredited by Colorado Department of Higher Education, Division of Private Occupational Schools. Program calendar is divided into semesters. 12-month certificate in teacher training. 4-month certificate in personal chef training.

AREAS OF STUDY
Baking; business plan development; controlling costs in food service; convenience cookery; culinary skill development; energetic nutrition; food preparation; food purchasing; food service communication; food service math; gardening; international cuisine; introduction to food service; kitchen management; management and human resources; meal planning; menu and facilities design; nutrition; nutrition and food service; performance dinners; personal chef repertoire; sanitation; soup, stock, sauce, and starch production; vegan gastronomy.

FACILITIES
Food production kitchen; garden; gourmet dining room; laboratory; library; student lounge; teaching kitchen.

FACULTY
5 total: 2 full-time; 3 part-time. 4 are industry professionals; 1 is a culinary-certified teacher. Prominent faculty: Joanne Saltzman; Susan Jane Cheney; Michael Thibodeaux; Maia Cunningham. Faculty-student ratio: 1:10 lecture; 1:1 lab.

SPECIAL PROGRAMS
Internships for qualified graduates.

TYPICAL EXPENSES
Application fee: $75. Tuition: $16,700 per personal chef program; $17,500 for teacher training program. Program-related fee includes $5500 for supplies, books, uniforms (included in total program cost for Personal Chef Training-$11,200 tuition.

FINANCIAL AID
Program-specific awards include financial aid loan program for qualified applicants, work-study assistance. Employment placement assistance is available. Employment opportunities within the program are available.

HOUSING
Average off-campus housing cost per month: $400–$600.

APPLICATION INFORMATION
Students may begin participation in January and July. Application deadline for fall is April 30. Application

School of Natural Cookery *(continued)*

deadline for spring is October 30. In 2004, 20 applied. Applicants must interview; submit a formal application, an essay, and letters of reference.

CONTACT

Nancie Graebddinger, Student Admissions, Professional Course, The Main Course, PO Box 19466, Boulder, CO 80308. Telephone: 303-444-8068. E-mail: info@ naturalcookery.com. World Wide Web: http://www. naturalcookery.com.

UNIVERSITY OF DENVER

School of Hotel, Restaurant, and Tourism Management

Denver, Colorado

GENERAL INFORMATION

Private, coeducational, university. Urban campus. Founded in 1864. Accredited by North Central Association of Colleges and Schools.

PROGRAM INFORMATION

Offered since 1946. Program calendar is divided into quarters. 4-year bachelor's degree in hotel, restaurant, and tourism management.

PROGRAM AFFILIATION

American Hotel and Lodging Association; Colorado Hotel and Lodging Association; Colorado Restaurant Association; Council on Hotel, Restaurant, and Institutional Education; National Restaurant Association; National Restaurant Association Educational Foundation.

AREAS OF STUDY

Beverage management; culinary skill development; food preparation; food purchasing; introduction to food service; management and human resources; menu and facilities design; nutrition; sanitation.

FACILITIES

9 classrooms; learning resource center; 11 lecture rooms; student lounge; teaching kitchen; seminar room; 14 meeting rooms.

TYPICAL STUDENT PROFILE

30 full-time.

SPECIAL PROGRAMS

Internships.

FINANCIAL AID

Program-specific awards include special travel awards for industry conferences. Employment placement assistance is available. Employment opportunities within the program are available.

HOUSING

Coed and single-sex housing available.

APPLICATION INFORMATION

Students may begin participation in January and September. Application deadline for fall is January 15. Applicants must interview; submit a formal application, letters of reference, an essay, ACT or SAT scores.

CONTACT

Director of Admissions, School of Hotel, Restaurant, and Tourism Management, 2030 East Evans Avenue, Denver, CO 80208-2322. Telephone: 303-871-4473. Fax: 303-871-4466. World Wide Web: http://www.daniels.du.edu/hrtm.

CONNECTICUT

BRIARWOOD COLLEGE

Southington, Connecticut

GENERAL INFORMATION

Private, coeducational, two-year college. Rural campus. Founded in 1966. Accredited by New England Association of Schools and Colleges.

PROGRAM INFORMATION

Offered since 1986. Program calendar is divided into semesters. 2-year associate degree in hotel/restaurant management.

PROGRAM AFFILIATION

Connecticut Restaurant Association; Council on Hotel, Restaurant, and Institutional Education; National Restaurant Association; National Restaurant Association Educational Foundation.

AREAS OF STUDY

Beverage management; food preparation; food purchasing; international cuisine; restaurant opportunities; sanitation.

FACILITIES

5 catering services; learning resource center; 4 lecture rooms; library; student lounge.

STUDENT PROFILE

13 total: 10 full-time; 3 part-time. 13 are under 25 years old.

FACULTY

3 total: 1 full-time; 2 part-time. 2 are industry professionals; 1 is a culinary-certified teacher. Prominent faculty: Nancy Massari, RD; William Ricco, CHA; Melissa Conway, BA, MS. Faculty-student ratio: 1:4.

TYPICAL EXPENSES

Application fee: $25. Tuition: $15,200 per year full-time, $500 per credit part-time. Program-related fee includes $1000 for program costs.

FINANCIAL AID

Employment placement assistance is available. Employment opportunities within the program are available.

HOUSING

Apartment-style housing available.

APPLICATION INFORMATION

Students may begin participation in January and September. Applications are accepted continuously. Applicants must submit a formal application.

CONTACT

Donna Yamanis, Director of Enrollment Management, 2279 Mount Vernon Road, Southington, CT 06489. Telephone: 860-628-4751. Fax: 860-628-6444. E-mail: yamanisd@ briarwood.edu. World Wide Web: http://www.briarwood. edu.

CENTER FOR CULINARY ARTS

Culinary Arts

Cromwell, Connecticut

GENERAL INFORMATION

Private, coeducational, culinary institute. Suburban campus. Founded in 1997. Accredited by Accrediting Commission of Career Schools and Colleges of Technology.

PROGRAM INFORMATION

Offered since 1997. Accredited by American Culinary Federation Accrediting Commission. Program calendar is divided into quarters. 15-month diploma in culinary arts.

PROGRAM AFFILIATION

American Culinary Federation; James Beard Foundation, Inc.; National Restaurant Association; National Restaurant Association Educational Foundation.

AREAS OF STUDY

Baking; beverage management; buffet catering; controlling costs in food service; culinary French; culinary skill development; food preparation; food purchasing; food service communication; food service math; garde-manger; international cuisine; introduction to food service; kitchen management; management and human resources; meal planning; meat cutting; meat fabrication; menu and facilities design; nutrition; nutrition and food service; sanitation; saucier; seafood processing; soup, stock, sauce, and starch production; wines and spirits.

FACILITIES

2 bake shops; 3 classrooms; 3 computer laboratories; 3 food production kitchens; learning resource center; 3 lecture rooms; library; student lounge; 3 teaching kitchens.

STUDENT PROFILE

160 total: 100 full-time; 60 part-time. 80 are under 25 years old; 60 are between 25 and 44 years old; 20 are over 44 years old.

FACULTY

17 total: 7 full-time; 10 part-time. 16 are industry professionals; 1 is a culinary-certified teacher. Prominent faculty: Richard Moriarty; Billy L. Smith; Gary Costa, CEC; Richard Moore. Faculty-student ratio: 1:10.

SPECIAL PROGRAMS

Internship program, culinary competitions, visits to distributors, growers, restaurants and shows.

TYPICAL EXPENSES

Application fee: $50. Tuition: $24,149 per diploma program. Program-related fees include $900 for cutlery, tools, uniforms, shoes; $1200 for textbooks.

FINANCIAL AID

In 2005, 6 scholarships were awarded (average award was $500). Employment placement assistance is available. Employment opportunities within the program are available.

APPLICATION INFORMATION

Students may begin participation in January, April, May, July, September, and October. Applications are accepted continuously. In 2005, 210 applied; 190 were accepted. Applicants must interview; submit a formal application.

CONTACT

Domenic Busto, Admissions Representative, Culinary Arts, 106 Sebethe Drive, Cromwell, CT 06416. Telephone: 860-613-3350. Fax: 860-613-3353. World Wide Web: http://www.centerforculinaryarts.com.

CENTER FOR CULINARY ARTS, SHELTON

Culinary Arts

Shelton, Connecticut

GENERAL INFORMATION

Private, coeducational, culinary institute. Suburban campus. Founded in 1997. Accredited by Accrediting Commission of Career Schools and Colleges of Technology.

PROGRAM INFORMATION

Offered since 1997. Accredited by American Culinary Federation Accrediting Commission. Program calendar is divided into quarters. 15-month diploma in culinary arts.

PROGRAM AFFILIATION

American Culinary Federation; James Beard Foundation, Inc.; National Restaurant Association; National Restaurant Association Educational Foundation.

AREAS OF STUDY

Baking; beverage management; buffet catering; controlling costs in food service; culinary French; culinary skill development; food preparation; food purchasing; food service communication; food service math; garde-manger;

Center for Culinary Arts, Shelton *(continued)*

international cuisine; introduction to food service; kitchen management; management and human resources; meal planning; meat cutting; meat fabrication; menu and facilities design; nutrition; nutrition and food service; sanitation; saucier; seafood processing; soup, stock, sauce, and starch production; wines and spirits.

FACILITIES

3 classrooms; 2 computer laboratories; 3 demonstration laboratories; 3 food production kitchens; learning resource center; 3 lecture rooms; library; public restaurant; student lounge; 3 teaching kitchens.

STUDENT PROFILE

150 total: 90 full-time; 60 part-time. 90 are under 25 years old; 30 are between 25 and 44 years old; 30 are over 44 years old.

FACULTY

7 total: 5 full-time; 2 part-time. 7 are industry professionals. Prominent faculty: Billy L. Smith; Brad Stabinsky; William Paternoster. Faculty-student ratio: 1:10.

SPECIAL PROGRAMS

Internship program, culinary competitions, visits to distributors, growers, restaurants and shows.

TYPICAL EXPENSES

Application fee: $50. Tuition: $18,000 per diploma program. Program-related fees include $900 for cutlery, tools, uniforms, shoes; $1200 for textbooks.

FINANCIAL AID

In 2004, 4 scholarships were awarded (average award was $500). Employment placement assistance is available. Employment opportunities within the program are available.

APPLICATION INFORMATION

Students may begin participation in January, April, May, July, September, and October. In 2004, 190 applied; 160 were accepted. Applicants must interview; submit a formal application.

CONTACT

Joanna Lia, Admissions Representative, Culinary Arts, 8 Progress Drive, Shelton, CT 06484. Telephone: 203-929-0592. Fax: 203-929-0763. E-mail: jlia@netiedu.com. World Wide Web: http://www.centerforculinaryarts.com.

CONNECTICUT CULINARY INSTITUTE

Advanced Culinary Arts Program

Hartford, Connecticut

GENERAL INFORMATION

Private, coeducational, culinary institute. Suburban campus. Founded in 1987. Accredited by Accrediting Commission of Career Schools and Colleges of Technology.

PROGRAM INFORMATION

Offered since 1987. Accredited by American Culinary Federation (ACF). Program calendar is divided into quarters, year-round. 15-month diploma in advanced culinary arts. 35-week diploma in pastry arts.

PROGRAM AFFILIATION

American Culinary Federation; Connecticut Restaurant Association; International Association of Culinary Professionals; James Beard Foundation, Inc.; National Restaurant Association; National Restaurant Association Educational Foundation.

AREAS OF STUDY

Baking; beverage management; buffet catering; confectionery show pieces; controlling costs in food service; convenience cookery; culinary French; culinary skill development; culinary theory; food preparation; food purchasing; food service communication; food service math; garde-manger; ice carving; international cuisine; introduction to food service; kitchen equipment; kitchen management; management and human resources; meal planning; meat cutting; meat fabrication; menu and facilities design; nutrition; nutrition and food service; patisserie; restaurant opportunities; sanitation; saucier; seafood processing; soup, stock, sauce, and starch production; wines and spirits; world flavors.

FACILITIES

2 bake shops; 2 bakeries; cafeteria; catering service; 6 classrooms; computer laboratory; demonstration laboratory; 3 food production kitchens; garden; gourmet dining room; 2 learning resource centers; 7 lecture rooms; 2 libraries; public restaurant; student lounge; 4 teaching kitchens.

STUDENT PROFILE

550 total: 450 full-time; 100 part-time. 285 are under 25 years old; 195 are between 25 and 44 years old; 70 are over 44 years old.

FACULTY

31 total: 29 full-time; 2 part-time. 26 are industry professionals; 1 is a master baker; 8 are culinary-certified teachers; 3 are certified executive pastry chefs; 5 certified executive chefs. Prominent faculty: Chef Paul Montalto, CEC; Chef Bruno Neveu, CEC, CCE, CEPC; Chef Barbara Howe; Chef Paul Zdanis, CEC. Faculty-student ratio: 1:15.

SPECIAL PROGRAMS

6-month paid externship, hands-on learning in on-site café, field trips to restaurants and casinos.

TYPICAL EXPENSES

Application fee: $100. Tuition: $13,950–$20,900. Program-related fee includes $1545 for cutlery, textbooks, and uniforms.

FINANCIAL AID

In 2004, 20 scholarships were awarded (average award was $1000). Program-specific awards include James Beard Scholarships. Employment placement assistance is available. Employment opportunities within the program are available.

HOUSING

Coed and apartment-style housing available. Average on-campus housing cost per month: $400. Average off-campus housing cost per month: $600.

APPLICATION INFORMATION

Students may begin participation in February, May, August, and November. Application deadline for both programs: 30 days prior to start. In 2004, 560 applied; 485 were accepted. Applicants must interview; submit a formal application and achieve satisfactory score in school's pre-enrollment test of verbal and quantitative skills.

CONTACT

Johanne Jefferies, Admissions Department, Advanced Culinary Arts Program, 85 Sigourney St., Hartford, CT

06105. Telephone: 800-762-4337. Fax: 860-676-0679. E-mail: admissions@ctculinary.com. World Wide Web: http://www.ctculinary.edu.

GATEWAY COMMUNITY COLLEGE

Hospitality Management

New Haven, Connecticut

GENERAL INFORMATION

Public, coeducational, two-year college. Urban campus. Founded in 1968. Accredited by New England Association of Schools and Colleges.

PROGRAM INFORMATION

Offered since 1985. Accredited by Council on Hotel, Restaurant and Institutional Education. Program calendar is divided into semesters. 1-year certificate in culinary arts. 2-year associate degree in hotel management. 2-year associate degree in foodservice management.

PROGRAM AFFILIATION

Council on Hotel, Restaurant, and Institutional Education; Hospitality Sales and Marketing Association International.

Gateway Community College *(continued)*

AREAS OF STUDY

Baking; beverage management; buffet catering; confectionery show pieces; controlling costs in food service; convenience cookery; culinary skill development; food preparation; food purchasing; food service math; international cuisine; introduction to food service; kitchen management; management and human resources; meal planning; nutrition; nutrition and food service; restaurant opportunities; sanitation; seafood processing; soup, stock, sauce, and starch production; wines and spirits.

FACILITIES

Bake shop; 2 cafeterias; 2 catering services; 4 computer laboratories; demonstration laboratory; 2 food production kitchens; gourmet dining room; laboratory; 2 libraries; public restaurant; 2 student lounges; teaching kitchen.

STUDENT PROFILE

160 total: 110 full-time; 50 part-time. 56 are under 25 years old; 56 are between 25 and 44 years old; 48 are over 44 years old.

FACULTY

7 total: 2 full-time; 5 part-time. 5 are industry professionals; 1 is a master chef; 1 is a master baker. Prominent faculty: Stephen Fries; Andrew V. Randi. Faculty-student ratio: 1:15.

SPECIAL PROGRAMS

One-day visit to the International Hotel/Restaurant show in New York City, internships.

TYPICAL EXPENSES

Application fee: $20. In-state tuition: $1268 per semester full-time (in district), $339.50 per 3 credit hours part-time. Out-of-state tuition: $3784 per semester full-time, $1008.50 per 3 credit hours part-time. Program-related fees include $100 for uniforms; $400 for textbooks.

FINANCIAL AID

In 2004, individual loans were awarded at $1500. Employment placement assistance is available. Employment opportunities within the program are available.

HOUSING

Average off-campus housing cost per month: $450.

APPLICATION INFORMATION

Students may begin participation in January and September. Application deadline for fall is September 6. Application deadline for spring is January 16. In 2004, 140 applied; 140 were accepted. Applicants must submit a formal application.

CONTACT

Stephen Fries, Coordinator, Hospitality Management, 60 Sargent Drive, New Haven, CT 06511-5918. Telephone: 203-285-2175. Fax: 203-285-2180. E-mail: sfries@gwcc. commnet.edu. World Wide Web: http://www.gwctc. commnet.edu.

MANCHESTER COMMUNITY COLLEGE

Culinary Arts Department

Manchester, Connecticut

GENERAL INFORMATION

Public, coeducational, two-year college. Suburban campus. Founded in 1963. Accredited by New England Association of Schools and Colleges.

PROGRAM INFORMATION

Offered since 1967. Accredited by American Culinary Federation Accrediting Commission. Program calendar is divided into semesters. 1-year certificate in culinary arts. 16-week certificate in professional cook. 16-week certificate in professional baker. 2-year associate degree in food service management. 2-year associate degree in hotel tourism.

PROGRAM AFFILIATION

American Culinary Federation; American Dietetic Association; American Wine Society; Council on Hotel, Restaurant, and Institutional Education; National Restaurant Association; National Restaurant Association Educational Foundation.

AREAS OF STUDY

Baking; beverage management; buffet catering; confectionery show pieces; controlling costs in food service; culinary skill development; food preparation; food purchasing; food service math; garde-manger; international cuisine; introduction to food service; management and human resources; meal planning; menu and facilities design; nutrition; nutrition and food service; sanitation; seafood processing; soup, stock, sauce, and starch production; wines and spirits.

FACILITIES

Cafeteria; 20 classrooms; coffee shop; computer laboratory; 2 food production kitchens; garden; gourmet dining room; learning resource center; library; student lounge.

TYPICAL STUDENT PROFILE

200 total: 50 full-time; 150 part-time.

FINANCIAL AID

Employment placement assistance is available. Employment opportunities within the program are available.

APPLICATION INFORMATION

Students may begin participation in January and September. Applications are accepted continuously. Applicants must submit a formal application.

CONTACT

Director of Admissions, Culinary Arts Department, Great Path, MS #17, Manchester, CT 06045-1046. Telephone: 860-512-2785. Fax: 860-512-2621. World Wide Web: http://www.mcc.commnet.edu/dept/hospitality.

NAUGATUCK VALLEY COMMUNITY COLLEGE

Hospitality Management Programs

Waterbury, Connecticut

GENERAL INFORMATION
Public, coeducational, two-year college. Urban campus. Founded in 1967. Accredited by New England Association of Schools and Colleges.

PROGRAM INFORMATION
Offered since 1982. Program calendar is divided into semesters. 1-semester certificate in dietary supervisor. 1-year certificate in culinary arts. 2-year associate degree in foodservice management. 2-year associate degree in hotel management.

PROGRAM AFFILIATION
American Wine Society; Council on Hotel, Restaurant, and Institutional Education; Institute of Food Technologists; National Restaurant Association; National Restaurant Association Educational Foundation.

AREAS OF STUDY
Buffet catering; controlling costs in food service; culinary skill development; food preparation; food purchasing; food service communication; food service math; garde-manger; international cuisine; introduction to food service; kitchen management; management and human resources; meal planning; menu and facilities design; nutrition; nutrition and food service; restaurant opportunities; sanitation; soup, stock, sauce, and starch production; wines and viniculture.

FACILITIES
Catering service; 2 classrooms; 6 computer laboratories; demonstration laboratory; food production kitchen; gourmet dining room; laboratory; learning resource center; library; student lounge; teaching kitchen; vineyard.

STUDENT PROFILE
115 total: 77 full-time; 38 part-time. 65 are under 25 years old; 35 are between 25 and 44 years old.

FACULTY
9 total: 3 full-time; 6 part-time. 9 are industry professionals; 3 are culinary-certified teachers. Prominent faculty: Todd Jones; Karen Rotella; Peter Cisek; Robert DeZinno. Faculty-student ratio: 1:12.

SPECIAL PROGRAMS
Cooperative education/work experience, international trips with student catering and sommelier clubs.

TYPICAL EXPENSES
Application fee: $20. Tuition: $2536 per year full-time (in district), $339 per 3-credit course part-time.

FINANCIAL AID
In 2004, 2 scholarships were awarded (average award was $500). Employment placement assistance is available. Employment opportunities within the program are available.

APPLICATION INFORMATION
Students may begin participation in January, May, and September. Applications are accepted continuously. Applicants must submit a formal application, high school transcript, immunization record.

CONTACT
Karen Rotella, Program Coordinator, Hospitality Management Programs, 750 Chase Parkway, Business Division, Waterbury, CT 06708. Telephone: 203-596-8739. Fax: 203-596-8767. E-mail: krotella@nvcc.commnet.edu. World Wide Web: http://www.nvctc.commnet.edu.

NORWALK COMMUNITY COLLEGE

Hospitality Management and Culinary Art Programs

Norwalk, Connecticut

GENERAL INFORMATION
Public, coeducational, two-year college. Suburban campus. Founded in 1961. Accredited by New England Association of Schools and Colleges.

PROGRAM INFORMATION
Offered since 1992. Program calendar is divided into semesters. 1- to 2-year certificate in culinary arts (part-time). 2-year associate degree in hotel/lodging management. 2-year associate degree in restaurant/food service management. 9-month certificate in culinary arts (full-time).

PROGRAM AFFILIATION
American Culinary Federation; American Institute of Wine & Food; Connecticut Restaurant Association; Council on Hotel, Restaurant, and Institutional Education; Foodservice Educators Network International; National Restaurant Association; National Restaurant Association Educational Foundation.

AREAS OF STUDY
Baking; beverage management; buffet catering; controlling costs in food service; culinary skill development; food preparation; food purchasing; food service math; garde-manger; international cuisine; introduction to food service; management and human resources; meal planning; nutrition and food service; sanitation; soup, stock, sauce, and starch production; wines and spirits.

FACILITIES
Bakery; catering service; 2 classrooms; computer laboratory; demonstration laboratory; food production kitchen;

Norwalk Community College *(continued)*

gourmet dining room; laboratory; 2 lecture rooms; library; snack shop; student lounge; teaching kitchen.

TYPICAL STUDENT PROFILE
150 total: 50 full-time; 100 part-time.

SPECIAL PROGRAMS
Educational exchange program with two French culinary schools, educational exchange program with schools in Greece and Italy.

FINANCIAL AID
Program-specific awards include full scholarship awarded to freshman student with the highest GPA (donated by the Connecticut Chapter of the American Institute of Wine and Food). Employment placement assistance is available. Employment opportunities within the program are available.

APPLICATION INFORMATION
Students may begin participation in January and September. Application deadline for fall is August 30. Application deadline for spring is January 21. Applicants must submit a formal application and take placement test in math and English.

CONTACT
Director of Admissions, Hospitality Management and Culinary Art Programs, 188 Richards Avenue, Norwalk, CT 06854-1655. Telephone: 203-857-7355. Fax: 203-857-3327. World Wide Web: http://www.ncc.commnet.edu/.

UNIVERSITY OF NEW HAVEN

Tagliatela School of Hospitality and Tourism

West Haven, Connecticut

GENERAL INFORMATION
Private, coeducational, four-year college. Suburban campus. Founded in 1920. Accredited by New England Association of Schools and Colleges.

PROGRAM INFORMATION
Offered since 1974. Program calendar is divided into semesters. 14-month master's degree in hospitality and tourism. 2-year associate degree in hotel-restaurant management. 4-year bachelor's degree in hotel-restaurant management.

PROGRAM AFFILIATION
American Institute of Wine & Food; Council on Hotel, Restaurant, and Institutional Education; National Restaurant Association; National Restaurant Association Educational Foundation.

AREAS OF STUDY
Baking; beverage management; controlling costs in food service; culinary French; culinary skill development; entrepreneurial marketing; food preparation; food purchasing; garde-manger; international cuisine; introduction to food service; kitchen management; leadership in hospitality; management and human resources; marketing for hospitality; meal planning; meat cutting; menu and facilities design; nutrition; nutrition and food service; restaurant opportunities; sanitation; saucier; soup, stock, sauce, and starch production; wines and spirits.

FACILITIES
Cafeteria; 6 classrooms; computer laboratory; demonstration laboratory; 2 food production kitchens; laboratory; learning resource center; library; teaching kitchen.

TYPICAL STUDENT PROFILE
88 total: 72 full-time; 16 part-time.

SPECIAL PROGRAMS
400-hour paid internships, 600-hour food practicums.

FINANCIAL AID
Program-specific awards include renewable "No Hassel Scholarship" (up to 50% of tuition based on grade point average). Employment placement assistance is available.

HOUSING
Coed housing available.

APPLICATION INFORMATION
Students may begin participation in January and August. Application deadline for fall is August 1. Application deadline for spring is January 3. Applicants must interview; submit a formal application and high school transcript.

CONTACT
Director of Admissions, Tagliatela School of Hospitality and Tourism, 300 Orange Avenue, West Haven, CT 06516. Telephone: 203-932-7391. Fax: 203-932-7083. World Wide Web: http://www.newhaven.edu/.

DELAWARE

DELAWARE TECHNICAL AND COMMUNITY COLLEGE

Culinary Arts/Food Service Management

Newark, Delaware

GENERAL INFORMATION
Public, coeducational, two-year college. Suburban campus. Founded in 1967. Accredited by Middle States Association of Colleges and Schools.

PROGRAM INFORMATION
Offered since 1993. Program calendar is divided into semesters. 1-year diploma in food service management.

2-year associate degree in culinary arts. 2-year associate degree in food service management.

PROGRAM AFFILIATION

American Culinary Federation; National Restaurant Association; National Restaurant Association Educational Foundation.

AREAS OF STUDY

Baking; beverage management; buffet catering; controlling costs in food service; convenience cookery; culinary skill development; food preparation; food purchasing; food service communication; food service math; garde-manger; international cuisine; introduction to food service; kitchen management; management and human resources; meal planning; meat cutting; meat fabrication; menu and facilities design; nutrition; nutrition and food service; patisserie; restaurant opportunities; sanitation; saucier; seafood processing; soup, stock, sauce, and starch production.

FACILITIES

Cafeteria; 10 classrooms; 20 computer laboratories; food production kitchen; gourmet dining room; learning resource center; lecture room; library; student lounge; teaching kitchen.

STUDENT PROFILE

75 full-time.

FACULTY

5 total: 3 full-time; 2 part-time. 5 are industry professionals; 1 is a culinary-certified teacher. Prominent faculty: David Nolker, CCE; Ed Hennessy, CEC, AAC; Ron Leounes; Liz Marden. Faculty-student ratio: 1:12.

TYPICAL EXPENSES

Application fee: $10. In-state tuition: $978 per semester full-time (in district), $81.50 per credit part-time. Out-of-state tuition: $2445 per semester full-time, $203.15 per credit part-time. Program-related fees include $4.50 for materials; $260 for lab fees (per credit hour).

FINANCIAL AID

Employment placement assistance is available. Employment opportunities within the program are available.

APPLICATION INFORMATION

Students may begin participation in January, June, and August. Application deadline for fall is April 15. Application deadline for spring is November 15. Applicants must submit a formal application and letters of reference.

CONTACT

Admission Department, Culinary Arts/Food Service Management, 400 Christiana-Stanton Road, Newark, DE 19713-2197. Telephone: 302-454-3954. Fax: 302-368-6620. World Wide Web: http://www.dtcc.edu.

UNIVERSITY OF DELAWARE

Hotel, Restaurant, and Institutional Management

Newark, Delaware

GENERAL INFORMATION

Public, coeducational, university. Urban campus. Founded in 1743. Accredited by Middle States Association of Colleges and Schools.

PROGRAM INFORMATION

Offered since 1988. Program calendar is divided into semesters. 2-year master's degree in hospitality information management. 4-year bachelor's degree in hotel, restaurant, and institutional management.

PROGRAM AFFILIATION

Council on Hotel, Restaurant, and Institutional Education.

AREAS OF STUDY

Beverage management; culinary skill development; food preparation; food purchasing; food service communication; introduction to food service; management and human resources; meal planning; menu and facilities design; restaurant opportunities.

FACILITIES

Gourmet dining room; public restaurant; Marriott Teaching Hotel.

TYPICAL STUDENT PROFILE

390 full-time.

FINANCIAL AID

Employment placement assistance is available. Employment opportunities within the program are available.

HOUSING

Coed and single-sex housing available.

APPLICATION INFORMATION

Students may begin participation in February and August. Application deadline for fall is January 15. Application deadline for spring is November 15. Applicants must submit a formal application.

CONTACT

Director of Admissions, Hotel, Restaurant, and Institutional Management, Raub Hall, 14 West Main Street, Newark, DE 19716. Telephone: 302-831-6077. Fax: 302-831-6395. World Wide Web: http://www.udel.edu/HRIM.

DISTRICT OF COLUMBIA

HOWARD UNIVERSITY

Center for Hospitality Management Education

Washington, District of Columbia

GENERAL INFORMATION
Private, coeducational, university. Urban campus. Founded in 1867. Accredited by Middle States Association of Colleges and Schools.

PROGRAM INFORMATION
Offered since 1970. Program calendar is divided into semesters. 4-year bachelor's degree in hospitality management.

FACILITIES
Classroom; computer laboratory; learning resource center; lecture room; library; student lounge.

TYPICAL STUDENT PROFILE
36 total: 32 full-time; 4 part-time. 36 are under 25 years old.

SPECIAL PROGRAMS
Internships, field trips.

FINANCIAL AID
Employment placement assistance is available. Employment opportunities within the program are available.

HOUSING
Coed and apartment-style housing available.

APPLICATION INFORMATION
Students may begin participation in January and August. Application deadline for fall is March 1. Application deadline for spring is November 1. Application deadline for summer session is April 1. Applicants must submit a formal application and letters of recommendation (helpful).

CONTACT
Director of Admissions, Center for Hospitality Management Education, School of Business, 2600 6th Street, NW, Washington, DC 20059. Telephone: 202-806-2753. Fax: 202-806-4465. World Wide Web: http://www.bschool.howard.edu/Programs/hospmgt.htm.

FLORIDA

THE ART INSTITUTE OF FORT LAUDERDALE

School of Culinary Arts

Fort Lauderdale, Florida

GENERAL INFORMATION
Private, coeducational, four-year college. Urban campus. Founded in 1968. Accredited by Accrediting Council for Independent Colleges and Schools.

PROGRAM INFORMATION
Offered since 1991. Accredited by American Culinary Federation Accrediting Commission. Program calendar is divided into quarters. 1-year diploma in culinary arts. 18-month associate degree in culinary arts. 3-year bachelor's degree in culinary management.

PROGRAM AFFILIATION
American Culinary Federation; Confrerie de la Chaine des Rotisseurs; Council on Hotel, Restaurant, and Institutional Education; Florida Restaurant Association; National Restaurant Association; Women Chefs and Restaurateurs.

AREAS OF STUDY
American regional cuisine; baking; beverage management; controlling costs in food service; cooking for the television camera; culinary skill development; food preparation; food purchasing; food service math; food styling; garde-manger; international cuisine; introduction to food service; kitchen management; management and human resources; menu and facilities design; nutrition; patisserie; sanitation; saucier; soup, stock, sauce, and starch production; wines and spirits.

FACILITIES
Bake shop; 2 classrooms; 2 computer laboratories; food production kitchen; learning resource center; library; public restaurant; 2 snack shops; student lounge; 2 teaching kitchens.

STUDENT PROFILE
360 full-time. 180 are under 25 years old; 170 are between 25 and 44 years old; 10 are over 44 years old.

FACULTY
15 total: 10 full-time; 5 part-time. 15 are industry professionals; 1 is a master chef; 10 are culinary-certified teachers. Prominent faculty: Klaus Friedenreich, CMC; Pamela Williams, CEC; Robert Sobkowski, CEPC. Faculty-student ratio: 1:20.

SPECIAL PROGRAMS
Culinary competitions, study abroad in France.

TYPICAL EXPENSES

Application fee: $50. Tuition: $375 per credit. Program-related fees include $200–$250 for lab fees (per quarter); $860 for culinary kit (includes uniforms).

FINANCIAL AID

In 2004, 4–6 scholarships were awarded (average award was $15,000). Employment placement assistance is available. Employment opportunities within the program are available.

HOUSING

Coed housing available. Average on-campus housing cost per month: $300. Average off-campus housing cost per month: $500.

APPLICATION INFORMATION

Students may begin participation in January, April, July, and October. Applications are accepted continuously. In 2004, 350 applied; 200 were accepted. Applicants must submit a formal application, an essay, have a high school diploma or GED.

CONTACT

Eileen Northrop, Director of Admissions, School of Culinary Arts, 1799 Southeast 17th Street Causeway, Fort Lauderdale, FL 33316-3000. Telephone: 800-275-7603 Ext. 2149. Fax: 954-728-8637. E-mail: northroe@aii.edu. World Wide Web: http://www.aifl.edu.

See color display following page 380.

THE ART INSTITUTE OF TAMPA

Culinary Arts Program

Tampa, Florida

GENERAL INFORMATION

Private, coeducational, two-year college. Urban campus. Accredited by Southern Association of Colleges and Schools.

PROGRAM INFORMATION

Program calendar is divided into quarters. 77-week associate degree in culinary arts program.

AREAS OF STUDY

Baking; beverage management; buffet catering; food preparation; food purchasing; food service communication; garde-manger; kitchen management; nutrition; sanitation; wines and spirits.

TYPICAL EXPENSES

Application fee: $50. Tuition: $385 per per credit hour. Program-related fees include $100 for enrollment fee; $850 for starting supply kit; $285 for lab fee (per quarter).

CONTACT

Director of Admissions, Culinary Arts Program, 4401 North Himes Avenue, Suite 150, Tampa, FL 33614. World Wide Web: http://www.aita.artinstitutes.edu.

See color display following page 380.

ATLANTIC TECHNICAL CENTER

Coconut Creek, Florida

GENERAL INFORMATION

Public, coeducational, technical institute. Suburban campus. Founded in 1970. Accredited by Council on Occupational Education.

PROGRAM INFORMATION

Offered since 1970. Accredited by American Culinary Federation Accrediting Commission. Program calendar is continuous. 1500-hour certificate in commercial foods/culinary arts.

PROGRAM AFFILIATION

American Culinary Federation; National Restaurant Association.

AREAS OF STUDY

Baking; beverage management; convenience cookery; culinary skill development; food preparation; food purchasing; food service math; garde-manger; international cuisine; introduction to food service; kitchen management; management and human resources; meal planning; meat cutting; nutrition; patisserie; restaurant opportunities; sanitation; saucier; seafood processing; soup, stock, sauce, and starch production; wines and spirits.

FACILITIES

Bakery; cafeteria; 3 classrooms; computer laboratory; demonstration laboratory; 2 food production kitchens; gourmet dining room; learning resource center; library; public restaurant.

STUDENT PROFILE

201 total: 96 full-time; 105 part-time.

FACULTY

7 total: 5 full-time; 2 part-time. 5 are industry professionals; 1 is a master baker; 4 are culinary-certified teachers. Prominent faculty: Martin Wilcox, CEC, CCE; Stephen Williamson, CMB; Christie Stainer; Joanne Fahey. Faculty-student ratio: 1:17.

SPECIAL PROGRAMS

Culinary competitions.

TYPICAL EXPENSES

Tuition: $3012 per certificate. Program-related fee includes $8 for supply fee.

FINANCIAL AID

Employment placement assistance is available. Employment opportunities within the program are available.

Atlantic Technical Center *(continued)*

APPLICATION INFORMATION
Students may begin participation in January, April, June, August, and November. Applications are accepted continuously. Applicants must interview, and take Test of Adult Basic Education.

CONTACT
Karen Russo, Counselor, 4700 Coconut Creek Parkway, Coconut Creek, FL 33063. Telephone: 754-321-5100 Ext. 2046. Fax: 754-321-5134. World Wide Web: http://www. atlantictechcenter.com.

BETHUNE-COOKMAN COLLEGE

Hospitality Management Program

Daytona Beach, Florida

GENERAL INFORMATION
Private, coeducational, four-year college. Small-town setting. Founded in 1904. Accredited by Southern Association of Colleges and Schools.

PROGRAM INFORMATION
Offered since 1982. Accredited by Council on Hotel, Restaurant and Institutional Education, Accreditation Commission for Programs in Hospitality Administration. Program calendar is divided into semesters. 4-year bachelor's degree in hospitality management (travel and tourism concentration). 4-year bachelor's degree in hospitality management (lodging concentration). 4-year bachelor's degree in hospitality management (food and beverage concentration). 4-year bachelor's degree in hospitality management.

PROGRAM AFFILIATION
American Culinary Federation; Council on Hotel, Restaurant, and Institutional Education; Multicultural Food Service and Hospitality Alliance; National Restaurant Association; National Restaurant Association Educational Foundation.

AREAS OF STUDY
Beverage management; culinary skill development; kitchen management; restaurant opportunities.

FACILITIES
Classroom; computer laboratory; food production kitchen; gourmet dining room; learning resource center; 2 lecture rooms; teaching kitchen.

STUDENT PROFILE
55 total: 50 full-time; 5 part-time. 51 are under 25 years old; 4 are between 25 and 44 years old.

FACULTY
3 total: 3 full-time. 2 are industry professionals; 1 is a culinary-certified teacher; 1 is a certified executive chef.

Prominent faculty: Ernest P. Boger, CHA, FMP, CHE; Leonard Jackson, CHAE, CHE. Faculty-student ratio: 1:15.

SPECIAL PROGRAMS
10-day international study tour, summer internships, culinary competition.

TYPICAL EXPENSES
Application fee: $25. Tuition: $5570 per semester full-time, $464 per credit hour part-time.

FINANCIAL AID
In 2004, 6 scholarships were awarded (average award was $1000). Program-specific awards include National Restaurant Association scholarships. Employment placement assistance is available. Employment opportunities within the program are available.

HOUSING
Single-sex housing available. Average on-campus housing cost per month: $670. Average off-campus housing cost per month: $830.

APPLICATION INFORMATION
Students may begin participation in January, May, and August. Application deadline for fall is June 30. Application deadline for spring is November 30. Application deadline for summer is April 15. In 2004, 95 applied; 71 were accepted. Applicants must submit a formal application, letters of reference, high school transcript or GED, SAT or ACT scores.

CONTACT
Ernest P. Boger, Department Head, Hospitality Management Program, 640 Dr. Mary McLeod Bethune Boulevard, Daytona Beach, FL 32114-3099. Telephone: 386-481-2871. Fax: 386-481-2980. E-mail: bogere@ cookman.edu. World Wide Web: http://www.bethune. cookman.edu.

BROWARD COMMUNITY COLLEGE

Restaurant Management Program

Davie, Florida

GENERAL INFORMATION
Public, coeducational, two-year college. Suburban campus. Founded in 1968. Accredited by Southern Association of Colleges and Schools.

PROGRAM INFORMATION
Program calendar is divided into semesters. 2-year associate degree in hospitality management. 2-year associate degree in restaurant management.

PROGRAM AFFILIATION
Council on Hotel, Restaurant, and Institutional Education.

AREAS OF STUDY

Beverage management; buffet catering; controlling costs in food service; culinary skill development; food preparation; food purchasing; international cuisine; introduction to food service.

FACILITIES

Classroom; demonstration laboratory; food production kitchen; gourmet dining room.

TYPICAL STUDENT PROFILE

45 total: 9 full-time; 36 part-time.

APPLICATION INFORMATION

Students may begin participation in January and August. Applications are accepted continuously. Applicants must submit a formal application and have high school diploma or GED.

CONTACT

Director of Admissions, Restaurant Management Program, 3501 Southwest Davie Road, Davie, FL 33314. Telephone: 954-201-6710. Fax: 954-201-6594. World Wide Web: http://www.broward.edu.

CAPITAL CULINARY INSTITUTE OF KEISER COLLEGE

Tallahassee, Florida

GENERAL INFORMATION

Private, coeducational, two-year college. Urban campus. Founded in 1977. Accredited by Southern Association of Colleges and Schools.

PROGRAM INFORMATION

Offered since 1998. Accredited by American Culinary Federation Accrediting Commission. Program calendar is 3 semesters per year. 20-month associate degree in baking and pastry arts. 20-month associate degree in culinary arts.

PROGRAM AFFILIATION

American Culinary Federation; American Dietetic Association; American Institute of Baking; National Restaurant Association; Women Chefs and Restaurateurs.

AREAS OF STUDY

Baking; confectionery show pieces; culinary French; culinary skill development; food preparation; food purchasing; food service communication; food service math; garde-manger; international cuisine; management and human resources; meat cutting; meat fabrication; menu and facilities design; nutrition; patisserie; sanitation; saucier; seafood processing; soup, stock, sauce, and starch production; wines and spirits.

FACILITIES

Bake shop; classroom; 3 food production kitchens; gourmet dining room.

TYPICAL STUDENT PROFILE

115 full-time. 58 are under 25 years old; 56 are between 25 and 44 years old; 1 is over 44 years old.

SPECIAL PROGRAMS

4-month paid externship, culinary competitions.

APPLICATION INFORMATION

Students may begin participation in January, March, May, July, September, and November. Applications are accepted continuously. Applicants must interview.

CONTACT

Director of Admissions, 1700 Halstead Boulevard, Building 2, Tallahassee, FL 32309. Telephone: 877-CHEF-123. Fax: 850-906-9497. World Wide Web: http://www. capitalculinaryinstitute.com.

See display on page 130.

CHARLOTTE TECHNICAL CENTER

Culinary Arts Program

Port Charlotte, Florida

GENERAL INFORMATION

Public, coeducational, technical college. Urban campus. Founded in 1980. Accredited by Council on Occupational Education.

PROGRAM INFORMATION

Offered since 1980. Program calendar is divided into quarters. 1500-hour certificate in commercial foods and culinary arts.

PROGRAM AFFILIATION

American Culinary Federation; International Foodservice Editorial Council.

AREAS OF STUDY

Baking; buffet catering; controlling costs in food service; convenience cookery; culinary French; culinary skill development; food preparation; food purchasing; food service communication; food service math; garde-manger; ice sculpture; international cuisine; introduction to food service; kitchen management; management and human resources; meal planning; menu and facilities design; nutrition; patisserie; restaurant opportunities; safety and first aid; sanitation; saucier; seafood processing; soup, stock, sauce, and starch production; wines and spirits.

FACILITIES

Bake shop; cafeteria; catering service; classroom; computer laboratory; demonstration laboratory; food production kitchen; gourmet dining room; laboratory; learning resource center; library; public restaurant; snack shop; teaching kitchen.

Your Chef's Career Starts Here

Earn your degree in Culinary Arts and begin your dream career in this creative and dynamic field

Capital Culinary Institute of Keiser College provides:
- Practical experience in fully-equipped kitchens, plus solid academics
- Hands – on training in a professional environment by faculty with extensive industry experience

Culinary Arts, Associate of Science Degree

The A.S. Degree in Culinary Arts program has a comprehensive curriculum that includes of food service production, food service sanitation, nutrition, stock and sauces, American regional cuisine, dining room management, introduction to baking & pastry, storeroom operations, meat cutting, international cuisine, and French cuisine.

Baking & Pastry Arts, Associate of Science Degree

The Associate of Science degree in Baking and Pastry Arts provides instruction in the art and science of the baking profession. Students in this program will use a variety of tools and equipment to produce items such as quick breads, yeast breads, cakes, frozen desserts, centerpieces, candies, cookies and various pastries.

MONTHLY CLASS STARTS
For more information contact admissions at:

Tallahassee, 850-906-9494
Melbourne, 321-409-4800
Sarasota, 941-907-3900
or visit our website at
www.CapitalCulinaryInstitute.com

STUDENT PROFILE

61 total: 21 full-time; 40 part-time. 40 are under 25 years old; 13 are between 25 and 44 years old; 8 are over 44 years old.

FACULTY

8 total: 3 full-time; 5 part-time. 2 are industry professionals; 1 is a culinary-certified teacher; 2 are para-pro. Prominent faculty: Ann Stout; Larry Berkel; Bill Seibert. Faculty-student ratio: 1:7 adults; 1:8 part time.

SPECIAL PROGRAMS

Annual tour and lecture at Ritz Carlton (Naples), culinary competitions.

TYPICAL EXPENSES

Application fee: $5. In-state tuition: $1.87 per per hour: $2805 for 1500 hours full-time (out-of-district), $1.87 per per hour; $280.50 for every 150 hours part-time (out-of-district). Out-of-state tuition: $1.87 per per hour; $2805 for 1500 hours full-time, $1.87 per per hour; $280.50 for every 150 hours part-time. Tuition for international students: $1.87 per per hour; $2805 for 1500 hours full-time, $1.87 per per hour; $280.50 for every 150 hours part-time. Program-related fees include $21 for consumable supplies; $100 for uniforms; $125 for books; $13 for classroom supplies.

FINANCIAL AID

In 2004, 12 scholarships were awarded (average award was $600). Program-specific awards include Pell Grants, Florida Vocational Tuition Assistant, Charlotte Technical Center Scholarship. Employment placement assistance is available. Employment opportunities within the program are available.

HOUSING

Average off-campus housing cost per month: $700.

APPLICATION INFORMATION

Students may begin participation in January, March, July, and October. Application deadline for summer term is July 30. Application deadline for fall term is September 30. Application deadline for winter term is December 30. Application deadline for spring term is March 30. In 2004, 63 applied. Applicants must be at least 16 years of age and pass entrance exam.

CONTACT

Dick Santello, Admissions Counselor, Culinary Arts Program, 18300 Toledo Blade Boulevard, Port Charlotte, FL 33948. Telephone: 941-255-7500 Ext. 115. Fax: 941-255-7509. E-mail: richard_santello@ccps.k12.fl.us.

DAYTONA BEACH COMMUNITY COLLEGE

Culinary Management/Hospitality Management

Daytona Beach, Florida

GENERAL INFORMATION

Public, coeducational, two-year college. Urban campus. Founded in 1958. Accredited by Southern Association of Colleges and Schools.

PROGRAM INFORMATION

Offered since 1997. Program calendar is divided into semesters. 2-year associate degree in hospitality management. 2-year associate degree in culinary management.

AREAS OF STUDY

Baking; beverage management; buffet catering; controlling costs in food service; culinary skill development; food preparation; food purchasing; food service communication; food service math; garde-manger; hospitality law; international cuisine; introduction to food service; kitchen management; management and human resources; meat cutting; meat fabrication; menu and facilities design; nutrition; restaurant opportunities; sanitation; saucier; seafood processing; soup, stock, sauce, and starch production; wines and spirits.

FACILITIES

Classroom; computer laboratory; lecture room; teaching kitchen.

TYPICAL STUDENT PROFILE

220 total: 154 full-time; 66 part-time.

APPLICATION INFORMATION

Students may begin participation in January and August. Applications are accepted continuously. Applicants must submit a formal application.

CONTACT

Director of Admissions, Culinary Management/Hospitality Management, PO Box 2811, Daytona Beach, FL 32120. Telephone: 386-254-3000 Ext. 3735. World Wide Web: http://www.dbcc.cc.fl.us.

FLORIDA COMMUNITY COLLEGE AT JACKSONVILLE

Culinary Management

Jacksonville, Florida

GENERAL INFORMATION
Public, coeducational, two-year college. Urban campus. Founded in 1963. Accredited by Southern Association of Colleges and Schools.

PROGRAM INFORMATION
Offered since 1989. Accredited by American Culinary Federation Accrediting Commission, Council on Hotel, Restaurant and Institutional Education. Program calendar is divided into semesters. 1-year certificate in catering. 2-year associate degree in restaurant management. 2-year associate degree in dietetic technician. 2-year associate degree in hospitality management. 2-year associate degree in culinary management.

PROGRAM AFFILIATION
American Culinary Federation; American Dietetic Association; American Hotel and Lodging Association; Council on Hotel, Restaurant, and Institutional Education; Foodservice Educators Network International; National Restaurant Association; National Restaurant Association Educational Foundation.

AREAS OF STUDY
American regional; baking; buffet catering; controlling costs in food service; culinary skill development; food preparation; food purchasing; garde-manger; international cuisine; introduction to food service; management and human resources; meal planning; menu and facilities design; nutrition; nutrition and food service; restaurant opportunities; sanitation; saucier; seafood processing; soup, stock, sauce, and starch production; wines and spirits.

FACILITIES
Bake shop; cafeteria; 5 classrooms; computer laboratory; 2 food production kitchens; gourmet dining room; 2 learning resource centers; library; public restaurant; student lounge; teaching kitchen.

TYPICAL STUDENT PROFILE
215 total: 180 full-time; 35 part-time. 54 are under 25 years old; 150 are between 25 and 44 years old; 11 are over 44 years old.

FINANCIAL AID
Employment opportunities within the program are available.

APPLICATION INFORMATION
Students may begin participation in January, May, and August. Applications are accepted continuously. Applicants must submit a formal application, high school transcript or GED, and take college placement test.

CONTACT
Director of Admissions, Culinary Management, 4501 Capper Road, Jacksonville, FL 32218. Telephone: 904-766-6703. Fax: 904-713-4858. World Wide Web: http://www.fccj.cc.fl.us/.

FLORIDA CULINARY INSTITUTE

West Palm Beach, Florida

GENERAL INFORMATION
Private, coeducational, culinary institute. Urban campus. Founded in 1983. Accredited by Accrediting Council for Independent Colleges and Schools.

PROGRAM INFORMATION
Offered since 1987. Accredited by American Culinary Federation Accrediting Commission. Program calendar is divided into quarters. 12-month diploma in food and beverage management. 12-month diploma in baking and pastry essentials. 12-month diploma in culinary nutrition. 12-month diploma in culinary essentials. 18-month associate degree in food and beverage management. 18-month associate degree in international baking and pastry. 18-month associate degree in culinary nutrition. 18-month associate degree in culinary arts. 24-month associate degree in international bakery and pastry with food and beverage management. 24-month associate degree in culinary arts with food and beverage management. 36-month bachelor's degree in culinary management.

PROGRAM AFFILIATION
American Culinary Federation; Confrerie de la Chaine des Rotisseurs; Foodservice Educators Network International; National Restaurant Association; National Restaurant Association Educational Foundation.

AREAS OF STUDY
Baking; beverage management; buffet catering; confectionery show pieces; controlling costs in food service; culinary French; culinary skill development; food preparation; food purchasing; food service math; garde-manger; international cuisine; introduction to food service; kitchen management; management and human resources; meal planning; meat cutting; meat fabrication; menu and facilities design; nutrition; nutrition and food service; patisserie; restaurant opportunities; sanitation; saucier; seafood processing; soup, stock, sauce, and starch production; wines and spirits.

FACILITIES
2 bake shops; 9 classrooms; computer laboratory; garden; gourmet dining room; learning resource center; lecture room; library; public restaurant; 5 teaching kitchens.

STUDENT PROFILE
500 full-time.

FACULTY

19 total: 17 full-time; 2 part-time. 17 are industry professionals; 2 are master bakers; 6 are culinary-certified teachers; 8 are certified executive chefs/pastry chefs. Prominent faculty: John Carlino, CEC, CCE, FMP; Manfred Schmidtke, CMB; Walter Tanner, CMB; August Carreiro, CEC, CCE. Faculty-student ratio: 1:18.

SPECIAL PROGRAMS

Culinary competitions.

TYPICAL EXPENSES

Application fee: $25. Tuition: $25,200 per 18 month AS degree full-time, $16,700 per 18 month diploma part-time. Program-related fees include $400 for lab fees (per quarter); $275 for cutlery; $100 for uniforms; $400 for text books and materials.

FINANCIAL AID

Employment placement assistance is available.

HOUSING

Average off-campus housing cost per month: $345.

APPLICATION INFORMATION

Students may begin participation in January, April, July, and October. Applications are accepted continuously. Applicants must submit a formal application and high school diploma/GED or take Test of Adult Basic Education.

CONTACT

David Conway, Associate Director of Admissions, 2400 Metrocentre Boulevard, West Palm Beach, FL 33407. Telephone: 561-842-8324 Ext. 202. Fax: 561-688-9882. E-mail: info@floridaculinary.com. World Wide Web: http://www.floridaculinary.com.

See color display following page 188.

FLORIDA STATE UNIVERSITY

Dedman School of Hospitality

Tallahassee, Florida

GENERAL INFORMATION

Public, coeducational, university. Urban campus. Founded in 1851. Accredited by Southern Association of Colleges and Schools.

PROGRAM INFORMATION

Offered since 1947. Accredited by AACSB. Program calendar is divided into semesters. 4-year bachelor's degree in hospitality administration. 4-year bachelor's degree in professional golf management.

PROGRAM AFFILIATION

American Academy of Chefs; American Dietetic Association; American Hotel and Lodging Association; American Institute of Wine & Food; Club Managers Association of America; Council on Hotel, Restaurant, and Institutional Education; National Restaurant Association; National Restaurant Association Educational Foundation; Society of Wine Educators.

AREAS OF STUDY

Beverage management; buffet catering; controlling costs in food service; food preparation; food purchasing; international hospitality management; introduction to food service; management and human resources; sanitation; senior services management; wines and spirits.

FACILITIES

Bakery; catering service; 5 classrooms; computer laboratory; 2 food production kitchens; gourmet dining room; learning resource center; lecture room; 2 libraries; public restaurant; teaching kitchen.

STUDENT PROFILE

225 full-time. 200 are under 25 years old; 25 are between 25 and 44 years old.

FACULTY

12 total: 10 full-time; 2 part-time. 3 are industry professionals. Prominent faculty: Robert H. Bosselman, FMP, RD; Jim Riscigno, CCM; Ernest Lanford, PGA. Faculty-student ratio: 1:20.

SPECIAL PROGRAMS

Summer study in Switzerland, international studies in London, Valencia (Spain), Panama City, Florence (Italy), summer program in resort management.

TYPICAL EXPENSES

Application fee: $20. In-state tuition: $2800 per year full-time (in district), $84 per credit hour part-time. Out-of-state tuition: $6000 per year full-time, $350 per credit hour part-time.

FINANCIAL AID

In 2004, 40 scholarships were awarded (average award was $1000). Program-specific awards include 20 Dedman Scholars Awards (up to $2500). Employment placement assistance is available. Employment opportunities within the program are available.

HOUSING

Coed, apartment-style, and single-sex housing available. Average on-campus housing cost per month: $330. Average off-campus housing cost per month: $500–$600.

APPLICATION INFORMATION

Students may begin participation in January, May, and August. Application deadline for spring is November 1. Application deadline for summer is March 3. Application deadline for fall is March 3. In 2004, 325 applied; 50 were accepted. Applicants must submit a formal application.

CONTACT

Dr. Robert H. Bosselman, Director, Dedman School of Hospitality, Dedman School of Hospitality, 1 Champions Way, Suite 4100, Tallahassee, FL 32306-2541. Telephone: 850-644-8243. Fax: 850-644-5565. E-mail: rbosselm@cob.fsu.edu. World Wide Web: http://www.cob.fsu.edu/dsh.

GULF COAST COMMUNITY COLLEGE

Culinary Management

Panama City, Florida

GENERAL INFORMATION
Public, coeducational, two-year college. Small-town setting. Founded in 1957. Accredited by Southern Association of Colleges and Schools.

PROGRAM INFORMATION
Offered since 1987. Accredited by American Culinary Federation Accrediting Commission. Program calendar is divided into semesters. 2-year associate degree in culinary management.

PROGRAM AFFILIATION
American Culinary Federation; Confrerie de la Chaine des Rotisseurs; Florida Restaurant Association; National Restaurant Association; Retailer's Bakery Association; The Bread Bakers Guild of America.

AREAS OF STUDY
Baking; beverage management; buffet catering; confectionery show pieces; controlling costs in food service; convenience cookery; culinary French; culinary skill development; food preparation; food purchasing; food service communication; food service math; garde-manger; international cuisine; introduction to food service; kitchen management; management and human resources; meal planning; meat cutting; meat fabrication; menu and facilities design; nutrition; nutrition and food service; patisserie; restaurant opportunities; sanitation; saucier; seafood processing; soup, stock, sauce, and starch production; wines and spirits.

FACILITIES
2 bake shops; 2 classrooms; 3 demonstration laboratories; 2 food production kitchens; gourmet dining room; learning resource center; lecture room; library; public restaurant; teaching kitchen.

TYPICAL STUDENT PROFILE
73 total: 58 full-time; 15 part-time.

SPECIAL PROGRAMS
French exchange (8 weeks), American Culinary Federation competitions.

FINANCIAL AID
Employment placement assistance is available. Employment opportunities within the program are available.

APPLICATION INFORMATION
Students may begin participation in January and August. Applications are accepted continuously. Applicants must interview; submit a formal application, essay, academic transcripts, and take placement test.

CONTACT
Director of Admissions, Culinary Management, 5230 West Highway 98, Panama City, FL 32401-1058. Telephone: 850-872-3839. Fax: 850-747-3259. World Wide Web: http://culinary.gulfcoast.edu.

HILLSBOROUGH COMMUNITY COLLEGE

Hospitality Management

Tampa, Florida

GENERAL INFORMATION
Public, coeducational, two-year college. Urban campus. Founded in 1968. Accredited by Southern Association of Colleges and Schools.

PROGRAM INFORMATION
Offered since 1985. Accredited by American Culinary Federation Accrediting Commission. Program calendar is divided into semesters. 1-year certificate in food and beverage management. 2-year associate degree in hotel management. 2-year associate degree in restaurant management. 2-year associate degree in culinary arts.

PROGRAM AFFILIATION
American Culinary Federation; Confrerie de la Chaine des Rotisseurs; National Restaurant Association; National Restaurant Association Educational Foundation.

AREAS OF STUDY
Baking; beverage management; controlling costs in food service; culinary skill development; food preparation; food purchasing; food service math; garde-manger; international cuisine; introduction to food service; kitchen management; management and human resources; meal planning; menu and facilities design; nutrition; nutrition and food service; sanitation; saucier; seafood processing; wines and spirits.

FACILITIES
Bake shop; cafeteria; classroom; computer laboratory; demonstration laboratory; food production kitchen; laboratory; learning resource center; lecture room; library; public restaurant; snack shop; student lounge; teaching kitchen.

STUDENT PROFILE
204 full-time.

FACULTY
5 total: 2 full-time; 3 part-time. 2 are industry professionals; 2 are culinary-certified teachers. Prominent faculty: George J. Pastor, EdD, CEC, CCE, AAC; Frederick Jaeger, MS. Faculty-student ratio: 1:12.

SPECIAL PROGRAMS
2-year paid internship, culinary competitions.

TYPICAL EXPENSES

Application fee: $20. In-state tuition: $66.11 per per credit hour full-time (in district), $66.11 per credit hour part-time. Out-of-state tuition: $241.05 per per credit hour full-time, $241.05 per credit hour part-time. Program-related fees include $15 for food prep for managers class (FSS 1223); $15 for food specialties (baking) class (FSS 1246C); $15 for food specialties class (FSS 1248C); $15 for food specialties III class (FSS 1249C).

FINANCIAL AID

In 2004, 4 scholarships were awarded (average award was $500). Employment placement assistance is available. Employment opportunities within the program are available.

APPLICATION INFORMATION

Students may begin participation in January, May, and August. Applications are accepted continuously. In 2004, 204 applied. Applicants must submit a formal application and high school diploma or GED.

CONTACT

George J. Pastor, Program Manager, Hospitality Management, PO Box 30030, Tampa, FL 33630. Telephone: 813-253-7316. Fax: 813-253-7400. E-mail: gpastor@hccfl. edu. World Wide Web: http://www.hccfl.edu.

INDIAN RIVER COMMUNITY COLLEGE

Fort Pierce, Florida

GENERAL INFORMATION

Public, coeducational, two-year college. Small-town setting. Founded in 1960. Accredited by Southern Association of Colleges and Schools.

PROGRAM INFORMATION

Offered since 1994. Accredited by American Culinary Federation Accrediting Commission. Program calendar is divided into semesters. 2-year associate degree in restaurant management and culinary arts.

PROGRAM AFFILIATION

American Culinary Federation.

AREAS OF STUDY

Baking; controlling costs in food service; garde-manger; introduction to food service; management and human resources; meal planning; meat cutting; meat fabrication; menu and facilities design; nutrition and food service; sanitation; saucier; seafood processing; soup, stock, sauce, and starch production.

FACILITIES

3 bake shops; 4 classrooms; 3 demonstration laboratories; 3 food production kitchens; 3 laboratories; learning resource center.

TYPICAL STUDENT PROFILE

125 full-time. 62 are under 25 years old; 60 are between 25 and 44 years old; 3 are over 44 years old.

SPECIAL PROGRAMS

Tuition-free Apprenticeship Program.

FINANCIAL AID

Employment placement assistance is available. Employment opportunities within the program are available.

HOUSING

Apartment-style housing available.

APPLICATION INFORMATION

Students may begin participation in January, May, and August. Applications are accepted continuously. Applicants must submit a formal application and an essay.

CONTACT

Director of Admissions, 3209 Virginia Avenue, Fort Pierce, FL 34981. Telephone: 772-462-4225. World Wide Web: http://www.ircc.edu.

JOHNSON & WALES UNIVERSITY

College of Culinary Arts

North Miami, Florida

GENERAL INFORMATION

Private, coeducational, four-year college. Urban campus. Founded in 1992. Accredited by New England Association of Schools and Colleges.

PROGRAM INFORMATION

Offered since 1992. Program calendar is divided into quarters. 2-year associate degree in baking and pastry arts. 2-year associate degree in culinary arts. 4-year bachelor's degree in food service management. 4-year bachelor's degree in culinary arts.

PROGRAM AFFILIATION

American Culinary Federation; American Dietetic Association; American Institute of Baking; American Institute of Wine & Food; Confrerie de la Chaine des Rotisseurs; Council on Hotel, Restaurant, and Institutional Education; Institute of Food Technologists; International Association of Culinary Professionals; International Food Service Executives Association; International Foodservice Editorial Council; James Beard Foundation, Inc.; National Restaurant Association; National Restaurant Association Educational Foundation; Oldways Preservation and Exchange Trust; Sommelier Society of America; Tasters Guild International.

AREAS OF STUDY

Baking; beverage management; buffet catering; confectionery show pieces; controlling costs in food service; convenience cookery; culinary French; culinary skill development; food preparation; food purchasing; food

Johnson & Wales University *(continued)*

service communication; food service math; garde-manger; international cuisine; introduction to food service; kitchen management; management and human resources; meat cutting; meat fabrication; menu and facilities design; nutrition; nutrition and food service; patisserie; restaurant opportunities; sanitation; saucier; seafood processing; soup, stock, sauce, and starch production.

FACILITIES
Bake shop; cafeteria; 15 classrooms; 2 computer laboratories; 8 food production kitchens; 2 gourmet dining rooms; learning resource center; 6 lecture rooms; library; public restaurant; 2 student lounges; pastry shop; meatroom/butcher shop; beverage lab; garde-manger kitchen; 5 hot kitchens.

STUDENT PROFILE
951 total: 894 full-time; 57 part-time. 788 are under 25 years old; 135 are between 25 and 44 years old; 28 are over 44 years old.

FACULTY
32 total: 27 full-time; 5 part-time. 20 are industry professionals; 2 are master chefs; 2 are culinary-certified teachers; 1 is a certified executive pastry chef; 1 certified chef de cuisine; 1 certified executive chef. Prominent faculty: Drue Brandenburg, MS, CEC, CCE; Patricia Wilson, PhD; Felicia Pritchett; Todd Tonova, PhD. Faculty-student ratio: 1:20.

SPECIAL PROGRAMS
3-month internship.

TYPICAL EXPENSES
Tuition: $19,875 per year. Program-related fees include $951 for general fee; $250 for orientation fee; $954 for weekend meal plan.

FINANCIAL AID
In 2005, 285 scholarships were awarded (average award was $1207). Employment placement assistance is available. Employment opportunities within the program are available.

HOUSING
Coed and apartment-style housing available. Average on-campus housing cost per month: $1000. Average off-campus housing cost per month: $950.

APPLICATION INFORMATION
Students may begin participation in March, June, July, September, and December. Applications are accepted continuously. In 2005, 1939 applied; 1446 were accepted. Applicants must submit a formal application.

CONTACT
Jeffrey Greenip, Director of Admissions, College of Culinary Arts, 170 NE 127th Street, North Miami, FL

33181. Telephone: 800-BEA-CHEF. Fax: 305-892-7020. E-mail: admissions@jwu.edu. World Wide Web: http://culinary.jwu.edu.
See color display following page 332.

LINDSEY HOPKINS TECHNICAL EDUCATION CENTER

Commercial Foods and Culinary Arts

Miami, Florida

GENERAL INFORMATION
Public, coeducational, technical institute. Urban campus. Founded in 1937. Accredited by Council on Occupational Education.

PROGRAM INFORMATION
Program calendar is divided into trimesters. 1500-hour certificate in culinary arts.

PROGRAM AFFILIATION
National Restaurant Association; National Restaurant Association Educational Foundation.

AREAS OF STUDY
Baking; buffet catering; confectionery show pieces; convenience cookery; culinary French; culinary skill development; food preparation; food purchasing; food service communication; food service math; garde-manger; international cuisine; introduction to food service; kitchen management; meal planning; meat cutting; patisserie; restaurant opportunities; sanitation; saucier; seafood processing; soup, stock, sauce, and starch production.

FACILITIES
Bake shop; bakery; cafeteria; catering service; classroom; 3 computer laboratories; 2 demonstration laboratories; 2 food production kitchens; 2 gourmet dining rooms; 2 learning resource centers; library.

TYPICAL STUDENT PROFILE
60 total: 40 full-time; 20 part-time. 18 are under 25 years old; 16 are between 25 and 44 years old; 6 are over 44 years old.

SPECIAL PROGRAMS
VICA and Calle Ocho competitions, Florida Restaurant Association Show.

FINANCIAL AID
Program-specific awards include SAVES (Skills for Academic, Vocational, and English Studies) scholarships. Employment placement assistance is available. Employment opportunities within the program are available.

APPLICATION INFORMATION
Students may begin participation in January, May, and September. Applications are accepted continuously.

Applicants must interview; submit a formal application and take Test of Adult Basic Education.

CONTACT

Director of Admissions, Commercial Foods and Culinary Arts, 750 Northwest 20th Street, Miami, FL 33127. Telephone: 305-324-6070 Ext. 8007. Fax: 305-545-6397. World Wide Web: http://lindsey.dadeschools.net.

LORENZO WALKER INSTITUTE OF TECHNOLOGY

Naples, Florida

GENERAL INFORMATION

Public, coeducational institution. Urban campus. Founded in 1974. Accredited by Council on Occupational Education.

PROGRAM INFORMATION

Accredited by American Culinary Federation Accrediting Commission. Program calendar is continuous. 1500-hour certificate in culinary arts.

PROGRAM AFFILIATION

American Culinary Federation; National Restaurant Association.

AREAS OF STUDY

Baking; buffet catering; controlling costs in food service; convenience cookery; culinary skill development; food preparation; food purchasing; garde-manger; kitchen management; meal planning; nutrition; patisserie; sanitation; saucier; soup, stock, sauce, and starch production.

FACILITIES

Bake shop; bakery; cafeteria; catering service; classroom; coffee shop; computer laboratory; demonstration laboratory; food production kitchen; garden; learning resource center; lecture room; public restaurant.

TYPICAL STUDENT PROFILE

47 total: 24 full-time; 23 part-time. 44 are under 25 years old; 2 are between 25 and 44 years old; 1 is over 44 years old.

SPECIAL PROGRAMS

Culinary competitions, articulation agreement with Johnson and Wales University, food activities (community service).

FINANCIAL AID

Program-specific awards include ACF Scholarships, LWIT Foundation Scholarships, Florida Restaurant Association Scholarships. Employment placement assistance is available. Employment opportunities within the program are available.

APPLICATION INFORMATION

Students may begin participation in January, June, and August. Applications are accepted continuously. Applicants must interview; submit a formal application.

CONTACT

Director of Admissions, 3702 Estey Avenue, Naples, FL 34104-4498. Telephone: 239-430-6900 Ext. 2024. Fax: 239-430-6922. World Wide Web: http://www.collier.k12.fl.us/workforce/lwit/index.html.

McFATTER TECHNICAL CENTER

Commercial Foods and Culinary Arts

Davie, Florida

GENERAL INFORMATION

Public, coeducational institution. Suburban campus. Founded in 1985. Accredited by Council on Occupational Education.

PROGRAM INFORMATION

Offered since 1996. Accredited by American Culinary Federation Accrediting Commission. Program calendar is divided into quarters. 1-year certificate in culinary arts.

PROGRAM AFFILIATION

American Culinary Federation; Florida Restaurant Association; National Restaurant Association.

AREAS OF STUDY

Baking; beverage management; buffet catering; controlling costs in food service; convenience cookery; culinary French; culinary skill development; food preparation; food purchasing; food service communication; food service math; garde-manger; international cuisine; introduction to food service; kitchen management; management and human resources; meal planning; meat cutting; meat fabrication; menu and facilities design; nutrition; nutrition and food service; patisserie; restaurant opportunities; sanitation; saucier; seafood processing; soup, stock, sauce, and starch production.

FACILITIES

Bake shop; cafeteria; catering service; 3 classrooms; coffee shop; computer laboratory; food production kitchen; garden; gourmet dining room; learning resource center; library; public restaurant; snack shop; teaching kitchen.

TYPICAL STUDENT PROFILE

65 full-time. 20 are under 25 years old; 40 are between 25 and 44 years old; 5 are over 44 years old.

SPECIAL PROGRAMS

VICA and ACF competitions.

FINANCIAL AID

Employment placement assistance is available. Employment opportunities within the program are available.

APPLICATION INFORMATION

Students may begin participation in January, April, June, August, and November. Applications are accepted continuously. Applicants must interview, and attend orientation.

McFatter Technical Center *(continued)*

CONTACT

Director of Admissions, Commercial Foods and Culinary Arts, 6500 Nova Drive, Davie, FL 33317. Telephone: 954-382-6543. Fax: 954-370-1647. World Wide Web: http://www.mcfattertech.com.

MIAMI LAKES EDUCATION CENTER

Commercial Foods and Culinary Arts Department

Miami Lakes, Florida

GENERAL INFORMATION

Public, coeducational, technical institute. Urban campus. Founded in 1979. Accredited by Council on Occupational Education.

PROGRAM INFORMATION

Offered since 1979. Program calendar is divided into trimesters. 1550-hour certificate in commercial foods.

PROGRAM AFFILIATION

American Culinary Federation; Council on Hotel, Restaurant, and Institutional Education; International Food Service Executives Association.

AREAS OF STUDY

Baking; controlling costs in food service; food preparation; garde-manger; introduction to food service; kitchen management; patisserie; sanitation; soup, stock, sauce, and starch production.

FACILITIES

Bake shop; computer laboratory; food production kitchen; learning resource center; lecture room.

TYPICAL STUDENT PROFILE

63 total: 29 full-time; 34 part-time. 34 are under 25 years old; 24 are between 25 and 44 years old; 5 are over 44 years old.

SPECIAL PROGRAMS

Culinary competitions.

FINANCIAL AID

Employment placement assistance is available.

APPLICATION INFORMATION

Students may begin participation year-round. Applications are accepted continuously. Applicants must submit a formal application and take the Test of Adult Basic Education.

CONTACT

Director of Admissions, Commercial Foods and Culinary Arts Department, 5780 Northwest 158th Street, Miami Lakes, FL 33014. Telephone: 305-557-1100 Ext. 2252. Fax: 305-557-7391. World Wide Web: http://pweb.netcom.com/~jwlovell/MLEC/index.html.

NORTHWOOD UNIVERSITY, FLORIDA CAMPUS

Hotel, Restaurant, and Resort Management

West Palm Beach, Florida

GENERAL INFORMATION

Private, coeducational, four-year college. Urban campus. Founded in 1982. Accredited by North Central Association of Colleges and Schools.

PROGRAM INFORMATION

Offered since 1984. Program calendar is divided into quarters. 2-year associate degree in hotel, restaurant, resort management. 4-year bachelor's degree in hotel, restaurant, resort management.

PROGRAM AFFILIATION

Council on Hotel, Restaurant, and Institutional Education; National Restaurant Association; National Restaurant Association Educational Foundation; Palm Beach County Hotel and Lodging Association.

AREAS OF STUDY

Beverage management; food preparation; food purchasing; introduction to food service; menu and facilities design; restaurant opportunities; sanitation.

FACILITIES

Classroom; demonstration laboratory; lecture room.

STUDENT PROFILE

47 full-time. 44 are under 25 years old; 3 are between 25 and 44 years old.

FACULTY

2 total: 1 full-time; 1 part-time. 2 are industry professionals. Prominent faculty: Dr. Janice Scarinci. Faculty-student ratio: 1:24.

SPECIAL PROGRAMS

400-hour paid internship, attendance at National Restaurant Association trade show in Chicago, participation in Palm Beach County Hotel and Lodging Association trade show and job fair.

TYPICAL EXPENSES

Application fee: $25. Tuition: $14,625 per year full-time, $304 per credit hour part-time.

FINANCIAL AID

Employment placement assistance is available. Employment opportunities within the program are available.

HOUSING

Single-sex housing available. Average on-campus housing cost per month: $410.

APPLICATION INFORMATION

Students may begin participation in March, June, September, and December. Applications are accepted continuously. In 2004, 118 applied; 82 were accepted. Applicants must submit a formal application and an essay.

CONTACT
Jack Letvinchuk, Director of Admissions, Hotel, Restaurant, and Resort Management, 2600 North Military Trail, West Palm Beach, FL 33409-2911. Telephone: 800-458-8325. Fax: 561-478-5500. E-mail: fladmit@northwood.edu. World Wide Web: http://www.northwood.edu.

NOTTER SCHOOL OF PASTRY ARTS

Orlando, Florida

GENERAL INFORMATION
Private, coeducational institution. Suburban campus. Founded in 1982.

PROGRAM INFORMATION
Offered since 1982. Accredited by American Culinary Federation Accrediting Commission. Program calendar is divided into weeks. 1-week certificate in cakes and desserts. 1-week certificate in wedding cake. 1-week certificate in advanced chocolate decoration. 1-week certificate in advanced sugar decoration. 1-week certificate in chocolate decoration. 1-week certificate in sugar blowing and pulling showplace class.

AREAS OF STUDY
Confectionery show pieces; patisserie.

FACILITIES
Classroom; student lounge; teaching kitchen.

APPLICATION INFORMATION
Students may begin participation in January, February, March, April, May, June, July, August, September, October, and November.

CONTACT
Director of Admissions, 8204 Crystal Clear Lane, #1600, Orlando, FL 32809. World Wide Web: http://www.notterschool.com/.

PALM BEACH COMMUNITY COLLEGE

Hospitality Management

Lake Worth, Florida

GENERAL INFORMATION
Public, coeducational, two-year college. Urban campus. Founded in 1933. Accredited by Southern Association of Colleges and Schools.

PROGRAM INFORMATION
Program calendar is divided into semesters. 2-year associate degree in hospitality and tourism management.

PROGRAM AFFILIATION
American Hotel and Lodging Association.

AREAS OF STUDY
Beverage management; menu and facilities design.

STUDENT PROFILE
47 part-time.

FACULTY
6 total: 1 full-time; 5 part-time. Faculty-student ratio: 1:25.

TYPICAL EXPENSES
Application fee: $20. In-state tuition: $1890 per fall and spring full-time (in district), $63 per credit hour part-time. Out-of-state tuition: $6892.50 per fall and spring full-time, $229.75 per credit hour part-time. Tuition for international students: $229.75 per credit hour part-time.

APPLICATION INFORMATION
Students may begin participation in January, May, and August. Applications are accepted continuously.

CONTACT
Robin Johnson, Director of Outreach and Recruitment, Hospitality Management, 4200 Congress Avenue, Lake Worth, FL 33461-4796. Telephone: 561-868-3377. Fax: 561-868-3584. E-mail: johnsor@pbcc.edu. World Wide Web: http://www.pbcc.edu.

PENSACOLA JUNIOR COLLEGE

Hospitality and Tourism Management/Culinary Management

Pensacola, Florida

GENERAL INFORMATION
Public, coeducational, two-year college. Suburban campus. Founded in 1948. Accredited by Southern Association of Colleges and Schools.

PROGRAM INFORMATION
Offered since 1995. Accredited by American Culinary Federation Accrediting Commission. Program calendar is divided into semesters. 2-year associate degree in hospitality and tourism management. 2-year associate degree in culinary management.

PROGRAM AFFILIATION
American Culinary Federation; Council on Hotel, Restaurant, and Institutional Education.

AREAS OF STUDY
Baking; beverage management; buffet catering; confectionery show pieces; controlling costs in food service; culinary skill development; dining room management; food preparation; food purchasing; food service math; garde-manger; international cuisine; introduction to food service; kitchen management; management and human resources;

Pensacola Junior College *(continued)*

meal planning; menu and facilities design; nutrition; patisserie; sanitation; saucier; soup, stock, sauce, and starch production.

FACILITIES
Bake shop; classroom; computer laboratory; food production kitchen; gourmet dining room; learning resource center; public restaurant; student lounge; teaching kitchen.

TYPICAL STUDENT PROFILE
62 full-time.

SPECIAL PROGRAMS
Mystery box competitions.

FINANCIAL AID
Program-specific awards include private scholarships. Employment placement assistance is available. Employment opportunities within the program are available.

APPLICATION INFORMATION
Students may begin participation in January, May, and August. Applications are accepted continuously. Applicants must submit a formal application.

CONTACT
Director of Admissions, Hospitality and Tourism Management/Culinary Management, 1000 College Boulevard, Pensacola, FL 32504-8998. Telephone: 850-484-2506. Fax: 850-484-1543. World Wide Web: http://www.pjc.edu.

PINELLAS TECHNICAL EDUCATION CENTER–CLEARWATER CAMPUS

Culinary Arts/Commercial Food

Clearwater, Florida

GENERAL INFORMATION
Public, coeducational, two-year college. Urban campus. Founded in 1969. Accredited by Council on Occupational Education.

PROGRAM INFORMATION
Offered since 1969. Accredited by American Culinary Federation Accrediting Commission. Program calendar is divided into quarters. 1500-hour certificate in culinary arts/commercial foods.

PROGRAM AFFILIATION
American Dietetic Association; Florida Restaurant Association; National Restaurant Association; National Restaurant Association Educational Foundation.

AREAS OF STUDY
Baking; buffet catering; convenience cookery; culinary skill development; food preparation; food purchasing; food

service communication; food service math; garde-manger; international cuisine; introduction to food service; kitchen management; management and human resources; meal planning; meat fabrication; nutrition; nutrition and food service; sanitation; saucier; soup, stock, sauce, and starch production.

FACILITIES
Bake shop; bakery; cafeteria; catering service; 2 classrooms; computer laboratory; demonstration laboratory; 2 food production kitchens; gourmet dining room; 3 laboratories; learning resource center; lecture room; library; teaching kitchen.

STUDENT PROFILE
46 total: 28 full-time; 18 part-time.

FACULTY
3 total: 2 full-time; 1 part-time. 2 are industry professionals; 1 is a culinary-certified teacher. Prominent faculty: Vincent Calandra, CCE; Brian Min Kin; Rose Audibert. Faculty-student ratio: 1:15.

SPECIAL PROGRAMS
Visits to industry, culinary competitions, field trips to food expositions.

TYPICAL EXPENSES
Application fee: $15. Tuition: $180 per school year. Program-related fee includes $520 for lab fee/cost of food.

FINANCIAL AID
In 2004, 2 scholarships were awarded (average award was $300). Program-specific awards include American Culinary Federation scholarships, Andrew's Scholarship, Florida Restaurant Association scholarship. Employment placement assistance is available.

HOUSING
Average off-campus housing cost per month: $600.

APPLICATION INFORMATION
Students may begin participation in January, April, August, and October. Applications are accepted continuously. Applicants must interview, and interview; submit a formal application.

CONTACT
Vincent Calandra, Department Chair, Culinary Arts/Commercial Food, 6100 154th Avenue N, Clearwater, FL 33760. Telephone: 727-538-7167 Ext. 1140. Fax: 727-509-4246. E-mail: vcalandra@ptec.pinellas.k12.fl.us. World Wide Web: http://www.ptec.pinellas.k12.fl.us.

St. Thomas University

Tourism and Hospitality Management

Miami Gardens, Florida

GENERAL INFORMATION
Private, coeducational, university. Urban campus. Founded in 1961. Accredited by Southern Association of Colleges and Schools.

PROGRAM INFORMATION
Program calendar is divided into semesters. 2-year master of business administration in sports administration. 4-year bachelor's degree in sports administration. 4-year bachelor's degree in health care service. 4-year bachelor's degree in tourism and hospitality management.

PROGRAM AFFILIATION
Council on Hotel, Restaurant, and Institutional Education; Florida Restaurant Association; Greater Miami Conventions and Visitors Bureau; International Food Service Executives Association; International Society of Travel and Tourism Educators; National Restaurant Association.

AREAS OF STUDY
Beverage management; convention and trade management; food preparation; food purchasing; introduction to food service; kitchen management; management and human resources; menu and facilities design; restaurant opportunities.

FACILITIES
Classroom; computer laboratory; garden; learning resource center; lecture room; library.

STUDENT PROFILE
32 total: 30 full-time; 2 part-time. 27 are under 25 years old; 5 are between 25 and 44 years old.

FACULTY
14 total: 10 full-time; 4 part-time. MPS, PhD, EdD, DBA. Prominent faculty: Paul-Michael Klein, MPS; Seok Ho Song, PhD; Jan Bell, EdD. Faculty-student ratio: 1:18.

SPECIAL PROGRAMS
Internships, experiential learning.

TYPICAL EXPENSES
Application fee: $40. Tuition: $17,850 per year full-time, $595 per credit part-time. In-state tuition: $17,850 per year full-time (out-of-district), $595 per credit part-time (out-of-district). Out-of-state tuition: $17,850 per year full-time, $595 per credit part-time. Tuition for international students: $17,850 per year full-time, $595 per credit part-time.

FINANCIAL AID
In 2004, 2 scholarships were awarded (average award was $9000). Program-specific awards include donor scholarships, PIT employment. Employment opportunities within the program are available.

HOUSING
Single-sex housing available.

APPLICATION INFORMATION
Students may begin participation in January and August. Applications are accepted continuously. In 2004, 24 applied. Applicants must submit a formal application, letters of reference, and an essay.

CONTACT
Andre Lightbourn, Director of Admissions, Tourism and Hospitality Management, 16401 NW 37th Avenue, Miami Gardens, FL 33054. Telephone: 305-628-6712. Fax: 305-628-6591. E-mail: alightbo@stu.edu. World Wide Web: http://www.stu.edu.

Sheridan Technical Center

Commercial Foods and Culinary Arts Program

Hollywood, Florida

GENERAL INFORMATION
Public, coeducational, technical institute. Urban campus. Founded in 1967. Accredited by Council on Occupational Education.

PROGRAM INFORMATION
Offered since 1968. Accredited by American Culinary Federation Accrediting Commission. Program calendar is divided into quarters. 1500-hour certificate in commercial foods and culinary arts.

PROGRAM AFFILIATION
American Culinary Federation.

AREAS OF STUDY
Baking; beverage management; controlling costs in food service; food preparation; food purchasing; food service communication; food service math; garde-manger; international cuisine; introduction to food service; kitchen management; management and human resources; meal planning; meat cutting; meat fabrication; menu and facilities design; nutrition; nutrition and food service; restaurant opportunities; sanitation; saucier; seafood processing; soup, stock, sauce, and starch production.

FACILITIES
3 classrooms; 2 computer laboratories; demonstration laboratory; food production kitchen; gourmet dining room; laboratory; learning resource center; 3 lecture rooms; library; snack shop; student lounge; teaching kitchen.

TYPICAL STUDENT PROFILE
100 total: 50 full-time; 50 part-time.

SPECIAL PROGRAMS
Internships, culinary competitions.

Sheridan Technical Center *(continued)*

FINANCIAL AID

Employment placement assistance is available. Employment opportunities within the program are available.

APPLICATION INFORMATION

Students may begin participation in January, March, June, August, and November. Applications are accepted continuously. Applicants must attend orientation program and take Test of Adult Basic Education.

CONTACT

Director of Admissions, Commercial Foods and Culinary Arts Program, 5400 Sheridan Street, Hollywood, FL 33021. Telephone: 954-985-3245. Fax: 954-986-8228. World Wide Web: http://www.SheridanTechnical.com.

THE SOUTHEAST INSTITUTE OF THE CULINARY ARTS

Commercial Foods/Culinary Arts

St. Augustine, Florida

GENERAL INFORMATION

Public, coeducational, culinary institute. Urban campus. Founded in 1970. Accredited by Southern Association of Colleges and Schools.

PROGRAM INFORMATION

Offered since 1970. Accredited by American Culinary Federation Accrediting Commission. 1500-hour diploma in culinary arts. 18-week diploma in baking/pastry. 30-hour certificate in management/hospitality. 30-hour certificate in sanitation/nutrition.

PROGRAM AFFILIATION

American Culinary Federation; National Restaurant Association Educational Foundation.

AREAS OF STUDY

Baking; buffet catering; confectionery show pieces; controlling costs in food service; culinary French; culinary skill development; food preparation; food purchasing; food service communication; food service math; garde-manger; ice carving; international cuisine; introduction to food service; kitchen management; management and human resources; meal planning; meat cutting; meat fabrication; meat fabrication; nutrition; nutrition and food service; patisserie; restaurant opportunities; sanitation; saucier; seafood processing; soup, stock, sauce, and starch production.

FACILITIES

Bake shop; bakery; cafeteria; catering service; classroom; computer laboratory; demonstration laboratory; food production kitchen; garden; gourmet dining room; laboratory; learning resource center; lecture room; library; public restaurant; teaching kitchen.

STUDENT PROFILE

410 total: 110 full-time; 300 part-time. 62 are under 25 years old; 327 are between 25 and 44 years old; 21 are over 44 years old.

FACULTY

14 total: 12 full-time; 2 part-time. 2 are industry professionals; 13 are culinary-certified teachers. Prominent faculty: Anthony Lowman, CCC, CCE; Noel Ridsdale, CEC, CCA; Marvin Berube; Dan Lundberg, CCC, CCE. Faculty-student ratio: 1:15.

SPECIAL PROGRAMS

Culinary competitions, paid externships, food shows/seminars, certificate courses in conjunction with U.S. Navy.

TYPICAL EXPENSES

Application fee: $15. Tuition: $515 per 9 weeks. Program-related fees include $620 for text books; $124 for uniforms; $176 for tools.

FINANCIAL AID

In 2004, 10 scholarships were awarded (average award was $150). Employment placement assistance is available. Employment opportunities within the program are available.

HOUSING

Average off-campus housing cost per month: $600.

APPLICATION INFORMATION

Students may begin participation in January, March, June, August, and October. Applications are accepted continuously. In 2004, 440 applied; 400 were accepted. Applicants must submit a formal application and take the Test of Adult Basic Education.

CONTACT

Noel Ridsdale, Program Director, Commercial Foods/Culinary Arts, 2980 Collins Avenue, St. Augustine, FL 32084. Telephone: 904-829-1060. Fax: 904-829-1089. E-mail: ridsdan@fcti.org. World Wide Web: http://www.fcti.org.

SOUTH FLORIDA COMMUNITY COLLEGE

Avon Park, Florida

GENERAL INFORMATION

Public, coeducational, two-year college. Rural campus. Founded in 1965. Accredited by Southern Association of Colleges and Schools.

PROGRAM INFORMATION
Program calendar is divided into semesters. 10-month certificate in food management, production and services. 2-year associate degree in hospitality and tourism management.

PROGRAM AFFILIATION
National Restaurant Association Educational Foundation.

AREAS OF STUDY
Baking; beverage management; controlling costs in food service; culinary skill development; food preparation; food purchasing; food service communication; food service math; garde-manger; introduction to food service; kitchen management; management and human resources; meal planning; sanitation.

FACILITIES
Catering service; classroom; computer laboratory; demonstration laboratory; food production kitchen; gourmet dining room; laboratory; learning resource center; lecture room; library; public restaurant; student lounge; teaching kitchen.

TYPICAL STUDENT PROFILE
23 full-time. 20 are under 25 years old; 2 are between 25 and 44 years old; 1 is over 44 years old.

FINANCIAL AID
Employment placement assistance is available. Employment opportunities within the program are available.

HOUSING
Coed housing available.

APPLICATION INFORMATION
Students may begin participation in January, May, and August. Applications are accepted continuously. Applicants must submit a formal application.

CONTACT
Director of Admissions, 600 West College Drive, Avon Park, FL 33825-9356. Telephone: 863-382-6900. World Wide Web: http://www.sfcc.cc.fl.us/.

UNIVERSITY OF CENTRAL FLORIDA

Rosen School of Hospitality Management

Orlando, Florida

GENERAL INFORMATION
Public, coeducational, university. Suburban campus. Founded in 1963. Accredited by Southern Association of Colleges and Schools.

PROGRAM INFORMATION
Offered since 1983. Accredited by Council on Hotel, Restaurant and Institutional Education. Program calendar is divided into semesters. 2-year master's degree in hospitality management. 4-year bachelor's degree in restaurant management. 4-year bachelor's degree in hospitality management.

PROGRAM AFFILIATION
Council on Hotel, Restaurant, and Institutional Education; National Restaurant Association; National Restaurant Association Educational Foundation.

AREAS OF STUDY
Food service management; restaurant operations.

FACILITIES
Cafeteria; 23 classrooms; coffee shop; 3 computer laboratories; demonstration laboratory; 2 food production kitchens; gourmet dining room; lecture room; library; student lounge; teaching kitchen.

STUDENT PROFILE
1700 full-time. 1600 are under 25 years old; 100 are between 25 and 44 years old.

FACULTY
54 total: 32 full-time; 22 part-time. 20 are industry professionals; 2 are master chefs; 3 are culinary-certified teachers. Prominent faculty: Abraham Pizam, PhD; Stephen LeBruto, EdD, CPA, CHAE; William Fisher, PhD; Chris Muller, PhD. Faculty-student ratio: 1:16.

SPECIAL PROGRAMS
Semester study abroad in France, 800-hour cooperative work experience, distinguished lectures series.

TYPICAL EXPENSES
Application fee: $30. In-state tuition: $3339 per year full-time (in district), $104.70 per credit hour part-time. Out-of-state tuition: $16,470 per year full-time, $542.42 per credit hour part-time.

FINANCIAL AID
In 2004, 100 scholarships were awarded (average award was $2500). Employment placement assistance is available. Employment opportunities within the program are available.

HOUSING
Coed and apartment-style housing available.

APPLICATION INFORMATION
Students may begin participation in January, May, June, and August. Application deadline for fall is May 1. Application deadline for spring is November 1. Application deadline for summer is March 1. Applicants must submit a formal application and SAT or ACT scores.

CONTACT
Chris Fletcher, Academic Relations, Rosen School of Hospitality Management, 9907 Universal Boulevard, Orlando, FL 32819. Telephone: 407-823-4447. Fax: 407-823-1110. E-mail: cfletche@mail.ucf.edu. World Wide Web: http://www.hospitality.ucf.edu.

VALENCIA COMMUNITY COLLEGE

Culinary Management

Orlando, Florida

GENERAL INFORMATION
Public, coeducational, two-year college. Urban campus. Founded in 1967. Accredited by Southern Association of Colleges and Schools.

PROGRAM INFORMATION
Offered since 1997. Program calendar is divided into semesters. 2-year associate degree in baking and pastry management. 2-year associate degree in hospitality management. 2-year associate degree in restaurant management. 2-year associate degree in culinary management. 35-credit certificate in baking and pastry arts. 35-credit certificate in culinary arts.

PROGRAM AFFILIATION
American Culinary Federation; Council on Hotel, Restaurant, and Institutional Education; Florida Restaurant Association; National Restaurant Association; National Restaurant Association Educational Foundation; Women Chefs and Restaurateurs.

AREAS OF STUDY
Baking; buffet catering; controlling costs in food service; convenience cookery; culinary French; culinary skill development; food preparation; food purchasing; food service communication; food service math; garde-manger; international cuisine; management and human resources; meal planning; meat cutting; meat fabrication; menu and facilities design; nutrition; nutrition and food service; patisserie; sanitation; saucier; seafood processing; soup, stock, sauce, and starch production; wines and spirits.

FACILITIES
Bakery; 6 classrooms; computer laboratory; demonstration laboratory; food production kitchen; gourmet dining room; learning resource center; library; teaching kitchen.

TYPICAL STUDENT PROFILE
213 total: 71 full-time; 142 part-time. 43 are under 25 years old; 149 are between 25 and 44 years old; 21 are over 44 years old.

SPECIAL PROGRAMS
Participation in Florida Restaurant Association Southeast EXPO (assisting in culinary competitions), paid internship, participation in Walt Disney Food and Wine Festival at the Epcot Center.

FINANCIAL AID
Employment placement assistance is available. Employment opportunities within the program are available.

APPLICATION INFORMATION
Students may begin participation in January, May, and August. Application deadline for fall is July 1. Application deadline for spring is November 1. Application deadline for summer is April 1. Applicants must submit a formal application and a high school diploma or GED.

CONTACT
Director of Admissions, Culinary Management, PO Box 3028, Orlando, FL 32802-3028. Telephone: 407-532-1880. Fax: 407-582-1900. World Wide Web: http://www.valencia.cc.fl.us.

WEBBER INTERNATIONAL UNIVERSITY

Hospitality Business Management

Babson Park, Florida

GENERAL INFORMATION
Private, coeducational, comprehensive institution. Rural campus. Founded in 1927. Accredited by Southern Association of Colleges and Schools.

PROGRAM INFORMATION
Offered since 1972. Accredited by Council on Hotel, Restaurant and Institutional Education. Program calendar is divided into semesters. 2-year associate degree in hospitality business management. 4-year bachelor's degree in hospitality business management.

PROGRAM AFFILIATION
Council on Hotel, Restaurant, and Institutional Education; National Restaurant Association; National Restaurant Association Educational Foundation.

AREAS OF STUDY
Beverage management; controlling costs in food service; food purchasing; introduction to food service; kitchen management; management and human resources; restaurant opportunities.

FACILITIES
Cafeteria; 2 classrooms; 2 computer laboratories; food production kitchen; learning resource center; library; snack shop; student lounge.

STUDENT PROFILE
43 total: 37 full-time; 6 part-time.

FACULTY
2 total: 1 full-time; 1 part-time. 1 is an industry professional; 1 is a culinary-certified teacher. Prominent faculty: Oscar A. Sampedro, CHA, CHE, FMP, MS. Faculty-student ratio: 1:20.

SPECIAL PROGRAMS
2 internship opportunities worldwide, trip to International Hotel and Lodging Show (New York), trip to National Restaurant Association Food Service Show (Chicago).

TYPICAL EXPENSES

Application fee: $35. Tuition: $13,150 per year full-time, $170 per hour part-time. Program-related fee includes $20 for lab fee.

FINANCIAL AID

In 2004, 12 scholarships were awarded (average award was $1700). Program-specific awards include Pro Start Scholarship-$2000 to graduate of high school culinary program who meets requirements, Entrance Exam Award-$1000 to student with SAT of 1090 or higher, renewable. Employment placement assistance is available. Employment opportunities within the program are available.

HOUSING

Coed housing available. Average on-campus housing cost per month: $325. Average off-campus housing cost per month: $400.

APPLICATION INFORMATION

Students may begin participation in January, May, and September. Application deadline for fall is August 1. Application deadline for spring is December 1. Application deadline for summer is April 1. Applicants must submit a formal application, letters of reference, an essay, SAT scores.

CONTACT

Ms. Julie Ragans, Director of Admissions, Hospitality Business Management, PO Box 96, Babson Park, FL 33827. Telephone: 800-741-1844. Fax: 863-638-1591. E-mail: admissions@webber.edu. World Wide Web: http://webber.edu.

GEORGIA

THE ART INSTITUTE OF ATLANTA

Culinary Arts and Culinary Arts Management

Atlanta, Georgia

GENERAL INFORMATION

Private, coeducational, four-year college. Suburban campus. Founded in 1949. Accredited by Southern Association of Colleges and Schools.

PROGRAM INFORMATION

Offered since 1991. Accredited by ACF American Culinary Federation. Program calendar is divided into quarters. 12-quarter bachelor's degree in culinary arts management. 3-quarter diploma in basic skills. 4-quarter diploma in baking and pastry. 7-quarter associate degree in culinary arts. 8-quarter associate degree in culinary arts with a concentration in baking and pastry.

PROGRAM AFFILIATION

American Culinary Federation; American Institute of Wine & Food; National Restaurant Association; National Restaurant Association Educational Foundation.

AREAS OF STUDY

Baking; beverage management; buffet catering; catering; confectionery show pieces; controlling costs in food service; convenience cookery; culinary French; culinary skill development; customer service; dining room operation; food preparation; food purchasing; food service communication; food service management; food service math; food styling; garde-manger; international cuisine; introduction to food service; kitchen management; management; management and human resources; marketing; meal planning; meat cutting; meat fabrication; menu and facilities design; nutrition; nutrition and food service; patisserie; personal chef repertoire; restaurant opportunities; sanitation; saucier; seafood processing; soup, stock, sauce, and starch production; wines and spirits.

FACILITIES

2 bake shops; cafeteria; 10 classrooms; coffee shop; 14 computer laboratories; 3 food production kitchens; gourmet dining room; 5 laboratories; learning resource center; 10 lecture rooms; library; snack shop; student lounge; 5 teaching kitchens.

STUDENT PROFILE

495 total: 375 full-time; 120 part-time. 94 are under 25 years old; 282 are between 25 and 44 years old; 94 are over 44 years old.

FACULTY

42 total: 12 full-time; 30 part-time. 32 are industry professionals; 9 are culinary-certified teachers. Prominent faculty: Sarah Gorham, MS, CEC; Marc Jolis; Daryl Shular, CCC; Audrie Clark. Faculty-student ratio: 1:16.

SPECIAL PROGRAMS

1-day workshops in specialized culinary subjects, Study Abroad Odyssey Program, culinary competitions, International Sommelier Guild Level 1 and 2 and Diploma.

TYPICAL EXPENSES

Application fee: $50. Tuition: $6320 per quarter full-time, $395 per credit hour part-time. Out-of-state tuition: $6320 full-time, $395 part-time. Tuition for international students: $6320 full-time, $395 part-time. Program-related fees include $1000 for culinary kit (cutlery, uniform, and textbooks); $285 for food and supplies for labs in some courses.

FINANCIAL AID

In 2005, 12 scholarships were awarded. Program-specific awards include full/partial tuition scholarship for high school seniors through competition, Art Institutes Best Teen Chef Competition scholarship, scholarships through articulation agreement with ProStart high schools (nationwide). Employment placement assistance is available. Employment opportunities within the program are available.

The Art Institute of Atlanta (*continued*)

HOUSING
Coed and apartment-style housing available. Average off-campus housing cost per month: $750–$850.

APPLICATION INFORMATION
Students may begin participation in January, April, July, and October. Applications are accepted continuously. Applicants must interview; submit a formal application, an essay, academic transcripts.

CONTACT
Office of Admissions, The Art Institute of Atlanta, Culinary Arts and Culinary Arts Management, 6600 Peachtree Dunwoody Road, 100 Embassy Row, Atlanta, GA 30328. Telephone: 800-275-4242. Fax: 770-394-0008. E-mail: aiaadm@aii.edu. World Wide Web: http://www.artinstitutes.edu/atlanta/.

See color display following page 380.

ATLANTA TECHNICAL COLLEGE

Culinary Arts Program

Atlanta, Georgia

GENERAL INFORMATION
Public, coeducational, two-year college. Urban campus. Founded in 1965. Accredited by Council on Occupational Education.

PROGRAM INFORMATION
Offered since 1965. Program calendar is divided into quarters. 1.5-year diploma in culinary arts.

PROGRAM AFFILIATION
American Culinary Federation; National Restaurant Association Educational Foundation.

AREAS OF STUDY
Baking; beverage management; buffet catering; controlling costs in food service; convenience cookery; food preparation; food purchasing; food service communication; food service math; garde-manger; international cuisine; introduction to food service; kitchen management; management and human resources; meal planning; meat cutting; menu and facilities design; nutrition; restaurant opportunities; sanitation; saucier; seafood processing; soup, stock, sauce, and starch production; wines and spirits.

FACILITIES
Cafeteria; catering service; 3 computer laboratories; gourmet dining room; 2 lecture rooms; 2 snack shops.

TYPICAL STUDENT PROFILE
90 total: 80 full-time; 10 part-time.

FINANCIAL AID
Employment placement assistance is available. Employment opportunities within the program are available.

APPLICATION INFORMATION
Students may begin participation in January, April, June, and September. Applications are accepted continuously. Applicants must submit a formal application and have a high school diploma or GED.

CONTACT
Director of Admissions, Culinary Arts Program, 1560 Metropolitan Parkway, Atlanta, GA 30310. Telephone: 404-756-4962. Fax: 404-756-3727. World Wide Web: http://www.atlantatech.org.

AUGUSTA TECHNICAL COLLEGE

Culinary Arts

Augusta, Georgia

GENERAL INFORMATION
Public, coeducational, two-year college. Suburban campus. Founded in 1961. Accredited by Southern Association of Colleges and Schools.

PROGRAM INFORMATION
Offered since 1984. Program calendar is divided into quarters. 2-quarter certificate in food service (evening). 6-quarter diploma in culinary arts.

PROGRAM AFFILIATION
American Culinary Federation; National Restaurant Association; National Restaurant Association Educational Foundation.

AREAS OF STUDY
Baking; buffet catering; food preparation; food purchasing; garde-manger; menu and facilities design; nutrition and food service; sanitation; soup, stock, sauce, and starch production.

FACILITIES
Bake shop; cafeteria; catering service; 2 classrooms; demonstration laboratory; food production kitchen; gourmet dining room; laboratory; learning resource center; library; teaching kitchen.

TYPICAL STUDENT PROFILE
52 full-time.

SPECIAL PROGRAMS
Exchange program with Grand Canary Island (Spain).

FINANCIAL AID
Program-specific awards include ProMgmt. scholarship, American Culinary Federation scholarship. Employment placement assistance is available.

APPLICATION INFORMATION
Students may begin participation in March and September. Applications are accepted continuously. Applicants must submit a formal application.

CONTACT

Director of Admissions, Culinary Arts, 3200 Augusta Tech Drive, Augusta, GA 30906. Telephone: 706-771-4084. Fax: 706-771-4016. World Wide Web: http://www.augusta.tec.ga.us.

CHATTAHOOCHEE TECHNICAL COLLEGE

Culinary Arts

Marietta, Georgia

GENERAL INFORMATION

Public, coeducational, two-year college. Suburban campus. Founded in 1961. Accredited by Southern Association of Colleges and Schools.

PROGRAM INFORMATION

Offered since 2001. Accredited by American Culinary Federation Accrediting Commission. Program calendar is divided into quarters. 12-month diploma in culinary arts. 24-month associate degree in culinary arts.

PROGRAM AFFILIATION

International Association of Culinary Professionals; James Beard Foundation, Inc.; National Restaurant Association; National Restaurant Association Educational Foundation.

AREAS OF STUDY

Baking; beverage management; buffet catering; controlling costs in food service; culinary skill development; food preparation; food purchasing; food service math; garde-manger; international cuisine; introduction to food service; kitchen management; management and human resources; meat fabrication; menu and facilities design; nutrition and food service; sanitation; soup, stock, sauce, and starch production; wines and spirits.

FACILITIES

Bake shop; catering service; classroom; computer laboratory; demonstration laboratory; food production kitchen; gourmet dining room; 2 lecture rooms; library; public restaurant; student lounge; teaching kitchen.

STUDENT PROFILE

170 total: 150 full-time; 20 part-time. 30 are under 25 years old; 119 are between 25 and 44 years old; 15 are over 44 years old.

FACULTY

6 total: 3 full-time; 3 part-time. 4 are industry professionals; 1 is a master chef; 1 is a culinary-certified teacher. Prominent faculty: Michael P. Bologna, CEC, CCE, AAC; Kevin Walker, CMC; Hillary Gallagher; Gary Slivenik. Faculty-student ratio: 1:15.

SPECIAL PROGRAMS

Culinary competitions, twelve-day cooking tour of Italy.

TYPICAL EXPENSES

Application fee: $15. In-state tuition: $372 per quarter full-time (in district), $31 per credit hour part-time. Out-of-state tuition: $744 per quarter full-time, $62 per credit hour part-time. Tuition for international students: $1488 per quarter full-time, $124 per credit hour part-time. Program-related fees include $80 for uniforms; $350 for cutlery (knife kit).

FINANCIAL AID

Employment placement assistance is available. Employment opportunities within the program are available.

HOUSING

Average off-campus housing cost per month: $650.

APPLICATION INFORMATION

Students may begin participation in January, March, July, and October. Applications are accepted continuously. In 2004, 100 applied; 75 were accepted. Applicants must interview; submit a formal application, letters of reference, an essay, official transcript from high school and/or college or original GED certificate.

CONTACT

Carolyn B. Hall, Dean, Culinary Arts, 2680 Gordy Parkway, Marietta, GA 30066. Telephone: 770-509-6310. Fax: 770-509-6345. E-mail: chall@chattcollege.com. World Wide Web: http://www.chattcollege.com.

COASTAL GEORGIA COMMUNITY COLLEGE

Culinary Arts

Brunswick, Georgia

GENERAL INFORMATION

Public, coeducational, two-year college. Small-town setting. Founded in 1961. Accredited by Southern Association of Colleges and Schools.

PROGRAM INFORMATION

Offered since 1994. Program calendar is divided into semesters. 18-month technical certificate in culinary arts. 24-month certificate in culinary arts.

PROGRAM AFFILIATION

American Hotel and Lodging Association.

AREAS OF STUDY

Baking; beverage management; buffet catering; business math; culinary skill development; food preparation; food purchasing; garde-manger; introduction to food service; management and human resources; meal planning; menu and facilities design; nutrition; nutrition and food service; sanitation; soup, stock, sauce, and starch production.

Coastal Georgia Community College *(continued)*

FACILITIES

3 classrooms; computer laboratory; food production kitchen; 2 learning resource centers; 2 libraries; student lounge; teaching kitchen.

STUDENT PROFILE

70 part-time. 15 are under 25 years old; 40 are between 25 and 44 years old; 15 are over 44 years old.

FACULTY

2 total: 2 full-time. 1 is an industry professional; 1 is a master chef. Prominent faculty: Walter Wright, CHA, CHE; Steven Ingersoll. Faculty-student ratio: 1:35.

TYPICAL EXPENSES

Application fee: $20. In-state tuition: $877 per semester full-time (in district), $65 per credit hour part-time. Out-of-state tuition: $3189 per semester full-time, $257 per credit hour part-time. Program-related fee includes $150 for uniforms and knives.

FINANCIAL AID

Employment placement assistance is available. Employment opportunities within the program are available.

APPLICATION INFORMATION

Students may begin participation in January, May, and August. Applications are accepted continuously. Applicants must submit a formal application and take COMPASS test.

CONTACT

Walter Wright, Instructor, Hospitality and Culinary Programs, Culinary Arts, 3700 Altama Avenue, Brunswick, GA 31520-3644. Telephone: 912-280-6899. Fax: 912-262-3283. E-mail: wwright@cgcc.edu. World Wide Web: http://www.cgcc.edu.

GEORGIA SOUTHERN UNIVERSITY

Department of Family and Consumer Sciences

Statesboro, Georgia

GENERAL INFORMATION

Public, coeducational, comprehensive institution. Small-town setting. Founded in 1906. Accredited by Southern Association of Colleges and Schools.

PROGRAM INFORMATION

Offered since 1989. Accredited by American Dietetic Association. Program calendar is divided into semesters. 4-year bachelor's degree in nutrition and food science. 4-year bachelor's degree in hotel and restaurant management.

PROGRAM AFFILIATION

American Culinary Federation; American Dietetic Association; Confrerie de la Chaine des Rotisseurs; Council on Hotel, Restaurant, and Institutional Education; National Restaurant Association; National Restaurant Association Educational Foundation.

AREAS OF STUDY

Beverage management; buffet catering; controlling costs in food service; convenience cookery; culinary French; culinary skill development; food preparation; food purchasing; food service communication; food service math; international cuisine; introduction to food service; kitchen management; management and human resources; meal planning; menu and facilities design; nutrition; nutrition and food service; restaurant opportunities; saucier; soup, stock, sauce, and starch production.

FACILITIES

6 classrooms; computer laboratory; demonstration laboratory; food production kitchen; gourmet dining room; laboratory; learning resource center; 6 lecture rooms; library; public restaurant; teaching kitchen.

STUDENT PROFILE

273 total: 228 full-time; 45 part-time. 252 are under 25 years old; 21 are between 25 and 44 years old.

FACULTY

3 total: 3 full-time. 3 are industry professionals; 1 is a culinary-certified teacher; 1 is a food service management professional. Prominent faculty: Jeffrey N. Brown, CEC, CCE, FMP; Dr. Larry Stalcup; Dr. Leslie Furr; Stephen Minton. Faculty-student ratio: 1:16.

SPECIAL PROGRAMS

New York Hotel Show (fall), Georgia Hotel Tourism Convention (fall/spring).

TYPICAL EXPENSES

Application fee: $20. In-state tuition: $2232 per year full-time (in district), $97 per semester hour part-time. Out-of-state tuition: $9290 per year full-time, $388 per semester hour part-time.

FINANCIAL AID

In 2004, 4 scholarships were awarded (average award was $2500). Program-specific awards include Georgia Hospitality and Tourism Association Scholarship. Employment placement assistance is available.

HOUSING

Coed, apartment-style, and single-sex housing available. Average on-campus housing cost per month: $289. Average off-campus housing cost per month: $250.

APPLICATION INFORMATION

Students may begin participation in January and August. Application deadline for fall is July 1. Application deadline for spring is December 1. Applicants must submit a formal application.

CONTACT

Mrs. Susan Braxton Davies, Director of Admissions, Department of Family and Consumer Sciences, PO Box 8024, Statesboro, GA 30460. Telephone: 912-681-5391. Fax:

912-486-7240. World Wide Web: http://chhs. georgiasouthern.edu/v_fam_consumer_sci.html.

GEORGIA STATE UNIVERSITY

Cecil B. Day School of Hospitality Administration

Atlanta, Georgia

GENERAL INFORMATION
Public, coeducational, university. Urban campus. Founded in 1913. Accredited by Southern Association of Colleges and Schools.

PROGRAM INFORMATION
Offered since 1974. Accredited by Council on Hotel, Restaurant and Institutional Education. Program calendar is divided into semesters. 1-year certificate in hospitality. 2-year master of business administration in hospitality operations. 4-year bachelor's degree in hospitality administration.

PROGRAM AFFILIATION
American Hotel and Lodging Association; Council on Hotel, Restaurant, and Institutional Education; National Restaurant Association; National Restaurant Association Educational Foundation.

AREAS OF STUDY
Controlling costs in food service; food preparation; food purchasing; food service communication; kitchen management; management and human resources; meal planning; menu and facilities design; restaurant opportunities; sanitation.

FACILITIES
Classroom; computer laboratory; food production kitchen; learning resource center; lecture room; library; teaching kitchen.

TYPICAL STUDENT PROFILE
235 full-time.

SPECIAL PROGRAMS
Student exchange program with European hospitality schools (semester), mentorship with industry executives (1 year), paid internships (semester).

FINANCIAL AID
Program-specific awards include scholarships from American Lodging Association, Days Inns, and GSU Foundation. Employment opportunities within the program are available.

HOUSING
Apartment-style housing available.

APPLICATION INFORMATION
Students may begin participation in January, June, and August. Application deadline for fall is June 1. Application deadline for spring is November 15. Application deadline for summer is April 1. Applicants must submit a formal application and high school transcripts, SAT or ACT scores.

CONTACT
Director of Admissions, Cecil B. Day School of Hospitality Administration, 35 Broad Street, Suite 215, Atlanta, GA 30303-3083. Telephone: 404-651-3672. Fax: 404-651-3670. World Wide Web: http://www.robinson.gsu/hospitality.

NORTH GEORGIA TECHNICAL COLLEGE

Culinary Arts and Hotel/Restaurant/Tourism Management

Blairsville, Georgia

GENERAL INFORMATION
Public, coeducational, two-year college. Rural campus. Founded in 1907. Accredited by Council on Occupational Education.

PROGRAM INFORMATION
Offered since 1998. Program calendar is divided into quarters. 2- to 3-quarter technical certificate in restaurant baking. 2- to 3-quarter technical certificate in culinary arts fundamentals. 2- to 3-quarter technical certificate in hospitality industry fundamentals. 4- to 5-quarter diploma in hotel/restaurant/tourism management. 5-quarter diploma in culinary arts. 7-quarter associate degree in culinary arts.

PROGRAM AFFILIATION
American Culinary Federation; National Restaurant Association Educational Foundation; Research Chefs Association.

AREAS OF STUDY
Baking; beverage management; buffet catering; convenience cookery; culinary skill development; food preparation; food purchasing; garde-manger; introduction to food service; management and human resources; meal planning; nutrition; nutrition and food service; restaurant opportunities; sanitation; soup, stock, sauce, and starch production.

FACILITIES
Bakery; catering service; 2 classrooms; coffee shop; 3 computer laboratories; demonstration laboratory; food production kitchen; gourmet dining room; learning resource center; lecture room; library; student lounge; teaching kitchen.

SPECIAL PROGRAMS
Culinary competitions, paid externships.

FINANCIAL AID
Employment placement assistance is available. Employment opportunities within the program are available.

North Georgia Technical College *(continued)*

APPLICATION INFORMATION

Students may begin participation in January, April, July, and October. Applications are accepted continuously. Applicants must submit a formal application and take ASSET Test.

CONTACT

Director of Admissions, Culinary Arts and Hotel/Restaurant/Tourism Management, 434 Meeks Avenue, Blairsville, GA 30512. Telephone: 706-781-2316. Fax: 706-781-2307. World Wide Web: http://www. ngtcollege.org.

SAVANNAH TECHNICAL COLLEGE

Culinary Arts Program

Savannah, Georgia

GENERAL INFORMATION

Public, coeducational, two-year college. Urban campus. Founded in 1929. Accredited by Southern Association of Colleges and Schools.

PROGRAM INFORMATION

Offered since 1981. Accredited by American Culinary Federation Accrediting Commission. Program calendar is divided into quarters. 18-month associate degree in culinary arts. 18-month diploma in culinary arts.

PROGRAM AFFILIATION

American Culinary Federation; Georgia Hospitality Association; Savannah Tourism leadership Council.

AREAS OF STUDY

Baking; buffet catering; controlling costs in food service; culinary skill development; dining room/guest services; food preparation; food purchasing; food service math; garde-manger; international cuisine; introduction to food service; kitchen management; management and human resources; meal planning; meat fabrication; nutrition; restaurant opportunities; sanitation; saucier; soup, stock, sauce, and starch production.

FACILITIES

Bake shop; catering service; classroom; coffee shop; computer laboratory; demonstration laboratory; food production kitchen; garden; gourmet dining room; laboratory; lecture room; library; public restaurant; student lounge; teaching kitchen.

STUDENT PROFILE

135 total: 75 full-time; 60 part-time. 3 are under 25 years old; 132 are between 25 and 44 years old.

FACULTY

2 total: 2 full-time. 1 is an industry professional; 1 is a culinary-certified teacher. Faculty-student ratio: 1:20.

SPECIAL PROGRAMS

Field trips (restaurants, vendor warehouses, food processing plants), special food production presentations, culinary competitions.

TYPICAL EXPENSES

Application fee: $15. In-state tuition: $372 per quarter full-time (in district), $31 per credit hour part-time. Out-of-state tuition: $744 per quarter full-time, $62 per credit hour part-time. Tuition for international students: $1488 per quarter. Program-related fees include $185 for knives; $150 for uniforms; $300 for books (per quarter).

FINANCIAL AID

In 2004, 2 scholarships were awarded (average award was $1500). Program-specific awards include Hector Boiardi scholarship, CAP (career assistance program), faculty and staff scholarships. Employment placement assistance is available.

HOUSING

Average off-campus housing cost per month: $600.

APPLICATION INFORMATION

Students may begin participation in April and October. Application deadline for all sessions: 30 days prior to start of each quarter. In 2004, 150 applied; 150 were accepted. Applicants must submit a formal application, have a high school diploma or GED and ASSET or SAT scores.

CONTACT

Student Services, Culinary Arts Program, 5717 White Bluff Road, Savannah, GA 31405-5521. Telephone: 912-443-5518. Fax: 912-303-1781. World Wide Web: http://www. savannahtech.edu.

WEST GEORGIA TECHNICAL COLLEGE

La Grange, Georgia

GENERAL INFORMATION

Public, coeducational, two-year college. Small-town setting. Founded in 1966. Accredited by Council on Occupational Education.

PROGRAM INFORMATION

Offered since 1996. Program calendar is divided into quarters. 18-month diploma in culinary arts.

AREAS OF STUDY

Beverage management; convenience cookery; food service communication; international cuisine; meat fabrication; menu and facilities design; nutrition; restaurant opportunities; wines and spirits.

FACILITIES

Classroom; library; student lounge; teaching kitchen.

TYPICAL STUDENT PROFILE
15 full-time. 10 are under 25 years old; 5 are between 25 and 44 years old.

SPECIAL PROGRAMS
NRA ServSafe certification, Culinary Food and Equipment Show of Atlanta, Sysco/US Food Service (local) Food and Equipment Show.

FINANCIAL AID
Employment placement assistance is available.

APPLICATION INFORMATION
Students may begin participation in January, April, July, and October. Applications are accepted continuously. Applicants must submit a formal application.

CONTACT
Director of Admissions, 303 Fort Drive, La Grange, GA 30240. Telephone: 706-837-4246. Fax: 706-845-4340. World Wide Web: http://www.westga.tec.ga.us.

HAWAII

LEEWARD COMMUNITY COLLEGE

Culinary Institute of the Pacific

Pearl City, Hawaii

GENERAL INFORMATION
Public, coeducational, two-year college. Suburban campus. Founded in 1968. Accredited by Western Association of Schools and Colleges.

PROGRAM INFORMATION
Offered since 1972. Accredited by American Culinary Federation Accrediting Commission. Program calendar is divided into semesters. 1-semester certificate of completion in food service. 1-semester certificate in prep cook. 1.5-semester certificate in dining room service. 1.5-semester certificate in baking. 2-semester certificate of achievement in food service. 2-year associate degree in food service.

PROGRAM AFFILIATION
American Culinary Federation.

AREAS OF STUDY
Baking; beverage management; controlling costs in food service; culinary skill development; food preparation; food purchasing; food service math; garde-manger; international cuisine; introduction to food service; management and human resources; nutrition and food service; sanitation; soup, stock, sauce, and starch production.

FACILITIES
Bake shop; cafeteria; 3 classrooms; coffee shop; 3 food production kitchens; gourmet dining room.

STUDENT PROFILE
150 total: 100 full-time; 50 part-time.

FACULTY
7 total: 5 full-time; 2 part-time. 3 are industry professionals; 3 are master chefs; 1 is a master baker; 5 are culinary-certified teachers. Prominent faculty: Ian Riseley, Executive Chef; Tommylynn Benavente, CCE; David Miller, Executive Chef; Linda Yamada, Executive Chef. Faculty-student ratio: 1:20.

SPECIAL PROGRAMS
Taste of the Stars, Japan study-abroad course in nutrition, networking opportunities with Hawaii's best chefs.

TYPICAL EXPENSES
In-state tuition: $43 per credit hour. Out-of-state tuition: $242 per credit hour.

FINANCIAL AID
In 2004, 10 scholarships were awarded (average award was $500). Program-specific awards include Scholarship Branch Awards, Industry Scholarships. Employment placement assistance is available. Employment opportunities within the program are available.

HOUSING
Average off-campus housing cost per month: $800.

APPLICATION INFORMATION
Students may begin participation in January and August. Application deadline for fall is July 15. Application deadline for spring is December 1. In 2004, 50 applied; 25 were accepted. Applicants must submit a formal application.

CONTACT
Tommylynn Benavente, Program Coordinator, Culinary Institute of the Pacific, 96-045 Ala Ike, Pearl City, HI 96782. Telephone: 808-455-0298. Fax: 808-455-0559. E-mail: tlbenave@hawaii.edu. World Wide Web: http://www.lcc.hawaii.edu/.

MAUI COMMUNITY COLLEGE

Food Service Program

Kahului, Hawaii

GENERAL INFORMATION
Public, coeducational, two-year college. Small-town setting. Founded in 1967. Accredited by Western Association of Schools and Colleges.

PROGRAM INFORMATION
Offered since 1977. Accredited by American Culinary Federation Accrediting Commission. Program calendar is divided into semesters. 1-year certificate in culinary arts. 2-year associate degree in food service/restaurant supervision. 2-year associate degree in food service-culinary arts specialty. 2-year associate degree in food service-baking specialty.

Maui Community College *(continued)*

PROGRAM AFFILIATION
American Culinary Federation; Confrerie de la Chaine des Rotisseurs; National Restaurant Association.

AREAS OF STUDY
Baking; beverage management; buffet catering; controlling costs in food service; culinary skill development; food preparation; food purchasing; food service communication; food service math; garde-manger; international cuisine; introduction to food service; management and human resources; menu and facilities design; nutrition; patisserie; restaurant opportunities; sanitation; soup, stock, sauce, and starch production; wines and spirits.

FACILITIES
Bake shop; cafeteria; catering service; classroom; computer laboratory; food production kitchen; garden; gourmet dining room; laboratory; lecture room; library; public restaurant; snack shop; teaching kitchen.

STUDENT PROFILE
155 total: 130 full-time; 25 part-time. 100 are under 25 years old; 20 are between 25 and 44 years old; 10 are over 44 years old.

FACULTY
10 total: 7 full-time; 3 part-time. 6 are industry professionals; 2 are culinary-certified teachers. Faculty-student ratio: 1:20.

SPECIAL PROGRAMS
Culinary competitions, field experiences, fellowships.

TYPICAL EXPENSES
In-state tuition: $549 per semester full-time (in district), $49.50 per credit part-time. Out-of-state tuition: $2913 per semester full-time, $246.50 per credit part-time. Tuition for international students: $2913 per semester full-time, $246.50 per credit part-time. Program-related fees include $150 for cooking and baking supplies; $250 for uniforms and shoes; $150 for books.

FINANCIAL AID
In 2004, 15 scholarships were awarded (average award was $300–$500). Employment placement assistance is available. Employment opportunities within the program are available.

HOUSING
Coed housing available. Average on-campus housing cost per month: $400. Average off-campus housing cost per month: $700.

APPLICATION INFORMATION
Students may begin participation in January, June, and August. Applications are accepted continuously. In 2004, 70 applied; 70 were accepted. Applicants must submit a formal application and submit a formal application.

CONTACT
Robert R. Santos, Coordinator, Food Service Program, 310 Kaahumanu Avenue, Kahului, HI 96732. Telephone: 808-984-3225. Fax: 808-984-3314. E-mail: santosro@hawaii.edu.

UNIVERSITY OF HAWAII-KAPIOLANI COMMUNITY COLLEGE

Culinary Institute of the Pacific

Honolulu, Hawaii

GENERAL INFORMATION
Public, coeducational, two-year college. Urban campus. Founded in 1957. Accredited by Western Association of Schools and Colleges.

PROGRAM INFORMATION
Offered since 1965. Accredited by American Culinary Federation Accrediting Commission, Commission on Accreditation of Hospitality Management Programs (CAHM). Program calendar is divided into semesters. 18-month certificate in culinary arts. 2-year associate degree in culinary arts. 2-year associate degree in patisserie. 4-month certificate in patisserie. 4-month certificate in culinary arts.

PROGRAM AFFILIATION
American Culinary Federation; American Dietetic Association; Confrerie de la Chaine des Rotisseurs; Council on Hotel, Restaurant, and Institutional Education; International Food Service Executives Association; National Restaurant Association; National Restaurant Association Educational Foundation.

AREAS OF STUDY
Asian Pacific cookery; baking; beverage management; confectionery show pieces; controlling costs in food service; food preparation; food service math; garde-manger; international cuisine; introduction to culinary arts; introduction to food service; management and human resources; meal planning; menu and facilities design; nutrition and food service; patisserie; sanitation; soup, stock, sauce, and starch production.

FACILITIES
2 bake shops; bakery; cafeteria; 12 classrooms; coffee shop; computer laboratory; demonstration laboratory; 4 food production kitchens; garden; 2 gourmet dining rooms; learning resource center; lecture room; library; 3 public restaurants; snack shop; student lounge; teaching kitchen.

STUDENT PROFILE
400 total: 200 full-time; 200 part-time. 150 are under 25 years old; 200 are between 25 and 44 years old; 50 are over 44 years old.

FACULTY

22 total: 14 full-time; 8 part-time. 15 are industry professionals; 7 are culinary-certified teachers. Faculty-student ratio: 1:35 lecture; 1:24 lab.

SPECIAL PROGRAMS

2-week Christmas break paid internships on neighbor islands, Walt Disney World College internship.

TYPICAL EXPENSES

Application fee: $25. In-state tuition: $49 per credit hour. Out-of-state tuition: $242 per credit hour. Program-related fee includes $250 for uniforms and cutlery.

FINANCIAL AID

In 2004, 45 scholarships were awarded (average award was $600); 250 loans were granted (average loan was $1200). Program-specific awards include Native Hawaiian student scholarships, culinary recipe scholarships. Employment placement assistance is available. Employment opportunities within the program are available.

HOUSING

Coed and apartment-style housing available. Average on-campus housing cost per month: $1000. Average off-campus housing cost per month: $900.

APPLICATION INFORMATION

Students may begin participation in January, March, May, July, August, and October. Application deadline for fall is July 1. Application deadline for spring is November 15. Application deadline for summer is April 15. In 2004, 400 applied; 400 were accepted. Applicants must submit a formal application.

CONTACT

Lori Maehara, Associate Professor/Counselor, Culinary Institute of the Pacific, 4303 Diamond Head Road, Honolulu, HI 96816. Telephone: 808-734-9466. Fax: 808-734-9212. E-mail: lmaehara@hawaii.edu. World Wide Web: http://www.kcc.hawaii.edu.

IDAHO

BOISE STATE UNIVERSITY

Culinary Arts Program

Boise, Idaho

GENERAL INFORMATION

Public, coeducational, comprehensive institution. Urban campus. Founded in 1932. Accredited by Northwest Association of Schools and Colleges.

PROGRAM INFORMATION

Offered since 1979. Accredited by American Culinary Federation Accrediting Commission. Program calendar is divided into semesters. 12-month certificate in culinary arts. 18-month certificate in culinary arts. 2-year associate degree in culinary arts. 6-month certificate in culinary arts.

PROGRAM AFFILIATION

American Culinary Federation.

AREAS OF STUDY

Baking; beverage management; controlling costs in food service; culinary skill development; food preparation; food purchasing; food service math; garde-manger; international cuisine; kitchen management; meat fabrication; nutrition; patisserie; sanitation; soup, stock, sauce, and starch production; wines and spirits.

FACILITIES

Bake shop; bakery; catering service; 3 classrooms; 2 demonstration laboratories; food production kitchen; 3 laboratories; learning resource center; 3 lecture rooms; library; public restaurant; snack shop; student lounge; teaching kitchen.

STUDENT PROFILE

46 total: 40 full-time; 6 part-time.

FACULTY

5 total: 4 full-time; 1 part-time. 2 are industry professionals; 2 are culinary-certified teachers. Prominent faculty: Julie Hosman-Kulm, CEC, CCE; Vern Hickman, CCC, CCE; Kelli Dever; Marie Edwards. Faculty-student ratio: 1:8.

SPECIAL PROGRAMS

One-semester paid internship.

TYPICAL EXPENSES

Application fee: $20. In-state tuition: $1765 per semester. Out-of-state tuition: $4365 per semester. Program-related fees include $30 for lab fee; $60 for uniform fee.

FINANCIAL AID

In 2004, 4 scholarships were awarded (average award was $300).

HOUSING

Coed, apartment-style, and single-sex housing available.

APPLICATION INFORMATION

Students may begin participation in January and August. Applications are accepted continuously. Applicants must submit a formal application and complete an entrance test.

CONTACT

Student Services Department, Culinary Arts Program, 1910 University Drive, Boise, ID 83725-0399. Telephone: 208-426-1431. World Wide Web: http://www.idbsu.edu/.

BRIGHAM YOUNG UNIVERSITY–IDAHO

Culinary Arts

Rexburg, Idaho

GENERAL INFORMATION
Private, coeducational, four-year college. Small-town setting. Founded in 1888. Accredited by Northwest Association of Schools and Colleges.

PROGRAM INFORMATION
Offered since 1990. Program calendar is divided into semesters. 2-year associate degree in culinary arts. 4-year bachelor's degree in applied management.

PROGRAM AFFILIATION
American Culinary Federation; American Dietetic Association.

AREAS OF STUDY
Baking; beverage management; buffet catering; controlling costs in food service; convenience cookery; culinary skill development; food preparation; food purchasing; food service math; garde-manger; international cuisine; introduction to food service; kitchen management; meal planning; menu and facilities design; nutrition; nutrition and food service; patisserie; sanitation; soup, stock, sauce, and starch production.

FACILITIES
Bakery; 3 classrooms; computer laboratory; 2 food production kitchens; garden; gourmet dining room; learning resource center; lecture room.

TYPICAL STUDENT PROFILE
49 total: 45 full-time; 4 part-time. 46 are under 25 years old; 2 are between 25 and 44 years old; 1 is over 44 years old.

SPECIAL PROGRAMS
4-year bachelor's degree in culinary arts management available in conjunction with Utah State University.

FINANCIAL AID
Employment placement assistance is available. Employment opportunities within the program are available.

HOUSING
Single-sex housing available.

APPLICATION INFORMATION
Students may begin participation in August. Application deadline for fall is March 1. Applicants must submit a formal application and culinary arts-specific application.

CONTACT
Director of Admissions, Culinary Arts, 352 Clarke Building, Rexburg, ID 83460-0615. Telephone: 208-496-1371. Fax: 208-496-5371. World Wide Web: http://www.byui.edu.

COLLEGE OF SOUTHERN IDAHO

Culinary and Pastry Arts

Twin Falls, Idaho

GENERAL INFORMATION
Public, coeducational, two-year college. Rural campus. Founded in 1964. Accredited by Northwest Association of Schools and Colleges.

PROGRAM INFORMATION
Offered since 1993. Program calendar is divided into semesters. 18-month associate degree in culinary and pastry arts. 9-month technical certificate in culinary and pastry arts.

PROGRAM AFFILIATION
American Culinary Federation.

AREAS OF STUDY
Baking; beverage management; controlling costs in food service; culinary skill development; food preparation; food purchasing; food service communication; food service math; garde-manger; introduction to food service; kitchen management; meal planning; meat cutting; menu and facilities design; nutrition; nutrition and food service; sanitation; saucier; soup, stock, sauce, and starch production.

FACILITIES
Bake shop; bakery; cafeteria; catering service; 3 classrooms; coffee shop; 2 computer laboratories; demonstration laboratory; food production kitchen; teaching kitchen.

TYPICAL STUDENT PROFILE
25 total: 20 full-time; 5 part-time.

SPECIAL PROGRAMS
Paid summer internships with local restaurants and at national venues including Disney World, 5-day tour of Las Vegas hotel and restaurant establishments, field trips to food service buying shows.

FINANCIAL AID
Employment placement assistance is available.

HOUSING
Coed housing available.

APPLICATION INFORMATION
Students may begin participation in August. Applications are accepted continuously. Applicants must submit a formal application and high school/college transcripts, take COMPASS test, and have high school diploma or GED.

CONTACT
Director of Admissions, Culinary and Pastry Arts, PO Box 1238, Twin Falls, ID 83303-1238. Telephone: 208-732-6231. Fax: 208-732-3014. World Wide Web: http://www.csi.edu.

IDAHO STATE UNIVERSITY

Culinary Arts Technology Program

Pocatello, Idaho

GENERAL INFORMATION
Public, coeducational, university. Rural campus. Founded in 1901. Accredited by Northwest Association of Schools and Colleges.

PROGRAM INFORMATION
Offered since 1967. Accredited by American Culinary Federation Accrediting Commission. Program calendar is divided into semesters. 1-year certificate in culinary management. 1-year certificate in culinary arts. 2-year associate degree in restaurant management. 2-year associate degree in culinary management. 2-year associate degree in culinary arts.

PROGRAM AFFILIATION
American Culinary Federation; Council on Hotel, Restaurant, and Institutional Education.

AREAS OF STUDY
Baking; beverage management; buffet catering; controlling costs in food service; convenience cookery; culinary skill development; food preparation; food purchasing; food service math; garde-manger; international cuisine; introduction to food service; kitchen management; management and human resources; meal planning; meat cutting; menu and facilities design; nutrition and food service; patisserie; restaurant opportunities; sanitation; saucier; seafood processing; soup, stock, sauce, and starch production; wines and spirits.

FACILITIES
Bake shop; catering service; classroom; coffee shop; computer laboratory; food production kitchen; learning resource center; lecture room; library.

STUDENT PROFILE
21 total: 20 full-time; 1 part-time. 15 are under 25 years old; 3 are between 25 and 44 years old; 2 are over 44 years old.

FACULTY
2 total: 2 full-time. 2 are industry professionals. Prominent faculty: David B. Miller; Josh Jackson. Faculty-student ratio: 1:8.

SPECIAL PROGRAMS
One-semester internship, culinary competitions.

TYPICAL EXPENSES
Application fee: $40. In-state tuition: $2075 per semester full-time (in district), $200 per credit part-time. Out-of-state tuition: $5925 per semester full-time, $310 per credit part-time. Program-related fee includes $75 for lab fee (per semester).

FINANCIAL AID
Employment placement assistance is available.

HOUSING
Coed housing available. Average on-campus housing cost per month: $300. Average off-campus housing cost per month: $500.

APPLICATION INFORMATION
Students may begin participation in January, May, and August. Application deadline for fall is August 20. Application deadline for spring is January 10. Application deadline for summer is May 20. Applicants must submit a formal application.

CONTACT
David B. Miller, Coordinator, Culinary Arts Technology Program, Box 8380, Pocatello, ID 83209. Telephone: 208-282-3327. Fax: 208-282-2105. E-mail: milldav1@isu.edu. World Wide Web: http://www.isu.edu.

ILLINOIS

COLLEGE OF DUPAGE

Culinary Arts/Pastry Arts

Glen Ellyn, Illinois

GENERAL INFORMATION
Public, coeducational, two-year college. Suburban campus. Founded in 1967. Accredited by North Central Association of Colleges and Schools.

PROGRAM INFORMATION
Offered since 1967. Accredited by American Culinary Federation Accrediting Commission. Program calendar is divided into semesters. 1-year certificate in food service administration. 1-year certificate in beverage management. 1-year certificate in pastry. 1-year certificate in culinary arts. 2-year associate degree in baking and pastry. 2-year associate degree in culinary arts. 2-year associate degree in food service administration.

PROGRAM AFFILIATION
American Culinary Federation; American Institute of Baking; Council on Hotel, Restaurant, and Institutional Education; International Food Service Executives Association; National Restaurant Association; National Restaurant Association Educational Foundation; Retailer's Bakery Association.

AREAS OF STUDY
Baking; beverage management; buffet catering; confectionery show pieces; controlling costs in food service; culinary skill development; food preparation; food purchasing; food service math; garde-manger; international cuisine; introduction to food service; kitchen management; management and human resources; menu and facilities design; nutrition; nutrition and food service; oriental

College of DuPage (continued)

cuisine; patisserie; sanitation; saucier; seafood processing; soup, stock, sauce, and starch production; wines and spirits.

FACILITIES

Bake shop; cafeteria; 2 classrooms; 3 computer laboratories; demonstration laboratory; food production kitchen; gourmet dining room; 2 laboratories; learning resource center; 2 lecture rooms; library; public restaurant; snack shop; student lounge; teaching kitchen.

STUDENT PROFILE

400 total: 160 full-time; 240 part-time. 160 are under 25 years old; 200 are between 25 and 44 years old; 40 are over 44 years old.

FACULTY

25 total: 5 full-time; 20 part-time. 13 are industry professionals; 6 are culinary-certified teachers. Prominent faculty: George Macht, CHA, CFE, FMP; Chris Thielman, CEC, CCE; David Kramer, CEC; Timothy Meyers, CCC, CCE. Faculty-student ratio: 1:18.

SPECIAL PROGRAMS

2-week culinary tour in Tuscany (Italy), one-week summer culinary tour in Provence (France), one-week wine and food tour of France.

TYPICAL EXPENSES

Application fee: $10. In-state tuition: $87 per credit hour. Out-of-state tuition: $286 per credit hour. Tuition for international students: $286 per credit hour. Program-related fees include $70 for knives; $75 for uniforms; $50 for supplies; $75 for class-specific tools; $50 for lab fees.

FINANCIAL AID

In 2004, 15 scholarships were awarded (average award was $200). Employment placement assistance is available. Employment opportunities within the program are available.

HOUSING

Average off-campus housing cost per month: $1000.

APPLICATION INFORMATION

Students may begin participation in January, May, and August. Applications are accepted continuously. In 2004, 200 applied; 200 were accepted. Applicants must submit a formal application.

CONTACT

George Macht, Coordinator, Culinary Arts/Pastry Arts, 425 Fawell Boulevard, Glen Ellyn, IL 60137. Telephone: 630-942-2315. Fax: 630-858-9399. E-mail: machtg@cdnet.cod.edu. World Wide Web: http://www.cod.edu/.

COLLEGE OF LAKE COUNTY

Food Service Program

Grayslake, Illinois

GENERAL INFORMATION

Public, coeducational, two-year college. Suburban campus. Founded in 1967. Accredited by North Central Association of Colleges and Schools.

PROGRAM INFORMATION

Offered since 1987. Program calendar is divided into semesters. 1-semester certificate in cooking. 1-year certificate in food service management. 1-year certificate in culinary arts. 2-year associate degree in food service management.

PROGRAM AFFILIATION

American Culinary Federation; American Dietetic Association; Council on Hotel, Restaurant, and Institutional Education; National Restaurant Association; National Restaurant Association Educational Foundation.

AREAS OF STUDY

Baking; buffet catering; controlling costs in food service; convenience cookery; culinary skill development; food preparation; food purchasing; food service communication; food service math; garde-manger; international cuisine; introduction to food service; kitchen management; management and human resources; meal planning; menu and facilities design; nutrition; restaurant opportunities; sanitation; saucier; soup, stock, sauce, and starch production.

FACILITIES

Bake shop; cafeteria; catering service; 4 classrooms; 12 computer laboratories; 2 demonstration laboratories; 2 food production kitchens; learning resource center; library; 2 public restaurants; snack shop.

STUDENT PROFILE

150 total: 50 full-time; 100 part-time. 40 are under 25 years old; 40 are between 25 and 44 years old; 20 are over 44 years old.

FACULTY

9 total: 1 full-time; 8 part-time. 4 are industry professionals; 3 are culinary-certified teachers. Prominent faculty: Tom Maguire; Jeanette Keyes; Jack Bress; Cliff Wener. Faculty-student ratio: 1:18.

SPECIAL PROGRAMS

Applied Food Service Sanitation Refresher Course, Basset Course.

TYPICAL EXPENSES

In-state tuition: $75 per credit hour full-time (in district), $75 per credit hour part-time (in district), $225 per credit hour full-time (out-of-district), $225 per credit hour part-time (out-of-district). Out-of-state tuition: $300 per credit hour full-time, $300 per credit hour part-time. Program-related fees include $150 for tools and equipment; $50 for uniforms; $50 for lab fee.

FINANCIAL AID

In 2004, 2 scholarships were awarded (average award was $1000); 50 loans were granted (average loan was $500). Employment placement assistance is available. Employment opportunities within the program are available.

HOUSING

Average off-campus housing cost per month: $600.

APPLICATION INFORMATION

Students may begin participation in January, June, and August. Applications are accepted continuously. In 2004, 50 applied; 50 were accepted. Applicants must submit a formal application.

CONTACT

Cliff Wener, Coordinator, Food Service Program, 19351 West Washington, Grayslake. Telephone: 847-543-2823. Fax: 847-223-7248. E-mail: crwener-fsm@clcillinois.edu. World Wide Web: http://www.clcillinois.edu.

THE COOKING AND HOSPITALITY INSTITUTE OF CHICAGO

Chicago, Illinois

GENERAL INFORMATION

Private, coeducational, two-year college. Urban campus. Founded in 1983. Accredited by Accrediting Commission of Career Schools and Colleges of Technology.

PROGRAM INFORMATION

Offered since 1991. Accredited by American Culinary Federation Accrediting Commission. Program calendar is divided into semesters. 16-month associate degree in patisserie and baking. 16-month associate degree in culinary arts.

PROGRAM AFFILIATION

American Culinary Federation; American Institute of Wine & Food; International Association of Culinary Professionals; National Restaurant Association; National Restaurant Association Educational Foundation.

AREAS OF STUDY

Baking; beverage management; confectionery show pieces; controlling costs in food service; culinary French; culinary skill development; food preparation; food purchasing; food service math; garde-manger; international cuisine;

The Cooking and Hospitality Institute of Chicago
(continued)

introduction to food service; kitchen management; management and human resources; meal planning; meat cutting; meat fabrication; menu and facilities design; nutrition; patisserie; restaurant opportunities; sanitation; saucier; seafood processing; soup, stock, sauce, and starch production.

FACILITIES
11 classrooms; computer laboratory; 4 demonstration laboratories; 8 food production kitchens; learning resource center; library; public restaurant; student lounge.

TYPICAL STUDENT PROFILE
978 full-time. 408 are under 25 years old; 505 are between 25 and 44 years old; 65 are over 44 years old.

SPECIAL PROGRAMS
Graduates with AAS receive Le Cordon Bleu Diplôme.

FINANCIAL AID
Program-specific awards include Alternative Educational Loans. Employment placement assistance is available. Employment opportunities within the program are available.

APPLICATION INFORMATION
Students may begin participation in January, March, May, July, September, and October. Applications are accepted continuously. Applicants must submit a formal application.

CONTACT
Director of Admissions, 361 West Chestnut Street, Chicago, IL 60610-3050. Telephone: 312-873-2064. Fax: 312-944-8557. World Wide Web: http://www.chic.edu.

ELGIN COMMUNITY COLLEGE

Culinary Management

Elgin, Illinois

GENERAL INFORMATION
Public, coeducational, two-year college. Suburban campus. Founded in 1949. Accredited by North Central Association of Colleges and Schools.

PROGRAM INFORMATION
Offered since 1971. Accredited by American Culinary Federation Accrediting Commission. Program calendar is divided into semesters. 1-semester certificate in baking assistant. 1-semester certificate in lead baker. 1-year certificate in cook's helper. 2-year associate degree in pastry chef. 2-year associate degree in culinary arts. 2-year associate degree in restaurant management. 3-semester certificate in pastry chef assistant.

PROGRAM AFFILIATION
American Culinary Federation; American Institute of Baking; Council on Hotel, Restaurant, and Institutional Education; National Restaurant Association; National Restaurant Association Educational Foundation.

AREAS OF STUDY
Baking; beverage management; controlling costs in food service; culinary French; culinary skill development; food preparation; food purchasing; food service math; garde-manger; introduction to food service; management and human resources; meat cutting; meat fabrication; menu and facilities design; nutrition; patisserie; restaurant opportunities; sanitation; saucier; seafood processing; soup, stock, sauce, and starch production.

FACILITIES
Bakery; cafeteria; catering service; 3 classrooms; computer laboratory; 4 demonstration laboratories; 5 food production kitchens; gourmet dining room; 5 laboratories; learning resource center; 5 lecture rooms; library; 2 public restaurants; snack shop; student lounge; business conference center.

STUDENT PROFILE
450 total: 300 full-time; 150 part-time.

FACULTY
15 total: 5 full-time; 10 part-time. 9 are industry professionals; 8 are culinary-certified teachers. Prominent faculty: Michael Zema, CCE, FMP; Stephanie Johnson, FMP, CEPC; Mark Bosanac, CEC; Kimberly Rother, MS. Faculty-student ratio: 1:30 lectures; 1:15 production classes.

SPECIAL PROGRAMS
International exchange with Hotelfaschule (Austria) and internship opportunities, employment at Western Open Golf Tournament, culinary internships with Disney World.

TYPICAL EXPENSES
Application fee: $20. In-state tuition: $77 per credit hour part-time (in district), $265.33 per credit hour part-time (out-of-district). Out-of-state tuition: $327.46 per credit hour part-time. Program-related fees include $100 for lab fees; $200 for smallwares, toolbox, uniforms.

FINANCIAL AID
Program-specific awards include 5 National Restaurant Association scholarships per semester. Employment placement assistance is available. Employment opportunities within the program are available.

HOUSING
Average off-campus housing cost per month: $300.

APPLICATION INFORMATION
Students may begin participation in January, May, and August. Applications are accepted continuously. In 2004, 300 applied. Applicants must submit a formal application and have a high school diploma or GED.

CONTACT
Michael Zema, Coordinator, Culinary Management, 1700 Spartan Drive, Room C AC 105A, Elgin, IL 60123.

Telephone: 847-214-7461. Fax: 847-214-7510. E-mail: mzema@elgin.edu. World Wide Web: http://www.elgin.edu.

THE ILLINOIS INSTITUTE OF ART–CHICAGO

Culinary Arts
Chicago, Illinois

GENERAL INFORMATION
Private, coeducational, four-year college. Urban campus. Founded in 1916. Accredited by Accrediting Commission of Career Schools and Colleges of Technology.

PROGRAM INFORMATION
Offered since 1999. Accredited by ACF. Program calendar is divided into quarters. 12-month certificate in professional cooking. 12-month certificate in baking and pastry. 18-month associate degree in culinary arts. 36-month bachelor's degree in culinary management.

PROGRAM AFFILIATION
American Culinary Federation; National Restaurant Association.

AREAS OF STUDY
À la carte; baking; catering; controlling costs in food service; culinary skill development; dining room operation; food and beverage management; food service communication; garde-manger; international cuisine; kitchen management; nutrition; sanitation.

FACILITIES
Learning resource center; 10 lecture rooms; library; public restaurant; 2 student lounges; 6 teaching kitchens.

FACULTY
16 total: 10 full-time; 6 part-time. Faculty-student ratio: 1:30.

SPECIAL PROGRAMS
Student-run restaurant, culinary competitions, student ambassadors.

TYPICAL EXPENSES
Application fee: $100. Tuition: $390 per credit hour part-time. Program-related fee includes $660 for starting kit (one time fee).

FINANCIAL AID
Employment placement assistance is available.

APPLICATION INFORMATION
Students may begin participation in January, February, April, May, July, August, September, October, and November. Applications are accepted continuously. Applicants must interview, and submit 150-word essay and have a high school diploma or equivalent.

CONTACT
Janis Anton, Vice President, Director of Admissions, Culinary Arts, 350 N. Orleans, Chicago, IL 60601. Telephone: 800-351-3450. Fax: 312-280-8562. E-mail: antonj@aii.edu. World Wide Web: http://www.ilic. artinstitute.edu.

JOLIET JUNIOR COLLEGE

Culinary Arts/Hospitality Management
Joliet, Illinois

GENERAL INFORMATION
Public, coeducational, two-year college. Suburban campus. Founded in 1901. Accredited by North Central Association of Colleges and Schools.

PROGRAM INFORMATION
Offered since 1970. Accredited by American Culinary Federation Accrediting Commission. Program calendar is divided into semesters. 1-year certificate in pastry arts. 1-year certificate in baking. 1-year certificate in culinary arts. 2-year associate degree in hospitality management. 2-year associate degree in culinary arts.

PROGRAM AFFILIATION
American Culinary Federation; American Institute of Wine & Food; Council on Hotel, Restaurant, and Institutional Education; International Association of Culinary Professionals; National Restaurant Association; National Restaurant Association Educational Foundation; Women Chefs and Restaurateurs.

AREAS OF STUDY
Baking; controlling costs in food service; culinary French; culinary skill development; food preparation; garde-manger; ice carving; management and human resources; sanitation; wines and spirits.

FACILITIES
3 bake shops; bakery; 2 cafeterias; 2 catering services; 10 classrooms; 2 coffee shops; computer laboratory; 2 demonstration laboratories; 3 food production kitchens; 2 gourmet dining rooms; learning resource center; 5 lecture rooms; 2 libraries; 2 public restaurants; snack shop; student lounge; 2 teaching kitchens; ice carving room.

TYPICAL STUDENT PROFILE
217 total: 118 full-time; 99 part-time. 144 are under 25 years old; 55 are between 25 and 44 years old; 18 are over 44 years old.

SPECIAL PROGRAMS
Culinary competitions, 1-year paid internships in U.S. and Germany, two-week trip to Europe to visit food and hotel venues.

Joliet Junior College *(continued)*

FINANCIAL AID
Employment placement assistance is available. Employment opportunities within the program are available.

HOUSING
Coed and apartment-style housing available.

APPLICATION INFORMATION
Students may begin participation in January, May, and August. Applications are accepted continuously. Applicants must have a high school diploma or GED.

CONTACT
Director of Admissions, Culinary Arts/Hospitality Management, 1215 Houbolt Road, Joliet, IL 60431-9352. Telephone: 815-280-2639. Fax: 815-280-2696. World Wide Web: http://www.jjc.edu.

KENDALL COLLEGE

School of Culinary Arts and School of Hotel Management

Chicago, Illinois

GENERAL INFORMATION
Private, coeducational, four-year college. Urban campus. Founded in 1934. Accredited by North Central Association of Colleges and Schools.

PROGRAM INFORMATION
Offered since 1985. Accredited by American Culinary Federation Accrediting Commission, Council on Hotel, Restaurant and Institutional Education, CFA, Higher Learning Commission of NCA. Program calendar is divided into quarters. 12-quarter bachelor's degree in culinary arts. 15-quarter bachelor's degree in hospitality management. 4-quarter certificate in catering. 4-quarter certificate in personal chef. 4-quarter certificate in baking and pastry arts. 4-quarter certificate in culinary arts/professional cookery. 5-quarter associate degree in culinary arts accelerated program. 6-quarter associate degree in baking and pastry arts. 6-quarter associate degree in culinary arts.

PROGRAM AFFILIATION
American Culinary Federation; American Institute of Baking; American Institute of Wine & Food; Council on Hotel, Restaurant, and Institutional Education; Hospitality Business Alliance; Illinois Restaurant Association; International Association of Culinary Professionals; National Restaurant Association; National Restaurant Association Educational Foundation; Northern Illinois Food Service Executives Association; Northern Illinois Hospitality Educators Association; The Bread Bakers Guild of America; Women Chefs and Restaurateurs.

AREAS OF STUDY
Baking; beverage management; buffet catering; confectionery show pieces; controlling costs in food service; convenience cookery; culinary French; culinary skill development; food preparation; food purchasing; food service communication; food service math; garde-manger; international cuisine; introduction to food service; kitchen management; management and human resources; meal planning; meat cutting; meat fabrication; menu and facilities design; nutrition; nutrition and food service; patisserie; restaurant opportunities; sanitation; saucier; seafood processing; soup, stock, sauce, and starch production; techniques of healthy cooking; wines and spirits.

FACILITIES
2 bake shops; cafeteria; catering service; 2 computer laboratories; 3 demonstration laboratories; 11 food production kitchens; garden; gourmet dining room; learning resource center; library; public restaurant; snack shop; student lounge; 11 teaching kitchens.

TYPICAL STUDENT PROFILE
628 total: 454 full-time; 174 part-time.

SPECIAL PROGRAMS
Internships (1–5 quarters), Culinary Competition Team, exchange programs in Marseille and Nice (France), Bluche (Switzerland), Montreal (Canada) and Tel Aviv (Israel).

FINANCIAL AID
Program-specific awards include graduate assistant appointments, college work-study positions in Culinary Arts Department, Hospitality Department and others. Employment placement assistance is available. Employment opportunities within the program are available.

HOUSING
Apartment-style housing available.

APPLICATION INFORMATION
Students may begin participation in January, March, June, and September. Applications are accepted continuously. Applicants must interview; submit a formal application, an essay, official transcripts, and ACT/SAT scores (freshmen).

CONTACT
Director of Admissions, School of Culinary Arts and School of Hotel Management, 900 N. North Branch Street, Chicago, IL 60622. Telephone: 877-588-8860. Fax: 312-752-2021. World Wide Web: http://www.kendall.edu/.

See display on page 161.

LEXINGTON COLLEGE

Chicago, Illinois

GENERAL INFORMATION
Private, four-year college. Urban campus. Founded in 1977. Accredited by North Central Association of Colleges and Schools.

PROGRAM INFORMATION
Offered since 1977. Program calendar is divided into semesters. 2-year associate degree in hospitality management. 4-year bachelor's degree in hospitality management.

PROGRAM AFFILIATION
American Culinary Federation; Council on Hotel, Restaurant, and Institutional Education; Illinois Restaurant Association; National Restaurant Association; Women Chefs and Restaurateurs; Women's Foodservice Forum.

AREAS OF STUDY
Culinary skill development; events management; hotel and restaurant management; management and human resources.

FACILITIES
4 classrooms; computer laboratory; demonstration laboratory; library; student lounge; teaching kitchen.

STUDENT PROFILE
49 total: 39 full-time; 10 part-time. 33 are under 25 years old; 12 are between 25 and 44 years old; 4 are over 44 years old.

FACULTY
16 total: 4 full-time; 12 part-time. 8 are industry professionals. Prominent faculty: Linda Rosner, CEC; Marta Elvira, PhD. Faculty-student ratio: 1:8.

SPECIAL PROGRAMS
Summer internships (paid).

TYPICAL EXPENSES
Application fee: $30. Tuition: $8050 per semester full-time, $530 per credit hour part-time. Program-related fee includes $400 for culinary lab.

FINANCIAL AID
In 2004, 25 scholarships were awarded (average award was $1396); 39 loans were granted (average loan was $2425). Employment placement assistance is available. Employment opportunities within the program are available.

HOUSING
Average off-campus housing cost per month: $800.

APPLICATION INFORMATION
Students may begin participation in January and August. Applications are accepted continuously. In 2004, 48 applied; 46 were accepted. Applicants must submit a formal application, letters of reference, an essay, ACT or SAT scores.

CONTACT
Elizabeth Searby, Admissions Representative, 310 South Peoria Street, Chicago, IL 60607. Telephone: 312-226-6294. Fax: 312-226-6405. E-mail: admissions@lexingtoncollege. edu. World Wide Web: http://www.lexingtoncollege.edu.

LINCOLN LAND COMMUNITY COLLEGE

Hospitality Management

Springfield, Illinois

GENERAL INFORMATION
Public, coeducational, two-year college. Urban campus. Founded in 1967. Accredited by North Central Association of Colleges and Schools.

PROGRAM INFORMATION
Offered since 1994. Accredited by Council on Hotel, Restaurant and Institutional Education. Program calendar is divided into semesters. 1-year certificate in certified dietary manager. 1-year certificate in lodging management. 1-year certificate in culinary arts. 1-year certificate in pastry. 2-year associate degree in hospitality management.

PROGRAM AFFILIATION
American Culinary Federation; American Dietetic Association; American Vegan Society; Confrerie de la Chaine des Rotisseurs; Council on Hotel, Restaurant, and Institutional Education; Dietary Managers Association; Illinois Restaurant Association; National Restaurant Association; National Restaurant Association Educational Foundation.

AREAS OF STUDY
Baking; buffet catering; controlling costs in food service; culinary French; culinary skill development; food preparation; food purchasing; food service communication; food service math; garde-manger; international cuisine; introduction to food service; kitchen management; management and human resources; meal planning; nutrition; nutrition and food service; patisserie; restaurant opportunities; sanitation; soup, stock, sauce, and starch production; wines and spirits.

FACILITIES
Bake shop; bakery; cafeteria; catering service; classroom; computer laboratory; demonstration laboratory; food production kitchen; garden; laboratory; learning resource center; lecture room; library; public restaurant; snack shop; student lounge; teaching kitchen.

STUDENT PROFILE
130 total: 30 full-time; 100 part-time. 45 are under 25 years old; 45 are between 25 and 44 years old; 40 are over 44 years old.

FACULTY

13 total: 1 full-time; 12 part-time. 12 are industry professionals; 3 are master chefs; 1 is a master baker; 4 are culinary-certified teachers. Prominent faculty: David Radwine; Howard Seidel, CEC; Raven Pulliam, CEC; Michael Higgins. Faculty-student ratio: 1:18.

SPECIAL PROGRAMS

Paid internships, participation in culinary society events, membership in ACF chapter.

TYPICAL EXPENSES

Tuition: $900 per semester full-time (in district), $225 per semester part-time. Program-related fees include $20 for materials; $25 for chef's jacket.

FINANCIAL AID

In 2004, 6 scholarships were awarded (average award was $500); 10 loans were granted (average loan was $1000). Employment placement assistance is available. Employment opportunities within the program are available.

HOUSING

Average off-campus housing cost per month: $400.

APPLICATION INFORMATION

Students may begin participation in January and August. Applications are accepted continuously. Applicants must submit a formal application.

CONTACT

Jay Kitterman, Program Coordinator, Hospitality Management, 5250 Shepherd Road, Springfield, IL 62794. Telephone: 217-786-2772. Fax: 217-786-2339. E-mail: jay.kitterman@llcc.edu. World Wide Web: http://www.llcc.edu.

NORTHWESTERN BUSINESS COLLEGE

Hospitality Tourism Management

Chicago, Illinois

GENERAL INFORMATION

Private, coeducational, two-year college. Urban campus. Founded in 1902. Accredited by North Central Association of Colleges and Schools.

PROGRAM INFORMATION

Offered since 1987. Accredited by Council on Hotel, Restaurant and Institutional Education. Program calendar is divided into quarters. 2-year associate degree in hospitality management.

PROGRAM AFFILIATION

Council on Hotel, Restaurant, and Institutional Education; National Restaurant Association Educational Foundation.

AREAS OF STUDY

Beverage management; introduction to food service; management and human resources; restaurant opportunities.

FACILITIES

4 classrooms; 4 computer laboratories; 2 libraries; 2 student lounges.

TYPICAL STUDENT PROFILE

18 total: 12 full-time; 6 part-time.

SPECIAL PROGRAMS

3-month internships, field trips.

FINANCIAL AID

Employment placement assistance is available.

APPLICATION INFORMATION

Students may begin participation in March, June, September, and December. Applications are accepted continuously. Applicants must interview; submit a formal application, letters of reference, an essay, take COMPASS test.

CONTACT

Director of Admissions, Hospitality Tourism Management, 4829 North Lipps Avenue, Chicago, IL 60630-2298. Telephone: 773-481-3756. Fax: 773-205-2124. World Wide Web: http://www.northwesternbc.edu.

PARKLAND COLLEGE

Hospitality Industry

Champaign, Illinois

GENERAL INFORMATION

Public, coeducational, two-year college. Small-town setting. Founded in 1967. Accredited by North Central Association of Colleges and Schools.

PROGRAM INFORMATION

Offered since 1981. Accredited by Council on Hotel, Restaurant and Institutional Education, Commission on Accreditation of Hospitality Management Programs. Program calendar is divided into semesters. 1-year certificate in hospitality industry: food service. 2-year associate degree in hospitality industry: restaurant management.

PROGRAM AFFILIATION

Council on Hotel, Restaurant, and Institutional Education; International Food Service Executives Association; National Restaurant Association; National Restaurant Association Educational Foundation.

AREAS OF STUDY

Baking; beverage management; buffet catering; controlling costs in food service; convenience cookery; culinary skill development; food preparation; food purchasing; food service communication; food service math; introduction to food service; kitchen management; management and human resources; meal planning; meat fabrication; menu

Parkland College *(continued)*

and facilities design; nutrition; restaurant opportunities; sanitation; soup, stock, sauce, and starch production; wines and spirits.

FACILITIES

Classroom; demonstration laboratory; food production kitchen; learning resource center; lecture room; teaching kitchen.

TYPICAL STUDENT PROFILE

62 total: 18 full-time; 44 part-time. 35 are under 25 years old; 20 are between 25 and 44 years old; 7 are over 44 years old.

SPECIAL PROGRAMS

Food Service Sanitation Certification, semester or summer internships.

FINANCIAL AID

Program-specific awards include Arby's Foodservice/ Restaurant Management Career Grant ($1000), William P. Myers Foundation Awards ($1000). Employment placement assistance is available. Employment opportunities within the program are available.

APPLICATION INFORMATION

Students may begin participation in January and August. Applications are accepted continuously. Applicants must submit a formal application.

CONTACT

Director of Admissions, Hospitality Industry, 2400 West Bradley Avenue, Champaign, IL 61821-1806. Telephone: 217-351-2378. Fax: 217-373-3896. World Wide Web: http://www.parkland.edu.

REND LAKE COLLEGE

Culinary Arts Management

Ina, Illinois

GENERAL INFORMATION

Public, coeducational, two-year college. Rural campus. Founded in 1967. Accredited by North Central Association of Colleges and Schools.

PROGRAM INFORMATION

Program calendar is divided into semesters. 1-year certificate in culinary arts management. 2-year associate degree in culinary arts management.

PROGRAM AFFILIATION

National Restaurant Association Educational Foundation.

AREAS OF STUDY

Culinary skill development; food purchasing; food service management; restaurant management.

FACILITIES

Bakery; catering service; classroom; computer laboratory; gourmet dining room; laboratory; learning resource center; lecture room; library; public restaurant; student lounge; teaching kitchen.

TYPICAL STUDENT PROFILE

50 total: 40 full-time; 10 part-time.

SPECIAL PROGRAMS

Culinary competitions.

FINANCIAL AID

Employment placement assistance is available. Employment opportunities within the program are available.

APPLICATION INFORMATION

Students may begin participation in January and August. Applications are accepted continuously. Applicants must submit a formal application.

CONTACT

Director of Admissions, Culinary Arts Management, 468 North Ken Gray Parkway, Ina, IL 62846. Telephone: 618-437-5321 Ext. 1332. Fax: 618-437-5356. World Wide Web: http://www.ric.edu.

ROBERT MORRIS COLLEGE

Institute of Culinary Arts

Aurora, Chicago, and Orland Park, Illinois

GENERAL INFORMATION

Private, coeducational, four-year college. Suburban campus. Founded in 1913. Accredited by North Central Association of Colleges and Schools.

PROGRAM INFORMATION

Offered since 2003. Program calendar is divided into quarters, 5 ten-week academic sessions per year. 15-month associate degree in Culinary Arts. 3-year bachelor's degree in Hospitality Management.

PROGRAM AFFILIATION

American Culinary Federation; International Association of Culinary Professionals; National Restaurant Association; National Restaurant Association Educational Foundation; Women Chefs and Restaurateurs.

AREAS OF STUDY

Baking; beverage management; buffet catering; controlling costs in food service; convenience cookery; culinary French; culinary skill development; food preparation; food purchasing; food service communication; food service math; garde-manger; international cuisine; introduction to food service; kitchen management; management and human resources; meal planning; meat cutting; meat fabrication; menu and facilities design; nutrition; restaurant opportunities; sanitation; saucier; seafood processing; soup, stock, sauce, and starch production; wines and spirits.

Robert Morris College *(continued)*

FACILITIES
32 computer laboratories; 3 learning resource centers; 32 lecture rooms; 6 teaching kitchens.

STUDENT PROFILE
293 total: 277 full-time; 16 part-time.

FACULTY
29 total: 6 full-time; 23 part-time. 23 are industry professionals; 12 are culinary-certified teachers. Prominent faculty: Kevin Appleton; Jennifer Bucko; John Hudac; Scott Nitsche, CEC. Faculty-student ratio: 1:16.

SPECIAL PROGRAMS
Culinary competitions, paid internships, international experience with Italian and French culinary schools.

TYPICAL EXPENSES
Application fee: $30. Tuition: $16,800 per year full-time, $1700 per course part-time. Program-related fees include $850 for lab fee (per session); $275 for knife kit; $180 for 3 uniforms.

FINANCIAL AID
In 2005, 20 scholarships were awarded (average award was $30,000). Program-specific awards include 85% of students receive some type of financial aid. Employment placement assistance is available. Employment opportunities within the program are available.

HOUSING
Coed and apartment-style housing available. Average on-campus housing cost per month: $800.

APPLICATION INFORMATION
Students may begin participation in February, July, and September. Applications are accepted continuously. In 2005, 495 applied; 373 were accepted. Applicants must interview; submit a formal application and proof of high school graduation or GED completion.

CONTACT
Nancy Rotunno, Executive Director, Institute of Culinary Arts, 401 South State Street, Chicago, IL 60605. Telephone: 312-935-6800. Fax: 312-935-6930. World Wide Web: http://www.robertmorris.edu/.

See display on page 165.

SOUTHWESTERN ILLINOIS COLLEGE

Hospitality and Food Service Management

Belleville, Illinois

GENERAL INFORMATION
Public, coeducational, two-year college. Suburban campus. Founded in 1946. Accredited by North Central Association of Colleges and Schools.

PROGRAM INFORMATION
Accredited by American Culinary Federation Accrediting Commission. Program calendar is divided into semesters. 1-year certificate in food management. 2-year associate degree in culinary arts and food management. 3-semester certificate in culinary arts/food management. 8-month certificate in culinary arts.

PROGRAM AFFILIATION
American Culinary Federation; National Restaurant Association.

AREAS OF STUDY
Baking; beverage management; controlling costs in food service; culinary skill development; food preparation; food purchasing; food service math; garde-manger; international cuisine; international cuisine; introduction to food service; kitchen management; meal planning; meat cutting; nutrition; nutrition and food service; restaurant opportunities; sanitation; soup, stock, sauce, and starch production.

FACILITIES
2 bake shops; 2 bakeries; 2 classrooms; 4 computer laboratories; 2 demonstration laboratories; 2 food production kitchens; 2 laboratories; 2 learning resource centers; 2 lecture rooms; 2 libraries; 2 public restaurants; 2 snack shops; 2 student lounges; 2 teaching kitchens.

STUDENT PROFILE
150 total: 50 full-time; 100 part-time.

FACULTY
10 total: 1 full-time; 9 part-time. 5 are industry professionals; 4 are culinary-certified teachers; 3 are certified executive chefs, 1 dietitian. Prominent faculty: Ollie Sommer, CEC, AAC; Tom Noonan, CEC; Lee Conway, CEC; Steve Nigg, MS, FMP, CHE. Faculty-student ratio: 1:12.

SPECIAL PROGRAMS
Semester internships, trip to National Restaurant Association show.

TYPICAL EXPENSES
Application fee: $10. In-state tuition: $4060 per degree full-time (in district), $58 per credit hour (for certificate) part-time (in district), $10,990 per degree full-time (out-of-district), $157 per credit hour (for certificate) part-time (out-of-district). Out-of-state tuition: $17,430 per degree full-time, $249 per credit hour (for certificate) part-time. Program-related fee includes $700 for supplies.

FINANCIAL AID
In 2004, 1 scholarship was awarded (award was $1000). Program-specific awards include National Restaurant Association scholarships. Employment placement assistance is available. Employment opportunities within the program are available.

APPLICATION INFORMATION

Students may begin participation in January, June, and August. Applications are accepted continuously. Applicants must submit a formal application and have high school diploma or GED.

CONTACT

Steve Nigg, Program Coordinator, Hospitality and Food Service Management, 4950 Maryville Road, Granite City, IL 62040. Telephone: 618-222-5436. Fax: 618-222-8964. E-mail: steve.nigg@swic.edu. World Wide Web: http://www.southwestern.cc.il.us.

TRITON COLLEGE

Hospitality Industry Administration

River Grove, Illinois

GENERAL INFORMATION

Public, coeducational, two-year college. Suburban campus. Founded in 1964. Accredited by North Central Association of Colleges and Schools.

PROGRAM INFORMATION

Offered since 1972. Accredited by American Culinary Federation Accrediting Commission, Council on Hotel, Restaurant and Institutional Education. Program calendar is divided into semesters. 1-year certificate in baking and pastry. 1-year certificate in hotel/motel management. 1-year certificate in restaurant management. 1-year certificate in culinary arts. 2-year associate degree in hotel/motel management. 2-year associate degree in restaurant management. 2-year associate degree in culinary arts.

PROGRAM AFFILIATION

American Culinary Federation; American Institute of Baking; American Institute of Wine & Food; American Wine Society; Council on Hotel, Restaurant, and Institutional Education; Institute of Food Technologists; International Wine & Food Society; National Association for the Specialty Food Trade, Inc.; National Restaurant Association; National Restaurant Association Educational Foundation.

AREAS OF STUDY

Baking; beverage management; buffet catering; controlling costs in food service; convenience cookery; culinary French; culinary skill development; food preparation; food purchasing; food service communication; garde-manger; international cuisine; introduction to food service; kitchen management; management and human resources; meal planning; meat cutting; meat fabrication; nutrition; nutrition and food service; patisserie; sanitation; saucier; seafood processing; soup, stock, sauce, and starch production; wines and spirits.

FACILITIES

Bake shop; bakery; 2 cafeterias; catering service; 4 classrooms; coffee shop; computer laboratory; 2 demonstration laboratories; 2 food production kitchens; 2 gardens; gourmet dining room; 2 laboratories; learning resource center; 3 lecture rooms; library; public restaurant; snack shop; 2 student lounges; teaching kitchen.

TYPICAL STUDENT PROFILE

400 total: 310 full-time; 90 part-time.

SPECIAL PROGRAMS

Culinary competitions, ice carving classes, student-operated restaurant and catering facility.

FINANCIAL AID

Program-specific awards include work-study program, tutoring opportunities. Employment placement assistance is available. Employment opportunities within the program are available.

APPLICATION INFORMATION

Students may begin participation in January and August. Application deadline for fall is August 30. Application deadline for spring is January 20. Applicants must submit a formal application.

CONTACT

Director of Admissions, Hospitality Industry Administration, 2000 5th Avenue, River Grove, IL 60171-9983. Telephone: 708-456-0300 Ext. 3624. Fax: 708-583-3317. World Wide Web: http://www.triton.cc.il.us/.

UNIVERSITY OF ILLINOIS AT URBANA–CHAMPAIGN

Hospitality Management/Department of Food Science and Human Nutrition

Urbana, Illinois

GENERAL INFORMATION

Public, coeducational, university. Urban campus. Founded in 1867. Accredited by North Central Association of Colleges and Schools.

PROGRAM INFORMATION

Offered since 1952. Accredited by American Dietetic Association. Program calendar is divided into semesters. 4-year bachelor's degree in hospitality management.

PROGRAM AFFILIATION

American Dietetic Association; Council on Hotel, Restaurant, and Institutional Education; Illinois Restaurant Association; Institute of Food Technologists.

AREAS OF STUDY

Buffet catering; controlling costs in food service; food preparation; food purchasing; food science; kitchen management; management and human resources; meat cutting; meat fabrication; nutrition; restaurant opportunities; sanitation.

University of Illinois at Urbana–Champaign *(continued)*

FACILITIES

Cafeteria; catering service; classroom; computer laboratory; food production kitchen; gourmet dining room; laboratory; lecture room; student lounge; teaching kitchen.

STUDENT PROFILE

106 full-time. 106 are under 25 years old.

FACULTY

2 total: 2 full-time. 2 are industry professionals. Prominent faculty: Elizabeth F. Reutter, MEd; Jill North, MS. Faculty-student ratio: 1:53.

SPECIAL PROGRAMS

Practical Work Experience, Professional Work Experience.

TYPICAL EXPENSES

Application fee: $40. In-state tuition: $3521 per semester. Out-of-state tuition: $10,564 per semester. Program-related fee includes $80 for materials.

FINANCIAL AID

In 2004, 8 scholarships were awarded (average award was $1200). Program-specific awards include two 4-year work-study scholarships ($2000 per year plus hourly wage). Employment placement assistance is available. Employment opportunities within the program are available.

HOUSING

Coed, apartment-style, and single-sex housing available.

APPLICATION INFORMATION

Students may begin participation in August. Application deadline for fall is January 1. In 2004, 51 applied; 32 were accepted. Applicants must submit a formal application, an essay, ACT scores.

CONTACT

Admissions and Records, Hospitality Management/ Department of Food Science and Human Nutrition, 901 West Illinois Street, Urbana, IL 61801. Telephone: 217-333-0302. E-mail: undergraduate@admissions.uiuc.edu. World Wide Web: http://www.ag.uiuc.edu/~food-lab/index.html.

WASHBURNE CULINARY INSTITUTE

Chicago, Illinois

GENERAL INFORMATION

Public, coeducational, culinary institute. Urban campus. Founded in 1937. Accredited by North Central Association of Colleges and Schools.

PROGRAM INFORMATION

Offered since 1937. Program calendar is divided into semesters, sixteen-weeks cycle. 16-week certificate in culinary arts. 16-week certificate in baking and pastry. 48-week advanced certificate in culinary arts. 80-week associate degree in culinary arts.

AREAS OF STUDY

Baking; controlling costs in food service; culinary skill development; food preparation; food purchasing; food service communication; food service math; garde-manger; international cuisine; introduction to food service; kitchen management; management and human resources; meal planning; meat cutting; meat fabrication; menu and facilities design; nutrition; nutrition and food service; restaurant opportunities; sanitation; saucier; seafood processing; soup, stock, sauce, and starch production.

FACILITIES

Bake shop; cafeteria; catering service; 3 classrooms; 2 computer laboratories; demonstration laboratory; 2 food production kitchens; 2 learning resource centers; 3 lecture rooms; 2 libraries; public restaurant; 2 student lounges; 2 teaching kitchens.

STUDENT PROFILE

110 full-time. 33 are under 25 years old; 55 are between 25 and 44 years old; 22 are over 44 years old.

FACULTY

9 total: 5 full-time; 4 part-time. 9 are industry professionals; 1 is a master chef; 3 are culinary-certified teachers. Prominent faculty: Alex Dering, CEC; Eugene Wrzesinski; Alex Erdmann, CMC; Lee Jamison. Faculty-student ratio: 1:12.

TYPICAL EXPENSES

Application fee: $100. In-state tuition: $11,163 per 80 weeks (in district), $22,199 per 80 weeks (out-of-district). Out-of-state tuition: $27,858 per 80 weeks. Tuition for international students: $27,858 per 80 weeks.

FINANCIAL AID

In 2004, 16 scholarships were awarded (average award was $1000). Employment placement assistance is available. Employment opportunities within the program are available.

HOUSING

Average off-campus housing cost per month: $600.

APPLICATION INFORMATION

Students may begin participation in January, May, August, and September. Applications are accepted continuously. In 2004, 100 applied; 95 were accepted. Applicants must have high school diploma or GED, be 18 years of age or older, and take entrance examination (reading and math).

CONTACT

Anne McDougal, Office Manager, 7059 S South Shore Drive, Chicago, IL 60649. Telephone: 773-602-5487. Fax: 773-602-5452. E-mail: amcdougal@ccc.edu. World Wide Web: http://www.ccc.edu/washburne/index.html.

WILLIAM RAINEY HARPER COLLEGE

Hospitality Management

Palatine, Illinois

GENERAL INFORMATION
Public, coeducational, two-year college. Suburban campus. Founded in 1965. Accredited by North Central Association of Colleges and Schools.

PROGRAM INFORMATION
Offered since 1970. Program calendar is divided into semesters. 12-month certificate in bread and pastry arts. 12-month certificate in culinary arts. 2-year associate degree in hospitality management. 9-month certificate in food service management. 9-month certificate in hotel management.

PROGRAM AFFILIATION
American Culinary Federation; Council on Hotel, Restaurant, and Institutional Education; International Association of Culinary Professionals; International Food Service Executives Association; National Restaurant Association; National Restaurant Association Educational Foundation; Retailer's Bakery Association.

AREAS OF STUDY
Baking; buffet catering; confectionery show pieces; controlling costs in food service; convenience cookery; food preparation; food purchasing; garde-manger; introduction to food service; management and human resources; meal planning; meat cutting; menu and facilities design; nutrition; patisserie; restaurant opportunities; sanitation; saucier; seafood processing; soup, stock, sauce, and starch production; wines and spirits.

FACILITIES
Bakery; cafeteria; catering service; 6 classrooms; demonstration laboratory; food production kitchen; laboratory; learning resource center; lecture room; library; public restaurant; teaching kitchen.

TYPICAL STUDENT PROFILE
210 total: 70 full-time; 140 part-time. 70 are under 25 years old; 70 are between 25 and 44 years old; 70 are over 44 years old.

SPECIAL PROGRAMS
Local and French guest chefs, culinary competition class, extensive cooperative work with Chicago area hospitality industry.

FINANCIAL AID
Program-specific awards include professional management and "ProStart" scholarships. Employment placement assistance is available. Employment opportunities within the program are available.

APPLICATION INFORMATION
Students may begin participation in January and August. Applications are accepted continuously. Applicants must submit a formal application.

CONTACT
Director of Admissions, Hospitality Management, 1200 West Algonquin Road, Palatine, IL 60067-7398. Telephone: 847-925-6206. Fax: 847-925-6044. World Wide Web: http://www.harpercollege.edu.

WILTON SCHOOL OF CAKE DECORATING AND CONFECTIONERY ARTS

Darien, Illinois

GENERAL INFORMATION
Private, coeducational, culinary institute. Suburban campus. Founded in 1929.

PROGRAM INFORMATION
Offered since 1929. Program calendar is continuous. 1-week certificate in candy making. 2-week certificate in cake decorating.

PROGRAM AFFILIATION
American Institute of Wine & Food; International Association of Culinary Professionals.

AREAS OF STUDY
Cake decorating; candy making.

FACILITIES
Classroom; demonstration laboratory; food production kitchen.

TYPICAL STUDENT PROFILE
520 part-time.

APPLICATION INFORMATION
Students may begin participation year-round. Applications are accepted continuously. Applicants must submit a formal application.

CONTACT
Director of Admissions, 2240 West 75th Street, Woodridge, IL 60517. Telephone: 630-810-2211. Fax: 630-810-2710. World Wide Web: http://www.school.wilton.com.

Indiana

Ball State University

Department of Family and Consumer Sciences

Muncie, Indiana

GENERAL INFORMATION
Public, coeducational, university. Urban campus. Founded in 1918. Accredited by North Central Association of Colleges and Schools.

PROGRAM INFORMATION
Offered since 1975. Program calendar is divided into semesters. 2-year associate degree in hospitality and food management. 4-year bachelor's degree in hospitality and food management.

PROGRAM AFFILIATION
American Culinary Federation; Council on Hotel, Restaurant, and Institutional Education.

AREAS OF STUDY
Beverage management; buffet catering; controlling costs in food service; convenience cookery; culinary skill development; customer relations; food preparation; food purchasing; introduction to food service; kitchen management; management and human resources; meal planning; nutrition; nutrition and food service; restaurant opportunities; sanitation.

FACILITIES
5 classrooms; computer laboratory; food production kitchen; gourmet dining room; 3 laboratories; learning resource center; lecture room; library; public restaurant; student lounge; teaching kitchen.

STUDENT PROFILE
75 full-time. 65 are under 25 years old; 10 are between 25 and 44 years old.

FACULTY
7 total: 3 full-time; 4 part-time. 4 are industry professionals; 1 is a culinary-certified teacher. Prominent faculty: Lois Altman, CEC, EdD; Deborah Foster; James Kew. Faculty-student ratio: 1:13.

SPECIAL PROGRAMS
Paid internships.

TYPICAL EXPENSES
Application fee: $50. In-state tuition: $4320 per year. Out-of-state tuition: $12,100 per year.

FINANCIAL AID
In 2004, 3 scholarships were awarded (average award was $750). Program-specific awards include 5 Moore Scholarships ($10,000). Employment placement assistance is available. Employment opportunities within the program are available.

HOUSING
Coed, apartment-style, and single-sex housing available.

APPLICATION INFORMATION
Students may begin participation in January, May, and August. Applications are accepted continuously. In 2004, 30 applied. Applicants must submit a formal application and letters of reference.

CONTACT
Lois A. Altman, Program Director, Department of Family and Consumer Sciences, AT 150 D, Ball State University, Muncie, IN. Telephone: 765-285-5956. Fax: 765-285-2314. E-mail: loisaltman@bsu.edu. World Wide Web: http://www.bsu.edu/.

Indiana University–Purdue University Fort Wayne

Hospitality Management

Fort Wayne, Indiana

GENERAL INFORMATION
Public, coeducational, comprehensive institution. Suburban campus. Founded in 1917. Accredited by North Central Association of Colleges and Schools.

PROGRAM INFORMATION
Offered since 1976. Program calendar is divided into semesters. 2-year associate degree in hotel, restaurant, and tourism management. 4-year bachelor's degree in hospitality and tourism management.

PROGRAM AFFILIATION
Confrerie de la Chaine des Rotisseurs; Council on Hotel, Restaurant, and Institutional Education; National Restaurant Association Educational Foundation.

AREAS OF STUDY
Beverage management; buffet catering; controlling costs in food service; convenience cookery; culinary French; culinary skill development; food preparation; food purchasing; food service communication; food service math; introduction to food service; kitchen management; management and human resources; meal planning; menu and facilities design; nutrition; nutrition and food service; restaurant opportunities; sanitation; soup, stock, sauce, and starch production; tourism; wines and spirits.

FACILITIES
5 computer laboratories; demonstration laboratory; food production kitchen; learning resource center; library; 6 student lounges; ballroom.

STUDENT PROFILE
100 total: 80 full-time; 20 part-time.

FACULTY

7 total: 1 full-time; 6 part-time. 6 are industry professionals. Prominent faculty: John B. Knight, CFBE; Linda Lolkus. Faculty-student ratio: 1:30.

SPECIAL PROGRAMS

Annual visits to New York, Las Vegas, Chicago, Walt Disney World, and international venues, opportunity for students to serve dining public in local hotels and restaurants.

TYPICAL EXPENSES

In-state tuition: $182.15 per credit hour part-time. Out-of-state tuition: $432.80 per credit hour part-time.

FINANCIAL AID

In 2004, 4 scholarships were awarded (average award was $500). Employment placement assistance is available.

HOUSING

Apartment-style housing available. Average on-campus housing cost per month: $570.

APPLICATION INFORMATION

Students may begin participation in January and August. Applications are accepted continuously. Applicants must submit a formal application.

CONTACT

Dr. John B. Knight, Director, Hospitality Management, Neff Hall, Room 330B, Fort Wayne, IN 46805-1499. Telephone: 260-481-6562. Fax: 260-481-5767. World Wide Web: http://www.ipfw.edu/cfs/dinner1.htm.

IVY TECH COMMUNITY COLLEGE–CENTRAL INDIANA

Hospitality Administration Program

Indianapolis, Indiana

GENERAL INFORMATION

Public, coeducational, two-year college. Urban campus. Founded in 1963. Accredited by North Central Association of Colleges and Schools.

PROGRAM INFORMATION

Offered since 1981. Accredited by Council on Hotel, Restaurant and Institutional Education, American Culinary Federation Foundation (ACFF), Commission on Accreditation on Hospitality Management (CAHM). Program calendar is divided into semesters. 2-year associate degree in restaurant management. 2-year associate degree in hotel management specialty. 2-year associate degree in event management specialty. 2-year associate degree in hospitality administration degree. 2-year associate degree in baking and pastry arts specialty. 2-year associate degree in culinary arts specialty. 3-year associate degree in culinary arts (with apprenticeship). 8-month certificate in baking/pastry arts. 8-month certificate in culinary arts. 8-month certificate in hospitality management.

PROGRAM AFFILIATION

American Culinary Federation; Council on Hotel, Restaurant, and Institutional Education; National Restaurant Association; National Restaurant Association Educational Foundation; Retailer's Bakery Association; Society of Wine Educators; Women Chefs and Restaurateurs.

AREAS OF STUDY

Baking; beverage management; controlling costs in food service; culinary French; culinary skill development; food preparation; food purchasing; food service communication; food service math; garde-manger; international cuisine; introduction to food service; kitchen management; management and human resources; meat cutting; meat fabrication; menu and facilities design; nutrition; nutrition and food service; patisserie; restaurant opportunities; sanitation; saucier; seafood processing; soup, stock, sauce, and starch production; wines and spirits.

FACILITIES

Cafeteria; catering service; 20 classrooms; 3 computer laboratories; 2 food production kitchens; 2 laboratories; 3 lecture rooms; library; student lounge; 2 teaching kitchens.

STUDENT PROFILE

450 total: 180 full-time; 270 part-time.

FACULTY

25 total: 4 full-time; 21 part-time. 20 are industry professionals; 16 are culinary-certified teachers. Prominent faculty: Lauri Griffin, CEC; Jeff Bricker, CEC; Thom England; Paul Vida. Faculty-student ratio: 1:25 lectures; 1:15 labs.

SPECIAL PROGRAMS

2-week program at cooking school in Europe, culinary competitions, ACF student chapter-club.

TYPICAL EXPENSES

In-state tuition: $83.95 per credit hour full-time (in district), $83.95 per credit hour part-time. Out-of-state tuition: $170.25 per credit hour full-time, $170.25 per credit hour part-time. Program-related fees include $192 for culinary/baking tool kit; $85 for student uniform.

FINANCIAL AID

Employment placement assistance is available. Employment opportunities within the program are available.

HOUSING

Average off-campus housing cost per month: $425.

APPLICATION INFORMATION

Students may begin participation in January, May, and August. Applications are accepted continuously. Applicants must submit a formal application and have a high school diploma, GED, or equivalent.

Ivy Tech Community College–Central Indiana
(continued)

CONTACT

Jeff Bricker, Chairperson, Hospitality Administration Program, 50 West Fall Creek Parkway, N. Drive, Indianapolis, IN 46208. Telephone: 317-921-4516. Fax: 317-921-4203. E-mail: jbricker@ivytech.edu. World Wide Web: http://www.ivytech.edu/indianapolis.

IVY TECH COMMUNITY COLLEGE–NORTHEAST

Hospitality Administration

Fort Wayne, Indiana

GENERAL INFORMATION

Public, coeducational, two-year college. Suburban campus. Founded in 1969. Accredited by North Central Association of Colleges and Schools.

PROGRAM INFORMATION

Offered since 1969. Accredited by American Culinary Federation Accrediting Commission. Program calendar is divided into semesters. 2-year associate degree in baking/pastry arts. 2-year associate degree in culinary arts.

PROGRAM AFFILIATION

American Culinary Federation.

AREAS OF STUDY

Baking; confectionery show pieces; controlling costs in food service; food preparation; food purchasing; garde-manger; international cuisine; kitchen management; management and human resources; meat cutting; meat fabrication; nutrition; patisserie; sanitation; seafood processing; soup, stock, sauce, and starch production; wines and spirits.

FACILITIES

Bake shop; bakery; catering service; 4 classrooms; 2 computer laboratories; demonstration laboratory; food production kitchen; gourmet dining room; 3 laboratories; 3 lecture rooms; library; 2 student lounges; teaching kitchen.

STUDENT PROFILE

242 total: 78 full-time; 164 part-time.

FACULTY

15 total: 3 full-time; 12 part-time. 10 are industry professionals; 1 is a master chef; 1 is a master baker; 3 are culinary-certified teachers. Prominent faculty: Robert Kelty, CCE; Meshele Wyneken, RD; G. Alan Eyler, CFBM. Faculty-student ratio: 1:13.

SPECIAL PROGRAMS

10-day European culinary study tour.

TYPICAL EXPENSES

In-state tuition: $83.95 per credit hour. Out-of-state tuition: $170.25 per credit hour. Program-related fees include $175 for knife kit; $185 for baking kit.

FINANCIAL AID

In 2004, 8 scholarships were awarded (average award was $2600). Program-specific awards include scholarships funded by Boiardi Endowment. Employment placement assistance is available.

HOUSING

Average off-campus housing cost per month: $600.

APPLICATION INFORMATION

Students may begin participation in January, May, and August. Application deadline for fall is August 15. Application deadline for spring is December 15. Application deadline for summer is April 30. Applicants must submit a formal application.

CONTACT

Alan Eyler, Program Chairperson, Hospitality Administration, 3800 North Anthony Boulevard, Ft. Wayne, IN 46805. Telephone: 219-480-4240. Fax: 219-480-2051. E-mail: aeyler@ivytech.edu. World Wide Web: http://www.ivytech.edu.

IVY TECH COMMUNITY COLLEGE–NORTHWEST

Hospitality Administration

Gary, Indiana

GENERAL INFORMATION

Public, coeducational, two-year college. Urban campus. Founded in 1963. Accredited by North Central Association of Colleges and Schools.

PROGRAM INFORMATION

Offered since 1985. Accredited by American Culinary Federation Accrediting Commission. Program calendar is divided into semesters. 1-year certificate in culinary arts. 2-year associate degree in convention management. 2-year associate degree in restaurant management. 2-year associate degree in hotel/restaurant management. 2-year associate degree in bakery and pastry arts. 2-year associate degree in culinary arts.

PROGRAM AFFILIATION

American Culinary Federation; National Restaurant Association; National Restaurant Association Educational Foundation; Women Chefs and Restaurateurs.

AREAS OF STUDY

Baking; buffet catering; controlling costs in food service; culinary French; culinary skill development; food preparation; food purchasing; garde-manger; international cuisine; introduction to food service; management and human resources; meal planning; meat cutting; meat fabrication; menu and facilities design; nutrition; patisserie; sanitation; saucier; seafood processing; soup, stock, sauce, and starch production; wines and spirits.

FACILITIES
Bake shop; 2 computer laboratories; 2 demonstration laboratories; gourmet dining room; learning resource center; library; student lounge; teaching kitchen.

TYPICAL STUDENT PROFILE
96 total: 75 full-time; 21 part-time.

SPECIAL PROGRAMS
National Restaurant Association shows, 2-week trip to France, National Convention for the American Culinary Education.

FINANCIAL AID
Employment placement assistance is available.

APPLICATION INFORMATION
Students may begin participation in January, May, and August. Applications are accepted continuously. Applicants must submit a formal application and have a high school diploma or GED.

CONTACT
Director of Admissions, Hospitality Administration, 1440 East 35th Avenue, Gary, IN 46409-1499. Telephone: 219-981-1111 Ext. 4400. Fax: 219-981-4415. World Wide Web: http://www.ivytech.edu.

IOWA

DES MOINES AREA COMMUNITY COLLEGE

Culinary Arts Department

Ankeny, Iowa

GENERAL INFORMATION
Public, coeducational, two-year college. Urban campus. Founded in 1966. Accredited by North Central Association of Colleges and Schools.

PROGRAM INFORMATION
Offered since 1975. Accredited by American Culinary Federation Accrediting Commission. Program calendar is divided into semesters. 2-year associate degree in hotel/restaurant management. 2-year associate degree in culinary arts.

PROGRAM AFFILIATION
American Culinary Federation; National Restaurant Association.

AREAS OF STUDY
Baking; beverage management; buffet catering; culinary French; culinary skill development; food preparation; food purchasing; garde-manger; international cuisine; introduction to food service; menu and facilities design; nutrition; sanitation; soup, stock, sauce, and starch production; wines and spirits.

FACILITIES
Bake shop; cafeteria; 3 classrooms; computer laboratory; demonstration laboratory; 2 food production kitchens; gourmet dining room; learning resource center; lecture room; library.

TYPICAL STUDENT PROFILE
95 total: 90 full-time; 5 part-time. 48 are under 25 years old; 47 are between 25 and 44 years old.

SPECIAL PROGRAMS
French culinary exchange, field study tour of Chicago.

FINANCIAL AID
Employment placement assistance is available.

HOUSING
Apartment-style housing available.

APPLICATION INFORMATION
Students may begin participation in January and September. Application deadline for spring is January 5. Application deadline for fall is August 1. Applicants must submit a formal application.

CONTACT
Director of Admissions, Culinary Arts Department, 2006 South Ankeny Boulevard, Building #7, Ankeny, IA 50021-8995. Telephone: 515-964-6532. Fax: 515-965-7129. World Wide Web: http://dmacc.edu.

IOWA LAKES COMMUNITY COLLEGE

Hotel and Restaurant Management Program

Emmetsburg, Iowa

GENERAL INFORMATION
Public, coeducational, two-year college. Rural campus. Founded in 1967. Accredited by North Central Association of Colleges and Schools.

PROGRAM INFORMATION
Offered since 1973. Accredited by Council on Hotel, Restaurant and Institutional Education. Program calendar is divided into semesters. 1-year diploma in hospitality technology program. 2-year associate degree in dietary management program. 2-year associate degree in hotel and restaurant management program.

PROGRAM AFFILIATION
American Hotel and Lodging Association; Council on Hotel, Restaurant, and Institutional Education; Dietary

Iowa Lakes Community College *(continued)*

Managers Association; Iowa Hospitality Association; Iowa Lodging Association; National Restaurant Association; National Restaurant Association Educational Foundation.

AREAS OF STUDY

Baking; beverage management; buffet catering; controlling costs in food service; convenience cookery; culinary skill development; food preparation; food purchasing; food service communication; food service math; garde-manger; hospitality law; international cuisine; introduction to food service; kitchen management; management and human resources; marketing; meal planning; menu and facilities design; nutrition; nutrition and food service; restaurant opportunities; sanitation; saucier; soup, stock, sauce, and starch production; wines and spirits.

FACILITIES

Bakery; 2 cafeterias; 3 catering services; 3 classrooms; coffee shop; 5 computer laboratories; demonstration laboratory; 2 food production kitchens; gourmet dining room; 2 laboratories; 3 learning resource centers; 2 lecture rooms; 3 libraries; public restaurant; snack shop; student lounge; teaching kitchen.

TYPICAL STUDENT PROFILE

45 total: 40 full-time; 5 part-time.

SPECIAL PROGRAMS

Iowa Hospitality Show in Des Moines, Midwest Hospitality Show in Minneapolis, Las Vegas Hospitality Show.

FINANCIAL AID

Program-specific awards include National Restaurant Association scholarships, scholarships for freshmen and sophomores ($150), American Hotel and Lodging Association Scholarship. Employment placement assistance is available. Employment opportunities within the program are available.

HOUSING

Coed and apartment-style housing available.

APPLICATION INFORMATION

Students may begin participation in January, May, and August. Application deadline for fall is August 1. Application deadline for spring is January 1. Application deadline for summer is May 1. Applicants must interview; submit a formal application.

CONTACT

Director of Admissions, Hotel and Restaurant Management Program, 3200 College Drive, Emmetsburg, IA 50536-1098. Telephone: 712-852-5256. Fax: 712-852-2152. World Wide Web: http://www.ilcc.cc.ia.us.

IOWA STATE UNIVERSITY OF SCIENCE AND TECHNOLOGY

Hotel, Restaurant, and Institution Management

Ames, Iowa

GENERAL INFORMATION

Public, coeducational, university. Small-town setting. Founded in 1858. Accredited by North Central Association of Colleges and Schools.

PROGRAM INFORMATION

Offered since 1924. Accredited by Accreditation Commission for Programs in Hospitality Administration. Program calendar is divided into semesters. 2-year master's degree in hotel and restaurant management. 3-year doctoral degree in hotel and restaurant management. 4-year bachelor's degree in hotel and restaurant management.

PROGRAM AFFILIATION

Council on Hotel, Restaurant, and Institutional Education.

AREAS OF STUDY

Beverage management; controlling costs in food service; food preparation; food purchasing; introduction to food service; management and human resources; nutrition and food service; sanitation; wines and spirits.

FACILITIES

2 classrooms; computer laboratory; food production kitchen; laboratory; learning resource center; library; teaching kitchen.

STUDENT PROFILE

220 total: 210 full-time; 10 part-time.

FACULTY

11 total: 8 full-time; 3 part-time. Prominent faculty: Jennie Sneed, PhD; Haemoon Oh, PhD; Shirley Gilmore, PhD; Mary Gregoire, PhD. Faculty-student ratio: 1:20.

TYPICAL EXPENSES

Application fee: $30. In-state tuition: $2445 per semester (undergraduate) $2854 per semester (graduate), $4890 year. Out-of-state tuition: $7490 per semester (undergraduate) $7860 per semester (graduate), $14,980 year.

FINANCIAL AID

In 2004, 27 scholarships were awarded (average award was $1000). Employment placement assistance is available. Employment opportunities within the program are available.

HOUSING

Coed, apartment-style, and single-sex housing available.

APPLICATION INFORMATION

Students may begin participation in January, June, and August. Applications are accepted continuously. In 2004, 65 applied; 50 were accepted. Applicants must submit a formal application, SAT or ACT scores, TOEFL scores (international applicants), and academic transcripts.

CONTACT
Dr. Shirley Gilmore, Undergraduate Program Coordinator, Hotel, Restaurant, and Institution Management, 31 Mackay Hall, Ames, IA 50011-1120. Telephone: 515-294-7474. Fax: 515-294-6364. E-mail: hrimdept@iastate.edu. World Wide Web: http://www.iastate.edu.

KIRKWOOD COMMUNITY COLLEGE

Hospitality Programs

Cedar Rapids, Iowa

GENERAL INFORMATION
Public, coeducational, two-year college. Urban campus. Founded in 1966. Accredited by North Central Association of Colleges and Schools.

PROGRAM INFORMATION
Offered since 1968. Accredited by American Culinary Federation Accrediting Commission. Program calendar is divided into semesters. 1-year certificate in bakery. 1-year diploma in food service training. 2-year associate degree in lodging management. 2-year associate degree in restaurant management. 2-year associate degree in culinary arts.

PROGRAM AFFILIATION
National Restaurant Association; National Restaurant Association Educational Foundation.

AREAS OF STUDY
Baking; beverage management; buffet catering; controlling costs in food service; culinary competition; culinary skill development; food and culture; food preparation; food purchasing; food service communication; food service math; garde-manger; international cuisine; kitchen management; management and human resources; meal planning; meat fabrication; menu and facilities design; nutrition; sanitation; soup, stock, sauce, and starch production; wines and spirits.

FACILITIES
Bakery; catering service; 2 classrooms; computer laboratory; demonstration laboratory; food production kitchen; gourmet dining room; 2 laboratories; learning resource center; 2 lecture rooms; library; public restaurant.

STUDENT PROFILE
230 total: 165 full-time; 65 part-time.

FACULTY
10 total: 6 full-time; 4 part-time. 5 are industry professionals; 2 are dietitians. Prominent faculty: Mary Jane German, MS, RD; Mary Rhiner, MS, RD; David Dettman, AAS; Amy Wyss, AAS. Faculty-student ratio: 1:35 lecture; 1:16 lab.

SPECIAL PROGRAMS
Professional meetings and conventions (local, state, national), international study tours (offered periodically), culinary competition.

TYPICAL EXPENSES
In-state tuition: $95 per credit hour full-time (in district), $95 per credit hour part-time. Out-of-state tuition: $180 per credit hour full-time, $180 per credit hour part-time. Program-related fees include $240 for knives; $200–$300 for uniforms.

FINANCIAL AID
In 2004, 20 scholarships were awarded (average award was $200–$500). Program-specific awards include Study Abroad Travel Scholarships. Employment opportunities within the program are available.

HOUSING
Average off-campus housing cost per month: $300–$400.

APPLICATION INFORMATION
Students may begin participation in January and August. Applications are accepted continuously. Applicants must submit a formal application, take placement tests, and attend a program conference.

CONTACT
Mary Jane German, Associate Professor/Coordinator, Hospitality Programs, 6301 Kirkwood Boulevard SW, Cedar Rapids, IA 52403. Telephone: 319-398-4981. Fax: 319-398-1244. E-mail: mgerman@kirkwood.edu. World Wide Web: http://www.kirkwood.edu.

KANSAS

AMERICAN INSTITUTE OF BAKING

Baking Science and Technology

Manhattan, Kansas

GENERAL INFORMATION
Private, coeducational institution. Small-town setting. Founded in 1919. Accredited by North Central Association of Colleges and Schools.

PROGRAM INFORMATION
Offered since 1919. Program calendar is divided into semesters. 2.5-month certificate in maintenance engineering. 5-month certificate in baking science and technology.

PROGRAM AFFILIATION
American Institute of Baking.

AREAS OF STUDY
Baking; maintenance engineering.

FACILITIES
4 bake shops; bakery; 4 classrooms; computer laboratory; 4 demonstration laboratories; laboratory; library; student lounge; cookie-cracker production line.

American Institute of Baking *(continued)*

STUDENT PROFILE
150 full-time.

FACULTY
10 total: 8 full-time; 2 part-time. 8 are industry professionals; 1 is a master baker. Prominent faculty: Michael Moore; Jeff Rootring, BS; Kirk O'Donnell, PhD; Debi Rogers, PhD, AACC. Faculty-student ratio: 1:5.

SPECIAL PROGRAMS
Half-day tours of grain elevator, flour mill, and Kansas wheat farm, half-day tours of commercial wholesale bakeries, 50-lesson correspondence course in science of baking.

TYPICAL EXPENSES
Application fee: $45. Tuition: $7200 per certificate (baking science); $4600 per certificate (maintenance engineering).

FINANCIAL AID
In 2004, 25 scholarships were awarded (average award was $2500); 15 loans were granted (average loan was $2000). Program-specific awards include full-tuition scholarships for food science graduates. Employment placement assistance is available.

HOUSING
Coed housing available. Average off-campus housing cost per month: $550.

APPLICATION INFORMATION
Students may begin participation in February, July, August, and September. Applications are accepted continuously. Applicants must submit a formal application, letters of reference, an essay, and have a college degree, or 2 years of work experience, or completion of baking science course.

CONTACT
Ken Embers, Director of Admissions and Financial Aid, Baking Science and Technology, 1213 Bakers Way, Manhattan, KS 66502. Telephone: 800-633-5137. Fax: 785-537-1493. E-mail: kembers@aibonline.org. World Wide Web: http://www.aibonline.org.

JOHNSON COUNTY COMMUNITY COLLEGE

Overland Park, Kansas

GENERAL INFORMATION
Public, coeducational, two-year college. Suburban campus. Founded in 1967. Accredited by North Central Association of Colleges and Schools.

PROGRAM INFORMATION
Offered since 1975. Accredited by American Culinary Federation Accrediting Commission. Program calendar is divided into semesters. 2-year associate degree in hotel management. 2-year associate degree in food and beverage management. 3-year associate degree in chef apprenticeship.

PROGRAM AFFILIATION
American Culinary Federation; American Institute of Wine & Food; Council on Hotel, Restaurant, and Institutional Education; Hotel/Motel Association of Kansas City; Kansas Restaurant Hospitality Association; Missouri Restaurant Association; National Restaurant Association.

AREAS OF STUDY
Baking; beverage management; buffet catering; confectionery show pieces; controlling costs in food service; convenience cookery; culinary skill development; food preparation; food purchasing; garde-manger; international cuisine; introduction to food service; management and human resources; meal planning; menu and facilities design; nutrition and food service; sanitation; saucier; seafood processing; soup, stock, sauce, and starch production; wines and spirits.

FACILITIES
Bake shop; 2 demonstration laboratories; food production kitchen; gourmet dining room; learning resource center; 4 lecture rooms; library; 2 teaching kitchens.

STUDENT PROFILE
490 total: 150 full-time; 340 part-time.

FACULTY
19 total: 10 full-time; 9 part-time. 5 are industry professionals; 5 are culinary-certified teachers; 2 are certified hospitality educators. Prominent faculty: Jerry Marcellus, CEC, CCE; Felix Sturmer; John Head, CCC; Robert Sobierja. Faculty-student ratio: 1:16.

SPECIAL PROGRAMS
National culinary competitions, ACF Knowledge Bowl competitions, trips to New York Hotel Show and NRA show in Chicago.

TYPICAL EXPENSES
In-state tuition: $63 per credit hour full-time (in district), $63 per credit hour part-time. Out-of-state tuition: $144 per credit hour full-time, $144 per credit hour part-time.

FINANCIAL AID
In 2004, 20 scholarships were awarded (average award was $500). Program-specific awards include paid apprenticeship program. Employment placement assistance is available.

HOUSING
Average off-campus housing cost per month: $600.

APPLICATION INFORMATION
Students may begin participation in January, June, and August. Application deadline for fall is August 15. Application deadline for spring is January 15. Application deadline for summer is May 1. In 2004, 144 applied; 144 were accepted. Applicants must submit a formal application.

CONTACT
Lindy Robinson, Assistant Dean, Hospitality Management, 12345 College Boulevard, Overland Park, KS 66210. Telephone: 913-469-8500 Ext. 3250. Fax: 913-469-2560. E-mail: lrobinsn@jccc.edu. World Wide Web: http://www. johnco.cc.ks.us/.

KANSAS CITY KANSAS AREA TECHNICAL SCHOOL

Professional Cooking

Kansas City, Kansas

GENERAL INFORMATION
Public, coeducational, adult vocational school. Urban campus. Founded in 1972. Accredited by North Central Association of Colleges and Schools.

PROGRAM INFORMATION
Offered since 1972. Program calendar is continuous, year-round. 6-month certificate in food service.

AREAS OF STUDY
Baking; catering; culinary skill development; dining room service; food preparation; food purchasing; food service management; garde-manger; introduction to food service; meal planning; patisserie; restaurant opportunities; sanitation; soup, stock, sauce, and starch production.

FACILITIES
Cafeteria; classroom; computer laboratory; food production kitchen; gourmet dining room; learning resource center; lecture room; library; snack shop.

STUDENT PROFILE
22 total: 10 full-time; 12 part-time.

FACULTY
3 total: 2 full-time; 1 part-time.

TYPICAL EXPENSES
In-state tuition: $1120 per certificate. Out-of-state tuition: $7226 per certificate. Program-related fee includes $150 for textbooks.

FINANCIAL AID
Employment placement assistance is available. Employment opportunities within the program are available.

HOUSING
Average off-campus housing cost per month: $700.

APPLICATION INFORMATION
Students may begin participation in January, February, March, April, May, June, August, September, October, November, and December. Applications are accepted continuously. Applicants must have a high school diploma or GED.

CONTACT
Mary Lynn Seeley, Admissions Counselor, Professional Cooking, 2220 North 59th Street, Kansas City, KS 66104. Telephone: 913-627-4100. World Wide Web: http://www. kckats.com/professionalcooking/index.htm.

KANSAS STATE UNIVERSITY

Hotel and Restaurant Management

Manhattan, Kansas

GENERAL INFORMATION
Public, coeducational, university. Small-town setting. Founded in 1863. Accredited by North Central Association of Colleges and Schools.

PROGRAM INFORMATION
Offered since 1952. Accredited by American Dietetic Association, Council on Hotel, Restaurant and Institutional Education. Program calendar is divided into semesters. 2-year master's degree in institution management. 3-year doctoral degree in foodservice and hospitality management. 4-year bachelor's degree in hotel and restaurant management.

PROGRAM AFFILIATION
American Dietetic Association; American Hotel and Lodging Association; Council on Hotel, Restaurant, and Institutional Education; National Restaurant Association.

AREAS OF STUDY
Beverage management; controlling costs in food service; food preparation; food purchasing; management and human resources; meat cutting; menu and facilities design; nutrition; wines and spirits.

FACILITIES
Bake shop; bakery; 4 cafeterias; catering service; 3 classrooms; coffee shop; computer laboratory; demonstration laboratory; 4 food production kitchens; 3 lecture rooms; library; public restaurant; 2 snack shops; student lounge.

TYPICAL STUDENT PROFILE
362 full-time.

SPECIAL PROGRAMS
Principles of Food Production Management (distance education).

FINANCIAL AID
Employment placement assistance is available.

HOUSING
Coed housing available.

APPLICATION INFORMATION
Students may begin participation in January, June, and August. Application deadline for fall is May 1. Application

Kansas State University *(continued)*

deadline for spring is December 1. Applicants must submit a formal application and SAT or ACT scores.

CONTACT

Director of Admissions, Hotel and Restaurant Management, Department of HRIMD, 103 Justin Hall, Manhattan, KS 66506-1404. Telephone: 785-532-2210. Fax: 785-532-5522. World Wide Web: http://www.ksu.edu/humec/hrimd/hrimd.htm.

WICHITA AREA TECHNICAL COLLEGE

Food Service Education

Wichita, Kansas

GENERAL INFORMATION

Public, coeducational institution. Urban campus. Accredited by Council on Occupational Education.

PROGRAM INFORMATION

Offered since 1979. Program calendar is divided into semesters. 2-year associate degree in food service management. 9-month diploma in food service production.

PROGRAM AFFILIATION

American Culinary Federation; National Restaurant Association.

AREAS OF STUDY

Baking; buffet catering; controlling costs in food service; culinary skill development; food preparation; food purchasing; food service math; garde-manger; international cuisine; introduction to food service; kitchen management; management and human resources; meal planning; nutrition and food service; restaurant opportunities; sanitation; soup, stock, sauce, and starch production.

FACILITIES

Bake shop; cafeteria; classroom; computer laboratory; food production kitchen; learning resource center; library.

TYPICAL STUDENT PROFILE

24 full-time.

FINANCIAL AID

Employment placement assistance is available.

APPLICATION INFORMATION

Students may begin participation in August. Applications are accepted continuously. Applicants must submit a formal application.

CONTACT

Director of Admissions, Food Service Education, 324 North Emporia, Wichita, KS 67217. Telephone: 316-677-1362. Fax: 316-677-1332. World Wide Web: http://www.wichitatech.com.

KENTUCKY

ELIZABETHTOWN COMMUNITY AND TECHNICAL COLLEGE

Culinary Arts

Elizabethtown, Kentucky

GENERAL INFORMATION

Public, coeducational, two-year college. Small-town setting. Founded in 1966. Accredited by Southern Association of Colleges and Schools.

PROGRAM INFORMATION

Offered since 1975. Program calendar is divided into semesters. 12-month degree in food and beverage management. 12-month degree in culinary arts. 12-month degree in catering. 18-month diploma in food and beverage management. 18-month diploma in culinary arts. 18-month diploma in catering. 6-12-month certificate in professional development. 6-12-month certificate in culinary arts. 6-12-month certificate in catering.

PROGRAM AFFILIATION

International Association of Culinary Professionals; National Restaurant Association; National Restaurant Association Educational Foundation; Retailer's Bakery Association.

AREAS OF STUDY

Baking; beverage management; buffet catering; confectionery show pieces; controlling costs in food service; culinary skill development; food preparation; food purchasing; food service communication; food service math; garde-manger; international cuisine; introduction to food service; kitchen management; management and human resources; meal planning; menu and facilities design; nutrition; nutrition and food service; restaurant opportunities; sanitation; soup, stock, sauce, and starch production.

FACILITIES

Bake shop; cafeteria; catering service; classroom; computer laboratory; food production kitchen; learning resource center; library; teaching kitchen.

STUDENT PROFILE

38 total: 28 full-time; 10 part-time. 20 are under 25 years old; 18 are between 25 and 44 years old.

FACULTY

4 total: 2 full-time; 2 part-time. 3 are industry professionals; 1 is a master chef; 2 are culinary-certified teachers. Prominent faculty: Jane Masse; Susie Swink. Faculty-student ratio: 1:15.

SPECIAL PROGRAMS

Field trips, public food demonstrations, culinary competitions.

TYPICAL EXPENSES

In-state tuition: $1470 per 15 credit hours per semester full-time (in district), $98 per credit hour part-time (in district), $118 per credit hour part-time (out-of-district). Out-of-state tuition: $294 per credit hour part-time. Program-related fees include $200 for uniforms; $500 for books; $300 for general supplies.

FINANCIAL AID

Program-specific awards include scholarships available through local organizations. Employment placement assistance is available. Employment opportunities within the program are available.

HOUSING

Average off-campus housing cost per month: $600.

APPLICATION INFORMATION

Students may begin participation in January and August. Application deadline for fall is July 1. Application deadline for spring is November 30. In 2004, 30 applied; 30 were accepted. Applicants must submit a formal application and submit a formal application, academic transcripts, and take the COMPASS Test.

CONTACT

Susie Swink, Program Coordinator, Culinary Arts, 620 College Street Road, Elizabethtown, KY 42701. Telephone: 270-706-8732. Fax: 270-766-5131. E-mail: susie.leblanc@ kctcs.edu.

JEFFERSON COMMUNITY AND TECHNICAL COLLEGE

Culinary Arts

Louisville, Kentucky

GENERAL INFORMATION

Public, coeducational, two-year college. Urban campus. Founded in 1968. Accredited by Southern Association of Colleges and Schools.

PROGRAM INFORMATION

Offered since 1974. Accredited by American Culinary Federation Accrediting Commission. Program calendar is divided into semesters. 2-year associate degree in catering. 2-year associate degree in foodservice management. 2-year associate degree in culinary arts. 2-year certificate in culinary arts.

PROGRAM AFFILIATION

American Culinary Federation; National Restaurant Association; National Restaurant Association Educational Foundation; Women Chefs and Restaurateurs.

AREAS OF STUDY

Baking; buffet catering; controlling costs in food service; culinary skill development; food preparation; food service communication; garde-manger; human resource management; international cuisine; kitchen management; management; marketing; meat cutting; menu and facilities design; nutrition; patisserie; sanitation; seafood processing.

FACILITIES

Bake shop; cafeteria; classroom; computer laboratory; demonstration laboratory; food production kitchen; gourmet dining room; laboratory; learning resource center; 3 lecture rooms; library; student lounge; teaching kitchen.

TYPICAL STUDENT PROFILE

80 total: 40 full-time; 40 part-time.

SPECIAL PROGRAMS

Paid internships.

FINANCIAL AID

Program-specific awards include 5 Kentucky Restaurant Association Scholarships ($725), James Edwards Scholarship. Employment placement assistance is available.

APPLICATION INFORMATION

Students may begin participation in January and August. Applications are accepted continuously. Applicants must interview; submit a formal application.

CONTACT

Director of Admissions, Culinary Arts, 109 East Broadway, Louisville, KY 40202-2005. Telephone: 502-213-2317. Fax: 502-213-2414. World Wide Web: http://www.jctc.kctcs.net.

SULLIVAN UNIVERSITY

National Center for Hospitality Studies

Louisville, Kentucky

GENERAL INFORMATION

Private, coeducational, comprehensive institution. Suburban campus. Founded in 1962. Accredited by Southern Association of Colleges and Schools.

PROGRAM INFORMATION

Offered since 1987. Accredited by American Culinary Federation Accrediting Commission. Program calendar is divided into quarters. 12-month diploma in professional cook. 18-month associate degree in travel and tourism. 18-month associate degree in professional catering. 18-month associate degree in hotel and restaurant management. 18-month associate degree in baking and pastry arts. 18-month associate degree in culinary arts. 36-month bachelor's degree in hospitality management. 9-month diploma in travel and tourism. 9-month diploma in professional baker.

PROGRAM AFFILIATION

American Culinary Federation; American Dietetic Association; American Institute of Wine & Food; Confrerie de la Chaine des Rotisseurs; Council on Hotel, Restaurant, and Institutional Education; International Association of Culinary Professionals; International Food Service

Sullivan University *(continued)*

Executives Association; James Beard Foundation, Inc.; Kentucky Restaurant Association; National Restaurant Association; National Restaurant Association Educational Foundation; United States Personal Chef Association; Women Chefs and Restaurateurs.

AREAS OF STUDY
Baking; beverage management; buffet catering; confectionery show pieces; controlling costs in food service; culinary French; culinary skill development; food preparation; food purchasing; food service math; garde-manger; hotel restaurant management; international cuisine; introduction to food service; kitchen management; management and human resources; meat cutting; menu and facilities design; nutrition; patisserie; professional catering; restaurant opportunities; sanitation; saucier; seafood processing; soup, stock, sauce, and starch production; travel and tourism; wines and spirits.

FACILITIES
5 bake shops; bakery; cafeteria; catering service; 41 classrooms; 7 computer laboratories; demonstration laboratory; 13 food production kitchens; garden; gourmet dining room; 3 laboratories; library; public restaurant; student lounge.

STUDENT PROFILE
960 total: 850 full-time; 110 part-time. 375 are under 25 years old; 375 are between 25 and 44 years old; 210 are over 44 years old.

FACULTY
28 total: 26 full-time; 2 part-time. 26 are industry professionals; 1 is a master chef; 12 are culinary-certified teachers. Prominent faculty: Thomas Hickey, CEC, CCE, CFE, CHE; Derek Spendlove, CEPC, CCE, AAC; David H. Dodd, MBE, CEC, CCE; Walter Rhea, CMPC, CCE, CEC, AAC. Faculty-student ratio: 1:19.

SPECIAL PROGRAMS
3-month restaurant practicum, culinary competitions, trip to Boston, MA and one-week cruise for hospitality (hotel-restaurant) majors.

TYPICAL EXPENSES
Application fee: $90. Tuition: $27,900 per 18 months. Program-related fee includes $845 for general fees.

FINANCIAL AID
In 2004, 8 scholarships were awarded (average award was $6000). Employment placement assistance is available. Employment opportunities within the program are available.

HOUSING
Apartment-style housing available. Average on-campus housing cost per month: $440.

APPLICATION INFORMATION
Students may begin participation in January, March, June, and September. Application deadline for fall is September 15. Application deadline for winter is December 15. Application deadline for spring is March 15. Application deadline for summer is June 15. In 2004, 940 applied; 860 were accepted. Applicants must interview; submit a formal application and CPAT, SAT, or ACT scores; TOEFL score for international applicants.

CONTACT
Greg Cawthon, Director of Admissions, National Center for Hospitality Studies, 3101 Bardstown Road, Louisville, KY 40205. Telephone: 502-456-6505. Fax: 502-456-0040. E-mail: admissions@sullivan.edu. World Wide Web: http://www.sullivan.edu.

See color display following page 188.

WESTERN KENTUCKY UNIVERSITY

Hotel, Restaurant, and Tourism Management

Bowling Green, Kentucky

GENERAL INFORMATION
Public, coeducational, comprehensive institution. Small-town setting. Founded in 1906. Accredited by Southern Association of Colleges and Schools.

PROGRAM INFORMATION
Offered since 1969. Accredited by American Dietetic Association. Program calendar is divided into semesters. 4-year bachelor's degree in hotel, restaurant, and tourism management.

PROGRAM AFFILIATION
American Dietetic Association; Council on Hotel, Restaurant, and Institutional Education; National Restaurant Association; National Restaurant Association Educational Foundation.

AREAS OF STUDY
Beverage management; buffet catering; controlling costs in food service; food preparation; food purchasing; international cuisine; introduction to food service; kitchen management; management and human resources; meal planning; nutrition; nutrition and food service; restaurant management; restaurant opportunities; sanitation.

FACILITIES
2 classrooms; computer laboratory; demonstration laboratory; food production kitchen; gourmet dining room; laboratory; learning resource center; 2 libraries; teaching kitchen.

STUDENT PROFILE
120 total: 114 full-time; 6 part-time. 110 are under 25 years old; 9 are between 25 and 44 years old; 1 is over 44 years old.

FACULTY
6 total: 5 full-time; 1 part-time. 6 are industry professionals. Prominent faculty: Richard F. Patterson,

EdD, RD; Patty J. Silfies, MHRIM; Danita Kelley, PhD, RD; Karen Mason, PhD, RD. Faculty-student ratio: 1:24.

SPECIAL PROGRAMS
2 semesters of paid internships.

TYPICAL EXPENSES
Application fee: $35. In-state tuition: $2736 per semester full-time (in district), $228 per credit hour part-time. Out-of-state tuition: $6744 per semester full-time, $537 per credit hour part-time. Program-related fee includes $50 for food preparation lab fee.

FINANCIAL AID
In 2004, 2 scholarships were awarded (average award was $500). Program-specific awards include Rafferty Restaurant Scholarship, Kentucky Restaurant Association Scholarship, Bowling Green/Warren County Lodging Scholarship. Employment placement assistance is available. Employment opportunities within the program are available.

HOUSING
Coed and single-sex housing available. Average on-campus housing cost per month: $275. Average off-campus housing cost per month: $393.

APPLICATION INFORMATION
Students may begin participation in January and August. Application deadline for fall is August 1. Application deadline for spring is January 1. In 2004, 49 applied; 46 were accepted. Applicants must submit a formal application.

CONTACT
Dr. Richard F. Patterson, Associate Professor, Hotel, Restaurant, and Tourism Management, Department of Consumer and Family Sciences, 1906 College Heights Boulevard, #11037, Bowling Green, KY 42101-1037. Telephone: 270-745-4031. Fax: 270-745-3999. E-mail: rich. patterson@wku.edu. World Wide Web: http://www.wku. edu/hospitality.

LOUISIANA

CULINARY INSTITUTE OF NEW ORLEANS

New Orleans, Louisiana

GENERAL INFORMATION
Private, coeducational, culinary institute. Urban campus. Founded in 1984. Accredited by Council on Occupational Education.

PROGRAM INFORMATION
Offered since 1984. Accredited by American Culinary Federation Accrediting Commission. Program calendar is continuous. 1,800-hour diploma in culinary arts. 14-month associate degree in culinary arts. 7-month certificate in

restaurant management. 900-hour certificate in culinary arts cooking theory, food science. 900-hour certificate in culinary arts-ethnic cuisine's II. 900-hour certificate in culinary arts-intermediate cooking theory. 900-hour certificate in culinary arts-professional baking. 900-hour certificate in culinary arts-ethnic cuisine's I. 900-hour certificate in culinary arts.

PROGRAM AFFILIATION
National Restaurant Association.

AREAS OF STUDY
Baking; beverage management; buffet catering; confectionery show pieces; controlling costs in food service; culinary French; culinary skill development; food preparation; food purchasing; food service communication; food service math; garde-manger; international cuisine; introduction to food service; kitchen management; management and human resources; meal planning; meat cutting; meat fabrication; menu and facilities design; nutrition; nutrition and food service; patisserie; restaurant opportunities; sanitation; saucier; seafood processing; soup, stock, sauce, and starch production; wines and spirits.

FACILITIES
3 bake shops; bakery; 2 cafeterias; 3 catering services; 8 classrooms; computer laboratory; 3 demonstration laboratories; 3 food production kitchens; 3 gardens; 3 gourmet dining rooms; learning resource center; 6 lecture rooms; library; 3 public restaurants; 2 snack shops; student lounge; 3 teaching kitchens; 2 vineyards.

TYPICAL STUDENT PROFILE
275 full-time.

SPECIAL PROGRAMS
Paid externship, tour of festivals of Louisiana, national PBS television cooking show exposure.

FINANCIAL AID
Employment placement assistance is available. Employment opportunities within the program are available.

APPLICATION INFORMATION
Students may begin participation year-round. Applications are accepted continuously. Applicants must interview; submit a formal application.

CONTACT
Director of Admissions, 2100 Saint Charles Avenue, Number One, New Orleans, LA 70140. Telephone: 504-525-2433. Fax: 504-525-2466. World Wide Web: http://www.ci-no.com.

DELGADO COMMUNITY COLLEGE

Culinary Arts Department

New Orleans, Louisiana

GENERAL INFORMATION

Public, coeducational, two-year college. Urban campus. Founded in 1921. Accredited by Southern Association of Colleges and Schools.

PROGRAM INFORMATION

Offered since 1939. Accredited by American Culinary Federation Accrediting Commission. Program calendar is divided into semesters. 1-year certificate of completion in culinary arts. 2-semester certificate in hospitality. 2-semester certificate in pastry arts. 2-semester diploma in NRA Management Development Program. 3-year associate degree in culinary arts apprenticeship. 4-semester associate degree in hospitality.

PROGRAM AFFILIATION

American Culinary Federation; American Dietetic Association; American Institute of Wine & Food; Confrerie de la Chaine des Rotisseurs; Council on Hotel, Restaurant, and Institutional Education; International Association of Culinary Professionals; James Beard Foundation, Inc.; National Restaurant Association; National Restaurant Association Educational Foundation; Retailer's Bakery Association.

AREAS OF STUDY

Baking; beverage management; confectionery show pieces; controlling costs in food service; culinary skill development; food preparation; food purchasing; food service math; garde-manger; introduction to food service; management and human resources; meal planning; meat fabrication; menu and facilities design; nutrition; nutrition and food service; patisserie; restaurant opportunities; sanitation; seafood processing; soup, stock, sauce, and starch production; wines and spirits.

FACILITIES

Bake shop; 3 classrooms; computer laboratory; food production kitchen; garden; learning resource center; library; snack shop; student lounge; teaching kitchen.

TYPICAL STUDENT PROFILE

200 full-time.

SPECIAL PROGRAMS

ACF student competitions.

FINANCIAL AID

Employment opportunities within the program are available.

APPLICATION INFORMATION

Students may begin participation in August. Application deadline for fall is March 30. Applicants must interview; submit a formal application, letters of reference, college transcript or ACT scores, high school diploma or GED.

CONTACT

Director of Admissions, Culinary Arts Department, 615 City Park Avenue, New Orleans, LA 70119. Telephone: 504-483-4208. Fax: 504-483-4893. World Wide Web: http://www.dcc.edu.

ELAINE P. NUNEZ COMMUNITY COLLEGE

Culinary Arts Program, Business and Technology Division

Chalmette, Louisiana

GENERAL INFORMATION

Public, coeducational, two-year college. Suburban campus. Founded in 1992. Accredited by Southern Association of Colleges and Schools.

PROGRAM INFORMATION

Offered since 1992. Program calendar is divided into semesters. 1-year certificate in culinary arts and occupations. 2-year associate degree in culinary arts and occupations.

PROGRAM AFFILIATION

American Culinary Federation; National Restaurant Association.

AREAS OF STUDY

Baking; beverage management; buffet catering; controlling costs in food service; culinary French; food preparation; food purchasing; food service communication; food service math; garde-manger; international cuisine; introduction to food service; kitchen management; management and human resources; meal planning; meat cutting; meat fabrication; nutrition; nutrition and food service; patisserie; sanitation; saucier; seafood processing; soup, stock, sauce, and starch production; wines and spirits.

FACILITIES

Bake shop; cafeteria; classroom; computer laboratory; demonstration laboratory; food production kitchen; gourmet dining room; learning resource center; lecture room; library; teaching kitchen.

TYPICAL STUDENT PROFILE

50 total: 27 full-time; 23 part-time.

SPECIAL PROGRAMS

Culinary competitions.

FINANCIAL AID

Employment placement assistance is available. Employment opportunities within the program are available.

APPLICATION INFORMATION

Students may begin participation in January, June, and August. Application deadline for fall is July 31. Application deadline for spring is December 31. Application deadline for summer is May 1. Applicants must submit a formal application.

CONTACT

Director of Admissions, Culinary Arts Program, Business and Technology Division, 3710 Paris Road, Chalmette, LA 70043-1249. Telephone: 504-680-2376. Fax: 504-680-2274. World Wide Web: http://www.nunez.cc.edu.

LOUISIANA CULINARY INSTITUTE, LLC

Professional Cooking and Culinary Arts

Baton Rouge, Louisiana

GENERAL INFORMATION

Private, coeducational, culinary institute. Urban campus. Founded in 2002.

PROGRAM INFORMATION

Offered since 2002. Accredited by Council on Occupational Education. Program calendar is divided into quarters. 18-month associate degree in professional cooking and culinary arts.

PROGRAM AFFILIATION

American Culinary Federation; International Association of Culinary Professionals; National Restaurant Association; National Restaurant Association Educational Foundation.

AREAS OF STUDY

Baking; beverage management; controlling costs in food service; convenience cookery; culinary French; culinary skill development; food preparation; food purchasing; food service communication; food service math; garde-manger; international cuisine; introduction to food service; kitchen management; management and human resources; meal planning; meat cutting; meat fabrication; menu and facilities design; nutrition; nutrition and food service; patisserie; sanitation; saucier; seafood processing; soup, stock, sauce, and starch production; wines and spirits.

FACILITIES

Bake shop; cafeteria; 3 classrooms; coffee shop; 4 computer laboratories; 2 demonstration laboratories; food production kitchen; garden; gourmet dining room; learning resource center; lecture room; library; student lounge; teaching kitchen.

STUDENT PROFILE

90 full-time. 40 are under 25 years old; 40 are between 25 and 44 years old; 10 are over 44 years old.

Louisiana Culinary Institute, LLC *(continued)*

FACULTY

7 total: 5 full-time; 2 part-time. 1 is an industry professional; 6 are culinary-certified teachers. Prominent faculty: Ross Headlee, FMP, CCP. Faculty-student ratio: 1:13.

SPECIAL PROGRAMS

Two-day "stage" at Commander's Palace or Mausur's on the Boulevarde, Home Plate Classic and Chefs' Bowl culinary competitions, tours of McIlhenny's Tabasco plant, Tony Chechere's spice plant, and many others.

TYPICAL EXPENSES

Tuition: $22,500 per year. Program-related fee includes $100 for registration (refundable).

FINANCIAL AID

In 2005, 19 scholarships were awarded (average award was $1000); 4 loans were granted (average loan was $14,750). Program-specific awards include sponsored professional education program ($2500), pro-start scholarship, Foundation for Culinary Excellence Scholarships. Employment placement assistance is available. Employment opportunities within the program are available.

HOUSING

Coed housing available. Average on-campus housing cost per month: $300. Average off-campus housing cost per month: $320.

APPLICATION INFORMATION

Students may begin participation in February, May, August, and November. Application deadline for spring is March 5. Application deadline for summer is June 11. Application deadline for fall is September 10. Application deadline for winter is December 10. In 2005, 180 applied; 60 were accepted. Applicants must interview; submit a formal application, letters of reference, an essay, high school diploma or GED; state required skills test (if no college transcripts).

CONTACT

Jordan Lewis, Public Affairs, Professional Cooking and Culinary Arts, 5837 Essen Lane, Baton Rouge, LA 70810. Telephone: 877-769-8820. Fax: 225-769-8792. E-mail: admissions@louisianaculinary.com. World Wide Web: http://www.louisianaculinary.com.

LOUISIANA TECHNICAL COLLEGE–BATON ROUGE CAMPUS

Culinary Arts and Occupations

Baton Rouge, Louisiana

GENERAL INFORMATION

Public, coeducational, technical institute. Urban campus. Founded in 1974.

PROGRAM INFORMATION

Offered since 1974. Program calendar is divided into quarters. 18-month diploma in culinary arts and occupations. 3-month certificate in nutrition. 3-month certificate in supervision. 3-month certificate in sanitation.

PROGRAM AFFILIATION

American Culinary Federation; Louisiana Restaurant Association; National Restaurant Association Educational Foundation.

AREAS OF STUDY

Baking; controlling costs in food service; culinary skill development; food preparation; food purchasing; food service communication; food service math; kitchen management; nutrition and food service; sanitation; soup, stock, sauce, and starch production.

FACILITIES

Bake shop; cafeteria; classroom; computer laboratory; food production kitchen.

TYPICAL STUDENT PROFILE

22 total: 20 full-time; 2 part-time.

FINANCIAL AID

Employment placement assistance is available. Employment opportunities within the program are available.

APPLICATION INFORMATION

Students may begin participation in March, May, August, and November. Applications are accepted continuously. Applicants must submit a formal application and complete an entrance test.

CONTACT

Director of Admissions, Culinary Arts and Occupations, 3250 North Acadian Thruway, East, Baton Rouge, LA 70805. Telephone: 225-359-9226. Fax: 225-359-9296. World Wide Web: http://www.brti.tec.la.us.

Louisiana Technical College–Jefferson Campus

Culinary Arts and Occupations

Metairie, Louisiana

GENERAL INFORMATION
Public, coeducational, two-year college. Urban campus. Accredited by Council on Occupational Education.

PROGRAM INFORMATION
Accredited by American Culinary Federation Accrediting Commission. Program calendar is divided into semesters. 4-semester diploma in culinary arts.

PROGRAM AFFILIATION
American Culinary Federation.

AREAS OF STUDY
Baking; beverage management; culinary skill development; food preparation; food service math; garde-manger; introduction to food service; management and human resources; meat fabrication; nutrition; restaurant opportunities; sanitation.

FACILITIES
Bake shop; cafeteria; catering service; classroom; computer laboratory; demonstration laboratory; food production kitchen; garden; laboratory; lecture room; library; snack shop; teaching kitchen.

TYPICAL STUDENT PROFILE
100 total: 85 full-time; 15 part-time.

SPECIAL PROGRAMS
Food show competitions, apprenticeships and externships.

FINANCIAL AID
Employment placement assistance is available. Employment opportunities within the program are available.

APPLICATION INFORMATION
Students may begin participation in January, May, and August. Applications are accepted continuously. Applicants must submit a formal application and take Test of Adult Basic Education.

CONTACT
Director of Admissions, Culinary Arts and Occupations, 5200 Blair Drive, Metairie, LA 70001. Telephone: 504-736-7081. Fax: 504-736-7120. World Wide Web: http://www.jeff.tec.la.us.

Louisiana Technical College–Lafayette Campus

Culinary Arts and Occupations

Lafayette, Louisiana

GENERAL INFORMATION
Public, coeducational institution. Urban campus. Founded in 1978. Accredited by Council on Occupational Education.

PROGRAM INFORMATION
Offered since 1979. Accredited by American Culinary Federation Accrediting Commission. Program calendar is divided into semesters. 18-month diploma in culinary arts and occupations.

PROGRAM AFFILIATION
American Culinary Federation.

AREAS OF STUDY
Baking; beverage management; buffet catering; controlling costs in food service; convenience cookery; culinary French; culinary skill development; food preparation; food purchasing; food service communication; food service math; garde-manger; international cuisine; introduction to food service; kitchen management; management and human resources; meal planning; meat fabrication; menu and facilities design; nutrition; nutrition and food service; patisserie; restaurant opportunities; sanitation; saucier; seafood processing; soup, stock, sauce, and starch production.

FACILITIES
Bake shop; catering service; food production kitchen; gourmet dining room; lecture room.

TYPICAL STUDENT PROFILE
80 full-time.

FINANCIAL AID
Employment placement assistance is available.

APPLICATION INFORMATION
Students may begin participation in January, May, and August. Applications are accepted continuously. Applicants must submit a formal application and complete an entrance exam.

CONTACT
Director of Admissions, Culinary Arts and Occupations, 1101 Bertrand Drive, Lafayette, LA 70506. Telephone: 318-262-5962 Ext. 232. Fax: 318-262-5122. World Wide Web: http://www.lafayette.tec.la.us.

LOUISIANA TECHNICAL COLLEGE–SIDNEY N. COLLIER CAMPUS

Culinary Arts

New Orleans, Louisiana

GENERAL INFORMATION
Public, coeducational, two-year college. Suburban campus. Founded in 1952.

PROGRAM INFORMATION
Offered since 1952. Program calendar is divided into quarters. 18-month diploma in culinary arts. 5-month certificate in fine dining. 6-month certificate in culinary arts.

PROGRAM AFFILIATION
American Culinary Federation.

AREAS OF STUDY
Baking; beverage management; buffet catering; controlling costs in food service; convenience cookery; culinary French; culinary skill development; food preparation; food purchasing; food service communication; food service math; garde-manger; international cuisine; introduction to food service; kitchen management; management and human resources; meal planning; meat cutting; meat fabrication; menu and facilities design; nutrition; nutrition and food service; patisserie; restaurant opportunities; sanitation; saucier; seafood processing; soup, stock, sauce, and starch production.

FACILITIES
Bake shop; bakery; cafeteria; classroom; computer laboratory; demonstration laboratory; food production kitchen; learning resource center; lecture room; library; student lounge; teaching kitchen.

TYPICAL STUDENT PROFILE
15 total: 11 full-time; 4 part-time.

FINANCIAL AID
Employment placement assistance is available.

APPLICATION INFORMATION
Students may begin participation year-round. Applications are accepted continuously. Applicants must submit a formal application and take Test of Adult Basic Education.

CONTACT
Director of Admissions, Culinary Arts, 3727 Louisa Street, New Orleans, LA 70126. Telephone: 504-942-8333 Ext. 134. Fax: 504-942-8337.

LOUISIANA TECHNICAL COLLEGE–SOWELA CAMPUS

Culinary Arts and Occupations

Lake Charles, Louisiana

GENERAL INFORMATION
Public, coeducational, two-year college. Suburban campus. Founded in 1940. Accredited by Council on Occupational Education.

PROGRAM INFORMATION
Offered since 1977. Program calendar is divided into quarters. 18-month diploma in culinary arts and occupations.

PROGRAM AFFILIATION
National Restaurant Association Educational Foundation.

AREAS OF STUDY
Baking; basic accounting; buffet catering; controlling costs in food service; convenience cookery; culinary skill development; food and beverage service; food preparation; food purchasing; food service communication; food service math; garde-manger; international cuisine; introduction to food service; kitchen management; management and human resources; meal planning; meat fabrication; nutrition; nutrition and food service; sanitation; saucier; soup, stock, sauce, and starch production.

FACILITIES
Bakery; cafeteria; classroom; computer laboratory; demonstration laboratory; food production kitchen; garden; gourmet dining room; laboratory; learning resource center; lecture room; library; snack shop; student lounge; teaching kitchen.

TYPICAL STUDENT PROFILE
100 full-time.

SPECIAL PROGRAMS
Culinary competitions, food shows in New Orleans or Houston, ServSafe course.

FINANCIAL AID
Program-specific awards include Rotary Club scholarship ($500), casino scholarships. Employment placement assistance is available.

APPLICATION INFORMATION
Students may begin participation year-round. Applications are accepted continuously. Applicants must submit a formal application and take entrance exam.

CONTACT
Director of Admissions, Culinary Arts and Occupations, 3820 J. Bennett Johnston Avenue, Lake Charles, LA 70615. Telephone: 337-491-2687. Fax: 337-491-2135.

NICHOLLS STATE UNIVERSITY

Chef John Folse Culinary Institute

Thibodaux, Louisiana

GENERAL INFORMATION
Public, coeducational, comprehensive institution. Rural campus. Founded in 1948. Accredited by Southern Association of Colleges and Schools.

PROGRAM INFORMATION
Offered since 1994. Program calendar is divided into semesters. 2-year associate degree in culinary arts. 4-year bachelor's degree in culinary arts.

PROGRAM AFFILIATION
American Culinary Federation; Council on Hotel, Restaurant, and Institutional Education; National Restaurant Association; Research Chefs Association; Society for the Advancement of Food Service Research.

AREAS OF STUDY
Baking; beverage management; buffet catering; confectionery show pieces; controlling costs in food service; convenience cookery; culinary entrepreneurship; culinary French; culinary skill development; food preparation; food purchasing; garde-manger; international cuisine; introduction to food service; kitchen management; management and human resources; meal planning; meat cutting; meat fabrication; menu and facilities design; nutrition; nutrition and food service; patisserie; restaurant opportunities; sanitation; saucier; seafood processing; soup, stock, sauce, and starch production; wines and spirits.

FACILITIES
Bakery; cafeteria; catering service; 3 classrooms; 2 computer laboratories; demonstration laboratory; food production kitchen; gourmet dining room; 3 laboratories; 2 learning resource centers; 3 lecture rooms; library; public restaurant; snack shop; student lounge; 2 teaching kitchens.

TYPICAL STUDENT PROFILE
240 total: 204 full-time; 36 part-time.

SPECIAL PROGRAMS
State and regional culinary competitions.

FINANCIAL AID
Employment placement assistance is available.

HOUSING
Coed, apartment-style, and single-sex housing available.

APPLICATION INFORMATION
Students may begin participation in January and August. Application deadline for fall is July 15. Application deadline for spring is November 15. Applicants must submit a formal application and high school transcript, minimum 2.5 high school GPA.

CONTACT
Director of Admissions, Chef John Folse Culinary Institute, PO Box 2099, Thibodaux, LA 70310. Telephone: 985-449-7091. Fax: 985-449-7089. World Wide Web: http://www.nicholls.edu/jfolse.

SCLAFANI COOKING SCHOOL, INC.

Commercial Cook/Baker

Metairie, Louisiana

GENERAL INFORMATION
Private, coeducational, culinary institute. Suburban campus. Founded in 1987.

PROGRAM INFORMATION
Offered since 1987. Program calendar is divided into months, months. 4-week certificate in commercial cooking/baking.

PROGRAM AFFILIATION
Foodservice Management Professionals; Louisiana Restaurant Association; National Association of Catering Executives.

AREAS OF STUDY
Baking; controlling costs in food service; culinary skill development; food preparation; food service math; garde-manger; introduction to food service; kitchen management; management and human resources; meal planning; restaurant opportunities; sanitation; saucier; soup, stock, sauce, and starch production.

FACILITIES
Bake shop; bakery; classroom; computer laboratory; demonstration laboratory; food production kitchen; lecture room; library; teaching kitchen.

TYPICAL STUDENT PROFILE
110 full-time. 23 are under 25 years old; 70 are between 25 and 44 years old; 17 are over 44 years old.

SPECIAL PROGRAMS
ServSafe certification program and exam.

FINANCIAL AID
Employment placement assistance is available.

APPLICATION INFORMATION
Students may begin participation year-round. Applications are accepted continuously. Applicants must interview; submit a formal application and pass the Wonderlic aptitude test.

CONTACT
Director of Admissions, Commercial Cook/Baker, 107 Gennaro Place, Metairie, LA 70001. Telephone: 504-833-7861. Fax: 504-833-7872. World Wide Web: http://www.sclafanicookingschool.com.

SOUTHERN UNIVERSITY AT SHREVEPORT

Shreveport, Louisiana

GENERAL INFORMATION
Public, coeducational, two-year college. Urban campus. Founded in 1964. Accredited by Southern Association of Colleges and Schools.

PROGRAM INFORMATION
Offered since 1984. Accredited by Student can earn an industry certificate in hospitality from the Educational Institute of the American Hotel and Motel Association for each course in hospitality. Program calendar is divided into semesters. 1-year certificate in food and beverage management. 1-year certificate in hospitality operation. 2-year associate degree in hospitality.

PROGRAM AFFILIATION
Council on Hotel, Restaurant, and Institutional Education; Educational Institute American Hotel and Motel Association.

AREAS OF STUDY
Baking; beverage management; controlling costs in food service; convenience cookery; culinary French; food preparation; food purchasing; food service communication; food service math; international cuisine; kitchen management; management and human resources; meal planning; menu and facilities design; nutrition and food service; restaurant opportunities; sanitation.

FACILITIES
Catering service; classroom; computer laboratory; demonstration laboratory; gourmet dining room; laboratory; lecture room; library; snack shop; vineyard.

STUDENT PROFILE
16 full-time. 3 are under 25 years old; 9 are between 25 and 44 years old; 4 are over 44 years old.

FACULTY
4 total: 1 full-time; 3 part-time. 3 are industry professionals. Prominent faculty: George Lewis, III, MBA; Scott Lane, MBA, CHE, CFBE, FMP; Randy Randolph, MBA; Debra Reed, MBA. Faculty-student ratio: 1:8.

SPECIAL PROGRAMS
Field trips to area food shows, Internships with hospitality partners.

TYPICAL EXPENSES
Application fee: $5. In-state tuition: $1126 per semester full-time (in district), $624 per 1- to 5-credit hours part-time. Out-of-state tuition: $1691 per semester full-time, $1189 per 1- to 5-credit hours part-time.

FINANCIAL AID
In 2004, 2 scholarships were awarded (average award was $800). Program-specific awards include Industry Scholarships. Employment placement assistance is available.

HOUSING
Average off-campus housing cost per month: $300.

APPLICATION INFORMATION
Students may begin participation in January, June, and August. Application deadline for fall is August 30. Application deadline for spring is January 15. Application deadline for summer is June 6. In 2004, 16 applied; 16 were accepted. Applicants must submit a formal application and high school transcript/diploma or equivalent.

CONTACT
Scott Lane, Hospitality Coordinator, Division of Business Studies, Shreveport, LA 71107. Telephone: 318-429-7236. Fax: 318-674-3313. E-mail: slane@susla.edu. World Wide Web: http://www.susla.edu.

UNIVERSITY OF LOUISIANA AT LAFAYETTE

College of Applied Life Sciences

Lafayette, Louisiana

GENERAL INFORMATION
Public, coeducational, university. Urban campus. Founded in 1898. Accredited by Southern Association of Colleges and Schools.

PROGRAM INFORMATION
Offered since 1950. Accredited by American Dietetic Association. Program calendar is divided into semesters. 4-year bachelor's degree in hospitality management.

PROGRAM AFFILIATION
American Culinary Federation; American Dietetic Association; Confrerie de la Chaine des Rotisseurs; Council on Hotel, Restaurant, and Institutional Education; National Restaurant Association; National Restaurant Association Educational Foundation.

AREAS OF STUDY
Beverage management; controlling costs in food service; food purchasing; food service communication; hotel and restaurant management; kitchen management; management and human resources; meal planning; tourism management.

FACILITIES
Catering service; computer laboratory; food production kitchen; gourmet dining room; laboratory; library; public restaurant; teaching kitchen.

STUDENT PROFILE
95 total: 86 full-time; 9 part-time. 76 are under 25 years old; 18 are between 25 and 44 years old; 1 is over 44 years old.

Sullivan University..

The Sullivan University Advantage

Sullivan University has earned a reputation as one of the most successful culinary schools in America by offering students a unique opportunity to prepare for a rewarding career in today's professional hospitality world.

Sullivan University's National Center for Hospitality Studies has been listed among the *top culinary schools in the nation.* The Baking & Pastry Arts and Culinary Arts degree programs in Louisville are accredited by the American Culinary Federation Accrediting Commission. The University is regionally accredited by the Commission on Colleges of the Southern Association of Colleges and Schools to award associate, bachelor's and master's degrees.

The main campus, located in Louisville, Kentucky, and the branch campus in Lexington, Kentucky, provide its students with access to more than 1,200 restaurants, as well as numerous other hospitality and travel related industries.

Modern, furnished apartments near each campus are available for non-resident students. Each apartment has access to laundry rooms, club house and the swimming pool. Daily transportation is provided by the University.

A Wide Range of Options

Sullivan offers students eight different undergraduate diplomas, associate degrees and bachelor's degree programs (*not all programs are offered at the Lexington campus*).

- **Professional Baker**
- **Professional Cook**
- **Baking & Pastry Arts**
- **Culinary Arts**
- **Professional Catering**
- **Hotel/Restaurant Management**
- **Hospitality Management (online)**
- **Travel, Tourism & Event Management**

A World Class Faculty

Sullivan's hospitality division has grown to more than 1000 students from 38 states and a number of foreign countries who choose to attend Sullivan for their career training. Our faculty includes *three International Culinary Olympic Gold-Medal winners*, two chef-instructors are London Guild trained and one holds the Certified Master Pastry Chef designation. The faculty bring over two hundred years of culinary, hospitality and hotel experience to their students.

Award-Winning Culinary Team

Sullivan University's Culinary Salon Competition Team provides an opportunity for team members to display their artistic talents in a highly competitive national environment. Sullivan students have won more than **360 Gold, Silver and Bronze medals and awards** in regional, national and international competitions. Including:

- **15 Best of Show Awards**
- **13 Special Judges Awards**
- **2 Baron Galand Awards**
- **3 Grand Prize Pastry Awards**
- **People's Choice Award and more!**

Difference!

Real-World Training

Sullivan students receive real-world training at the University's on-campus gourmet restaurant. **Winston's**, rated three-and-one-half stars, is a fine dining restaurant operated by senior students. It is open to the public on the weekend.

Baking and Pastry Arts majors get hands-on training and experience as well as the opportunity to develop their special artistic skills at **The Bakery**, Sullivan University's retail bakery and laboratory training facility.

Professional Catering and Culinary Arts students gain valuable insights and trade knowledge from their experience with **Juleps Catering**, a professional division of Sullivan University. The National Association of Catering Executives (NACE) recently awarded Sullivan's Professional Catering Program the *National Chapter Education Program of the Year*.

100% Graduate Employment Success

Sullivan University provides its graduates with a Graduate Employment Services Department. Companies that place job requests for Sullivan hospitality graduates include such nationally known firms as Hyatt Hotels, Hilton Hotels, Caesars World, Clipper Cruise Lines, and ARA Services. Resorts such as Walt Disney World, airlines and numerous nationally recognized restaurants including Wolfgang Puck's Spago's in Beverly Hills, Nick's Fishmarkets in Hawaii and other cities, Emeril's in Atlanta and Orlando, and many others are among the additional businesses that seek out Sullivan's hospitality graduates. With a 100% graduate employment success record in recent years, the professional staff at Sullivan University matches graduates with employment needs – locally, nationally and internationally.

Let Sullivan University be your entry into a successful hospitality career.

Sullivan University
National Center for Hospitality Studies

Main Campus: 3101 Bardstown Road • Louisville, Kentucky 40205 - Branch Campus: 2355 Harrodsburg Road • Lexington, Kentucky 40504

BALTIMORE INTERNATIONAL COLLEGE

Baltimore International College is your key to success in the hospitality industry. Whether your goal is to own a restaurant, be an Executive Chef, or manage a hotel, Baltimore International College can provide you with the skills and knowledge needed to jump start your career.

The college offers master's, bachelors, and associates degrees plus certificate programs. Students received hands-on instruction from chefs who have decades of real-world experience as well as the opportunity to study abroad at the college's campus in Ireland.

Scholarships and financial aid are available to those that qualify.

FACULTY
3 total: 2 full-time; 1 part-time. 1 is an industry professional. Prominent faculty: Jerome Agrusa, PhD; Linda M. Vincent, EdD; Becky Gaspard.

SPECIAL PROGRAMS
Senior level 15-week internship, required 1500 hours of work experience, trips to NRA and AMLA shows in New York, Chicago, and New Orleans.

TYPICAL EXPENSES
Application fee: $20. In-state tuition: $2699.50 per year full-time (in district), $85.42 per credit hour part-time. Out-of-state tuition: $8959.50 per year full-time, $257.50 per credit hour part-time. Tuition for international students: $9095.50 per year.

FINANCIAL AID
In 2004, 38 scholarships were awarded (average award was $872). Employment placement assistance is available. Employment opportunities within the program are available.

HOUSING
Apartment-style and single-sex housing available. Average off-campus housing cost per month: $400.

APPLICATION INFORMATION
Students may begin participation in January, June, and August. Applications are accepted continuously. In 2004, 43 applied; 40 were accepted. Applicants must submit a formal application and ACT or SAT scores.

CONTACT
Dr. Rachel Fournet, Director, School of Human Resources, College of Applied Life Sciences, PO Box 40399, Lafayette, LA 70504. Telephone: 337-482-5724. Fax: 337-482-5395. World Wide Web: http://www.louisiana.edu.

MAINE

EASTERN MAINE COMMUNITY COLLEGE

Culinary Arts Department

Bangor, Maine

GENERAL INFORMATION
Public, coeducational, two-year college. Small-town setting. Founded in 1966. Accredited by New England Association of Schools and Colleges.

PROGRAM INFORMATION
Program calendar is divided into semesters. 1-year certificate in food service specialist. 2-year associate degree in culinary arts.

PROGRAM AFFILIATION
American Culinary Federation; International Association of Culinary Professionals; Maine Restaurant Association; National Restaurant Association; National Restaurant Association Educational Foundation.

FACILITIES
Bake shop; 2 bakeries; cafeteria; catering service; 2 classrooms; 5 computer laboratories; food production kitchen; garden; gourmet dining room; learning resource center; 2 lecture rooms; 2 libraries; public restaurant; snack shop; 3 student lounges; teaching kitchen.

TYPICAL STUDENT PROFILE
67 total: 60 full-time; 7 part-time.

SPECIAL PROGRAMS
Exchange program, culinary competitions, food shows.

FINANCIAL AID
Employment placement assistance is available.

HOUSING
Coed housing available.

APPLICATION INFORMATION
Students may begin participation in January and August. Applications are accepted continuously. Applicants must interview; submit a formal application and an essay.

CONTACT
Director of Admissions, Culinary Arts Department, 354 Hogan Road, Bangor, ME 04401. Telephone: 207-974-4680. Fax: 207-974-4683. World Wide Web: http://www.emtc.org.

SOUTHERN MAINE COMMUNITY COLLEGE

Culinary Arts

South Portland, Maine

GENERAL INFORMATION
Public, coeducational, two-year college. Suburban campus. Founded in 1946. Accredited by New England Association of Schools and Colleges.

PROGRAM INFORMATION
Offered since 1958. Program calendar is divided into semesters. 2-year associate degree in culinary arts/applied science.

PROGRAM AFFILIATION
American Culinary Federation; American Institute of Baking; Council on Hotel, Restaurant, and Institutional Education; Foodservice Educators Network International; International Association of Culinary Professionals; Maine Restaurant Association; National Restaurant Association; National Restaurant Association Educational Foundation.

Southern Maine Community College *(continued)*

AREAS OF STUDY

Baking; beverage management; buffet catering; confectionery show pieces; controlling costs in food service; culinary skill development; food preparation; food purchasing; food service communication; food service math; garde-manger; international cuisine; introduction to food service; kitchen management; management and human resources; meal planning; meat cutting; meat fabrication; menu and facilities design; nutrition; nutrition and food service; restaurant opportunities; sanitation; saucier; seafood processing; soup, stock, sauce, and starch production.

FACILITIES

Bake shop; bakery; 7 classrooms; computer laboratory; demonstration laboratory; 4 food production kitchens; gourmet dining room; 3 laboratories; learning resource center; lecture room; library; public restaurant; student lounge; 2 teaching kitchens.

STUDENT PROFILE

140 total: 97 full-time; 43 part-time. 111 are under 25 years old; 27 are between 25 and 44 years old; 2 are over 44 years old.

FACULTY

9 total: 4 full-time; 5 part-time. 4 are industry professionals; 2 are culinary-certified teachers; 2 are culinary arts instructors; 2 are dietetic instructors; 2 are hospitality management instructors. Prominent faculty: David Libby, MSEd; Paul Charpentier, MS, CCE, CEC; Wilfred Beriau, MS, CCE, CEC, AAC; Maurice Leavitt, BA. Faculty-student ratio: 1:15.

SPECIAL PROGRAMS

Tours of food service establishments, guest lectures, study abroad program in Austria/Italy.

TYPICAL EXPENSES

Application fee: $20. In-state tuition: $1565 per semester. Out-of-state tuition: $2780 per semester. Program-related fees include $400 for uniforms, knives, and equipment; $900–$1000 for texts (for two years).

FINANCIAL AID

In 2004, 8 scholarships were awarded (average award was $500). Employment placement assistance is available. Employment opportunities within the program are available.

HOUSING

Coed housing available. Average on-campus housing cost per month: $350–$650. Average off-campus housing cost per month: $550.

APPLICATION INFORMATION

Students may begin participation in January and August. Applications are accepted continuously. In 2004, 174 applied; 81 were accepted. Applicants must submit a formal application.

CONTACT

David Tracy, Assistant Dean of Enrollment Services, Culinary Arts, Fort Road, South Portland, ME 04106. Telephone: 207-741-5800. Fax: 207-741-5760. E-mail: menrollmentservices@smccme.edu. World Wide Web: http://www.smccme.edu.

YORK COUNTY COMMUNITY COLLEGE

Wells, Maine

GENERAL INFORMATION

Public, coeducational, two-year college. Small-town setting. Founded in 1994. Accredited by New England Association of Schools and Colleges.

PROGRAM INFORMATION

Offered since 1995. Program calendar is divided into semesters. 1-year certificate in food service specialist. 1-year certificate in lodging operations. 1-year certificate in food and beverage operations. 2-year associate degree in hotel/restaurant operations. 2-year associate degree in culinary arts.

PROGRAM AFFILIATION

Council on Hotel, Restaurant, and Institutional Education; National Restaurant Association; National Restaurant Association Educational Foundation.

AREAS OF STUDY

Baking; beverage management; controlling costs in food service; culinary skill development; food preparation; food purchasing; food service communication; food service math; garde-manger; international cuisine; kitchen management; management and human resources; meal planning; meat fabrication; menu and facilities design; nutrition and food service; sanitation; saucier; seafood processing; soup, stock, sauce, and starch production; wines and spirits.

FACILITIES

Bake shop; catering service; classroom; computer laboratory; demonstration laboratory; food production kitchen; learning resource center; library; student lounge; teaching kitchen.

TYPICAL STUDENT PROFILE

52 total: 26 full-time; 26 part-time.

SPECIAL PROGRAMS

Culinary competitions through the Maine Restaurant Association, Austria Exchange Program through Maine Technical College System.

FINANCIAL AID

Employment placement assistance is available.

APPLICATION INFORMATION

Students may begin participation in January, May, and September. Applications are accepted continuously. Applicants must submit a formal application, an essay, high school transcript or GED, and take assessment test (administered by college).

CONTACT

Director of Admissions, 112 College Drive, Wells, ME 04090. Telephone: 207-646-9282. Fax: 207-641-0837. World Wide Web: http://www.yccc.edu.

MARYLAND

ALLEGANY COLLEGE OF MARYLAND

School of Hospitality, Tourism, and Culinary Arts

Cumberland, Maryland

GENERAL INFORMATION

Public, coeducational, two-year college. Suburban campus. Founded in 1961. Accredited by Middle States Association of Colleges and Schools.

PROGRAM INFORMATION

Offered since 1998. Program calendar is divided into semesters. 2-term (11 credit) letter of recognition in baking essentials. 2-term (11 credit) letter of recognition in culinary essential. 2-year associate degree in culinary arts.

PROGRAM AFFILIATION

American Culinary Federation; American Dietetic Association.

AREAS OF STUDY

Culinary skill development; kitchen management; restaurant opportunities.

FACILITIES

Bake shop; classroom; computer laboratory; food production kitchen; gourmet dining room; learning resource center; library; public restaurant; student lounge; teaching kitchen.

STUDENT PROFILE

40 total: 16 full-time; 24 part-time. 34 are under 25 years old; 5 are between 25 and 44 years old; 1 is over 44 years old.

FACULTY

8 total: 3 full-time; 5 part-time. 3 are industry professionals. Prominent faculty: Debra Frank, RD; David L. Sanford, CCC; Bill Hand. Faculty-student ratio: 1:13.

SPECIAL PROGRAMS

Responsibility for student-operated restaurant.

TYPICAL EXPENSES

In-state tuition: $2970 per year full-time (in district), $90 per credit hour part-time (in district), $5676 per year full-time (out-of-district), $172 per credit hour part-time (out-of-district). Out-of-state tuition: $6666 per year full-time, $202 per credit hour part-time. Program-related fees include $135 for cutlery kit; $72 for lab fee (per course); $100 for uniform.

FINANCIAL AID

In 2004, 1 scholarship was awarded (award was $1000). Program-specific awards include Culinary Arts is a statewide designated program. Employment placement assistance is available.

HOUSING

Apartment-style housing available. Average on-campus housing cost per month: $500. Average off-campus housing cost per month: $350.

APPLICATION INFORMATION

Students may begin participation in January and August. Applications are accepted continuously. In 2004, 77 applied; 74 were accepted. Applicants must interview; submit a formal application, an essay, separate culinary arts application.

CONTACT

Mrs. Cathy Nolan, Director of Admissions and Registration, School of Hospitality, Tourism, and Culinary Arts, 12401 Willowbrook Road, SE, Cumberland, MD 21502. Telephone: 301-784-5000. Fax: 301-784-5027. E-mail: cnolan@allegany.edu. World Wide Web: http://www.allegany.edu.

ANNE ARUNDEL COMMUNITY COLLEGE

Hospitality, Culinary Arts, and Tourism Institute

Arnold, Maryland

GENERAL INFORMATION

Public, coeducational, two-year college. Suburban campus. Founded in 1961. Accredited by Middle States Association of Colleges and Schools.

PROGRAM INFORMATION

Offered since 1988. Program calendar is divided into semesters. 1-year certificate in catering. 1-year certificate in baking and pastry arts. 1-year certificate in culinary arts option. 1-year certificate in hospitality management option. 2-year associate degree in culinary arts. 2-year associate degree in residential life management. 2-year associate degree in hotel management. 2-year associate degree in food and beverage management. 3-year associate degree in chef apprenticeship with option in pastry chef. 6-month certificate in hotel front desk management.

Anne Arundel Community College *(continued)*

PROGRAM AFFILIATION
American Culinary Federation; Council on Hotel, Restaurant, and Institutional Education; International Food Service Executives Association; National Restaurant Association; National Restaurant Association Educational Foundation; Women Chefs and Restaurateurs.

AREAS OF STUDY
Baking; beverage management; buffet catering; confectionery show pieces; controlling costs in food service; convenience cookery; culinary French; culinary skill development; food preparation; food purchasing; food service math; garde-manger; international cuisine; introduction to food service; kitchen management; management and human resources; meal planning; meat fabrication; menu and facilities design; nutrition; nutrition and food service; patisserie; sanitation; saucier; soup, stock, sauce, and starch production; wines and spirits.

FACILITIES
Bake shop; 5 classrooms; computer laboratory; 4 food production kitchens; learning resource center; student lounge.

TYPICAL STUDENT PROFILE
491 total: 135 full-time; 356 part-time.

SPECIAL PROGRAMS
Junior Culinary Team, international internships, international and national travel study opportunities.

FINANCIAL AID
Employment placement assistance is available. Employment opportunities within the program are available.

APPLICATION INFORMATION
Students may begin participation in January, June, and September. Application deadline for each session: 30 days prior to start of program. Applicants must submit a formal application and letters of reference and essay (for apprenticeship program only).

CONTACT
Director of Admissions, Hospitality, Culinary Arts, and Tourism Institute, 101 College Parkway, Arnold, MD 21012. Telephone: 410-777-2065. Fax: 410-777-1143. World Wide Web: http://www.aacc.cc.md.us.

BALTIMORE INTERNATIONAL COLLEGE

School of Culinary Arts

Baltimore, Maryland

GENERAL INFORMATION
Private, coeducational, four-year college. Urban campus. Founded in 1972. Accredited by Middle States Association of Colleges and Schools.

PROGRAM INFORMATION
Offered since 1972. Program calendar is divided into semesters. 12-month certificate in professional culinary arts. 2-year associate degree in professional cooking and baking. 2-year associate degree in professional cooking. 2-year associate degree in professional baking and pastry. 22-month certificate in culinary arts-evening program. 4-year bachelor's degree in hospitality/business management. 4-year bachelor's degree in hospitality/business management with marketing concentration. 4-year bachelor's degree in culinary management.

PROGRAM AFFILIATION
American Culinary Federation; Council on Hotel, Restaurant, and Institutional Education; International Association of Culinary Professionals; National Restaurant Association.

AREAS OF STUDY
Baking; beverage management; buffet catering; classical cuisine; confectionery show pieces; controlling costs in food service; convenience cookery; culinary skill development; food preparation; food purchasing; food service communication; garde-manger; hotel operations; international cuisine; introduction to food service; kitchen management; management and human resources; marketing; meal planning; meat fabrication; menu and facilities design; nutrition; patisserie; restaurant operations; sanitation; saucier; seafood processing; soup, stock, sauce, and starch production; wines and spirits.

FACILITIES
21 classrooms; 2 computer laboratories; garden; gourmet dining room; learning resource center; library; public restaurant; snack shop; student lounge; 7 teaching kitchens; 2 public hotels; auditorium; student parking lot.

STUDENT PROFILE
800 full-time.

FACULTY
35 total: 15 full-time; 20 part-time. 5 are industry professionals; 1 is a master baker; 9 are culinary-certified teachers. Prominent faculty: Jan Bandula, CMPC, CCE, AAC; Charles Talucci, CEC; Greg Wentz, CEC; Faith Kling, CEC. Faculty-student ratio: 1:18.

SPECIAL PROGRAMS
Externships, participation in honors program at campus in Ireland for qualified students, accelerated programs.

TYPICAL EXPENSES
Application fee: $35. Tuition: $7744 per semester.

FINANCIAL AID
In 2005, 582 scholarships were awarded (average award was $3862). Program-specific awards include scholarships for alumni returning to complete bachelor's degree, Career Opportunity Grant, Leadership Grant. Employment placement assistance is available. Employment opportunities within the program are available.

HOUSING
Coed housing available.

APPLICATION INFORMATION
Students may begin participation in January, May, July, and September. Applications are accepted continuously. Applicants must submit a formal application and submit a formal application, academic transcripts, SAT or ACT scores.

CONTACT
Kristin Ciarlo, Director of Admissions, School of Culinary Arts, 17 Commerce Street, Baltimore, MD 21202-3230. Telephone: 410-752-4710 Ext. 120. Fax: 410-752-3730. E-mail: admissions@bic.edu. World Wide Web: http://www. bic.edu.

See color display following page 188.

L'ACADEMIE DE CUISINE

Gaithersburg, Maryland

GENERAL INFORMATION
Private, coeducational, culinary institute. Suburban campus. Founded in 1976. Accredited by Accrediting Council for Continuing Education and Training.

PROGRAM INFORMATION
Offered since 1976. Program calendar is continuous, year-round. 34-week certificate in pastry arts. 48-week certificate in culinary arts.

PROGRAM AFFILIATION
American Institute of Wine & Food; Confrerie de la Chaine des Rotisseurs; International Association of Culinary Professionals; Les Dames d'Escoffier; National Restaurant Association; National Restaurant Association Educational Foundation; The Bread Bakers Guild of America; Women Chefs and Restaurateurs.

AREAS OF STUDY
Baking; buffet catering; controlling costs in food service; culinary French; culinary skill development; food preparation; food purchasing; food service math; garde-manger; international cuisine; kitchen management; meal planning; meat cutting; meat fabrication; menu and facilities design; nutrition; nutrition and food service; patisserie; sanitation; saucier; seafood processing; soup, stock, sauce, and starch production; wines and spirits.

FACILITIES
Demonstration laboratory; 2 food production kitchens; library; student lounge.

TYPICAL STUDENT PROFILE
100 total: 70 full-time; 30 part-time.

SPECIAL PROGRAMS
1-week culinary tour in Gascony, France.

FINANCIAL AID
Employment placement assistance is available.

APPLICATION INFORMATION
Students may begin participation in January, March, July, and September. Applications are accepted continuously. Applicants must interview; submit a formal application, letters of reference, an essay, resume, proof of high school graduation, and proof of age (18 or older).

CONTACT
Director of Admissions, 16006 Industrial Drive, Gaithersburg, MD 20877-1414. Telephone: 301-670-8670. Fax: 301-670-0450. World Wide Web: http://www. lacademie.com.

UNIVERSITY OF MARYLAND EASTERN SHORE

Department of Hotel and Restaurant Management

Princess Anne, Maryland

GENERAL INFORMATION
Public, coeducational, university. Small-town setting. Founded in 1886. Accredited by Middle States Association of Colleges and Schools.

PROGRAM INFORMATION
Program calendar is divided into semesters. 4-year bachelor's degree in hotel and restaurant management.

PROGRAM AFFILIATION
Council on Hotel, Restaurant, and Institutional Education.

TYPICAL STUDENT PROFILE
150 full-time.

SPECIAL PROGRAMS
Paid internships.

FINANCIAL AID
Employment placement assistance is available.

HOUSING
Coed, apartment-style, and single-sex housing available.

APPLICATION INFORMATION
Students may begin participation in January and September. Application deadline for fall is July 15.

University of Maryland Eastern Shore *(continued)*

Application deadline for spring is December 1. Applicants must submit a formal application and ACT/SAT score, high school/college transcripts.

CONTACT
Director of Admissions, Department of Hotel and Restaurant Management, Richard A. Hanson Center, Room 2100, Princess Anne, MD 21853. Telephone: 410-651-6567. Fax: 410-651-6273. World Wide Web: http://www.umes.edu/hrm.

WOR-WIC COMMUNITY COLLEGE

Hotel/Motel/Restaurant Management

Berlin, Maryland

GENERAL INFORMATION
Public, coeducational, two-year college. Small-town setting. Founded in 1975. Accredited by Middle States Association of Colleges and Schools.

PROGRAM INFORMATION
Offered since 1976. Program calendar is divided into semesters. 1-year certificate in restaurant management. 1-year certificate in hotel/motel management. 2-year associate degree in hotel/motel/restaurant management.

PROGRAM AFFILIATION
Council on Hotel, Restaurant, and Institutional Education; National Restaurant Association; Ocean City Hotel-Motel-Restaurant Association.

AREAS OF STUDY
Beverage management; controlling costs in food service; food preparation; food purchasing; introduction to food service; management and human resources; menu and facilities design; nutrition; sanitation.

FACILITIES
3 classrooms; computer laboratory; learning resource center; 2 lecture rooms; teaching kitchen.

STUDENT PROFILE
70 total: 23 full-time; 47 part-time. 46 are under 25 years old; 20 are between 25 and 44 years old; 4 are over 44 years old.

FACULTY
3 total: 1 full-time; 2 part-time. Prominent faculty: Scott D. Dahlberg, EdD. Faculty-student ratio: 1:23.

SPECIAL PROGRAMS
Trade shows, guest chefs, access to many resort hotels in Ocean City for tours.

TYPICAL EXPENSES
In-state tuition: $876 per semester full-time (in district), $73 per credit hour part-time (in district), $2208 per semester full-time (out-of-district), $184 per credit hour part-time (out-of-district). Out-of-state tuition: $2580 per semester full-time, $215 per credit hour part-time. Program-related fee includes $35 for materials for food preparation class.

FINANCIAL AID
In 2004, 3 scholarships were awarded (average award was $1000).

HOUSING
Average off-campus housing cost per month: $750.

APPLICATION INFORMATION
Students may begin participation in January, May, July, and September. Applications are accepted continuously. In 2004, 114 applied; 114 were accepted. Applicants must submit a formal application.

CONTACT
Richard C. Webster, Director of Admissions, Hotel/Motel/Restaurant Management, 32000 Campus Drive, Salisbury, MD 21804. Telephone: 410-334-2895. Fax: 410-334-2954. E-mail: admissions@worwic.edu. World Wide Web: http://www.worwic.edu.

MASSACHUSETTS

BOSTON UNIVERSITY

Certificate Program in the Culinary Arts

Boston, Massachusetts

GENERAL INFORMATION
Private, coeducational, university. Urban campus. Founded in 1839. Accredited by New England Association of Schools and Colleges.

PROGRAM INFORMATION
Offered since 1989. Program calendar is divided into semesters. 1-year diploma in wine (WSET). 2-year master's degree in gastronomy. 4-month certificate in culinary arts. 8-week certificate in cheese. 8- to 13-week certificate in wine (WSET).

PROGRAM AFFILIATION
American Institute of Wine & Food; Culinary Historians; International Association of Culinary Professionals; James Beard Foundation, Inc.; New England Culinary Guild; Oldways Preservation and Exchange Trust; Women Chefs and Restaurateurs.

AREAS OF STUDY
Baking; buffet catering; confectionery show pieces; controlling costs in food service; convenience cookery; culinary French; culinary skill development; food preparation; food purchasing; garde-manger; international cuisine; introduction to food service; kitchen management; management and human resources; meal planning; meat cutting; menu and facilities design; nutrition; nutrition and

food service; patisserie; restaurant opportunities; sanitation; saucier; seafood processing; soup, stock, sauce, and starch production; wines and spirits.

FACILITIES

4 classrooms; demonstration laboratory; 8 food production kitchens; 8 laboratories; learning resource center; lecture room; library; student lounge; teaching kitchen.

TYPICAL STUDENT PROFILE

1,027 total: 27 full-time; 1000 part-time.

SPECIAL PROGRAMS

Culture and gastronomy tours, certification in wine courses with WSET.

FINANCIAL AID

Employment placement assistance is available. Employment opportunities within the program are available.

APPLICATION INFORMATION

Students may begin participation in January and September. Application deadline for fall is July 16. Application deadline for spring is December 16. Applicants must interview; submit a formal application, an essay, letters of reference, and have prior food industry employment.

CONTACT

Director of Admissions, Certificate Program in the Culinary Arts, 808 Commonwealth Avenue, Boston, MA 02215. Telephone: 617-353-9852. Fax: 617-353-4130. World Wide Web: http://www.bu.edu/lifelong.

BRISTOL COMMUNITY COLLEGE

Culinary Arts Department

Fall River, Massachusetts

GENERAL INFORMATION

Public, coeducational, two-year college. Suburban campus. Founded in 1965. Accredited by New England Association of Schools and Colleges.

PROGRAM INFORMATION

Offered since 1985. Program calendar is divided into semesters. 2-semester certificate of proficiency in bakery for retail outlets. 2-year associate degree in culinary arts.

AREAS OF STUDY

Baking; beverage management; buffet catering; confectionery show pieces; controlling costs in food service; culinary skill development; food preparation; food service math; garde-manger; international cuisine; introduction to food service; meal planning; nutrition; patisserie; sanitation; saucier; soup, stock, sauce, and starch production; wines and spirits.

FACILITIES

Bake shop; cafeteria; catering service; classroom; computer laboratory; food production kitchen; gourmet dining room; learning resource center; lecture room; library; teaching kitchen; bar/lounge.

TYPICAL STUDENT PROFILE

41 total: 39 full-time; 2 part-time.

FINANCIAL AID

Program-specific awards include scholarships for second-year students. Employment placement assistance is available. Employment opportunities within the program are available.

APPLICATION INFORMATION

Students may begin participation in September. Applications are accepted continuously. Applicants must interview; submit a formal application.

CONTACT

Director of Admissions, Culinary Arts Department, 777 Elsbree Street, Fall River, MA 02720-7395. Telephone: 508-678-2811 Ext. 2111. Fax: 508-730-3290. World Wide Web: http://www.bristol.mass.edu.

BUNKER HILL COMMUNITY COLLEGE

Culinary Arts Program

Boston, Massachusetts

GENERAL INFORMATION

Public, coeducational, two-year college. Urban campus. Founded in 1973. Accredited by New England Association of Schools and Colleges.

PROGRAM INFORMATION

Offered since 1978. Program calendar is divided into semesters. 1-year certificate in culinary arts. 2-year associate degree in culinary arts.

PROGRAM AFFILIATION

American Culinary Federation; Council on Hotel, Restaurant, and Institutional Education; Food Service Consultants International; National Restaurant Association; National Restaurant Association Educational Foundation.

Bunker Hill Community College *(continued)*

AREAS OF STUDY

Baking; bar and beverage management; beverage management; buffet catering; café/bistro cuisine; controlling costs in food service; convenience cookery; culinary French; culinary skill development; dining room management; dining room service; food preparation; food purchasing; food service communication; food service math; garde-manger; hospitality law; international cuisine; introduction to food service; kitchen management; management and human resources; meal planning; meat cutting; menu and facilities design; nutrition; nutrition and food service; patisserie; sanitation; saucier; seafood processing; soup, stock, sauce, and starch production; wines and spirits.

FACILITIES

Bake shop; bakery; catering service; classroom; demonstration laboratory; food production kitchen; gourmet dining room; learning resource center; lecture room; library; public restaurant; teaching kitchen.

STUDENT PROFILE

280 total: 252 full-time; 28 part-time.

FACULTY

6 total: 4 full-time; 2 part-time. 2 are industry professionals; 4 are culinary-certified teachers. Faculty-student ratio: 1:12 lab; 1:20 classroom.

SPECIAL PROGRAMS

Culinary competitions.

TYPICAL EXPENSES

Application fee: $10. In-state tuition: $100 per credit; $112 per credit (participants in the New England Regional Student Program) full-time (in district), $100 per credit; $112 per credit (participants in the New England Regional Student Program) part-time. Out-of-state tuition: $306 per credit full-time, $306 per credit part-time. Program-related fees include $150 for knives; $60 for uniforms.

FINANCIAL AID

In 2004, 3 scholarships were awarded (average award was $500). Employment placement assistance is available. Employment opportunities within the program are available.

APPLICATION INFORMATION

Students may begin participation in January and September. Applications are accepted continuously. In 2004, 71 applied. Applicants must submit a formal application.

CONTACT

Cheryl A. Senato, Professor, Culinary Arts Program, 250 New Rutherford Avenue, Boston, MA 02129. Telephone: 617-228-2171. Fax: 617-228-2052. E-mail: csenato@bhcc.mass.edu. World Wide Web: http://www.bhcc.mass.edu.

THE CAMBRIDGE SCHOOL OF CULINARY ARTS

Professional Chef's Program

Cambridge, Massachusetts

GENERAL INFORMATION

Private, coeducational, culinary institute. Urban campus. Founded in 1974. Accredited by Accrediting Commission of Career Schools and Colleges of Technology.

PROGRAM INFORMATION

Offered since 1974. Program calendar is divided into quarters. 15-week certificate in culinary training. 37-week diploma in professional chefs training.

PROGRAM AFFILIATION

American Institute of Wine & Food; International Association of Culinary Professionals; James Beard Foundation, Inc.; National Restaurant Association; Oldways Preservation and Exchange Trust; Women Chefs and Restaurateurs.

AREAS OF STUDY

Baking; buffet catering; confectionery show pieces; controlling costs in food service; convenience cookery; culinary French; culinary skill development; food preparation; food purchasing; food service math; garde-manger; international cuisine; introduction to food service; kitchen management; management and human resources; meal planning; meat cutting; meat fabrication; nutrition; nutrition and food service; patisserie; restaurant opportunities; sanitation; saucier; soup, stock, sauce, and starch production; wines and spirits.

FACILITIES

4 lecture rooms; library; student lounge; 4 teaching kitchens.

TYPICAL STUDENT PROFILE

165 full-time. 36 are under 25 years old; 109 are between 25 and 44 years old; 20 are over 44 years old.

SPECIAL PROGRAMS

International culinary excursions, culinary competitions, externships and internships.

FINANCIAL AID

Program-specific awards include The Anthony Spinazzola Foundation Awards. Employment placement assistance is available. Employment opportunities within the program are available.

APPLICATION INFORMATION

Students may begin participation in January, May, and September. Application deadline for fall is August 1. Application deadline for winter is December 1. Application deadline for spring (certificate) is April 1. Applicants must interview; submit a formal application, letters of reference, an essay, resume, educational records.

CONTACT
Director of Admissions, Professional Chef's Program, 2020 Massachusetts Avenue, Cambridge, MA 02140-2104. Telephone: 617-354-2020. Fax: 617-576-1963. World Wide Web: http://www.cambridgeculinary.com.

CAPE COD COMMUNITY COLLEGE

Hotel and Restaurant Management/Culinary Arts

West Barnstable, Massachusetts

GENERAL INFORMATION
Public, coeducational, two-year college. Small-town setting. Founded in 1961. Accredited by New England Association of Schools and Colleges.

PROGRAM INFORMATION
Offered since 1971. Accredited by Council on Hotel, Restaurant and Institutional Education. Program calendar is divided into semesters. 1-year certificate in culinary arts. 2-year associate degree in hotel/restaurant management.

PROGRAM AFFILIATION
American Culinary Federation; Council on Hotel, Restaurant, and Institutional Education; Les Amis d'Escoffier Society; Massachusetts Restaurant Association; National Restaurant Association.

AREAS OF STUDY
Baking; beverage management; controlling costs in food service; culinary French; culinary skill development; food preparation; food purchasing; food service math; garde-manger; introduction to food service; kitchen management; management and human resources; meal planning; nutrition and food service; sanitation; seafood processing; soup, stock, sauce, and starch production.

FACILITIES
Cafeteria; classroom; coffee shop; computer laboratory; demonstration laboratory; food production kitchen; learning resource center; lecture room; library.

SPECIAL PROGRAMS
Work cooperative experience.

APPLICATION INFORMATION
Students may begin participation in January and September. Applications are accepted continuously. Applicants must submit a formal application and proof of high school graduation or the equivalent.

CONTACT
Director of Admissions, Hotel and Restaurant Management/Culinary Arts, Route 132, West Barnstable, MA 02668. Telephone: 877-846-3672. Fax: 508-362-3988. World Wide Web: http://www.capecod.mass.edu.

ENDICOTT COLLEGE

Hotel and Tourism Administration

Beverly, Massachusetts

GENERAL INFORMATION
Private, coeducational, comprehensive institution. Suburban campus. Founded in 1939. Accredited by New England Association of Schools and Colleges.

PROGRAM INFORMATION
Offered since 1994. Program calendar is divided into semesters. Bachelor's degree in senior community manager. Bachelor's degree in events management. 4-year bachelor's degree in hospitality and tourism administration.

PROGRAM AFFILIATION
American Culinary Federation; American Hotel and Lodging Association; Club Managers Association of America; Council on Hotel, Restaurant, and Institutional Education; International Hotel and Restaurant Association; Massachusetts Restaurant Association; National Restaurant Association; National Restaurant Association Educational Foundation.

AREAS OF STUDY
Beverage management; buffet catering; controlling costs in food service; culinary French; culinary skill development; food preparation; food purchasing; food service communication; garde-manger; international cuisine; introduction to food service; kitchen management; management and human resources; meal planning; menu and facilities design; nutrition; restaurant opportunities; sanitation; soup, stock, sauce, and starch production; wines and spirits.

FACILITIES
Cafeteria; 2 classrooms; computer laboratory; food production kitchen; gourmet dining room; learning resource center; public restaurant; student lounge; teaching kitchen.

STUDENT PROFILE
120 full-time. 115 are under 25 years old; 5 are between 25 and 44 years old.

FACULTY
10 total: 6 full-time; 4 part-time. 5 are industry professionals; 1 is a master chef; 1 is a culinary-certified teacher. Prominent faculty: Brendan Cronin; Peter Jenner; Patricia McCaughey; William H. Samerfink. Faculty-student ratio: 1:15.

SPECIAL PROGRAMS
Community service activities, 1-semester internship, study abroad opportunities.

TYPICAL EXPENSES
Application fee: $40. Tuition: $19,690 per year full-time, $615 per credit part-time. Program-related fee includes $50–$65 for food and wine.

FINANCIAL AID
In 2004, 4 scholarships were awarded (average award was $1500-$2000). Employment placement assistance is available.

HOUSING
Coed, apartment-style, and single-sex housing available. Average on-campus housing cost per month: $856.

APPLICATION INFORMATION
Students may begin participation in February and September. Applications are accepted continuously. In 2004, 151 applied; 91 were accepted. Applicants must submit a formal application, an essay, letters of reference, academic transcripts, and SAT scores.

CONTACT
Thomas Redman, Vice President of Admission and Financial Aid, Hotel and Tourism Administration, 376 Hale Street, Beverly, MA 01915-2096. Telephone: 978-921-1000. Fax: 978-232-2520. E-mail: admissio@endicott.edu. World Wide Web: http://www.endicott.edu/.

INTERNATIONAL INSTITUTE OF CULINARY ARTS

Fall River, Massachusetts

GENERAL INFORMATION
Private, coeducational, culinary institute. Urban campus. Founded in 1997.

PROGRAM INFORMATION
Offered since 1997. Program calendar is divided into semesters. 1-year certificate in culinary. 1-year diploma in baking. 2-year grand diploma in culinary arts/restaurant hospitality.

PROGRAM AFFILIATION
The Bread Bakers Guild of America.

AREAS OF STUDY
Baking; beverage management; buffet catering; confectionery show pieces; controlling costs in food service; convenience cookery; culinary French; culinary skill development; food preparation; food purchasing; food service communication; food service math; garde-manger; international cuisine; introduction to food service; kitchen management; management and human resources; meal planning; meat cutting; meat fabrication; menu and facilities design; nutrition; nutrition and food service; patisserie; restaurant opportunities; sanitation; saucier; seafood processing; soup, stock, sauce, and starch production; wines and spirits.

FACILITIES
Bake shop; 4 classrooms; computer laboratory; 6 food production kitchens; garden; 4 gourmet dining rooms; 5 lecture rooms; 2 libraries; 5 public restaurants; snack shop; student lounge.

STUDENT PROFILE

20 full-time. 18 are under 25 years old; 2 are between 25 and 44 years old.

FACULTY

5 total: 4 full-time; 1 part-time. 4 are industry professionals; 1 is a master chef; 4 are culinary-certified teachers. Prominent faculty: George Karousos, Master Chef; Theodore Karousos, BA; Michael Petit Bon, AD; Robert Castagna, MA. Faculty-student ratio: 1:10.

TYPICAL EXPENSES

Application fee: $45. Tuition: $11,500 per year for grand diploma, diploma, or certificate. Program-related fee includes $1800 for uniform, equipment, fees, publications, commencement and labs.

FINANCIAL AID

In 2005, 10 scholarships were awarded (average award was $11,500); 8 loans were granted (average loan was $11,000). Employment placement assistance is available. Employment opportunities within the program are available.

APPLICATION INFORMATION

Students may begin participation in January and September. Applications are accepted continuously. In 2005, 70 applied; 25 were accepted. Applicants must submit letters of reference, an essay, formal application, letters of reference, and academic transcripts.

CONTACT

Theodore Karousas, Director of Admissions, 100 Rock Street, Fall River, MA 02720. Telephone: 508-675-9305. Fax: 508-678-5214. E-mail: culinaryarts@meganet.net. World Wide Web: http://www.iicaculinary.com.

MASSASOIT COMMUNITY COLLEGE

Culinary Arts Program

Brockton, Massachusetts

GENERAL INFORMATION

Public, coeducational, two-year college. Urban campus. Founded in 1966. Accredited by New England Association of Schools and Colleges.

PROGRAM INFORMATION

Offered since 1982. Program calendar is divided into semesters. 2-semester certificate in food production. 2-year associate degree in culinary arts.

PROGRAM AFFILIATION

National Restaurant Association; National Restaurant Association Educational Foundation.

Massasoit Community College *(continued)*

AREAS OF STUDY
Baking; introduction to food service; soup, stock, sauce, and starch production; storeroom and inventory procedures.

FACILITIES
Bakery; classroom; computer laboratory; demonstration laboratory; food production kitchen; gourmet dining room; lecture room; library; student lounge; teaching kitchen.

STUDENT PROFILE
68 total: 44 full-time; 24 part-time. 50 are under 25 years old; 15 are between 25 and 44 years old; 3 are over 44 years old.

FACULTY
4 total: 4 full-time. 4 are culinary-certified teachers; 1 is a master pastry chef. Faculty-student ratio: 1:13.

TYPICAL EXPENSES
In-state tuition: $1332 per 12 credits full-time (in district), $111 per credit part-time. Out-of-state tuition: $3804 per 12 credits full-time, $317 per credit part-time. Tuition for international students: $3804 per 12 credits full-time, $317 per credit part-time. Program-related fees include $70 for uniforms; $100 for knives.

FINANCIAL AID
Employment placement assistance is available.

APPLICATION INFORMATION
Students may begin participation in January and September. Applications are accepted continuously. Applicants must submit a formal application.

CONTACT
Michelle Hughes, Director of Admissions, Culinary Arts Program, One Massasoit Boulevard, Brockton, MA 02402-3996. Telephone: 508-588-9100 Ext. 1411. E-mail: admoffice@massasoit.mass.edu. World Wide Web: http://www.massasoit.mass.edu.

MIDDLESEX COMMUNITY COLLEGE

Lowell, Massachusetts

GENERAL INFORMATION
Public, coeducational, two-year college. Urban campus. Founded in 1970. Accredited by New England Association of Schools and Colleges.

PROGRAM INFORMATION
Accredited by NEASC. Program calendar is divided into semesters. 1-year certificate in culinary arts. 2-year associate degree in hospitality management-culinary arts option.

PROGRAM AFFILIATION
Council on Hotel, Restaurant, and Institutional Education; National Restaurant Association; National Restaurant Association Educational Foundation.

AREAS OF STUDY
Baking; beverage management; buffet catering; confectionery show pieces; culinary skill development; food preparation; food purchasing; food service math; introduction to food service; kitchen management; management and human resources; menu and facilities design; nutrition and food service; patisserie; sanitation; soup, stock, sauce, and starch production; wines and spirits.

FACILITIES
Bake shop; bakery; classroom; computer laboratory; demonstration laboratory; food production kitchen; lecture room; library.

STUDENT PROFILE
25 total: 20 full-time; 5 part-time. 20 are under 25 years old; 5 are between 25 and 44 years old.

FACULTY
13 total: 9 full-time; 4 part-time. 4 are industry professionals; 2 are culinary-certified teachers. Prominent faculty: Barbara Dexter-Smith, CTC; Scott Plath; Meg Castello. Faculty-student ratio: 1:20.

TYPICAL EXPENSES
In-state tuition: $3300 per 1 academic year full-time (in district), $1650 per 1 academic year part-time. Out-of-state tuition: $7858 per 1 academic year full-time, $3929 per 1 academic year part-time. Tuition for international students: $7858 per 1 academic year full-time, $3929 per 1 academic year part-time. Program-related fee includes $100 for uniform.

FINANCIAL AID
Program-specific awards include local industry scholarships-through the Massachusetts Lodging Association. Employment placement assistance is available. Employment opportunities within the program are available.

APPLICATION INFORMATION
Students may begin participation in January and September. Application deadline for fall is September 6. In 2004, 25 applied; 25 were accepted. Applicants must submit a formal application.

CONTACT
Barbara Dexter-Smith, Program Coordinator, Hospitality, Travel and Culinary Arts, 33, Kearney Square, Lowell, MA 01852-1987. Telephone: 978-656-3170. Fax: 978-656-3150. E-mail: dextersmithb@middlesex.mass.edu. World Wide Web: http://www.middlesex.mass.edu.

NEWBURY COLLEGE

Brookline, Massachusetts

GENERAL INFORMATION
Private, coeducational, four-year college. Suburban campus. Founded in 1962. Accredited by New England Association of Schools and Colleges.

PROGRAM INFORMATION
Offered since 1983. Accredited by Council on Hotel, Restaurant and Institutional Education. Program calendar is divided into semesters. 11-month certificate in hotel and resort management. 11-month certificate in pastry arts. 11-month certificate in buffet catering. 11-month certificate in food service and restaurant management. 2-year associate degree in food service and restaurant management. 2-year associate degree in hotel and resort management. 2-year associate degree in culinary arts. 4-year bachelor's degree in culinary management. 4-year bachelor's degree in hotel, restaurant, and service management.

PROGRAM AFFILIATION
Council on Hotel, Restaurant, and Institutional Education; National Restaurant Association Educational Foundation; Retailer's Bakery Association.

AREAS OF STUDY
Baking; buffet catering; controlling costs in food service; culinary French; culinary skill development; food preparation; food purchasing; garde-manger; international cuisine; introduction to food service; meal planning; meat cutting; menu and facilities design; nutrition; patisserie; sanitation; saucier; soup, stock, sauce, and starch production; wines and spirits.

FACILITIES
2 bake shops; cafeteria; 3 computer laboratories; 2 food production kitchens; gourmet dining room; learning resource center; library; student lounge; 6 teaching kitchens.

STUDENT PROFILE
320 total: 200 full-time; 120 part-time.

FACULTY
17 total: 6 full-time; 11 part-time. 17 are industry professionals. Prominent faculty: Damon Revelas, Dean. Faculty-student ratio: 1:15.

SPECIAL PROGRAMS
1-2 year internship, Boston Food Show, operation of college's own restaurant.

Creating Culinary Careers!

The School of
Arts, Science and Technology

The School of
Business and Management

The Roger A. Saunders
School of Hotel and
Restaurant Management

Culinary Arts

Culinary Management

Food Service &
Restaurant Management

Hotel Administration

Hotel & Resort
Management

Newbury College
129 Fisher Avenue
Brookline, MA 02445
www.newbury.edu
1-800-NEWBURY

NEWBURY
COLLEGE

Why Newbury?
- Excellent location, with access to Boston's finest restaurants and hotels.
- Taught by chefs, each with at least 10 years of Newbury experience.
- Professional hands-on environment.
- Small classes in fully-equipped teaching kitchens.
- 96% placement in excellent positions in the field.

Newbury College *(continued)*

TYPICAL EXPENSES
Application fee: $50. Tuition: $17,000 per year full-time, $300 per credit hour part-time. Program-related fee includes $500 for culinary arts uniforms and tools.

FINANCIAL AID
In 2004, 4 scholarships were awarded (average award was $4000). Employment placement assistance is available.

HOUSING
Coed housing available. Average on-campus housing cost per month: $650. Average off-campus housing cost per month: $700.

APPLICATION INFORMATION
Students may begin participation in January and September. Applications are accepted continuously. In 2004, 1000 applied; 950 were accepted. Applicants must submit a formal application, letters of reference, an essay, transcripts.

CONTACT
Salvadore Liberto, Vice President of Enrollment, 129 Fisher Avenue, Brookline, MA 02445. Telephone: 617-730-7007. Fax: 617-731-9618. E-mail: info@newbury.edu. World Wide Web: http://www.newbury.edu.

NORTH SHORE COMMUNITY COLLEGE

Culinary Arts and Food Science

Danvers, Massachusetts

GENERAL INFORMATION
Public, coeducational, two-year college. Suburban campus. Founded in 1965. Accredited by New England Association of Schools and Colleges.

PROGRAM INFORMATION
Offered since 1965. Program calendar is divided into semesters. 1-year certificate in culinary arts and food science. 2-year associate degree in culinary arts and food science.

PROGRAM AFFILIATION
American Institute of Baking; Massachusetts Restaurant Association.

AREAS OF STUDY
Baking; beverage management; buffet catering; confectionery show pieces; controlling costs in food service; culinary skill development; food preparation; food purchasing; food service communication; food service math; garde-manger; international cuisine; introduction to food service; kitchen management; management and human resources; meal planning; meat cutting; meat fabrication; menu and facilities design; nutrition; nutrition

and food service; patisserie; restaurant opportunities; sanitation; soup, stock, sauce, and starch production.

FACILITIES
Bake shop; 5 classrooms; computer laboratory; 3 demonstration laboratories; food production kitchen; 4 laboratories; learning resource center; 3 lecture rooms; library; public restaurant; student lounge; teaching kitchen.

TYPICAL STUDENT PROFILE
40 full-time.

FINANCIAL AID
Employment placement assistance is available.

APPLICATION INFORMATION
Students may begin participation in January and September. Application deadline for fall is September 5. Application deadline for spring is January 21. Applicants must submit a formal application.

CONTACT
Director of Admissions, Culinary Arts and Food Science, One Ferncroft Road, PO Box 3340, Danvers, MA 01923. Telephone: 978-762-4000 Ext. 4356. Fax: 978-762-4015. World Wide Web: http://www.nscc.mass.edu.

MICHIGAN

BAKER COLLEGE OF MUSKEGON

Culinary Arts and Food and Beverage Management

Muskegon, Michigan

GENERAL INFORMATION
Private, coeducational, four-year college. Suburban campus. Founded in 1888. Accredited by North Central Association of Colleges and Schools.

PROGRAM INFORMATION
Offered since 1997. Accredited by American Culinary Federation Accrediting Commission. Program calendar is divided into quarters. 1-year certificate in baking and pastry. 2-year associate degree in food and beverage management. 2-year associate degree in culinary arts. 4-year bachelor's degree in food and beverage management.

PROGRAM AFFILIATION
American Culinary Federation; Council on Hotel, Restaurant, and Institutional Education; National Restaurant Association; National Restaurant Association Educational Foundation; Tasters Guild International.

AREAS OF STUDY
Baking; beverage management; buffet catering; confectionery show pieces; controlling costs in food service; convenience cookery; culinary French; culinary skill development; food preparation; food purchasing; food

service math; garde-manger; international cuisine; introduction to food service; kitchen management; management and human resources; meal planning; meat cutting; meat fabrication; menu and facilities design; nutrition; nutrition and food service; patisserie; restaurant opportunities; sanitation; saucier; seafood processing; soup, stock, sauce, and starch production; wines and spirits.

FACILITIES
Bake shop; catering service; 5 classrooms; 10 computer laboratories; demonstration laboratory; food production kitchen; garden; gourmet dining room; learning resource center; 105 lecture rooms; library; public restaurant; student lounge; teaching kitchen.

STUDENT PROFILE
330 full-time.

FACULTY
20 total: 3 full-time; 17 part-time. 7 are industry professionals; 2 are culinary-certified teachers. Prominent faculty: Robb White, CEC; Luis Amado, CEPC. Faculty-student ratio: 1:8.

SPECIAL PROGRAMS
Culinary competitions, ice carving, international competitions and overseas excursions.

TYPICAL EXPENSES
Application fee: $20. Tuition: $100–$180 per credit hour. Program-related fees include $425 for cutlery; $150 for uniforms.

FINANCIAL AID
In 2004, individual scholarships were awarded at $2000. Program-specific awards include National Restaurant Association scholarships ($2000), Warren A. Husid Memorial Scholarships ($2000). Employment placement assistance is available. Employment opportunities within the program are available.

HOUSING
Coed and apartment-style housing available. Average off-campus housing cost per month: $600–$700.

APPLICATION INFORMATION
Students may begin participation in January, April, and September. Applications are accepted continuously. In 2004, 112 applied; 112 were accepted. Applicants must submit a formal application and have high school diploma or GED.

CONTACT
Kathy Jacobson, Vice President of Admissions, Culinary Arts and Food and Beverage Management, 1903 Marquette Avenue, Muskegon, MT 49442. Telephone: 231-777-5207. Fax: 231-777-5256. E-mail: kathy.jacobson@baker.edu. World Wide Web: http://www.baker.edu.

CENTRAL MICHIGAN UNIVERSITY

Mt. Pleasant, Michigan

GENERAL INFORMATION
Public, coeducational, university. Small-town setting. Founded in 1892. Accredited by North Central Association of Colleges and Schools.

PROGRAM INFORMATION
Offered since 1892. Accredited by American Dietetic Association. Program calendar is divided into semesters. 4-year bachelor's degree in food service administration. 4-year bachelor's degree in hospitality services administration-hospitality services.

PROGRAM AFFILIATION
American Vegan Society; International Food Service Executives Association.

AREAS OF STUDY
Beverage management; food preparation; food purchasing; food service communication; management and human resources; meal planning; menu and facilities design; nutrition; nutrition and food service; sanitation.

FACILITIES
Catering service; 14 classrooms; coffee shop; 8 computer laboratories; 17 lecture rooms; library.

STUDENT PROFILE
70 total: 63 full-time; 7 part-time. 64 are under 25 years old; 6 are between 25 and 44 years old.

FACULTY
9 total: 9 full-time. Prominent faculty: Wesley Luckhardt, RD; Christine Henries-Zerbe, RD. Faculty-student ratio: 1:7.

SPECIAL PROGRAMS
Food service internship, hospitality internship.

TYPICAL EXPENSES
Application fee: $35. In-state tuition: $5868 per 2 semesters full-time (in district), $195.60 per credit hour part-time. Out-of-state tuition: $13,632 per 2 semesters full-time, $454.40 per credit hour part-time.

FINANCIAL AID
Employment placement assistance is available.

HOUSING
Coed, apartment-style, and single-sex housing available. Average on-campus housing cost per month: $708. Average off-campus housing cost per month: $550.

APPLICATION INFORMATION
Students may begin participation in January, May, July, and August. Applications are accepted continuously. Applicants must submit a formal application and have high school diploma or GED.

CONTACT
Betty Wagner, Director of Admissions, Warriner Hall 102, Mt. Pleasant, MI 48859. Telephone: 989-774-3076. Fax:

Central Michigan University *(continued)*

989-774-7267. E-mail: cmuadmit@cmich.edu. World Wide Web: http://nutrition.cmich.edu.

FERRIS STATE UNIVERSITY

Hospitality Programs

Big Rapids, Michigan

GENERAL INFORMATION
Public, coeducational, comprehensive institution. Small-town setting. Founded in 1884. Accredited by North Central Association of Colleges and Schools.

PROGRAM INFORMATION
Offered since 1963. Program calendar is divided into semesters. 2-year associate degree in restaurant food industry management. 4-class certificate in club management. 4-class certificate in hotel management. 4-class certificate in restaurant food industry management. 4-year bachelor's degree in hotel management.

PROGRAM AFFILIATION
American Hotel and Motel Association; Council on Hotel, Restaurant, and Institutional Education; International Food Service Executives Association; National Restaurant Association; National Restaurant Association Educational Foundation.

AREAS OF STUDY
Beverage management; buffet catering; club management; facilities operations management; lodging.

FACILITIES
Classroom; computer laboratory; demonstration laboratory; food production kitchen; laboratory; learning resource center; lecture room; library; teaching kitchen.

TYPICAL STUDENT PROFILE
125 total: 100 full-time; 25 part-time. 105 are under 25 years old; 19 are between 25 and 44 years old; 1 is over 44 years old.

SPECIAL PROGRAMS
2-6 month paid internships, Salute to Excellence, 3-day tour of Chicago's restaurants and hotels.

FINANCIAL AID
Employment placement assistance is available. Employment opportunities within the program are available.

HOUSING
Coed, apartment-style, and single-sex housing available.

APPLICATION INFORMATION
Students may begin participation in January, May, and August. Applications are accepted continuously. Applicants must submit a formal application.

CONTACT
Director of Admissions, Hospitality Programs, 1319 Cramer Circle, W-C, Big Rapids, MI 49307. Telephone: 231-591-2385. Fax: 231-591-2998. World Wide Web: http://www.ferris.edu/hospitality.

GRAND RAPIDS COMMUNITY COLLEGE

Hospitality Education Department

Grand Rapids, Michigan

GENERAL INFORMATION
Public, coeducational, two-year college. Urban campus. Founded in 1914. Accredited by North Central Association of Colleges and Schools.

PROGRAM INFORMATION
Offered since 1980. Accredited by American Culinary Federation Accrediting Commission, American Culinary Federation. Program calendar is divided into semesters. 12-month certificate in baking and pastry arts. 21-month associate degree in culinary arts. 21-month associate degree in culinary management.

PROGRAM AFFILIATION
American Culinary Federation; American Institute of Baking; American Vegan Society; Confrerie de la Chaine des Rotisseurs; Council on Hotel, Restaurant, and Institutional Education; Foodservice Educators Network International; International Food Service Executives Association; National Restaurant Association; National Restaurant Association Educational Foundation; North American Vegetarian Society; Retailer's Bakery Association; Society of Wine Educators; Tasters Guild International.

AREAS OF STUDY
Baking; beverage management; buffet catering; cake decorating; confectionery show pieces; controlling costs in food service; culinary skill development; deli-bakery operations; food preparation; food purchasing; food service math; garde-manger; ice carving; international cuisine; introduction to food service; kitchen management; management and human resources; meat fabrication; menu and facilities design; nutrition; nutrition and food service; patisserie; restaurant opportunities; sanitation; saucier; seafood processing; soup, stock, sauce, and starch production; table service; vegetarian and vegan cooking; wines and spirits.

FACILITIES
3 bake shops; cafeteria; catering service; 3 classrooms; coffee shop; computer laboratory; 2 demonstration laboratories; 3 food production kitchens; garden; 3 gourmet dining rooms; learning resource center; 3 lecture rooms; library; public restaurant; snack shop; student lounge; 6 teaching kitchens; 6 banquet rooms; beverage lab; wine education classroom.

Grand Rapids Community College Hospitality Education

the choice is yours...

Hospitality Education students choose from among three programs:

Baking and Pastry Arts

Our certificate-granting program can prepare you for a rewarding
career as a baker, pastry chef, deli-bakery manager or the proprietor
of your own bakery.

Culinary Arts or Culinary Management

Our associate degree-granting programs in Applied Arts and Sciences
can prepare you for an exciting career as a food and beverage director,
executive chef, caterer, or the proprietor of your own foodservice operation.

Grand Rapids
Community
College

- See our listing in this edition of *Peterson's Culinary Schools*
- Visit our Web Site – www.grcc.edu
- Contact us for more information at (616) 234-3690
- Visit our Center for Culinary Education, 151 Fountain St, NE
  Grand Rapids, MI 49503-3263

Grand Rapids Community College is an equal opportunity institution.

Grand Rapids Community College *(continued)*

STUDENT PROFILE
495 total: 300 full-time; 195 part-time. 352 are under 25 years old; 118 are between 25 and 44 years old; 25 are over 44 years old.

FACULTY
22 total: 12 full-time; 10 part-time. 17 are industry professionals; 2 are master chefs; 2 are culinary-certified teachers. Prominent faculty: Robert Garlough; Jim Muth; Angus Campbell; Randy Sahajdack. Faculty-student ratio: 1:18.

SPECIAL PROGRAMS
International exchange program, international culinary study tours, culinary competition.

TYPICAL EXPENSES
Application fee: $20. In-state tuition: $73.50 per contact hour full-time (in district), $73.50 per contact hour part-time (in district), $142 per contact hour full-time (out-of-district), $142 per contact hour part-time (out-of-district). Out-of-state tuition: $202 per contact hour full-time, $202 per contact hour part-time. Program-related fees include $260 for knife kit; $300 for uniforms; $1000 for textbooks.

FINANCIAL AID
In 2005, 19 scholarships were awarded (average award was $1000). Employment placement assistance is available. Employment opportunities within the program are available.

HOUSING
Average off-campus housing cost per month: $400.

APPLICATION INFORMATION
Students may begin participation in January and September. Applications are accepted continuously. In 2005, 170 applied; 160 were accepted. Applicants must submit a formal application and ASSET or ACT scores.

CONTACT
Mr. Randy Sahajdack, Program Director, Hospitality Education Department, 143 Paostwick, NE, Grand Rapids, MI 49503. Telephone: 616-234-3690. Fax: 616-234-3698. E-mail: marp@grcc.edu. World Wide Web: http://www.grcc.edu.

See display on page 205.

HENRY FORD COMMUNITY COLLEGE

Hospitality Studies/Culinary Arts and Hotel Restaurant Management

Dearborn, Michigan

GENERAL INFORMATION
Public, coeducational, two-year college. Suburban campus. Founded in 1938. Accredited by North Central Association of Colleges and Schools.

PROGRAM INFORMATION
Offered since 1972. Accredited by American Culinary Federation Accrediting Commission. Program calendar is divided into semesters. 1-year certificate in hospitality professional management. 1-year certificate in hospitality service career. 1-year certificate in culinary arts supervisor. 1-year certificate in culinary skills. 1-year certificate in culinary/baking. 2-year associate degree in culinary arts. 2-year associate degree in hotel/restaurant management.

PROGRAM AFFILIATION
American Culinary Federation; American Institute of Baking; Council on Hotel, Restaurant, and Institutional Education; International Food Service Executives Association; Michigan Lodging and Tourism Association; Michigan Restaurant Association; National Restaurant Association; National Restaurant Association Educational Foundation.

AREAS OF STUDY
Baking; beverage management; confectionery show pieces; controlling costs in food service; culinary skill development; food preparation; food purchasing; food service communication; food service math; garde-manger; international cuisine; introduction to food service; kitchen management; management and human resources; meal planning; meat cutting; meat fabrication; menu and facilities design; nutrition; patisserie; sanitation; saucier; seafood processing; soup, stock, sauce, and starch production; wines and spirits.

FACILITIES
Bake shop; bakery; cafeteria; catering service; classroom; computer laboratory; 2 food production kitchens; gourmet dining room; laboratory; learning resource center; lecture room; library; public restaurant; snack shop; student lounge; teaching kitchen.

STUDENT PROFILE
225 full-time.

FACULTY
18 total: 6 full-time; 12 part-time. 6 are industry professionals; 2 are master bakers; 4 are culinary-certified teachers; 1 is a sanitarian. Prominent faculty: Richard Teeple, CEC, CCE; Eric Gackenback, CEC; Jeff Click; Mark Scofield, CEC.

SPECIAL PROGRAMS
Culinary competitions, ice carving.

TYPICAL EXPENSES

Application fee: $30. In-state tuition: $855 per semester full-time (in district), $57 per credit hour part-time (in district), $1568 per semester full-time (out-of-district), $112 per credit hour part-time (out-of-district). Out-of-state tuition: $1680 per semester full-time, $120 per credit hour part-time. Program-related fees include $100 for uniforms; $300 for lab fee; $108 for service fee; $24 for technology fee.

FINANCIAL AID

In 2004, 8 scholarships were awarded (average award was $500); 100 loans were granted (average loan was $3000). Employment placement assistance is available. Employment opportunities within the program are available.

HOUSING

Average off-campus housing cost per month: $350–$400.

APPLICATION INFORMATION

Students may begin participation in January, May, July, and August. Applications are accepted continuously. In 2004, 175 applied; 175 were accepted. Applicants must submit a formal application and have a high school diploma or GED.

CONTACT

Dennis Konarski, Culinary Director, Hospitality Studies/Culinary Arts and Hotel Restaurant Management, 5101 Evergreen Road, Dearborn, MI 48128-1495. Telephone: 313-845-6390. Fax: 313-845-9784. E-mail: dennis@hfcc.edu. World Wide Web: http://www.henryford.cc.mi.us/.

MACOMB COMMUNITY COLLEGE

Macomb Culinary Institute

Clinton Township, Michigan

GENERAL INFORMATION

Public, coeducational, two-year college. Suburban campus. Founded in 1954.

PROGRAM INFORMATION

Offered since 1969. Accredited by American Culinary Federation. Program calendar is divided into semesters. 1-year certificate in culinary management. 1-year certificate in pastry arts. 2-year associate degree in culinary arts. 2-year associate degree in hospitality management. 2-year associate degree in restaurant management. 2-year certificate in certified culinarian.

PROGRAM AFFILIATION

American Culinary Federation; Council on Hotel, Restaurant, and Institutional Education; Michigan Restaurant Association; National Restaurant Association; National Restaurant Association Educational Foundation.

AREAS OF STUDY

Baking; beverage management; buffet catering; confectionery show pieces; controlling costs in food service; culinary skill development; food preparation; food purchasing; food service communication; food service math; garde-manger; international cuisine; kitchen management; management and human resources; meal planning; meat cutting; meat fabrication; menu and facilities design; nutrition; nutrition and food service; patisserie; restaurant opportunities; sanitation; saucier; seafood processing; soup, stock, sauce, and starch production; wines and spirits.

FACILITIES

Bake shop; 4 classrooms; computer laboratory; demonstration laboratory; food production kitchen; gourmet dining room; learning resource center; lecture room; library; public restaurant; student lounge; 3 teaching kitchens.

STUDENT PROFILE

320 total: 160 full-time; 160 part-time.

FACULTY

16 total: 4 full-time; 12 part-time. 8 are industry professionals; 8 are culinary-certified teachers; 1 is a ServSafe-Alcohol. Prominent faculty: David F. Schneider, CEC, CCE; Francois Faloppa, CEPC, CCE; Jeff Wolf; Scott O'Farrell, CEC, CEPC, CCA. Faculty-student ratio: 1:30 lecture; 1:15 lab.

SPECIAL PROGRAMS

Apprenticeship program with ACF Blue Water Chefs Association, IKA Culinary Olympics (every 4 years); Hot/Cold/Ice/Gingerbread/Skills USA competitions, culinary tour of France.

TYPICAL EXPENSES

In-state tuition: $68 per credit hour (in district), $104 per credit hour (out-of-district). Out-of-state tuition: $135 per credit hour. Program-related fees include $130 for kitchen classes; $150 for cutlery; $60 for uniforms.

FINANCIAL AID

In 2005, 3 scholarships were awarded (average award was $300). Employment placement assistance is available. Employment opportunities within the program are available.

HOUSING

Average off-campus housing cost per month: $600–$800.

APPLICATION INFORMATION

Students may begin participation in January and August. Applications are accepted continuously. Applicants must submit a formal application.

CONTACT

David F. Schneider, Department Coordinator, Macomb Culinary Institute, 44575 Garfield Road, Clinton Township, MI 48038. Telephone: 586-286-2088. Fax: 586-226-4725. World Wide Web: http://www.macomb.edu.

MICHIGAN STATE UNIVERSITY

The School of Hospitality Business

East Lansing, Michigan

GENERAL INFORMATION
Public, coeducational, university. Suburban campus. Founded in 1855. Accredited by North Central Association of Colleges and Schools.

PROGRAM INFORMATION
Offered since 1927. Program calendar is divided into semesters. 1- to 2-year master's degree in foodservice management. 2-year master of business administration in hospitality business. 4-year bachelor's degree in hospitality business.

PROGRAM AFFILIATION
American Culinary Federation; American Hotel and Lodging Association; Council on Hotel, Restaurant, and Institutional Education; International Association of Culinary Professionals; International Food Service Executives Association; National Restaurant Association; Society for Foodservice Management; Society of Wine Educators.

AREAS OF STUDY
Accounting; beverage management; controlling costs in food service; finance; food preparation; food purchasing; food service math; foodservice management; human resource management; introduction to food service; kitchen management; management and human resources; marketing; nutrition and food service; restaurant opportunities; sanitation; wines and spirits.

FACILITIES
6 classrooms; 4 computer laboratories; demonstration laboratory; 2 food production kitchens; gourmet dining room.

FACULTY
13 total: 11 full-time; 2 part-time. 1 is an industry professional; 2 are culinary-certified teachers; 2 are certified food and beverage executives; 1 is a certified chef. Prominent faculty: Robert Nelson, CEC, CCE, CFBE; Michael Kasavana, PhD; Ray Schmidgall, PhD; Ronald Cichy, PhD, CFBE. Faculty-student ratio: 1:30.

SPECIAL PROGRAMS
Paid internships, student club visits to program-related venues.

TYPICAL EXPENSES
Application fee: $30. In-state tuition: $197–$291 per credit hour. Out-of-state tuition: $529–$589 per credit hour.

FINANCIAL AID
Program-specific awards include industry-sponsored scholarships. Employment placement assistance is available. Employment opportunities within the program are available.

HOUSING
Coed, apartment-style, and single-sex housing available. Average on-campus housing cost per month: $300–$600.

APPLICATION INFORMATION
Students may begin participation in January, May, and August. Applications are accepted continuously. Applicants must submit a formal application, an essay, letters of reference, and SAT, GRE, or GMAT scores.

CONTACT
Dr. Ronald F. Cichy, Director, The School of Hospitality Business, 232 Eppley Center, East Lansing, MI 48824-1121. Telephone: 517-355-5080. E-mail: cichy@msu.edu. World Wide Web: http://www.bus.msu.edu/shb/.

MOTT COMMUNITY COLLEGE

Culinary Arts Program

Flint, Michigan

GENERAL INFORMATION
Public, coeducational, two-year college. Urban campus. Founded in 1923. Accredited by North Central Association of Colleges and Schools.

PROGRAM INFORMATION
Offered since 1984. Program calendar is divided into semesters. 1-year certificate in baking and pastry arts. 2-year associate degree in culinary arts. 2-year associate degree in food service management.

PROGRAM AFFILIATION
Flint/Saginaw Valley Chefs Association; National Restaurant Association; National Restaurant Association Educational Foundation.

AREAS OF STUDY
À la carte dining; baking; beverage management; controlling costs in food service; culinary skill development; food preparation; food purchasing; food service math; garde-manger; introduction to food service; kitchen management; management and human resources; meal planning; meat cutting; meat fabrication; menu and facilities design; nutrition; patisserie; sanitation; specialty desserts.

FACILITIES
Bake shop; cafeteria; catering service; 5 classrooms; computer laboratory; demonstration laboratory; food production kitchen; gourmet dining room; laboratory.

TYPICAL STUDENT PROFILE
170 total: 115 full-time; 55 part-time.

SPECIAL PROGRAMS
Internships, culinary competitions.

FINANCIAL AID
Employment placement assistance is available. Employment opportunities within the program are available.

APPLICATION INFORMATION
Students may begin participation in January and September. Applications are accepted continuously. Applicants must submit a formal application.

CONTACT
Director of Admissions, Culinary Arts Program, 1401 East Court Street, Flint, MI 48503-2089. Telephone: 810-232-7845. Fax: 810-232-6744. World Wide Web: http://www.mcc.edu/.

NORTHERN MICHIGAN UNIVERSITY

Hospitality Management

Marquette, Michigan

GENERAL INFORMATION
Public, coeducational, comprehensive institution. Rural campus. Founded in 1899. Accredited by North Central Association of Colleges and Schools.

PROGRAM INFORMATION
Offered since 1980. Program calendar is divided into semesters. 2-year associate degree in food service management. 4-year bachelor's degree in hospitality management.

PROGRAM AFFILIATION
American Culinary Federation; American Institute of Baking; Council on Hotel, Restaurant, and Institutional Education; National Restaurant Association; National Restaurant Association Educational Foundation.

AREAS OF STUDY
Hotel and restaurant management; kitchen management.

FACILITIES
Bake shop; cafeteria; catering service; 4 classrooms; computer laboratory; food production kitchen; garden; 3 laboratories; learning resource center; library; public restaurant; teaching kitchen.

STUDENT PROFILE
160 total: 140 full-time; 20 part-time. 75 are under 25 years old; 25 are between 25 and 44 years old.

FACULTY
4 total: 3 full-time; 1 part-time. 4 are industry professionals; 2 are culinary-certified teachers. Prominent faculty: Christopher Kibit, CCE, CHE; Yvonne Lee, CHE; Leslie Cory; Deborah Pearce. Faculty-student ratio: 1:20.

SPECIAL PROGRAMS
Paid internships, international study.

TYPICAL EXPENSES
Application fee: $25. In-state tuition: $222 per credit hour. Out-of-state tuition: $320 per credit hour. Program-related fee includes $100 for uniforms.

FINANCIAL AID
In 2004, 6 scholarships were awarded (average award was $500). Program-specific awards include ProMgmt. Scholarships, ACF Upper Michigan Chapter scholarships, Thaddeus Bogdan scholarships. Employment placement assistance is available. Employment opportunities within the program are available.

HOUSING
Coed, apartment-style, and single-sex housing available. Average off-campus housing cost per month: $350.

APPLICATION INFORMATION
Students may begin participation in January and August. Application deadline for fall is July 1. Application deadline for spring is November 1. In 2004, 47 applied; 47 were accepted. Applicants must submit a formal application.

CONTACT
Kathy Solka, Administrative Assistant, Hospitality Management, 1401 Presque Isle Avenue, Marquette, MI 49855-5366. Telephone: 906-227-2135. Fax: 906-227-1549. E-mail: ksolka@nmu.edu. World Wide Web: http://www.nmu.edu/.

NORTHWESTERN MICHIGAN COLLEGE

Great Lakes Culinary Institute

Traverse City, Michigan

GENERAL INFORMATION
Public, coeducational, two-year college. Small-town setting. Founded in 1951. Accredited by North Central Association of Colleges and Schools.

PROGRAM INFORMATION
Offered since 1992. Accredited by American Culinary Federation Accrediting Commission. Program calendar is divided into semesters. 2-year associate degree in culinary arts.

PROGRAM AFFILIATION
American Culinary Federation; Council on Hotel, Restaurant, and Institutional Education; National Restaurant Association; National Restaurant Association Educational Foundation; Tasters Guild International.

AREAS OF STUDY
Baking; buffet catering; controlling costs in food service; culinary skill development; food preparation; food purchasing; food service communication; food service math; garde-manger; international cuisine; introduction to food service; kitchen management; management and

Northwestern Michigan College *(continued)*

human resources; meal planning; nutrition; nutrition and food service; patisserie; sanitation; soup, stock, sauce, and starch production.

FACILITIES
Bake shop; bakery; cafeteria; catering service; 3 classrooms; 2 computer laboratories; demonstration laboratory; food production kitchen; laboratory; 2 learning resource centers; 2 lecture rooms; library; public restaurant; student lounge; teaching kitchen; vineyard.

TYPICAL STUDENT PROFILE
130 total: 100 full-time; 30 part-time.

SPECIAL PROGRAMS
6-month paid internship.

FINANCIAL AID
Program-specific awards include industry scholarships. Employment placement assistance is available. Employment opportunities within the program are available.

HOUSING
Coed, apartment-style, and single-sex housing available.

APPLICATION INFORMATION
Students may begin participation in January and August. Application deadline for fall is August 15. Application deadline for spring is December 15. Applicants must submit a formal application.

CONTACT
Director of Admissions, Great Lakes Culinary Institute, 1701 East Front Street, Traverse City, MI 49686-3061. Telephone: 800-748-0566 Ext. 1197. Fax: 231-995-1134. World Wide Web: http://www.nmc.edu/.

NORTHWOOD UNIVERSITY

Hotel, Restaurant, and Resort Management

Midland, Michigan

GENERAL INFORMATION
Private, coeducational, four-year college. Suburban campus. Founded in 1959. Accredited by North Central Association of Colleges and Schools.

PROGRAM INFORMATION
Offered since 1966. Program calendar is divided into quarters. 2-year associate degree in hotel/restaurant/resort management. 4-year bachelor's degree in hotel/restaurant/resort management.

PROGRAM AFFILIATION
Council on Hotel, Restaurant, and Institutional Education; Institute of Food Technologists; National Restaurant Association; National Restaurant Association Educational Foundation.

AREAS OF STUDY
Beverage management; food preparation; food purchasing; introduction to food service; kitchen management; management and human resources; meal planning; menu and facilities design; nutrition; sanitation; wines and spirits.

FACILITIES
Classroom; demonstration laboratory; food production kitchen; gourmet dining room; lecture room; teaching kitchen.

STUDENT PROFILE
98 full-time. 95 are under 25 years old; 3 are between 25 and 44 years old.

FACULTY
5 total: 2 full-time; 3 part-time. 2 are industry professionals. Prominent faculty: William E. Spaulding, MBA, CHA; Karla H. Shaw. Faculty-student ratio: 1:20.

SPECIAL PROGRAMS
3-month faculty-supervised internships, trips to AHLA show in New York and NRA show in Chicago, annual "live-in weekend" at Zehnders of Frankemuth.

TYPICAL EXPENSES
Application fee: $25. Tuition: $14,625 per year full-time, $304 per credit hour part-time. Program-related fees include $50 for wine/beverage seminars fees; $50 for food lab fees.

FINANCIAL AID
In 2004, 34 scholarships were awarded (average award was $400). Employment placement assistance is available. Employment opportunities within the program are available.

HOUSING
Single-sex housing available. Average on-campus housing cost per month: $378.

APPLICATION INFORMATION
Students may begin participation in March, September, and December. Applications are accepted continuously. In 2004, 88 applied; 69 were accepted. Applicants must submit a formal application and an essay.

CONTACT
Dan Toland, Dean of Admissions, Hotel, Restaurant, and Resort Management, 4000 Whiting Drive, Midland, MI 48640. Telephone: 989-837-4273. Fax: 989-837-4490. E-mail: miadmit@northwood.edu. World Wide Web: http://www.northwood.edu.

OAKLAND COMMUNITY COLLEGE

Culinary Studies Institute

Farmington Hills, Michigan

GENERAL INFORMATION
Public, coeducational, two-year college. Suburban campus. Founded in 1964. Accredited by North Central Association of Colleges and Schools.

PROGRAM INFORMATION
Offered since 1965. Accredited by American Culinary Federation Accrediting Commission. Program calendar is divided into semesters. Associate degree in hotel management. 1-year certificate in baking and pastry arts. 2-year associate degree in restaurant management. 2-year associate degree in culinary arts. 3-year certificate in culinary apprentice.

PROGRAM AFFILIATION
American Culinary Federation; American Dietetic Association; American Institute of Baking; Council on Hotel, Restaurant, and Institutional Education; National Restaurant Association; National Restaurant Association Educational Foundation; Tasters Guild International.

AREAS OF STUDY
Baking; beverage management; buffet catering; confectionery show pieces; controlling costs in food service; culinary skill development; food preparation; food purchasing; garde-manger; international cuisine; management and human resources; meat cutting; meat fabrication; menu and facilities design; nutrition; patisserie; sanitation; saucier; seafood processing; soup, stock, sauce, and starch production; wines and spirits.

FACILITIES
2 bake shops; cafeteria; catering service; 3 classrooms; computer laboratory; demonstration laboratory; 3 food production kitchens; 2 gourmet dining rooms; 4 laboratories; learning resource center; 2 lecture rooms; library; public restaurant; teaching kitchen; bakery retail center.

STUDENT PROFILE
225 total: 150 full-time; 75 part-time.

FACULTY
18 total: 8 full-time; 10 part-time. 5 are culinary-certified teachers; 2 are food management professionals. Prominent faculty: Kevin Enright, CEC, CCE; Doug Ganhs, CEC; Roger Holden, CEPC, CCE; Darlene Levinson, FMP. Faculty-student ratio: 1:12.

SPECIAL PROGRAMS
Ice carving/sugar artistry/culinary competitions.

TYPICAL EXPENSES
In-state tuition: $55.15 per credit hour part-time. Out-of-state tuition: $93.35 per credit hour part-time. Tuition for international students: $130.90 per credit hour part-time.

Program-related fee includes $50–100 lab fee (per course), food product used in classes, small equipment.

FINANCIAL AID
In 2004, 5 scholarships were awarded (average award was $500). Employment placement assistance is available. Employment opportunities within the program are available.

APPLICATION INFORMATION
Students may begin participation in January, May, and September. Application deadline for fall is July 15. Application deadline for winter is November 15. Application deadline for spring is April 15. Applicants must interview; submit a formal application.

CONTACT
Susan Baier, Program Coordinator, Culinary Studies Institute, 27055 Orchard Lake Road, Farmington Hills, MI 48334. Telephone: 248-522-3700. Fax: 248-522-3706. E-mail: smbaier@oaklandcc.edu. World Wide Web: http://www.oaklandcc.edu.

SCHOOLCRAFT COLLEGE

Culinary Arts

Livonia, Michigan

GENERAL INFORMATION
Public, coeducational, two-year college. Suburban campus. Founded in 1961. Accredited by North Central Association of Colleges and Schools.

PROGRAM INFORMATION
Offered since 1964. Program calendar is divided into semesters. 1-year certificate in baking and pastry culinary arts. 1-year certificate in culinary arts. 2-year associate degree in culinary arts.

PROGRAM AFFILIATION
American Culinary Federation; Michigan Restaurant Association; National Restaurant Association; National Restaurant Association Educational Foundation.

AREAS OF STUDY
Baking; buffet catering; confectionery show pieces; controlling costs in food service; culinary French; culinary skill development; food preparation; food purchasing; food service math; garde-manger; ice carving; international cuisine; introduction to food service; kitchen management; management and human resources; meal planning; meat cutting; meat fabrication; menu and facilities design; nutrition; patisserie; restaurant opportunities; salon competition; sanitation; saucier; seafood processing; soup, stock, sauce, and starch production; wines and spirits.

FACILITIES
Bake shop; bakery; cafeteria; 8 classrooms; computer laboratory; demonstration laboratory; 6 food production

Everything about our program is world-class.

The faculty

- Six Certified Master and Executive Chefs, each an industry leader in his own right.

The facility

- Part of a $27 million culinary education/ business training/ conference center.

- Six specialized teaching kitchens: Restaurant, Production, Charcuterie, Bake Shop, Pastry, and Demonstration.

- Student-run gourmet restaurant and retail café.

The students

- American Culinary Federation National Champions in Salon Hot Food and Culinary Knowledge Bowl competitions.

The curriculum

- Certificate and associate degree programs have trained thousands of graduates who now enjoy career success in America and abroad.

- Escoffier-inspired Brigade advanced culinary skills program for aspiring chefs.

- Baking and Pastry one-year certificate program.

Schoolcraft College
18600 Haggerty Road
Livonia, MI 48152-2696
734-462-4426
admissions@schoolcraft.edu

kitchens; garden; gourmet dining room; learning resource center; library; public restaurant; student lounge; 6 teaching kitchens.

STUDENT PROFILE
400 full-time.

FACULTY
21 total: 6 full-time; 15 part-time. 17 are industry professionals; 4 are master chefs; 5 are certified executive chefs. Prominent faculty: Kevin Gawronski, CMC; Jeff Gabriel, CMC; Dan Hugelier, CMC; Joe Decker, CMPC. Faculty-student ratio: 1:16.

SPECIAL PROGRAMS
Salon competitions, local culinary competitions.

TYPICAL EXPENSES
In-state tuition: $68 per credit hour (in district), $100 per credit hour (out-of-district). Out-of-state tuition: $149 per credit hour. Program-related fee includes $1900 for lab fees for instruction.

FINANCIAL AID
In 2005, 2 scholarships were awarded (average award was $500). Employment placement assistance is available. Employment opportunities within the program are available.

HOUSING
Average off-campus housing cost per month: $600.

APPLICATION INFORMATION
Students may begin participation in January and August. Applications are accepted continuously. Applicants must submit a formal application and complete prerequisite course.

CONTACT
Office of Admissions, Culinary Arts, 18600 Haggerty Road, Livonia, MI 48152-2696. Telephone: 734-462-4426. Fax: 734-462-4553. E-mail: admissions@schoolcraft.edu. World Wide Web: http://www.schoolcraft.edu.

See display on page 212.

MINNESOTA

THE ART INSTITUTES INTERNATIONAL MINNESOTA

Culinary Arts

Minneapolis, Minnesota

GENERAL INFORMATION
Private, coeducational, four-year college. Urban campus. Founded in 1997. Accredited by Accrediting Council for Independent Colleges and Schools.

PROGRAM INFORMATION
Offered since 1998. Accredited by American Culinary Federation (ACF). Program calendar is divided into quarters. 1-year certificate in baking and pastry. 1-year certificate in art of cooking. 21-month associate degree in baking and pastry. 21-month associate degree in culinary arts. 3-year bachelor's degree in culinary management.

PROGRAM AFFILIATION
American Culinary Federation; American Dietetic Association; Confrerie de la Chaine des Rotisseurs; International Association of Culinary Professionals; International Sommelier Guild; National Restaurant Association; National Restaurant Association Educational Foundation; The Bread Bakers Guild of America.

AREAS OF STUDY
Baking; beverage management; controlling costs in food service; culinary skill development; food preparation; food purchasing; food service math; garde-manger; international cuisine; kitchen management; management and human resources; meal planning; menu and facilities design; nutrition; patisserie; sanitation; saucier; seafood processing; soup, stock, sauce, and starch production; wines and spirits.

FACILITIES
Bake shop; bakery; catering service; classroom; computer laboratory; demonstration laboratory; food production kitchen; gourmet dining room; laboratory; learning resource center; lecture room; library; public restaurant; student lounge; teaching kitchen.

STUDENT PROFILE
237 total: 101 full-time; 136 part-time.

FACULTY
12 total: 11 full-time; 1 part-time. 3 are industry professionals; 9 are culinary-certified teachers. Prominent faculty: David Cappaccioli, CEC; Amy Carter, CEPC; Byron Korus, CEC, AAC, CCE, ' Sommelier. Faculty-student ratio: 1:20.

SPECIAL PROGRAMS
Culinary competitions, student-run restaurant, specialized catering, hospitality-related industry tours.

TYPICAL EXPENSES
Application fee: $150. Tuition: $24,448 per academic year full-time, $382 per credit hour part-time. Program-related fees include $850 for supply kit (first quarter textbooks, cutlery, uniforms); $300 for consumables lab fee (per quarter); $150 for textbooks (per quarter).

FINANCIAL AID
In 2005, 5 scholarships were awarded; 6 loans were granted (average loan was $10,800). Employment placement assistance is available. Employment opportunities within the program are available.

HOUSING
Apartment-style housing available. Average on-campus housing cost per month: $596.66.

The Art Institutes International Minnesota *(continued)*

APPLICATION INFORMATION
Students may begin participation in January, April, July, and October. Applications are accepted continuously. In 2005, 322 applied; 203 were accepted. Applicants must interview; submit a formal application and an essay.

CONTACT
Director of Admissions, Culinary Arts, 15 South Ninth Street, Minneapolis, MN 55402-3137. Telephone: 612-332-3361. Fax: 612-332-3934. E-mail: aimadm@aii.edu. World Wide Web: http://www.aim.artinstitutes.edu.
See color display following page 380.

HENNEPIN TECHNICAL COLLEGE

Culinary Arts Department

Brooklyn Park, Minnesota

GENERAL INFORMATION
Public, coeducational, two-year college. Suburban campus. Founded in 1972. Accredited by North Central Association of Colleges and Schools.

PROGRAM INFORMATION
Offered since 1972. Accredited by American Culinary Federation Accrediting Commission. Program calendar is divided into semesters. 1.5-year diploma in culinary arts. 15-month certificate in culinary arts. 2-year associate degree in culinary arts.

PROGRAM AFFILIATION
American Culinary Federation.

AREAS OF STUDY
Baking; bar and beverage management; buffet catering; confectionery show pieces; controlling costs in food service; convenience cookery; culinary French; culinary skill development; food preparation; food purchasing; food service communication; food service math; garde-manger; hospitality law; hospitality marketing; international cuisine; introduction to food service; kitchen management; meal planning; meat cutting; meat fabrication; menu and facilities design; nutrition; nutrition and food service; restaurant opportunities; sanitation; saucier; seafood processing; soup, stock, sauce, and starch production; sugar work; wines and spirits.

FACILITIES
4 bake shops; 2 cafeterias; 2 catering services; 4 classrooms; coffee shop; 6 computer laboratories; 3 demonstration laboratories; 3 food production kitchens; 2 gourmet dining rooms; 4 laboratories; 3 learning resource centers; 4 lecture rooms; 2 libraries; 2 public restaurants; snack shop; 2 student lounges; 4 teaching kitchens.

TYPICAL STUDENT PROFILE
87 full-time.

SPECIAL PROGRAMS
Specialized labs with individual students, culinary competitions, 1-year paid internships.

FINANCIAL AID
Program-specific awards include 3 Minneapolis ACF Scholarships ($500), Toby Landgraf Scholarships ($500). Employment placement assistance is available. Employment opportunities within the program are available.

APPLICATION INFORMATION
Students may begin participation in January and August. Application deadline for fall is October 1. Application deadline for spring is February 1. Applicants must interview; submit a formal application.

CONTACT
Director of Admissions, Culinary Arts Department, 9000 Brooklyn Boulevard, Brooklyn Park, MN 55445. Telephone: 763-425-3800 Ext. 2463. World Wide Web: http://www.htc.mnscu.edu/.

HIBBING COMMUNITY COLLEGE

Culinary Arts

Hibbing, Minnesota

GENERAL INFORMATION
Public, coeducational, two-year college. Small-town setting. Founded in 1916. Accredited by North Central Association of Colleges and Schools.

PROGRAM INFORMATION
Program calendar is divided into semesters. 1-year diploma in culinary arts. 2-year diploma in food service and management. 5-semester associate degree in culinary arts.

PROGRAM AFFILIATION
National Restaurant Association.

AREAS OF STUDY
Baking; buffet catering; controlling costs in food service; culinary skill development; food preparation; food purchasing; food service management; food service math; international cuisine; introduction to food service; kitchen management; management and human resources; meal planning; meat cutting; meat fabrication; menu and facilities design; nutrition and food service; restaurant opportunities; sanitation; saucier; seafood processing; soup, stock, sauce, and starch production.

FACILITIES
Bake shop; bakery; cafeteria; 2 classrooms; coffee shop; 3 computer laboratories; demonstration laboratory; 2 food production kitchens; gourmet dining room; 2 laboratories; 3 learning resource centers; lecture room; 2 libraries; public restaurant; 3 student lounges; teaching kitchen.

TYPICAL STUDENT PROFILE
22 full-time.

SPECIAL PROGRAMS
Upper Midwest Hospitality Show, tours of food service distribution facilities (Sysco, Alliant).

FINANCIAL AID
Employment placement assistance is available. Employment opportunities within the program are available.

HOUSING
Apartment-style housing available.

APPLICATION INFORMATION
Students may begin participation in September. Applications are accepted continuously. Applicants must submit a formal application.

CONTACT
Director of Admissions, Culinary Arts, 1515 East 25th Street, Hibbing, MN 55746. Telephone: 218-262-7207. Fax: 218-262-6717. World Wide Web: http://www.hcc.mnscu.edu.

LE CORDON BLEU MINNEAPOLIS/ ST. PAUL

Le Cordon Bleu Culinary Program

Mendota Heights, Minnesota

GENERAL INFORMATION
Private, coeducational, culinary institute. Suburban campus. Founded in 1946. Accredited by Accrediting Commission of Career Schools and Colleges of Technology.

PROGRAM INFORMATION
Offered since 1999. Accredited by American Culinary Federation. Program calendar is divided into quarters. 15-month associate degree in Patisserie and Baking. 15-month associate degree in Le Cordon Bleu Culinary Program.

PROGRAM AFFILIATION
American Culinary Federation.

AREAS OF STUDY
Baking; controlling costs in food service; culinary French; culinary skill development; food preparation; food purchasing; food service math; garde-manger; international cuisine; introduction to food service; kitchen management; meal planning; meat cutting; nutrition; patisserie; restaurant opportunities; sanitation; saucier; soup, stock, sauce, and starch production; wines and spirits.

FACILITIES
3 bakeries; cafeteria; 7 classrooms; 3 computer laboratories; 3 demonstration laboratories; 4 food production kitchens; gourmet dining room; learning resource center; 8 lecture rooms; library; public restaurant; 2 snack shops; student lounge; 6 teaching kitchens.

STUDENT PROFILE
650 full-time.

FACULTY
49 total: 35 full-time; 14 part-time. 29 are industry professionals; 1 is a master chef; 1 is a master baker; 1 is a culinary-certified teacher. Prominent faculty: Chef Toufik Halimi; Chef Walter Whitwen; Chef Gil Gaiton; Chef William Niemer, CEC, CCE. Faculty-student ratio: 1:20.

SPECIAL PROGRAMS
Culinary competitions, internship opportunities, clubs and organizations.

TYPICAL EXPENSES
Application fee: $50. Tuition: $37,500 per program. Program-related fee includes $1622 for knife kits, uniforms, books, and supplies.

FINANCIAL AID
In 2005, 25 scholarships were awarded (average award was $2000). Employment placement assistance is available. Employment opportunities within the program are available.

HOUSING
Average off-campus housing cost per month: $450.

APPLICATION INFORMATION
Students may begin participation in January, February, April, June, July, August, October, and November. Applications are accepted continuously. Applicants must interview; submit a formal application.

CONTACT
Abby Norbin, Director of Admissions, Le Cordon Bleu Culinary Program, 1315 Mendota Heights Road, Mendota Heights, MN 55120. Telephone: 651-675-4700. Fax: 651-452-5282. E-mail: info@twincitiesculinary.com. World Wide Web: http://www.twincitiesculinary.com/.
See color display following page 380.

NORMANDALE COMMUNITY COLLEGE

Hospitality Management Program

Bloomington, Minnesota

GENERAL INFORMATION
Public, coeducational, two-year college. Suburban campus. Founded in 1968. Accredited by North Central Association of Colleges and Schools.

PROGRAM INFORMATION
Offered since 1968. Accredited by Council on Hotel, Restaurant and Institutional Education. Program calendar is divided into semesters. 2-year associate degree in hotel and restaurant management.

Normandale Community College *(continued)*

PROGRAM AFFILIATION
American Dietetic Association; American Institute of Wine & Food; Council on Hotel, Restaurant, and Institutional Education; National Restaurant Association; National Restaurant Association Educational Foundation.

AREAS OF STUDY
Baking; beverage management; controlling costs in food service; culinary French; culinary skill development; food preparation; food purchasing; food service math; introduction to food service; kitchen management; management and human resources; meal planning; meat cutting; meat fabrication; menu and facilities design; nutrition; nutrition and food service; restaurant opportunities; sanitation; saucier; seafood processing; soup, stock, sauce, and starch production; wines and spirits.

FACILITIES
Bakery; cafeteria; catering service; 3 classrooms; coffee shop; 3 computer laboratories; demonstration laboratory; food production kitchen; laboratory; learning resource center; 3 lecture rooms; library.

TYPICAL STUDENT PROFILE
120 total: 80 full-time; 40 part-time.

SPECIAL PROGRAMS
Paid internships (international), annual professional development tours.

FINANCIAL AID
Employment placement assistance is available. Employment opportunities within the program are available.

APPLICATION INFORMATION
Students may begin participation in January, June, and August. Application deadline for fall is August 25. Application deadline for spring is January 3. Application deadline for summer is May 25. Applicants must interview; submit a formal application and minimum TOEFL score of 500 for international applicants.

CONTACT
Director of Admissions, Hospitality Management Program, 9700 France Avenue South, Bloomington, MN 55431. Telephone: 952-487-8160. Fax: 952-487-8101. World Wide Web: http://www.nr.cc.mn.us/.

ST. CLOUD TECHNICAL COLLEGE

St. Cloud, Minnesota

GENERAL INFORMATION
Public, coeducational, two-year college. Suburban campus. Founded in 1948. Accredited by North Central Association of Colleges and Schools.

PROGRAM INFORMATION
Offered since 1973. Program calendar is divided into semesters. 32-week diploma in culinary arts.

PROGRAM AFFILIATION
American Culinary Federation.

AREAS OF STUDY
Baking; buffet catering; controlling costs in food service; culinary French; culinary skill development; food preparation; food purchasing; food service communication; food service math; garde-manger; international cuisine; introduction to food service; meal planning; meat cutting; nutrition; patisserie; sanitation; saucier; seafood processing; soup, stock, sauce, and starch production.

FACILITIES
Cafeteria; catering service; 2 classrooms; computer laboratory; demonstration laboratory; food production kitchen; gourmet dining room; learning resource center; lecture room; library; student lounge; teaching kitchen.

TYPICAL STUDENT PROFILE
25 full-time.

SPECIAL PROGRAMS
Culinary competitions, food shows.

FINANCIAL AID
Employment placement assistance is available. Employment opportunities within the program are available.

APPLICATION INFORMATION
Students may begin participation in August. Application deadline for fall is August 10. Applicants must submit a formal application and have high school diploma or GED.

CONTACT
Director of Admissions, 1540 Northway Drive, St. Cloud, MN 56303-1240. Telephone: 320-308-5037. Fax: 320-308-5981. World Wide Web: http://www.sctconline.com/html/home.htm.

SAINT PAUL COLLEGE–A COMMUNITY & TECHNICAL COLLEGE

Culinary Arts

St. Paul, Minnesota

GENERAL INFORMATION
Public, coeducational, two-year college. Urban campus. Founded in 1922. Accredited by North Central Association of Colleges and Schools.

PROGRAM INFORMATION
Offered since 1958. Accredited by American Culinary Federation Accrediting Commission. Program calendar is divided into semesters. 1.5-year diploma in culinary arts.

2-year associate degree in culinary arts. 24-week certificate in baking. 6-month certificate in short order/grill cook.

PROGRAM AFFILIATION
American Culinary Federation; National Restaurant Association.

AREAS OF STUDY
Baking; beverage management; confectionery show pieces; controlling costs in food service; convenience cookery; culinary skill development; food preparation; food service communication; food service math; garde-manger; international cuisine; introduction to food service; kitchen management; management and human resources; meal planning; meat cutting; meat fabrication; menu and facilities design; nutrition; nutrition and food service; restaurant opportunities; sanitation; saucier; seafood processing; soup, stock, sauce, and starch production; wines and spirits.

FACILITIES
3 bake shops; cafeteria; catering service; 4 classrooms; 4 computer laboratories; demonstration laboratory; 3 food production kitchens; gourmet dining room; learning resource center; 4 lecture rooms; library; public restaurant; 2 student lounges; 3 teaching kitchens.

TYPICAL STUDENT PROFILE
68 total: 59 full-time; 9 part-time.

FINANCIAL AID
Program-specific awards include Toby Landgraf Scholarships ($750), Eberhard Wertmann Scholarship ($500–$1000). Employment placement assistance is available. Employment opportunities within the program are available.

APPLICATION INFORMATION
Students may begin participation in January and August. Applications are accepted continuously. Applicants must submit a formal application and high school diploma or GED.

CONTACT
Director of Admissions, Culinary Arts, 235 Marshall Avenue, St. Paul, MN 55102-1800. Telephone: 651-846-1398. Fax: 651-221-1416. World Wide Web: http://www.saintpaul.edu.

SOUTH CENTRAL COLLEGE

Culinary Arts

North Mankato, Minnesota

GENERAL INFORMATION
Public, coeducational, two-year college. Urban campus. Founded in 1968. Accredited by North Central Association of Colleges and Schools.

PROGRAM INFORMATION
Offered since 1968. Program calendar is divided into semesters. 18-month diploma in culinary arts. 2-year associate degree in restaurant management. 2-year associate degree in culinary arts.

PROGRAM AFFILIATION
Council on Hotel, Restaurant, and Institutional Education; National Restaurant Association; National Restaurant Association Educational Foundation; Retailer's Bakery Association.

AREAS OF STUDY
Baking; buffet catering; classical pastries; controlling costs in food service; culinary skill development; food preparation; food purchasing; food service math; garde-manger; ice carving; introduction to food service; kitchen management; management and human resources; meal planning; meat cutting; meat fabrication; menu and facilities design; nutrition; sanitation; saucier; seafood processing; soup, stock, sauce, and starch production.

FACILITIES
Bake shop; cafeteria; 2 catering services; 2 classrooms; 2 computer laboratories; demonstration laboratory; 2 food production kitchens; learning resource center; lecture room; library; public restaurant; snack shop; student lounge; 2 teaching kitchens.

TYPICAL STUDENT PROFILE
25 total: 22 full-time; 3 part-time.

SPECIAL PROGRAMS
Culinary competitions.

FINANCIAL AID
Program-specific awards include work-study program. Employment placement assistance is available. Employment opportunities within the program are available.

APPLICATION INFORMATION
Students may begin participation in January, May, and August. Applications are accepted continuously. Applicants must submit a formal application.

CONTACT
Director of Admissions, Culinary Arts, 1920 Lee Boulevard, North Mankato, MN 56003. Telephone: 507-389-7229. Fax: 507-388-9951. World Wide Web: http://www.sctc.mnscu.edu.

UNIVERSITY OF MINNESOTA, CROOKSTON

Hotel, Restaurant, and Institutional Management

Crookston, Minnesota

GENERAL INFORMATION
Public, coeducational, four-year college. Rural campus. Founded in 1966. Accredited by North Central Association of Colleges and Schools.

PROGRAM INFORMATION
Program calendar is divided into semesters. 2-year associate degree in hotel, restaurant, and institutional management. 4-year bachelor's degree in hotel, restaurant, and institutional management.

AREAS OF STUDY
Beverage management; buffet catering; confectionery show pieces; controlling costs in food service; convenience cookery; kitchen management; management and human resources; menu and facilities design; nutrition; nutrition and food service; restaurant opportunities; sanitation.

FACILITIES
Classroom; demonstration laboratory; learning resource center; library; snack shop; student lounge.

TYPICAL STUDENT PROFILE
70 full-time.

FINANCIAL AID
Employment placement assistance is available. Employment opportunities within the program are available.

HOUSING
Coed and single-sex housing available.

APPLICATION INFORMATION
Students may begin participation in January and August. Application deadline for fall (priority date) is February 1. Applicants must submit a formal application.

CONTACT
Director of Admissions, Hotel, Restaurant, and Institutional Management, 2900 University Avenue, Crookston, MN 56716-5001. Telephone: 218-281-8200. Fax: 218-281-8250. World Wide Web: http://www.crk.umn.edu/academics/HRI/index.htm.

MISSISSIPPI

COPIAH-LINCOLN COMMUNITY COLLEGE

Food Production and Management Technology

Wesson, Mississippi

GENERAL INFORMATION
Public, coeducational, two-year college. Rural campus. Founded in 1928. Accredited by Southern Association of Colleges and Schools.

PROGRAM INFORMATION
Offered since 1979. Program calendar is divided into semesters. 4-semester associate degree in food production and management technology. 4-semester certificate in food production and management.

PROGRAM AFFILIATION
National Restaurant Association; National Restaurant Association Educational Foundation.

AREAS OF STUDY
Baking; buffet catering; controlling costs in food service; culinary skill development; food preparation; food purchasing; food service communication; food service math; introduction to food service; kitchen management; management and human resources; meal planning; nutrition; nutrition and food service; sanitation.

FACILITIES
Cafeteria; classroom; computer laboratory; food production kitchen; laboratory; learning resource center; lecture room; library; public restaurant; snack shop; student lounge.

TYPICAL STUDENT PROFILE
21 full-time.

SPECIAL PROGRAMS
15-week internship, Skills USA competition.

FINANCIAL AID
Program-specific awards include National Restaurant Association scholarship ($2000). Employment placement assistance is available.

HOUSING
Single-sex housing available.

APPLICATION INFORMATION
Students may begin participation in January and August. Application deadline for fall is August 18. Application deadline for spring is January 7. Applicants must submit a formal application.

CONTACT
Director of Admissions, Food Production and Management Technology, PO Box 649, Wesson, MS 39191-0649. Telephone: 601-643-8388. Fax: 601-643-8214. World Wide Web: http://www.colin.edu.

EAST MISSISSIPPI COMMUNITY COLLEGE

Hotel and Restaurant Management Technology

Scooba, Mississippi

GENERAL INFORMATION
Public, coeducational, two-year college. Rural campus. Founded in 1927. Accredited by Southern Association of Colleges and Schools.

PROGRAM INFORMATION
Offered since 1997. Program calendar is divided into semesters. 2-year associate degree in hotel and restaurant management technology.

PROGRAM AFFILIATION
Dietary Managers Association; Educational Institute American Hotel and Motel Association; National Restaurant Association Educational Foundation.

AREAS OF STUDY
Beverage management; buffet catering; controlling costs in food service; culinary skill development; food preparation; food purchasing; food service math; hotel and restaurant management; kitchen management; management and human resources; menu and facilities design; nutrition; sanitation.

FACILITIES
Cafeteria; catering service; classroom; computer laboratory; food production kitchen; gourmet dining room; learning resource center; lecture room; library; snack shop; student lounge; teaching kitchen.

SPECIAL PROGRAMS
Opportunity to attend Mississippi Hotel and Motel Association Convention and Trade Show, supervised work experience and work-based learning, competitions sponsored by Delta Epsilon Chi Career Development Conference.

FINANCIAL AID
Employment placement assistance is available.

APPLICATION INFORMATION
Students may begin participation in January and August. Applications are accepted continuously. Applicants must submit a formal application and high school transcript or GED.

CONTACT
Director of Admissions, Hotel and Restaurant Management Technology, PO Box 158, Scooba, MS 39358. Telephone: 662-243-1926. Fax: 662-243-1952. World Wide Web: http://www.emcc.cc.ms.us.

HINDS COMMUNITY COLLEGE

Hospitality and Tourism Management

Jackson, Mississippi

GENERAL INFORMATION
Public, coeducational, two-year college. Suburban campus. Founded in 1917. Accredited by Southern Association of Colleges and Schools.

PROGRAM INFORMATION
Offered since 1970. Program calendar is divided into semesters. 2-year associate degree in travel and tourism management. 2-year associate degree in hotel/restaurant management. 2-year associate degree in culinary arts.

PROGRAM AFFILIATION
James Beard Foundation, Inc.; Mississippi Lodging Association; Mississippi Restaurant Association.

AREAS OF STUDY
Baking; beverage management; buffet catering; controlling costs in food service; culinary French; culinary skill development; food preparation; food purchasing; food service communication; food service math; garde-manger; international cuisine; introduction to food service; management and human resources; meat cutting; meat fabrication; menu and facilities design; nutrition; restaurant opportunities; sanitation; saucier; seafood processing; soup, stock, sauce, and starch production; wines and spirits.

FACILITIES
Bake shop; 4 classrooms; computer laboratory; demonstration laboratory; food production kitchen; gourmet dining room; learning resource center; 3 lecture rooms; student lounge; teaching kitchen.

TYPICAL STUDENT PROFILE
64 total: 62 full-time; 2 part-time.

FINANCIAL AID
Employment placement assistance is available. Employment opportunities within the program are available.

HOUSING
Single-sex housing available.

APPLICATION INFORMATION
Students may begin participation in January and August. Applications are accepted continuously. Applicants must submit a formal application.

CONTACT
Director of Admissions, Hospitality and Tourism Management, 3925 Sunset Drive, Jackson, MS 39213. Telephone: 601-987-8155. Fax: 601-982-5804. World Wide Web: http://www.hindscc.edu.

MERIDIAN COMMUNITY COLLEGE

Hotel and Restaurant Management Technology

Meridian, Mississippi

GENERAL INFORMATION
Public, coeducational, two-year college. Small-town setting. Founded in 1937. Accredited by Southern Association of Colleges and Schools.

PROGRAM INFORMATION
Offered since 1970. Program calendar is divided into semesters. 2-year associate degree in hotel and restaurant management.

PROGRAM AFFILIATION
American Hotel and Lodging Association; Mississippi Hotel and Motel Association; National Restaurant Association.

AREAS OF STUDY
Baking; beverage management; buffet catering; controlling costs in food service; convenience cookery; culinary skill development; food preparation; food purchasing; food service communication; food service math; garde-manger; international cuisine; introduction to food service; kitchen management; management and human resources; meal planning; meat cutting; meat fabrication; menu and facilities design; nutrition and food service; restaurant opportunities; sanitation; saucier; soup, stock, sauce, and starch production; wines and spirits.

FACILITIES
Classroom; computer laboratory; demonstration laboratory; food production kitchen; learning resource center; lecture room; teaching kitchen.

STUDENT PROFILE
33 full-time. 19 are under 25 years old; 12 are between 25 and 44 years old; 2 are over 44 years old.

FACULTY
1 total: 1 full-time. 1 is an industry professional. Prominent faculty: Mark A. Chandler. Faculty-student ratio: 1:33.

SPECIAL PROGRAMS
Mississippi Hotel and Lodging Association Convention and Trade Show, DEX-DECA Management Skills Competition.

TYPICAL EXPENSES
Application fee: $73. In-state tuition: $725 per semester full-time (in district), $80 per semester hour part-time. Out-of-state tuition: $1320 per semester full-time, $137 per semester hour part-time. Tuition for international students: $1570 per semester full-time, $157 per semester hour part-time. Program-related fee includes $15 for DEX-DECA membership (optional).

FINANCIAL AID
In 2004, 1 scholarship was awarded (award was $1500). Employment placement assistance is available.

HOUSING
Coed, apartment-style, and single-sex housing available. Average on-campus housing cost per month: $300. Average off-campus housing cost per month: $450.

APPLICATION INFORMATION
Students may begin participation in January and August. Application deadline for fall is August 30. Application deadline for spring is January 12. In 2004, 28 applied; 28 were accepted. Applicants must submit a formal application.

CONTACT
Mark A. Chandler, Coordinator/Instructor, Hotel and Restaurant Management Technology, 910 Hwy 19 North, Meridan, MS 39307. Telephone: 601-484-8825. Fax: 601-484-8824. E-mail: mchandle@mcc.cc.ms.us. World Wide Web: http://www.mcc.cc.ms.us.

MISSISSIPPI GULF COAST COMMUNITY COLLEGE

Perkinston, Mississippi

GENERAL INFORMATION
Public, coeducational, two-year college. Suburban campus. Founded in 1911. Accredited by Southern Association of Colleges and Schools.

PROGRAM INFORMATION
Program calendar is divided into semesters. 1-year diploma in food production and management technology.

AREAS OF STUDY
Baking; buffet catering; controlling costs in food service; fast foods; food preparation; food purchasing; food service math; meal planning; nutrition; quantity foods; sanitation.

FACILITIES
2 cafeterias; 2 classrooms; 2 food production kitchens.

STUDENT PROFILE
23 total: 15 full-time; 8 part-time.

FACULTY
2 total: 1 full-time; 1 part-time. 2 are industry professionals. Faculty-student ratio: 1:20.

SPECIAL PROGRAMS
Internship (up to 3 semesters).

TYPICAL EXPENSES
In-state tuition: $745 per semester full-time (in district), $75 per semester hour part-time. Out-of-state tuition: $1668 per semester full-time, $152 per semester hour part-time.

FINANCIAL AID
Employment placement assistance is available.

HOUSING
Single-sex housing available.

APPLICATION INFORMATION
Students may begin participation in January and August. Applications are accepted continuously. In 2004, 23 applied; 23 were accepted. Applicants must submit a formal application.

CONTACT
Shelly Caro, Recruiter, PO Box 609, Perkinston, MS 39573. Telephone: 601-928-6381. Fax: 601-928-6279. E-mail: shelly.caro@mgccc.edu. World Wide Web: http://www.mgccc.cc.ms.us.

MISSISSIPPI UNIVERSITY FOR WOMEN

Culinary Arts Institute

Columbus, Mississippi

GENERAL INFORMATION
Public, coeducational, comprehensive institution. Small-town setting. Founded in 1884. Accredited by Southern Association of Colleges and Schools.

PROGRAM INFORMATION
Offered since 1997. Program calendar is divided into semesters. 1-year certificate in culinary arts. 4-year bachelor's degree in culinary arts.

PROGRAM AFFILIATION
International Association of Culinary Professionals; National Restaurant Association; Southern Foodways Alliance.

AREAS OF STUDY
Baking; buffet catering; controlling costs in food service; culinary skill development; food for special diets; food preparation; food purchasing; food service communication; food service math; garde-manger; international cuisine; introduction to food service; kitchen management; meal planning; meat fabrication; nutrition; patisserie; sanitation; saucier; soup, stock, sauce, and starch production.

FACILITIES
Bake shop; classroom; demonstration laboratory; 2 food production kitchens; garden; library; teaching kitchen; food photography kitchen.

STUDENT PROFILE
204 total: 94 full-time; 110 part-time.

Mississippi University for Women (*continued*)

FACULTY

15 total: 4 full-time; 11 part-time. 3 are culinary-certified teachers; 2 are registered dietitians. Prominent faculty: James Fitzgerald, PhD, CCP; W. Scott McKenzie; Rebecca Kelly; Erich Ogle. Faculty-student ratio: 1:7.

SPECIAL PROGRAMS

3-month paid internship, international internship.

TYPICAL EXPENSES

In-state tuition: $1747.50 per semester full-time (in district), $145.67 per credit hour part-time. Out-of-state tuition: $2636.50 per semester full-time, $331.85 per credit hour part-time. Program-related fee includes $100 for food for each food preparation course.

FINANCIAL AID

In 2004, 3 scholarships were awarded (average award was $500); 2 loans were granted (average loan was $500). Employment placement assistance is available. Employment opportunities within the program are available.

HOUSING

Single-sex housing available. Average on-campus housing cost per month: $378. Average off-campus housing cost per month: $450.

APPLICATION INFORMATION

Students may begin participation in January, June, and August. Application deadline for fall is August 25. Application deadline for spring is January 20. Applicants must submit a formal application, SAT or ACT scores, and academic transcripts.

CONTACT

W. Scott McKenzie, Director, Culinary Arts Institute, 1100 College Street MUW 1639, Columbus, MS 39701. Telephone: 662-241-7472. Fax: 662-241-7627. E-mail: cularts@muw.edu. World Wide Web: http://www.muw.edu/interdisc.

NORTHEAST MISSISSIPPI COMMUNITY COLLEGE

Hotel and Restaurant Management Technology

Booneville, Mississippi

GENERAL INFORMATION

Public, coeducational, two-year college. Small-town setting. Founded in 1948. Accredited by Southern Association of Colleges and Schools.

PROGRAM INFORMATION

Offered since 1974. Program calendar is divided into semesters. 2-year associate degree in hotel and restaurant management.

PROGRAM AFFILIATION

American Hotel and Lodging Association; National Restaurant Association; National Restaurant Association Educational Foundation.

FACILITIES

Catering service; classroom; computer laboratory; food production kitchen; laboratory; lecture room; teaching kitchen; bed and breakfast.

TYPICAL STUDENT PROFILE

18 full-time. 9 are under 25 years old; 8 are between 25 and 44 years old; 1 is over 44 years old.

FINANCIAL AID

Employment placement assistance is available. Employment opportunities within the program are available.

HOUSING

Single-sex housing available.

APPLICATION INFORMATION

Students may begin participation in January and August. Applications are accepted continuously. Applicants must submit a formal application.

CONTACT

Director of Admissions, Hotel and Restaurant Management Technology, 101 Cunningham Boulevard, Booneville, MS 38829. Telephone: 662-720-7233. Fax: 662-728-1165. World Wide Web: http://www.necc.cc.ms.us.

MISSOURI

COLLEGE OF THE OZARKS

Point Lookout, Missouri

GENERAL INFORMATION

Private, coeducational, four-year college. Small-town setting. Founded in 1906. Accredited by North Central Association of Colleges and Schools.

PROGRAM INFORMATION

Offered since 1993. Accredited by American Dietetic Association. Program calendar is divided into semesters. 4-year bachelor's degree in HRM: professional food service emphasis. 4-year bachelor's degree in food and nutrition. 4-year bachelor's degree in dietetics. 4-year bachelor's degree in hotel and restaurant management.

PROGRAM AFFILIATION

American Culinary Federation; American Dietetic Association; Council on Hotel, Restaurant, and Institutional Education; Missouri Hotel and Motel Association; National Restaurant Association.

AREAS OF STUDY

Baking; controlling costs in food service; culinary skill development; food preparation; food purchasing; garde-manger; international cuisine; introduction to food service; kitchen management; management and human resources; meal planning; menu and facilities design; nutrition; nutrition and food service; restaurant opportunities; sanitation; seafood processing; soup, stock, sauce, and starch production.

FACILITIES
Bake shop; cafeteria; catering service; 5 classrooms; computer laboratory; demonstration laboratory; food production kitchen; laboratory; learning resource center; lecture room; public restaurant; snack shop; student lounge; teaching kitchen.

STUDENT PROFILE
54 full-time. 52 are under 25 years old; 1 is between 25 and 44 years old; 1 is over 44 years old.

FACULTY
5 total: 2 full-time; 3 part-time. 3 are industry professionals; 2 are culinary-certified teachers. Faculty-student ratio: 1:14.

SPECIAL PROGRAMS
Paid internships, travel to regional program-related events and shows, leadership opportunities through student organizations.

TYPICAL EXPENSES
Tuition: Use Pell or other grants and college scholarships full-time, $275 per per credit hour part-time.

FINANCIAL AID
Employment placement assistance is available.

HOUSING
Single-sex housing available.

APPLICATION INFORMATION
Students may begin participation in August. Application deadline for fall is February 15. Application deadline for spring a year in advance is January 1. Applicants must interview; submit a formal application, letters of reference, an essay, ACT score, financial information (FAFSA form), all required to interview.

CONTACT
Jerry J. Shackette, Associate Professor, Hotel/Restaurant Management, PO Box 17, Point Lookout, MO 65726. Telephone: 417-239-1900 Ext. 119. Fax: 417-335-8140. E-mail: shackette@cofo.edu. World Wide Web: http://www.cofo.edu.

EAST CENTRAL COLLEGE

Hospitality Program

Union, Missouri

GENERAL INFORMATION
Public, coeducational, two-year college. Suburban campus. Founded in 1959. Accredited by North Central Association of Colleges and Schools.

PROGRAM INFORMATION
Offered since 1991. Program calendar is divided into semesters. 1-year certificate in culinary arts. 2-year associate degree in culinary arts.

PROGRAM AFFILIATION
American Culinary Federation; National Restaurant Association; National Restaurant Association Educational Foundation.

AREAS OF STUDY
Baking; buffet catering; controlling costs in food service; culinary skill development; food preparation; food purchasing; kitchen management; management and human resources; menu and facilities design; restaurant opportunities; sanitation.

FACILITIES
Bake shop; 4 classrooms; 2 computer laboratories; demonstration laboratory; food production kitchen; garden; gourmet dining room; lecture room; teaching kitchen.

TYPICAL STUDENT PROFILE
25 full-time.

FINANCIAL AID
Employment placement assistance is available. Employment opportunities within the program are available.

APPLICATION INFORMATION
Students may begin participation in August. Applications are accepted continuously. Applicants must submit a formal application and have high school transcript or GED.

CONTACT
Director of Admissions, Hospitality Program, 1964 Prairie Dell Road, Union, MO 63084. Telephone: 636-583-5195 Ext. 2401. Fax: 636-583-1897. World Wide Web: http://www.eastcentral.edu.

MISSOURI STATE UNIVERSITY

Hospitality and Restaurant Administration

Springfield, Missouri

GENERAL INFORMATION
Public, coeducational, comprehensive institution. Urban campus. Founded in 1905. Accredited by North Central Association of Colleges and Schools.

Missouri State University *(continued)*

PROGRAM INFORMATION
Offered since 1985. Accredited by Council on Hotel, Restaurant and Institutional Education. Program calendar is divided into semesters. 4-year bachelor's degree in hospitality and restaurant administration.

PROGRAM AFFILIATION
Council on Hotel, Restaurant, and Institutional Education; National Restaurant Association; National Restaurant Association Educational Foundation.

AREAS OF STUDY
Baking; beverage management; buffet catering; controlling costs in food service; culinary skill development; food preparation; food purchasing; food service communication; gaming; garde-manger; international cuisine; introduction to food service; kitchen management; management and human resources; menu and facilities design; nutrition; nutrition and food service; patisserie; restaurant opportunities; sanitation; soup, stock, sauce, and starch production; wines and spirits.

FACILITIES
Bake shop; 2 classrooms; computer laboratory; demonstration laboratory; food production kitchen; gourmet dining room; laboratory; learning resource center; 2 lecture rooms; library; public restaurant; teaching kitchen.

TYPICAL STUDENT PROFILE
250 total: 225 full-time; 25 part-time.

SPECIAL PROGRAMS
National Restaurant Association Annual Convention, American Hotel Association Annual Convention.

FINANCIAL AID
Employment placement assistance is available. Employment opportunities within the program are available.

HOUSING
Coed, apartment-style, and single-sex housing available.

APPLICATION INFORMATION
Students may begin participation in January and August. Application deadline for program: 3 weeks prior to beginning of semester. Applicants must submit a formal application and ACT or SAT score.

CONTACT
Director of Admissions, Hospitality and Restaurant Administration, 901 South National, Springfield, MO 65804. Telephone: 417-836-4908. Fax: 417-836-7673. World Wide Web: http://www.smsu.edu/hra.

OZARKS TECHNICAL COMMUNITY COLLEGE

Culinary Arts

Springfield, Missouri

GENERAL INFORMATION
Public, coeducational, two-year college. Urban campus. Founded in 1990. Accredited by North Central Association of Colleges and Schools.

PROGRAM INFORMATION
Offered since 1990. Accredited by American Culinary Federation Accrediting Commission. Program calendar is divided into semesters. 2-year associate degree in restaurant management. 2-year associate degree in culinary arts. 2-year associate degree in hospitality management.

PROGRAM AFFILIATION
American Culinary Federation; Missouri Restaurant Association; National Restaurant Association; National Restaurant Association Educational Foundation; Retailer's Bakery Association.

AREAS OF STUDY
Baking; beverage management; buffet catering; controlling costs in food service; culinary French; culinary skill development; food preparation; food purchasing; food service communication; food service math; garde-manger; international cuisine; introduction to food service; kitchen management; management and human resources; meal planning; meat cutting; meat fabrication; menu and facilities design; nutrition; nutrition and food service; patisserie; restaurant opportunities; sanitation; saucier; seafood processing; soup, stock, sauce, and starch production; wines and spirits.

FACILITIES
2 bake shops; bakery; cafeteria; catering service; 10 classrooms; coffee shop; computer laboratory; demonstration laboratory; 3 food production kitchens; gourmet dining room; learning resource center; library; public restaurant.

TYPICAL STUDENT PROFILE
190 total: 70 full-time; 120 part-time. 100 are under 25 years old; 60 are between 25 and 44 years old; 30 are over 44 years old.

SPECIAL PROGRAMS
Junior Culinary Team competitions, Junior BBQ Competition Team.

FINANCIAL AID
Employment placement assistance is available. Employment opportunities within the program are available.

APPLICATION INFORMATION
Students may begin participation in January and August. Applications are accepted continuously. Applicants must interview; submit a formal application.

CONTACT
Director of Admissions, Culinary Arts, PO Box 5958, Springfield, MO 65801. Telephone: 417-895-7282. Fax: 417-895-7264. World Wide Web: http://www.otc.edu.

PENN VALLEY COMMUNITY COLLEGE

Lodging and Food Service Department

Kansas City, Missouri

GENERAL INFORMATION
Public, coeducational, two-year college. Urban campus. Founded in 1975. Accredited by North Central Association of Colleges and Schools.

PROGRAM INFORMATION
Program calendar is divided into semesters. 4-semester associate degree in food and beverage. 6-semester associate degree in chef apprenticeship (both programs offered jointly with Johnson County Community College).

STUDENT PROFILE
9 total: 1 full-time; 8 part-time. 6 are under 25 years old; 3 are between 25 and 44 years old.

TYPICAL EXPENSES
In-state tuition: $2130 per 1 year full-time (in district), $71 per credit hour part-time (in district), $3870 per 1 year full-time (out-of-district), $129 per credit hour part-time (out-of-district). Out-of-state tuition: $5250 per 1 year full-time, $175 per credit hour part-time. Tuition for international students: $6210 per 1 year full-time, $207 per credit hour part-time.

APPLICATION INFORMATION
Students may begin participation in January and August. Applications are accepted continuously. In 2004, 9 applied; 7 were accepted. Applicants must submit a formal application.

CONTACT
Johnson County Community College, Lodging and Food Service Department, 12345 College Boulevard, Overland Park, KS 66210. Telephone: 913-469-8500. E-mail: jhaas@jccc.edu. World Wide Web: http://www.kcmetro.edu.

ST. LOUIS COMMUNITY COLLEGE AT FOREST PARK

Hospitality Studies

St. Louis, Missouri

GENERAL INFORMATION
Public, coeducational, two-year college. Urban campus. Founded in 1962. Accredited by North Central Association of Colleges and Schools.

PROGRAM INFORMATION
Offered since 1964. Program calendar is divided into semesters. 1-year certificate in baking and pastry. 2-year associate degree in hotel restaurant management. 2-year associate degree in culinary arts.

PROGRAM AFFILIATION
American Culinary Federation; Council on Hotel, Restaurant, and Institutional Education; Missouri Restaurant Association; National Restaurant Association; National Restaurant Association Educational Foundation.

AREAS OF STUDY
Baking; beverage management; buffet catering; confectionery show pieces; controlling costs in food service; culinary skill development; food preparation; food purchasing; food service math; garde-manger; international cuisine; introduction to food service; kitchen management; management and human resources; meal planning; menu and facilities design; nutrition; nutrition and food service; restaurant opportunities; sanitation; saucier; seafood processing; soup, stock, sauce, and starch production; wines and spirits.

FACILITIES
Bake shop; 3 classrooms; computer laboratory; demonstration laboratory; food production kitchen; garden; gourmet dining room; learning resource center; library; public restaurant; student lounge; teaching kitchen; full-service restaurant and kitchen.

TYPICAL STUDENT PROFILE
550 total: 275 full-time; 275 part-time.

SPECIAL PROGRAMS
Culinary competitions, paid internships.

FINANCIAL AID
Employment placement assistance is available. Employment opportunities within the program are available.

APPLICATION INFORMATION
Students may begin participation in January, June, and August. Application deadline for fall is August 21. Application deadline for spring is January 5. Application deadline for summer is June 4. Applicants must submit a formal application.

St. Louis Community College at Forest Park *(continued)*

CONTACT
Director of Admissions, Hospitality Studies, 5600 Oakland Avenue, St. Louis, MO 63110-1316. Telephone: 314-644-9276. Fax: 314-644-9011. World Wide Web: http://www.stlcc.edu.

SAINT LOUIS UNIVERSITY

Department of Nutrition and Dietetics

St. Louis, Missouri

GENERAL INFORMATION
Private, coeducational, university. Urban campus. Founded in 1818. Accredited by North Central Association of Colleges and Schools.

PROGRAM INFORMATION
Offered since 2002. Accredited by American Dietetic Association. Program calendar is divided into semesters. Verification statement in didactic program in dietetics. Verification statement in didactic program in dietetics with special emphasis in culinary arts. 10-month verification statement in dietetic internship. 36- to 42-credit hour master's degree in nutrition and dietetics with emphasis in nutrition and physical performance. 37-credit hour verification statement in medical dietetics. 4-year bachelor's degree in nutrition and dietetics and physician assistant scholars. 4-year bachelor's degree in nutrition and dietetics and preprofessional studies. 4-year bachelor's degree in nutrition and dietetics. 4-year bachelor's degree in nutrition and dietetics with special emphasis in culinary arts. 53-credit hour master's degree in nutrition and dietetics and public health.

PROGRAM AFFILIATION
American Culinary Federation; American Dietetic Association.

AREAS OF STUDY
Baking; beverage management; buffet catering; controlling costs in food service; culinary skill development; food preparation; food purchasing; food service math; garde-manger; international cuisine; introduction to food service; kitchen management; management and human resources; meal planning; meat cutting; meat fabrication; menu and facilities design; nutrition; nutrition and food service; patisserie; restaurant opportunities; sanitation; saucier; seafood processing; soup, stock, sauce, and starch production; sustainable food systems.

FACILITIES
Bake shop; bakery; cafeteria; 2 catering services; 4 classrooms; computer laboratory; demonstration laboratory; food production kitchen; garden; gourmet dining room; laboratory; learning resource center; 4 lecture rooms; 2 libraries; public restaurant; teaching kitchen.

TYPICAL STUDENT PROFILE
14 full-time. 14 are under 25 years old.

SPECIAL PROGRAMS
Practicum (required) at local country club, student-run booth at Clayton Farmer's Market, sustainable university garden in collaboration with the Missouri Botanical Garden.

FINANCIAL AID
Program-specific awards include The Sr. Mary Carolla Sellmeyer Scholarship, The Healthy Futures Minority Scholarship. Employment placement assistance is available. Employment opportunities within the program are available.

HOUSING
Coed and apartment-style housing available.

APPLICATION INFORMATION
Students may begin participation in January, May, and August. Application deadline for fall is August 1. Application deadline for spring is December 1. Application deadline for summer is May 1. Applicants must submit a formal application, letters of reference, an essay, ACT or SAT score (for freshman applicants).

CONTACT
Director of Admissions, Department of Nutrition and Dietetics, 3437 Caroline Street, Room 3076, St. Louis, MO 63104. Telephone: 314-977-8523. Fax: 314-977-8520. World Wide Web: http://www.slu.edu/colleges/AH/ND.

UNIVERSITY OF CENTRAL MISSOURI

Department of Health and Human Performance

Warrensburg, Missouri

GENERAL INFORMATION
Public, coeducational, comprehensive institution. Small-town setting. Founded in 1871. Accredited by North Central Association of Colleges and Schools.

PROGRAM INFORMATION
Offered since 1976. Accredited by American Dietetic Association. Program calendar is divided into semesters. 4-year bachelor's degree in hotel and restaurant administration.

PROGRAM AFFILIATION
American Dietetic Association; Council on Hotel, Restaurant, and Institutional Education; National Restaurant Association.

AREAS OF STUDY
Beverage management; controlling costs in food service; food preparation; food purchasing; food service communication; food service math; international cuisine;

introduction to food service; meal planning; menu and facilities design; nutrition; restaurant opportunities; sanitation.

FACILITIES
5 classrooms; demonstration laboratory; 4 food production kitchens; library; teaching kitchen.

TYPICAL STUDENT PROFILE
55 full-time.

SPECIAL PROGRAMS
Employer-paid internships.

FINANCIAL AID
Employment placement assistance is available.

HOUSING
Coed, apartment-style, and single-sex housing available.

APPLICATION INFORMATION
Students may begin participation in January and August. Applications are accepted continuously.

CONTACT
Director of Admissions, Department of Health and Human Performance, Grinstead 247, Warrensburg, MO 64093. Telephone: 660-543-4361. Fax: 660-543-8847. World Wide Web: http://www.cmsu.edu.

UNIVERSITY OF MISSOURI– COLUMBIA

Hotel and Restaurant Management

Columbia, Missouri

GENERAL INFORMATION
Public, coeducational, university. Small-town setting. Founded in 1839. Accredited by North Central Association of Colleges and Schools.

PROGRAM INFORMATION
Offered since 1971. Accredited by Council on Hotel, Restaurant and Institutional Education. Program calendar is divided into semesters. 2-Year master's degree in food science/hotel and restaurant management. 4-Year bachelor's degree in hotel and restaurant management.

PROGRAM AFFILIATION
Council on Hotel, Restaurant, and Institutional Education; Educational Institute-American Hotel and Motel Association; Institute of Food Technologists; National Restaurant Association; National Restaurant Association Educational Foundation.

AREAS OF STUDY
Beverage management; controlling costs in food service; food preparation; food purchasing; introduction to food service; management and human resources; meal planning; nutrition; restaurant opportunities; sanitation.

FACILITIES
3 classrooms; 2 computer laboratories; 2 demonstration laboratories; 2 food production kitchens; lecture room; library; public restaurant; student lounge; 2 teaching kitchens.

TYPICAL STUDENT PROFILE
196 total: 181 full-time; 15 part-time. 196 are under 25 years old.

SPECIAL PROGRAMS
600-hour internship (paid by industry).

HOUSING
Coed and single-sex housing available.

APPLICATION INFORMATION
Students may begin participation in January, June, and August. Applications are accepted continuously. Applicants must submit a formal application.

CONTACT
Director of Admissions, Hotel and Restaurant Management, 122 Eckles Hall, Columbia, MO 65211. Telephone: 573-882-4114. Fax: 573-882-0596. World Wide Web: http://www.fse.missouri.edu/hrm.

MONTANA

FLATHEAD VALLEY COMMUNITY COLLEGE

Hospitality Management

Kalispell, Montana

GENERAL INFORMATION
Public, coeducational, two-year college. Rural campus. Founded in 1967. Accredited by Northwest Association of Schools and Colleges.

PROGRAM INFORMATION
Offered since 1996. Program calendar is divided into semesters. 1-year certificate in culinary arts. 2-year associate degree in hospitality and tourism.

AREAS OF STUDY
Baking; culinary skill development; food preparation.

TYPICAL STUDENT PROFILE
10 total: 6 full-time; 4 part-time. 5 are under 25 years old; 4 are between 25 and 44 years old; 1 is over 44 years old.

FINANCIAL AID
Employment placement assistance is available.

APPLICATION INFORMATION
Students may begin participation in January, June, and September. Applications are accepted continuously. Applicants must submit a formal application.

Flathead Valley Community College (*continued*)

CONTACT
Director of Admissions, Hospitality Management, 777 Grandview Drive, Kalispell, MT 59901. Telephone: 406-756-3865. Fax: 406-756-3815. World Wide Web: http://www.fvcc.edu.

THE UNIVERSITY OF MONTANA– MISSOULA

Culinary Arts Department/Food Service Management

Missoula, Montana

GENERAL INFORMATION
Public, coeducational, university. Suburban campus. Founded in 1893. Accredited by Northwest Association of Schools and Colleges.

PROGRAM INFORMATION
Offered since 1974. Accredited by American Culinary Federation Accrediting Commission. Program calendar is divided into semesters. 1-year certificate in culinary arts. 2-year associate degree in food service management. 4-year bachelor's degree in food service management.

PROGRAM AFFILIATION
American Culinary Federation; Council on Hotel, Restaurant, and Institutional Education; International Food Service Executives Association; National Association of College and University Food Service; National Restaurant Association; National Restaurant Association Educational Foundation.

AREAS OF STUDY
Baking; beverage management; buffet catering; confectionery show pieces; controlling costs in food service; convenience cookery; culinary skill development; food preparation; food purchasing; food service communication; food service math; garde-manger; international cuisine; introduction to food service; kitchen management; management and human resources; meal planning; meat cutting; meat fabrication; menu and facilities design; nutrition; nutrition and food service; patisserie; restaurant opportunities; sanitation; saucier; seafood processing; soup, stock, sauce, and starch production; wines and spirits.

FACILITIES
2 bakeries; 2 cafeterias; catering service; 3 classrooms; 2 coffee shops; computer laboratory; demonstration laboratory; 4 food production kitchens; 2 gourmet dining rooms; 3 laboratories; learning resource center; 11 lecture rooms; 2 libraries; 5 public restaurants; 2 snack shops; student lounge; 3 teaching kitchens.

TYPICAL STUDENT PROFILE
40 full-time.

SPECIAL PROGRAMS
Specialized internships at local, regional, and national sites.

FINANCIAL AID
Employment placement assistance is available. Employment opportunities within the program are available.

HOUSING
Coed, apartment-style, and single-sex housing available.

APPLICATION INFORMATION
Students may begin participation in January and September. Applications are accepted continuously. Applicants must submit a formal application.

CONTACT
Director of Admissions, Culinary Arts Department/Food Service Management, 909 South Avenue West, Missoula, MT 59801-7910. Telephone: 406-243-7811. Fax: 406-243-7899. World Wide Web: http://www.umt.edu/.

NEBRASKA

CENTRAL COMMUNITY COLLEGE– HASTINGS CAMPUS

Hospitality Management and Culinary Arts

Hastings, Nebraska

GENERAL INFORMATION
Public, coeducational, two-year college. Small-town setting. Founded in 1966. Accredited by North Central Association of Colleges and Schools.

PROGRAM INFORMATION
Offered since 1970. Program calendar is semester plus 6-week summer session. 1-year diploma in culinary arts. 2-year associate degree in hotel management. 2-year associate degree in culinary arts. 2-year associate degree in restaurant management.

PROGRAM AFFILIATION
Council on Hotel, Restaurant, and Institutional Education; National Restaurant Association.

AREAS OF STUDY
Baking; beverage management; confectionery show pieces; controlling costs in food service; culinary skill development; food preparation; food purchasing; food service math; garde-manger; international cuisine; introduction to food service; kitchen management; management and human resources; meal planning; menu and facilities design; nutrition and food service; patisserie; sanitation; saucier; soup, stock, sauce, and starch production.

FACILITIES

Bake shop; cafeteria; catering service; 3 classrooms; 2 computer laboratories; food production kitchen; learning resource center; 2 lecture rooms; library; public restaurant; teaching kitchen.

TYPICAL STUDENT PROFILE

45 total: 30 full-time; 15 part-time. 25 are under 25 years old; 15 are between 25 and 44 years old; 5 are over 44 years old.

FINANCIAL AID

Employment placement assistance is available.

HOUSING

Coed and single-sex housing available.

APPLICATION INFORMATION

Students may begin participation in January, February, March, April, May, June, August, September, October, November, and December. Applications are accepted continuously. Applicants must submit a formal application.

CONTACT

Director of Admissions, Hospitality Management and Culinary Arts, PO Box 1024, Hastings, NE 68902-1024. Telephone: 402-463-9811. Fax: 402-461-2506. World Wide Web: http://www.cccneb.edu/Hastings.

METROPOLITAN COMMUNITY COLLEGE

Institute for the Culinary Arts

Omaha, Nebraska

GENERAL INFORMATION

Public, coeducational, two-year college. Urban campus. Founded in 1974. Accredited by North Central Association of Colleges and Schools.

PROGRAM INFORMATION

Offered since 1974. Accredited by American Culinary Federation Accrediting Commission, Council on Hotel, Restaurant and Institutional Education. Program calendar is divided into quarters. 2-year associate degree in culinary management. 2-year associate degree in bakery arts. 2-year associate degree in Culinology (TM). 2-year associate degree in culinary arts. 2-year associate degree in foodservice management. 3-year associate degree in chef apprentice.

PROGRAM AFFILIATION

American Culinary Federation; American Institute of Baking; American Wine Society; Council on Hotel, Restaurant, and Institutional Education; International Wine & Food Society; National Restaurant Association; National Restaurant Association Educational Foundation; Research Chefs Association; The Bread Bakers Guild of America; United States Personal Chef Association.

AREAS OF STUDY

Baking; beverage management; buffet catering; controlling costs in food service; convenience cookery; culinary skill development; food preparation; food purchasing; food service communication; food service math; garde-manger; international cuisine; introduction to food service; kitchen management; management and human resources; meal planning; meat fabrication; menu and facilities design; nutrition; nutrition and food service; patisserie; restaurant opportunities; sanitation; saucier; seafood processing; soup, stock, sauce, and starch production.

FACILITIES

Bake shop; bakery; cafeteria; catering service; 4 classrooms; 2 coffee shops; computer laboratory; demonstration laboratory; food production kitchen; garden; 2 gourmet dining rooms; 2 laboratories; learning resource center; 4 lecture rooms; library; public restaurant; teaching kitchen.

STUDENT PROFILE

550 total: 250 full-time; 300 part-time.

FACULTY

26 total: 4 full-time; 22 part-time. 20 are industry professionals; 1 is a master baker; 5 are culinary-certified teachers. Prominent faculty: James E. Trebbien, CCE; Janet Mar, PhD; Tina Powers, CCE, CEC, CMB; Guy Sockrider, CEC. Faculty-student ratio: 1:18.

SPECIAL PROGRAMS

Study tour to annual NRA convention in Chicago, participation in local, regional, and national SkillsUSA competition, paid research and development projects for local food manufacturing companies.

TYPICAL EXPENSES

In-state tuition: $38.50 per credit hour part-time. Out-of-state tuition: $58 per credit hour part-time. Tuition for international students: $100 per credit hour part-time. Program-related fee includes $300 for uniforms and knives.

FINANCIAL AID

In 2004, 18 scholarships were awarded (average award was $1000). Program-specific awards include Omaha Restaurant Association scholarships (up to $1000), Con Agra scholarships ($1000), International Food & Wine Society Scholarship (up to $1000). Employment placement assistance is available. Employment opportunities within the program are available.

HOUSING

Coed housing available. Average on-campus housing cost per month: $450. Average off-campus housing cost per month: $450–$600.

APPLICATION INFORMATION

Students may begin participation in March, June, September, and December. Applications are accepted continuously. In 2004, 550 applied; 550 were accepted. Applicants must submit a formal application.

Metropolitan Community College *(continued)*

CONTACT

James Trebbien, Culinary Academic Director, Institute for the Culinary Arts, PO Box 3777, Omaha, NE 68103-0777. Telephone: 402-457-2510. Fax: 402-457-2984. E-mail: jtrebbien@mccneb.edu. World Wide Web: http://business.mccneb.edu/culinaryarts.

SOUTHEAST COMMUNITY COLLEGE, LINCOLN CAMPUS

Food Service Program

Lincoln, Nebraska

GENERAL INFORMATION

Public, coeducational, two-year college. Urban campus. Founded in 1973. Accredited by North Central Association of Colleges and Schools.

PROGRAM INFORMATION

Offered since 1973. Accredited by American Culinary Federation Accrediting Commission, American Dietetic Association. Program calendar is divided into quarters. 18-month associate degree in food service management. 18-month associate degree in culinary arts. 18-month associate degree in dietetic technology.

PROGRAM AFFILIATION

American Culinary Federation; American Dietetic Association; Council on Hotel, Restaurant, and Institutional Education; Dietary Managers Association; National Restaurant Association; National Restaurant Association Educational Foundation.

AREAS OF STUDY

Baking; beverage management; buffet catering; controlling costs in food service; culinary French; culinary skill development; food preparation; food purchasing; food service math; garde-manger; introduction to food service; kitchen management; management and human resources; meal planning; meat fabrication; menu and facilities design; nutrition; sanitation; saucier; soup, stock, sauce, and starch production.

FACILITIES

Bakery; cafeteria; catering service; 4 classrooms; computer laboratory; food production kitchen; gourmet dining room; laboratory; learning resource center; 2 lecture rooms; library; public restaurant; student lounge.

STUDENT PROFILE

135 total: 88 full-time; 47 part-time.

FACULTY

8 total: 3 full-time; 5 part-time. 4 are industry professionals; 1 is a culinary-certified teacher; 2 are registered dietitians. Prominent faculty: Jo Taylor, RD, LMNT, MA; Gerrine Schrek Kirby, CEC, CCE; Lois Cockerham, CDM; Erin Caudill, RD, LMNT, MS. Faculty-student ratio: 1:18.

SPECIAL PROGRAMS

Trip to the National Restaurant Association show, culinary competitions.

TYPICAL EXPENSES

Application fee: $25. In-state tuition: $39 per credit hour part-time. Out-of-state tuition: $47.50 per credit hour part-time. Program-related fee includes $300 for uniform and knives.

FINANCIAL AID

In 2004, 4 scholarships were awarded (average award was $300). Employment placement assistance is available. Employment opportunities within the program are available.

HOUSING

Average off-campus housing cost per month: $350.

APPLICATION INFORMATION

Students may begin participation in January, March, July, and October. Application deadline for fall is September 1. Application deadline for winter is November 23. Application deadline for spring is February 22. Application deadline for summer is May 17. Applicants must submit a formal application and have high school diploma or GED.

CONTACT

Jo Taylor, Program Chair, Food Service Program, 8800 O Street, Lincoln, NE 68520-1299. Telephone: 402-437-2465. Fax: 402-437-2404. E-mail: jtaylor@southeast.edu. World Wide Web: http://www.college.sccm.cc.ne.us.

NEVADA

THE ART INSTITUTE OF LAS VEGAS

Henderson, Nevada

GENERAL INFORMATION

Private, coeducational, two-year college. Urban campus. Founded in 2001. Accredited by Accrediting Commission of Career Schools and Colleges of Technology.

PROGRAM INFORMATION

Offered since 2002. Program calendar is divided into quarters. 3-quarter diploma in art of cooking. 7-quarter associate degree in culinary arts.

AREAS OF STUDY

Baking; controlling costs in food service; dining room operation; food purchasing; garde-manger; international cuisine; introduction to food service; kitchen management; management and human resources; menu and facilities design; nutrition; nutrition and food service; patisserie; restaurant opportunities; sanitation.

FACILITIES
Bake shop; 2 classrooms; computer laboratory; 2 food production kitchens; learning resource center; student lounge; teaching kitchen.

SPECIAL PROGRAMS
Internship, culinary competitions.

APPLICATION INFORMATION
Students may begin participation in January, April, July, and October. Applications are accepted continuously. Applicants must interview; submit a formal application and high school diploma or GED.

CONTACT
Director of Admissions, 2350 Corporate Circle, Henderson, NV 89074. Telephone: 702-369-9944. Fax: 702-992-8458. World Wide Web: http://www.ailv.artinstitutes.edu.
See color display following page 380.

COMMUNITY COLLEGE OF SOUTHERN NEVADA

Hotel, Restaurant, and Casino Management

North Las Vegas, Nevada

GENERAL INFORMATION
Public, coeducational, two-year college. Urban campus. Founded in 1971. Accredited by Northwest Association of Schools and Colleges.

PROGRAM INFORMATION
Offered since 1990. Accredited by American Culinary Federation Accrediting Commission, Council for Accreditation for Hospitality Associates. Program calendar is divided into semesters. 1-year certificate in hotel, restaurant, and casino management with emphasis in culinary arts, pastry, or food and beverage. 2-year associate degree in hotel, restaurant, and casino management with emphasis in culinary arts, pastry, or food and beverage.

PROGRAM AFFILIATION
American Culinary Federation; Council on Hotel, Restaurant, and Institutional Education; National Restaurant Association Educational Foundation.

AREAS OF STUDY
Beverage management; culinary skill development; food preparation; introduction to food service; management and human resources; restaurant opportunities.

FACILITIES
2 bake shops; catering service; 15 classrooms; 2 computer laboratories; demonstration laboratory; 2 food production kitchens; garden; gourmet dining room; learning resource center; 8 lecture rooms; public restaurant; student lounge; teaching kitchen; wine cellar; bistro.

TYPICAL STUDENT PROFILE
630 total: 450 full-time; 180 part-time.

SPECIAL PROGRAMS
Culinary competitions, membership in Junior American Culinary Federation.

FINANCIAL AID
Employment placement assistance is available. Employment opportunities within the program are available.

APPLICATION INFORMATION
Students may begin participation in January, June, and September. Applications are accepted continuously. Applicants must submit a formal application.

CONTACT
Director of Admissions, Hotel, Restaurant, and Casino Management, 3200 East Cheyenne Avenue, North Las Vegas, NV 89030. Telephone: 702-651-4818. Fax: 702-651-4116. World Wide Web: http://www.ccsn.edu.

TRUCKEE MEADOWS COMMUNITY COLLEGE

Culinary Arts

Reno, Nevada

GENERAL INFORMATION
Public, coeducational, two-year college. Urban campus. Founded in 1971. Accredited by Northwest Association of Schools and Colleges.

PROGRAM INFORMATION
Offered since 1979. Accredited by American Culinary Federation Accrediting Commission. Program calendar is divided into semesters. Certificate of achievement in baking and pastry. Certificate of achievement in culinary arts. 2-year associate degree in culinary arts.

PROGRAM AFFILIATION
American Culinary Federation; Council on Hotel, Restaurant, and Institutional Education; National Restaurant Association Educational Foundation; Nevada Restaurant Association; Oldways Preservation and Exchange Trust; Retailer's Bakery Association; The Bread Bakers Guild of America.

AREAS OF STUDY
Baking; beverage management; buffet catering; controlling costs in food service; convenience cookery; culinary skill development; food preparation; food purchasing; food service math; garde-manger; international cuisine; introduction to food service; kitchen management; management and human resources; meal planning; meat cutting; meat fabrication; menu and facilities design; nutrition; nutrition and food service; patisserie; retail

Truckee Meadows Community College *(continued)*

deli/bakery operations; sanitation; saucier; seafood processing; soup, stock, sauce, and starch production; wines and spirits.

FACILITIES
Bake shop; bakery; cafeteria; catering service; 3 classrooms; 4 computer laboratories; food production kitchen; gourmet dining room; laboratory; learning resource center; 3 lecture rooms; 2 libraries; public restaurant; snack shop; student lounge; teaching kitchen.

TYPICAL STUDENT PROFILE
175 total: 44 full-time; 131 part-time.

SPECIAL PROGRAMS
2-day tours to wineries and/or food production operations, instructional assistant opportunities.

FINANCIAL AID
Employment placement assistance is available. Employment opportunities within the program are available.

APPLICATION INFORMATION
Students may begin participation in January and August. Applications are accepted continuously. Applicants must submit a formal application.

CONTACT
Director of Admissions, Culinary Arts, 7000 Dandini Boulevard, RDMT 207-0, Reno, NV 89512-3999. Telephone: 775-674-7917. Fax: 775-674-7980. World Wide Web: http://www.tmcc.edu/.

UNIVERSITY OF NEVADA, LAS VEGAS

Department of Food and Beverage Management

Las Vegas, Nevada

GENERAL INFORMATION
Public, coeducational, university. Urban campus. Founded in 1957. Accredited by Northwest Association of Schools and Colleges.

PROGRAM INFORMATION
Offered since 1967. Program calendar is divided into semesters. 4-year bachelor's degree in culinary arts management.

PROGRAM AFFILIATION
American Culinary Federation; American Dietetic Association; Council on Hotel, Restaurant, and Institutional Education; National Restaurant Association; National Restaurant Association Educational Foundation; Nevada Restaurant Association; Research Chefs Association.

AREAS OF STUDY
Baking; beers; beverage management; buffet catering; concessions; controlling costs in food service; culinary skill development; culture and cuisine; food preparation; food purchasing; food science; food service communication; food service math; garde-manger; in-flight food service; introduction to food service; kitchen management; management and human resources; meal planning; menu and facilities design; noncommercial food service; nutrition; nutrition and food service; operations management; quantity foods; quick service; restaurant opportunities; sanitation; saucier; soup, stock, sauce, and starch production; wines and spirits.

FACILITIES
Bake shop; catering service; 25 classrooms; computer laboratory; demonstration laboratory; 2 food production kitchens; 3 gourmet dining rooms; 4 laboratories; 25 lecture rooms; library; 2 teaching kitchens; bar/lounge.

STUDENT PROFILE
185 total: 160 full-time; 25 part-time.

FACULTY
87 total: 55 full-time; 32 part-time. 12 are industry professionals; 1 is a master baker; 5 are culinary-certified teachers. Prominent faculty: Claude Lambertz, CHE; John Stefanelli, PhD; Jean Hertzman, CCE; Don Bell, PhD. Faculty-student ratio: 1:24.

SPECIAL PROGRAMS
5-week summer studies in Switzerland and Australia, local and national internships, local and national conferences and trade shows.

TYPICAL EXPENSES
Application fee: $90. In-state tuition: $98 per per semester hour full-time (in district), $98 per semester hour (up to 6 hours) part-time (in district), $206 per semester hour (up to 6 hours) part-time (out-of-district). Out-of-state tuition: $4735 per per semester; $98 per semester hour full-time, $206 per semester hour (up to 6 hours) part-time. Tuition for international students: $4735 per per semester; $98 per semester hour. Program-related fees include $30–$135 for supplies-per class for lab classes; $20 for internship administration; $156 for student activities fee per semester; $100 for international student fee per semester.

FINANCIAL AID
In 2004, 140 scholarships were awarded (average award was $1500). Employment placement assistance is available.

HOUSING
Coed housing available. Average on-campus housing cost per month: $485. Average off-campus housing cost per month: $650.

APPLICATION INFORMATION
Students may begin participation in January, May, and August. Application deadline for fall is February 1. Application deadline for spring is October 1. Application deadline for summer is February 1. Applicants must submit a formal application.

CONTACT
Sherri Theriault, Advising Coordinator, Department of Food and Beverage Management, Harrah Hotel College; Office for Student Advising, Las Vegas, NV 89154-6039.

Telephone: 702-895-3616. Fax: 702-895-3127. E-mail: hoaadviz@nevada.edu. World Wide Web: http://www.unlv.edu.

NEW HAMPSHIRE

ATLANTIC CULINARY ACADEMY AT McINTOSH COLLEGE

Dover, New Hampshire

GENERAL INFORMATION
Private, coeducational, two-year college. Small-town setting. Accredited by New England Association of Schools and Colleges.

PROGRAM INFORMATION
Offered since 2000. Program calendar is continuous. 18-month associate degree in culinary arts (Le Cordon Bleu).

PROGRAM AFFILIATION
American Culinary Federation; National Restaurant Association.

AREAS OF STUDY
Baking; beverage management; confectionery show pieces; controlling costs in food service; convenience cookery; culinary French; culinary skill development; food preparation; food purchasing; food service math; garde-manger; international cuisine; introduction to food service; kitchen management; meat cutting; meat fabrication; nutrition; nutrition and food service; patisserie; sanitation; saucier; soup, stock, sauce, and starch production; wines and spirits.

FACILITIES
Bake shop; bakery; cafeteria; coffee shop; computer laboratory; demonstration laboratory; food production kitchen; gourmet dining room; laboratory; lecture room; library; public restaurant; snack shop; teaching kitchen.

TYPICAL STUDENT PROFILE
360 full-time. 200 are under 25 years old; 137 are between 25 and 44 years old; 23 are over 44 years old.

SPECIAL PROGRAMS
12-week internship.

FINANCIAL AID
Employment placement assistance is available.

HOUSING
Coed housing available.

APPLICATION INFORMATION
Applications are accepted continuously. Applicants must interview; submit a formal application.

CONTACT
Director of Admissions, 181 Silver Street, Dover, NH 03820. Telephone: 877-628-1222. Fax: 603-749-0837. World Wide Web: http://www.atlanticculinary.com.

NEW HAMPSHIRE COMMUNITY TECHNICAL COLLEGE

Culinary Arts Department

Berlin, New Hampshire

GENERAL INFORMATION
Public, coeducational, two-year college. Rural campus. Founded in 1966. Accredited by New England Association of Schools and Colleges.

PROGRAM INFORMATION
Program calendar is divided into semesters. 1-year certificate in culinary arts. 1-year diploma in culinary arts (basic). 2-year associate degree in culinary arts.

PROGRAM AFFILIATION
American Culinary Federation; Institute of Food Technologists; National Restaurant Association.

AREAS OF STUDY
Baking; beverage management; buffet catering; confectionery show pieces; controlling costs in food service; culinary skill development; food preparation; food purchasing; food service communication; food service math; garde-manger; international cuisine; introduction to food service; kitchen management; management and human resources; meal planning; meat cutting; meat fabrication; menu and facilities design; nutrition; nutrition and food service; patisserie; restaurant opportunities; sanitation; saucier; seafood processing; soup, stock, sauce, and starch production; wines and spirits.

FACILITIES
Bakery; cafeteria; catering service; 5 computer laboratories; 2 demonstration laboratories; 2 food production kitchens; gourmet dining room; 2 laboratories; learning resource center; 3 lecture rooms; library; student lounge.

TYPICAL STUDENT PROFILE
50 total: 48 full-time; 2 part-time.

SPECIAL PROGRAMS
2-semester externship at area restaurants, apprenticeship with Balsams Hotel.

FINANCIAL AID
Employment placement assistance is available.

New Hampshire Community Technical College
(continued)

APPLICATION INFORMATION

Students may begin participation in January and September. Applications are accepted continuously. Applicants must submit a formal application and high school transcript.

CONTACT

Director of Admissions, Culinary Arts Department, 2020 Riverside Drive, Berlin, NH 03570-3717. Telephone: 603-752-1113. Fax: 603-752-6335. World Wide Web: http://www.berl.tec.nh.us.

SOUTHERN NEW HAMPSHIRE UNIVERSITY

The School of Hospitality, Tourism, and Culinary Management

Manchester, New Hampshire

GENERAL INFORMATION

Private, coeducational, comprehensive institution. Suburban campus. Founded in 1932. Accredited by New England Association of Schools and Colleges.

PROGRAM INFORMATION

Offered since 1983. Accredited by American Culinary Federation Accrediting Commission. Program calendar is divided into semesters. 2-year associate degree in baking and pastry arts. 2-year associate degree in culinary arts. 2-year master's degree in hospitality. 4-year bachelor's degree in food and beverage management. 4-year bachelor's degree in hospitality administration. 9-month certificate in culinary arts. 9-month certificate in baking and pastry arts.

PROGRAM AFFILIATION

Council on Hotel, Restaurant, and Institutional Education; National Restaurant Association; Retailer's Bakery Association; Women Chefs and Restaurateurs.

AREAS OF STUDY

Advanced pastry; bakery management; bakeshop; baking; beverage management; buffet catering; classic cuisine; confectionery show pieces; controlling costs in food service; culinary competition; culinary French; culinary skill development; food preparation; food purchasing; food service communication; food service math; garde-manger; holiday baking; international baking; international cuisine; introduction to culinary arts; introduction to food service; kitchen management; meal planning; meat cutting; menu and facilities design; new American cuisine; nutrition; nutrition and food service; patisserie; principles of supervision; regional American cooking; restaurant opportunities; sanitation; saucier; soup, stock, sauce, and starch production; spa cuisine; table service; wines and spirits.

FACILITIES

2 bake shops; bakery; cafeteria; catering service; 5 classrooms; coffee shop; 2 computer laboratories; 5 demonstration laboratories; 4 food production kitchens; garden; gourmet dining room; 2 laboratories; learning resource center; 9 lecture rooms; library; public restaurant; snack shop; student lounge; 4 teaching kitchens.

STUDENT PROFILE

140 total: 130 full-time; 10 part-time. 106 are under 25 years old; 20 are between 25 and 44 years old; 4 are over 44 years old.

FACULTY

13 total: 6 full-time; 7 part-time. 5 are industry professionals; 1 is a master baker; 7 are culinary-certified teachers. Prominent faculty: Perrin Long, CEC, CHE, AAC, CCE; J. Desmond Keefe, III, CHE; Mary Brigid Flanigan, CHE. Faculty-student ratio: 1:10.

SPECIAL PROGRAMS

Internships at various locations in the United States, student culinary organizations and associations.

TYPICAL EXPENSES

Application fee: $35. Tuition: $21,384 per year full-time, $791 per credit part-time. Program-related fees include $125 for uniforms; $300 for knives; $550 for books (2 semesters).

FINANCIAL AID

In 2005, 31 scholarships were awarded (average award was $7000). Employment placement assistance is available. Employment opportunities within the program are available.

HOUSING

Coed, apartment-style, and single-sex housing available.

APPLICATION INFORMATION

Students may begin participation in September. Applications are accepted continuously. In 2005, 157 applied; 125 were accepted. Applicants must submit a formal application, an essay, letters of reference, and academic transcripts.

CONTACT

Sam Mahra, Senior Assistant Director of Admission/Culinary Coordinator, The School of Hospitality, Tourism, and Culinary Management, 2500 North River Road, Manchester, NH 03106-1045. Telephone: 800-642-4968. Fax: 603-645-9693. World Wide Web: http://www.snhu.edu.

See display on page 235.

UNIVERSITY OF NEW HAMPSHIRE

Food Services Management, Thompson School of Applied Science

Durham, New Hampshire

GENERAL INFORMATION
Public, coeducational, university. Small-town setting. Founded in 1866. Accredited by New England Association of Schools and Colleges.

PROGRAM INFORMATION
Offered since 1964. Accredited by American Dietetic Association. Program calendar is divided into semesters. 2-year associate degree in dietetic technician, registered. 2-year associate degree in restaurant management.

PROGRAM AFFILIATION
American Culinary Federation; American Dietetic Association; Council on Hotel, Restaurant, and Institutional Education; National Restaurant Association; National Restaurant Association Educational Foundation.

AREAS OF STUDY
Beverage management; buffet catering; controlling costs in food service; convenience cookery; culinary skill development; food preparation; food purchasing; food service math; introduction to food service; kitchen management; management and human resources; meal planning; menu and facilities design; nutrition; nutrition and food service; restaurant opportunities; sanitation; wines and spirits.

FACILITIES
Bake shop; bakery; 2 cafeterias; 2 catering services; 6 classrooms; coffee shop; computer laboratory; demonstration laboratory; 2 food production kitchens; garden; gourmet dining room; 2 laboratories; learning resource center; 6 lecture rooms; 2 libraries; 3 public restaurants; snack shop; student lounge; 2 teaching kitchens; vineyard.

STUDENT PROFILE
31 total: 27 full-time; 4 part-time.

FACULTY
3 total: 3 full-time. 2 are industry professionals; 1 is a culinary-certified teacher. Prominent faculty: Charles A. Caramihalis, MOE, CCE; Nancy Johnson, MEd, RD; Eugene Alibrio, MS, CHE. Faculty-student ratio: 1:11.

SPECIAL PROGRAMS
Summer internships (required), independent studies with food and beverage facilities, career services internships at Disney World and other national and international resorts.

TYPICAL EXPENSES
Application fee: $45. In-state tuition: $9778 per year full-time (in district), $235 per 1 credit hour up to 12 credits part-time. Out-of-state tuition: $21,498 per year full-time, $259 per credit hour part-time. Program-related fee includes $400 for computer use, field trips, and uniforms.

FINANCIAL AID
In 2004, 1 scholarship was awarded (award was $500). Employment placement assistance is available. Employment opportunities within the program are available.

HOUSING
Coed, apartment-style, and single-sex housing available. Average on-campus housing cost per month: $600. Average off-campus housing cost per month: $800–$1000.

APPLICATION INFORMATION
Students may begin participation in January and August. Applications are accepted continuously. In 2004, 33 applied; 27 were accepted. Applicants must submit a formal application, letters of reference, an essay, SAT scores, and have a high school transcript or GED.

CONTACT
Deborah Pack, Admissions Coordinator, Food Services Management, Thompson School of Applied Science, Cole Hall, Durham, NH 03824. Telephone: 603-862-1025. Fax: 603-862-2915. E-mail: tsas.admit@unh.edu. World Wide Web: http://www.unh.edu/thompson-school.

NEW JERSEY

ATLANTIC CAPE COMMUNITY COLLEGE

Academy of Culinary Arts

Mays Landing, New Jersey

GENERAL INFORMATION
Public, coeducational, two-year college. Small-town setting. Founded in 1964. Accredited by Middle States Association of Colleges and Schools.

PROGRAM INFORMATION
Offered since 1981. Program calendar is divided into semesters. 1-year certificate of specialization in pastry/baking. 2-year associate degree in pastry/baking. 2-year associate degree in food service management. 2-year associate degree in culinary arts. 3-semester certificate in food service management. 3-semester certificate in baking/pastry. 3-semester certificate in culinary arts. 9-month certificate of specialization in catering. 9-month certificate of specialization in food service management. 9-month certificate of specialization in hot foods.

PROGRAM AFFILIATION
American Culinary Federation; Foodservice Educators Network International; National Restaurant Association;

National Restaurant Association Educational Foundation; New Jersey Restaurant Association; Retailer's Bakery Association.

AREAS OF STUDY

American regional; baking; buffet catering; charcuterie; confectionery show pieces; controlling costs in food service; culinary skill development; food preparation; food purchasing; food service math; garde-manger; international cuisine; introduction to food service; Italian regional and traditional cooking; kitchen management; meal planning; meat cutting; meat fabrication; menu and facilities design; nutrition; patisserie; restaurant operations; sanitation; saucier; soup, stock, sauce, and starch production; vegetarian cooking; wines and spirits.

FACILITIES

2 bake shops; 4 classrooms; computer laboratory; food production kitchen; gourmet dining room; learning resource center; 4 lecture rooms; library; public restaurant; 5 teaching kitchens; banquet room.

STUDENT PROFILE

363 total: 249 full-time; 114 part-time. 263 are under 25 years old; 77 are between 25 and 44 years old; 23 are over 44 years old.

FACULTY

18 total: 13 full-time; 5 part-time. 18 are industry professionals; 6 are culinary-certified teachers; 1 is a licensed dietitian. Prominent faculty: Mary Theresa McCann, MS, CEPC; Marsha Patrick, MS, RD; Philip Cragg, CEC, CCE, AAC; Annmarie Chelius, CCE, CWPC, BS. Faculty-student ratio: 1:20.

SPECIAL PROGRAMS

400-hour cooperative education program, culinary competitions, study abroad.

TYPICAL EXPENSES

Application fee: $35. In-state tuition: $5600 per semester full-time (in district), $1400 per course part-time (in district), $6552 per semester full-time (out-of-district), $1638 per course part-time (out-of-district). Out-of-state tuition: $7975 per semester full-time, $1994 per course part-time. Program-related fees include $300 for knives and specialty tools; $400 for textbooks; $350 for uniforms.

FINANCIAL AID

In 2005, 139 scholarships were awarded (average award was $1034); 138 loans were granted (average loan was $2206). Program-specific awards include Press of Atlantic City Restaurant Gala Scholarships. Employment placement assistance is available. Employment opportunities within the program are available.

APPLICATION INFORMATION

Students may begin participation in January and August. Applications are accepted continuously. In 2005, 390 applied; 390 were accepted. Applicants must submit a formal application.

Atlantic Cape Community College (*continued*)

CONTACT

Linda McLeod, Assistant Director for College Recruitment, Academy of Culinary Arts, 5100 Black Horse Pike, Mays Landing, NJ 08330-2699. Telephone: 609-343-5009. Fax: 609-343-4921. E-mail: accadmit@atlantic.edu. World Wide Web: http://www.atlantic.edu/aca.

BERGEN COMMUNITY COLLEGE

Hotel/Restaurant/Hospitality

Paramus, New Jersey

GENERAL INFORMATION

Public, coeducational, two-year college. Suburban campus. Founded in 1965. Accredited by Middle States Association of Colleges and Schools.

PROGRAM INFORMATION

Offered since 1974. Program calendar is divided into semesters. 1-semester certificate of achievement in professional cooking. 1-year certificate in hospitality management. 1-year certificate in culinary arts. 2-year associate degree in catering/ banquet management. 2-year associate degree in hospitality management.

PROGRAM AFFILIATION

Council on Hotel, Restaurant, and Institutional Education; National Restaurant Association; National Restaurant Association Educational Foundation; New Jersey Restaurant Association.

AREAS OF STUDY

Baking; beverage management; buffet catering; controlling costs in food service; culinary skill development; food preparation; food purchasing; garde-manger; international cuisine; introduction to food service; kitchen management; meal planning; nutrition; sanitation; soup, stock, sauce, and starch production; wines and spirits.

FACILITIES

Cafeteria; 6 classrooms; 2 computer laboratories; 2 food production kitchens; gourmet dining room; learning resource center; library; public restaurant; snack shop; 2 student lounges; teaching kitchen.

STUDENT PROFILE

230 total: 170 full-time; 60 part-time. 70 are under 25 years old; 100 are between 25 and 44 years old; 60 are over 44 years old.

FACULTY

4 total: 4 full-time. 4 are industry professionals; 1 is a culinary-certified teacher; 1 is a executive chef. Prominent faculty: Arthur P. Tolve, Coordinator. Faculty-student ratio: 1:57.

SPECIAL PROGRAMS

Co-op work experience.

TYPICAL EXPENSES

Application fee: $25. In-state tuition: $82.60 per credit hour (in district), $171 per credit hour (out-of-district). Out-of-state tuition: $181 per credit hour. Tuition for international students: $171 per credit hour. Program-related fee includes $30 for lab fees (per course).

FINANCIAL AID

Employment placement assistance is available. Employment opportunities within the program are available.

HOUSING

Average off-campus housing cost per month: $800–$1200.

APPLICATION INFORMATION

Students may begin participation in January and September. Application deadline for fall is August 31. Application deadline for spring is January 14. In 2004, 230 applied; 230 were accepted. Applicants must interview; submit a formal application.

CONTACT

Arthur P. Tolve, Coordinator Hotel, Restaurant, Hospitality, Hotel/Restaurant/Hospitality, 400 Paramus Road-E185A, Paramus, NJ 07052-1595. Telephone: 201-447-7192. Fax: 201-612-5240. E-mail: atolve@bergen.edu. World Wide Web: http://www.bergen.edu.

BROOKDALE COMMUNITY COLLEGE

Asbury Park, New Jersey

GENERAL INFORMATION

Public, coeducational, two-year college. Founded in 1967. Accredited by Middle States Association of Colleges and Schools.

PROGRAM INFORMATION

Program calendar is divided into semesters. 2-year associate degree in culinary arts. 30.5-credit certificate in pastry arts. 36.5-credit certificate in culinary arts.

AREAS OF STUDY

Baking; beverage management; culinary skill development; food preparation; food purchasing; food service communication; food service math; garde-manger; international cuisine; introduction to food service; kitchen management; meal planning; meat cutting; nutrition; nutrition and food service; patisserie; sanitation; seafood processing; soup, stock, sauce, and starch production; wines and spirits.

TYPICAL STUDENT PROFILE

51 total: 32 full-time; 19 part-time.

SPECIAL PROGRAMS

Student exchange programs in Scotland, Netherlands, and France, internships, field trips and guest lecturers.

APPLICATION INFORMATION

Application deadline for all sessions: one week before term begins.

CONTACT
Director of Admissions, 131B, Lincroft, NJ 07738.
Telephone: 732-774-3782.

BURLINGTON COUNTY COLLEGE

Food Service and Hospitality Management

Pemberton, New Jersey

GENERAL INFORMATION
Public, coeducational, two-year college. Suburban campus.
Founded in 1966. Accredited by Middle States Association
of Colleges and Schools.

PROGRAM INFORMATION
Offered since 1997. Program calendar is semester plus 2
summer terms. 1-year certificate in food service and
hospitality management. 1.5-year certificate in cooking and
baking. 2-year associate degree in food service and
hospitality management.

PROGRAM AFFILIATION
National Restaurant Association Educational Foundation.

AREAS OF STUDY
Baking; controlling costs in food service; food preparation;
food purchasing; food service math; introduction to food
service; management and human resources; managing
quantity food service; marketing for hospitality; menu and
facilities design; nutrition; nutrition and food service;
quality service; sanitation.

FACILITIES
Classroom; food production kitchen; lecture room.

STUDENT PROFILE
30 total: 10 full-time; 20 part-time. 10 are under 25 years
old; 20 are between 25 and 44 years old.

FACULTY
2 total: 1 full-time; 1 part-time. registered dietitian/certified
hospitality educator. Prominent faculty: Steven F.
Bergonzoni, MPA, RD, CHE; Paula Carlson. Faculty-
student ratio: 1:10.

TYPICAL EXPENSES
Application fee: $20. In-state tuition: $858 per semester
full-time (in district), $66 per credit hour part-time (in
district), $85 per credit hour part-time (out-of-district).
Out-of-state tuition: $150 per credit hour part-time.
Program-related fees include $300 for culinary arts courses;
$200 for baking courses.

FINANCIAL AID
Employment placement assistance is available. Employment
opportunities within the program are available.

APPLICATION INFORMATION
Students may begin participation in January, May, July,
and September. Application deadline for fall is August 25.

Application deadline for spring is January 25. Application
deadline for summer is May 25. Applicants must submit a
formal application.

CONTACT
Steven F. Bergonzoni, Director, Food Service and
Hospitality Management, Route 530, Pemberton, NJ
08068-1599. Telephone: 609-894-9311 Ext. 2750. Fax:
609-726-0442. E-mail: sbergonz@bcc.edu. World Wide Web:
http://www.bcc.edu/html/FoodServHospManCert.html.

COUNTY COLLEGE OF MORRIS

Hospitality Management Program

Randolph, New Jersey

GENERAL INFORMATION
Public, coeducational, two-year college. Suburban campus.
Founded in 1965. Accredited by Middle States Association
of Colleges and Schools.

PROGRAM INFORMATION
Offered since 1986. Program calendar is divided into
semesters. 1-year certificate in culinary arts. 2-year associate
degree in hospitality management.

PROGRAM AFFILIATION
National Restaurant Association.

AREAS OF STUDY
Baking; beverage management; buffet catering; controlling
costs in food service; convenience cookery; culinary French;
culinary skill development; food preparation; food
purchasing; kitchen management; sanitation; saucier; soup,
stock, sauce, and starch production; wines and spirits.

FACILITIES
Bake shop; catering service; classroom; computer
laboratory; food production kitchen; laboratory; learning
resource center; lecture room; library; student lounge;
teaching kitchen.

TYPICAL STUDENT PROFILE
87 total: 54 full-time; 33 part-time.

FINANCIAL AID
Employment opportunities within the program are
available.

APPLICATION INFORMATION
Students may begin participation in January and August.
Applications are accepted continuously. Applicants must
submit a formal application.

CONTACT
Director of Admissions, Hospitality Management Program,
214 Center Grove Road, Randolph, NJ 07869. Telephone:
973-328-5669. Fax: 973-328-5676. World Wide Web: http://
www.ccm.edu.

CULINARY EDUCATION CENTER OF MONMOUTH COUNTY

Asbury Park, New Jersey

GENERAL INFORMATION
Public, coeducational, two-year college. Urban campus. Founded in 1999. Accredited by Middle States Association of Colleges and Schools.

PROGRAM INFORMATION
Offered since 1999. Program calendar is divided into semesters. 1-year certificate in pastry arts. 1-year certificate in culinary arts. 2-year associate degree in culinary arts.

PROGRAM AFFILIATION
American Culinary Federation; American Institute of Baking; National Restaurant Association; The Bread Bakers Guild of America.

AREAS OF STUDY
Baking; beverage management; buffet catering; confectionery show pieces; controlling costs in food service; culinary skill development; food preparation; food purchasing; food service communication; food service math; garde-manger; international cuisine; introduction to food service; kitchen management; management and human resources; meal planning; meat cutting; meat fabrication; menu and facilities design; nutrition; nutrition and food service; patisserie; restaurant opportunities; sanitation; saucier; seafood processing; soup, stock, sauce, and starch production; wines and spirits.

FACILITIES
Bakery; 4 classrooms; computer laboratory; 3 food production kitchens; learning resource center; 2 public restaurants; student lounge.

TYPICAL STUDENT PROFILE
106 full-time.

SPECIAL PROGRAMS
350–400 hour paid externships in the U.S. and abroad, culinary competitions.

FINANCIAL AID
Employment placement assistance is available. Employment opportunities within the program are available.

APPLICATION INFORMATION
Students may begin participation in January, February, March, April, September, October, November, and December. Applications are accepted continuously. Applicants must submit a formal application and an essay.

CONTACT
Director of Admissions, 601 Grand Avenue, Asbury Park, NJ 07712. Telephone: 732-774-3782. Fax: 732-774-7556. World Wide Web: http://www.brookdale.cc.nj.us/content. php?ID=136.

HUDSON COUNTY COMMUNITY COLLEGE

Culinary Arts Institute

Jersey City, New Jersey

GENERAL INFORMATION
Public, coeducational, two-year college. Urban campus. Founded in 1974. Accredited by Middle States Association of Colleges and Schools.

PROGRAM INFORMATION
Offered since 1983. Accredited by American Culinary Federation Accrediting Commission. Program calendar is divided into semesters. 1-semester certificate in hot food production. 1-semester certificate in garde manger. 1-semester certificate in baking. 1-year certificate in hospitality management. 1-year certificate in culinary arts. 2-year associate degree in hospitality management-catering management option. 2-year associate degree in hospitality management. 2-year associate degree in culinary arts.

PROGRAM AFFILIATION
American Culinary Federation; Confrerie de la Chaine des Rotisseurs; Council on Hotel, Restaurant, and Institutional Education; James Beard Foundation, Inc.; Les Amis d'Escoffier Society; National Restaurant Association; National Restaurant Association Educational Foundation.

AREAS OF STUDY
Baking; beverage management; buffet catering; confectionery show pieces; controlling costs in food service; convenience cookery; culinary French; culinary skill development; food preparation; food purchasing; garde-manger; international cuisine; introduction to food service; menu and facilities design; nutrition; patisserie; sanitation; saucier; soup, stock, sauce, and starch production; table service; wines and spirits.

FACILITIES
2 bake shops; bakery; catering service; 14 classrooms; 8 computer laboratories; 4 food production kitchens; gourmet dining room; 2 learning resource centers; 14 lecture rooms; 2 libraries; student lounge; 8 teaching kitchens.

STUDENT PROFILE
423 total: 219 full-time; 204 part-time. 254 are under 25 years old; 127 are between 25 and 44 years old; 42 are over 44 years old.

FACULTY
26 total: 9 full-time; 17 part-time. 14 are industry professionals; 12 are culinary-certified teachers. Prominent faculty: Arnold Trzepacz, CEC, CPC; Paul Dillon; Kevin O'Malley; Siroun Meguerditchian. Faculty-student ratio: 1:15.

SPECIAL PROGRAMS
Société Culinaire Philanthropique Show, exchange program abroad.

Award-Winning Culinary Program

ASSOCIATE IN APPLIED SCIENCE & CERTIFICATE PROGRAMS OFFERED

- New Culinary Arts Institute/Business Conference Center/ Classroom Building with state-of-the-art classrooms and elegant banquet facilities
- Fully accredited by the American Culinary Federation
- Award-winning chef instructors
- Extensive externship requirement with some of the most prominent hotels, country clubs, restaurants, and other food service establishments in the country
- Student to faculty ratio of 12:1
- Individualized instruction
- "Hands-On" classroom instruction
- Exchange programs available overseas
- Culinary education providing the total dining experience
- Operating restaurant as a part of the curriculum
- State-of-the-art equipment and kitchen designs
- 99% job placement
- Several articulation agreements with four-year college and universities
- Culinary Arts Club - Winner of several awards in food competitions

Specialized Programs offered at The Culinary Arts Institute

- **Bakeshop**
- **Garde Manger**
- **Hot Food Production**

- **10 minutes by PATH to NYC**

- **1 block from Journal Square PATH Station**

- **Financial Aid Available**

- **Full-time and Part-time options**

CULINARY ARTS INSTITUTE OF HUDSON COUNTY COMMUNITY COLLEGE
161 Newkirk Street • Jersey City, NJ • 201-360-4639
www.hccc.edu

Hudson County Community College *(continued)*

TYPICAL EXPENSES

Application fee: $15. In-state tuition: $5740 per associate degree; $2706 per certificate full-time (in district), $82 per credit part-time (in district), $11,480 per associate degree; $5442 per certificate full-time (out-of-district), $164 per credit part-time (out-of-district). Out-of-state tuition: $17,220 per associate degree; $8118 per certificate full-time, $246 per credit part-time. Program-related fees include $920 for lab fees (per semester); $206 for knife kit; $194 for uniforms.

FINANCIAL AID

In 2005, 8 scholarships were awarded (average award was $3000); 6 loans were granted (average loan was $500). Employment placement assistance is available. Employment opportunities within the program are available.

HOUSING

Average off-campus housing cost per month: $800.

APPLICATION INFORMATION

Students may begin participation in January, May, and September. Application deadline for fall is August 5. Application deadline for spring is January 5. Application deadline for summer is May 5. In 2005, 400 applied; 260 were accepted. Applicants must submit a formal application.

CONTACT

Dennis Baumeyer, Executive Director, Culinary Arts Institute, 161 Newkirk Street, Jersey City, NJ 07306. Telephone: 201-360-4631. Fax: 201-795-4641. E-mail: dbaumeyer@hccc.edu. World Wide Web: http://www.hccc.edu.

See display on page 241.

MIDDLESEX COUNTY COLLEGE

Hotel Restaurant and Institution Management

Edison, New Jersey

GENERAL INFORMATION

Public, coeducational, two-year college. Suburban campus. Founded in 1964. Accredited by Middle States Association of Colleges and Schools.

PROGRAM INFORMATION

Offered since 1964. Program calendar is divided into semesters. Certificate of achievement in culinary arts. 2-year associate degree in hotel, restaurant, and institution management (with culinary arts option).

PROGRAM AFFILIATION

American Dietetic Association; American Hotel and Lodging Association; Council on Hotel, Restaurant, and Institutional Education; Institute of Food Technologists; National Association for the Specialty Food Trade, Inc.; National Restaurant Association; National Restaurant Association Educational Foundation.

AREAS OF STUDY

Baking; beverage management; controlling costs in food service; culinary skill development; facilities layout and design; food preparation; food purchasing; food service communication; food service math; garde-manger; international cuisine; introduction to food service; kitchen management; management and human resources; meal planning; meat fabrication; menu and facilities design; nutrition; nutrition and food service; restaurant opportunities; sanitation; soup, stock, sauce, and starch production; wines and spirits.

FACILITIES

Bake shop; cafeteria; catering service; 2 classrooms; computer laboratory; demonstration laboratory; food production kitchen; laboratory; learning resource center; 2 lecture rooms; library; public restaurant; teaching kitchen.

STUDENT PROFILE

200 total: 125 full-time; 75 part-time.

FACULTY

10 total: 6 full-time; 4 part-time. 7 are industry professionals; 2 are culinary-certified teachers. Prominent faculty: Ralph Tellone, MBA, CHE, CHA; Deborah Keenan Lynch; Joseph Vastano, MS, RD; Marilyn Laskowski-Sachnoff, MA, RD. Faculty-student ratio: 1:16.

SPECIAL PROGRAMS

Externships, cooperative work experiences, Walt Disney World College Program (practicum).

TYPICAL EXPENSES

Application fee: $25. In-state tuition: $79.25 per credit. Out-of-state tuition: $158.50 per credit. Tuition for international students: $158.50 per credit. Program-related fees include $145 for equipment and uniforms; $275 for course fees.

FINANCIAL AID

Employment placement assistance is available. Employment opportunities within the program are available.

APPLICATION INFORMATION

Students may begin participation in January, May, and August. Application deadline for fall is August 1. Application deadline for spring is December 31. Application deadline for summer is May 1. Applicants must submit a formal application.

CONTACT

Marilyn Laskowski-Sachnoff, Chairman, Hotel Restaurant and Institution Management, 2600 Woodbridge Avenue, PO Box 3050, Edison, NJ 08818-3050. Telephone: 732-906-2538. Fax: 732-906-7745. E-mail: m_laskowski_sachnoff@middlesexcc.edu. World Wide Web: http://www.middlesexcc.edu.

MORRIS COUNTY SCHOOL OF TECHNOLOGY

Culinary Arts

Denville, New Jersey

GENERAL INFORMATION
Public, coeducational institution. Suburban campus. Founded in 1970. Accredited by Middle States Association of Colleges and Schools.

PROGRAM INFORMATION
Offered since 1970. 1,000-hour certificate in culinary arts.

PROGRAM AFFILIATION
American Culinary Federation; Foodservice Educators Network International; National Restaurant Association; National Restaurant Association Educational Foundation.

AREAS OF STUDY
Baking; buffet catering; controlling costs in food service; culinary skill development; food preparation; food purchasing; food service math; garde-manger; hospitality management; international cuisine; introduction to food service; kitchen management; management and human resources; menu and facilities design; restaurant opportunities; sanitation; soup, stock, sauce, and starch production.

FACILITIES
Bake shop; cafeteria; 3 classrooms; computer laboratory; 2 food production kitchens; gourmet dining room; learning resource center; 3 lecture rooms; student lounge; 2 teaching kitchens.

TYPICAL STUDENT PROFILE
66 part-time.

SPECIAL PROGRAMS
Cross training for supermarkets industry for take-home, chef express, and baking departments, technical internships and mentorships with industry members, preparation of cafeteria foods.

FINANCIAL AID
Employment placement assistance is available. Employment opportunities within the program are available.

APPLICATION INFORMATION
Students may begin participation in September. Application deadline for fall is July 1. Applicants must interview; submit a formal application and academic transcripts.

CONTACT
Director of Admissions, Culinary Arts, 400 East Main Street, Denville, NJ 07834. Telephone: 973-627-4600 Ext. 220. Fax: 973-627-6979. World Wide Web: http://www.mcvts.org.

TECHNICAL INSTITUTE OF CAMDEN COUNTY

Culinary Arts

Sicklerville, New Jersey

GENERAL INFORMATION
Public, coeducational, technical institute. Rural campus. Founded in 1927. Accredited by Middle States Association of Colleges and Schools.

PROGRAM INFORMATION
Program calendar is divided into semesters. 1-year diploma in culinary arts.

PROGRAM AFFILIATION
National Restaurant Association Educational Foundation.

AREAS OF STUDY
Buffet catering; convenience cookery; culinary French; culinary skill development; food preparation; food purchasing; food service communication; food service math; garde-manger; international cuisine; introduction to food service; meal planning; meat cutting; meat fabrication; menu and facilities design; nutrition; nutrition and food service; sanitation; saucier; seafood processing; soup, stock, sauce, and starch production.

FACILITIES
Cafeteria; 2 classrooms; coffee shop; demonstration laboratory; food production kitchen; gourmet dining room; lecture room; public restaurant; 2 teaching kitchens.

STUDENT PROFILE
21 full-time. 10 are under 25 years old; 9 are between 25 and 44 years old; 2 are over 44 years old.

FACULTY
3 total: 3 part-time. 3 are culinary-certified teachers. Prominent faculty: Barry Galasso; Anthony Marrocco; William Washart. Faculty-student ratio: 1:10.

TYPICAL EXPENSES
Application fee: $10. In-state tuition: $1642 per year (in district), $1762 per year (out-of-district). Out-of-state tuition: $3222 per year. Program-related fees include $290 for uniforms and books; $100 for administrative fee.

FINANCIAL AID
Employment placement assistance is available.

APPLICATION INFORMATION
Students may begin participation in September. Application deadline for fall is October 15. In 2005, 52 applied; 30 were accepted. Applicants must submit a formal application.

CONTACT
Gayle S. Butler, Director of Student Personnel Services, Culinary Arts, 343 Berlin Cross Keys Road, Sicklerville, NJ 08081. Telephone: 856-767-7002. Fax: 856-767-4278. E-mail: gbutler@ccts.tec.nj.us.

THOMAS EDISON STATE COLLEGE

Hotel/Motel/Restaurant Management

Trenton, New Jersey

GENERAL INFORMATION
Public, coeducational, comprehensive institution. Urban campus. Founded in 1972. Accredited by Middle States Association of Colleges and Schools.

PROGRAM INFORMATION
Offered since 1981. Program calendar is continuous. Associate degree in hotel/motel/restaurant management. Bachelor's degree in hotel/motel/restaurant management.

STUDENT PROFILE
36 part-time. 3 are under 25 years old; 23 are between 25 and 44 years old; 8 are over 44 years old.

TYPICAL EXPENSES
Application fee: $75. In-state tuition: $3780 per year part-time. Out-of-state tuition: $5400 per year part-time. Tuition for international students: $5400 per year part-time.

APPLICATION INFORMATION
Students may begin participation year-round. Applications are accepted continuously. In 2004, 24 applied; 24 were accepted. Applicants must submit a formal application.

CONTACT
Mr. Gordon Holly, Director of Admissions, Hotel/Motel/Restaurant Management, 101 West State Street, Trenton, NJ 08608-1176. Telephone: 888-442-8372. Fax: 609-984-8447. E-mail: info@tesc.edu. World Wide Web: http://www.tesc.edu.

UNION COUNTY COLLEGE

Cranford, New Jersey

GENERAL INFORMATION
Public, coeducational, two-year college. Suburban campus. Founded in 1933. Accredited by Middle States Association of Colleges and Schools.

PROGRAM INFORMATION
Offered since 1996. Program calendar is divided into semesters. 2-year associate degree in restaurant management (offered jointly with Fairleigh Dickinson University).

TYPICAL STUDENT PROFILE
19 total: 12 full-time; 7 part-time. 12 are under 25 years old; 5 are between 25 and 44 years old; 2 are over 44 years old.

SPECIAL PROGRAMS
Opportunity to transfer to a four-year program in hospitality management.

APPLICATION INFORMATION
Applications are accepted continuously. Applicants must submit a formal application.

CONTACT
Director of Admissions, 1033 Springfield Avenue, Cranford, NJ 07016. Telephone: 908-709-7596. Fax: 908-709-7131. World Wide Web: http://www.ucc.edu.

NEW MEXICO

CENTRAL NEW MEXICO COMMUNITY COLLEGE

Culinary Arts Program

Albuquerque, New Mexico

GENERAL INFORMATION
Public, coeducational, two-year college. Urban campus. Founded in 1965. Accredited by North Central Association of Colleges and Schools.

PROGRAM INFORMATION
Offered since 1973. Accredited by American Culinary Federation Accrediting Commission. Program calendar is divided into trimesters. 1-trimester certificate in food service management. 2-trimester certificate in professional cooking. 2-trimester certificate in baking. 2-year associate degree in culinary arts.

PROGRAM AFFILIATION
American Culinary Federation; American Institute of Baking; New Mexico Restaurant Association; Retailer's Bakery Association.

AREAS OF STUDY
Baking; beverage management; buffet catering; communications; confectionery show pieces; controlling costs in food service; convenience cookery; culinary French; culinary skill development; food preparation; food purchasing; food service math; garde-manger; international cuisine; introduction to food service; kitchen management; management and human resources; meal planning; meat cutting; meat fabrication; menu and facilities design; nutrition; nutrition and food service; patisserie; restaurant opportunities; sanitation; saucier; seafood processing; soup, stock, sauce, and starch production; wines and spirits.

FACILITIES
Bake shop; bakery; 2 cafeterias; catering service; 10 classrooms; computer laboratory; demonstration laboratory; 2 food production kitchens; garden; gourmet dining room; 3 laboratories; learning resource center; 5 lecture rooms; 2 libraries; 3 public restaurants; snack shop; 3 student lounges; 2 teaching kitchens.

TYPICAL STUDENT PROFILE
210 total: 160 full-time; 50 part-time. 103 are under 25 years old; 78 are between 25 and 44 years old; 29 are over 44 years old.

SPECIAL PROGRAMS
Cooperative education, field trips, service learning.

FINANCIAL AID
Program-specific awards include New Mexico Restaurant Association scholarships, 3-5 International Food Services Executive Association scholarships ($500), Culinary Arts Foundation Endowment awards. Employment placement assistance is available. Employment opportunities within the program are available.

APPLICATION INFORMATION
Students may begin participation in January, May, and August. Applications are accepted continuously. Applicants must submit a formal application.

CONTACT
Director of Admissions, Culinary Arts Program, Student Services Building, 900 University Boulevard, SE, Albuquerque, NM 87106. Telephone: 505-224-3194. World Wide Web: http://www.tvi.cc.nm.us/.

CULINARY BUSINESS ACADEMY

Rio Rancho, New Mexico

GENERAL INFORMATION
Private, coeducational institution. Urban campus. Founded in 1991.

PROGRAM INFORMATION
Offered since 1991. Program calendar is divided into months. 100-hour certificate in personal chef (quick start). 100-hour certificate in personal chef (home study). 50-hour certificate in personal chef (mentorship).

PROGRAM AFFILIATION
United States Personal Chef Association.

AREAS OF STUDY
Controlling costs in food service; food purchasing; kitchen management; meal planning; sanitation.

FACILITIES
Classroom; food production kitchen.

STUDENT PROFILE
500 full-time. 25 are under 25 years old; 275 are between 25 and 44 years old; 200 are over 44 years old.

FACULTY
8 total: 8 part-time. 8 are industry professionals. Faculty-student ratio: 1:3.

SPECIAL PROGRAMS
USPCA National Conference.

TYPICAL EXPENSES
Tuition: $2495 per course.

APPLICATION INFORMATION
Students may begin participation year-round. Applications are accepted continuously. In 2004, 500 applied; 500 were accepted. Applicants must have ability to cook.

CONTACT
Phil Ellison, Director of Admissions, 481 Rio Rancho Boulevard, Rio Rancho, NM 87124. Telephone: 800-747-2433. Fax: 505-994-6399. E-mail: info@culinarybusiness.com. World Wide Web: http://www.culinarybusiness.com.

INSTITUTE FOR CULINARY AWAKENING

Vegan Culinary Arts Training Program

Santa Fe, New Mexico

GENERAL INFORMATION
Private, coeducational institution. Urban campus. Founded in 1993.

PROGRAM INFORMATION
Offered since 1993. 5- to 12-day certificate in organic plant-based cuisine.

PROGRAM AFFILIATION
American Vegan Society; Chefs Collaborative 2000; North American Vegetarian Society; Vegetarian Resource Group; Vegetarian Union of North America.

AREAS OF STUDY
Baking; culinary skill development; food preparation; international cuisine.

TYPICAL STUDENT PROFILE
7 full-time.

SPECIAL PROGRAMS
Public consultations, public speaking services, workshops, and training programs.

FINANCIAL AID
Employment placement assistance is available.

APPLICATION INFORMATION
Applications are accepted continuously.

CONTACT
Director of Admissions, Vegan Culinary Arts Training Program, 7 Avenue Vista Grande, 316, Santa Fe, NM 87505-9199. Telephone: 505-466-4597. World Wide Web: http://www.chefal.org.

NEW MEXICO STATE UNIVERSITY

Hotel, Restaurant, and Tourism Management

Las Cruces, New Mexico

GENERAL INFORMATION
Public, coeducational, university. Suburban campus. Founded in 1888. Accredited by North Central Association of Colleges and Schools.

PROGRAM INFORMATION
Offered since 1988. Program calendar is divided into semesters. 4-year bachelor's degree in hotel, restaurant, and tourism management.

PROGRAM AFFILIATION
Council on Hotel, Restaurant, and Institutional Education; National Restaurant Association; National Restaurant Association Educational Foundation.

AREAS OF STUDY
Beverage management; controlling costs in food service; culinary skill development; food preparation; food purchasing; food service math; introduction to food service; management and human resources; meal planning; restaurant opportunities; sanitation; soup, stock, sauce, and starch production; wines and spirits.

STUDENT PROFILE
290 total: 263 full-time; 27 part-time. 246 are under 25 years old; 38 are between 25 and 44 years old; 6 are over 44 years old.

FACULTY
11 total: 5 full-time; 6 part-time.

TYPICAL EXPENSES
Application fee: $15. In-state tuition: $3666 per year full-time (in district), $152.75 per credit part-time. Out-of-state tuition: $12,210 per year full-time, $508.75 per credit part-time. Program-related fees include $35 for cutlery, lab coats; $30 for sanitation fee for certification; $25 for additional booklets.

FINANCIAL AID
In 2004, 29 scholarships were awarded (average award was $500). Employment placement assistance is available. Employment opportunities within the program are available.

HOUSING
Coed, apartment-style, and single-sex housing available.

APPLICATION INFORMATION
Students may begin participation in January and August. Applicants must submit a formal application.

CONTACT
Angela Mora-Riley, Office of Admissions, Hotel, Restaurant, and Tourism Management, PO Box 30001, MSC 3A, Las Cruces, NM 88003-8001. Telephone: 505-646-3121. Fax: 505-646-6330. E-mail: hrtm@nmsu.edu. World Wide Web: http://www.NMSU.edu/~hrtm/Resources/htmlHRTM/index.html.

SANTA FE COMMUNITY COLLEGE

Culinary Arts/Hospitality Department

Santa Fe, New Mexico

GENERAL INFORMATION
Public, coeducational, two-year college. Small-town setting. Founded in 1983. Accredited by North Central Association of Colleges and Schools.

PROGRAM INFORMATION
Offered since 1985. Program calendar is divided into semesters. 2-year associate degree in hotel/restaurant management. 2-year associate degree in culinary arts. 3-year associate degree in ACF apprenticeship program. 32-credit certificate of achievement in patisserie. 8-week certificate in commercial baking. 8-week certificate in cake making.

PROGRAM AFFILIATION
American Culinary Federation; Educational Institute American Hotel and Motel Association; National Restaurant Association Educational Foundation.

AREAS OF STUDY
Baking; beverage management; buffet catering; confectionery show pieces; controlling costs in food service; convenience cookery; culinary French; culinary skill development; food preparation; food purchasing; food service communication; food service math; garde-manger; international cuisine; introduction to food service; kitchen management; management and human resources; meal planning; meat cutting; meat fabrication; menu and facilities design; nutrition; nutrition and food service; patisserie; restaurant opportunities; sanitation; saucier; seafood processing; soup, stock, sauce, and starch production; Southwest cuisine; wines and spirits.

FACILITIES
Classroom; computer laboratory; demonstration laboratory; food production kitchen; garden; laboratory; learning resource center; lecture room; library; student lounge; teaching kitchen.

TYPICAL STUDENT PROFILE
78 total: 23 full-time; 55 part-time.

SPECIAL PROGRAMS
Paid internship program.

FINANCIAL AID
Employment placement assistance is available. Employment opportunities within the program are available.

APPLICATION INFORMATION

Students may begin participation in January, May, and August. Applications are accepted continuously. Applicants must submit a formal application.

CONTACT

Director of Admissions, Culinary Arts/Hospitality Department, 6401 Richards Avenue, Santa Fe, NM 87505. Telephone: 505-428-1435. Fax: 505-428-1237. World Wide Web: http://www.santa-fe.cc.nm.us/.

SOUTHWESTERN INDIAN POLYTECHNIC INSTITUTE

Culinary Arts Program

Albuquerque, New Mexico

GENERAL INFORMATION

Public, coeducational, two-year college. Urban campus. Founded in 1971. Accredited by North Central Association of Colleges and Schools.

PROGRAM INFORMATION

Offered since 1971. Program calendar is divided into trimesters. 3-trimester certificate in culinary arts. 5-trimester associate degree in hospitality. 5-trimester associate degree in culinary arts.

PROGRAM AFFILIATION

American Culinary Federation; International Food Service Executives Association; National Restaurant Association; National Restaurant Association Educational Foundation.

AREAS OF STUDY

Baking; convenience cookery; culinary skill development; food preparation; food service math; kitchen management; meal planning; nutrition; sanitation.

FACILITIES

Bake shop; cafeteria; 2 classrooms; computer laboratory; demonstration laboratory; food production kitchen; library; snack shop; pantry.

TYPICAL STUDENT PROFILE

48 full-time.

FINANCIAL AID

Employment placement assistance is available. Employment opportunities within the program are available.

HOUSING

Coed housing available.

APPLICATION INFORMATION

Students may begin participation in January, May, and August. Applications are accepted continuously. Applicants must submit a formal application, ACT scores, and be a high school graduate.

CONTACT

Director of Admissions, Culinary Arts Program, 9169 Coors, NW, Box 10146, Albuquerque, NM 87184-0146. Telephone: 505-346-2349. World Wide Web: http://www.sipi.bia.edu/culinaryarts.htm.

NEW YORK

THE ART INSTITUTE OF NEW YORK CITY

Culinary Arts and Restaurant Management

New York, New York

GENERAL INFORMATION

Private, coeducational, two-year college. Urban campus. Founded in 1980. Accredited by Accrediting Council for Independent Colleges and Schools.

PROGRAM INFORMATION

Offered since 1980. Program calendar is divided into quarters, 6-week terms. 3- to 4-quarter certificate in restaurant management. 3- to 4-quarter certificate in pastry arts. 4-quarter certificate in restaurant management (part-time). 4-quarter certificate in pastry arts (part-time). 4- to 6-quarter certificate in culinary arts. 6-quarter certificate in culinary arts (part-time). 6- to 8-quarter associate degree in culinary arts and restaurant management. 8-quarter associate degree in culinary arts and restaurant management (part-time).

PROGRAM AFFILIATION

American Culinary Federation; American Institute of Wine & Food; International Association of Culinary Professionals; James Beard Foundation, Inc.; National Restaurant Association; National Restaurant Association Educational Foundation; New York State Restaurant Association; United States Personal Chef Association; Women Chefs and Restaurateurs.

AREAS OF STUDY

Baking; beverage management; buffet catering; confectionery show pieces; controlling costs in food service; convenience cookery; culinary French; culinary skill development; food preparation; food purchasing; food service communication; food service math; garde-manger; international cuisine; introduction to food service; kitchen management; management and human resources; meal planning; meat cutting; meat fabrication; menu and facilities design; nutrition; nutrition and food service; patisserie; restaurant opportunities; sanitation; saucier; seafood processing; soup, stock, sauce, and starch production; wines and spirits.

The Art Institute of New York City *(continued)*

FACILITIES

10 classrooms; 2 computer laboratories; 9 food production kitchens; gourmet dining room; 14 lecture rooms; library; 3 student lounges.

STUDENT PROFILE

2,313 total: 1318 full-time; 995 part-time. 1573 are under 25 years old; 671 are between 25 and 44 years old; 69 are over 44 years old.

FACULTY

68 total: 60 full-time; 8 part-time. 20 are culinary-certified teachers. Prominent faculty: George Conte, CC; Eric Pellizzari, CEC; Michael Vignapiano, CCE, CHE; Tony D'Onofrio, CHE. Faculty-student ratio: 1:21; 1:25 labs.

SPECIAL PROGRAMS

198-hour externship (for students in culinary arts and pastry programs), culinary competition, ACF Junior Memberships.

TYPICAL EXPENSES

Application fee: $50. Tuition: $452 per credit. Program-related fee includes $100 for registration.

FINANCIAL AID

In 2005, 5 scholarships were awarded (average award was $18,000). Program-specific awards include scholarships for high school seniors. Employment placement assistance is available. Employment opportunities within the program are available.

HOUSING

Coed housing available. Average on-campus housing cost per month: $1200. Average off-campus housing cost per month: $800.

APPLICATION INFORMATION

Students may begin participation in January, April, July, and October. Applications are accepted continuously. Applicants must interview; submit a formal application, an essay, high school diploma or GED.

CONTACT

Lauren Malone, Director of Admissions, Culinary Arts and Restaurant Management, 75 Varick Street, 16th Floor, New York, NY 10013. Telephone: 212-226-5500 Ext. 6080. Fax: 212-625-6065. E-mail: lmalon@aii.edu. World Wide Web: http://www.artinstitutes.edu/newyork/.

See color display following page 380.

BROOME COMMUNITY COLLEGE

Hotel Restaurant Management

Binghamton, New York

GENERAL INFORMATION

Public, coeducational, two-year college. Suburban campus. Founded in 1946. Accredited by Middle States Association of Colleges and Schools.

PROGRAM INFORMATION

Offered since 1986. Program calendar is divided into semesters. 1-year certificate in dietary management. 2-year associate degree in hotel restaurant management.

PROGRAM AFFILIATION

Council on Hotel, Restaurant, and Institutional Education; National Restaurant Association; National Restaurant Association Educational Foundation; New York State Hospitality and Tourism Association.

AREAS OF STUDY

Controlling costs in food service; convenience cookery; culinary skill development; food preparation; food service math; management and human resources.

FACILITIES

3 classrooms; computer laboratory; demonstration laboratory; food production kitchen; laboratory; lecture room; teaching kitchen.

STUDENT PROFILE

86 total: 66 full-time; 20 part-time. 58 are under 25 years old; 23 are between 25 and 44 years old; 5 are over 44 years old.

FACULTY

1 is an industry professional; 2 are culinary-certified teachers. Faculty-student ratio: 1:28.

SPECIAL PROGRAMS

American Hotel and Lodging Association and foodservice trade shows, internship opportunities for credit (one year), study abroad and international internship opportunities.

TYPICAL EXPENSES

In-state tuition: $2814 per year full-time (in district), $118 per credit hour part-time. Out-of-state tuition: $5628 per year full-time, $236 per credit hour part-time.

FINANCIAL AID

Employment placement assistance is available.

HOUSING

Average off-campus housing cost per month: $300–$400.

APPLICATION INFORMATION

Students may begin participation in January and September. Applications are accepted continuously.

CONTACT

Mr. Reynald C. Wojdat, Dean, Division of Business and Business Technology, Hotel Restaurant Management, PO

Box 1017, Binghamton, NY 13902. Telephone: 607-778-5008. E-mail: lopez_v@sunybroome.edu. World Wide Web: http://www.sunybroome.edu.

BUFFALO STATE COLLEGE, STATE UNIVERSITY OF NEW YORK

Hospitality Administration

Buffalo, New York

GENERAL INFORMATION
Public, coeducational, comprehensive institution. Urban campus. Founded in 1867. Accredited by Middle States Association of Colleges and Schools.

PROGRAM INFORMATION
Offered since 1989. Accredited by American Dietetic Association, Council on Hotel, Restaurant and Institutional Education, Accreditation Commission for Programs in Hospitality Administration. Program calendar is divided into semesters. 1-semester certificate in sanitation. 1-semester certificate in hospitality training. 1-semester certificate in hospitality law. 4-year bachelor's degree in hospitality administration.

PROGRAM AFFILIATION
Council on Hotel, Restaurant, and Institutional Education.

AREAS OF STUDY
Food preparation; management and human resources; sanitation.

FACILITIES
6 classrooms; computer laboratory; food production kitchen; gourmet dining room; 6 lecture rooms; library; teaching kitchen.

TYPICAL STUDENT PROFILE
104 total: 88 full-time; 16 part-time. 77 are under 25 years old; 25 are between 25 and 44 years old; 2 are over 44 years old.

SPECIAL PROGRAMS
Walt Disney World co-op experiences (paid), two-year paid internship in hotel management, 6 credit hours of hands-on, lab-based operations and management.

FINANCIAL AID
Employment placement assistance is available.

HOUSING
Coed and apartment-style housing available.

APPLICATION INFORMATION
Students may begin participation in January and September. Applications are accepted continuously. Applicants must submit a formal application and high school and college transcripts.

CONTACT
Director of Admissions, Hospitality Administration, 1300 Elmwood Avenue, Buffalo, NY 14222. Telephone: 716-878-5913. Fax: 716-878-5834. World Wide Web: http://www.buffalostate.edu/depts/hospitality.

CULINARY ACADEMY OF LONG ISLAND

Westbury, New York

GENERAL INFORMATION
Private, coeducational, culinary institute. Suburban campus. Founded in 1996. Accredited by Accrediting Commission of Career Schools and Colleges of Technology.

PROGRAM INFORMATION
Offered since 1996. Program calendar is continuous. 13-session certificate in advanced baking pastry arts. 13-session certificate in basic baking pastry arts. 9-month certificate in restaurant management (evening courses available). 9-month certificate in culinary arts (evening courses available).

PROGRAM AFFILIATION
American Culinary Federation; National Restaurant Association Educational Foundation.

AREAS OF STUDY
Baking; buffet catering; culinary skill development; food preparation; food purchasing; food service math; garde-manger; meal planning; meat cutting; meat fabrication; menu and facilities design; nutrition; nutrition and food service; sanitation; seafood processing; soup, stock, sauce, and starch production.

FACILITIES
Classroom; library; student lounge; 2 teaching kitchens.

TYPICAL STUDENT PROFILE
217 total: 162 full-time; 55 part-time. 87 are under 25 years old; 121 are between 25 and 44 years old; 9 are over 44 years old.

SPECIAL PROGRAMS
Evening of Good Taste (culinary competitions), ACF Student Competition.

FINANCIAL AID
Employment placement assistance is available.

APPLICATION INFORMATION
Students may begin participation in January, February, March, May, June, July, September, November, and December. Applications are accepted continuously. Applicants must interview.

CONTACT
Director of Admissions, 141 Post Avenue, Westbury, NY 11590. Telephone: 516-876-8888. Fax: 516-846-8488. World Wide Web: http://www.culinaryacademyli.com.

THE CULINARY INSTITUTE OF AMERICA

Hyde Park, New York

GENERAL INFORMATION
Private, coeducational, four-year college. Small-town setting. Founded in 1946. Accredited by Middle States Association of Colleges and Schools.

PROGRAM INFORMATION
Offered since 1946. Program calendar is continuous. 2-year associate degree in baking and pastry arts. 2-year associate degree in culinary arts. 4-year bachelor's degree in baking and pastry arts management. 4-year bachelor's degree in culinary arts management.

PROGRAM AFFILIATION
American Culinary Federation; American Dietetic Association; American Institute of Baking; American Institute of Wine & Food; Confrerie de la Chaine des Rotisseurs; Council on Hotel, Restaurant, and Institutional Education; International Association of Culinary Professionals; International Foodservice Editorial Council; James Beard Foundation, Inc.; Napa Valley Wine Library Association; National Association for the Specialty Food Trade, Inc.; National Restaurant Association; Oldways Preservation and Exchange Trust; Society of Wine Educators; Sommelier Society of America; The Bread Bakers Guild of America; Women Chefs and Restaurateurs.

AREAS OF STUDY
Baking; beverage management; buffet catering; confectionery show pieces; controlling costs in food service; culinary skill development; finance; food preparation; food service communication; food service math; garde-manger; gastronomy; international cuisine; introduction to food service; Italian cuisine; kitchen management; management and human resources; marketing; meat cutting; meat fabrication; menu and facilities design; nutrition; nutrition and food service; patisserie; restaurant operations; sanitation; saucier; seafood processing; soup, stock, sauce, and starch production; wines and spirits.

FACILITIES
9 bake shops; bakery; 33 classrooms; 8 computer laboratories; 2 demonstration laboratories; 2 food production kitchens; 2 gardens; 4 gourmet dining rooms; laboratory; learning resource center; 4 lecture rooms; library; 5 public restaurants; snack shop; 2 student lounges; 32 teaching kitchens; 2 amphitheaters.

STUDENT PROFILE
2713 full-time.

FACULTY
148 total: 120 full-time; 28 part-time. 15 are industry professionals; 10 are master chefs; 8 are master bakers; 102 are culinary-certified teachers; 2 are European master chefs, 1 certified master pastry chef. Prominent faculty: Thomas Vaccaro, CEPC; Eve Felder, CEC, CHC; Kate Covatti, CMB, CHE; Oliver Andreini, CMC, CHE. Faculty-student ratio: 1:18.

SPECIAL PROGRAMS
3-week tour of wine country and restaurants in California, 18-week externship, hands-on experience in some of the five on-campus public restaurants.

TYPICAL EXPENSES
Application fee: $30. Tuition: $20,300 per full academic year. Program-related fees include $1395 for books and supplies; $7170 for room and board (mandatory); $360 for externship.

FINANCIAL AID
In 2005, 2258 scholarships were awarded (average award was $2000). Program-specific awards include Cream of the Crop Scholarships (up to $20,000), MFK Fisher Scholarships (available to incoming students based on writing ability). Employment placement assistance is available. Employment opportunities within the program are available.

HOUSING
Coed housing available. Average on-campus housing cost per month: $550.

APPLICATION INFORMATION
Students may begin participation year-round. Applications are accepted continuously. In 2005, 2098 applied; 1692 were accepted. Applicants must submit a formal application, letters of reference, an essay, academic transcript, interview (for bachelor's degree).

CONTACT
Rachel Birchwood, Director of Admissions, 1946 Campus Drive, Hyde Park, NY 12538. Telephone: 800-CULINARY. Fax: 845-451-1068. E-mail: admissions@culinary.edu. World Wide Web: http://www.ciachef.edu.

See display on page 251.

ERIE COMMUNITY COLLEGE, CITY CAMPUS

Culinary Arts

Buffalo, New York

GENERAL INFORMATION
Public, coeducational, two-year college. Urban campus. Founded in 1971. Accredited by Middle States Association of Colleges and Schools.

PROGRAM INFORMATION
Offered since 1984. Program calendar is divided into semesters. 1-year certificate in baking and pastry arts. 2-year associate degree in culinary arts.

VOL AU VENTS?

New brand of Swedish spring water?

Actually it means "flying in the wind" – but foodies around the world know it as a puff pastry shell that's, you guessed it, incredibly light. At The Culinary Institute of America, we speak food, and our knowledge of this international language draws from an appetite ingrained in the fingertips, taste buds, and imagination of our students, professors, and alumni. It's expression, it's love – it's life.

THE WORLD'S PREMIER CULINARY COLLEGE

Visit **www.ciachef.edu** and find out how you can mold your passion for cooking and baking into a profession good enough to eat.

At the CIA – the world's premier culinary college – not only will you master the art of fine food, but you'll also gain the business savvy to succeed in today's competitive market. Our determined students, impassioned instructors, state-of-the-art facilities, and decorated alumni will help you get where you want to be – on the restaurant floor, in test kitchens, at corporate headquarters, behind a writer's desk, on TV, or anywhere else you dream of going.

APPLY NOW! 1-800-CULINARY (285-4627).
Bachelor's & Associate Degrees
Ninety-two percent of students receive financial aid | Financial aid available for those who qualify

Erie Community College, City Campus *(continued)*

PROGRAM AFFILIATION
Council on Hotel, Restaurant, and Institutional Education; National Restaurant Association; National Restaurant Association Educational Foundation.

AREAS OF STUDY
Baking; beverage management; buffet catering; confectionery show pieces; controlling costs in food service; culinary skill development; food preparation; food purchasing; food service math; garde-manger; international cuisine; introduction to food service; kitchen management; management and human resources; meal planning; menu and facilities design; nutrition; sanitation; soup, stock, sauce, and starch production; wines and spirits.

FACILITIES
Bake shop; bakery; cafeteria; 3 classrooms; coffee shop; computer laboratory; demonstration laboratory; food production kitchen; gourmet dining room; learning resource center; library; public restaurant; teaching kitchen.

STUDENT PROFILE
109 total: 99 full-time; 10 part-time. 64 are under 25 years old; 32 are between 25 and 44 years old; 13 are over 44 years old.

FACULTY
11 total: 3 full-time; 8 part-time. 10 are industry professionals; 1 is a master baker; 3 are culinary-certified teachers. Prominent faculty: Paul J. Cannamela, CCE, AAC; Anthony Songin, CPC. Faculty-student ratio: 1:16.

TYPICAL EXPENSES
Application fee: $25. In-state tuition: $1450 per semester full-time (in district), $121 per credit hour part-time (in district), $2900 per semester full-time (out-of-district), $242 per credit hour part-time (out-of-district). Out-of-state tuition: $2900 per semester full-time, $242 per credit hour part-time. Tuition for international students: $2900 per semester full-time, $242 per credit hour part-time. Program-related fees include $175 for knives; $500 for books; $150 for uniforms.

FINANCIAL AID
In 2004, 50 scholarships were awarded (average award was $500); 40 loans were granted (average loan was $1500). Employment placement assistance is available. Employment opportunities within the program are available.

APPLICATION INFORMATION
Students may begin participation in January and September. Applications are accepted continuously. In 2004, 116 applied; 91 were accepted. Applicants must submit a formal application.

CONTACT
Richard Mills, Professor, Culinary Arts, 121 Ellicott Street, Buffalo, NY 14203-2698. Telephone: 716-851-1034. Fax: 716-851-1133. E-mail: millsr@ecc.edu. World Wide Web: http://www.ecc.edu.

ERIE COMMUNITY COLLEGE, NORTH CAMPUS

Food Service Administration/Restaurant Management

Williamsville, New York

GENERAL INFORMATION
Public, coeducational, two-year college. Suburban campus. Founded in 1946. Accredited by Middle States Association of Colleges and Schools.

PROGRAM INFORMATION
Offered since 1953. Accredited by American Dietetic Association, Council on Hotel, Restaurant and Institutional Education, Commission on Accreditation of Hospitality Management Programs. Program calendar is divided into semesters. 2-year associate degree in culinary arts. 2-year associate degree in food service administration: dietetic technology/nutrition. 2-year associate degree in hotel/restaurant management.

PROGRAM AFFILIATION
American Culinary Federation; American Dietetic Association; Confrerie de la Chaine des Rotisseurs; Council on Hotel, Restaurant, and Institutional Education; International Food Service Executives Association; International Foodservice Editorial Council; National Restaurant Association; National Restaurant Association Educational Foundation; New York State Restaurant Association.

AREAS OF STUDY
Baking; beverage management; buffet catering; controlling costs in food service; culinary skill development; food preparation; food purchasing; food service communication; food service math; garde-manger; international cuisine; introduction to food service; kitchen management; management and human resources; meal planning; menu and facilities design; nutrition; nutrition and food service; sanitation; soup, stock, sauce, and starch production; wines and spirits.

FACILITIES
Bake shop; bakery; cafeteria; 2 classrooms; computer laboratory; demonstration laboratory; 3 food production kitchens; gourmet dining room; laboratory; lecture room; library; 2 public restaurants; student lounge; teaching kitchen.

STUDENT PROFILE
233 total: 175 full-time; 58 part-time. 176 are under 25 years old; 48 are between 25 and 44 years old; 9 are over 44 years old.

FACULTY
36 total: 8 full-time; 28 part-time. 18 are industry professionals; 2 are master chefs; 1 is a master baker; 4 are culinary-certified teachers. Prominent faculty: Terance

McDonough; Jane Myers-Reitmeier; Mark Wright, CEC; Donald Spasiano. Faculty-student ratio: 1:16.

SPECIAL PROGRAMS
8-week off-campus internship, culinary competitions.

TYPICAL EXPENSES
Application fee: $25. In-state tuition: $1450 per semester full-time (in district), $121 per credit hour part-time (in district), $2900 per semester full-time (out-of-district), $242 per credit hour part-time (out-of-district). Out-of-state tuition: $2900 per semester full-time, $242 per credit hour part-time. Tuition for international students: $2900 per semester full-time, $242 per credit hour part-time. Program-related fees include $30 for lab fee (per semester); $150 for cutlery; $100 for uniforms.

FINANCIAL AID
In 2004, 50 scholarships were awarded (average award was $500–$750). Program-specific awards include Erie Community College Foundation scholarships; American Dietetic Association Scholarship, Gertrude Chrymko Memorial Scholarship, Statler Foundation Scholarships, New York State Restaurant Association Scholarships. Employment placement assistance is available. Employment opportunities within the program are available.

APPLICATION INFORMATION
Students may begin participation in January and September. Applications are accepted continuously. In 2004, 162 applied; 149 were accepted. Applicants must submit a formal application.

CONTACT
Jane Reitmeier, (culinary arts/hotel restaurant), Margaret Garfoot (dietetics), Food Service Administration/Restaurant Management, 6205 Main Street, Williamsville, NY 14221. Telephone: 716-851-1394. Fax: 716-851-1429. E-mail: reitmeier@ecc.edu or garfoot@ecc.edu. World Wide Web: http://www.ecc.edu.

THE FRENCH CULINARY INSTITUTE AT THE INTERNATIONAL CULINARY CENTER

Classic Culinary Arts

New York, New York

GENERAL INFORMATION
Private, coeducational, culinary institute. Urban campus. Founded in 1984. Accredited by Accrediting Commission of Career Schools and Colleges of Technology.

PROGRAM INFORMATION
Offered since 1984. Accredited by Accrediting Commission of Career Schools and Colleges of Technology. Program calendar is continuous, six-week cycles. 10-hour certificate in Tapas Essentials (cooking clinic). 100-hour certificate in

essentials of pastry (amateur). 110-hour certificate in La Technique (amateur culinary). 12-hour certificate in Parisian Breads (cooking clinic). 12-hour certificate in Whole Grain Breads (cooking clinic). 15-week certificate in opening and running a restaurant. 225-hour certificate in fundamentals of Italian cooking. 25-hour certificate in Fondant and Royal Icing (cooking clinic). 25-hour certificate in Chocolate (cooking clinic). 29-week diploma in Italian Culinary Experience. 30-hour certificate in essentials of artisanal bread baking (amateur). 4-week certificate in classic European breads. 40-hour certificate in Essentials of Italian Cooking II. 40-hour certificate in Essentials of Italian Cooking III. 40-hour certificate in Essentials of Italian Cooking I. 6-month diploma in classic pastry arts. 6-month diploma in classic culinary arts. 6-week certificate in great wine and food made simple (amateur). 6-week certificate in The Craft of Food Writing. 6-week diploma in art of international bread baking. 60-hour certificate in La Technique ll (amateur culinary). 8-week certificate in fundamentals of wine. 8-week certificate in essentials of fine cooking (amateur).

PROGRAM AFFILIATION
American Institute of Baking; American Institute of Wine & Food; Chefs Collaborative 2000; Council on Hotel, Restaurant, and Institutional Education; Federation of Dining Rooms Professionals; International Association of Culinary Professionals; James Beard Foundation, Inc.; National Restaurant Association; National Restaurant Association Educational Foundation; Slow Food International; The Bread Bakers Guild of America; Women Chefs and Restaurateurs.

AREAS OF STUDY
Baking; beverage management; buffet catering; confectionery show pieces; culinary French; culinary skill development; food preparation; food purchasing; garde-manger; introduction to food service; kitchen management; management and human resources; meal planning; meat cutting; menu and facilities design; nutrition and food service; patisserie; restaurant opportunities; sanitation; saucier; seafood processing; soup, stock, sauce, and starch production; wines and spirits.

FACILITIES
12 classrooms; computer laboratory; demonstration laboratory; food production kitchen; gourmet dining room; 4 lecture rooms; library; public restaurant; student lounge; 6 teaching kitchens.

STUDENT PROFILE
1,084 total: 436 full-time; 648 part-time. 437 are under 25 years old; 627 are between 25 and 44 years old; 20 are over 44 years old.

FACULTY
55 total: 55 full-time. 10 are industry professionals; 5 are master chefs; 1 is a master baker; 55 are culinary-certified teachers; 1 is a Master Sommelier. Prominent faculty: Jacques Pépin; André Soltner; Alain Sailhac; Jacques Torres; Andrea Robison; Alan Richman; Cesare Casella. Faculty-student ratio: 1:12.

The French Culinary Institute at the International Culinary Center *(continued)*

SPECIAL PROGRAMS
Demonstrations in International Culinary Theater, internships, student clubs and activities: Supper Club, Wine Club, Career Avenues, Forager Club, International Student Club.

TYPICAL EXPENSES
Application fee: $100. Tuition: Tuition varies by program. Contact school directly for current costs. Program-related fees include $10 for insurance; $40–$700 for books, tools, and uniforms.

FINANCIAL AID
In 2005, 32 scholarships were awarded (average award was $4125.63); 521 loans were granted (average loan was $22,307). Employment placement assistance is available. Employment opportunities within the program are available.

HOUSING
Coed and apartment-style housing available. Average on-campus housing cost per month: $1060. Average off-campus housing cost per month: $2000.

APPLICATION INFORMATION
Students may begin participation year-round. Applications are accepted continuously. In 2005, 1918 applied; 1905 were accepted. Applicants must interview; submit a formal application, an essay, proof of high school graduation or equivalent and resume (career programs only).

CONTACT
Judy Currie-Hellmann, Director of Admission, Classic Culinary Arts, 462 Broadway, 4th Floor, New York, NY 10013. Telephone: 888-324-CHEF. Fax: 212-431-3065. E-mail: admission@frenchculinary.com. World Wide Web: http://www.frenchculinary.com.
See color display following page 236.

FULTON-MONTGOMERY COMMUNITY COLLEGE

Hospitality Management

Johnstown, New York

GENERAL INFORMATION
Public, coeducational, two-year college. Small-town setting. Founded in 1964. Accredited by Middle States Association of Colleges and Schools.

PROGRAM INFORMATION
Offered since 1972. Accredited by American Culinary Federation Accrediting Commission, Council on Hotel, Restaurant and Institutional Education. Program calendar is divided into semesters. 2-year associate degree in restaurant management. 2-year associate degree in food service administration.

PROGRAM AFFILIATION
Council on Hotel, Restaurant, and Institutional Education; National Restaurant Association; National Restaurant Association Educational Foundation.

AREAS OF STUDY
Baking; beverage management; controlling costs in food service; culinary skill development; food preparation; food purchasing; food service math; introduction to food service; menu and facilities design; nutrition; nutrition and food service; restaurant opportunities; sanitation.

FACILITIES
Food production kitchen; gourmet dining room; lecture room.

TYPICAL STUDENT PROFILE
28 total: 18 full-time; 10 part-time.

SPECIAL PROGRAMS
Opportunity to prepare food for local fundraising events, field trips, flexible internships, participation in local restaurant surveys and marketing.

FINANCIAL AID
Employment placement assistance is available. Employment opportunities within the program are available.

APPLICATION INFORMATION
Students may begin participation in January and September. Application deadline for fall is September 1. Application deadline for spring is January 15. Applicants must submit a formal application.

CONTACT
Director of Admissions, Hospitality Management, 2805 State Highway 67, Johnstown, NY 12095. Telephone: 518-762-4651 Ext. 2404. Fax: 518-762-4334. World Wide Web: http://fmcc.suny.edu/.

GENESEE COMMUNITY COLLEGE

Hospitality Management

Batavia, New York

GENERAL INFORMATION
Public, coeducational, two-year college. Small-town setting. Founded in 1966. Accredited by Middle States Association of Colleges and Schools.

PROGRAM INFORMATION
Offered since 1967. Program calendar is divided into semesters. 2-year associate degree in hospitality management.

AREAS OF STUDY
Management and human resources.

STUDENT PROFILE
58 total: 48 full-time; 10 part-time.

FACULTY
3 total: 1 full-time; 2 part-time. Faculty-student ratio: 1:17.

TYPICAL EXPENSES
In-state tuition: $3390 per year full-time (in district), $137 per per credit hour part-time. Out-of-state tuition: $3790 per year full-time, $147 per per credit hour part-time.

HOUSING
Coed housing available. Average on-campus housing cost per month: $450. Average off-campus housing cost per month: $450.

APPLICATION INFORMATION
Students may begin participation in January and September. In 2004, 42 applied.

CONTACT
Tanya Lane-Martin, Admission Office, Hospitality Management, 1 College Road, Batavia, NY 14020-9704. Telephone: 866-CALLGCC. Fax: 716-345-6810. E-mail: tmlanemartin@genesee.edu. World Wide Web: http://www.genesee.edu.

THE INSTITUTE OF CULINARY EDUCATION

New York, New York

GENERAL INFORMATION
Private, coeducational, culinary institute. Urban campus. Founded in 1975. Accredited by Accrediting Commission of Career Schools and Colleges of Technology.

PROGRAM INFORMATION
Offered since 1975. Accredited by Accrediting Commission of Career Schools and Colleges of Technology (ACCSCT). Program calendar is continuous. 26-week diploma in culinary management. 26-week diploma in full-time career culinary arts. 26-week diploma in full-time career pastry and baking arts. 31-week diploma in part-time career pastry and baking arts. 31-week diploma in part-time career culinary arts. 39-week diploma in weekend part-time career pastry and baking arts. 39-week diploma in weekend part-time culinary arts.

PROGRAM AFFILIATION
American Institute of Wine & Food; International Association of Culinary Professionals; International Wine & Food Society; James Beard Foundation, Inc.; National Restaurant Association; National Restaurant Association Educational Foundation; Society of Wine Educators; Sommelier Society of America; The Bread Bakers Guild of America; United States Personal Chef Association; Women Chefs and Restaurateurs.

AREAS OF STUDY
Baking; beverage management; buffet catering; controlling costs in food service; culinary French; culinary skill development; food preparation; food purchasing; food service communication; food service math; garde-manger; international cuisine; introduction to food service; kitchen management; management and human resources; meal planning; meat cutting; meat fabrication; menu and facilities design; nutrition; nutrition and food service; patisserie; restaurant opportunities; sanitation; seafood processing; soup, stock, sauce, and starch production; wines and spirits.

FACILITIES
Bake shop; catering service; 3 classrooms; 2 demonstration laboratories; food production kitchen; lecture room; library; 2 student lounges; 12 teaching kitchens.

STUDENT PROFILE
750 total: 586 full-time; 164 part-time. 201 are under 25 years old; 477 are between 25 and 44 years old; 72 are over 44 years old.

FACULTY
32 total: 24 full-time; 8 part-time. 32 are industry professionals; 32 are culinary-certified teachers. Prominent faculty: Nick Malgieri; Toba Garrett; Michael Handel, CCC, CCE; Chris Gesaldi. Faculty-student ratio: 1:14.

SPECIAL PROGRAMS
210-hour externship in a restaurant, pastry shop, or with a caterer in the United States, France, England, Spain, Italy, or Singapore, 9-day student trip to France including cooking and baking classes, market visits and vineyard tours, elective classes on specialized wine, baking, and cooking topics.

TYPICAL EXPENSES
Application fee: $25. Tuition: $24,067 for pastry diploma; $24,067 for culinary arts diploma; $12,900 for culinary management diploma.

FINANCIAL AID
In 2004, 40 scholarships were awarded (average award was $4000); 450 loans were granted (average loan was $24,000). Employment placement assistance is available.

HOUSING
Average off-campus housing cost per month: $600–$800.

APPLICATION INFORMATION
Students may begin participation year-round. Applications are accepted continuously. In 2004, 1167 applied; 750 were accepted. Applicants must interview; submit a formal application.

CONTACT
Stephen Tave, Vice President, Institute of Culinary Education, 50 West 23rd Street, New York, NY 10010. Telephone: 212-847-0711. Fax: 212-847-0726. E-mail: stave@iceculinary.com. World Wide Web: http://www.ICEculinary.com.
See color display following page 236.

Julie Sahni's School of Indian Cooking

Brooklyn, New York

General Information
Private, coeducational, culinary institute. Urban campus. Founded in 1974.

Program Information
Offered since 1974. Program calendar is divided into weekends, weekends. 3-day diploma in vegetarian cooking. 3-day diploma in Indian cooking. 3-day diploma in spices and herbs.

Program Affiliation
International Association of Culinary Professionals.

Areas of Study
Indian cooking; international cuisine; spices and herbs.

Faculty
1 total: 1 full-time. 1 is a master chef. Prominent faculty: Julie Sahni.

Typical Expenses
Application fee: $35. Tuition: $1195–$1695 per diploma; corporate rates available: $2000 (2 Days) $9000 (1 week).

Application Information
Students may begin participation in January, February, March, April, May, June, September, October, November, and December. Applications are accepted continuously. Applicants must submit a formal application.

Contact
Julie Sahni, President, PO Box 023792, Brooklyn, NY 11202-3792. Telephone: 718-625-3958. Fax: 718-625-3958. E-mail: jsicooking@aol.com.

Katharine Gibbs School

Hotel and Restaurant Management

New York, New York

General Information
Private, coeducational, two-year college. Urban campus. Founded in 1911. Accredited by Accrediting Council for Independent Colleges and Schools.

Program Information
Offered since 1987. Accredited by Council on Hotel, Restaurant and Institutional Education. Program calendar is divided into quarters. 18-month associate degree in hotel and restaurant management.

Program Affiliation
American Hotel and Lodging Association Educational Institute; Council on Hotel, Restaurant, and Institutional Education.

Areas of Study
Hotel and restaurant management.

Facilities
35 classrooms; 30 computer laboratories; learning resource center; library; student lounge.

Typical Student Profile
250 full-time. 220 are under 25 years old; 28 are between 25 and 44 years old; 2 are over 44 years old.

Special Programs
360-hour internship.

Financial Aid
Employment placement assistance is available.

Application Information
Students may begin participation in January, April, July, and October. Applications are accepted continuously. Applicants must interview; submit a formal application and take ACCUPLACER Test.

Contact
Director of Admissions, Hotel and Restaurant Management, 50 West 40th Street, New York, NY 10018. Telephone: 212-973-3130. World Wide Web: http://www.katharinegibbs.com.

Keuka College

Hospitality Management

Keuka Park, New York

General Information
Private, coeducational, four-year college. Rural campus. Founded in 1890. Accredited by Middle States Association of Colleges and Schools.

Program Information
Offered since 1990. Program calendar is divided into semesters. 4-year bachelor's degree in hospitality management.

Program Affiliation
Council on Hotel, Restaurant, and Institutional Education; National Restaurant Association.

Areas of Study
Beverage management; management and human resources; restaurant opportunities; wines and spirits.

Facilities
Cafeteria; catering service; 5 classrooms; 2 computer laboratories; food production kitchen; gourmet dining

room; learning resource center; lecture room; library; public restaurant; snack shop; student lounge; vineyard.

TYPICAL STUDENT PROFILE
15 full-time.

SPECIAL PROGRAMS
5-week internships at Finger Lakes wineries, summer internships.

FINANCIAL AID
Employment placement assistance is available. Employment opportunities within the program are available.

HOUSING
Coed and single-sex housing available.

APPLICATION INFORMATION
Students may begin participation in February and August. Applications are accepted continuously. Applicants must submit a formal application, letters of reference, and an essay.

CONTACT
Director of Admissions, Hospitality Management, Keuka Park, NY 14478-0098. Telephone: 800-33-KEUKA. World Wide Web: http://www.keuka.edu.

MOHAWK VALLEY COMMUNITY COLLEGE

Hospitality Programs

Rome, New York

GENERAL INFORMATION
Public, coeducational, two-year college. Urban campus. Founded in 1946. Accredited by Middle States Association of Colleges and Schools.

PROGRAM INFORMATION
Offered since 1980. Program calendar is divided into semesters. 1-year certificate in chef training. 2-year associate degree in hotel technology: meeting services management. 2-year associate degree in culinary arts management. 2-year associate degree in food service administration: restaurant management.

PROGRAM AFFILIATION
American Culinary Federation; Council on Hotel, Restaurant, and Institutional Education; International Food Service Executives Association; National Restaurant Association; National Restaurant Association Educational Foundation.

AREAS OF STUDY
Baking; beverage management; buffet catering; controlling costs in food service; culinary skill development; food preparation; food purchasing; food service math; garde-manger; international cuisine; kitchen management; management and human resources; meal planning; meat

cutting; meat fabrication; menu and facilities design; nutrition; patisserie; restaurant opportunities; sanitation; saucier; seafood processing; soup, stock, sauce, and starch production; wines and spirits.

FACILITIES
Bake shop; catering service; 6 classrooms; computer laboratory; demonstration laboratory; 2 food production kitchens; gourmet dining room; learning resource center; library; public restaurant; snack shop; student lounge; teaching kitchen; banquet room.

STUDENT PROFILE
120 total: 80 full-time; 40 part-time.

FACULTY
7 total: 4 full-time; 3 part-time. 7 are industry professionals; 2 are culinary-certified teachers; 1 is a food service management professional, 1 certified baker. Prominent faculty: Jo Ann Detraglia, MS; Andrew Glidden, MS, FMP, CB; David Hoffman, MS; Betty Milson, MS. Faculty-student ratio: 1:20.

SPECIAL PROGRAMS
Annual participation in National Restaurant Association and International Hotel and Motel Association shows, semester-long internship/co-op experience.

TYPICAL EXPENSES
Application fee: $30. In-state tuition: $1400 per semester full-time (in district), $115 per credit hour part-time. Out-of-state tuition: $2800 per semester full-time, $230 per credit hour part-time.

FINANCIAL AID
In 2004, 7 scholarships were awarded (average award was $350). Employment placement assistance is available. Employment opportunities within the program are available.

HOUSING
Average off-campus housing cost per month: $325.

APPLICATION INFORMATION
Students may begin participation in January, May, and August. Applications are accepted continuously. In 2004, 75 applied; 65 were accepted. Applicants must submit a formal application.

CONTACT
Ann Nicholson, Secretary, Hospitality Programs, 1101 Floyd Avenue, Rome, NY 13440. Telephone: 315-334-7702. World Wide Web: http://www.mvcc.edu.

Monroe College

Hospitality Management

Bronx, New York

General Information
Private, coeducational, four-year college. Urban campus. Founded in 1933. Accredited by Middle States Association of Colleges and Schools.

Program Information
Offered since 1993. Program calendar is divided into trimesters. 16-month associate degree in culinary arts. 16-month associate degree in hotel/restaurant management. 32-month bachelor's degree in hotel/restaurant management.

Program Affiliation
American Culinary Federation; American Hotel and Lodging Association; Caribbean Tourism Association; Council on Hotel, Restaurant, and Institutional Education; International Association of Culinary Professionals; James Beard Foundation, Inc.; National Restaurant Association; National Restaurant Association Educational Foundation; Sommelier Society of America; The Bread Bakers Guild of America; Women Chefs and Restaurateurs.

Areas of Study
Baking; confectionery show pieces; culinary skill development; food preparation; food purchasing; food service math; garde-manger; international cuisine; introduction to food service; kitchen management; management and human resources; menu and facilities design; patisserie; restaurant opportunities; sanitation; soup, stock, sauce, and starch production.

Facilities
Bake shop; bakery; 10 classrooms; 6 computer laboratories; demonstration laboratory; 2 food production kitchens; garden; gourmet dining room; 3 laboratories; 2 learning resource centers; 10 lecture rooms; 2 libraries; public restaurant; student lounge; 3 teaching kitchens.

Student Profile
465 total: 415 full-time; 50 part-time. 227 are under 25 years old; 208 are between 25 and 44 years old; 30 are over 44 years old.

Faculty
17 total: 5 full-time; 12 part-time. 16 are industry professionals. Prominent faculty: Luke Schultheis; Brian MacMenamin. Faculty-student ratio: 1:20.

Special Programs
Paid internships in New York City, Study Abroad in Parma, Italy, residential internships abroad.

Typical Expenses
Application fee: $35. Tuition: $4880 per semester full-time, $1135 per 3 credits part-time.

Financial Aid
In 2004, 40 scholarships were awarded (average award was $1500). Program-specific awards include industry scholarships, Trades Council (NYC Hotel) Scholarship. Employment placement assistance is available. Employment opportunities within the program are available.

Housing
Coed, apartment-style, and single-sex housing available. Average on-campus housing cost per month: $500. Average off-campus housing cost per month: $600.

Application Information
Students may begin participation in January, May, and September. Applications are accepted continuously. In 2004, 600 applied; 132 were accepted. Applicants must interview; submit a formal application and an essay.

Contact
Luke D. Schultheis, Chairperson, Department of Hospitality Management and The Culinary Arts, Hospitality Management, 2468 Jerome Avenue, Bronx, NY 10468. Telephone: 718-933-6700 Ext. 8250. Fax: 718-364-3552. E-mail: lschultheis@monroecollege.edu. World Wide Web: http://www.monroecollege.edu.

Monroe Community College

Department of Hospitality Management

Rochester, New York

General Information
Public, coeducational, two-year college. Suburban campus. Founded in 1961. Accredited by Middle States Association of Colleges and Schools.

Program Information
Offered since 1967. Program calendar is divided into semesters. 16-month certificate in food production. 16-month certificate in food management. 2-year associate degree in hospitality management-travel and tourism. 2-year associate degree in hospitality management-physical fitness. 2-year associate degree in hospitality management-golf management. 2-year associate degree in hospitality management-food service. 2-year associate degree in hospitality management-hotel.

Program Affiliation
American Culinary Federation; American Dietetic Association; Council on Hotel, Restaurant, and Institutional Education; International Food Service Executives Association; National Restaurant Association; National Restaurant Association Educational Foundation.

Areas of Study
Beverage management; buffet catering; controlling costs in food service; culinary French; culinary skill development; food preparation; food purchasing; introduction to food service; kitchen management; management and human

resources; meal planning; menu and facilities design; nutrition; nutrition and food service; restaurant opportunities; sanitation; soup, stock, sauce, and starch production.

FACILITIES
2 cafeterias; 2 catering services; coffee shop; 12 computer laboratories; 4 demonstration laboratories; 3 food production kitchens; gourmet dining room; 10 learning resource centers; 2 libraries; public restaurant; snack shop; 2 student lounges; 3 teaching kitchens.

TYPICAL STUDENT PROFILE
230 total: 140 full-time; 90 part-time. 115 are under 25 years old; 80 are between 25 and 44 years old; 35 are over 44 years old.

SPECIAL PROGRAMS
Visits to various culinary conventions.

FINANCIAL AID
Employment placement assistance is available. Employment opportunities within the program are available.

HOUSING
Coed housing available.

APPLICATION INFORMATION
Students may begin participation in January and September. Applications are accepted continuously. Applicants must submit a formal application.

CONTACT
Director of Admissions, Department of Hospitality Management, 1000 East Henrietta Road, Rochester, NY 14623-5780. Telephone: 585-292-2580. Fax: 585-292-3826. World Wide Web: http://www.monroecc.edu.

NASSAU COMMUNITY COLLEGE

Garden City, New York

GENERAL INFORMATION
Public, coeducational, two-year college. Suburban campus. Founded in 1959. Accredited by Middle States Association of Colleges and Schools.

PROGRAM INFORMATION
Offered since 1973. Program calendar is divided into semesters. 1-year certificate in restaurant management. 2-year associate degree in hotel management. 2-year associate degree in restaurant management.

PROGRAM AFFILIATION
American Culinary Federation; American Dietetic Association; Council on Hotel, Restaurant, and Institutional Education; National Restaurant Association; National Restaurant Association Educational Foundation.

AREAS OF STUDY
Baking; beverage management; buffet catering; controlling costs in food service; culinary skill development; food

preparation; food purchasing; garde-manger; international cuisine; introduction to food service; kitchen management; management and human resources; meal planning; meat cutting; meat fabrication; menu and facilities design; nutrition and food service; restaurant opportunities; sanitation; saucier; soup, stock, sauce, and starch production; wines and spirits.

FACILITIES
Bake shop; 3 cafeterias; catering service; 3 classrooms; 3 coffee shops; 2 computer laboratories; 3 demonstration laboratories; 4 food production kitchens; 2 laboratories; 5 learning resource centers; 6 lecture rooms; library; 2 snack shops; student lounge; 2 teaching kitchens.

TYPICAL STUDENT PROFILE
331 total: 216 full-time; 115 part-time. 264 are under 25 years old; 50 are between 25 and 44 years old; 17 are over 44 years old.

SPECIAL PROGRAMS
6-month internship at Walt Disney World, 2-week international study abroad (Italy), 4-6 month international work co-op (England).

FINANCIAL AID
Employment placement assistance is available. Employment opportunities within the program are available.

APPLICATION INFORMATION
Students may begin participation in January and September. Applications are accepted continuously.

CONTACT
Director of Admissions, Hotel/Restaurant Department, Garden City, NY 11530-6793. Telephone: 516-572-7344. Fax: 516-572-9739. World Wide Web: http://www.sunynassau.edu.

NEW YORK INSTITUTE OF TECHNOLOGY

Center for Hospitality and Culinary Arts

Central Islip, New York

GENERAL INFORMATION
Private, coeducational, comprehensive institution. Suburban campus. Founded in 1955. Accredited by Middle States Association of Colleges and Schools.

PROGRAM INFORMATION
Offered since 1985. Accredited by American Culinary Federation Accrediting Commission. Program calendar is divided into semesters. 2-year associate degree in culinary arts. 4-year bachelor's degree in hospitality management. 500-hour certificate in baking and pastry arts. 500-hour certificate in culinary arts.

New York Institute of Technology *(continued)*

PROGRAM AFFILIATION
American Culinary Federation; American Institute of Wine & Food; Council on Hotel, Restaurant, and Institutional Education; International Association of Culinary Professionals; National Restaurant Association; National Restaurant Association Educational Foundation; Oldways Preservation and Exchange Trust; Women Chefs and Restaurateurs.

AREAS OF STUDY
Allergy specific foods and service; artisanal breads; baking; beverage management; buffet catering; confectionery show pieces; controlling costs in food service; convenience cookery; culinary horticulture; culinary skill development; food preparation; food purchasing; food service communication; food service math; garde-manger; international cuisine; kitchen management; management and human resources; meal planning; meat cutting; meat fabrication; menu and facilities design; nutrition; patisserie; restaurant opportunities; sanitation; saucier; seafood processing; soup, stock, sauce, and starch production; wines and spirits.

FACILITIES
Bake shop; bakery; 2 cafeterias; catering service; 10 classrooms; coffee shop; 3 computer laboratories; demonstration laboratory; 2 food production kitchens; garden; gourmet dining room; learning resource center; library; public restaurant; snack shop; student lounge; 3 teaching kitchens; sugar and chocolate room; interactive synchronistic lab.

STUDENT PROFILE
142 total: 127 full-time; 15 part-time. 33 are under 25 years old; 101 are between 25 and 44 years old; 8 are over 44 years old.

FACULTY
17 total: 6 full-time; 11 part-time. 12 are industry professionals; 7 are certified executive chefs, 1 certified culinary educator. Prominent faculty: Susan Sykes Hendee, MS, MA, PhD; Gunter Grossmann, CEC; James Turley, Chairman-Division of Hospitality Programs; James Dunne, MA, JD. Faculty-student ratio: 1:15.

SPECIAL PROGRAMS
Summer program in Switzerland and Italy, 3-month paid externship, culinary competitions.

TYPICAL EXPENSES
Application fee: $50. Tuition: $9348 per semester full-time, $630 per credit part-time. Program-related fees include $700 for uniforms and knives (first-year); $110 for uniforms (second year); $1200 for comprehensive food fees (per year); $85 for ACFEI certification culinarian fee.

FINANCIAL AID
In 2004, 3 scholarships were awarded (average award was $1000); 3 loans were granted (average loan was $1500). Program-specific awards include Whitson's Scholarship ($500), J. King Scholarship ($1000), James Lewis Scholarship ($1000); Scotto Brothers Scholarship. Employment opportunities within the program are available.

HOUSING
Coed housing available. Average on-campus housing cost per month: $210. Average off-campus housing cost per month: $1200.

APPLICATION INFORMATION
Students may begin participation in January and September. Application deadline for fall is June 1. Application deadline for spring is December 1. Applicants must submit a formal application, an essay, and have a high school diploma and minimum combined SAT score of 800.

CONTACT
Admissions Office, Center for Hospitality and Culinary Arts, PO Box 8000, Old Westbury, NY 11568-8000. Telephone: 800-345-NYIT. Fax: 516-686-7516. E-mail: admissions@nyit.edu. World Wide Web: http://iris.nyit.edu/culinary.

NEW YORK UNIVERSITY

Department of Nutrition, Food Studies, and Public Health

New York, New York

GENERAL INFORMATION
Private, coeducational, university. Urban campus. Founded in 1831. Accredited by Middle States Association of Colleges and Schools.

PROGRAM INFORMATION
Accredited by American Dietetic Association, Council on Public Health. Program calendar is divided into semesters. 24-month master's degree in community public health. 24-month master's degree in nutrition and dietetics. 24-month master's degree in food studies. 24-month master's degree in food management. 4-year bachelor's degree in nutrition and dietetics. 4-year bachelor's degree in food and restaurant management. 4-year bachelor's degree in food studies. 5-year doctoral degree in public health. 5-year doctoral degree in nutrition and dietetics. 5-year doctoral degree in food studies and food management.

PROGRAM AFFILIATION
American Dietetic Association; Association for the Study of Food and Society.

AREAS OF STUDY
Community public health; food history and culture; food writing; introduction to food service; management and human resources; nutrition; nutrition and food service; public health nutrition.

FACILITIES

Classroom; computer laboratory; demonstration laboratory; food production kitchen; lecture room; library; teaching kitchen.

STUDENT PROFILE

400 total: 200 full-time; 200 part-time. 100 are under 25 years old; 250 are between 25 and 44 years old; 50 are over 44 years old.

FACULTY

59 total: 14 full-time; 45 part-time. 20 are industry professionals; 5 are culinary-certified teachers. Prominent faculty: Marion Nestle, PhD, MPH; Amy Bentley, PhD; Judith Gilbride PhD, RD; Sally Guttmacher, PhD; Sharon Dalton, PhD, RD. Faculty-student ratio: 1:7.

SPECIAL PROGRAMS

Internships in every program, summer graduate study in Italy and South Africa, intersession courses.

TYPICAL EXPENSES

Application fee: $50–$65. Tuition: $15,767 per semester (undergraduate); $1048 per credit (graduate) full-time, $929 per credit (undergraduate); $1048 per credit (graduate) part-time. Program-related fees include $299 for fall 2006 registration fee; $312 for spring 2007 registration fee.

FINANCIAL AID

In 2005, 200 scholarships were awarded. Program-specific awards include food studies scholarships, graduate assistantships, teaching fellowships. Employment placement assistance is available. Employment opportunities within the program are available.

HOUSING

Coed, apartment-style, and single-sex housing available. Average on-campus housing cost per month: $1300. Average off-campus housing cost per month: $1500.

APPLICATION INFORMATION

Students may begin participation in January, May, June, July, and September. Application deadline for fall (bachelor's and doctoral) is January 15. Application deadline for fall (master's) is February 1. Application deadline for spring (bachelor's and master's) is November 1. Applicants must submit a formal application, letters of reference, GRE score (MPH and doctoral applicants), MCAT score (alternate for MPH applicants) Transcripts.

CONTACT

Kelli Ranieri, Department Administrator, Department of Nutrition, Food Studies, and Public Health, 35 West 4th Street, Room 1077 I, New York, NY 10012. Telephone: 212-998-5580. Fax: 212-995-4194. E-mail: nutrition@nyu.edu. World Wide Web: http://www.steinhardt.nyu.edu/.

NIAGARA COUNTY COMMUNITY COLLEGE

Culinary Arts Program

Sanborn, New York

GENERAL INFORMATION

Public, coeducational, two-year college. Founded in 1962. Accredited by Middle States Association of Colleges and Schools.

PROGRAM INFORMATION

Offered since 1976. Accredited by American Culinary Federation Accrediting Commission. Program calendar is divided into semesters. 1-year certificate in casino operations. 1-year certificate in hospitality. 1-year certificate in food service. 1-year certificate in baking and pastry arts. 2-year associate degree in gaming and casino management. 2-year associate degree in hospitality management. 2-year associate degree in culinary arts.

PROGRAM AFFILIATION

American Culinary Federation; American Dietetic Association; National Restaurant Association.

AREAS OF STUDY

Baking; beverage management; controlling costs in food service; culinary French; food preparation; food purchasing; food service math; garde-manger; international cuisine; introduction to food service; management and human resources; meat cutting; menu and facilities design; nutrition; patisserie; sanitation; saucier; soup, stock, sauce, and starch production; wines and spirits.

FACILITIES

Bake shop; cafeteria; 3 classrooms; coffee shop; computer laboratory; demonstration laboratory; food production kitchen; 3 laboratories; learning resource center; 5 lecture rooms; library; snack shop; 2 food preparation laboratories; baking laboratory.

STUDENT PROFILE

176 total: 150 full-time; 26 part-time. 85 are under 25 years old; 69 are between 25 and 44 years old; 22 are over 44 years old.

FACULTY

7 total: 3 full-time; 4 part-time. 2 are culinary-certified teachers; 1 is a registered dietitian. Prominent faculty: Carl B. Heintz, Professor; Sam Sheusi, Professor; Mark Mistriner, Associate Professor. Faculty-student ratio: 1:16 lab; 1:30 lecture.

SPECIAL PROGRAMS

Two 6-month internships/cooperative education.

TYPICAL EXPENSES

In-state tuition: $2976 per year full-time (in district), $124 per credit hour part-time. Out-of-state tuition: $4464 per

Niagara County Community College *(continued)*

year full-time, $186 per credit hour part-time. Program-related fees include $60 for uniform; $150 for knives; $150–$200 for books.

FINANCIAL AID

In 2004, 2 scholarships were awarded (average award was $500). Program-specific awards include Statler Foundation scholarship, Antoncci scholarship. Employment placement assistance is available. Employment opportunities within the program are available.

APPLICATION INFORMATION

Students may begin participation in January, May, and September. Applications are accepted continuously. In 2004, 200 applied. Applicants must submit a formal application.

CONTACT

Kathy Saunders, Director of Admissions, Culinary Arts Program, 3111 Saunders Settlement Road, Sanborn, NY 14132. Telephone: 716-614-6201. Fax: 716-614-6820. E-mail: saunders@niagaracc.suny.edu. World Wide Web: http://www.niagaracc.suny.edu.

NIAGARA UNIVERSITY

College of Hospitality and Tourism Management

Niagara University, New York

GENERAL INFORMATION

Private, coeducational, comprehensive institution. Suburban campus. Founded in 1856. Accredited by Middle States Association of Colleges and Schools.

PROGRAM INFORMATION

Offered since 1968. Accredited by Council on Hotel, Restaurant and Institutional Education. Program calendar is divided into semesters. 4-year bachelor's degree in hotel and restaurant management-food service management. 4-year bachelor's degree in hotel and restaurant management-hotel planning and control. 4-year bachelor's degree in hotel and restaurant management-restaurant entrepreneurship.

PROGRAM AFFILIATION

Council on Hotel, Restaurant, and Institutional Education; National Restaurant Association; National Restaurant Association Educational Foundation.

AREAS OF STUDY

Beverage management; controlling costs in food service; food preparation; food purchasing; kitchen management; management and human resources; restaurant opportunities.

FACILITIES

2 cafeterias; catering service; 4 classrooms; 5 computer laboratories; demonstration laboratory; food production kitchen; gourmet dining room; learning resource center; lecture room; library; snack shop; 2 student lounges; teaching kitchen.

STUDENT PROFILE

365 total: 350 full-time; 15 part-time.

FACULTY

12 total: 8 full-time; 4 part-time. 4 are industry professionals. Faculty-student ratio: 1:20.

SPECIAL PROGRAMS

Work-based program in Como, Italy and co-ops across the country, 20 industry speakers/demonstrations per year, cruise course.

TYPICAL EXPENSES

Application fee: $30. Tuition: $19,000 per year full-time, $635 per credit hour part-time. Out-of-state tuition: $19,000 per year full-time, $635 per credit hour part-time. Tuition for international students: $19,000 per year full-time, $635 per credit hour part-time.

FINANCIAL AID

Program-specific awards include 1-3 Statler Foundation Scholarships of Excellence ($20,000), Statler Scholarships (up to $2000 per year), generous financial aid including transfer scholarships are available. Employment placement assistance is available. Employment opportunities within the program are available.

HOUSING

Coed, apartment-style, and single-sex housing available. Average on-campus housing cost per month: $940.

APPLICATION INFORMATION

Students may begin participation in January, May, and September. Applications are accepted continuously. In 2004, 300 applied; 200 were accepted. Applicants must submit a formal application, letters of reference, and an essay.

CONTACT

Dr. Gary D. Praetzel, Dean, College of Hospitality and Tourism Management, College of Hospitality and Tourism Management, Niagara University, NY 14109-2012. Telephone: 716-286-8272. Fax: 716-286-8277. E-mail: gdp@niagara.edu. World Wide Web: http://www.niagara.edu/hospitality.

ONONDAGA COMMUNITY COLLEGE

Food Service Administration/Restaurant Management/Professional Cooking

Syracuse, New York

GENERAL INFORMATION

Public, coeducational, two-year college. Suburban campus. Founded in 1962. Accredited by Middle States Association of Colleges and Schools.

PROGRAM INFORMATION
Offered since 1979. Program calendar is divided into semesters. 1-year certificate in professional cooking. 2-year associate degree in food service administration/restaurant management. 2-year associate degree in hotel technology.

PROGRAM AFFILIATION
American Culinary Federation; Council on Hotel, Restaurant, and Institutional Education; International Food Service Executives Association; National Restaurant Association; National Restaurant Association Educational Foundation.

AREAS OF STUDY
Buffet catering; controlling costs in food service; food preparation; food purchasing; food service math; international cuisine; management and human resources; meal planning; menu and facilities design; nutrition; nutrition and food service; patisserie; sanitation.

FACILITIES
Catering service; computer laboratory; 2 food production kitchens; garden; gourmet dining room; 2 laboratories; learning resource center; library; student lounge; 2 teaching kitchens.

STUDENT PROFILE
100 total: 80 full-time; 20 part-time.

FACULTY
10 total: 3 full-time; 7 part-time. 3 are industry professionals; 2 are master chefs; 2 are master bakers; 1 is a culinary-certified teacher; 1 is a registered dietitian. Prominent faculty: James P. Drake, MEd; Jillann Neely, MEd; Theresea O'Hare, AAS. Faculty-student ratio: 1:8 labs.

SPECIAL PROGRAMS
2-day trip to New York City, 5-day tour of restaurants, hotels, and casinos in Las Vegas, Walt Disney World College Program (internship).

TYPICAL EXPENSES
Application fee: $40. In-state tuition: $1590 per semester full-time (in district), $125 per credit hour part-time (in district), $3000 per per semester full-time (out-of-district), $300 per per credit hour part-time (out-of-district). Out-of-state tuition: $4770 per semester full-time, $375 per credit hour part-time. Program-related fees include $25 for lab fees; $150 for uniform.

FINANCIAL AID
In 2004, 4 scholarships were awarded (average award was $500–$1000). Employment placement assistance is available.

APPLICATION INFORMATION
Students may begin participation in January and August. In 2004, 86 applied; 80 were accepted. Applicants must submit a formal application.

CONTACT
Jillann Neely, Curriculum Coordinator, Food Service Administration/Restaurant Management/Professional Cooking, 4941 Onondaga Road, Syracuse, NY 13215.

Telephone: 315-498-2232. Fax: 315-498-2703. E-mail: neelyj@sunyocc.edu. World Wide Web: http://www.sunyocc.edu/.

PAUL SMITH'S COLLEGE OF ARTS AND SCIENCES

Paul Smiths, New York

GENERAL INFORMATION
Private, coeducational, four-year college. Rural campus. Founded in 1937. Accredited by Middle States Association of Colleges and Schools.

PROGRAM INFORMATION
Accredited by American Culinary Federation Accrediting Commission, Council on Hotel, Restaurant and Institutional Education. Program calendar is divided into semesters. 1-year certificate in baking and pastry arts. 2-year associate degree in hotel and restaurant management. 2-year associate degree in culinary arts. 2-year associate degree in culinary arts-baking track. 4-year bachelor's degree in hotel, resort, and tourism management. 4-year bachelor's degree in culinary arts and service management.

PROGRAM AFFILIATION
American Culinary Federation; Council on Hotel, Restaurant, and Institutional Education; National Restaurant Association; National Restaurant Association Educational Foundation; Retailer's Bakery Association.

AREAS OF STUDY
Baking; beverage management; buffet catering; confectionery show pieces; controlling costs in food service; culinary French; culinary skill development; food preparation; food purchasing; food service communication; food service math; garde-manger; international cuisine; introduction to food service; kitchen management; management and human resources; meal planning; meat cutting; meat fabrication; menu and facilities design; nutrition; nutrition and food service; patisserie; restaurant opportunities; sanitation; saucier; seafood processing; soup, stock, sauce, and starch production; wines and spirits.

FACILITIES
Bake shop; bakery; 15 classrooms; 5 computer laboratories; demonstration laboratory; gourmet dining room; 5 laboratories; learning resource center; lecture room; library; 2 public restaurants; snack shop; student lounge; 5 teaching kitchens; on-campus retail bakery; new Wally Ganzi, Jr. Restaurant Training Center (modeled after legendary Palm Restaurant Steakhouse).

FACULTY
23 total: 15 full-time; 8 part-time. 1 is a master baker; 3 are culinary-certified teachers. Prominent faculty: Lucille Banker; Robert Brown, CMB; Dave Gotzmer. Faculty-student ratio: 1:14.

Paul Smith's College of Arts and Sciences *(continued)*

SPECIAL PROGRAMS
International Student Exchange Program, Bakery operated 22 weeks a year, over 1100 externship opportunities.

TYPICAL EXPENSES
Application fee: $30. Tuition: $16,100 per year. Program-related fee includes $730 for uniforms, clothing, and equipment.

FINANCIAL AID
Program-specific awards include Cooking for Scholarships competition. Employment placement assistance is available. Employment opportunities within the program are available.

HOUSING
Coed and single-sex housing available.

APPLICATION INFORMATION
Students may begin participation in January and September. Applications are accepted continuously. Applicants must submit a formal application and high school or college transcripts, SAT/ACT scores, and letters of recommendation and a personal essay are recommended.

CONTACT
Admissions Office, Routes 86 and 30, PO Box 265, Paul Smiths, NY 12970. Telephone: 800-421-2605. Fax: 518-327-6016. E-mail: admiss@paulsmiths.edu. World Wide Web: http://www.paulsmiths.edu/.

PLATTSBURGH STATE UNIVERSITY OF NEW YORK

Hotel, Restaurant, and Tourism Management

Plattsburgh, New York

GENERAL INFORMATION
Public, coeducational, university. Suburban campus. Founded in 1889. Accredited by Middle States Association of Colleges and Schools.

PROGRAM INFORMATION
Offered since 1988. Program calendar is divided into semesters. 4-year bachelor's degree in hotel, restaurant, and tourism management.

PROGRAM AFFILIATION

American Hotel and Lodging Association; Council on Hotel, Restaurant, and Institutional Education; Hospitality Sales and Marketing Association International; National Restaurant Association; National Restaurant Association Educational Foundation; New York State Hospitality and Tourism Association.

AREAS OF STUDY

Beverage management; food preparation; introduction to food service; lodging; nutrition; nutrition and food service; restaurant opportunities; tourism.

FACILITIES

Classroom; computer laboratory; food production kitchen; lecture room.

STUDENT PROFILE

176 total: 167 full-time; 9 part-time. 174 are under 25 years old; 2 are between 25 and 44 years old.

FACULTY

6 total: 5 full-time; 1 part-time. 7 are industry professionals. Prominent faculty: Ray Guydosh, PhD; Kimberly Emery, CIA; Robert Rolf, MA; Mark Gultek, PhD. Faculty-student ratio: 1:26.

SPECIAL PROGRAMS

800 hours of field work, community-related projects, special dinners for nonprofit organizations.

TYPICAL EXPENSES

Application fee: $30. In-state tuition: $4350 per year full-time (in district), $181 per credit hour part-time. Out-of-state tuition: $10,610 per year full-time, $442 per credit hour part-time. Program-related fees include $100 for food lab; $50 for wine courses.

FINANCIAL AID

In 2004, 15 scholarships were awarded (average award was $883.06); 141 loans were granted (average loan was $4015.30). Program-specific awards include Marriott Corporation Award, Sodexo Award, Restaurants of New York Foundations Awards. Employment opportunities within the program are available.

HOUSING

Coed housing available. Average on-campus housing cost per month: $400. Average off-campus housing cost per month: $400.

APPLICATION INFORMATION

Students may begin participation in January and September. Application deadline for fall is August 1. Application deadline for spring is January 1. In 2004, 91 applied. Applicants must interview; submit a formal application and essay (recommended).

CONTACT

Richard Higgins, Director of Admissions, Hotel, Restaurant, and Tourism Management, Kehoe Building, Plattsburgh, NY 12901. Telephone: 518-564-2040. Fax: 518-564-2045. E-mail: higginrj@plattsburgh.edu. World Wide Web: http://www.plattsburgh.edu.

ROCHESTER INSTITUTE OF TECHNOLOGY

School of Hospitality and Service Management

Rochester, New York

GENERAL INFORMATION

Private, coeducational, comprehensive institution. Suburban campus. Founded in 1829. Accredited by Middle States Association of Colleges and Schools.

PROGRAM INFORMATION

Offered since 1891. Accredited by American Dietetic Association. Program calendar is divided into quarters. 12-month master's degree in service management. 12-month master's degree in hospitality and tourism management. 4-year bachelor's degree in nutrition management. 4-year bachelor's degree in hospitality and service management.

PROGRAM AFFILIATION

American Dietetic Association; Council on Hotel, Restaurant, and Institutional Education; Institute of Food Technologists; International Food Service Executives Association; National Restaurant Association; National Restaurant Association Educational Foundation.

AREAS OF STUDY

Beverage management; controlling costs in food service; food preparation; food purchasing; food service communication; food service math; international cuisine; introduction to food service; kitchen management; management and human resources; meal planning; menu and facilities design; nutrition; nutrition and food service; restaurant opportunities; sanitation; wines and spirits.

FACILITIES

Bakery; 3 classrooms; computer laboratory; demonstration laboratory; food production kitchen; gourmet dining room; laboratory; learning resource center; lecture room; library; public restaurant; teaching kitchen.

STUDENT PROFILE

225 total: 200 full-time; 25 part-time. 160 are under 25 years old; 35 are between 25 and 44 years old; 5 are over 44 years old.

FACULTY

45 total: 15 full-time; 30 part-time. 10 are industry professionals; 1 is a master chef. Prominent faculty: Carol Whitlock, PhD, RD; Barbra Cerio, RD; Elizabeth Kmiecinski, RD. Faculty-student ratio: 1:13.

SPECIAL PROGRAMS

Required cooperative education plan (provides salaried employment), operation of hotel and conference center on campus, international hospitality and food management program in Croatia.

Rochester Institute of Technology *(continued)*

TYPICAL EXPENSES

Application fee: $50. Tuition: $23,247 per year (undergraduate); $25,392 per year (graduate) full-time, $518 per credit hour (undergraduate); $712 per credit hour (graduate) part-time.

FINANCIAL AID

Program-specific awards include RIT achievement scholarship for hospitality and service management ($5000/year). Employment placement assistance is available. Employment opportunities within the program are available.

HOUSING

Coed, apartment-style, and single-sex housing available. Average on-campus housing cost per month: $540. Average off-campus housing cost per month: $550.

APPLICATION INFORMATION

Students may begin participation in March, June, September, and December. Applications are accepted continuously. In 2004, 177 applied; 119 were accepted. Applicants must submit a formal application and high school and/or college transcripts.

CONTACT

Daniel Shelley, Director of Undergraduate Admissions, School of Hospitality and Service Management, 60 Lomb Memorial Drive, Rochester, NY 14624. Telephone: 585-475-6631. Fax: 585-475-7428. E-mail: admissions@rit.edu. World Wide Web: http://www.rit.edu.

ST. JOHN'S UNIVERSITY

Division of Hotel, Restaurant, Sports, Travel, and Tourism

Queens and Staten Island, New York

GENERAL INFORMATION

Private, coeducational, university. Urban campus. Founded in 1870. Accredited by Middle States Association of Colleges and Schools.

PROGRAM INFORMATION

Offered since 1997. Accredited by Council on Hotel, Restaurant and Institutional Education, International Society of Travel and Tourism Edu, American Hotel and Lodging Association. Program calendar is divided into semesters. 4-year bachelor's degree in hospitality management.

PROGRAM AFFILIATION

Council on Hotel, Restaurant, and Institutional Education; National Restaurant Association.

AREAS OF STUDY

Beverage management; confectionery show pieces; food purchasing; international cuisine; introduction to food service; management and human resources; menu and facilities design; restaurant opportunities.

FACILITIES

2 cafeterias; catering service; 2 coffee shops; 2 computer laboratories; 2 gardens; learning resource center; lecture room; 2 libraries; student lounge.

STUDENT PROFILE

99 total: 95 full-time; 4 part-time. 89 are under 25 years old; 10 are between 25 and 44 years old.

FACULTY

8 total: 3 full-time; 5 part-time. 8 are industry professionals. Prominent faculty: Dr. Francis X. Brown; Dr. Charles Gladstone; Dr. Heidi Sung. Faculty-student ratio: 1:20.

SPECIAL PROGRAMS

Certificate Program in "Tourism Italy" at Perugia University (5 weeks summer), Study Abroad Program in "Event Management" at Leeds Metropolitan University UK.

TYPICAL EXPENSES

Application fee: $30. Tuition: $22,800 per year full-time, $760 per credit part-time. Tuition for international students: $22,800 per year full-time, $760 per credit part-time.

HOUSING

Coed housing available. Average on-campus housing cost per month: $1375.

APPLICATION INFORMATION

Students may begin participation in January, June, and September. Applications are accepted continuously. In 2004, 107 applied; 49 were accepted. Applicants must submit a formal application, letters of reference, an essay, SAT I or ACT scores, high school transcript.

CONTACT

Mr. Matthew Whelan, Director, Office of Admission, Division of Hotel, Restaurant, Sports, Travel, and Tourism, 8000 Utopia Parkway, Queens, NY 11439. Telephone: 718-990-2000. Fax: 718-990-5728. E-mail: admissions@stjohns.edu. World Wide Web: http://www.stjohns.edu.

SCHENECTADY COUNTY COMMUNITY COLLEGE

Hotel, Culinary Arts, and Tourism

Schenectady, New York

GENERAL INFORMATION
Public, coeducational, two-year college. Urban campus. Founded in 1969. Accredited by Middle States Association of Colleges and Schools.

PROGRAM INFORMATION
Offered since 1980. Accredited by American Culinary Federation Accrediting Commission. Program calendar is divided into semesters. 1-year certificate in tourism, sales, and convention management. 1-year certificate in assistant chef. 2-year associate degree in tourism and hospitality management. 2-year associate degree in food sales and distribution. 2-year associate degree in hotel and restaurant management. 2-year associate degree in culinary arts.

PROGRAM AFFILIATION
American Culinary Federation; Club Managers Association of America; Council on Hotel, Restaurant, and Institutional Education; National Restaurant Association; National Restaurant Association Educational Foundation; New York State Hospitality and Tourism Association; Retailer's Bakery Association; Society of Wine Educators; The Bread Bakers Guild of America.

AREAS OF STUDY
Baking; beverage management; buffet catering; confectionery show pieces; controlling costs in food service; culinary French; culinary skill development; food preparation; food purchasing; food service math; garde-manger; international cuisine; introduction to food service; kitchen management; management and human resources; meal planning; meat cutting; menu and facilities design; nutrition; patisserie; restaurant opportunities; sanitation; saucier; seafood processing; soup, stock, sauce, and starch production; wines and spirits.

FACILITIES
2 bake shops; catering service; computer laboratory; 5 food production kitchens; gourmet dining room; library.

TYPICAL STUDENT PROFILE
961 total: 574 full-time; 387 part-time.

SPECIAL PROGRAMS
4-10 day work experience at the Kentucky Derby, Belmont, and Saratoga, semester internships at Disney World.

FINANCIAL AID
Employment placement assistance is available. Employment opportunities within the program are available.

APPLICATION INFORMATION
Students may begin participation in January, June, and September. Applications are accepted continuously. Applicants must submit a formal application.

CONTACT
Director of Admissions, Hotel, Culinary Arts, and Tourism, 78 Washington Avenue, Schenectady, NY 12305-2294. Telephone: 518-381-1370. Fax: 518-346-0379. World Wide Web: http://www.sunysccc.edu/academic/arrays/AOScul.htm.

STATE UNIVERSITY OF NEW YORK COLLEGE AT COBLESKILL

Culinary Arts, Hospitality, and Tourism

Cobleskill, New York

GENERAL INFORMATION
Public, coeducational, four-year college. Rural campus. Founded in 1916. Accredited by Middle States Association of Colleges and Schools.

PROGRAM INFORMATION
Offered since 1971. Accredited by American Culinary Federation Accrediting Commission. Program calendar is divided into semesters. 1-year certificate in commercial cooking. 2-year associate degree in travel and resort marketing. 2-year associate degree in restaurant management. 2-year associate degree in institutional foods. 2-year associate degree in hotel technology. 2-year associate degree in culinary arts. 4-year bachelor's degree in culinary arts/technology management.

PROGRAM AFFILIATION
American Culinary Federation; American Dietetic Association; Chefs Collaborative 2000; Council on Hotel, Restaurant, and Institutional Education; Institute of Food Technologists; National Restaurant Association; National Restaurant Association Educational Foundation; The Bread Bakers Guild of America; Women Chefs and Restaurateurs.

AREAS OF STUDY
Beverage management; buffet catering; confectionery show pieces; controlling costs in food service; culinary French; culinary skill development; food preparation; food purchasing; food service math; garde-manger; hospitality law; international cuisine; management; management and human resources; marketing; meat cutting; menu and facilities design; nutrition; sanitation; wines and spirits.

FACILITIES
Catering service; 15 classrooms; 4 computer laboratories; demonstration laboratory; food production kitchen; gourmet dining room; learning resource center; 15 lecture rooms; library; public restaurant; 3 teaching kitchens; vineyard.

STUDENT PROFILE
132 total: 120 full-time; 12 part-time.

State University of New York College at Cobleskill
(continued)

FACULTY
11 total: 10 full-time; 1 part-time. 6 are industry professionals; 2 are culinary-certified teachers. Prominent faculty: Anne Rogan, PhD, RD, CND; Keith Buerker, CEC, CCE, CFBE; David Campbell, CHE, CCC, CCE; Robert Sielaff. Faculty-student ratio: 1:12.

SPECIAL PROGRAMS
Culinary competitions, student-run restaurant and catering facilities, internship in bachelor's program.

TYPICAL EXPENSES
Application fee: $40. In-state tuition: $181 per credit hour part-time, $4350 per year (out-of-district). Out-of-state tuition: $7210 per year full-time, $442 per credit hour part-time. Program-related fees include $120 for cutlery; $100 for uniforms; $150 for lab fee; $50 for travel/field trips.

FINANCIAL AID
In 2004, 10 scholarships were awarded (average award was $1500). Program-specific awards include on-campus work-study programs. Employment placement assistance is available.

HOUSING
Coed and single-sex housing available. Average on-campus housing cost per month: $500. Average off-campus housing cost per month: $500.

APPLICATION INFORMATION
Students may begin participation in January and August. Applications are accepted continuously. In 2004, 279 applied; 190 were accepted. Applicants must submit a formal application.

CONTACT
Christopher Tacea, Director of Admissions, Culinary Arts, Hospitality, and Tourism, Knapp Hall, Cobleskill, NY 12043. Telephone: 800-295-8988. Fax: 518-255-6769. E-mail: admissions@cobleskill.edu. World Wide Web: http://www.cobleskill.edu/.

STATE UNIVERSITY OF NEW YORK COLLEGE AT ONEONTA

Food Service and Restaurant Administration

Oneonta, New York

GENERAL INFORMATION
Public, coeducational, comprehensive institution. Small-town setting. Founded in 1889. Accredited by Middle States Association of Colleges and Schools.

PROGRAM INFORMATION
Offered since 1974. Accredited by American Association of Family and Consumer Sciences. Program calendar is divided into semesters. 4-year bachelor's degree in food service/restaurant administration.

PROGRAM AFFILIATION
American Dietetic Association; Council on Hotel, Restaurant, and Institutional Education; National Restaurant Association.

AREAS OF STUDY
Buffet catering; controlling costs in food service; food preparation; food purchasing; food service communication; food service math; introduction to food service; management and human resources; meal planning; menu and facilities design; nutrition; nutrition and food service; restaurant opportunities; sanitation.

FACILITIES
3 classrooms; computer laboratory; demonstration laboratory; food production kitchen; gourmet dining room; laboratory; learning resource center; 3 lecture rooms; student lounge; teaching kitchen.

TYPICAL STUDENT PROFILE
58 total: 53 full-time; 5 part-time. 57 are under 25 years old; 1 is between 25 and 44 years old.

SPECIAL PROGRAMS
Food and Nutrition Association, field trips to food shows in the Northeast and speakers from the profession, Nutrition Awareness Week.

FINANCIAL AID
Employment placement assistance is available. Employment opportunities within the program are available.

HOUSING
Coed housing available.

APPLICATION INFORMATION
Students may begin participation in January and August. Applications are accepted continuously. Applicants must submit a formal application and an essay.

CONTACT
Director of Admissions, Food Service and Restaurant Administration, Human Ecology Department, Oneonta, NY 13820. Telephone: 607-436-2071. Fax: 607-436-2051. World Wide Web: http://www.oneonta.edu.

At our **Penn State** affiliate, you can choose a program of study that best suits your career goals.

School of Hospitality

Culinary Arts and Systems
(Bachelor of Science)

Baking and Pastry Arts Technology
(Associate of Applied Science)

Culinary Arts Technology
(Associate of Applied Science)

Hospitality Management
(Associate of Applied Science)

Penn College is a special mission affiliate of Penn State, committed to applied technology education. With more than 6,000 students, Penn College has the second highest enrollment in the Penn State system.

Scholarships and financial aid for eligible students

College's Le Jeune Chef restaurant offers fine dining and Wine Spectator awarded wine list.

Nationally recognized visiting chefs

ACF-certified culinary instructors

Professionally equipped kitchens

On-campus housing

Pennsylvania College of Technology

PENNSTATE

1855

www.pct.edu/peter
(800) 367-9222

Penn College is located in **Williamsport**

An affiliate of The Pennsylvania State University

Penn College operates on a nondiscriminatory basis.

STATE UNIVERSITY OF NEW YORK COLLEGE OF AGRICULTURE AND TECHNOLOGY AT MORRISVILLE

Restaurant Management

Morrisville, New York

GENERAL INFORMATION
Public, coeducational, two-year college. Small-town setting. Founded in 1908. Accredited by Middle States Association of Colleges and Schools.

PROGRAM INFORMATION
Offered since 1908. Accredited by American Dietetic Association. Program calendar is divided into semesters. 2-year associate degree in food service administration. 2-year associate degree in restaurant management. 4-year bachelor's degree in resort and recreation service management.

PROGRAM AFFILIATION
Council on Hotel, Restaurant, and Institutional Education; International Food Service Executives Association; National Restaurant Association; National Restaurant Association Educational Foundation.

AREAS OF STUDY
Beverage management; buffet catering; controlling costs in food service; culinary skill development; food preparation; food purchasing; food service math; international cuisine; introduction to food service; kitchen management; management and human resources; meal planning; menu and facilities design; nutrition; nutrition and food service; sanitation; soup, stock, sauce, and starch production.

FACILITIES
Bake shop; cafeteria; catering service; classroom; computer laboratory; demonstration laboratory; food production kitchen; laboratory; learning resource center; lecture room; library; public restaurant; snack shop; student lounge; teaching kitchen.

TYPICAL STUDENT PROFILE
125 total: 100 full-time; 25 part-time. 80 are under 25 years old; 30 are between 25 and 44 years old; 15 are over 44 years old.

SPECIAL PROGRAMS
320-hour paid internship, attendance at International Food Service Executives Association Conference.

FINANCIAL AID
Employment placement assistance is available. Employment opportunities within the program are available.

HOUSING
Coed housing available.

APPLICATION INFORMATION
Students may begin participation in January and August. Applications are accepted continuously. Applicants must submit a formal application.

CONTACT
Director of Admissions, Restaurant Management, Brooks Hall, Morrisville, NY 13408. Telephone: 315-684-6232. Fax: 315-684-6225. World Wide Web: http://www.morrisville.edu.

STATE UNIVERSITY OF NEW YORK COLLEGE OF TECHNOLOGY AT ALFRED

Culinary Arts Program

Wellsville, New York

GENERAL INFORMATION
Public, coeducational, two-year college. Small-town setting. Founded in 1908. Accredited by Middle States Association of Colleges and Schools.

PROGRAM INFORMATION
Offered since 1966. Program calendar is divided into semesters. 2-year associate degree in baking production and management. 2-year associate degree in culinary arts and foods.

PROGRAM AFFILIATION
American Culinary Federation; Council on Hotel, Restaurant, and Institutional Education; National Restaurant Association; National Restaurant Association Educational Foundation; New York State Restaurant Association.

AREAS OF STUDY
Baking; beverage management; buffet catering; confectionery show pieces; controlling costs in food service; culinary French; culinary skill development; food preparation; food purchasing; food service math; garde-manger; international cuisine; introduction to food service; kitchen management; management and human resources; meal planning; meat cutting; menu and facilities design; nutrition; nutrition and food service; sanitation; seafood processing; soup, stock, sauce, and starch production; wines and spirits.

FACILITIES
2 bake shops; bakery; cafeteria; catering service; 3 classrooms; coffee shop; computer laboratory; 3 demonstration laboratories; 2 food production kitchens; gourmet dining room; laboratory; learning resource center; 3 lecture rooms; 2 libraries; public restaurant; student lounge; 2 teaching kitchens.

State University of New York College of Technology at Alfred *(continued)*

TYPICAL STUDENT PROFILE

62 full-time. 59 are under 25 years old; 3 are between 25 and 44 years old.

SPECIAL PROGRAMS

Annual Culinary Arts Food Show, regional ACF Hot Foods and Team Competitions at SUNY Delhi, senior class fine dining excursion and training seminar.

FINANCIAL AID

Employment placement assistance is available.

HOUSING

Coed housing available.

APPLICATION INFORMATION

Students may begin participation in August. Applications are accepted continuously. Applicants must submit a formal application.

CONTACT

Director of Admissions, Culinary Arts Program, 10 Upper College Drive, Alfred, NY 14802. Telephone: 800-4-ALFRED. Fax: 607-587-3166. World Wide Web: http://www.alfredstate.edu.

STATE UNIVERSITY OF NEW YORK COLLEGE OF TECHNOLOGY AT DELHI

Hospitality Management

Delhi, New York

GENERAL INFORMATION

Public, coeducational, two-year college. Rural campus. Founded in 1913. Accredited by Middle States Association of Colleges and Schools.

PROGRAM INFORMATION

Offered since 1994. Accredited by American Culinary Federation Accrediting Commission. Program calendar is divided into semesters. 2-year associate degree in restaurant management. 2-year associate degree in culinary arts. 4-year bachelor's degree in restaurant management. 4-year bachelor's degree in culinary arts management.

PROGRAM AFFILIATION

American Culinary Federation; Council on Hotel, Restaurant, and Institutional Education; International Food Service Executives Association; International Hotel and Motel Association; National Restaurant Association; New York State Hospitality and Tourism Association; Society of Wine Educators.

AREAS OF STUDY

Baking; beverage management; buffet catering; confectionery show pieces; controlling costs in food service; convenience cookery; culinary competition; culinary French; culinary skill development; food preparation; food purchasing; food service communication; food service math; garde-manger; ice carving; international cuisine; introduction to food service; kitchen management; management and human resources; meal planning; meat cutting; meat fabrication; menu and facilities design; nutrition; patisserie; restaurant management; restaurant opportunities; salt carving; sanitation; saucier; seafood processing; soup, stock, sauce, and starch production; wines and spirits.

FACILITIES

Bakery; catering service; 2 classrooms; computer laboratory; demonstration laboratory; 2 food production kitchens; gourmet dining room; laboratory; learning resource center; 2 lecture rooms; library; public restaurant; 2 teaching kitchens; beverage lounge; charcuterie.

STUDENT PROFILE

173 full-time. 158 are under 25 years old; 15 are between 25 and 44 years old.

FACULTY

12 total: 11 full-time; 1 part-time. 8 are industry professionals; 3 are culinary-certified teachers. Prominent faculty: Thomas Recinella, CEC; Michael Petrillose, PhD; Julee Miller,CEC; Jamie Rotter, CEC.

SPECIAL PROGRAMS

Culinary competitions, organized trips to food shows and businesses.

TYPICAL EXPENSES

Application fee: $30. In-state tuition: $2175 per semester full-time (in district), $181 per credit hour part-time. Out-of-state tuition: $3605 per semester full-time, $300 per credit hour part-time. Program-related fee includes $130 for lab fees.

FINANCIAL AID

In 2005, 6 scholarships were awarded (average award was $300). Employment placement assistance is available. Employment opportunities within the program are available.

HOUSING

Coed and single-sex housing available. Average on-campus housing cost per month: $350. Average off-campus housing cost per month: $350.

APPLICATION INFORMATION

Students may begin participation in January and September. Applications are accepted continuously. In 2005, 334 applied; 218 were accepted. Applicants must submit a formal application.

CONTACT

Craig Wesley, Dean of Enrollment Services, Hospitality Management, 119 Bush Hall, Main Street, Delhi, NY 13753.

Telephone: 607-746-4556. Fax: 607-746-4104. E-mail: enroll@delhi.edu. World Wide Web: http://www.delhi.edu/.

SUFFOLK COUNTY COMMUNITY COLLEGE

Culinary Arts

Riverhead, New York

GENERAL INFORMATION
Public, coeducational, two-year college. Rural campus. Founded in 1959. Accredited by Middle States Association of Colleges and Schools.

PROGRAM INFORMATION
Offered since 2001. Program calendar is divided into semesters. 2-year associate degree in culinary arts. 2-year associate degree in dietetic technician.

PROGRAM AFFILIATION
American Culinary Federation; National Restaurant Association; National Restaurant Association Educational Foundation.

AREAS OF STUDY
Baking; beverage management; buffet catering; confectionery show pieces; controlling costs in food service; culinary French; culinary skill development; food preparation; food purchasing; food service math; garde-manger; international cuisine; introduction to food service; kitchen management; management and human resources; meal planning; meat cutting; menu and facilities design; nutrition; nutrition and food service; patisserie; restaurant opportunities; sanitation; seafood processing; soup, stock, sauce, and starch production; wines and spirits.

FACILITIES
Bake shop; cafeteria; 4 classrooms; computer laboratory; demonstration laboratory; food production kitchen; gourmet dining room; learning resource center; lecture room; library; teaching kitchen; 2 vineyards.

TYPICAL STUDENT PROFILE
65 total: 40 full-time; 25 part-time. 45 are under 25 years old; 20 are between 25 and 44 years old.

SPECIAL PROGRAMS
200-hour culinary arts internship/cooperative education.

FINANCIAL AID
Employment opportunities within the program are available.

APPLICATION INFORMATION
Students may begin participation in January and September. Application deadline for fall is August 1. Application deadline for spring is January 1. Applicants must submit a formal application.

CONTACT
Director of Admissions, Culinary Arts, 121 Speonk Riverhead Road, Riverhead, NY 11901. Telephone: 631-548-2512. Fax: 631-548-2504. World Wide Web: http://www.sunysuffolk.edu.

SULLIVAN COUNTY COMMUNITY COLLEGE

Culinary Arts Division

Loch Sheldrake, New York

GENERAL INFORMATION
Public, coeducational, two-year college. Rural campus. Founded in 1962. Accredited by Middle States Association of Colleges and Schools.

PROGRAM INFORMATION
Offered since 1965. Accredited by American Culinary Federation Accrediting Commission. Program calendar is divided into semesters. 1-year certificate in food service. 2-year associate degree in culinary arts. 2-year associate degree in hospitality management. 2-year associate degree in professional chef.

PROGRAM AFFILIATION
American Culinary Federation; Council on Hotel, Restaurant, and Institutional Education; National Restaurant Association; National Restaurant Association Educational Foundation; The Bread Bakers Guild of America.

AREAS OF STUDY
Baking; beverage management; buffet catering; confectionery show pieces; controlling costs in food service; convenience cookery; culinary French; culinary skill development; food preparation; food purchasing; food service math; garde-manger; international cuisine; introduction to food service; kitchen management; management and human resources; meat cutting; meat fabrication; menu and facilities design; nutrition; nutrition and food service; patisserie; restaurant opportunities; sanitation; saucier; seafood processing; soup, stock, sauce, and starch production; wines and spirits.

FACILITIES
2 bake shops; classroom; 3 demonstration laboratories; 2 food production kitchens; gourmet dining room.

TYPICAL STUDENT PROFILE
100 total: 75 full-time; 25 part-time.

FINANCIAL AID
Employment placement assistance is available. Employment opportunities within the program are available.

HOUSING
Coed housing available.

Sullivan County Community College *(continued)*

APPLICATION INFORMATION
Students may begin participation in January and September. Applications are accepted continuously. Applicants must submit a formal application.

CONTACT
Director of Admissions, Culinary Arts Division, 112 College Road, Loch Sheldrake, NY 12759. Telephone: 800-577-5243. Fax: 845-434-4806. World Wide Web: http://www.sullivan.suny.edu/.

SYRACUSE UNIVERSITY

Hospitality and Food Service Management

Syracuse, New York

GENERAL INFORMATION
Private, coeducational, university. Urban campus. Founded in 1870. Accredited by Middle States Association of Colleges and Schools.

PROGRAM INFORMATION
Offered since 1986. Accredited by American Dietetic Association. Program calendar is divided into semesters. 4-year bachelor's degree in hospitality and food service management. 4-year bachelor's degree in nutrition science. 4-year bachelor's degree in coordinated dietetics. 4-year bachelor's degree in nutrition.

PROGRAM AFFILIATION
American Dietetic Association; Council on Hotel, Restaurant, and Institutional Education; National Restaurant Association; National Restaurant Association Educational Foundation.

AREAS OF STUDY
Baking; beverage management; buffet catering; controlling costs in food service; culinary skill development; food preparation; food purchasing; introduction to food service; kitchen management; management and human resources; menu and facilities design; nutrition; nutrition and food service; restaurant development; sanitation; wines and spirits.

FACILITIES
Bake shop; bakery; 8 cafeterias; catering service; 25 classrooms; coffee shop; 5 computer laboratories; 2 demonstration laboratories; 2 food production kitchens; 2 gardens; gourmet dining room; 5 learning resource centers; 12 lecture rooms; 8 libraries; 2 public restaurants; 6 snack shops; 9 student lounges; 2 teaching kitchens.

STUDENT PROFILE
148 total: 145 full-time; 3 part-time.

FACULTY
14 total: 6 full-time; 8 part-time. 3 are industry professionals; 1 is a master chef; 2 are culinary-certified teachers. Prominent faculty: Norm Faiola, PhD, MPS; Sarah Short, PhD, RD; Brad Beran, PhD, MBA; Kay Sterns Breuning, PhD, RD. Faculty-student ratio: 1:10.

SPECIAL PROGRAMS
ServSafe Program.

TYPICAL EXPENSES
Application fee: $40. Tuition: $24,500 per year.

FINANCIAL AID
In 2004, 2 scholarships were awarded (average award was $500). Employment placement assistance is available.

HOUSING
Coed, apartment-style, and single-sex housing available.

APPLICATION INFORMATION
Students may begin participation in January and August. Application deadline for fall is January 15. Application deadline for spring is November 15. Applicants must submit a formal application and letters of reference.

CONTACT
Bradley Beran, Director, Hospitality and Food Service Management, 034 Slocum Hall, Syracuse, NY 13244. Telephone: 315-443-2386. Fax: 315-443-2735. E-mail: bcberan@syr.edu. World Wide Web: http://www.syr.edu/.

TOMPKINS CORTLAND COMMUNITY COLLEGE

Hotel and Restaurant Management

Dryden, New York

GENERAL INFORMATION
Public, coeducational, two-year college. Small-town setting. Founded in 1969. Accredited by Middle States Association of Colleges and Schools.

PROGRAM INFORMATION
Offered since 1970. Program calendar is divided into semesters. 2-year associate degree in hotel and restaurant management.

PROGRAM AFFILIATION
Council on Hotel, Restaurant, and Institutional Education; National Restaurant Association.

AREAS OF STUDY
Beverage management; food preparation; food purchasing; food service math; introduction to food service; management and human resources; nutrition; sanitation; soup, stock, sauce, and starch production; wines and spirits.

FACILITIES
5 classrooms; 3 computer laboratories; demonstration laboratory; learning resource center; lecture room.

STUDENT PROFILE

42 total: 33 full-time; 9 part-time. 28 are under 25 years old; 9 are between 25 and 44 years old; 5 are over 44 years old.

FACULTY

4 total: 1 full-time; 3 part-time. 4 are industry professionals. Prominent faculty: John N. Martindale; Raymond C. Quick; John Parmelee; Susan Stafford. Faculty-student ratio: 1:13.

SPECIAL PROGRAMS

AAS degree program available online.

TYPICAL EXPENSES

Application fee: $15. In-state tuition: $3100 per year full-time (in district), $120 per credit part-time. Out-of-state tuition: $6500 per year full-time, $250 per credit part-time. Program-related fees include $10 for food purchases; $150 for alcoholic beverage purchases.

FINANCIAL AID

Employment placement assistance is available. Employment opportunities within the program are available.

HOUSING

Apartment-style housing available. Average on-campus housing cost per month: $627.

APPLICATION INFORMATION

Students may begin participation in January and August. Applications are accepted continuously. In 2004, 56 applied; 56 were accepted. Applicants must submit a formal application.

CONTACT

Sandy Drumluk, Director of Admissions, Hotel and Restaurant Management, 170 North Street, PO Box 139, Dryden, NY 13053-0139. Telephone: 607-844-6580. Fax: 607-844-6541. E-mail: admissions@sunytccc.edu. World Wide Web: http://www.sunytccc.edu.

WESTCHESTER COMMUNITY COLLEGE

Restaurant Management

Valhalla, New York

GENERAL INFORMATION

Public, coeducational, two-year college. Suburban campus. Founded in 1946. Accredited by Middle States Association of Colleges and Schools.

PROGRAM INFORMATION

Offered since 1946. Program calendar is divided into semesters. 2-year associate degree in food service administration: restaurant management.

PROGRAM AFFILIATION

American Dietetic Association; Council on Hotel, Restaurant, and Institutional Education; National Restaurant Association; National Restaurant Association Educational Foundation.

AREAS OF STUDY

Baking; beverage management; buffet catering; controlling costs in food service; culinary skill development; food preparation; food purchasing; food service math; garde-manger; international cuisine; introduction to food service; kitchen management; management and human resources; meal planning; menu and facilities design; nutrition; nutrition and food service; patisserie; restaurant opportunities; sanitation; soup, stock, sauce, and starch production; wines and spirits.

FACILITIES

Catering service; classroom; computer laboratory; demonstration laboratory; 2 food production kitchens; gourmet dining room; 2 laboratories; learning resource center; lecture room; library; public restaurant; student lounge; 2 teaching kitchens.

TYPICAL STUDENT PROFILE

120 total: 70 full-time; 50 part-time. 60 are under 25 years old; 48 are between 25 and 44 years old; 12 are over 44 years old.

FINANCIAL AID

Employment placement assistance is available. Employment opportunities within the program are available.

APPLICATION INFORMATION

Students may begin participation in January, May, and September. Applications are accepted continuously. Applicants must submit a formal application.

CONTACT

Director of Admissions, Restaurant Management, 75 Grasslands Road, Valhalla, NY 10595-1698. Telephone: 914-785-6551. Fax: 914-785-6423. World Wide Web: http://www.sunywcc.edu.

NORTH CAROLINA

ALAMANCE COMMUNITY COLLEGE

Culinary Technology

Graham, North Carolina

GENERAL INFORMATION

Public, coeducational, two-year college. Small-town setting. Founded in 1959. Accredited by Southern Association of Colleges and Schools.

Alamance Community College *(continued)*

PROGRAM INFORMATION
Offered since 1978. Program calendar is divided into semesters. 12-month diploma in culinary professional. 24-month associate degree in culinary technology. 6-month certificate in culinary specialist.

PROGRAM AFFILIATION
Council on Hotel, Restaurant, and Institutional Education.

AREAS OF STUDY
Baking; beverage management; buffet catering; confectionery show pieces; controlling costs in food service; convenience cookery; culinary French; culinary skill development; food preparation; food purchasing; food service communication; food service math; garde-manger; international cuisine; kitchen management; management and human resources; meal planning; menu and facilities design; nutrition; nutrition and food service; patisserie; restaurant opportunities; sanitation; saucier; soup, stock, sauce, and starch production.

FACILITIES
Bake shop; catering service; classroom; computer laboratory; food production kitchen; gourmet dining room; laboratory; lecture room; teaching kitchen; herb garden.

TYPICAL STUDENT PROFILE
60 total: 40 full-time; 20 part-time. 30 are under 25 years old; 20 are between 25 and 44 years old; 10 are over 44 years old.

SPECIAL PROGRAMS
Culinary competitions, online continuing education courses for ACF, online nutrition and hospitality supervision courses (3 credits).

FINANCIAL AID
Employment placement assistance is available.

APPLICATION INFORMATION
Students may begin participation in January, May, and August. Applications are accepted continuously. Applicants must submit a formal application.

CONTACT
Director of Admissions, Culinary Technology, 1247 Jimmie Kerr Road, Graham, NC 27253. Telephone: 336-506-4241. Fax: 336-578-1987. World Wide Web: http://www.alamance.cc.nc.us.

THE ART INSTITUTE OF CHARLOTTE
Culinary Arts

Charlotte, North Carolina

GENERAL INFORMATION
Private, coeducational, two-year college. Suburban campus. Founded in 1999. Accredited by Accrediting Council for Independent Colleges and Schools.

PROGRAM INFORMATION
Offered since 2000. Program calendar is divided into quarters. 21-month associate degree in culinary arts. 36-month bachelor's degree in culinary arts.

PROGRAM AFFILIATION
American Culinary Federation; National Restaurant Association; Slow Food International.

AREAS OF STUDY
Baking; controlling costs in food service; culinary skill development; food preparation; food purchasing; garde-manger; international cuisine; kitchen management; management and human resources; menu and facilities design; nutrition; sanitation; soup, stock, sauce, and starch production.

FACILITIES
Bake shop; 6 computer laboratories; food production kitchen; garden; gourmet dining room; 10 lecture rooms; library; public restaurant; snack shop; student lounge; 4 teaching kitchens.

STUDENT PROFILE
132 total: 117 full-time; 15 part-time.

FACULTY
12 total: 8 full-time; 4 part-time. 2 are industry professionals; 1 is a culinary-certified teacher. Prominent faculty: Joseph Bonaparte, CCC, CCE, MHM. Faculty-student ratio: 1:18.

SPECIAL PROGRAMS
7-10 day culinary tours with hands-on classes to Italy, Paris, China, Culinary Competition Team, guest chefs.

TYPICAL EXPENSES
Application fee: $50. Tuition: $365 per credit hour (112 hours for associate and 188 hours for bachelor). Program-related fee includes $265 for food cost per quarter.

FINANCIAL AID
Employment placement assistance is available. Employment opportunities within the program are available.

HOUSING
Apartment-style housing available.

APPLICATION INFORMATION
Students may begin participation in January, February, April, May, July, August, and October. Applications are accepted continuously. Applicants must interview; submit a formal application and an essay.

CONTACT
Director of Admissions, Culinary Arts, Three Lake Pointe Plaza, 2110 Water Ridge Parkway, Charlotte, NC 28217-4536. Telephone: 800-872-4417. Fax: 704-357-1133. E-mail: aichadm@aii.edu. World Wide Web: http://www.aich.artinstitutes.edu.

See color display following page 380.

ASHEVILLE-BUNCOMBE TECHNICAL COMMUNITY COLLEGE

Culinary Technology

Asheville, North Carolina

GENERAL INFORMATION
Public, coeducational, two-year college. Urban campus. Founded in 1959. Accredited by Southern Association of Colleges and Schools.

PROGRAM INFORMATION
Offered since 1967. Accredited by Culinary Technology program accredited by the American Culinary Federation. Program calendar is divided into semesters. 2-year associate degree in baking and pastry arts. 2-year associate degree in culinary technology. 2-year associate degree in hotel and restaurant management.

PROGRAM AFFILIATION
Council on Hotel, Restaurant, and Institutional Education; National Restaurant Association; National Restaurant Association Educational Foundation; Women Chefs and Restaurateurs.

AREAS OF STUDY
American regional cuisine; baking; beverage management; classical cuisine; confectionery show pieces; controlling costs in food service; culinary French; culinary skill development; food preparation; food purchasing; food service math; garde-manger; international cuisine; introduction to food service; management and human resources; meal planning; meat cutting; meat fabrication; menu and facilities design; nutrition; nutrition and food service; patisserie; restaurant opportunities; sanitation; saucier; seafood processing; soup, stock, sauce, and starch production; wines and spirits.

FACILITIES
Bake shop; 4 classrooms; computer laboratory; demonstration laboratory; food production kitchen; garden; 2 gourmet dining rooms; laboratory; learning resource center; 4 lecture rooms; library; public restaurant; snack shop; student lounge; 2 teaching kitchens; hotel.

STUDENT PROFILE
110 total: 70 full-time; 40 part-time.

FACULTY
13 total: 7 full-time; 6 part-time. 2 are industry professionals; 5 are culinary-certified teachers. Prominent faculty: Mark Moritz; Vincent Donatelli; Sheila Tillman; Gary Schwartz, JD. Faculty-student ratio: 1:10.

SPECIAL PROGRAMS
Culinary competitions, paid internship.

TYPICAL EXPENSES
In-state tuition: $608 per semester full-time (in district), $38 per credit part-time. Out-of-state tuition: $3376 per semester full-time, $211 per credit part-time.

FINANCIAL AID
In 2004, 10 scholarships were awarded (average award was $700). Employment placement assistance is available. Employment opportunities within the program are available.

APPLICATION INFORMATION
Students may begin participation in January, May, and August. Applications are accepted continuously. In 2004, 120 applied; 60 were accepted. Applicants must submit a formal application and computerized placement test.

CONTACT
Sheila Tillman, Chairperson, Culinary Technology, 340 Victoria Road, Asheville, NC 28801. Telephone: 828-254-1921 Ext. 232. Fax: 828-281-9794. E-mail: stillman@abtech.edu. World Wide Web: http://www.abtech.edu.

CENTRAL PIEDMONT COMMUNITY COLLEGE

Hospitality Education Division

Charlotte, North Carolina

GENERAL INFORMATION
Public, coeducational, two-year college. Urban campus. Founded in 1963. Accredited by Southern Association of Colleges and Schools.

PROGRAM INFORMATION
Offered since 1977. Program calendar is divided into semesters. 1-year certificate in management skills. 1-year certificate in beverage operations. 1-year certificate in restaurant management. 1-year certificate in garde manger. 1-year certificate in hot foods. 1-year certificate in baking. 1-year certificate in culinary. 1- to 2-year diploma in restaurant management. 1- to 2-year diploma in hotel management. 2-year associate degree in hotel and restaurant management. 2-year associate degree in culinary technology.

PROGRAM AFFILIATION
American Culinary Federation; National Association of Catering Executives; National Restaurant Association; National Restaurant Association Educational Foundation.

Central Piedmont Community College *(continued)*

AREAS OF STUDY

Baking; beverage management; confectionery show pieces; controlling costs in food service; culinary skill development; food preparation; food purchasing; food service communication; garde-manger; international cuisine; introduction to food service; kitchen management; management and human resources; meal planning; meat cutting; nutrition; patisserie; restaurant opportunities; sanitation; soup, stock, sauce, and starch production; wines and spirits.

FACILITIES

2 bake shops; 4 classrooms; demonstration laboratory; 2 food production kitchens; gourmet dining room; learning resource center; 2 lecture rooms; library; public restaurant.

TYPICAL STUDENT PROFILE

390 full-time.

FINANCIAL AID

Employment placement assistance is available.

APPLICATION INFORMATION

Students may begin participation in January and August. Applications are accepted continuously. Applicants must submit a formal application, have a high school diploma or GED, and take placement test.

CONTACT

Director of Admissions, Hospitality Education Division, PO Box 35009, Charlotte, NC 28235-5009. Telephone: 704-330-6721. Fax: 704-330-6581. World Wide Web: http://www.cpcc.cc.nc.us/.

EAST CAROLINA UNIVERSITY

Department of Nutrition and Hospitality Management

Greenville, North Carolina

GENERAL INFORMATION

Public, coeducational, university. Small-town setting. Founded in 1907. Accredited by Southern Association of Colleges and Schools.

PROGRAM INFORMATION

Offered since 1988. Program calendar is divided into semesters. 1- to 2-year master of business administration in hospitality management (concentration). 4-year bachelor's degree in hospitality management.

PROGRAM AFFILIATION

American Dietetic Association; Council on Hotel, Restaurant, and Institutional Education; National Restaurant Association; National Restaurant Association Educational Foundation.

AREAS OF STUDY

Hotel and restaurant management.

FACILITIES

4 classrooms; computer laboratory; demonstration laboratory; food production kitchen; 2 teaching kitchens.

STUDENT PROFILE

236 total: 201 full-time; 35 part-time. 208 are under 25 years old; 25 are between 25 and 44 years old; 3 are over 44 years old.

FACULTY

17 total: 13 full-time; 4 part-time. 1 is a master chef. Prominent faculty: Dori Finley, PhD, RD, LDN; Jim Chandler, PhD, CHA, CHE; Mel Weber, PhD; David Rivera, PhD. Faculty-student ratio: 1:13.

SPECIAL PROGRAMS

Paid internship, international study abroad program, tours of North Carolina wineries, including Biltmore Estates and Childres wineries.

TYPICAL EXPENSES

Application fee: $45. In-state tuition: $2135 per year full-time (in district), $889 per up to 10 hours part-time (in district), $889 per up to 10 hours part-time (out-of-district). Out-of-state tuition: $12,349 per year full-time, $5145 per up to 10 hours part-time. Tuition for international students: $12,349 per year.

FINANCIAL AID

In 2005, 12 scholarships were awarded (average award was $1500). Program-specific awards include paid internship with Red Lobster, ARAMARK, Biltmore Estates, Pinehurst Resorts and Kingsmill Resort. Employment placement assistance is available. Employment opportunities within the program are available.

HOUSING

Coed, apartment-style, and single-sex housing available. Average on-campus housing cost per month: $369.

APPLICATION INFORMATION

Students may begin participation in January, May, July, and August. Application deadline for summer and fall is March 15. Application deadline for spring is November 1. Application deadline for transfers (summer and fall) is April 15. Applicants must submit a formal application and letters of reference.

CONTACT

William Forsythe, Chair, Department of Nutrition and Hospitality Management, Rivers Building Room 148, Greenville, NC 27858. Telephone: 252-328-6850. Fax: 252-328-4276. E-mail: forsythew@ecu.edu. World Wide Web: http://www.ecu.edu/che/nuhm.

GUILFORD TECHNICAL COMMUNITY COLLEGE

Culinary Technology

Jamestown, North Carolina

GENERAL INFORMATION
Public, coeducational, two-year college. Suburban campus. Founded in 1958. Accredited by Southern Association of Colleges and Schools.

PROGRAM INFORMATION
Offered since 1976. Accredited by American Culinary Federation Accrediting Commission. Program calendar is divided into semesters. 1-year certificate in culinary technology. 1-year diploma in culinary technology. 2-year associate degree in culinary technology.

PROGRAM AFFILIATION
American Culinary Federation; Culinary Hospitality and Tourism Educators Association of North Carolina; Foodservice Educators Network International; International Food Service Executives Association; National Restaurant Association Educational Foundation.

AREAS OF STUDY
Baking; controlling costs in food service; culinary skill development; food and beverage service; food preparation; food purchasing; food service communication; food service math; garde-manger; international cuisine; introduction to food service; kitchen management; management and human resources; meal planning; meat cutting; meat fabrication; menu and facilities design; nutrition; patisserie; restaurant opportunities; sanitation; saucier; seafood processing; soup, stock, sauce, and starch production; wines and spirits.

FACILITIES
Bake shop; 4 classrooms; demonstration laboratory; 2 food production kitchens; garden; gourmet dining room; public restaurant; student lounge; teaching kitchen; garde-manger kitchen.

TYPICAL STUDENT PROFILE
100 total: 60 full-time; 40 part-time. 25 are under 25 years old; 60 are between 25 and 44 years old; 15 are over 44 years old.

FINANCIAL AID
Employment placement assistance is available. Employment opportunities within the program are available.

APPLICATION INFORMATION
Students may begin participation in January and August. Applications are accepted continuously. Applicants must interview; submit a formal application.

CONTACT
Director of Admissions, Culinary Technology, PO Box 309, Jamestown, NC 27282-0309. Telephone: 336-454-1126 Ext. 2302. Fax: 336-819-2032. World Wide Web: http://technet.gtcc.cc.nc.us/.

JOHNSON & WALES UNIVERSITY

College of Culinary Arts

Charlotte, North Carolina

GENERAL INFORMATION
Private, coeducational, university. Urban campus. Founded in 1914. Accredited by New England Association of Schools and Colleges.

PROGRAM INFORMATION
Offered since 2004. Program calendar is divided into quarters. 2-year associate degree in baking and pastry arts. 2-year associate degree in culinary arts. 4-year bachelor's degree in food service management.

PROGRAM AFFILIATION
American Culinary Federation; American Institute of Wine & Food; Institute of Food Technologists; International Association of Culinary Professionals; National Restaurant Association; National Restaurant Association Educational Foundation; Research Chefs Association; The Bread Bakers Guild of America; Women Chefs and Restaurateurs.

AREAS OF STUDY
Baking; beverage management; confectionery show pieces; controlling costs in food service; culinary skill development; food preparation; food purchasing; food service math; garde-manger; international cuisine; introduction to food service; meat cutting; meat fabrication; menu and facilities design; nutrition; patisserie; sanitation; saucier; seafood processing; soup, stock, sauce, and starch production; wines and spirits.

FACILITIES
6 bake shops; cafeteria; 12 classrooms; 4 computer laboratories; demonstration laboratory; food production kitchen; 3 gourmet dining rooms; learning resource center; lecture room; library; snack shop; 2 student lounges; 11 teaching kitchens; storeroom.

STUDENT PROFILE
1,268 total: 1267 full-time; 1 part-time. 1081 are under 25 years old; 163 are between 25 and 44 years old; 18 are over 44 years old.

FACULTY
24 total: 23 full-time; 1 part-time. Prominent faculty: Ed Batten, BS, CEC, CCE, FMP, CCI; Susan Batten, BS, CEC, CCE, FMP, CCI; Frances Burnett, CMB, CEPC; Michael Calenda, CEC. Faculty-student ratio: 1:18.

Johnson & Wales University (*continued*)

SPECIAL PROGRAMS
Summer tour abroad (Germany, France, or Singapore), Inter-Campus Hot Food Competition.

TYPICAL EXPENSES
Tuition: $19,875 per year. Program-related fees include $951 for general fee; $250 for orientation fee; $954 for optional weekend meal plan.

FINANCIAL AID
In 2005, 293 scholarships were awarded (average award was $2572); 727 loans were granted (average loan was $6013). Employment placement assistance is available.

HOUSING
Coed housing available. Average on-campus housing cost per month: $1000.

APPLICATION INFORMATION
Students may begin participation in March, September, and December. Applications are accepted continuously. In 2005, 2219 applied; 1893 were accepted. Applicants must submit a formal application.

CONTACT
Brian Stanley, Director of Admissions, College of Culinary Arts, 901 West Trade Street, Charlotte, NC 28202. Telephone: 980-598-1100. Fax: 980-598-1111. E-mail: charlotte.admissions@jwu.edu. World Wide Web: http://culinary.jwu.edu.
See color display following page 332.

SANDHILLS COMMUNITY COLLEGE

Culinary Technology

Pinehurst, North Carolina

GENERAL INFORMATION
Public, coeducational, two-year college. Small-town setting. Founded in 1963. Accredited by Southern Association of Colleges and Schools.

PROGRAM INFORMATION
Offered since 1993. Program calendar is divided into semesters. 2-year associate degree in hotel restaurant management. 2-year associate degree in culinary technology.

PROGRAM AFFILIATION
American Culinary Federation; American Hotel and Lodging Association; International Food Service Executives Association; National Restaurant Association; National Restaurant Association Educational Foundation.

AREAS OF STUDY
Baking; beverage management; buffet catering; confectionery show pieces; controlling costs in food service; culinary skill development; food preparation; food

purchasing; garde-manger; international cuisine; introduction to food service; kitchen management; management and human resources; meal planning; meat cutting; meat fabrication; menu and facilities design; nutrition; patisserie; restaurant opportunities; sanitation; saucier; seafood processing; soup, stock, sauce, and starch production; wines and spirits.

FACILITIES
Bake shop; cafeteria; 5 classrooms; 3 computer laboratories; demonstration laboratory; food production kitchen; garden; laboratory; learning resource center; lecture room; library; student lounge; 2 teaching kitchens.

TYPICAL STUDENT PROFILE
110 total: 70 full-time; 40 part-time.

SPECIAL PROGRAMS
5-month internship at leading resorts, 2-3 year paid apprenticeship at a leading resort.

FINANCIAL AID
Program-specific awards include Hospitality Club scholarships. Employment placement assistance is available.

APPLICATION INFORMATION
Students may begin participation in January, May, and August. Application deadline for fall is August 16. Application deadline for spring is January 7. Application deadline for summer is May 18. Applicants must submit a formal application.

CONTACT
Director of Admissions, Culinary Technology, 3395 Airport Road, Pinehurst, NC 28374-8299. Telephone: 910-695-3756. Fax: 910-695-1823. World Wide Web: http://www.sandhills.cc.nc.us/Sandhills/.

SOUTHWESTERN COMMUNITY COLLEGE

Culinary Technology

Sylva, North Carolina

GENERAL INFORMATION
Public, coeducational, two-year college. Small-town setting. Founded in 1964. Accredited by Southern Association of Colleges and Schools.

PROGRAM INFORMATION
Offered since 1973. Program calendar is divided into semesters. 2-semester certificate in culinary technology. 5-semester associate degree in culinary technology.

PROGRAM AFFILIATION
National Restaurant Association Educational Foundation.

FACILITIES
Classroom; teaching kitchen.

TYPICAL STUDENT PROFILE

22 total: 9 full-time; 13 part-time. 16 are under 25 years old; 4 are between 25 and 44 years old; 2 are over 44 years old.

SPECIAL PROGRAMS

Annual gingerbread house competition at Grove Park Inn.

FINANCIAL AID

Program-specific awards include E.M. Moulton scholarships ($200).

APPLICATION INFORMATION

Students may begin participation in January, May, and August. Applications are accepted continuously. Applicants must submit a formal application.

CONTACT

Director of Admissions, Culinary Technology, 447 College Drive, Sylva, NC 28779. Telephone: 828-586-4091 Ext. 253. Fax: 828-586-3129. World Wide Web: http://www.southwest.cc.nc.us.

THE UNIVERSITY OF NORTH CAROLINA AT GREENSBORO

Greensboro, North Carolina

GENERAL INFORMATION

Public, coeducational, university. Urban campus. Founded in 1891. Accredited by Southern Association of Colleges and Schools.

PROGRAM INFORMATION

Accredited by American Dietetic Association. Program calendar is divided into semesters. 37- to 40-hour master's degree in nutrition. 4-year bachelor's degree in nutrition and food service systems. 63-hour doctoral degree in nutrition.

PROGRAM AFFILIATION

American Dietetic Association.

AREAS OF STUDY

Hospitality management; nutrition; nutrition and food service; restaurant opportunities.

FACILITIES

Classroom; computer laboratory; demonstration laboratory; lecture room; library; student lounge.

STUDENT PROFILE

181 total: 140 full-time; 41 part-time. 128 are under 25 years old; 48 are between 25 and 44 years old; 5 are over 44 years old.

FACULTY

12 total: 8 full-time; 4 part-time. Faculty-student ratio: 1:7.

SPECIAL PROGRAMS

Dietetic Internship.

TYPICAL EXPENSES

Application fee: $35. In-state tuition: $3038 per year full-time (in district), $356 per 3 hours part-time. Out-of-state tuition: $13,412 per year full-time, $1652 per 3 hours part-time.

HOUSING

Coed, apartment-style, and single-sex housing available. Average on-campus housing cost per month: $354. Average off-campus housing cost per month: $576.

APPLICATION INFORMATION

Students may begin participation in January and August. Application deadline for fall is August 1. Application deadline for spring is December 1. Applicants must submit a formal application and SAT or ACT scores.

CONTACT

Office of Admissions, 123 Mossman Building, PO Box 26166, Greensboro, NC 27402. Telephone: 336-334-5243. Fax: 336-334-4180. E-mail: undergrad_admissions@uncg.edu. World Wide Web: http://www.uncg.edu.

WAKE TECHNICAL COMMUNITY COLLEGE

Culinary Technology, Hotel/Restaurant Management

Raleigh, North Carolina

GENERAL INFORMATION

Public, coeducational, two-year college. Suburban campus. Founded in 1958. Accredited by Southern Association of Colleges and Schools.

PROGRAM INFORMATION

Offered since 1983. Program calendar is divided into semesters. 2-year associate degree in hotel/restaurant management. 2-year associate degree in culinary technology.

PROGRAM AFFILIATION

American Culinary Federation; American Institute of Baking; American Institute of Wine & Food; Council on Hotel, Restaurant, and Institutional Education; National Restaurant Association; National Restaurant Association Educational Foundation; North Carolina Culinary, Hospitality, and Tourism Alliance; North Carolina Restaurant and Hotel Management Association.

AREAS OF STUDY

Baking; beverage management; buffet catering; confectionery show pieces; controlling costs in food service; culinary French; culinary skill development; food preparation; food purchasing; food service communication; food service math; garde-manger; hotel operations; international cuisine; introduction to food service; kitchen management; management and human resources; meal

Wake Technical Community College *(continued)*

planning; meat cutting; meat fabrication; menu and facilities design; nutrition; nutrition and food service; patisserie; restaurant opportunities; sanitation; saucier; seafood processing; soup, stock, sauce, and starch production; table service; wines and spirits.

FACILITIES

Bake shop; 2 classrooms; computer laboratory; demonstration laboratory; 4 food production kitchens; gourmet dining room; learning resource center; 2 lecture rooms; library; public restaurant; student lounge; 7 teaching kitchens.

STUDENT PROFILE

172 total: 160 full-time; 12 part-time.

FACULTY

10 total: 6 full-time; 4 part-time. 5 are industry professionals; 2 are culinary-certified teachers; certified hospitality educators. Prominent faculty: Fredi Mort; Caralyn House; Richard Roberts; John Berardi. Faculty-student ratio: 1:15.

SPECIAL PROGRAMS

3-week work-study in France, American Culinary Federation Hot Food Competition.

TYPICAL EXPENSES

In-state tuition: $35.50 per credit hour. Out-of-state tuition: $197 per credit hour.

FINANCIAL AID

In 2004, 4 scholarships were awarded (average award was $1500); 1 loan was granted (loan was $1500). Employment placement assistance is available. Employment opportunities within the program are available.

APPLICATION INFORMATION

Students may begin participation in January, May, and August. Applications are accepted continuously. In 2004, 125 applied; 90 were accepted. Applicants must submit a formal application and SAT scores or equivalent.

CONTACT

Office of the Registrar, Culinary Technology, Hotel/Restaurant Management, 9101 Fayetteville Road, Raleigh, NC 27603-5696. Telephone: 919-662-3400. World Wide Web: http://www.waketech.edu.

WILKES COMMUNITY COLLEGE

Culinary Technology and Baking and Pastry Arts

Wilkesboro, North Carolina

GENERAL INFORMATION

Public, coeducational, two-year college. Rural campus. Founded in 1965. Accredited by Southern Association of Colleges and Schools.

PROGRAM INFORMATION

Offered since 1997. Program calendar is divided into semesters. 2-year associate degree in baking and pastry arts. 2-year associate degree in culinary technology. 4-month certificate in line cook.

PROGRAM AFFILIATION

Chefs Collaborative 2000.

AREAS OF STUDY

Artisanal breads; baking; beverage management; buffet catering; controlling costs in food service; convenience cookery; culinary skill development; food preparation; food purchasing; garde-manger; international cuisine; introduction to food service; kitchen management; nutrition; pastry cooking.

FACILITIES

Bake shop; classroom; food production kitchen; public restaurant; teaching kitchen.

STUDENT PROFILE

30 total: 24 full-time; 6 part-time. 14 are under 25 years old; 11 are between 25 and 44 years old; 5 are over 44 years old.

FACULTY

3 total: 1 full-time; 2 part-time. 1 is an industry professional; 2 are culinary-certified teachers. Prominent faculty: Kimrey Jordan; William Bullock; Chris Magee. Faculty-student ratio: 1:10.

SPECIAL PROGRAMS

Participation in providing food for Merlefest (bluegrass festival), student-run Tory Oak Restaurant on campus, trip to Paris to work in Alain Ducasse, Michael Rostang, and Grand Cascade restaurants.

TYPICAL EXPENSES

In-state tuition: $1264 per year full-time (in district), $39.50 per credit hour part-time. Out-of-state tuition: $7024 per year full-time, $219.50 per credit hour part-time. Program-related fee includes $200 for uniforms and cutlery.

FINANCIAL AID

In 2004, 10 scholarships were awarded (average award was $1000). Program-specific awards include participation in Ye Host Culinary Club (provides full tuition for up to four semesters). Employment placement assistance is available. Employment opportunities within the program are available.

HOUSING

Average off-campus housing cost per month: $500.

APPLICATION INFORMATION

Students may begin participation in January and August. Applications are accepted continuously. In 2004, 29 applied; 29 were accepted. Applicants must submit a formal application.

CONTACT

C. Mac Warren, Director of Admissions, Culinary Technology and Baking and Pastry Arts, PO Box 120, Wilkesboro, NC 28677. Telephone: 336-838-6141. Fax: 336-838-6547. E-mail: mac.warren@wilkescc.edu. World Wide Web: http://www.wilkescc.edu.

NORTH DAKOTA

BISMARCK STATE COLLEGE

Hotel/Restaurant Management

Bismarck, North Dakota

GENERAL INFORMATION

Public, coeducational, two-year college. Urban campus. Founded in 1939. Accredited by North Central Association of Colleges and Schools.

PROGRAM INFORMATION

Program calendar is divided into semesters. 11-month certificate in basic hotel management. 11-month certificate in basic restaurant management. 5-semester associate degree in hotel/restaurant management.

AREAS OF STUDY

Beverage management; culinary skill development; food preparation; food purchasing; food service math; introduction to food service; management and human resources; meal planning; sanitation.

FACILITIES

Cafeteria; catering service; classroom; food production kitchen; lecture room.

TYPICAL STUDENT PROFILE

25 full-time.

SPECIAL PROGRAMS

On-the-job experience.

FINANCIAL AID

Employment placement assistance is available.

HOUSING

Single-sex housing available.

APPLICATION INFORMATION

Students may begin participation in January, June, and August. Applications are accepted continuously. Applicants must submit a formal application.

CONTACT

Director of Admissions, Hotel/Restaurant Management, PO Box 5587, 1500 Edwards Avenue, Bismarck, ND 58506-5587. Telephone: 701-224-5497. Fax: 701-224-5643. World Wide Web: http://www.bismarckstate.edu.

NORTH DAKOTA STATE COLLEGE OF SCIENCE

Culinary Arts

Wahpeton, North Dakota

GENERAL INFORMATION

Public, coeducational, two-year college. Small-town setting. Founded in 1903. Accredited by North Central Association of Colleges and Schools.

PROGRAM INFORMATION

Offered since 1971. Program calendar is divided into semesters. 2-year associate degree in restaurant management. 2-year associate degree in chef training and management technology. 2-year diploma in chef training and management technology.

PROGRAM AFFILIATION

American Culinary Federation; National Restaurant Association; North Dakota Hospitality Association.

AREAS OF STUDY

Baking; buffet catering; controlling costs in food service; culinary skill development; food preparation; food purchasing; food service math; garde-manger; introduction to food service; kitchen management; management and human resources; meal planning; meat cutting; meat fabrication; menu and facilities design; nutrition and food service; patisserie; sanitation; saucier; seafood processing; soup, stock, sauce, and starch production.

FACILITIES

Bake shop; bakery; cafeteria; catering service; classroom; coffee shop; 7 computer laboratories; demonstration laboratory; food production kitchen; laboratory; learning resource center; lecture room; 2 libraries; public restaurant; snack shop; 3 student lounges; teaching kitchen.

STUDENT PROFILE

30 full-time. 27 are under 25 years old; 3 are between 25 and 44 years old.

FACULTY

2 total: 2 full-time. 2 are industry professionals. Prominent faculty: Kyle Armitage; Mary Uhren. Faculty-student ratio: 1:15.

SPECIAL PROGRAMS

Cooperative Education Program (paid internship).

TYPICAL EXPENSES

Application fee: $25. In-state tuition: $2225 per year full-time (in district), $84.37 per credit part-time. Out-of-state tuition: $2835 per year full-time, $109.79 per credit part-time. Program-related fees include $290 for uniforms; $170 for cutlery; $75 for laboratory supply fees (per semester); $300 for program fees.

North Dakota State College of Science *(continued)*

FINANCIAL AID
In 2004, 4 scholarships were awarded (average award was $500). Employment placement assistance is available.

HOUSING
Coed, apartment-style, and single-sex housing available. Average on-campus housing cost per month: $96. Average off-campus housing cost per month: $250.

APPLICATION INFORMATION
Students may begin participation in January and August. Application deadline for fall is August 24. Application deadline for spring is January 8. In 2004, 30 applied; 30 were accepted. Applicants must submit a formal application and ACT scores.

CONTACT
Mary Uhren, Director, Culinary Arts, 800 North Sixth Street, Wahpeton, ND 58076. Telephone: 701-671-2842. Fax: 701-671-2774. E-mail: mary.uhren@ndscs.nodak.edu. World Wide Web: http://www.ndscs.nodak.edu/instruct/cul_arts.

NORTH DAKOTA STATE UNIVERSITY

Human Development and Education

Fargo, North Dakota

GENERAL INFORMATION
Public, coeducational, university. Small-town setting. Founded in 1980. Accredited by North Central Association of Colleges and Schools.

PROGRAM INFORMATION
Accredited by American Dietetic Association. Program calendar is divided into semesters. 4-year bachelor's degree in hospitality and tourism management. 4-year bachelor's degree in dietetics.

AREAS OF STUDY
Food preparation; kitchen management; meal planning; nutrition; nutrition and food service; sanitation.

HOUSING
Coed, apartment-style, and single-sex housing available.

APPLICATION INFORMATION
Application deadline for fall (recommended) is August 18. Applicants must high school transcript, SAT or ACT scores.

CONTACT
Director of Admissions, Human Development and Education, Fargo, ND 58105. World Wide Web: http://www.ndsu.edu.

OHIO

THE ART INSTITUTE OF OHIO–CINCINNATI

Cincinnati, Ohio

GENERAL INFORMATION
Private, coeducational, two-year college.

PROGRAM INFORMATION
Program calendar is continuous. Associate degree in AAS Culinary Arts.

AREAS OF STUDY
Baking; controlling costs in food service; dining room operation; garde-manger; international and regional cusines; kitchen management; management and human resources; nutrition; purchasing and cost control; sanitation.

SPECIAL PROGRAMS
Experiential learning components such as field trips, externships, and internships.

CONTACT
Admissions Office, 1011 Glendale Road, Cincinnati, OH 45215. Telephone: 513-771-2821. World Wide Web: http://www.artinstitutes.edu/cincinnati/.

See color display following page 380.

ASHLAND UNIVERSITY

Ashland, Ohio

GENERAL INFORMATION
Private, coeducational, comprehensive institution. Rural campus. Founded in 1878. Accredited by North Central Association of Colleges and Schools.

PROGRAM INFORMATION
Accredited by Council on Hotel, Restaurant and Institutional Education. Program calendar is divided into semesters. 4-year bachelor's degree in hotel and restaurant management.

PROGRAM AFFILIATION
Council on Hotel, Restaurant, and Institutional Education; National Restaurant Association.

FACILITIES
Computer laboratory; demonstration laboratory; food production kitchen.

TYPICAL STUDENT PROFILE
37 total: 35 full-time; 2 part-time. 35 are under 25 years old; 2 are between 25 and 44 years old.

SPECIAL PROGRAMS
640-hour internship, semester at Disney (for credit), international internship opportunities.

FINANCIAL AID
Employment placement assistance is available.

HOUSING
Coed, apartment-style, and single-sex housing available.

APPLICATION INFORMATION
Students may begin participation in January and August. Application deadline for fall is August 25. Application deadline for spring is January 15. Applicants must submit a formal application, an essay, high school transcripts, ACT or SAT score.

CONTACT
Director of Admissions, 401 College Avenue, Ashland, OH 44805. Telephone: 800-882-1548. Fax: 419-289-5999. World Wide Web: http://www.ashland.edu.

CINCINNATI STATE TECHNICAL AND COMMUNITY COLLEGE

Business Division

Cincinnati, Ohio

GENERAL INFORMATION
Public, coeducational, two-year college. Urban campus. Founded in 1966. Accredited by North Central Association of Colleges and Schools.

PROGRAM INFORMATION
Offered since 1978. Accredited by American Culinary Federation Accrediting Commission. Program calendar is 5 ten-week terms. 1-year certificate in culinary arts. 2-year associate degree in hotel management. 2-year associate degree in restaurant management. 2-year associate degree in culinary arts.

PROGRAM AFFILIATION
American Culinary Federation; Council on Hotel, Restaurant, and Institutional Education; National Restaurant Association; National Restaurant Association Educational Foundation.

AREAS OF STUDY
Baking; beverage management; buffet catering; controlling costs in food service; culinary skill development; food preparation; food purchasing; garde-manger; international cuisine; management and human resources; meat cutting; menu and facilities design; nutrition; nutrition and food service; restaurant opportunities; sanitation; seafood processing; soup, stock, sauce, and starch production; wines and spirits.

FACILITIES
Demonstration laboratory; 2 food production kitchens; laboratory; lecture room; public restaurant; 2 teaching kitchens.

TYPICAL STUDENT PROFILE
200 total: 160 full-time; 40 part-time.

SPECIAL PROGRAMS
Cooperative education experience.

FINANCIAL AID
Employment placement assistance is available. Employment opportunities within the program are available.

APPLICATION INFORMATION
Students may begin participation in February, April, June, September, and November. Applications are accepted continuously. Applicants must submit a formal application and take entrance exam.

CONTACT
Director of Admissions, Business Division, 3520 Central Parkway, Cincinnati, OH 45223-2690. Telephone: 513-569-1637. Fax: 513-569-1467. World Wide Web: http://www.cinstate.cc.oh.us/.

COLUMBUS STATE COMMUNITY COLLEGE

Hospitality Management Department

Columbus, Ohio

GENERAL INFORMATION
Public, coeducational, two-year college. Urban campus. Founded in 1963. Accredited by North Central Association of Colleges and Schools.

PROGRAM INFORMATION
Offered since 1966. Accredited by American Culinary Federation Accrediting Commission, American Dietetic Association, Council on Hotel, Restaurant and Institutional Education. Program calendar is divided into quarters. 2-year associate degree in travel/tourism hotel management. 2-year associate degree in dietetic technician. 2-year associate degree in food service/restaurant management. 3-year associate degree in chef apprenticeship. 9-month certificate in dietary manager.

PROGRAM AFFILIATION
American Dietetic Association; Council on Hotel, Restaurant, and Institutional Education; National Restaurant Association; National Restaurant Association Educational Foundation; Ohio Hotel and Lodging Association; Retailer's Bakery Association.

AREAS OF STUDY
Baking; beverage management; catering services; controlling costs in food service; food preparation; food purchasing;

Columbus State Community College *(continued)*

food service math; garde-manger; introduction to food service; kitchen management; management and human resources; meal planning; menu and facilities design; nutrition; nutrition and food service; restaurant opportunities; sanitation; soup, stock, sauce, and starch production; wines and spirits.

FACILITIES

Catering service; 3 classrooms; computer laboratory; demonstration laboratory; 2 food production kitchens; 2 laboratories; learning resource center; 3 lecture rooms; library; 2 teaching kitchens.

STUDENT PROFILE

425 total: 200 full-time; 225 part-time.

FACULTY

13 total: 5 full-time; 8 part-time. 3 are industry professionals; 2 are culinary-certified teachers. Prominent faculty: Mokie Steiskal, PhD, CCE, RD, FMP; James Taylor, CEC, AAC; Jan Van Hor, MS, RDLD. Faculty-student ratio: 1:25 lecture; 1:15 lab.

SPECIAL PROGRAMS

Wine-food pairing competition-2 winners get trip to California wine country, culinary competitions and demonstrations, paid apprenticeship and cooperative work experiences.

TYPICAL EXPENSES

Application fee: $10. In-state tuition: $69 per quarter credit hour full-time (in district), $76 per quarter credit hour part-time. Out-of-state tuition: $152 per quarter credit hour full-time, $168 per quarter credit hour part-time. Tuition for international students: $183 per quarter credit hour full-time, $202 per quarter credit hour part-time. Program-related fee includes $150 for average food and non-food lab supplies (per year).

FINANCIAL AID

In 2004, 10 scholarships were awarded (average award was $1000). Employment placement assistance is available. Employment opportunities within the program are available.

HOUSING

Average off-campus housing cost per month: $375.

APPLICATION INFORMATION

Students may begin participation in January, March, June, and September. Application deadline for fall chef apprenticeships is May 15. Application deadline for spring chef apprenticeships; continuous for other majors is November 15. In 2004, 225 applied; 200 were accepted. Applicants must submit a formal application, 2 letters of reference, essay, and interview (chef apprentice option only).

CONTACT

Mokie Steiskal, Professor, Hospitality Management, Hospitality Management Department, 550 East Spring Street, Columbus, OH 43215. Telephone: 614-287-5126. Fax: 614-287-5973. E-mail: msteiska@cscc.edu. World Wide Web: http://www.cscc.edu/.

CUYAHOGA COMMUNITY COLLEGE, METROPOLITAN CAMPUS

Hospitality Management Department

Cleveland, Ohio

GENERAL INFORMATION

Public, coeducational, two-year college. Urban campus. Founded in 1963. Accredited by North Central Association of Colleges and Schools.

PROGRAM INFORMATION

Offered since 1976. Accredited by American Culinary Federation Accrediting Commission, Commission on Accreditation of Hospitality Management Programs. Program calendar is divided into semesters. 1-year certificate in food and beverage operations. 1-year certificate in culinarian/cook. 1-year certificate in professional baker. 2-year associate degree in restaurant/ food service management. 2-year associate degree in culinary arts.

PROGRAM AFFILIATION

American Culinary Federation; American Personal Chef Institute & Association; Council on Hotel, Restaurant, and Institutional Education; International Food Service Executives Association; National Restaurant Association; National Restaurant Association Educational Foundation.

AREAS OF STUDY

Baking; beverage management; buffet catering; controlling costs in food service; culinary skill development; food preparation; food purchasing; food service math; garde-manger; international cuisine; introduction to food service; kitchen management; management and human resources; meal planning; meat cutting; menu and facilities design; nutrition; nutrition and food service; sanitation; saucier; seafood processing; soup, stock, sauce, and starch production; wines and spirits.

FACILITIES

Bake shop; 4 classrooms; computer laboratory; demonstration laboratory; 2 food production kitchens; gourmet dining room; learning resource center; lecture room; library; public restaurant; snack shop; student lounge; 2 teaching kitchens.

FACULTY

9 total: 6 full-time; 3 part-time. 9 are industry professionals; 3 are culinary-certified teachers; 2 are certified executive chef. Prominent faculty: Richard Fulchiron, CEC, CCE, M.Ed.; Thomas Capretta, M.Ed., CEC, CCE; Paul Glatt, MBA. Faculty-student ratio: 1:14.

SPECIAL PROGRAMS
210-hour required practicum (associate degree), culinary competitions, personal chef.

TYPICAL EXPENSES
In-state tuition: $4986 per associate degree full-time (in district), $76.70 per credit hour part-time (in district), $6591 per associate degree full-time (out-of-district), $101.40 per credit hour part-time (out-of-district). Out-of-state tuition: $13,497.25 per associate degree full-time, $207.65 per credit hour part-time. Tuition for international students: $13,497.25 full-time, $207.65 per credit hour part-time. Program-related fees include $165 for lab fees (cooking/baking classes) (2 years); $80 for uniforms (2 years); $2000 for books (2 years).

FINANCIAL AID
In 2004, 20 scholarships were awarded (average award was $600). Program-specific awards include Chef Boirdee Scholarship, A. LoPresti Scholarship, Hospitality Student Club Scholarship-for books only. Employment placement assistance is available. Employment opportunities within the program are available.

HOUSING
Average off-campus housing cost per month: $500.

APPLICATION INFORMATION
Students may begin participation in January, March, May, August, and October. Applications are accepted continuously. In 2004, 231 applied; 231 were accepted. Applicants must interview, and be high school graduate or have GED, take college math and English placements tests.

CONTACT
Julia Patterson, Program Assistant, Hospitality Management Department, Hospitality Management, 2900 Community College Avenue, Cleveland, OH 44112. Telephone: 216-987-4081. Fax: 216-987-4086. E-mail: julia.patterson@tri-c.edu. World Wide Web: http://www.tri-c.edu/infoaccess.

HOCKING COLLEGE

Hospitality Department

Nelsonville, Ohio

GENERAL INFORMATION
Public, coeducational, two-year college. Rural campus. Founded in 1968. Accredited by North Central Association of Colleges and Schools.

PROGRAM INFORMATION
Offered since 1978. Accredited by American Culinary Federation Accrediting Commission. Program calendar is divided into quarters. 2-year associate degree in culinary arts. 2-year associate degree in hotel/restaurant management.

PROGRAM AFFILIATION
American Culinary Federation; American Hotel and Lodging Association; National Restaurant Association; National Restaurant Association Educational Foundation.

AREAS OF STUDY
Baking; beverage management; buffet catering; controlling costs in food service; culinary skill development; food preparation; food purchasing; garde-manger; international cuisine; introduction to food service; kitchen management; management and human resources; meal planning; meat cutting; meat fabrication; menu and facilities design; nutrition; patisserie; sanitation; seafood processing; soup, stock, sauce, and starch production; wines and spirits.

FACILITIES
Bake shop; bakery; 2 catering services; 5 classrooms; coffee shop; computer laboratory; demonstration laboratory; food production kitchen; garden; laboratory; learning resource center; 3 lecture rooms; library; public restaurant; student lounge; teaching kitchen.

TYPICAL STUDENT PROFILE
230 total: 200 full-time; 30 part-time.

SPECIAL PROGRAMS
Internships in the Caribbean and South America, ACF junior competitions, trip to Chicago Food Show and state, regional, and national ACF conferences.

FINANCIAL AID
Employment placement assistance is available. Employment opportunities within the program are available.

HOUSING
Coed and apartment-style housing available.

APPLICATION INFORMATION
Students may begin participation year-round. Applications are accepted continuously. Applicants must submit a formal application.

CONTACT
Director of Admissions, Hospitality Department, 3301 Hocking Parkway, Nelsonville, OH 45764-9588. Telephone: 740-753-3531 Ext. 310. Fax: 740-753-5286. World Wide Web: http://www.hocking.edu.

THE LORETTA PAGANINI SCHOOL OF COOKING

The International Culinary Arts and Sciences Institute

Chesterland, Ohio

GENERAL INFORMATION
Private, coeducational, culinary institute. Suburban campus. Founded in 1981.

The Loretta Paganini School of Cooking (*continued*)

PROGRAM INFORMATION
Offered since 1989. Program calendar is divided into quarters. 18-month diploma in pastry arts. 18-month diploma in culinary arts. 6-month certificate in pastry arts. 6-month certificate in culinary arts.

PROGRAM AFFILIATION
American Culinary Federation; American Institute of Wine & Food; International Association of Culinary Professionals.

AREAS OF STUDY
Baking; culinary skill development; food preparation; food purchasing; food service math; garde-manger; international cuisine; introduction to food service; meal planning; meat fabrication; menu and facilities design; nutrition; patisserie; sanitation; saucier; seafood processing; soup, stock, sauce, and starch production; wines and spirits.

FACILITIES
Bake shop; classroom; food production kitchen; garden; lecture room; library; 2 teaching kitchens.

TYPICAL STUDENT PROFILE
125 total: 75 full-time; 50 part-time. 10 are under 25 years old; 105 are between 25 and 44 years old; 10 are over 44 years old.

SPECIAL PROGRAMS
5-day cooking classes in Italy.

FINANCIAL AID
Employment placement assistance is available. Employment opportunities within the program are available.

APPLICATION INFORMATION
Students may begin participation in January, April, and September. Applications are accepted continuously. Applicants must interview; submit a formal application, letters of reference, an essay, and have high school diploma or GED.

CONTACT
Director of Admissions, The International Culinary Arts and Sciences Institute, 8623 Mayfield Road, Chesterland, OH 44026. Telephone: 440-729-7340. Fax: 440-729-4546. World Wide Web: http://www.icasi.net.

OWENS COMMUNITY COLLEGE

Hotel, Restaurant, and Institution Technology

Toledo, Ohio

GENERAL INFORMATION
Public, coeducational, two-year college. Suburban campus. Founded in 1965. Accredited by North Central Association of Colleges and Schools.

PROGRAM INFORMATION
Offered since 1968. Program calendar is divided into semesters. 1-year certificate in culinary arts. 2-year associate degree in hospitality management. 2-year associate degree in food service management.

PROGRAM AFFILIATION
National Restaurant Association; Ohio Restaurant Association.

AREAS OF STUDY
Advanced food production; baking; beverage management; buffet catering; controlling costs in food service; culinary skill development; food preparation; food purchasing; garde-manger; international cuisine; introduction to food service; management and human resources; meal planning; menu and facilities design; nutrition; restaurant opportunities; sanitation; soup, stock, sauce, and starch production; wines and spirits.

FACILITIES
Classroom; food production kitchen; public restaurant.

STUDENT PROFILE
150 total: 50 full-time; 100 part-time. 40 are under 25 years old; 100 are between 25 and 44 years old; 10 are over 44 years old.

FACULTY
12 total: 1 full-time; 11 part-time. 8 are industry professionals; 3 are culinary-certified teachers; 1 is a registered dietitian. Prominent faculty: William Powell, CCC. Faculty-student ratio: 1:12.

SPECIAL PROGRAMS
Cooperative work experience, department-run, Terrace View Café.

TYPICAL EXPENSES
In-state tuition: $1392 per semester full-time (in district), $116 per credit hour part-time. Out-of-state tuition: $2604 per semester full-time, $217 per credit hour part-time. Tuition for international students: $2604 per semester full-time, $217 per credit hour part-time. Program-related fees include $580 for lab fees, materials, and consumable supplies (food service management); $380 for lab fees, materials, and consumable supplies (culinary arts certificate); $280 for lab fees, materials, and consumable supplies (hospitality management).

FINANCIAL AID
In 2004, 4 scholarships were awarded (average award was $1200). Employment placement assistance is available.

HOUSING
Average off-campus housing cost per month: $500.

APPLICATION INFORMATION
Students may begin participation in January, June, and August. Applications are accepted continuously. In 2004, 75 applied; 5 were accepted. Applicants must submit a formal application.

CONTACT

William Powell, Chef Educator, HRI Technologies, Hotel, Restaurant, and Institution Technology, PO Box 10000, Oregon Road, Toledo, OH 43699-1947. Telephone: 567-661-7563. Fax: 567-661-7251. E-mail: william_powell@owens.edu. World Wide Web: http://www.owens.edu/academic_dept/health_tech/hri/index.html.

SINCLAIR COMMUNITY COLLEGE

Hospitality Management/Culinary Arts Option

Dayton, Ohio

GENERAL INFORMATION

Public, coeducational, two-year college. Urban campus. Founded in 1887. Accredited by North Central Association of Colleges and Schools.

PROGRAM INFORMATION

Offered since 1993. Accredited by American Culinary Federation Accrediting Commission, Commission on Accreditation of Hospitality Management Programs. Program calendar is divided into quarters. 1-year certificate in food service management. 2-year associate degree in culinary arts option. 2-year associate degree in hospitality management.

PROGRAM AFFILIATION

American Culinary Federation; American Institute of Baking; American Vegan Society; Council on Hotel, Restaurant, and Institutional Education; National Restaurant Association; National Restaurant Association Educational Foundation; North American Vegetarian Society; The Bread Bakers Guild of America.

AREAS OF STUDY

Baking; beverage management; buffet catering; controlling costs in food service; culinary skill development; food preparation; food purchasing; garde-manger; international cuisine; introduction to food service; management and human resources; meat cutting; meat fabrication; menu and facilities design; nutrition; patisserie; restaurant opportunities; sanitation; saucier; seafood processing; soup, stock, sauce, and starch production; wines and spirits.

FACILITIES

Bake shop; catering service; 2 classrooms; 5 computer laboratories; demonstration laboratory; food production kitchen; gourmet dining room; 3 laboratories; learning resource center; library; public restaurant; 3 snack shops; student lounge; 3 teaching kitchens.

STUDENT PROFILE

400 total: 100 full-time; 300 part-time.

FACULTY

14 total: 3 full-time; 11 part-time. 8 are industry professionals; 4 are culinary-certified teachers. Prominent faculty: Steven K. Cornelius, CCE, FMP, MSEd, CEC;

Frank Leibold, CEC, CWPC, CCE; Derek Allen, CHE, MBA; Malichi Sloan. Faculty-student ratio: 1:20.

SPECIAL PROGRAMS

Disney World Internship Program.

TYPICAL EXPENSES

Application fee: $10. In-state tuition: $42.45 per credit hour (in district), $69.35 per credit hour (out-of-district). Out-of-state tuition: $132 per credit hour. Tuition for international students: $132 per credit hour. Program-related fees include $50–$100 for lab fees for products used in demonstrations and training; $125–$200 for uniforms and knives.

FINANCIAL AID

In 2004, 7 scholarships were awarded (average award was $400). Employment placement assistance is available. Employment opportunities within the program are available.

APPLICATION INFORMATION

Students may begin participation in January, March, June, and September. Applications are accepted continuously. In 2004, 225 applied; 225 were accepted. Applicants must submit a formal application.

CONTACT

Steven Cornelius, Department Chair/Professor, Hospitality Management/Culinary Arts Option, 444 West Third Street, Dayton, OH 45402-1460. Telephone: 937-512-5197. Fax: 937-512-5396. E-mail: steve.cornelius@sinclair.edu. World Wide Web: http://www.sinclair.edu/academics/bus/departments/hmt/index.cfm.

THE UNIVERSITY OF AKRON

Hospitality Management

Akron, Ohio

GENERAL INFORMATION

Public, coeducational, university. Urban campus. Founded in 1870. Accredited by North Central Association of Colleges and Schools.

PROGRAM INFORMATION

Offered since 1974. Program calendar is divided into semesters. 1-year certificate in restaurant management. 1-year certificate in hotel/motel management. 1-year certificate in culinary arts. 2-year associate degree in culinary arts. 2-year associate degree in restaurant management. 2-year associate degree in hotel/motel management. 2-year associate degree in hospitality marketing and sales.

PROGRAM AFFILIATION

American Culinary Federation; Council on Hotel, Restaurant, and Institutional Education; National Restaurant Association; Ohio Hotel/Motel Association.

The University of Akron *(continued)*

AREAS OF STUDY

Baking; beverage management; controlling costs in food service; culinary skill development; food preparation; food purchasing; food service communication; food service math; garde-manger; international cuisine; introduction to food service; kitchen management; management and human resources; meal planning; menu and facilities design; nutrition; sanitation; soup, stock, sauce, and starch production; wines and spirits.

FACILITIES

Classroom; computer laboratory; food production kitchen; public restaurant.

TYPICAL STUDENT PROFILE

115 total: 40 full-time; 75 part-time. 80 are under 25 years old; 30 are between 25 and 44 years old; 5 are over 44 years old.

SPECIAL PROGRAMS

Internships, field trips to local and national professional shows.

FINANCIAL AID

Employment placement assistance is available. Employment opportunities within the program are available.

HOUSING

Coed and single-sex housing available.

APPLICATION INFORMATION

Students may begin participation in January and August. Applications are accepted continuously. Applicants must submit a formal application and have a high school diploma or GED.

CONTACT

Director of Admissions, Hospitality Management, Gallucci Hall. Telephone: 800-655-4884. World Wide Web: http://www.uakron.edu/.

ZANE STATE COLLEGE

Culinary Arts Program

Zanesville, Ohio

GENERAL INFORMATION

Public, coeducational, two-year college. Suburban campus. Founded in 1970. Accredited by North Central Association of Colleges and Schools.

PROGRAM INFORMATION

Offered since 1993. Accredited by American Culinary Federation Accrediting Commission. Program calendar is divided into quarters. 1-quarter certificate in safety and sanitation. 2-year associate degree in culinary arts.

PROGRAM AFFILIATION

American Culinary Federation; National Restaurant Association; National Restaurant Association Educational Foundation.

AREAS OF STUDY

Baking; culinary French; culinary skill development; food preparation; food purchasing; food service math; garde-manger; international cuisine; meat cutting; meat fabrication; menu and facilities design; nutrition and food service; sanitation; soup, stock, sauce, and starch production.

FACILITIES

Bake shop; cafeteria; classroom; 10 computer laboratories; demonstration laboratory; food production kitchen; learning resource center; lecture room; library; 4 public restaurants; 2 student lounges; teaching kitchen.

STUDENT PROFILE

30 total: 20 full-time; 10 part-time. 15 are under 25 years old; 10 are between 25 and 44 years old; 5 are over 44 years old.

FACULTY

4 total: 1 full-time; 3 part-time. Prominent faculty: Marco Adornetto, CEC; Trina Beem, CPC; Dave Roach, CC; Julie Nash, Registered Dietitian. Faculty-student ratio: 1:12.

TYPICAL EXPENSES

Application fee: $20. In-state tuition: $80.50 per credit hour. Out-of-state tuition: $161 per credit hour. Program-related fee includes $180 for cutlery.

FINANCIAL AID

In 2004, 2 scholarships were awarded (average award was $5000). Employment placement assistance is available.

APPLICATION INFORMATION

Students may begin participation in September. Applications are accepted continuously. In 2004, 40 applied; 30 were accepted. Applicants must submit a formal application.

CONTACT

Marco Adornetto, Chef/Instructor, Culinary Arts Program, 1555 Newark Road, Zanesville, OH 43701. Telephone: 740-588-1334. Fax: 740-454-0035. E-mail: madornetto@zanestate.edu. World Wide Web: http://www.matc.tec.oh.us/programs/programs/cul.htm.

OKLAHOMA

CARL ALBERT STATE COLLEGE

Poteau, Oklahoma

GENERAL INFORMATION
Public, coeducational, two-year college. Rural campus. Founded in 1934. Accredited by North Central Association of Colleges and Schools.

PROGRAM INFORMATION
Offered since 1981. Program calendar is divided into semesters. 1-year certificate in food handling management. 2-year associate degree in hotel/restaurant and tourism management.

AREAS OF STUDY
Food preparation; food purchasing; food service management; hospitality management; kitchen management; lodging; management and human resources; menu and facilities design; restaurant opportunities; sanitation; tourism.

FACILITIES
Cafeteria; 3 classrooms; 4 computer laboratories; food production kitchen; learning resource center; lecture room; library; student lounge; teaching kitchen.

TYPICAL STUDENT PROFILE
8 full-time.

HOUSING
Coed housing available.

APPLICATION INFORMATION
Students may begin participation in January, June, and August. Applications are accepted continuously. Applicants must submit a formal application.

CONTACT
Director of Admissions, 1507 South McKenna, Poteau, OK 74953. Telephone: 918-647-1425. Fax: 918-647-1426. World Wide Web: http://www.carlalbert.edu.

GREAT PLAINS AREA VOCATIONAL TECHNICAL CENTER

Commercial Foods

Lawton, Oklahoma

GENERAL INFORMATION
Public, coeducational, technical institute. Urban campus. Founded in 1971. Accredited by North Central Association of Colleges and Schools.

PROGRAM INFORMATION
Offered since 1971. Program calendar is divided into semesters. 18-month certificate in baker studies. 18-month certificate in cold food cook studies. 18-month certificate in hot food cook studies.

AREAS OF STUDY
Baking; beverage management; buffet catering; controlling costs in food service; food preparation; food purchasing; food service math; garde-manger; introduction to food service; kitchen management; management and human resources; meal planning; nutrition; sanitation; soup, stock, sauce, and starch production.

TYPICAL STUDENT PROFILE
70 total: 65 full-time; 5 part-time.

APPLICATION INFORMATION
Students may begin participation in January, February, March, April, May, August, September, October, November, and December. Applications are accepted continuously. Applicants must submit a formal application.

CONTACT
Director of Admissions, Commercial Foods, 4500 West Lee Boulevard, Lawton, OK 73505. Telephone: 405-250-5622. Fax: 405-250-5677. World Wide Web: http://www.gptech.org.

MERIDIAN TECHNOLOGY CENTER

Commercial Food Production

Stillwater, Oklahoma

GENERAL INFORMATION
Public, coeducational, two-year college. Rural campus. Founded in 1975. Accredited by North Central Association of Colleges and Schools.

PROGRAM INFORMATION
Offered since 1975. Program calendar is divided into semesters. 2-year certificate in culinary arts.

PROGRAM AFFILIATION
National Restaurant Association; Oklahoma Restaurant Association.

AREAS OF STUDY
Baking; buffet catering; controlling costs in food service; culinary skill development; food preparation; food purchasing; food service math; garde-manger; introduction to food service; kitchen management; management and human resources; meal planning; meat cutting; menu and facilities design; nutrition; restaurant opportunities; sanitation; soup, stock, sauce, and starch production.

FACILITIES
Bake shop; cafeteria; catering service; classroom; coffee shop; 2 computer laboratories; food production kitchen; 2

Meridian Technology Center *(continued)*

gourmet dining rooms; laboratory; learning resource center; lecture room; 2 public restaurants; snack shop; student lounge; teaching kitchen.

TYPICAL STUDENT PROFILE
54 total: 10 full-time; 44 part-time.

SPECIAL PROGRAMS
400-hour paid internship.

FINANCIAL AID
Employment placement assistance is available. Employment opportunities within the program are available.

APPLICATION INFORMATION
Students may begin participation in January and August. Applications are accepted continuously. Applicants must interview; submit a formal application.

CONTACT
Director of Admissions, Commercial Food Production, 1312 South Sangre Road, Stillwater, OK 74074. Telephone: 405-377-3333. World Wide Web: http://www.meridian-technology.com.

METRO AREA VOCATIONAL TECHNICAL SCHOOL DISTRICT 22

Oklahoma City, Oklahoma

GENERAL INFORMATION
Public, coeducational, technical institute. Urban campus. Founded in 1980.

PROGRAM INFORMATION
Offered since 1980. Program calendar is divided into quarters. 525- to 600-hour certificate in food service management/production. 525- to 600-hour certificate in food service production.

PROGRAM AFFILIATION
American Culinary Federation; National Restaurant Association; National Restaurant Association Educational Foundation; Oklahoma Restaurant Association.

AREAS OF STUDY
Baking; buffet catering; controlling costs in food service; food preparation; food purchasing; food service communication; food service math; introduction to food service; kitchen management; meal planning; nutrition; nutrition and food service; sanitation.

FACILITIES
Bake shop; cafeteria; classroom; demonstration laboratory; food production kitchen; learning resource center; library.

SPECIAL PROGRAMS
400-hour paid internship.

FINANCIAL AID
Employment placement assistance is available. Employment opportunities within the program are available.

APPLICATION INFORMATION
Students may begin participation in January, February, March, April, May, August, September, October, November, and December. Applications are accepted continuously. Applicants must submit a formal application.

CONTACT
Director of Admissions, 4901 South Bryant Avenue, Oklahoma City, OK 73129. Telephone: 405-605-2206. Fax: 405-670-6895. World Wide Web: http://www.metrotech.org.

OKLAHOMA STATE UNIVERSITY, OKMULGEE

Hospitality Services Department

Okmulgee, Oklahoma

GENERAL INFORMATION
Public, coeducational, two-year college. Rural campus. Founded in 1946. Accredited by North Central Association of Colleges and Schools.

PROGRAM INFORMATION
Offered since 1946. Program calendar is divided into trimesters. 79-hour associate degree in dietetic technology. 90-hour associate degree in culinary arts.

PROGRAM AFFILIATION
American Culinary Federation; American Dietetic Association; Greater Southwest Retail Bakers Association; International Food Service Executives Association; National Restaurant Association; National Restaurant Association Educational Foundation; Oklahoma Restaurant Association; Retailer's Bakery Association.

AREAS OF STUDY
Buffet catering; controlling costs in food service; culinary French; culinary skill development; food preparation; food purchasing; garde-manger; international cuisine; introduction to food service; kitchen management; management and human resources; meal planning; meat cutting; meat fabrication; menu and facilities design; nutrition; patisserie; sanitation; saucier; seafood processing; soup, stock, sauce, and starch production; wines and spirits.

FACILITIES
Cafeteria; 5 classrooms; coffee shop; computer laboratory; demonstration laboratory; 2 food production kitchens; gourmet dining room; learning resource center; library; 2 public restaurants; snack shop; student lounge; herb garden.

TYPICAL STUDENT PROFILE
205 total: 175 full-time; 30 part-time.

SPECIAL PROGRAMS
Trip to the National Restaurant Association Convention (Chicago), 8-week paid internships.

FINANCIAL AID
Program-specific awards include work-study programs, possible waiver of out-of-state tuition. Employment placement assistance is available. Employment opportunities within the program are available.

HOUSING
Coed and apartment-style housing available.

APPLICATION INFORMATION
Students may begin participation in January, April, and August. Application deadline for fall is August 30. Application deadline for spring is January 3. Application deadline for summer is April 25. Applicants must submit a formal application, ACT scores, and have a high school diploma or GED.

CONTACT
Director of Admissions, Hospitality Services Department, 1801 East Fourth Street, Okmulgee, OK 74447-3901. Telephone: 918-293-5296. Fax: 918-293-4628. World Wide Web: http://www.osu-okmulgee.edu/.

OREGON

CENTRAL OREGON COMMUNITY COLLEGE

Cascade Culinary Institute

Bend, Oregon

GENERAL INFORMATION
Public, coeducational, two-year college. Rural campus. Founded in 1949. Accredited by Northwest Association of Schools and Colleges.

PROGRAM INFORMATION
Offered since 1993. Accredited by American Culinary Federation Accrediting Commission, American Culinary Federation. Program calendar is divided into quarters. 4-term certificate in culinary arts. 6-term associate degree in hospitality/tourism/recreation management.

PROGRAM AFFILIATION
American Culinary Federation; American Dietetic Association; Council on Hotel, Restaurant, and Institutional Education; International Association of Culinary Professionals.

AREAS OF STUDY
Baking; controlling costs in food service; culinary skill development; food preparation; food purchasing; food service math; garde-manger; introduction to food service; kitchen management; management and human resources; meal planning; nutrition and food service; restaurant opportunities; sanitation; soup, stock, sauce, and starch production.

FACILITIES
Bake shop; cafeteria; catering service; 2 classrooms; computer laboratory; food production kitchen; 2 lecture rooms; library; public restaurant; snack shop; teaching kitchen.

STUDENT PROFILE
21 full-time.

FACULTY
7 total: 4 full-time; 3 part-time. 4 are industry professionals; 2 are culinary-certified teachers; 1 is a certified executive chef. Prominent faculty: Julian Darwin; Julie Hood. Faculty-student ratio: 1:18.

SPECIAL PROGRAMS
3-day tour of Napa Valley wineries and farm gardens, visit to fisheries on Oregon coast, food and cultural experience in Spain.

TYPICAL EXPENSES
Application fee: $25. In-state tuition: $61 per per credit, 4 term program (in district), $83 per per credit (out-of-district). Out-of-state tuition: $172 per per credit. Tuition for international students: $172 per per credit.

FINANCIAL AID
In 2004, 3 scholarships were awarded (average award was $1000); 18 loans were granted (average loan was $2100). Program-specific awards include Pine Tavern Award ($1800). Employment placement assistance is available. Employment opportunities within the program are available.

HOUSING
Coed housing available. Average on-campus housing cost per month: $250. Average off-campus housing cost per month: $400–$600.

APPLICATION INFORMATION
Students may begin participation in January, March, and September. Application deadline for fall is August 1. Application deadline for winter is November 1. Application deadline for spring is February 1. Applicants must interview; submit a formal application.

CONTACT
Jim Kress, Program Coordinator, Cascade Culinary Institute, 2600 Northwest College Way, Bend, OR 97701-5998. Telephone: 541-383-7712. Fax: 541-383-7508. E-mail: jkress@cocc.edu. World Wide Web: http://www.culinary.cocc.edu.

CHEMEKETA COMMUNITY COLLEGE

Hospitality Systems Management

Salem, Oregon

GENERAL INFORMATION
Public, coeducational, two-year college. Urban campus. Founded in 1955. Accredited by Northwest Association of Schools and Colleges.

PROGRAM INFORMATION
Offered since 1974. Program calendar is divided into quarters. 1-year certificate in tourism and travel management. 1-year certificate in hospitality management. 2-year associate degree in nutrition and food management with Oregon State University. 2-year associate degree in hotel and business management with Washington State University. 2-year associate degree in tourism and travel management. 2-year associate degree in hotel, restaurant, and resort management. 2-year associate degree in hospitality management.

PROGRAM AFFILIATION
American Hotel and Lodging Association; Council on Hotel, Restaurant, and Institutional Education; Hospitality Sales and Marketing Association International; National Restaurant Association; National Restaurant Association Educational Foundation; Oregon Lodging Association; Oregon Restaurant Educational Foundation; Portland Oregon Visitors Association.

AREAS OF STUDY
Beverage management; controlling costs in food service; cultural heritage tourism; gaming; introduction to food service; leisure/recreation; lodging; management and human resources; meal planning; meeting and event planning; nature-based tourism; nutrition; restaurant opportunities; sanitation; travel and tourism; wines and spirits.

FACILITIES
Classroom; computer laboratory; lecture room; library; vineyard.

STUDENT PROFILE
225 total: 125 full-time; 100 part-time.

FACULTY
15 total: 2 full-time; 13 part-time. 15 are industry professionals. Prominent faculty: Eric Aebi; Ben Gentile; Ann Raymon; Sandra Frank. Faculty-student ratio: 1:25.

SPECIAL PROGRAMS
Online classes-complete degree/certificate are available online, transfer degree to Washington State University School of Hospitality Business Management.

TYPICAL EXPENSES
In-state tuition: $744 per to $930 quarter, 12 to 15 credits full-time (in district), $62 per credit hour part-time. Out-of-state tuition: $2436 per to $3045 quarter, 12 to 15 credits full-time, $203 per credit hour part-time. Tuition for international students: $2436 per to $3045 quarter, 12 to 15 credits full-time, $203 per credit hour part-time. Program-related fee includes $50 for online fee (per course).

FINANCIAL AID
Employment placement assistance is available. Employment opportunities within the program are available.

HOUSING
Average off-campus housing cost per month: $400–$650.

APPLICATION INFORMATION
Students may begin participation in January, March, June, and September. Applications are accepted continuously. Applicants must submit a formal application and have high school diploma or GED, and take placement test.

CONTACT
Nancy Duncan, Program Coordinator, Hospitality Systems Management, 4000 Lancaster Drive NE, Salem, OR 97309. Telephone: 503-399-5296. Fax: 503-365-4770. E-mail: nduncan@chemeketa.edu. World Wide Web: http://www.hsm.org.

LANE COMMUNITY COLLEGE

Culinary Arts and Hospitality Management

Eugene, Oregon

GENERAL INFORMATION
Public, coeducational, two-year college. Suburban campus. Founded in 1964. Accredited by Northwest Association of Schools and Colleges.

PROGRAM INFORMATION
Offered since 1979. Accredited by American Culinary Federation. Program calendar is divided into quarters. 1-year certificate of completion in hospitality management. 2-year associate degree in culinary arts. 2-year associate degree in hospitality management.

PROGRAM AFFILIATION
Council on Hotel, Restaurant, and Institutional Education; Educational Institute-American Hotel and Motel Association; National Restaurant Association; National Restaurant Association Educational Foundation.

AREAS OF STUDY
Baking; beverage management; buffet catering; controlling costs in food service; culinary skill development; food preparation; food purchasing; food service math; garde-manger; international cuisine; introduction to food service; management and human resources; menu and facilities design; nutrition; sanitation; soup, stock, sauce, and starch production.

FACILITIES

3 classrooms; 3 demonstration laboratories; 2 food production kitchens; gourmet dining room; learning resource center; 3 lecture rooms; library; public restaurant; 3 teaching kitchens.

STUDENT PROFILE

105 total: 85 full-time; 20 part-time.

FACULTY

8 total: 4 full-time; 4 part-time. 8 are industry professionals; 2 are master bakers; 3 are culinary-certified teachers; 1 is a certified executive chef. Prominent faculty: Clive Wanstall, CEC; Duane Partain, MS; Chris Crosthwaite, CCCC; Joe McCully, MS, CHE. Faculty-student ratio: 1:18.

SPECIAL PROGRAMS

Culinary competition.

TYPICAL EXPENSES

Application fee: $275. In-state tuition: $67 per credit hour full-time (in district), $67 per credit hour part-time. Out-of-state tuition: $230 per credit hour full-time, $230 per credit hour part-time. Tuition for international students: $230 per credit hour full-time, $230 per credit hour part-time. Program-related fee includes $40–$150 for lab fees.

FINANCIAL AID

In 2004, 9 scholarships were awarded (average award was $1000). Employment placement assistance is available. Employment opportunities within the program are available.

HOUSING

Average off-campus housing cost per month: $350–$475.

APPLICATION INFORMATION

Students may begin participation in January, April, and September. Application deadline for fall is June 30. In 2004, 80 applied; 80 were accepted. Applicants must interview; submit a formal application, letters of reference, test scores.

CONTACT

Peg Allison, Director, Conference and Culinary Services, Culinary Arts and Hospitality Management, 4000 East 30th Avenue, Building 19 Room 202, Eugene, OR 97405. Telephone: 541-463-3510 Ext. 3510. Fax: 541-463-4738. E-mail: allisonp@lanecc.edu. World Wide Web: http://www.lanecc.edu.

LINN-BENTON COMMUNITY COLLEGE

Culinary Arts/Restaurant Management

Albany, Oregon

GENERAL INFORMATION

Public, coeducational, two-year college. Rural campus. Founded in 1966. Accredited by Northwest Association of Schools and Colleges.

PROGRAM INFORMATION

Offered since 1969. Program calendar is divided into quarters. 2-year associate degree in wine and food dynamics. 2-year associate degree in chef training. 2-year associate degree in pre-restaurant management.

PROGRAM AFFILIATION

American Culinary Federation; Council on Hotel, Restaurant, and Institutional Education; National Restaurant Association; Women Chefs and Restaurateurs.

AREAS OF STUDY

Baking; beverage management; buffet catering; confectionery show pieces; controlling costs in food service; culinary French; culinary skill development; food preparation; food purchasing; food service math; garde-manger; international cuisine; introduction to food service; kitchen management; management and human resources; meal planning; meat cutting; meat fabrication; menu and facilities design; nutrition; patisserie; sanitation; saucier; seafood processing; soup, stock, sauce, and starch production; wine and food; wines and spirits.

FACILITIES

Bake shop; bakery; cafeteria; catering service; classroom; coffee shop; computer laboratory; food production kitchen; garden; gourmet dining room; laboratory; learning resource center; lecture room; library; public restaurant; snack shop; student lounge.

TYPICAL STUDENT PROFILE

45 full-time. 15 are under 25 years old; 25 are between 25 and 44 years old; 5 are over 44 years old.

FINANCIAL AID

Program-specific awards include 36 credits of tuition waiver per year for program club officers. Employment placement assistance is available.

APPLICATION INFORMATION

Students may begin participation in September. Applications are accepted continuously. Applicants must submit a formal application.

CONTACT

Director of Admissions, Culinary Arts/Restaurant Management, 6500 Southwest Pacific Boulevard, Albany, OR 97321. Telephone: 541-917-4388. Fax: 541-917-4395. World Wide Web: http://www.lbcc.cc.or.us.

OREGON COAST CULINARY INSTITUTE

Coos Bay, Oregon

GENERAL INFORMATION
Public, coeducational, culinary institute. Small-town setting. Founded in 2000. Accredited by Northwest Association of Schools and Colleges.

PROGRAM INFORMATION
Offered since 2000. Program calendar is divided into quarters. 15-month associate degree in pastry and baking. 15-month associate degree in culinary arts management.

PROGRAM AFFILIATION
American Culinary Federation.

AREAS OF STUDY
Baking; beverage management; buffet catering; culinary skill development; food preparation; food purchasing; food service communication; food service math; garde-manger; international cuisine; introduction to food service; kitchen management; meal planning; meat cutting; menu and facilities design; Northwest cuisine; nutrition; nutrition and food service; restaurant opportunities; sanitation; saucier; seafood processing; soup, stock, sauce, and starch production; wines and spirits.

FACILITIES
Bakery; cafeteria; catering service; 3 classrooms; computer laboratory; demonstration laboratory; food production kitchen; gourmet dining room; learning resource center; 3 lecture rooms; library; student lounge; 2 teaching kitchens.

STUDENT PROFILE
60 full-time. 40 are under 25 years old; 20 are between 25 and 44 years old.

FACULTY
7 total: 7 full-time. 2 are culinary-certified teachers. Prominent faculty: Kevin Shaw, CEPC. Faculty-student ratio: 1:16.

SPECIAL PROGRAMS
Internships, two-week European Baking Tour (optional baking and pastry program), Culinary Competition, including team events.

TYPICAL EXPENSES
Application fee: $30. Tuition: $19,500 per 15-month program (includes textbooks, knife set, 2 sets of chef uniforms).

FINANCIAL AID
Employment placement assistance is available.

HOUSING
Coed and apartment-style housing available. Average off-campus housing cost per month: $500.

APPLICATION INFORMATION
Students may begin participation in January and September. Applications are accepted continuously. Applicants must submit a formal application.

CONTACT
Chris Johnson, Admissions Representative, 1988 Newmark Avenue, Coos Bay, OR 97420. Telephone: 877-895-CHEF. Fax: 541-888-7194. E-mail: cjohnson@socc.edu. World Wide Web: http://www.occi.net.

OREGON CULINARY INSTITUTE

Portland, Oregon

GENERAL INFORMATION
Private, coeducational, culinary institute. Urban campus. Founded in 2006. Accredited by Accrediting Council for Independent Colleges and Schools.

PROGRAM INFORMATION
Offered since 2006. Program calendar is divided into ten-week cycles. 40-academic week diploma in culinary arts. 70-academic week associate degree in Associate of Applied Science.

PROGRAM AFFILIATION
Chefs Collaborative; Oregon Culinary Tourism Board; Oregon Restaurant Association.

AREAS OF STUDY
Culinary skill development.

FACILITIES
3 classrooms; computer laboratory; 3 food production kitchens; gourmet dining room; library; student lounge.

FACULTY
11 total: 10 full-time; 1 part-time. Prominent faculty: Brian Wilke CEC, CCE; Dan Brophy, CEC, CCE; Robert Parks, CEPC; George Thompson.

SPECIAL PROGRAMS
10-week paid externship, optional weekly field trips.

TYPICAL EXPENSES
Application fee: $50. Tuition: $13,500 for the diploma program & $19,080 for the Associate of Applied Science (AAS) degree program. Program-related fees include $50 for graduation fee; $100 for registration fee; $400 for lab fee, uniforms, and knives.

FINANCIAL AID
Program-specific awards include Pell grants, Stafford Student Loans, Plus Loans, Alternative loans. Employment

Oregon Culinary Institute *(continued)*

placement assistance is available. Employment opportunities within the program are available.

HOUSING
Average off-campus housing cost per month: $500.

APPLICATION INFORMATION
Students may begin participation in February, April, July, September, and December. Applications are accepted continuously. Applicants must interview; submit a formal application and high school diploma or GED.

CONTACT
Mary Harris, Director of Admissions, 2140 SW Jefferson #100, Portland, OR 97201. Telephone: 888-OCI-CHEF. Fax: 503-961-6240. E-mail: mharris@pioneerpacific.edu. World Wide Web: http://www.oregonculinaryinstitute.com.

SOUTHERN OREGON UNIVERSITY

Hotel, Restaurant, and Resort Management Program

Ashland, Oregon

GENERAL INFORMATION
Public, coeducational, four-year college. Small-town setting. Founded in 1926. Accredited by Northwest Association of Schools and Colleges.

PROGRAM INFORMATION
Offered since 1992. Program calendar is divided into quarters. 4-year bachelor's degree in hotel, restaurant, and resort management.

AREAS OF STUDY
Beverage management; controlling costs in food service; food purchasing; food service communication; food service math; management and human resources; restaurant opportunities.

FACILITIES
Cafeteria; catering service; 10 classrooms; 2 computer laboratories; food production kitchen; library.

TYPICAL STUDENT PROFILE
40 full-time.

SPECIAL PROGRAMS
600 hours of hospitality/tourism experience.

FINANCIAL AID
Employment placement assistance is available. Employment opportunities within the program are available.

HOUSING
Coed housing available.

APPLICATION INFORMATION
Students may begin participation in January, April, June, and September. Applications are accepted continuously. Applicants must submit a formal application.

CONTACT
Director of Admissions, Hotel, Restaurant, and Resort Management Program, 1250 Siskiyou Boulevard, Ashland, OR 97520. Telephone: 541-552-6483. World Wide Web: http://www.sou.edu/business/hrrm/index.htm.

WESTERN CULINARY INSTITUTE

Le Cordon Bleu Programs at Western Culinary Institute

Portland, Oregon

GENERAL INFORMATION
Private, coeducational, culinary institute. Urban campus. Founded in 1983. Accredited by Accrediting Commission of Career Schools and Colleges of Technology.

PROGRAM INFORMATION
Offered since 1983. Accredited by American Culinary Federation Accrediting Commission. Program calendar is divided into six-week cycles, six-week cycles. 15-month associate degree in patisserie and baking. 15-month associate degree in hospitality and restaurant management. 15-month associate degree in culinary arts. 9-month diploma in culinary arts. 9-month diploma in patisserie and baking.

PROGRAM AFFILIATION
American Culinary Federation; California Restaurant Association; International Sommelier Guild; James Beard Foundation, Inc.; National Restaurant Association; National Restaurant Association Educational Foundation; Ontario Restaurant Association; Washington Restaurant Association; Women Chefs and Restaurateurs.

AREAS OF STUDY
Baking; beverage management; buffet catering; confectionery show pieces; controlling costs in food service; convenience cookery; culinary French; culinary skill development; food preparation; food purchasing; food service communication; food service math; garde-manger; international cuisine; introduction to food service; kitchen management; management and human resources; meal planning; meat cutting; meat fabrication; menu and facilities design; nutrition; nutrition and food service; patisserie; restaurant opportunities; sanitation; saucier; soup, stock, sauce, and starch production; wines and spirits.

FACILITIES
Bake shop; bakery; cafeteria; catering service; 7 classrooms; coffee shop; 3 computer laboratories; 2 demonstration laboratories; 13 food production kitchens; gourmet dining

room; learning resource center; 7 lecture rooms; library; 2 public restaurants; 2 student lounges; bakery/delicatessen.

STUDENT PROFILE
950 full-time.

FACULTY
51 total: 48 full-time; 3 part-time. 40 are industry professionals; 1 is a master baker; 7 are culinary-certified teachers. Prominent faculty: Glenda Murray, CEC; Jacky Bonnet, CCE, CEC; Ron Costa, CC; Tina Powers, CEC, CLE, CMB. Faculty-student ratio: 1:18 in culinary labs.

SPECIAL PROGRAMS
6 to 12 week internship required at U.S. or international location, culinary competitions, Opportunity for students to participate in a school-guided international culinary tour. Rules and restrictions apply. Contact WU for more information.

TYPICAL EXPENSES
Application fee: $50. Tuition: Contact school for costs.

FINANCIAL AID
In 2005, 93 scholarships were awarded. Employment placement assistance is available. Employment opportunities within the program are available.

APPLICATION INFORMATION
Students may begin participation in January, February, April, May, July, August, October, and November. Applications are accepted continuously. Applicants must submit a formal application and have a high school diploma.

CONTACT
Director of Admissions, Le Cordon Bleu Programs at Western Culinary Institute, 921 SW Morrison Street, Suite 400, Portland, OR 97205. Telephone: 888-848-3202. Fax: 503-223-5554. E-mail: info@wci.edu. World Wide Web: http://www.wci.edu.

See color display following page 284.

PENNSYLVANIA

THE ART INSTITUTE OF PHILADELPHIA

Culinary Arts

Philadelphia, Pennsylvania

GENERAL INFORMATION
Private, coeducational, two-year college. Urban campus. Founded in 1966. Accredited by Accrediting Council for Independent Colleges and Schools.

PROGRAM INFORMATION
Offered since 1997. Program calendar is divided into quarters. 12-month diploma in baking and pastry. 18-month associate degree in culinary arts.

PROGRAM AFFILIATION
American Culinary Federation; Council on Hotel, Restaurant, and Institutional Education; International Association of Culinary Professionals; National Restaurant Association; National Restaurant Association Educational Foundation.

AREAS OF STUDY
À la carte; baking; beverage management; controlling costs in food service; culinary French; culinary science; culinary skill development; food preparation; food purchasing; food service communication; food service math; garde-manger; international cuisine; introduction to food service; kitchen management; management and human resources; meat cutting; menu and facilities design; nutrition; patisserie; restaurant opportunities; safety; sanitation; saucier; seafood processing; soup, stock, sauce, and starch production; wines and spirits.

FACILITIES
Bake shop; 5 classrooms; 3 computer laboratories; gourmet dining room; learning resource center; library; public restaurant; 2 student lounges; 4 teaching kitchens; baking kitchen.

STUDENT PROFILE
400 total: 300 full-time; 100 part-time.

FACULTY
12 total: 8 full-time; 4 part-time. 7 are industry professionals; 5 are culinary-certified teachers. Prominent faculty: Carl Deutsch, CCC, CCE; Dan D'Angelo, CEC; William J. Tillinghast, CEC, AAC; Robert Axel. Faculty-student ratio: 1:18.

SPECIAL PROGRAMS
Individualized instruction, specialization through in-house internships and externships, culinary competitions.

TYPICAL EXPENSES
Application fee: $50. Tuition: $36,090 per associate degree; $14,436 for diploma. Program-related fee includes $250 for lab fees (per quarter).

FINANCIAL AID
Program-specific awards include Pennsylvania Restaurant Association scholarships, American Culinary Federation scholarships, International Food Service Executives scholarships. Employment placement assistance is available. Employment opportunities within the program are available.

HOUSING
Coed and apartment-style housing available. Average on-campus housing cost per month: $600. Average off-campus housing cost per month: $600.

The Art Institute of Philadelphia *(continued)*

APPLICATION INFORMATION
Students may begin participation in January, April, July, and October. Applications are accepted continuously. Applicants must interview; submit a formal application and letters of reference.

CONTACT
Larry McHugh, Director of Admissions, Culinary Arts, 1622 Chestnut Street, Philadelphia, PA 19103. Telephone: 800-275-2474. Fax: 215-405-6763. E-mail: aiphadm@aii.edu. World Wide Web: http://www.aiph.artinstitutes.edu.
See color display following page 380.

THE ART INSTITUTE OF PITTSBURGH

Pittsburgh, Pennsylvania

GENERAL INFORMATION
Private, coeducational, four-year college. Urban campus. Founded in 1921. Accredited by Accrediting Council for Independent Colleges and Schools.

PROGRAM INFORMATION
Offered since 2001. Program calendar is divided into quarters. 12-month diploma in art of cooking. 3-year bachelor's degree in culinary management. 7-quarter associate degree in culinary arts.

AREAS OF STUDY
Baking; garde-manger; international cuisine; kitchen management.

FACILITIES
Classroom; demonstration laboratory; food production kitchen; teaching kitchen.

TYPICAL STUDENT PROFILE
110 full-time.

SPECIAL PROGRAMS
Culinary competitions.

FINANCIAL AID
Employment placement assistance is available.

HOUSING
Apartment-style housing available.

APPLICATION INFORMATION
Students may begin participation in January, April, July, and October. Applications are accepted continuously. Applicants must interview; submit a formal application and an essay.

CONTACT
Director of Admissions, 420 Boulevard of the Allies, Pittsburgh, PA 15219. Telephone: 800-275-2470. Fax: 412-263-6667. World Wide Web: http://www.aip.aii.edu.
See color display following page 380.

THE ART INSTITUTE ONLINE

Pittsburgh, Pennsylvania

GENERAL INFORMATION
Private, coeducational, four-year college.

PROGRAM INFORMATION
Program calendar is divided into quarters. Bachelor's degree in Hotel and Restaurant Management. Bachelor's degree in Culinary Management.

SPECIAL PROGRAMS
Experiential learning components such as field trips, externships, and internships.

CONTACT
Admissions Office, 420 Boulevard of the Allies, Pittsburgh, PA 15219. Telephone: 877-872-8869. World Wide Web: http://www.aionline.edu/.
See color display following page 380.

BUCKS COUNTY COMMUNITY COLLEGE

Business Department

Newtown, Pennsylvania

GENERAL INFORMATION
Public, coeducational, two-year college. Suburban campus. Founded in 1964. Accredited by Middle States Association of Colleges and Schools.

PROGRAM INFORMATION
Offered since 1967. Program calendar is divided into semesters. 1-year associate degree in travel and event planning. 1-year certificate in travel and event planning. 1-year certificate in culinary/pastry and catering arts. 1-year certificate in hospitality/restaurant/institutional supervision. 2-year associate degree in tourism/hospitality/restaurant/ management. 3-year associate degree in chef apprenticeship-pastry emphasis. 3-year associate degree in chef apprenticeship-foods emphasis.

PROGRAM AFFILIATION
American Culinary Federation; Confrerie de la Chaine des Rotisseurs; International Association of Culinary Professionals; International Food Service Executives Association; National Restaurant Association; National Restaurant Association Educational Foundation.

AREAS OF STUDY
Baking; buffet catering; confectionery show pieces; controlling costs in food service; culinary skill development; food preparation; food purchasing; food service communication; food service math; garde-manger; introduction to food service; kitchen management; management and human resources; meal planning; meat

cutting; meat fabrication; menu and facilities design; nutrition; nutrition and food service; patisserie; restaurant opportunities; sanitation; saucier; seafood processing; soup, stock, sauce, and starch production.

FACILITIES

Cafeteria; 5 classrooms; computer laboratory; demonstration laboratory; 2 food production kitchens; gourmet dining room; laboratory; learning resource center; library; snack shop; student lounge; teaching kitchen; greenhouse.

FACULTY

8 total: 3 full-time; 5 part-time. 3 are industry professionals; 3 are culinary-certified teachers. Faculty-student ratio: 1:15 (labs); 1:25 (lecture).

SPECIAL PROGRAMS

Required paid cooperative education and paid summer internship in management.

TYPICAL EXPENSES

Application fee: $30. In-state tuition: $89 per credit (in district), $178 per credit (out-of-district). Out-of-state tuition: $267 per credit.

FINANCIAL AID

In 2004, 5 scholarships were awarded (average award was $500). Employment placement assistance is available. Employment opportunities within the program are available.

APPLICATION INFORMATION

Students may begin participation in January and August. Applicants must submit a formal application and an essay.

CONTACT

Earl R. Arrowood, Coordinator, Culinary Arts and Chef Apprenticeship, Business Department, 275 Swamp Road, Newton, PA 18901-4106. Telephone: 215-968-8241. Fax: 215-504-8509. E-mail: arrowood@bucks.edu. World Wide Web: http://www.bucks.edu.

CENTRAL PENNSYLVANIA COLLEGE

Hotel and Restaurant Management

Summerdale, Pennsylvania

GENERAL INFORMATION

Private, coeducational, four-year college. Small-town setting. Founded in 1881. Accredited by Middle States Association of Colleges and Schools.

PROGRAM INFORMATION

Offered since 1992. Program calendar is divided into trimesters. 20-month associate degree in hotel/restaurant management.

PROGRAM AFFILIATION

National Restaurant Association; National Restaurant Association Educational Foundation.

AREAS OF STUDY

Beverage management; buffet catering; controlling costs in food service; food preparation; food purchasing; food service communication; food service math; introduction to food service; kitchen management; management and human resources; meal planning; menu and facilities design; nutrition; nutrition and food service; restaurant opportunities; sanitation; wines and spirits.

FACILITIES

Cafeteria; catering service; classroom; 5 computer laboratories; demonstration laboratory; food production kitchen; learning resource center; lecture room; library; public restaurant; student lounge; teaching kitchen.

STUDENT PROFILE

24 full-time.

FACULTY

2 total: 2 full-time. 2 are industry professionals. Prominent faculty: Michael Di Vecchio. Faculty-student ratio: 1:15.

SPECIAL PROGRAMS

Internships, tour of greater metro area 4 star hotels, partnership with Hilton Hotel Corporation for restaurant use/training.

TYPICAL EXPENSES

Tuition: $10,980 per 3 quarters full-time, $305 per credit part-time.

FINANCIAL AID

Employment placement assistance is available. Employment opportunities within the program are available.

HOUSING

Coed and apartment-style housing available.

APPLICATION INFORMATION

Students may begin participation in January, April, July, and October. Applications are accepted continuously. Applicants must interview; submit a formal application.

CONTACT

Mike Di Vecchio, Professor, Hotel and Restaurant Management, College Hill and Valley Roads, Summerdale, PA 17093. Telephone: 717-728-2245. Fax: 717-732-5254. E-mail: mikedivecchio@centralpenn.edu. World Wide Web: http://www.centralpenn.edu.

COMMONWEALTH TECHNICAL INSTITUTE

Culinary Arts Program

Johnstown, Pennsylvania

GENERAL INFORMATION

Private, coeducational, technical institute. Suburban campus. Founded in 1959. Accredited by Accrediting Commission of Career Schools and Colleges of Technology.

Commonwealth Technical Institute *(continued)*

PROGRAM INFORMATION
Offered since 1974. Program calendar is divided into trimesters. 16-month associate degree in culinary arts. 8-month diploma in kitchen helper.

PROGRAM AFFILIATION
Council on Hotel, Restaurant, and Institutional Education.

AREAS OF STUDY
Baking; controlling costs in food service; food preparation; food purchasing; food service math; introduction to food service; management and human resources; meal planning; menu and facilities design; nutrition; sanitation; soup, stock, sauce, and starch production.

FACILITIES
Bake shop; cafeteria; 3 classrooms; 2 computer laboratories; food production kitchen; 2 laboratories; learning resource center; library; snack shop; teaching kitchen.

STUDENT PROFILE
74 full-time. 62 are under 25 years old; 7 are between 25 and 44 years old; 5 are over 44 years old.

FACULTY
3 total: 3 full-time. 1 is an industry professional; 2 are culinary-certified teachers. Prominent faculty: Noel B. Graham; Robert H. Lawson; Alexander M. McLachlan.

TYPICAL EXPENSES
Tuition: $5612 per 16 weeks.

FINANCIAL AID
Employment placement assistance is available.

HOUSING
Single-sex housing available.

APPLICATION INFORMATION
Students may begin participation in January, May, and September. Applications are accepted continuously. In 2004, 74 applied; 74 were accepted. Applicants must submit a formal application.

CONTACT
Rebecca Halza, Director of Admissions, Culinary Arts Program, 727 Goucher Street, Johnstown, PA 15905. Telephone: 814-255-8256. E-mail: rhalza@state.pa.us. World Wide Web: http://www.hgac.org.

DELAWARE COUNTY COMMUNITY COLLEGE

Hotel/Restaurant Management Program

Media, Pennsylvania

GENERAL INFORMATION
Public, coeducational, two-year college. Suburban campus. Founded in 1967. Accredited by Middle States Association of Colleges and Schools.

PROGRAM INFORMATION
Offered since 1973. Program calendar is divided into semesters. 2-year associate degree in hotel-restaurant management.

PROGRAM AFFILIATION
Council on Hotel, Restaurant, and Institutional Education; Greater Philadelphia Hotel Association; Greater Philadelphia Restaurant and Purveyor Association; National Restaurant Association; National Restaurant Association Educational Foundation.

AREAS OF STUDY
Beverage management; catering (management); controlling costs in food service; culinary skill development; food preparation; hotel/foodservice law; introduction to food service; management and human resources; nutrition; sanitation.

FACILITIES
Classroom; demonstration laboratory; food production kitchen.

TYPICAL STUDENT PROFILE
90 total: 60 full-time; 30 part-time.

SPECIAL PROGRAMS
Internships and co-ops, Disney World externships.

FINANCIAL AID
Employment placement assistance is available. Employment opportunities within the program are available.

APPLICATION INFORMATION
Students may begin participation in January, May, July, and September. Applications are accepted continuously. Applicants must submit a formal application and take placement test.

CONTACT
Director of Admissions, Hotel/Restaurant Management Program, 901 South Media Line Road, Media, PA 19063-1094. Telephone: 610-359-5267. World Wide Web: http://www.dccc.edu.

DREXEL UNIVERSITY

Hospitality Management and Culinary Arts

Philadelphia, Pennsylvania

GENERAL INFORMATION
Private, coeducational, university. Urban campus. Founded in 1891. Accredited by Middle States Association of Colleges and Schools.

PROGRAM INFORMATION
Offered since 1988. Accredited by Council on Hotel, Restaurant and Institutional Education, Commission on Accreditation of Hospitality Management Programs. Program calendar is divided into quarters. 4-year bachelor's degree in culinary arts. 4-year bachelor's degree in hospitality management.

PROGRAM AFFILIATION
American Culinary Federation; American Dietetic Association; American Institute of Wine & Food; American Vegan Society; American Wine Society; Confrerie de la Chaine des Rotisseurs; Council on Hotel, Restaurant, and Institutional Education; International Association of Culinary Professionals; International Wine & Food Society; James Beard Foundation, Inc.; National Restaurant Association; National Restaurant Association Educational Foundation; Society of Wine Educators; Women Chefs and Restaurateurs.

AREAS OF STUDY
Baking; beverage management; buffet catering; confectionery show pieces; controlling costs in food service; convenience cookery; culinary French; culinary skill development; food preparation; food purchasing; food service communication; garde-manger; international cuisine; kitchen management; management and human resources; meal planning; meat cutting; meat fabrication; menu and facilities design; nutrition; nutrition and food service; patisserie; restaurant opportunities; sanitation; saucier; seafood processing; soup, stock, sauce, and starch production; wines and spirits.

FACILITIES
Bake shop; bakery; catering service; 10 classrooms; coffee shop; 7 computer laboratories; demonstration laboratory; 3 food production kitchens; garden; 2 gourmet dining rooms; 4 laboratories; learning resource center; 2 lecture rooms; 2 libraries; public restaurant; snack shop; student lounge; 2 teaching kitchens.

STUDENT PROFILE
139 total: 125 full-time; 14 part-time.

FACULTY
22 total: 7 full-time; 15 part-time. 15 are industry professionals; 22 are culinary-certified teachers. Prominent faculty: Francis McFadden; Alan Segel; Georges Perrier; Christina Pirello. Faculty-student ratio: 1:12.

SPECIAL PROGRAMS
Study abroad in London, cooperative employment experience.

TYPICAL EXPENSES
Application fee: $50. Tuition: $27,100 per year full-time, $480 per credit part-time. Program-related fees include $200 for uniform; $350 for cutlery.

FINANCIAL AID
In 2004, 10 scholarships were awarded (average award was $4000). Employment placement assistance is available. Employment opportunities within the program are available.

HOUSING
Coed and apartment-style housing available. Average on-campus housing cost per month: $650.

APPLICATION INFORMATION
Students may begin participation in January, April, June, and September. Application deadline for fall is March 1. In 2004, 181 applied; 79 were accepted. Applicants must submit a formal application and letters of reference.

CONTACT
Maria McNichols, Program Manager, Hospitality Management and Culinary Arts, 33rd and Arch Street, Suite 110, Philadelphia, PA 19104. Telephone: 215-895-2836. Fax: 215-895-2426. E-mail: hospitality.mgt@drexel.edu. World Wide Web: http://www.drexel.edu.

See display on page 302.

HARRISBURG AREA COMMUNITY COLLEGE

Hospitality, Restaurant, and Institutional Management Department

Harrisburg, Pennsylvania

GENERAL INFORMATION
Public, coeducational, two-year college. Suburban campus. Founded in 1964. Accredited by Middle States Association of Colleges and Schools.

PROGRAM INFORMATION
Offered since 1989. Program calendar is divided into semesters. 1-year diploma in institutional food service. 1-year diploma in culinary arts/catering. 10-month diploma in dietary manager. 16-month certificate in restaurant food service management. 17-month certificate in culinary arts. 21-month associate degree in hotel and motel management. 21-month associate degree in health care food service. 21-month associate degree in restaurant food service management. 21-month associate degree in culinary arts.

UNIVERSITY

CULINARY ARTS AND HOSPITALITY MANAGEMENT

The Department of Hospitality Management at Goodwin College, Drexel University offers the following undergraduate degrees:

- **BS in Hospitality Management (HM) with concentrations in**
    - **Lodging Administration**
    - **Food & Beverage Management**
    - **Travel and Tourism Consulting**
- **BS in Culinary Arts (CULA) with a Business minor**

Both programs prepare students for leadership positions with a global perspective and offer the option of a BS/MBA.

Drexel's programs, among the technology-oriented leaders in the country, offer students exposure to cutting edge problem solving techniques and ideas. Distinguishing features include a 14,000 square-foot state-of-the-art commercial kitchen, The Academic Bistro (student run restaurant & lounge), Goodwin Technology Center, The Culinary Reference Library, The Center for the Study of Wine and Food and the Ross Commons Advisement Center, as well as a student-run kitchen garden.

Centrally located in the heart of Philadelphia, the campus is close to New York City, Baltimore, Washington and the Atlantic seacoast. This region includes hundreds of five star/diamond hotels, award-winning restaurants and resorts, many of which are active partners in our curriculum and in Drexel's Co-Operative Education Program. Programs offer the option to study at the London Campus for three months in the sophomore, junior or senior year.

Contact:
Drexel University
Department of Hospitality
229 N. 34th Street
Philadelphia, PA 19104
215-895-2411
hospitality.mgt@drexel.edu
www.drexel.edu/goodwin

PROGRAM AFFILIATION

American Culinary Federation; American Dietetic Association; College Restaurant Hospitality Institute Educators; Council on Hotel, Restaurant, and Institutional Education; National Restaurant Association; National Restaurant Association Educational Foundation.

AREAS OF STUDY

Baking; controlling costs in food service; culinary skill development; food preparation; food purchasing; introduction to hospitality; kitchen management; management and human resources; meal planning; meat cutting; menu and facilities design; nutrition; sanitation; soup, stock, sauce, and starch production.

FACILITIES

Classroom; computer laboratory; demonstration laboratory; food production kitchen; gourmet dining room; learning resource center; lecture room; library; teaching kitchen; herb garden.

TYPICAL STUDENT PROFILE

150 total: 75 full-time; 75 part-time. 83 are under 25 years old; 45 are between 25 and 44 years old; 22 are over 44 years old.

SPECIAL PROGRAMS

4-month paid internship, culinary competitions, participation in community charity events.

FINANCIAL AID

Employment placement assistance is available.

APPLICATION INFORMATION

Students may begin participation in January, May, and August. Application deadline for fall is May 1. Application deadline for spring is November 1. Applicants must interview; submit a formal application, an essay, letters of reference, and have a health certificate.

CONTACT

Director of Admissions, Hospitality, Restaurant, and Institutional Management Department, M250-A One HACC Drive, Harrisburg, PA 17110-2999. Telephone: 717-780-2674. Fax: 717-231-7670. World Wide Web: http://www.hacc.edu/.

INDIANA UNIVERSITY OF PENNSYLVANIA

Academy of Culinary Arts

Punxsutawney, Pennsylvania

GENERAL INFORMATION

Public, coeducational, university. Rural campus. Founded in 1875. Accredited by Middle States Association of Colleges and Schools.

PROGRAM INFORMATION

Offered since 1989. Accredited by American Culinary Federation Accrediting Commission. Program calendar is divided into semesters. 12-month certificate in baking and pastry arts. 16-month certificate in culinary arts. 2-year certificate in culinary arts and baking and pastry arts. 4-year bachelor's degree in food and nutrition. 4-year bachelor's degree in hotel, restaurant, and institutional management.

PROGRAM AFFILIATION

American Culinary Federation; American Dietetic Association; Confrerie de la Chaine des Rotisseurs; Council on Hotel, Restaurant, and Institutional Education; International Association of Culinary Professionals; National Restaurant Association; National Restaurant Association Educational Foundation.

AREAS OF STUDY

Baking; beverage management; buffet catering; confectionery show pieces; controlling costs in food service; convenience cookery; culinary French; culinary skill development; food preparation; food purchasing; food service communication; food service math; garde-manger; international cuisine; introduction to food service; kitchen management; management and human resources; meal planning; meat cutting; meat fabrication; menu and facilities design; nutrition; nutrition and food service; patisserie; restaurant opportunities; sanitation; saucier; seafood processing; soup, stock, sauce, and starch production; wines and spirits.

FACILITIES

Bake shop; cafeteria; 3 classrooms; computer laboratory; 2 demonstration laboratories; food production kitchen; garden; gourmet dining room; learning resource center; lecture room; library; student lounge; 2 teaching kitchens.

STUDENT PROFILE

98 full-time. 83 are under 25 years old; 13 are between 25 and 44 years old; 2 are over 44 years old.

FACULTY

9 total: 8 full-time; 1 part-time. 1 is an industry professional; 7 are culinary-certified teachers; 1 is a certified executive pastry chef; 6 certified executive chefs; 1 certified sous-chef; 1 registered dietetic technician. Prominent faculty: Albert Wutsch; Hilary DeMane. Faculty-student ratio: 1:14.

SPECIAL PROGRAMS

International externship option, international study tours.

TYPICAL EXPENSES

Application fee: $30. Tuition: $6606 per semester. Program-related fee includes $1500 for supply package.

FINANCIAL AID

In 2004, 16 scholarships were awarded (average award was $2300). Program-specific awards include private scholarship support for program students. Employment placement assistance is available. Employment opportunities within the program are available.

Indiana University of Pennsylvania *(continued)*

HOUSING

Coed, apartment-style, and single-sex housing available. Average on-campus housing cost per month: $295. Average off-campus housing cost per month: $350.

APPLICATION INFORMATION

Students may begin participation in September. Applications are accepted continuously. In 2004, 288 applied; 145 were accepted. Applicants must submit a formal application, letters of reference, an essay, official high school transcript or GED certificate, and visit school.

CONTACT

Lori Roles, Admissions Counselor, Academy of Culinary Arts, 1010 Winslow Street, Punxsutawney, PA 15767. Telephone: 800-438-6424. Fax: 814-938-1158. E-mail: culinary-arts@iup.edu. World Wide Web: http://www.iup.edu/culinary.

JNA INSTITUTE OF CULINARY ARTS

Philadelphia, Pennsylvania

GENERAL INFORMATION

Private, coeducational, culinary institute. Urban campus. Founded in 1988. Accredited by Accrediting Commission of Career Schools and Colleges of Technology.

PROGRAM INFORMATION

Offered since 1988. Program calendar is divided into quarters, ten-week cycles. 30-week diploma in specialized food service management. 30-week diploma in food service training/professional cooking. 60-week associate degree in culinary arts/restaurant management.

PROGRAM AFFILIATION

American Culinary Federation; Foodservice Educators Network International; International Food Service Executives Association; National Restaurant Association; National Restaurant Association Educational Foundation.

AREAS OF STUDY

Baking; beverage management; buffet catering; controlling costs in food service; culinary French; culinary skill development; food preparation; food purchasing; food service communication; food service math; garde-manger; international cuisine; introduction to food service; kitchen management; management and human resources; meal planning; meat cutting; menu and facilities design; nutrition; nutrition and food service; patisserie; restaurant opportunities; sanitation; saucier; seafood processing; soup, stock, sauce, and starch production; wines and spirits.

FACILITIES

Bake shop; cafeteria; catering service; 4 classrooms; computer laboratory; demonstration laboratory; food production kitchen; learning resource center; lecture room; library; public restaurant; student lounge; teaching kitchen.

STUDENT PROFILE
80 total: 74 full-time; 6 part-time.

FACULTY
10 total: 7 full-time; 3 part-time. 10 are industry professionals. Prominent faculty: Joseph DiGironimo, CFE, FMP; Michael DeLuca, FMP; Roland Pasche; Michael Gilletto, MCFE, FMP. Faculty-student ratio: 1:12.

SPECIAL PROGRAMS
Paid externships, student clubs (wine club, culinary club), culinary competitions.

TYPICAL EXPENSES
Tuition: $7000 per diploma; $14,000 per degree full-time, $150 per credit part-time. Program-related fees include $75 for registration; $115 for knives.

FINANCIAL AID
In 2004, 1 scholarship was awarded (award was $5000); 51 loans were granted (average loan was $3000). Employment placement assistance is available. Employment opportunities within the program are available.

HOUSING
Average off-campus housing cost per month: $650.

APPLICATION INFORMATION
Students may begin participation in January, April, July, and October. Applications are accepted continuously. In 2004, 110 applied; 86 were accepted. Applicants must submit a formal application and schedule an interview or provide letters of reference.

CONTACT
Darrence DuBose, Admissions Department, 1212 South Broad Street, Philadelphia, PA 19146. Telephone: 215-468-8800. Fax: 215-468-8838. E-mail: admissions@culinaryarts.com. World Wide Web: http://www.culinaryarts.com.

KEYSTONE COLLEGE

Culinary Arts

La Plume, Pennsylvania

GENERAL INFORMATION
Private, coeducational, two-year college. Rural campus. Founded in 1868. Accredited by Middle States Association of Colleges and Schools.

PROGRAM INFORMATION
Offered since 1995. Program calendar is divided into semesters. 1-year certificate in culinary arts. 2-year associate degree in culinary arts. 2-year associate degree in restaurant/food service management.

PROGRAM AFFILIATION
American Culinary Federation; Council on Hotel, Restaurant, and Institutional Education.

AREAS OF STUDY
Baking; beverage management; controlling costs in food service; food preparation; food purchasing; garde-manger; introduction to food service; kitchen management; management and human resources; meal planning; meat cutting; nutrition; nutrition and food service; sanitation; saucier; soup, stock, sauce, and starch production; wines and spirits.

FACILITIES
Bakery; cafeteria; catering service; 4 classrooms; 3 coffee shops; 6 computer laboratories; 2 demonstration laboratories; food production kitchen; gourmet dining room; 5 laboratories; 2 learning resource centers; library; snack shop; 6 student lounges; teaching kitchen.

TYPICAL STUDENT PROFILE
35 total: 26 full-time; 9 part-time. 27 are under 25 years old; 8 are between 25 and 44 years old.

SPECIAL PROGRAMS
500-hour internship between freshman and sophomore year.

FINANCIAL AID
Employment placement assistance is available. Employment opportunities within the program are available.

HOUSING
Coed, apartment-style, and single-sex housing available.

APPLICATION INFORMATION
Students may begin participation in January and August. Application deadline for fall is August 1. Application deadline for spring is January 2. Applicants must submit a formal application, letters of reference, and interview (if possible).

CONTACT
Director of Admissions, Culinary Arts, One College Green, La Plume, PA 18440. Telephone: 570-945-5141. Fax: 570-945-8006. World Wide Web: http://www.keystone.edu/.

LEHIGH CARBON COMMUNITY COLLEGE

Hotel/Restaurant Management and Culinary Arts

Allentown, Pennsylvania

GENERAL INFORMATION
Public, coeducational, two-year college. Suburban campus. Founded in 1967. Accredited by Middle States Association of Colleges and Schools.

PROGRAM INFORMATION
Offered since 1986. Program calendar is divided into semesters. 1-year certificate in culinary arts. 2-year associate degree in culinary arts. 2-year associate degree in hotel/restaurant management.

Lehigh Carbon Community College *(continued)*

PROGRAM AFFILIATION
American Culinary Federation; Council on Hotel, Restaurant, and Institutional Education; National Restaurant Association; National Restaurant Association Educational Foundation.

AREAS OF STUDY
Baking; beverage management; culinary skill development; dining room operation; food preparation; food purchasing; international cuisine; introduction to food service; management and human resources; meal planning; menu and facilities design; nutrition; nutrition and food service; sanitation; soup, stock, sauce, and starch production.

FACILITIES
Classroom; computer laboratory; lecture room; public restaurant; student lounge; teaching kitchen.

STUDENT PROFILE
88 total: 51 full-time; 37 part-time. 64 are under 25 years old; 16 are between 25 and 44 years old; 8 are over 44 years old.

FACULTY
8 total: 2 full-time; 6 part-time. 8 are industry professionals; 1 is a culinary-certified teacher. Prominent faculty: Timothy Gibbons, HTHM, CHE; Pamela Weldon, MEd, CHE. Faculty-student ratio: 1:15.

SPECIAL PROGRAMS
Paid Internships in all degree programs, for-credit participation in Walt Disney World College program.

TYPICAL EXPENSES
Application fee: $30. In-state tuition: $1350 per semester full-time (in district), $90 per credit part-time (in district), $2625 per semester full-time (out-of-district), $175 per credit part-time (out-of-district). Out-of-state tuition: $3900 per semester full-time, $260 per credit part-time. Tuition for international students: $3900 per semester full-time, $260 per credit part-time. Program-related fee includes $75 for lab fee (food costs for specific courses).

FINANCIAL AID
In 2004, 2 scholarships were awarded (average award was $250). Employment placement assistance is available.

APPLICATION INFORMATION
Students may begin participation in January and August. Applications are accepted continuously. In 2004, 49 applied. Applicants must submit a formal application.

CONTACT
Timothy J. Gibbons, Hospitality Education Coordinator, Hotel/Restaurant Management and Culinary Arts, ICCC Hospitality Training Center, 4234 Dorney Park Road, Allentown, PA 18104. Telephone: 610-530-7818. E-mail: tgibbons@lccc.edu. World Wide Web: http://www.lccc.edu.

LUZERNE COUNTY COMMUNITY COLLEGE

Food Production Management

Nanticoke, Pennsylvania

GENERAL INFORMATION
Public, coeducational, two-year college. Suburban campus. Founded in 1966. Accredited by Middle States Association of Colleges and Schools.

PROGRAM INFORMATION
Accredited by Council on Hotel, Restaurant and Institutional Education. Program calendar is divided into semesters. 1-semester diploma in food production. 1-year certificate in hotel and restaurant management. 1-year certificate of specialization in food production management. 2-year associate degree in hotel and restaurant management. 2-year associate degree in pastry arts. 2-year associate degree in food production management.

PROGRAM AFFILIATION
American Culinary Federation; American Dietetic Association; Council on Hotel, Restaurant, and Institutional Education; International Association of Culinary Professionals; National Restaurant Association; National Restaurant Association Educational Foundation; Pocono Mountain Professional Chefs.

AREAS OF STUDY
Baking; beverage management; buffet catering; confectionery show pieces; controlling costs in food service; food preparation; food purchasing; food service communication; food service math; garde-manger; kitchen management; management and human resources; meal planning; meat cutting; meat fabrication; menu and facilities design; nutrition; nutrition and food service; patisserie; sanitation; saucier; seafood processing; soup, stock, sauce, and starch production.

FACILITIES
Bake shop; bakery; cafeteria; catering service; classroom; coffee shop; computer laboratory; demonstration laboratory; food production kitchen; laboratory; lecture room; library; student lounge; teaching kitchen.

TYPICAL STUDENT PROFILE
110 total: 66 full-time; 44 part-time. 61 are under 25 years old; 22 are between 25 and 44 years old; 27 are over 44 years old.

SPECIAL PROGRAMS
Culinary competitions, Walt Disney World internship, Pennsylvania and New York State brewery and winery tours.

FINANCIAL AID
Employment placement assistance is available. Employment opportunities within the program are available.

APPLICATION INFORMATION

Students may begin participation in January and August. Applications are accepted continuously. Applicants must submit a formal application.

CONTACT

Director of Admissions, Food Production Management, 1333 South Prospect Street, Nanticoke, PA 18634-9804. Telephone: 570-740-0340. Fax: 570-740-0238. World Wide Web: http://www.luzerne.edu.

MARYWOOD UNIVERSITY

Scranton, Pennsylvania

GENERAL INFORMATION

Private, coeducational, comprehensive institution. Suburban campus. Founded in 1915. Accredited by Middle States Association of Colleges and Schools.

PROGRAM INFORMATION

Accredited by American Dietetic Association. Program calendar is divided into semesters. 35-credit certificate in nutrition and dietetics. 36-credit master's degree in food and nutrition. 4-year bachelor's degree in nutrition and dietetics. 4-year bachelor's degree in hotel and restaurant management.

PROGRAM AFFILIATION

American Dietetic Association; Council on Hotel, Restaurant, and Institutional Education; Institute of Food Technologists.

AREAS OF STUDY

Food preparation; food purchasing; management and human resources; menu and facilities design; nutrition; nutrition and food service; sanitation.

FACILITIES

3 classrooms; computer laboratory; demonstration laboratory; laboratory; teaching kitchen.

STUDENT PROFILE

137 total: 71 full-time; 66 part-time. 58 are under 25 years old; 58 are between 25 and 44 years old; 21 are over 44 years old.

FACULTY

12 total: 4 full-time; 8 part-time. Prominent faculty: Barbara Winters, PhD, RD; Alan M. Levine, PhD, RD, CMFC; Lee Harrison, PhD, RD, FADA, CNSD, CMFC; Marianne Borja, EdD, RD, FADA. Faculty-student ratio: 1:11.

SPECIAL PROGRAMS

Coordinated program in nutrition and dietetics, one-credit certificate in food safety.

TYPICAL EXPENSES

Application fee: $20. Tuition: $18,560 per year full-time, $580 per credit part-time. Program-related fee includes $285 for dietetics program fees.

FINANCIAL AID

In 2004, 5 scholarships were awarded (average award was $1000). Employment placement assistance is available.

HOUSING

Coed, apartment-style, and single-sex housing available. Average on-campus housing cost per month: $500. Average off-campus housing cost per month: $550.

APPLICATION INFORMATION

Students may begin participation in January, June, July, and September. Applications are accepted continuously. In 2004, 63 applied; 54 were accepted. Applicants must submit a formal application, letters of reference, transcripts, SAT or ACT scores.

CONTACT

Robert W. Reese, Director of Admissions, 2300 Adams Avenue, Scranton, PA 18509-1598. Telephone: 800-346-5014. Fax: 570-961-4763. E-mail: reese@marywood.edu. World Wide Web: http://www.marywood.edu.

MERCYHURST COLLEGE

The Culinary and Wine Institute of Mercyhurst North East

North East, Pennsylvania

GENERAL INFORMATION

Private, coeducational, comprehensive institution. Small-town setting. Founded in 1926. Accredited by Middle States Association of Colleges and Schools.

PROGRAM INFORMATION

Offered since 1995. Accredited by Accreditation Commission for Programs in Hospitality Administration (ACPHA). Program calendar is term 4-3-3. 2-year associate degree in culinary arts. 4-year bachelor's degree in hotel, restaurant, and institutional management (culinary arts concentration).

PROGRAM AFFILIATION

American Culinary Federation; Council on Hotel, Restaurant, and Institutional Education; National Restaurant Association.

AREAS OF STUDY

Baking; beverage management; buffet catering; controlling costs in food service; culinary skill development; food preparation; food purchasing; food service communication; food service math; garde-manger; international cuisine; introduction to food service; kitchen management; management and human resources; meal planning; meat cutting; meat fabrication; menu and facilities design; nutrition; nutrition and food service; patisserie; sanitation; saucier; seafood processing; soup, stock, sauce, and starch production; wine making; wines and spirits.

Mercyhurst College *(continued)*

FACILITIES
Bake shop; cafeteria; 4 classrooms; 2 computer laboratories; 3 demonstration laboratories; 3 food production kitchens; gourmet dining room; learning resource center; 2 lecture rooms; library; student lounge; 2 teaching kitchens; vineyard.

TYPICAL STUDENT PROFILE
55 total: 53 full-time; 2 part-time. 44 are under 25 years old; 10 are between 25 and 44 years old; 1 is over 44 years old.

SPECIAL PROGRAMS
400-hour culinary externship.

FINANCIAL AID
Program-specific awards include institution grants. Employment placement assistance is available.

HOUSING
Coed housing available.

APPLICATION INFORMATION
Students may begin participation in March, September, and November. Applications are accepted continuously. Applicants must submit a formal application and possess a high school diploma or GED.

CONTACT
Director of Admissions, The Culinary and Wine Institute of Mercyhurst North East, 16 West Division Street, North East, PA 16428. Telephone: 814-725-6144. Fax: 814-725-6251. World Wide Web: http://northeast.mercyhurst.edu.

NORTHAMPTON COUNTY AREA COMMUNITY COLLEGE

Culinary Arts

Bethlehem, Pennsylvania

GENERAL INFORMATION
Public, coeducational, two-year college. Suburban campus. Founded in 1967. Accredited by Middle States Association of Colleges and Schools.

PROGRAM INFORMATION
Offered since 1993. Program calendar is divided into semesters. 2-year associate degree in culinary arts. 2-year associate degree in restaurant/hotel management. 45-week diploma in culinary arts.

AREAS OF STUDY
Baking; beverage management; controlling costs in food service; culinary skill development; food preparation; food purchasing; garde-manger; introduction to food service; meat cutting; meat fabrication; nutrition; restaurant

opportunities; sanitation; seafood processing; soup, stock, sauce, and starch production; wines and spirits.

FACILITIES
Bakery; cafeteria; catering service; 10 computer laboratories; food production kitchen; gourmet dining room; learning resource center; lecture room; library; public restaurant; snack shop; student lounge; teaching kitchen.

TYPICAL STUDENT PROFILE
52 full-time. 20 are under 25 years old; 28 are between 25 and 44 years old; 4 are over 44 years old.

FINANCIAL AID
Employment placement assistance is available.

HOUSING
Coed and apartment-style housing available.

APPLICATION INFORMATION
Students may begin participation in March and September. Applications are accepted continuously. Applicants must submit a formal application.

CONTACT
Director of Admissions, Culinary Arts, 3835 Green Pond Road, Bethlehem, PA 18020. Telephone: 610-861-5593. Fax: 610-861-5093. World Wide Web: http://www.northampton.edu/academics/credprgs/hotlrest.html.

PENN FOSTER CAREER SCHOOL

Hospitality Management ASB

Scranton, Pennsylvania

GENERAL INFORMATION
Private, coeducational, two-year college. Suburban campus. Founded in 1975.

PROGRAM INFORMATION
Offered since 1994. Accredited by Distance Education and Training Council. Program calendar is divided into semesters. 2-year associate degree in hospitality management (program offered through distance learning only).

PROGRAM AFFILIATION
Council on Hotel, Restaurant, and Institutional Education.

AREAS OF STUDY
Beverage management; food purchasing; meal planning; nutrition; sanitation.

APPLICATION INFORMATION
Students may begin participation year-round. Applications are accepted continuously. Applicants must submit a formal application and have a high school diploma.

CONTACT
Director of Admissions, Hospitality Management ASB, 925 Oak Street, Scranton, PA 18515. Telephone: 570-342-7701. World Wide Web: http://www.educationdirect.com.

PENNSYLVANIA COLLEGE OF TECHNOLOGY

School of Hospitality

Williamsport, Pennsylvania

GENERAL INFORMATION
Public, coeducational, four-year college. Urban campus. Founded in 1965. Accredited by Middle States Association of Colleges and Schools.

PROGRAM INFORMATION
Offered since 1965. Accredited by American Culinary Federation Accrediting Commission, Council on Hotel, Restaurant and Institutional Education. Program calendar is divided into semesters. 2-year associate degree in hospitality management. 2-year associate degree in baking/pastry arts technology. 2-year associate degree in culinary arts technology. 4-year bachelor's degree in culinary arts technology. 8-month competency credential in professional cooking. 8-month competency credential in professional baking. 8-month competency credential in dining room service.

PROGRAM AFFILIATION
American Culinary Federation; American Institute of Baking; Council on Hotel, Restaurant, and Institutional Education; Dietary Managers Association; National Restaurant Association; National Restaurant Association Educational Foundation; Pennsylvania Travel Council; Retailer's Bakery Association; Sommelier Society of America; The Bread Bakers Guild of America; Women Chefs and Restaurateurs.

AREAS OF STUDY
Baking; beverage management; buffet catering; confectionery show pieces; controlling costs in food service; culinary French; culinary skill development; food preparation; food purchasing; garde-manger; international cuisine; introduction to food service; kitchen management; management and human resources; meal planning; meat cutting; meat fabrication; menu and facilities design; nutrition; nutrition and food service; patisserie; restaurant opportunities; sanitation; seafood processing; soup, stock, sauce, and starch production; wines and spirits.

FACILITIES
Bake shop; 2 bakeries; catering service; 3 classrooms; computer laboratory; demonstration laboratory; 4 food production kitchens; garden; 2 gourmet dining rooms; learning resource center; lecture room; library; public restaurant; teaching kitchen.

STUDENT PROFILE
196 total: 178 full-time; 18 part-time.

FACULTY
26 total: 9 full-time; 17 part-time. 18 are industry professionals; 3 are culinary-certified teachers. Prominent faculty: Paul Mach, CCC, CCE; Mike Ditchfield, CEC, CCC; Judith Shimp, CEC, CCC; Monica Lanczak. Faculty-student ratio: 1:24 lecture; 1:12 lab.

SPECIAL PROGRAMS
Semi-annual Distinguished Visiting Chefs/Pastry Chefs Series, Hunt County Vineyards/Finger Lakes Harvest Festival, You're the Chef (PBS television show).

TYPICAL EXPENSES
Application fee: $50. In-state tuition: $10,080 per year full-time (in district), $336 per credit part-time. Out-of-state tuition: $12,680 per year full-time, $422 per credit part-time. Program-related fees include $180 for knife kit; $300 for uniforms; $250 for tools.

FINANCIAL AID
In 2004, 16 scholarships were awarded (average award was $937). Program-specific awards include Stroehmann Scholarships, Boiaroi Scholarship, Distinguished Visiting Chef Scholarships. Employment placement assistance is available. Employment opportunities within the program are available.

HOUSING
Coed housing available. Average on-campus housing cost per month: $400. Average off-campus housing cost per month: $300.

APPLICATION INFORMATION
Students may begin participation in January and August. Application deadline for fall is July 1. In 2004, 298 applied; 251 were accepted. Applicants must submit a formal application.

CONTACT
Chester Schuman, Director of Admission, School of Hospitality, One College Avenue, Williamsport, PA 17701-5778. Telephone: 570-326-3761 Ext. 4671. Fax: 570-327-4503. E-mail: cschuman@pct.edu. World Wide Web: http://www.pct.edu/peter.

See color display following page 284.

PENNSYLVANIA CULINARY INSTITUTE

Le Cordon Bleu Culinary Arts

Pittsburgh, Pennsylvania

GENERAL INFORMATION
Private, coeducational, culinary institute. Urban campus. Founded in 1986. Accredited by Accrediting Commission of Career Schools and Colleges of Technology.

Pennsylvania Culinary Institute *(continued)*

PROGRAM INFORMATION

Offered since 1986. Accredited by ACFET American Culinary Federation. Program calendar is divided into semesters. 16-month associate degree in hospitality and restaurant management. 16-month associate degree in patisserie and baking. 16-month associate degree in culinary arts.

PROGRAM AFFILIATION

American Academy of Chefs; American Wine Society; Confrerie de la Chaine des Rotisseurs; Council on Hotel, Restaurant, and Institutional Education; National Restaurant Association; Pennsylvania Restaurant Association; The Bread Bakers Guild of America; Women Chefs and Restaurateurs; World Association of Chefs and Cooks.

AREAS OF STUDY

Baking; beverage management; buffet catering; confectionery show pieces; controlling costs in food service; convenience cookery; culinary French; culinary skill development; food preparation; food purchasing; food service communication; food service math; garde-manger; international cuisine; introduction to food service; kitchen management; management and human resources; meal planning; meat cutting; meat fabrication; menu and facilities design; nutrition; nutrition and food service; patisserie; restaurant opportunities; sanitation; saucier; seafood processing; soup, stock, sauce, and starch production; wines and spirits.

FACILITIES

Bake shop; cafeteria; 18 classrooms; 2 computer laboratories; demonstration laboratory; 10 food production kitchens; learning resource center; library; 7 student lounges; 9 teaching kitchens.

STUDENT PROFILE

1823 full-time.

FACULTY

50 total: 50 full-time. 18 are industry professionals; 29 are culinary-certified teachers. Prominent faculty: Bill Hunt, CEC; Dave Watson, CEPC; Andrea Schrenk, CEPC. Faculty-student ratio: 1:18.

SPECIAL PROGRAMS

4-month paid externship, culinary competitions, educational seminars (including ice carving), field trips.

TYPICAL EXPENSES

Application fee: $100. Tuition: $9275 per semester. Program-related fees include $521 for uniforms and shoes; $850 for cutlery; $766 for books; $1733 for materials.

FINANCIAL AID

In 2004, 2 scholarships were awarded (average award was $9275). Employment placement assistance is available. Employment opportunities within the program are available.

HOUSING

Coed and apartment-style housing available. Average on-campus housing cost per month: $515. Average off-campus housing cost per month: $575.

APPLICATION INFORMATION

Students may begin participation in January, March, May, July, September, and October. Applications are accepted continuously. Applicants must interview; submit a formal application and high school diploma/GED; reading assignment.

CONTACT

Chris O'Dell, Vice President of Marketing and Admissions, Le Cordon Bleu Culinary Arts, 717 Liberty Avenue, Pittsburgh, PA 15222-3500. Telephone: 800-432-2433. Fax: 412-566-2434. E-mail: Leads-PCl@paculinary.com. World Wide Web: http://www.pci.edu.

THE RESTAURANT SCHOOL AT WALNUT HILL COLLEGE

School of Hospitality Management/School of Culinary and Pastry Arts

Philadelphia, Pennsylvania

GENERAL INFORMATION

Private, coeducational, four-year college. Urban campus. Founded in 1974. Accredited by Accrediting Commission of Career Schools and Colleges of Technology.

PROGRAM INFORMATION

Offered since 1982. Program calendar is divided into semesters. 18-month associate degree in hotel management. 18-month associate degree in restaurant management. 18-month associate degree in pastry arts. 18-month associate degree in culinary arts. 36-month bachelor's degree in hotel management. 36-month bachelor's degree in restaurant management. 36-month bachelor's degree in pastry arts. 36-month bachelor's degree in culinary arts.

PROGRAM AFFILIATION

American Culinary Federation; American Institute of Wine & Food; Confrerie de la Chaine des Rotisseurs; Council on Hotel, Restaurant, and Institutional Education; International Association of Culinary Professionals; James Beard Foundation, Inc.; National Restaurant Association; National Restaurant Association Educational Foundation; Women Chefs and Restaurateurs.

AREAS OF STUDY

Baking; beverage management; buffet catering; confectionery show pieces; controlling costs in food service; culinary French; culinary skill development; food preparation; food purchasing; food service communication; food service math; garde-manger; international cuisine; introduction to food service; kitchen management; management and human resources; meal planning; meat cutting; meat fabrication; menu and facilities design; nutrition; nutrition and food service; patisserie; restaurant opportunities; sanitation; saucier; seafood processing; soup, stock, sauce, and starch production; wines and spirits.

FACILITIES

Bake shop; bakery; 2 classrooms; computer laboratory; 2 demonstration laboratories; 2 food production kitchens; gourmet dining room; learning resource center; 2 lecture rooms; library; 3 public restaurants; 2 student lounges; 6 teaching kitchens; wine laboratory; gourmet shop.

TYPICAL STUDENT PROFILE

706 total: 541 full-time; 165 part-time. 471 are under 25 years old; 181 are between 25 and 44 years old; 54 are over 44 years old.

SPECIAL PROGRAMS

8-day gastronomic tour of France (culinary students), 8-day Florida and Bahamas cruise and resort tour (management students), culinary competitions.

FINANCIAL AID

Program-specific awards include Culinary Society of Philadelphia Scholarships, Elaine Tait Scholarship Fund, two exclusive scholarships. Employment placement assistance is available. Employment opportunities within the program are available.

HOUSING

Coed and apartment-style housing available.

APPLICATION INFORMATION

Students may begin participation in January, May, September, and November. Applications are accepted continuously. Applicants must interview; submit a formal application, letters of reference, and an essay.

CONTACT

Director of Admissions, School of Hospitality Management/ School of Culinary and Pastry Arts, 4207 Walnut Street, Philadelphia, PA 19104-3518. Telephone: 215-222-4200 Ext. 3011. Fax: 215-222-2811. World Wide Web: http://www. walnuthillcollege.edu.

SETON HILL UNIVERSITY

Hospitality and Tourism; Dietetics

Greensburg, Pennsylvania

GENERAL INFORMATION

Private, coeducational, comprehensive institution. Small-town setting. Founded in 1883. Accredited by Middle States Association of Colleges and Schools.

PROGRAM INFORMATION

Accredited by American Dietetic Association. Program calendar is divided into semesters. 4-year bachelor's degree in dietetics. 4-year bachelor's degree in hospitality and tourism.

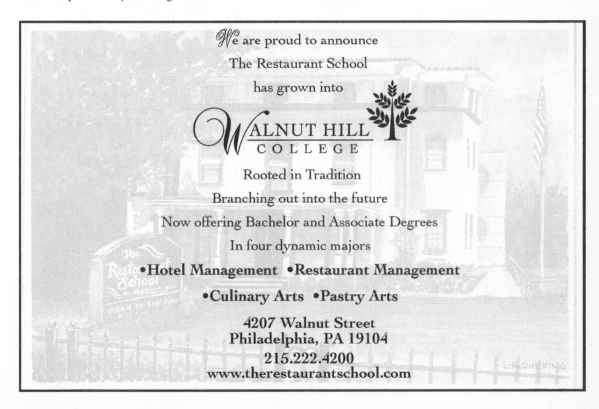

Seton Hill University *(continued)*

PROGRAM AFFILIATION

American Dietetic Association; Council on Hotel, Restaurant, and Institutional Education; National Restaurant Association; National Restaurant Association Educational Foundation.

AREAS OF STUDY

Controlling costs in food service; food preparation; food purchasing; food service math; introduction to food service; management and human resources; meal planning; menu and facilities design; nutrition; nutrition and food service; sanitation.

FACILITIES

Computer laboratory; demonstration laboratory; food production kitchen; 2 laboratories; learning resource center; teaching kitchen.

TYPICAL STUDENT PROFILE

20 total: 19 full-time; 1 part-time. 17 are under 25 years old; 3 are between 25 and 44 years old.

SPECIAL PROGRAMS

Internship (required), coordinated supervised practice.

FINANCIAL AID

Program-specific awards include dedicated scholarship for dietetics students. Employment placement assistance is available.

HOUSING

Coed and single-sex housing available.

APPLICATION INFORMATION

Students may begin participation in January and August. Application deadline for spring is October 1. Application deadline for fall is August 1. Applicants must submit transcripts, SAT or ACT scores.

CONTACT

Director of Admissions, Hospitality and Tourism; Dietetics, Seton Hill Drive, Greensburg, PA 15601. Telephone: 724-838-4255. Fax: 724-830-1294. World Wide Web: http://www.setonhill.edu.

WESTMORELAND COUNTY COMMUNITY COLLEGE

Hospitality Programs Department

Youngwood, Pennsylvania

GENERAL INFORMATION

Public, coeducational, two-year college. Rural campus. Founded in 1970. Accredited by Middle States Association of Colleges and Schools.

PROGRAM INFORMATION

Offered since 1980. Accredited by American Culinary Federation Accrediting Commission, American Dietetic Association. Program calendar is divided into semesters. 16-month associate degree in culinary arts-nonapprenticeship. 2-year associate degree in baking and pastry nonapprenticeship. 2-year associate degree in culinary-nonapprenticeship. 2-year associate degree in travel and tourism. 2-year associate degree in hotel/motel management. 2-year associate degree in restaurant and culinary management. 2-year associate degree in dietetic technician. 3-year associate degree in baking and pastry apprenticeship. 3-year associate degree in culinary arts-apprenticeship. 5-month certificate in hotel/motel management. 5-month certificate in dining room management. 5-month certificate in culinary arts. 5-month certificate in baking and pastry.

PROGRAM AFFILIATION

American Culinary Federation; American Dietetic Association; Council on Hotel, Restaurant, and Institutional Education; National Restaurant Association.

AREAS OF STUDY

Baking; beverage management; buffet catering; confectionery show pieces; controlling costs in food service; convenience cookery; culinary French; culinary skill development; food preparation; food purchasing; food service communication; food service math; garde-manger; international cuisine; introduction to food service; kitchen management; management and human resources; meal planning; menu and facilities design; nutrition; nutrition and food service; patisserie; restaurant opportunities; sanitation; saucier; seafood processing; soup, stock, sauce, and starch production; wines and spirits.

FACILITIES

2 bake shops; cafeteria; 10 classrooms; 4 computer laboratories; demonstration laboratory; food production kitchen; gourmet dining room; laboratory; learning resource center; lecture room; library; 2 student lounges; teaching kitchen.

STUDENT PROFILE

201 total: 131 full-time; 70 part-time. 135 are under 25 years old; 42 are between 25 and 44 years old; 24 are over 44 years old.

FACULTY

22 total: 4 full-time; 18 part-time. 17 are industry professionals; 5 are culinary-certified teachers. Prominent faculty: Mary Zappone, CCE, AAC, MS; Carl Dunkel, CCE, CEC; Cheryl Byers Shipley, MS, RD; Cindy Komarinski, CCC, CCE, MBA. Faculty-student ratio: 1:17.

SPECIAL PROGRAMS

10-day hospitality study tour of Italy, culinary competition, paid apprenticeship.

TYPICAL EXPENSES

Application fee: $10. In-state tuition: $780–$1170 per semester (12-18 credits) full-time (in district), $65 per credit part-time (in district), $1560–$2340 per semester

(12–18 credits) full-time (out-of-district), $130 per credit part-time (out-of-district). Out-of-state tuition: $2340–$3510 per semester 12/18 credits) full-time, $195 per credit part-time. Program-related fees include $150 for uniforms; $125 for knives; $200 for lab fees.

FINANCIAL AID
In 2004, 5 scholarships were awarded (average award was $900); 20 loans were granted (average loan was $1300). Employment placement assistance is available. Employment opportunities within the program are available.

APPLICATION INFORMATION
Students may begin participation in January, May, and August. Applications are accepted continuously. In 2004, 88 applied; 88 were accepted. Applicants must submit a formal application and take a physical exam.

CONTACT
Janice Grabowski, Director of Admissions, Hospitality Programs Department, 400 Armbrust Road, Youngwood, PA 15697. Telephone: 724-925-4064. Fax: 724-925-5802. E-mail: grabowskij@wccc-pa.edu. World Wide Web: http://www.wccc-pa.edu.

WIDENER UNIVERSITY

School of Hospitality Management

Chester, Pennsylvania

GENERAL INFORMATION
Private, coeducational, university. Suburban campus. Founded in 1821. Accredited by Middle States Association of Colleges and Schools.

PROGRAM INFORMATION
Offered since 1981. Accredited by Council on Hotel, Restaurant and Institutional Education. Program calendar is divided into semesters. 2-year master's degree in hospitality management. 4-year bachelor's degree in hospitality management.

PROGRAM AFFILIATION
American Dietetic Association; Council on Hotel, Restaurant, and Institutional Education; International Food Service Executives Association; National Restaurant Association; National Restaurant Association Educational Foundation; Society for Foodservice Management.

AREAS OF STUDY
Beverage management; controlling costs in food service; food preparation; food purchasing; hotel management; introduction to food service; management and human resources; menu and facilities design; nutrition; nutrition and food service; restaurant opportunities; sanitation; wines and spirits.

FACILITIES
Bake shop; 5 classrooms; computer laboratory; demonstration laboratory; food production kitchen; gourmet dining room; laboratory; lecture room; library; student lounge; teaching kitchen.

TYPICAL STUDENT PROFILE
180 total: 175 full-time; 5 part-time.

SPECIAL PROGRAMS
2 paid summer internships, paid cooperative education semester, study abroad program.

FINANCIAL AID
Employment placement assistance is available. Employment opportunities within the program are available.

HOUSING
Coed, apartment-style, and single-sex housing available.

APPLICATION INFORMATION
Students may begin participation in January and September. Applications are accepted continuously. Applicants must submit a formal application, an essay, SAT or ACT scores, and high school transcripts.

CONTACT
Director of Admissions, School of Hospitality Management, One University Place, Chester, PA 19013. Telephone: 610-499-4129. Fax: 610-499-4676. World Wide Web: http://www.widener.edu/soh/index.html.

WINNER INSTITUTE OF ARTS & SCIENCES CULINARY EDUCATION

Culinary Arts Program

Transfer, Pennsylvania

GENERAL INFORMATION
Private, coeducational, culinary institute. Rural campus. Founded in 1997. Accredited by Council on Occupational Education.

PROGRAM INFORMATION
Offered since 1997. Accredited by American Culinary Federation Accrediting Commission. Program calendar is divided into quarters. 60-week diploma in culinary arts.

PROGRAM AFFILIATION
American Culinary Federation; International Association of Culinary Professionals; National Restaurant Association; The Bread Bakers Guild of America.

AREAS OF STUDY
Baking; controlling costs in food service; culinary skill development; food preparation; food purchasing; food service communication; food service math; garde-manger; international cuisine; introduction to food service; kitchen management; meal planning; meat cutting; meat fabrication; menu and facilities design; nutrition; patisserie; sanitation; saucier; seafood processing; soup, stock, sauce, and starch production.

Winner Institute of Arts & Sciences Culinary Education
(continued)

FACILITIES
4 classrooms; computer laboratory; learning resource center; library; student lounge; 3 teaching kitchens.

TYPICAL STUDENT PROFILE
65 full-time.

SPECIAL PROGRAMS
Paid externships, culinary competitions.

FINANCIAL AID
Employment placement assistance is available.

HOUSING
Apartment-style housing available.

APPLICATION INFORMATION
Students may begin participation in January, April, July, and October. Application deadline for winter is January 3. Application deadline for spring is April 1. Application deadline for summer is July 5. Application deadline for fall is October 1. Applicants must interview; submit a formal application, an essay, and take an entrance exam.

CONTACT
Director of Admissions, Culinary Arts Program, One Winner Place, Transfer, PA 16154. Telephone: 888-414-CHEF. Fax: 724-646-0218. World Wide Web: http://www.winner-institute.com.

YORKTOWNE BUSINESS INSTITUTE

School of Culinary Arts

York, Pennsylvania

GENERAL INFORMATION
Private, coeducational, two-year college. Small-town setting. Founded in 1976. Accredited by Accrediting Council for Independent Colleges and Schools.

PROGRAM INFORMATION
Offered since 1998. Program calendar is divided into trimesters. 12-month diploma in professional baking and pastry. 12-month diploma in food service. 16-month associate degree in culinary arts. 6-week certificate in professional bartending.

PROGRAM AFFILIATION
American Culinary Federation; American Hotel and Lodging Association; National Restaurant Association; Pennsylvania Restaurant Association.

AREAS OF STUDY
Baking; beverage management; buffet catering; confectionery show pieces; controlling costs in food service; convenience cookery; culinary French; culinary skill development; food preparation; food purchasing; food service communication; food service math; garde-manger; international cuisine; introduction to food service; kitchen management; management and human resources; meal planning; meat cutting; meat fabrication; menu and facilities design; nutrition; nutrition and food service; patisserie; restaurant opportunities; sanitation; saucier; seafood processing; soup, stock, sauce, and starch production; wines and spirits.

FACILITIES
7 classrooms; 4 computer laboratories; 2 demonstration laboratories; 4 food production kitchens; garden; gourmet dining room; 3 learning resource centers; 2 lecture rooms; 2 libraries; public restaurant; student lounge; 4 teaching kitchens.

STUDENT PROFILE
124 full-time. 69 are under 25 years old; 39 are between 25 and 44 years old; 16 are over 44 years old.

FACULTY
9 total: 6 full-time; 3 part-time. 9 are industry professionals; 3 are culinary-certified teachers. Prominent faculty: David Haynes, CEC. Faculty-student ratio: 1:10.

SPECIAL PROGRAMS
6-week externship (including European locations), culinary competitions, participation in student-run restaurant.

TYPICAL EXPENSES
Application fee: $55. Tuition: $13,068 per baking and pastry 12-month diploma; $26,841 for culinary arts 16-month degree. Program-related fees include $500 for tool kit; $500 for facility fee; $195 for uniforms.

FINANCIAL AID
Program-specific awards include institutional grants. Employment placement assistance is available. Employment opportunities within the program are available.

HOUSING
Average off-campus housing cost per month: $600.

APPLICATION INFORMATION
Students may begin participation in February, June, and October. Application deadline for fall is October 1. Application deadline for spring is February 1. Application deadline for summer is May 15. In 2005, 152 applied; 135 were accepted. Applicants must interview; submit a formal application and take entrance exam.

CONTACT
Jane Regan, Director of Admissions, School of Culinary Arts, West 7th Avenue, York, PA 17404. Telephone: 800-840-1004. Fax: 717-848-4584. E-mail: info@ybi.edu. World Wide Web: http://www.yorkchef.com.

YTI CAREER INSTITUTE

YTI Career Institute

Lancaster, Pennsylvania

GENERAL INFORMATION
Private, coeducational, two-year college. Suburban campus. Founded in 1967. Accredited by Accrediting Commission of Career Schools and Colleges of Technology.

PROGRAM INFORMATION
Offered since 1999. Program calendar is continuous. 12-month diploma in pastry arts. 21-month associate degree in culinary arts/restaurant management.

PROGRAM AFFILIATION
American Culinary Federation; National Restaurant Association Educational Foundation; Pennsylvania Restaurant Association.

AREAS OF STUDY
Baking; beverage management; buffet catering; confectionery show pieces; controlling costs in food service; culinary skill development; food preparation; food purchasing; food service communication; food service math; garde-manger; international cuisine; introduction to food service; kitchen management; management and human resources; meal planning; meat fabrication; menu and facilities design; nutrition; patisserie; restaurant opportunities; sanitation; saucier; seafood processing; soup, stock, sauce, and starch production; wines and spirits.

FACILITIES
Bakery; 7 classrooms; computer laboratory; demonstration laboratory; 4 food production kitchens; gourmet dining room; learning resource center; 7 lecture rooms; library; student lounge.

STUDENT PROFILE
200 full-time.

FACULTY
15 total: 12 full-time; 3 part-time. 9 are industry professionals; 1 is a master chef; 1 is a master baker. Faculty-student ratio: 1:20.

TYPICAL EXPENSES
Application fee: $40. Tuition: $5710 per quarter (culinary arts, restaurant management); $5330 per quarter (pastry arts). Program-related fees include $2100 for books, kits and supplies (culinary arts/restaurant management); $1300 for books, kits and supplies (pastry arts).

FINANCIAL AID
Employment placement assistance is available. Employment opportunities within the program are available.

HOUSING

Average off-campus housing cost per month: $350.

APPLICATION INFORMATION

Students may begin participation in January, July, and October. Applications are accepted continuously. Applicants must interview; submit a formal application and transcript.

CONTACT

Craig Sobel, Director of Admissions, YTI Career Institute, Lancaster Campus, 3050 Hempland Road, Lancaster, PA 17601. Telephone: 866-984-4723. Fax: 717-295-1135. E-mail: sobec@yti.edu. World Wide Web: http://cuisine.yti.edu.

See display on page 316.

RHODE ISLAND

JOHNSON & WALES UNIVERSITY

College of Culinary Arts

Providence, Rhode Island

GENERAL INFORMATION

Private, coeducational, comprehensive institution. Urban campus. Founded in 1914. Accredited by New England Association of Schools and Colleges.

PROGRAM INFORMATION

Offered since 1973. Accredited by American Dietetic Association. Program calendar is divided into quarters. 1-year master's degree in hospitality administration. 2-year associate degree in baking and pastry arts. 2-year associate degree in culinary arts. 4-year bachelor's degree in food service management. 4-year bachelor's degree in food service entrepreneurship. 4-year bachelor's degree in food marketing. 4-year bachelor's degree in culinary nutrition. 4-year bachelor's degree in culinary arts. 4-year bachelor's degree in baking and pastry arts.

PROGRAM AFFILIATION

American Culinary Federation; American Dietetic Association; American Institute of Baking; American Institute of Wine & Food; Confrerie de la Chaine des Rotisseurs; Council on Hotel, Restaurant, and Institutional Education; Institute of Food Technologists; International Association of Culinary Professionals; International Food Service Executives Association; International Foodservice Editorial Council; James Beard Foundation, Inc.; National Restaurant Association; National Restaurant Association Educational Foundation; Oldways Preservation and Exchange Trust; Society of Wine Educators; The Bread Bakers Guild of America; Women Chefs and Restaurateurs.

AREAS OF STUDY

Baking; beverage management; buffet catering; confectionery show pieces; controlling costs in food service; convenience cookery; culinary French; culinary skill development; food preparation; food purchasing; food service communication; food service math; garde-manger; international cuisine; introduction to food service; kitchen management; management and human resources; meal planning; meat cutting; meat fabrication; menu and facilities design; nutrition; nutrition and food service; patisserie; sanitation; saucier; seafood processing; soup, stock, sauce, and starch production; wines and spirits.

FACILITIES

13 bake shops; bakery; 4 cafeterias; catering service; 22 classrooms; coffee shop; 4 computer laboratories; 27 demonstration laboratories; 30 food production kitchens; 2 gardens; 4 gourmet dining rooms; 3 laboratories; 2 learning resource centers; 22 lecture rooms; 2 libraries; 10 public restaurants; snack shop; 5 student lounges.

STUDENT PROFILE

2,413 total: 2246 full-time; 167 part-time. 2118 are under 25 years old; 247 are between 25 and 44 years old; 48 are over 44 years old.

FACULTY

81 total: 80 full-time; 1 part-time. 81 are industry professionals; 1 is a master chef; 28 are culinary-certified teachers. Prominent faculty: Frank Terranova, BS, CEC, CCE; Edward M. Korry, MA, Certified Wine Educator; George O'Palenick, MS, CEC, CCE, AAC; Martha Crawford, CEPC. Faculty-student ratio: 1:20.

SPECIAL PROGRAMS

Customized corporate and commercial training programs.

TYPICAL EXPENSES

Tuition: $19,875 per year. Program-related fees include $951 for general fee; $250 for orientation; $954 for optional weekend meal plan.

FINANCIAL AID

In 2005, 1105 scholarships were awarded (average award was $4455); 1855 loans were granted (average loan was $5575). Employment placement assistance is available. Employment opportunities within the program are available.

HOUSING

Coed housing available. Average on-campus housing cost per month: $1030.

APPLICATION INFORMATION

Students may begin participation in March, June, September, and December. Applications are accepted continuously. In 2005, 3027 applied; 2437 were accepted. Applicants must submit a formal application.

CONTACT

Amy Podbelski, Assistant Director of Admissions, College of Culinary Arts, 8 Abbott Park Place, Providence, RI 02903-3703. Telephone: 800-342-5598 Ext. 2370. Fax:

Johnson & Wales University *(continued)*

401-598-2948. E-mail: admissions.pvd@jwu.edu. World Wide Web: http://culinary.jwu.edu.

See color display following page 332.

SOUTH CAROLINA

THE CULINARY INSTITUTE OF CHARLESTON

Trident Technical College

Charleston, South Carolina

GENERAL INFORMATION
Public, coeducational, two-year college. Urban campus. Founded in 1964. Accredited by Southern Association of Colleges and Schools.

PROGRAM INFORMATION
Offered since 1988. Accredited by American Culinary Federation Accrediting Commission, Council on Hotel, Restaurant and Institutional Education, Commission on Accreditation of Hospitality Management Programs. Program calendar is divided into semesters. 1-year certificate in catering. 1-year certificate in hospitality industry service. 1-year certificate in baking and pastry. 1-year diploma in culinary arts. 2-year associate degree in culinary arts technology. 2-year associate degree in hospitality and tourism management.

PROGRAM AFFILIATION
American Culinary Federation; American Institute of Wine & Food; Council on Hotel, Restaurant, and Institutional Education; Federation of Dining Rooms Professionals; International Association of Culinary Professionals; National Association of Catering Executives; National Restaurant Association; National Restaurant Association Educational Foundation; Serve Safe Sanitation National Certification Association.

AREAS OF STUDY
Baking; beverage management; buffet catering; controlling costs in food service; convenience cookery; culinary skill development; food preparation; food purchasing; food service math; garde-manger; ice carving; introduction to food service; kitchen management; management and human resources; meal planning; meat cutting; meat fabrication; menu and facilities design; nutrition; nutrition and food service; patisserie; restaurant opportunities; sanitation; saucier; seafood processing; soup, stock, sauce, and starch production; wines and spirits.

FACILITIES
2 bake shops; catering service; 10 classrooms; computer laboratory; 5 demonstration laboratories; food production kitchen; garden; gourmet dining room; learning resource center; 6 lecture rooms; library; public restaurant; student lounge; 2 teaching kitchens; broadcast kitchen ampitheater.

STUDENT PROFILE
469 total: 305 full-time; 164 part-time. 263 are under 25 years old; 189 are between 25 and 44 years old; 17 are over 44 years old.

FACULTY
24 total: 10 full-time; 14 part-time. 10 are industry professionals; 1 is a master baker; 7 are culinary-certified teachers. Prominent faculty: Michael Carmel, CEC, CCE; Benjamin Black, CCC; Berndt Gronert, CMPC; Ward Morgan, CWC, CCE. Faculty-student ratio: 1:16.

SPECIAL PROGRAMS
Participation in Annual Chef's Fest Benefit for Lowcountry Food Bank for 900 guests, participation in formal, black tie Vintners Dinner for 600 guests, participation in annual Wine Expo with 1800 guests and 40 vinters.

TYPICAL EXPENSES
Application fee: $25. In-state tuition: $1557 per semester full-time (in district), $127 per credit hour part-time (in district), $1729 per semester full-time (out-of-district), $141 per credit hour part-time (out-of-district). Out-of-state tuition: $2949 per semester full-time, $243 per credit hour part-time. Program-related fees include $123–$139 for uniforms culinary; $231 for knife kit; $188 for pastry kit; $154–$194 for uniforms dining room.

FINANCIAL AID
In 2005, 8 scholarships were awarded (average award was $1000). Program-specific awards include Hotel and Restaurant Association scholarships, Scholarships sponsored by College Foundation; baking and pastry scholarship, Concierge Association of Charleston scholarship. Employment placement assistance is available. Employment opportunities within the program are available.

HOUSING
Average off-campus housing cost per month: $720.

APPLICATION INFORMATION
Students may begin participation in January, May, and August. Application deadline for fall 2006 is August 7. Application deadline for summer 2006 is May 26. Applicants must submit a formal application and placement tests.

CONTACT
Chef Michael Carmel, Department Head, Culinary, Trident Technical College, PO Box 118067, HT-M, Charleston, SC 29423-8067. Telephone: 843-820-5096. Fax: 843-820-5060. E-mail: michael.carmel@tridenttech.edu. World Wide Web: http://www.culinaryinstituteofcharleston.com/.

See color display following page 332.

GREENVILLE TECHNICAL COLLEGE

Hospitality Education

Greenville, South Carolina

GENERAL INFORMATION
Public, coeducational, two-year college. Suburban campus. Founded in 1962. Accredited by Southern Association of Colleges and Schools.

PROGRAM INFORMATION
Accredited by American Culinary Federation Accrediting Commission. Program calendar is divided into semesters. 1-year certificate in bakery and pastry. 1-year certificate in catering. 1-year certificate in restaurant management/hotel operations. 1-year certificate in dietary manager. 1-year certificate in culinary education. 2-year associate degree in food service management-culinary arts.

PROGRAM AFFILIATION
American Culinary Federation; American Dietetic Association; American Hotel and Lodging Association; Council on Hotel, Restaurant, and Institutional Education; Dietary Managers Association; National Restaurant Association.

AREAS OF STUDY
Baking; beverage management; buffet catering; controlling costs in food service; culinary skill development; food preparation; food purchasing; garde-manger; introduction to food service; kitchen management; management and human resources; meal planning; meat fabrication; menu and facilities design; nutrition; patisserie; restaurant opportunities; sanitation; seafood processing; soup, stock, sauce, and starch production.

FACILITIES
Classroom; computer laboratory; food production kitchen; gourmet dining room; laboratory; learning resource center; lecture room; library; snack shop; student lounge; teaching kitchen.

TYPICAL STUDENT PROFILE
210 total: 95 full-time; 115 part-time.

FINANCIAL AID
Employment placement assistance is available.

APPLICATION INFORMATION
Students may begin participation in January, May, and August. Applications are accepted continuously. Applicants must submit a formal application, ASSET and/or SAT scores.

CONTACT
Director of Admissions, Hospitality Education, PO Box 5616, Greenville, SC 29606-5616. Telephone: 864-250-8303. Fax: 864-250-8430. World Wide Web: http://www.greenvilletech.com/.

HORRY-GEORGETOWN TECHNICAL COLLEGE

Culinary Arts Department

Conway, South Carolina

GENERAL INFORMATION
Public, coeducational, two-year college. Suburban campus. Founded in 1965. Accredited by Southern Association of Colleges and Schools.

PROGRAM INFORMATION
Offered since 1987. Accredited by American Culinary Federation Accrediting Commission. Program calendar is divided into semesters. 1-semester certificate in culinary arts certification. 2-semester certificate in baking and pastry arts. 5-semester associate degree in culinary arts technology-business major.

PROGRAM AFFILIATION
American Culinary Federation; Council on Hotel, Restaurant, and Institutional Education; National Restaurant Association Educational Foundation.

AREAS OF STUDY
Baking; beverage management; buffet catering; controlling costs in food service; culinary French; food preparation; food purchasing; food service communication; food service math; garde-manger; international cuisine; introduction to food service; kitchen management; management and human resources; meat fabrication; menu and facilities design; nutrition; sanitation; saucier; seafood processing; soup, stock, sauce, and starch production.

FACILITIES
2 bake shops; cafeteria; 3 classrooms; computer laboratory; 2 demonstration laboratories; 4 food production kitchens; garden; 3 gourmet dining rooms; 2 learning resource centers; 2 lecture rooms; 2 libraries; 2 public restaurants; 2 student lounges; teaching kitchen.

STUDENT PROFILE
140 full-time.

FACULTY
12 total: 3 full-time; 9 part-time. 1 is an industry professional; 2 are culinary-certified teachers; 1 is a registered dietitian. Prominent faculty: Kathleen Gerba, CCE; Lindsey McInville; Eric Wagner, CEC. Faculty-student ratio: 1:25 lecture; 1:10 lab.

SPECIAL PROGRAMS
Student exchange program with Bahamas Hotel Training College, Nassau, Bahamas.

TYPICAL EXPENSES
Application fee: $25. In-state tuition: $1195 per semester (in district), $1795 per semester (out-of-district). Out-of-state tuition: $2400 per semester. Program-related fees include $185 for knives; $80 for uniforms; $250 for books (per semester); $60 for technology fee (per semester).

Horry-Georgetown Technical College *(continued)*

FINANCIAL AID
In 2004, 50 scholarships were awarded (average award was $680); 3 loans were granted (average loan was $300). Employment placement assistance is available.

APPLICATION INFORMATION
Students may begin participation in January, May, and August. Applications are accepted continuously. In 2004, 70 applied. Applicants must submit a formal application and SAT, CPT, or ACT scores.

CONTACT
Carmen Catino, Chair, Culinary Arts Department, 2050 Hwy 501 East, Conway, SC 29526. Telephone: 843-349-5333. Fax: 843-347-4207. E-mail: catino@hor.tec.sc.us. World Wide Web: http://www.hor.tec.sc.us/.

UNIVERSITY OF SOUTH CAROLINA

School of Hotel, Restaurant, and Tourism Management

Columbia, South Carolina

GENERAL INFORMATION
Public, coeducational, university. Urban campus. Founded in 1801. Accredited by Southern Association of Colleges and Schools.

PROGRAM INFORMATION
Offered since 1972. Accredited by Council on Hotel, Restaurant and Institutional Education. Program calendar is divided into semesters. 2-year master's degree in hotel, restaurant, and tourism management. 4-year bachelor's degree in hotel, restaurant, and tourism management.

PROGRAM AFFILIATION
Council on Hotel, Restaurant, and Institutional Education; National Restaurant Association.

AREAS OF STUDY
Beverage management; contract food service; food preparation; food purchasing; nutrition; wines and spirits.

FACILITIES
2 food production kitchens.

TYPICAL STUDENT PROFILE
340 full-time.

SPECIAL PROGRAMS
Overseas study in Germany, internships available at Hilton Head Island.

FINANCIAL AID
Employment placement assistance is available. Employment opportunities within the program are available.

HOUSING
Coed, apartment-style, and single-sex housing available.

APPLICATION INFORMATION
Students may begin participation in January, May, June, and August. Application deadline for fall is March 1. Applicants must submit a formal application.

CONTACT
Director of Admissions, School of Hotel, Restaurant, and Tourism Management, Columbia, SC 29208. Telephone: 803-777-6665. Fax: 803-777-1224. World Wide Web: http://www.csd.scarolina.edu/.

SOUTH DAKOTA

MITCHELL TECHNICAL INSTITUTE

Culinary Arts Program

Mitchell, South Dakota

GENERAL INFORMATION
Public, coeducational, two-year college. Rural campus. Founded in 1968. Accredited by North Central Association of Colleges and Schools.

PROGRAM INFORMATION
Offered since 1968. Program calendar is divided into semesters. 13.5- to 24-month diploma in culinary arts.

PROGRAM AFFILIATION
American Culinary Federation; National Restaurant Association; National Restaurant Association Educational Foundation.

AREAS OF STUDY
Baking; controlling costs in food service; culinary skill development; food preparation; food purchasing; food service math; introduction to food service; management and human resources; meal planning; meat cutting; meat fabrication; nutrition; patisserie; sanitation; saucier; seafood processing; soup, stock, sauce, and starch production.

FACILITIES
Bake shop; cafeteria; 2 classrooms; computer laboratory; demonstration laboratory; 2 food production kitchens; gourmet dining room; learning resource center; lecture room; public restaurant.

TYPICAL STUDENT PROFILE
29 full-time.

SPECIAL PROGRAMS
Trip to professional show in Minnesota in February, guest presenters, 12-week paid internship.

FINANCIAL AID
Employment placement assistance is available.

APPLICATION INFORMATION

Students may begin participation in January, June, and August. Applications are accepted continuously. Applicants must submit a formal application, high school/college transcripts.

CONTACT

Director of Admissions, Culinary Arts Program, 821 North Capital, Mitchell, SD 57301. Telephone: 605-995-3024. World Wide Web: http://mti.tec.sd.us/.

SOUTH DAKOTA STATE UNIVERSITY

Hotel and Foodservice Management

Brookings, South Dakota

GENERAL INFORMATION

Public, coeducational, university. Small-town setting. Founded in 1881. Accredited by North Central Association of Colleges and Schools.

PROGRAM INFORMATION

Program calendar is divided into semesters. 30-month master's degree in nutrition and food science. 4-year bachelor's degree in nutritional sciences. 4-year bachelor's degree in food science. 4-year bachelor's degree in dietetics. 4-year bachelor's degree in hotel and foodservice management. 48-month doctoral degree in nutrition and food science.

PROGRAM AFFILIATION

American Dietetic Association; Council on Hotel, Restaurant, and Institutional Education.

AREAS OF STUDY

Beverage management; casino management; controlling costs in food service; food preparation; food purchasing; food service communication; hotel operations; introduction to food service; kitchen management; management and human resources; meal planning; meat cutting; menu and facilities design; nutrition; nutrition and food service; restaurant opportunities; sanitation; seafood processing; wines and spirits.

FACILITIES

Cafeteria; catering service; 10 classrooms; 10 computer laboratories; demonstration laboratory; 2 food production kitchens; 2 laboratories; learning resource center; 2 lecture rooms; library; teaching kitchen.

STUDENT PROFILE

124 full-time. 111 are under 25 years old; 10 are between 25 and 44 years old; 3 are over 44 years old.

FACULTY

6 total: 4 full-time; 2 part-time. 1 is an industry professional; 1 is a culinary-certified teacher. Prominent faculty: Georgia Crews, PhD, RD; Gary Lee Frantz, PhD, FMP; Don Behrend, MS. Faculty-student ratio: 1:10.

SPECIAL PROGRAMS

Upper Midwest Food Purveyors Show, 2 practicum, Swiss study tour (2006).

TYPICAL EXPENSES

Application fee: $35. In-state tuition: $74.10 per credit. Out-of-state tuition: $233.55 per credit.

FINANCIAL AID

In 2004, 25 scholarships were awarded (average award was $2000). Employment placement assistance is available.

HOUSING

Coed and apartment-style housing available. Average on-campus housing cost per month: $250. Average off-campus housing cost per month: $275.

APPLICATION INFORMATION

Students may begin participation in January and September. Applications are accepted continuously. In 2004, 34 applied; 34 were accepted. Applicants must submit a formal application and high school transcript.

CONTACT

Admissions Counselor, Hotel and Foodservice Management, Box 2201, Brookings, SD 57007. Telephone: 800-952-3541. Fax: 605-688-6384. E-mail: sdsu_admissions@sdstate.edu. World Wide Web: http://www3.sdstate.edu.

TENNESSEE

THE ART INSTITUTE OF TENNESSEE–NASHVILLE

Nashville, Tennessee

GENERAL INFORMATION

Coeducational, four-year college.

PROGRAM INFORMATION

Diploma in Culinary Arts-Baking and Pastry. Diploma in Culinary Arts-Culinary Skills. Associate degree in Culinary Arts. Bachelor's degree in Culinary Arts Management.

SPECIAL PROGRAMS

Students compete every year in local, regional, or national competitions.

TYPICAL EXPENSES

Tuition: $44,240 Associate's program (total program tuition), $75,840 BS program (total program tuition) full-time, $395 per credit part-time.

CONTACT

Admissions Office, 100 CNA Drive, Nashville, TN 37214-3439. Telephone: 866-747-5770. World Wide Web: http://www.artinstitutes.edu/nashville/.

See color display following page 380.

NASHVILLE STATE TECHNICAL COMMUNITY COLLEGE

Culinary Arts

Nashville, Tennessee

GENERAL INFORMATION
Public, coeducational, two-year college. Suburban campus. Founded in 1970. Accredited by Southern Association of Colleges and Schools.

PROGRAM INFORMATION
Offered since 1996. Program calendar is divided into semesters. 1-year technical certificate in culinary arts. 2-year associate degree in culinary arts.

AREAS OF STUDY
Baking; beverage management; buffet catering; culinary French; culinary skill development; food preparation; food purchasing; food service communication; food service math; garde-manger; international cuisine; kitchen management; management and human resources; meal planning; meat cutting; menu and facilities design; nutrition; patisserie; sanitation; saucier; soup, stock, sauce, and starch production.

FACILITIES
Demonstration laboratory; food production kitchen; learning resource center; library; teaching kitchen.

STUDENT PROFILE
120 total: 70 full-time; 50 part-time.

FACULTY
7 total: 2 full-time; 5 part-time. 2 are industry professionals; 1 is a culinary-certified teacher. Prominent faculty: Kenneth P. Morlino, CEC, MBA; Tom Loftis, AAS. Faculty-student ratio: 1:12.

SPECIAL PROGRAMS
Paid internship.

TYPICAL EXPENSES
Application fee: $5. In-state tuition: $912 per semester full-time (in district), $78 per credit hour part-time. Out-of-state tuition: $3644 per semester full-time, $314 per credit hour part-time. Program-related fee includes $250 for knives and uniforms.

FINANCIAL AID
In 2004, 2 scholarships were awarded (average award was $500). Employment placement assistance is available.

HOUSING
Average off-campus housing cost per month: $500–$700.

APPLICATION INFORMATION
Students may begin participation in January and August. Applications are accepted continuously. Applicants must submit a formal application.

CONTACT
Kenneth P. Morlino, Program Coordinator, Culinary Arts, 120 White Bridge Road, Nashville, TN 37209. Telephone: 615-353-3419. Fax: 618-353-3428. E-mail: kenneth.morlino@nscc.edu. World Wide Web: http://www.nscc.edu.

WALTERS STATE COMMUNITY COLLEGE

Hospitality Business

Sevierville, Tennessee

GENERAL INFORMATION
Public, coeducational, two-year college. Small-town setting. Founded in 1970. Accredited by Southern Association of Colleges and Schools.

PROGRAM INFORMATION
Offered since 1997. Accredited by American Culinary Federation Accrediting Commission. Program calendar is divided into semesters. 1-year certificate in culinary arts. 2-year associate degree in hotel/restaurant management. 2-year associate degree in culinary arts.

PROGRAM AFFILIATION
American Culinary Federation; National Restaurant Association; Sevier County Hospitality Association; Tennessee Restaurant Association.

AREAS OF STUDY
Baking; beverage management; buffet catering; confectionery show pieces; controlling costs in food service; culinary French; culinary skill development; food preparation; food purchasing; food service communication; food service math; garde-manger; international cuisine; introduction to food service; kitchen management; management and human resources; meal planning; meat cutting; meat fabrication; menu and facilities design; nutrition and food service; patisserie; restaurant opportunities; sanitation; saucier; seafood processing; soup, stock, sauce, and starch production.

FACILITIES
Bake shop; catering service; 4 classrooms; 2 computer laboratories; demonstration laboratory; food production kitchen; gourmet dining room; lecture room; library; teaching kitchen; herb garden.

STUDENT PROFILE
115 total: 75 full-time; 40 part-time. 67 are under 25 years old; 30 are between 25 and 44 years old; 18 are over 44 years old.

FACULTY
9 total: 3 full-time; 6 part-time. 7 are industry professionals; 2 are culinary-certified teachers. Prominent faculty: Vanda Poyter, Chef Instructor; Catherine Hallman, CEPC; David Colburn, CEC. Faculty-student ratio: 1:13.

SPECIAL PROGRAMS

Culinary Competition Team, annual visit to National Restaurant Show (Chicago), biennial trips emphasizing the culinary industry.

TYPICAL EXPENSES

Application fee: $10. In-state tuition: $1190 per semester full-time (in district), $325 per 3 credit hours part-time. Out-of-state tuition: $4397 per semester full-time, $1159 per 3 credit hours part-time. Program-related fees include $70 for uniform (1); $175 for knife kit; $75 for American Culinary Federation membership.

FINANCIAL AID

In 2004, 6 scholarships were awarded (average award was $500). Program-specific awards include state and local tourism association scholarships. Employment placement assistance is available. Employment opportunities within the program are available.

HOUSING

Average off-campus housing cost per month: $550.

APPLICATION INFORMATION

Students may begin participation in January and August. Applications are accepted continuously. In 2004, 50 applied; 45 were accepted. Applicants must submit a formal application.

CONTACT

Kelli Campbell, Office of Enrollment Development, Hospitality Business, 500 South Davy Crockett Parkway, Morristown, TN 37813. Telephone: 423-585-2691. Fax: 423-585-6786. E-mail: kelli.campbell@ws.edu. World Wide Web: http://www.ws.edu.

TEXAS

THE ART INSTITUTE OF DALLAS

Dallas, Texas

GENERAL INFORMATION

Private, coeducational, two-year college. Urban campus. Founded in 1978. Accredited by Southern Association of Colleges and Schools.

PROGRAM INFORMATION

Offered since 1999. Accredited by American Culinary Federation Accrediting Commission. Program calendar is divided into quarters. 5-quarter certificate in culinary arts. 7-quarter associate degree in restaurant and catering management. 7-quarter associate degree in culinary arts.

PROGRAM AFFILIATION

American Culinary Federation; American Institute of Wine & Food.

AREAS OF STUDY

Baking; beverage management; buffet catering; confectionery show pieces; controlling costs in food service; culinary skill development; food preparation; food purchasing; food service communication; food service math; garde-manger; international cuisine; introduction to food service; kitchen management; management and human resources; meat cutting; meat fabrication; menu and facilities design; nutrition; nutrition and food service; patisserie; restaurant opportunities; sanitation; soup, stock, sauce, and starch production; wines and spirits.

FACILITIES

Bake shop; catering service; classroom; computer laboratory; food production kitchen; garden; gourmet dining room; learning resource center; lecture room; library; public restaurant; snack shop; student lounge; 3 teaching kitchens.

TYPICAL STUDENT PROFILE

297 total: 247 full-time; 50 part-time.

SPECIAL PROGRAMS

Yearly opportunities to travel outside the U.S., culinary competitions.

FINANCIAL AID

Employment placement assistance is available. Employment opportunities within the program are available.

HOUSING

Apartment-style housing available.

APPLICATION INFORMATION

Students may begin participation in January, April, July, and October. Applications are accepted continuously. Applicants must interview; submit a formal application, an essay, school transcripts, and take ASSET Test.

CONTACT

Director of Admissions, Two North Park East, 8080 Park Lane, Suite 100, Dallas, TX 75231. Telephone: 800-275-4243. Fax: 214-692-8080. World Wide Web: http://www.aid.edu.

See color display following page 380.

THE ART INSTITUTE OF HOUSTON

The School of Culinary Arts

Houston, Texas

GENERAL INFORMATION

Private, coeducational, two-year college. Urban campus. Founded in 1978. Accredited by Southern Association of Colleges and Schools.

PROGRAM INFORMATION

Offered since 1992. Accredited by American Culinary Federation Accrediting Commission. Program calendar is divided into quarters. 15-month diploma in culinary arts.

The Art Institute of Houston *(continued)*

18-month associate degree in restaurant and catering management. 21-month associate degree in culinary arts. 36-month bachelor's degree in culinary management.

PROGRAM AFFILIATION
American Culinary Federation; American Dietetic Association; Council on Hotel, Restaurant, and Institutional Education; International Association of Culinary Professionals; James Beard Foundation, Inc.; National Restaurant Association; National Restaurant Association Educational Foundation; Sommelier Society of America; Texas Restaurant Association.

AREAS OF STUDY
Baking; beverage management; buffet catering; controlling costs in food service; culinary French; culinary skill development; food preparation; food purchasing; food service math; garde-manger; international cuisine; introduction to food service; kitchen management; management and human resources; meal planning; meat cutting; menu and facilities design; nutrition; patisserie; restaurant opportunities; sanitation; saucier; seafood processing; soup, stock, sauce, and starch production; wines and spirits.

FACILITIES
Bakery; catering service; 3 classrooms; 3 computer laboratories; demonstration laboratory; food production kitchen; garden; gourmet dining room; learning resource center; 3 lecture rooms; library; public restaurant; snack shop; 2 student lounges; 4 teaching kitchens.

STUDENT PROFILE
1,489 total: 947 full-time; 542 part-time. 663 are under 25 years old; 229 are between 25 and 44 years old; 55 are over 44 years old.

FACULTY
20 total: 15 full-time; 5 part-time. 5 are industry professionals; 15 are culinary-certified teachers. Prominent faculty: Joe O'Donnell, BS, MA, CEC; Gary Eaton, MA; Peter Lehr, CEC, CCE; Pierre Gutknecht, BS, CEC. Faculty-student ratio: 1:20.

SPECIAL PROGRAMS
ACF Junior Competition Team, annual trip abroad to study international cuisines, 150-hour paid internship.

TYPICAL EXPENSES
Application fee: $50. Tuition: $403 per credit hour full-time, $403 per credit hour part-time. Program-related fees include $300 for lab fee (per quarter); $100 for tuition deposit.

FINANCIAL AID
Program-specific awards include culinary experience grant ($500), partnership grant, private scholarships. Employment placement assistance is available. Employment opportunities within the program are available.

HOUSING
Apartment-style and single-sex housing available. Average on-campus housing cost per month: $505–$820. Average off-campus housing cost per month: $600.

APPLICATION INFORMATION
Students may begin participation in January, April, July, and October. Application deadline for fall is October 6. Application deadline for winter is January 12. Application deadline for spring is April 5. Application deadline for summer is July 13. In 2005, 1422 applied; 560 were accepted. Applicants must interview; submit a formal application and high school transcripts or GED test scores, and ASSET/COMPASS scores.

CONTACT
Director of Admissions, The School of Culinary Arts, 1900 Yorktown, Houston, TX 77056. Telephone: 800-275-4244 Ext. 3612. Fax: 713-966-2797. E-mail: aihadm@aii.edu. World Wide Web: http://www.aih.aii.edu.

See color display following page 380.

AUSTIN COMMUNITY COLLEGE

Culinary Arts

Austin, Texas

GENERAL INFORMATION
Public, coeducational, two-year college. Urban campus. Founded in 1972. Accredited by Southern Association of Colleges and Schools.

PROGRAM INFORMATION
Accredited by American Culinary Federation Accrediting Commission. Program calendar is divided into semesters. 1-year certificate in hospitality management. 12-month certificate in culinary arts. 2-year associate degree in hospitality management. 2-year associate degree in culinary arts.

PROGRAM AFFILIATION
American Culinary Federation; American Institute of Baking; Council on Hotel, Restaurant, and Institutional Education; International Association of Culinary Professionals; International Foodservice Editorial Council; International Sommelier Guild; National Restaurant Association; National Restaurant Association Educational Foundation; Society of Wine Educators; The Bread Bakers Guild of America; Women Chefs and Restaurateurs.

AREAS OF STUDY
Beverage management; controlling costs in food service; culinary skill development; food service math; international cuisine; kitchen management; management and human resources; meat cutting; meat fabrication; nutrition; restaurant opportunities; sanitation; wines and spirits.

FACILITIES

10 classrooms; 4 computer laboratories; demonstration laboratory; food production kitchen; gourmet dining room; learning resource center; library; snack shop; student lounge.

STUDENT PROFILE

120 total: 45 full-time; 75 part-time. 25 are under 25 years old; 60 are between 25 and 44 years old; 15 are over 44 years old.

FACULTY

11 total: 3 full-time; 8 part-time. 7 are industry professionals; 2 are culinary-certified teachers. Faculty-student ratio: 1:12.

SPECIAL PROGRAMS

School trips (Napa Valley, New York), culinary competitions, internships/practicums.

TYPICAL EXPENSES

In-state tuition: $1800 per year full-time (in district), $160 per 3-credit hour class part-time. Out-of-state tuition: $3200 per year full-time, $280 per 3-credit hour class part-time. Program-related fees include $200 for equipment and uniforms; $150 for books (per semester).

FINANCIAL AID

In 2004, 5 scholarships were awarded (average award was $425). Employment opportunities within the program are available.

HOUSING

Average off-campus housing cost per month: $700.

APPLICATION INFORMATION

Students may begin participation in January, May, and August. Applications are accepted continuously. In 2004, 60 applied; 45 were accepted.

CONTACT

Brian Hay, Program Coordinator, Culinary Arts, 3401 Webberville Road, Austin, TX 78702. Telephone: 512-223-5173. Fax: 512-223-5125. E-mail: bhay@austincc.edu. World Wide Web: http://www2.austincc.edu/hospmgmt.

CENTRAL TEXAS COLLEGE

Hospitality Management/Culinary Arts

Killeen, Texas

GENERAL INFORMATION

Public, coeducational, two-year college. Small-town setting. Founded in 1967. Accredited by Southern Association of Colleges and Schools.

PROGRAM INFORMATION

Offered since 1970. Program calendar is divided into semesters. 16-month certificate in culinary arts. 16-month certificate in institutional food service operations. 2-year associate degree in food and beverage management. 2-year associate degree in food service management. 2-year associate degree in restaurant and culinary management. 9-month certificate in food and beverage management. 9-month certificate in restaurant skills.

PROGRAM AFFILIATION

American Culinary Federation; American Hotel and Lodging Association; Council on Hotel, Restaurant, and Institutional Education; Institute of Food Technologists; National Restaurant Association; National Restaurant Association Educational Foundation; Texas Restaurant Association; Texas State Food Servers Association.

AREAS OF STUDY

Baking; beverage management; buffet catering; confectionery show pieces; controlling costs in food service; culinary French; culinary skill development; food preparation; food purchasing; food service math; garde-manger; international cuisine; introduction to food service; kitchen management; management and human resources; meal planning; meat cutting; menu and facilities design; nutrition; nutrition and food service; restaurant opportunities; sanitation; saucier; seafood processing; soup, stock, sauce, and starch production; wines and spirits.

FACILITIES

Bake shop; bakery; cafeteria; catering service; 6 classrooms; 2 computer laboratories; demonstration laboratory; food production kitchen; gourmet dining room; laboratory; learning resource center; lecture room; library; snack shop; student lounge; teaching kitchen.

TYPICAL STUDENT PROFILE

300 total: 100 full-time; 200 part-time. 120 are under 25 years old; 120 are between 25 and 44 years old; 60 are over 44 years old.

SPECIAL PROGRAMS

Dual credit program for high school students.

FINANCIAL AID

Program-specific awards include Charles Leopard Scholarship.

HOUSING

Coed housing available.

APPLICATION INFORMATION

Students may begin participation in January, May, and August. Applications are accepted continuously. Applicants must interview; submit a formal application.

CONTACT

Director of Admissions, Hospitality Management/Culinary Arts, PO Box 1800, Killeen, TX 76540-1800. Telephone: 800-792-3348 Ext. 1539. Fax: 254-526-1841. World Wide Web: http://www.ctcd.cc.tx.us/.

COLLIN COUNTY COMMUNITY COLLEGE DISTRICT

Hotel/Restaurant Management

Plano, Texas

GENERAL INFORMATION
Public, coeducational, two-year college. Suburban campus. Founded in 1985. Accredited by Southern Association of Colleges and Schools.

PROGRAM INFORMATION
Offered since 1997. Program calendar is divided into semesters. 2-year associate degree in hotel/restaurant management. 2-year associate degree in culinary arts. 9-month certificate in culinary arts. 9-month certificate in hotel/restaurant management.

PROGRAM AFFILIATION
American Culinary Federation; Council on Hotel, Restaurant, and Institutional Education; Greater Dallas Hotel and Motel Association; Texas Chefs Association; Texas Restaurant Association.

AREAS OF STUDY
Baking; buffet catering; controlling costs in food service; culinary French; culinary skill development; food preparation; food purchasing; international cuisine; introduction to food service; kitchen management; management and human resources; meal planning; meat cutting; meat fabrication; menu and facilities design; nutrition; nutrition and food service; restaurant opportunities; sanitation.

FACILITIES
Bakery; 3 classrooms; 2 computer laboratories; 2 demonstration laboratories; food production kitchen; laboratory; 3 learning resource centers; 3 lecture rooms; public restaurant; 2 snack shops; 2 student lounges; teaching kitchen.

TYPICAL STUDENT PROFILE
110 total: 50 full-time; 60 part-time.

SPECIAL PROGRAMS
992 hours of on-the-job training, certification in ServSafe and Texas Food Protection Management.

FINANCIAL AID
Program-specific awards include paid co-op positions. Employment placement assistance is available. Employment opportunities within the program are available.

HOUSING
Apartment-style housing available.

APPLICATION INFORMATION
Students may begin participation in January, March, June, July, August, and October. Applications are accepted continuously.

CONTACT
Director of Admissions, Hotel/Restaurant Management, 9700 Wade Boulevard, Frisco, TX 78035. Telephone: 972-377-1672. Fax: 972-377-1511. World Wide Web: http://www.ccccd.edu.

CULINARY ACADEMY OF AUSTIN, INC.

Austin, Texas

GENERAL INFORMATION
Private, coeducational, culinary institute. Urban campus. Founded in 1998.

PROGRAM INFORMATION
Offered since 1998. Program calendar is divided into quarters. 15-month diploma in professional culinary arts. 4.5-month diploma in introduction to culinary arts and Italian cooking. 6-month diploma in professional pastry arts. 6-week certificate in introduction to culinary arts.

PROGRAM AFFILIATION
American Culinary Federation; Foodservice Educators Network International; International Association of Culinary Professionals; National Restaurant Association; Texas Restaurant Association.

AREAS OF STUDY
Baking; buffet catering; controlling costs in food service; convenience cookery; culinary skill development; food history and culture; food preparation; food service math; garde-manger; international cuisine; introduction to food service; meal planning; menu and facilities design; nutrition; nutrition and food service; patisserie; restaurant opportunities; sanitation; saucier; seafood processing; soup, stock, sauce, and starch production; wines and spirits.

FACILITIES
Bake shop; catering service; 2 classrooms; computer laboratory; food production kitchen; learning resource center; library.

SPECIAL PROGRAMS
International culinary programs in Italy, culinary competitions, food and drink symposium.

FINANCIAL AID
Program-specific awards include work study with professional catering company. Employment placement assistance is available. Employment opportunities within the program are available.

APPLICATION INFORMATION
Students may begin participation in January, April, July, and October. Applications are accepted continuously. Applicants must interview; submit a formal application and letters of reference.

CONTACT
Director of Admissions, 2823 Hancock Drive, Austin, TX 78731. Telephone: 512-451-5743. Fax: 512-467-9120. World Wide Web: http://www.culinaryacademyofaustin.com/.

CULINARY INSTITUTE ALAIN AND MARIE LENÔTRE

Houston, Texas

GENERAL INFORMATION
Private, coeducational, culinary institute. Urban campus. Founded in 1998. Accredited by Accrediting Commission of Career Schools and Colleges of Technology.

PROGRAM INFORMATION
Offered since 1998. Accredited by Accrediting Commission of Career Schools and Colleges of Technology (ACCSCT). Program calendar is continuous. 20- to 40-week diploma in Sous-Chef Patissier. 20- to 40-week diploma in Sous-Chef de Cuisine. 30- to 60-week diploma in culinary arts. 60- to 100-week associate degree in applied science degree in Baking and Pastry Arts. 60- to 100-week associate degree in applied science degree in Culinary Arts.

PROGRAM AFFILIATION
French Chef Association; Houston Professional Chef Association; Texas Chefs Association; Texas Restaurant Association.

AREAS OF STUDY
Bakery Operations; baking; beverage management; buffet catering; candy making; Career Exploration and Planning; chocolate; chocolate candy making; chocolate décor; confectionery show pieces; culinary French; culinary skill development; Dining Room service; food and beverage service; food and beverage service management; food preparation; garde-manger; hospitality marketing; human resource management; international cuisine; meat cutting; meat fabrication; Menu Management; patisserie; purchasing; sanitation; saucier; seafood processing; soup, stock, sauce, and starch production; wines and spirits.

FACILITIES
6 demonstration laboratories; gourmet dining room; 2 lecture rooms; library; student lounge; 3 teaching kitchens.

STUDENT PROFILE
120 total: 70 full-time; 50 part-time. 50 are under 25 years old; 50 are between 25 and 44 years old; 20 are over 44 years old.

Culinary Institute Alain and Marie LeNôtre *(continued)*

FACULTY
6 total: 6 full-time. 6 are industry professionals; 2 are master bakers; 1 is a culinary-certified teacher; 6 are French master chefs. Prominent faculty: Chef André Lemaire; Chef Philippe Richard; Chef Daniel Klein; Chef Bertrand Goutelon; Jean Rene Thiery; Chef Francis Fauquenot. Faculty-student ratio: 1:12.

SPECIAL PROGRAMS
Culinary internships in France, externships in Houston, business workshops, Summer camp for teenagers and adults.

TYPICAL EXPENSES
Application fee: $50. Tuition: $17,450 to $25,000 per 5 to 8 month morning classes or 10 to 16 month evening classes; $34,800 for each of the Associate degree programs. Program-related fees include $1100 for culinary arts program (tools, uniforms, textbooks); $2600 for Associate degree in culinary arts; $850 for sous-chef de cuisine program (tools, uniforms, textbooks); $890 for sous-chef Pâtissier program (tools, uniforms, textbooks); $2600 for Associate degree in Management (tools, uniform, textbooks).

FINANCIAL AID
In 2005, 25 scholarships were awarded (average award was $2000); 96 loans were granted (average loan was $21,000). Program-specific awards include High School Scholarship Competition, Hospitality Educators Association of Texas Scholarship, Institute has a full time Financial Aid director and full time Student Service and Job placement manager. Employment placement assistance is available. Employment opportunities within the program are available.

HOUSING
Average off-campus housing cost per month: $800.

APPLICATION INFORMATION
Students may begin participation year-round. Applications are accepted continuously. In 2005, 160 applied; 120 were accepted. Applicants must interview; submit a formal application, letters of reference, an essay, and have a high school diploma or GED; essay for scholarship consideration.

CONTACT
Pete Ghosh, Director of Admissions, 7070 Allensby, Houston, TX 77022. Telephone: 713-692-0077. Fax: 713-692-7399. E-mail: lenotre@wt.net. World Wide Web: http://www.ciaml.com.

DEL MAR COLLEGE
Department of Hospitality Management

Corpus Christi, Texas

GENERAL INFORMATION
Public, coeducational, two-year college. Urban campus. Founded in 1935. Accredited by Southern Association of Colleges and Schools.

PROGRAM INFORMATION
Offered since 1963. Accredited by American Culinary Federation Accrediting Commission. Program calendar is divided into semesters. 1-year certificate in certified. 1-year certificate in kitchen supervisor. 1-year certificate in restaurant supervisor. 2-year associate degree in baking pastry specialization. 2-year associate degree in culinary arts. 2-year associate degree in restaurant management specialization. 2-year degree. 9-month certificate in cook/baker.

PROGRAM AFFILIATION
American Culinary Federation; Coastal Bend HotelMotel Condominium Association; Coastal Bend Restaurant Association; Council on Hotel, Restaurant, and Institutional Education; National Restaurant Association; Texas Chefs Association; Texas Restaurant Association.

AREAS OF STUDY
Baking; beverage management; buffet catering; confectionery show pieces; controlling costs in food service; culinary skill development; food preparation; food purchasing; garde-manger; international cuisine; introduction to food service; kitchen management; management and human resources; menu and facilities design; nutrition; nutrition and food service; patisserie; restaurant opportunities; sanitation; saucier; soup, stock, sauce, and starch production.

FACILITIES
Bake shop; cafeteria; catering service; 4 classrooms; computer laboratory; 2 demonstration laboratories; 2 food production kitchens; gourmet dining room; 2 laboratories; learning resource center; 4 lecture rooms; 2 libraries; public restaurant; 2 teaching kitchens; herb garden; ice carving room.

STUDENT PROFILE
120 total: 24 full-time; 96 part-time. 24 are under 25 years old; 84 are between 25 and 44 years old; 12 are over 44 years old.

FACULTY
11 total: 2 full-time; 9 part-time. 8 are industry professionals; 1 is a culinary-certified teacher; 1 is a certified executive chef. Prominent faculty: Robert Ard; Mark Carpenter, CEC. Faculty-student ratio: 1:15.

SPECIAL PROGRAMS
Paid internships in local restaurants, hotels, and clubs, annual pastry and garde manger competition.

TYPICAL EXPENSES

In-state tuition: $1015 per semester full-time (in district), $325–$400 per 3-credit course part-time (in district), $1615 per semester full-time (out-of-district), $525–$600 per 3-credit course part-time (out-of-district). Out-of-state tuition: $2215 per semester full-time, $1000–$1100 per 3-credit course part-time. Tuition for international students: $2215 per semester full-time, $1000–$1100 per 3-credit course part-time. Program-related fee includes $24 for lab fees (per course).

FINANCIAL AID

In 2004, 5 scholarships were awarded (average award was $200). Employment placement assistance is available. Employment opportunities within the program are available.

HOUSING

Average off-campus housing cost per month: $1000.

APPLICATION INFORMATION

Students may begin participation in January, June, and September. Application deadline for fall is August 18. Application deadline for spring is January 15. Application deadline for summer is May 25. In 2004, 169 applied; 169 were accepted. Applicants must submit a formal application, academic transcripts, and test scores.

CONTACT

Robert Ard, Chairperson, Department of Hospitality Management, 101 Baldwin Boulevard, Corpus Christi, TX 78404-3897. Telephone: 361-698-1734. Fax: 361-698-1829. E-mail: bard@delmar.edu. World Wide Web: http://www.delmar.edu/hospmgmt.

EL PASO COMMUNITY COLLEGE

Hospitality and Travel Services

El Paso, Texas

GENERAL INFORMATION

Public, coeducational, two-year college. Urban campus. Founded in 1969. Accredited by Southern Association of Colleges and Schools.

PROGRAM INFORMATION

Offered since 1989. Program calendar is divided into semesters. 1-year certificate of completion in restaurant/food service management. 1-year certificate of completion in culinary arts. 2-year associate degree in culinary arts. 2-year associate degree in restaurant/food service management.

PROGRAM AFFILIATION

American Hotel and Lodging Association Educational Institute; Council on Hotel, Restaurant, and Institutional Education; National Restaurant Association Educational Foundation.

AREAS OF STUDY

Baking; confectionery show pieces; controlling costs in food service; culinary skill development; food and beverage management; food and beverage service; food preparation; food purchasing; garde-manger; international cuisine; introduction to food service; kitchen management; management and human resources; meal planning; meat cutting; menu and facilities design; nutrition; sanitation.

FACILITIES

Cafeteria; classroom; food production kitchen; 6 lecture rooms; library.

FINANCIAL AID

Employment placement assistance is available. Employment opportunities within the program are available.

APPLICATION INFORMATION

Students may begin participation in June and September. Application deadline for fall is July 22. Application deadline for spring is November 18. Application deadline for summer is May 4. Applicants must submit a formal application and have a high school diploma or GED.

CONTACT

Director of Admissions, Hospitality and Travel Services, 919 Hunter Drive, El Paso, TX 79915. Telephone: 915-831-5148. Fax: 915-831-5017. World Wide Web: http://www.epcc.edu/.

GALVESTON COLLEGE

Culinary Arts Academy

Galveston, Texas

GENERAL INFORMATION

Public, coeducational, two-year college. Urban campus. Founded in 1967. Accredited by Southern Association of Colleges and Schools.

PROGRAM INFORMATION

Offered since 1987. Program calendar is divided into semesters. 1-year certificate in culinary/hospitality management. 1-year certificate in culinary arts. 2-year associate degree in culinary arts/hospitality.

PROGRAM AFFILIATION

American Culinary Federation; Confrerie de la Chaine des Rotisseurs; International Association of Culinary Professionals; National Restaurant Association; National Restaurant Association Educational Foundation; Texas Chefs Association; Texas Restaurant Association.

AREAS OF STUDY

Baking; beverage management; culinary skill development; food preparation; food purchasing; garde-manger; international cuisine; kitchen management; menu and facilities design; nutrition; sanitation; soup, stock, sauce, and starch production.

Galveston College *(continued)*

FACILITIES
Bake shop; 3 classrooms; 2 computer laboratories; food production kitchen; learning resource center; library; snack shop; student lounge; teaching kitchen.

STUDENT PROFILE
50 total: 35 full-time; 15 part-time.

FACULTY
3 total: 1 full-time; 2 part-time. 3 are industry professionals; 1 is a culinary-certified teacher. Prominent faculty: Paul Mendoza; Mia Holsapple; Kaye Gable; Peter Mitchell, MHM. Faculty-student ratio: 1:20.

SPECIAL PROGRAMS
320-hour paid internships, ServSafe certification.

TYPICAL EXPENSES
In-state tuition: $750 per semester. Out-of-state tuition: $1230 per semester. Program-related fees include $275 for knives; $150 for books; $100 for uniforms; $192 for lab fee.

FINANCIAL AID
In 2004, 7 scholarships were awarded (average award was $200); 15 loans were granted (average loan was $750). Employment placement assistance is available.

APPLICATION INFORMATION
Students may begin participation in January, February, March, April, May, June, July, August, September, October, and November. Applications are accepted continuously. In 2004, 50 applied; 50 were accepted. Applicants must submit a formal application.

CONTACT
Paul Mendoza, Director, Culinary Arts Academy, 4015 Avenue Q, Galveston, TX 77550-7496. Telephone: 409-944-1304. Fax: 409-944-1511. E-mail: chef@gc.edu. World Wide Web: http://www.gc.edu/chef.

LAMAR UNIVERSITY

Family and Consumer Sciences - Hospitality Management

Beaumont, Texas

GENERAL INFORMATION
Public, coeducational, university. Urban campus. Founded in 1923. Accredited by Southern Association of Colleges and Schools.

PROGRAM INFORMATION
Offered since 1986. Accredited by American Culinary Federation Accrediting Commission, American Dietetic Association. Program calendar is divided into semesters. 2-year certificate in lodging. 2-year certificate in restaurant management. 2-year certificate in culinary arts. 2-year master's degree in family and consumer sciences. 4-year bachelor's degree in hospitality management.

PROGRAM AFFILIATION
American Dietetic Association; American Hotel and Lodging Association; Confrerie de la Chaine des Rotisseurs; Council on Hotel, Restaurant, and Institutional Education; International Food Service Executives Association; National Restaurant Association; National Restaurant Association Educational Foundation.

AREAS OF STUDY
Baking; beverage management; buffet catering; controlling costs in food service; culinary French; culinary skill development; food preparation; food purchasing; food service math; garde-manger; introduction to food service; kitchen management; management and human resources; meal planning; meat cutting; menu and facilities design; nutrition; nutrition and food service; patisserie; restaurant opportunities; sanitation; saucier; soup, stock, sauce, and starch production; wines and spirits.

FACILITIES
2 cafeterias; catering service; 6 classrooms; 2 computer laboratories; demonstration laboratory; food production kitchen; laboratory; 2 learning resource centers; 6 lecture rooms; library; teaching kitchen.

STUDENT PROFILE
70 total: 50 full-time; 20 part-time.

FACULTY
5 total: 4 full-time; 1 part-time. 3 are industry professionals; 1 is a culinary-certified teacher; 2 are registered dietitians. Prominent faculty: Molly J. Dahm, PhD; Charles Duit, CEC; Connie Ruiz, PhD, RD; Amy Shows, PhD, RD. Faculty-student ratio: 1:15.

SPECIAL PROGRAMS
Culinary competitions, paid internships with local properties.

TYPICAL EXPENSES
In-state tuition: $2200 per semester. Out-of-state tuition: $6000 per semester. Program-related fees include $100 for lab fee per class; $100 for cutlery; $40 for uniform.

FINANCIAL AID
In 2004, 14 scholarships were awarded (average award was $500–$1000). Employment placement assistance is available. Employment opportunities within the program are available.

HOUSING
Coed housing available. Average on-campus housing cost per month: $500.

APPLICATION INFORMATION
Students may begin participation in January and August. Applications are accepted continuously. In 2004, 20 applied; 14 were accepted. Applicants must submit a formal application and an essay.

CONTACT
Molly J. Dahm, Program Director, Hospitality Management, Family and Consumer Sciences - Hospitality Management, 211 Redbird Lane, Box 10035, Beaumont, TX 77710. Telephone: 409-880-1744. Fax: 409-880-8666. E-mail: dahmmj@hal.lamar.edu. World Wide Web: http://www.lamar.edu.

NORTHWOOD UNIVERSITY, TEXAS CAMPUS

Hotel, Restaurant, and Resort Management

Cedar Hill, Texas

GENERAL INFORMATION
Private, coeducational, four-year college. Suburban campus. Founded in 1965. Accredited by North Central Association of Colleges and Schools.

PROGRAM INFORMATION
Offered since 1966. Program calendar is divided into quarters. 2-year associate degree in hotel, restaurant, resort management. 4-year bachelor's degree in hotel, restaurant, resort management.

PROGRAM AFFILIATION
Council on Hotel, Restaurant, and Institutional Education; Institute of Food Technologists; National Restaurant Association; National Restaurant Association Educational Foundation.

AREAS OF STUDY
Beverage management; food preparation; food purchasing; food service communication; food service math; introduction to food service; kitchen management; management and human resources; meal planning; menu and facilities design; nutrition; nutrition and food service; restaurant opportunities; sanitation.

FACILITIES
Classroom; demonstration laboratory; lecture room.

STUDENT PROFILE
35 total: 34 full-time; 1 part-time. 33 are under 25 years old; 1 is between 25 and 44 years old.

FACULTY
2 total: 1 full-time; 1 part-time. 1 is an industry professional. Prominent faculty: Michael Lansing. Faculty-student ratio: 1:18.

SPECIAL PROGRAMS
Trip to NRA trade show in Chicago, FS/TEC 2005 International Food Service Technology Exhibition.

TYPICAL EXPENSES
Application fee: $25. Tuition: $14,625 per year full-time, $304 per credit hour part-time.

FINANCIAL AID
In 2004, 1 scholarship was awarded (award was $1250). Employment placement assistance is available. Employment opportunities within the program are available.

HOUSING
Single-sex housing available. Average on-campus housing cost per month: $378.

APPLICATION INFORMATION
Students may begin participation in March, September, and December. Applications are accepted continuously. In 2004, 39 applied; 26 were accepted. Applicants must submit a formal application and an essay.

CONTACT
Sylvia Correa, Director of Admissions, Hotel, Restaurant, and Resort Management, 1114 West FM 1382, Cedar Hill, TX 75104. Telephone: 800-927-9663. Fax: 972-291-3824. E-mail: xadmit@northwood.edu. World Wide Web: http://www.northwood.edu.

ODESSA COLLEGE

Culinary Arts

Odessa, Texas

GENERAL INFORMATION
Public, coeducational, two-year college. Urban campus. Founded in 1946. Accredited by Southern Association of Colleges and Schools.

PROGRAM INFORMATION
Offered since 1990. Program calendar is divided into semesters. 1-semester certificate in food preparation cook. 16-month associate degree in culinary arts. 2-semester certificate in food production cook.

PROGRAM AFFILIATION
Council on Hotel, Restaurant, and Institutional Education.

AREAS OF STUDY
Baking; beverage management; buffet catering; confectionery show pieces; controlling costs in food service; convenience cookery; culinary skill development; food preparation; food purchasing; food service communication; food service math; garde-manger; international cuisine; introduction to food service; kitchen management; management and human resources; meal planning; meat cutting; menu and facilities design; nutrition; nutrition and food service; patisserie; restaurant opportunities; sanitation; saucier; seafood processing; soup, stock, sauce, and starch production; wines and spirits.

FACILITIES
Bake shop; cafeteria; classroom; food production kitchen; gourmet dining room; laboratory; learning resource center; library; public restaurant.

Odessa College *(continued)*

TYPICAL STUDENT PROFILE
38 total: 30 full-time; 8 part-time.

SPECIAL PROGRAMS
4-day practicum in Las Vegas, Nevada.

FINANCIAL AID
Employment placement assistance is available. Employment opportunities within the program are available.

APPLICATION INFORMATION
Students may begin participation in January and August. Applications are accepted continuously. Applicants must submit a formal application.

CONTACT
Director of Admissions, Culinary Arts, 201 West University, Odessa, TX 79764-7127. Telephone: 915-335-6320. World Wide Web: http://www.odessa.edu.

ST. PHILIP'S COLLEGE

Department of Tourism, Hospitality, and Culinary Arts

San Antonio, Texas

GENERAL INFORMATION
Public, coeducational, two-year college. Urban campus. Founded in 1898. Accredited by Southern Association of Colleges and Schools.

PROGRAM INFORMATION
Offered since 1980. Accredited by American Culinary Federation Accrediting Commission, American Dietetic Association. Program calendar is divided into semesters. 1-year certificate in baking principles. 1-year certificate in culinary studies. 2-year associate degree in restaurant management. 2-year associate degree in culinary arts.

PROGRAM AFFILIATION
American Culinary Federation; American Dietetic Association; Confrerie de la Chaine des Rotisseurs; Council on Hotel, Restaurant, and Institutional Education; National Restaurant Association; National Restaurant Association Educational Foundation; Texas Hotel/Motel Association.

AREAS OF STUDY
Baking; beverage management; controlling costs in food service; culinary skill development; food preparation; food purchasing; garde-manger; international cuisine; kitchen management; nutrition; nutrition and food service; sanitation.

FACILITIES
Bake shop; 3 classrooms; computer laboratory; demonstration laboratory; food production kitchen; garden; 3 lecture rooms; library; public restaurant.

TYPICAL STUDENT PROFILE
450 total: 250 full-time; 200 part-time. 275 are under 25 years old; 125 are between 25 and 44 years old; 50 are over 44 years old.

SPECIAL PROGRAMS
Culinary competition, practicum work experience.

FINANCIAL AID
Employment placement assistance is available. Employment opportunities within the program are available.

APPLICATION INFORMATION
Students may begin participation in January, May, and August. Applications are accepted continuously. Applicants must submit a formal application.

CONTACT
Director of Admissions, Department of Tourism, Hospitality, and Culinary Arts, 1801 Martin Luther King Drive, San Antonio, TX 78203. Telephone: 210-531-3315. Fax: 210-531-3351. World Wide Web: http://www.accd.edu/spc.

SAN JACINTO COLLEGE–CENTRAL CAMPUS

Culinary Arts/Restaurant Management/Dietetic Technology

Pasadena, Texas

GENERAL INFORMATION
Public, coeducational, two-year college. Suburban campus. Founded in 1961. Accredited by Southern Association of Colleges and Schools.

PROGRAM INFORMATION
Program calendar is divided into semesters. 1-year certificate in dietetic technology. 1-year certificate in restaurant management. 1-year certificate in culinary arts. 2-year associate degree in dietetic technology. 2-year associate degree in culinary arts. 2-year associate degree in restaurant management.

PROGRAM AFFILIATION
Texas Restaurant Association.

AREAS OF STUDY
Baking; beverage management; buffet catering; confectionery show pieces; controlling costs in food service; convenience cookery; culinary French; culinary skill development; food preparation; food purchasing; food service communication; food service math; garde-manger; international cuisine; introduction to food service; kitchen management; management and human resources; meal planning; meat cutting; meat fabrication; menu and facilities design; nutrition; nutrition and food service;

patisserie; restaurant opportunities; sanitation; saucier; seafood processing; soup, stock, sauce, and starch production; wines and spirits.

FACILITIES
Cafeteria; catering service; 4 classrooms; food production kitchen; lecture room; library; snack shop.

TYPICAL STUDENT PROFILE
80 total: 45 full-time; 35 part-time.

SPECIAL PROGRAMS
Paid internships.

FINANCIAL AID
Employment placement assistance is available.

APPLICATION INFORMATION
Students may begin participation in January, June, and September. Applications are accepted continuously. Applicants must interview; submit a formal application and take the Texas Academic Skills Program test.

CONTACT
Director of Admissions, Culinary Arts/Restaurant Management/Dietetic Technology, 8060 Spencer Highway, Pasadena, TX 77501-2007. Telephone: 281-542-2099. Fax: 281-478-2790.

SOUTH TEXAS COLLEGE

McAllen, Texas

GENERAL INFORMATION
Public, coeducational, two-year college. Suburban campus. Founded in 1993. Accredited by Southern Association of Colleges and Schools.

PROGRAM INFORMATION
Offered since 1997. Program calendar is divided into semesters. 1-year certificate in commercial cooking. 2-year associate degree in restaurant management. 2-year associate degree in culinary arts.

AREAS OF STUDY
Baking; beverage management; buffet catering; controlling costs in food service; culinary skill development; food preparation; food purchasing; food service math; garde-manger; international cuisine; management and human resources; meat fabrication; menu and facilities design; nutrition and food service; patisserie; sanitation; saucier; soup, stock, sauce, and starch production.

FACILITIES
Cafeteria; food production kitchen; lecture room; library; teaching kitchen.

TYPICAL STUDENT PROFILE
60 total: 50 full-time; 10 part-time.

FINANCIAL AID
Employment placement assistance is available.

APPLICATION INFORMATION
Students may begin participation in January and August. Applications are accepted continuously. Applicants must submit a formal application.

CONTACT
Director of Admissions, PO Box 9701, McAllen, TX 78502-9701. Telephone: 956-928-3514. Fax: 956-688-2032. World Wide Web: http://www.stcc.cc.tx.us/culinary.

STEPHEN F. AUSTIN STATE UNIVERSITY

Department of Human Services

Nacogdoches, Texas

GENERAL INFORMATION
Public, coeducational, university. Small-town setting. Founded in 1923. Accredited by Southern Association of Colleges and Schools.

PROGRAM INFORMATION
Offered since 1992. Program calendar is divided into semesters. 18-month-2 year master's degree in food and nutrition. 4-year bachelor's degree in hospitality administration. 4- to 5-year bachelor's degree in food/nutrition/dietetics.

PROGRAM AFFILIATION
American Dietetic Association; Council on Hotel, Restaurant, and Institutional Education; Institute of Food Technologists.

AREAS OF STUDY
Food preparation; food purchasing; introduction to food service; management and human resources; menu and facilities design; nutrition; sanitation.

FACILITIES
Cafeteria; catering service; 2 classrooms; computer laboratory; 2 demonstration laboratories; 2 laboratories; 5 lecture rooms; library; 2 teaching kitchens.

TYPICAL STUDENT PROFILE
162 total: 153 full-time; 9 part-time.

SPECIAL PROGRAMS
Dietetic internship.

FINANCIAL AID
Employment placement assistance is available.

HOUSING
Coed, apartment-style, and single-sex housing available.

APPLICATION INFORMATION
Students may begin participation in January, June, and August. Applications are accepted continuously. Applicants must submit a formal application.

Stephen F. Austin State University (*continued*)

CONTACT
Director of Admissions, Department of Human Services, Box 13014, SFA Station, Nacogdoches, TX 75962. Telephone: 936-468-4502. Fax: 936-468-2140. World Wide Web: http://www.sfasu.edu/hms/department.

TEXAS A&M UNIVERSITY-KINGSVILLE

Food and Nutrition Science

Kingsville, Texas

GENERAL INFORMATION
Public, coeducational, university. Small-town setting. Founded in 1925. Accredited by Southern Association of Colleges and Schools.

PROGRAM INFORMATION
Accredited by American Dietetic Association. Program calendar is divided into semesters. 4-year bachelor's degree in food and nutrition science.

PROGRAM AFFILIATION
American Dietetic Association.

AREAS OF STUDY
Food preparation; food service communication; introduction to food service; kitchen management; management and human resources; meal planning; menu and facilities design; nutrition; nutrition and food service.

FACILITIES
Laboratory; lecture room; teaching kitchen.

TYPICAL STUDENT PROFILE
29 total: 21 full-time; 8 part-time. 21 are under 25 years old; 5 are between 25 and 44 years old; 3 are over 44 years old.

FINANCIAL AID
Employment opportunities within the program are available.

HOUSING
Coed, apartment-style, and single-sex housing available.

APPLICATION INFORMATION
Students may begin participation in January, June, July, and August. Applications are accepted continuously. Applicants must submit a formal application.

CONTACT
Director of Admissions, Food and Nutrition Science, MSC 105, Kingsville, TX 78363. Telephone: 361-593-2315. Fax: 361-593-2195. World Wide Web: http://www.tamuk.edu.

TEXAS CULINARY ACADEMY

Austin, Texas

GENERAL INFORMATION
Private, coeducational, culinary institute. Urban campus. Founded in 1981. Accredited by Council on Occupational Education.

PROGRAM INFORMATION
Offered since 2002. Program calendar is continuous. 15-month associate degree in Le Cordon Bleu Culinary Arts.

AREAS OF STUDY
Baking; beverage management; buffet catering; confectionery show pieces; controlling costs in food service; convenience cookery; culinary French; culinary skill development; food preparation; food purchasing; food service communication; food service math; garde-manger; international cuisine; introduction to food service; kitchen management; management and human resources; meal planning; meat cutting; meat fabrication; menu and facilities design; nutrition; nutrition and food service; patisserie; restaurant opportunities; sanitation; saucier; seafood processing; soup, stock, sauce, and starch production; wines and spirits.

FACILITIES
3 classrooms; computer laboratory; demonstration laboratory; 2 food production kitchens; gourmet dining room; learning resource center; lecture room; library; public restaurant; student lounge; 6 teaching kitchens.

SPECIAL PROGRAMS
270-hour paid externship, culinary competitions.

FINANCIAL AID
Program-specific awards include payment plans to be paid in full by graduation. Employment placement assistance is available. Employment opportunities within the program are available.

APPLICATION INFORMATION
Students may begin participation in January, February, April, May, July, August, October, and November. Applications are accepted continuously. Applicants must interview; submit a formal application and have a high school diploma or GED.

CONTACT
Director of Admissions, 11400 Burnet Road, Suite 2100, Austin, TX 78758. Telephone: 512-837-2665. Fax: 512-977-9753. World Wide Web: http://www.txca.com.

Texas State Technical College– Waco Campus

Culinary Arts/Food Service

Waco, Texas

GENERAL INFORMATION

Public, coeducational, two-year college. Suburban campus. Founded in 1965. Accredited by Southern Association of Colleges and Schools.

PROGRAM INFORMATION

Offered since 1968. Program calendar is divided into semesters. 12-month certificate in food service/culinary arts. 18-month associate degree in food service/culinary arts. 9-month diploma in dietary management.

PROGRAM AFFILIATION

Council on Hotel, Restaurant, and Institutional Education; National Restaurant Association; National Restaurant Association Educational Foundation; Texas Restaurant Association.

AREAS OF STUDY

Baking; buffet catering; controlling costs in food service; culinary skill development; food preparation; food purchasing; food service communication; food service math; garde-manger; introduction to food service; kitchen management; management and human resources; meal planning; meat cutting; meat fabrication; menu and facilities design; nutrition; nutrition and food service; sanitation; saucier; seafood processing; soup, stock, sauce, and starch production; wines and spirits.

FACILITIES

Bake shop; bakery; cafeteria; catering service; 3 classrooms; computer laboratory; demonstration laboratory; food production kitchen; gourmet dining room; laboratory; learning resource center; lecture room; library; public restaurant; teaching kitchen.

TYPICAL STUDENT PROFILE

48 total: 18 full-time; 30 part-time.

SPECIAL PROGRAMS

Cooperative education, culinary competitions, attendance at state and national trade shows.

FINANCIAL AID

Employment placement assistance is available.

HOUSING

Apartment-style and single-sex housing available.

APPLICATION INFORMATION

Students may begin participation in January, May, and September. Applications are accepted continuously. Applicants must submit a formal application.

CONTACT

Director of Admissions, Culinary Arts/Food Service, 3801 Campus Drive, Waco, TX 76705-1695. Telephone: 254-867-4868. Fax: 254-867-3663. World Wide Web: http://www.tstc.edu/.

University of Houston

Conrad N. Hilton College of Hotel and Restaurant Management

Houston, Texas

GENERAL INFORMATION

Public, coeducational, university. Urban campus. Founded in 1927. Accredited by Southern Association of Colleges and Schools.

PROGRAM INFORMATION

Offered since 1969. Accredited by Council on Hotel, Restaurant and Institutional Education. Program calendar is divided into semesters. 1-year certificate in wine and spirit management institute (commercial beverage management). 1- to 2-year master's degree in hospitality management. 4-year bachelor's degree in hotel and restaurant management.

PROGRAM AFFILIATION

American Hotel and Lodging Association; Confrerie de la Chaine des Rotisseurs; Council on Hotel, Restaurant, and Institutional Education; Greater Houston Restaurant Association; International Food Service Executives Association; International Hotel and Restaurant Association; National Restaurant Association; National Restaurant Association Educational Foundation; Society of Wine Educators; Texas Restaurant Association.

AREAS OF STUDY

Beverage management; buffet catering; catering (management); controlling costs in food service; culinary skill development; facilities layout and design; food and beverage management; food and beverage of gaming operation; food and beverage service; food preparation; food purchasing; food service communication; food service math; hotel food and beverage management; international cuisine; introduction to food service; kitchen management; management and human resources; meal planning; menu and facilities design; nutrition and food service; restaurant development; restaurant management; restaurant opportunities; sanitation; wines and spirits.

FACILITIES

Bake shop; cafeteria; catering service; 6 classrooms; coffee shop; 4 computer laboratories; 2 demonstration laboratories; 8 food production kitchens; gourmet dining room; 2 laboratories; learning resource center; library; 2 public restaurants; snack shop; student lounge; 2 teaching kitchens.

University of Houston (continued)

STUDENT PROFILE
703 total: 572 full-time; 131 part-time.

FACULTY
42 total: 22 full-time; 20 part-time. 25 are industry professionals; 1 is a culinary-certified teacher; 24 are certified hospitality educators; 1 registered dietitian; 2 certified hotel administrators; 1 certified lodging security director. Prominent faculty: John Bowen, PhD, CHE; Agnes L. DeFranco, EdD, CHE, CHAE; Clinton Rappole, PhD, CHE; Ronald Nykiel, PhD, CHE, CHA. Faculty-student ratio: 1:23.

SPECIAL PROGRAMS
Paid internships, summer programs in France and Mexico and Hong Kong, California, and Japan to study culture, tourism, and wine production and distribution, one-week study tours of casino operations in Nevada, New Jersey, and Mississippi, and cruise management (6-day cruise in Caribbean).

TYPICAL EXPENSES
Application fee: $50. In-state tuition: $1500 per year full-time (in district), $50 per credit hour (undergraduate); $100 per credit hour for graduate part-time. Out-of-state tuition: $9780 per year full-time, $326 per credit hour (undergraduate); $376 per credit hour (graduate) part-time. Program-related fees include $15–$90 for fees for food and beverage purchases in selected courses; $450 for college fees.

FINANCIAL AID
In 2004, 127 scholarships were awarded (average award was $2500). Program-specific awards include Conrad N. Hilton College Scholarships, teaching and research assistantships for graduate students. Employment placement assistance is available. Employment opportunities within the program are available.

HOUSING
Coed and apartment-style housing available. Average on-campus housing cost per month: $337–$450. Average off-campus housing cost per month: $350–$700.

APPLICATION INFORMATION
Students may begin participation in January, May, and August. Application deadline for summer/fall is May 1. Application deadline for spring is December 1. In 2004, 375 applied; 308 were accepted. Applicants must submit a formal application and letters of reference and essay (for master's program only).

CONTACT
Danny Arocha, Enrollment Manager, Conrad N. Hilton College of Hotel and Restaurant Management, 229 C. N. Hilton Hotel-College, Houston, TX 77204-3028. Telephone: 713-743-2446. Fax: 713-743-2581. E-mail: darocha@uh.edu. World Wide Web: http://www.hrm.uh.edu/.

UNIVERSITY OF NORTH TEXAS

Hospitality Management

Denton, Texas

GENERAL INFORMATION
Public, coeducational, university. Urban campus. Founded in 1890. Accredited by Southern Association of Colleges and Schools.

PROGRAM INFORMATION
Offered since 1985. Accredited by Council on Hotel, Restaurant and Institutional Education. Program calendar is divided into semesters. 2-year master's degree in hospitality management. 4-year bachelor's degree in hospitality management.

PROGRAM AFFILIATION
American Dietetic Association; American Hotel and Lodging Association; Council on Hotel, Restaurant, and Institutional Education; International Wine & Food Society; National Restaurant Association; National Restaurant Association Educational Foundation.

AREAS OF STUDY
Controlling costs in food service; food preparation; food purchasing; international cuisine; introduction to food service; kitchen management; management and human resources; menu and facilities design; nutrition; nutrition and food service; restaurant opportunities; sanitation; wines and spirits.

FACILITIES
4 classrooms; 6 computer laboratories; 2 demonstration laboratories; 2 food production kitchens; gourmet dining room; 2 laboratories; learning resource center; 4 lecture rooms; 2 libraries; public restaurant; 2 teaching kitchens.

STUDENT PROFILE
450 full-time.

FACULTY
15 total: 10 full-time; 5 part-time. 10 are industry professionals. Prominent faculty: Joan Marie Clay, PhD; Johnny Sue Reynolds, PhD, CFCS; Richard Tas, PhD; Lea R. Dopson, EdD.

SPECIAL PROGRAMS
Faculty-supervised internships, student-operated laboratory restaurant.

TYPICAL EXPENSES
Application fee: $25. In-state tuition: $131 per hour. Out-of-state tuition: $407 per hour.

FINANCIAL AID
In 2004, 35 scholarships were awarded (average award was $1100). Employment placement assistance is available.

HOUSING
Coed and apartment-style housing available. Average off-campus housing cost per month: $500.

APPLICATION INFORMATION

Students may begin participation in January, May, June, July, and August. Applications are accepted continuously. In 2004, 180 applied; 150 were accepted. Applicants must submit a formal application.

CONTACT

Lynne Hale, Academic Counselor, Hospitality Management, PO Box 311100, Denton, TX 75057. Telephone: 940-565-2436. Fax: 940-565-4348. E-mail: lhale@smhm.unt.edu. World Wide Web: http://www.smhm.unt.edu.

UTAH

SALT LAKE COMMUNITY COLLEGE

Apprenticeship Division

Salt Lake City, Utah

GENERAL INFORMATION

Public, coeducational, two-year college. Suburban campus. Founded in 1948. Accredited by Northwest Association of Schools and Colleges.

PROGRAM INFORMATION

Offered since 1985. Accredited by American Culinary Federation Accrediting Commission. Program calendar is divided into semesters. 2-year associate degree in apprentice chef. 2-year certificate in professional management development program.

PROGRAM AFFILIATION

American Culinary Federation; National Restaurant Association Educational Foundation.

AREAS OF STUDY

Baking; beverage management; buffet catering; controlling costs in food service; culinary French; culinary skill development; food preparation; food purchasing; food service math; garde-manger; international cuisine; introduction to food service; kitchen management; meal planning; meat cutting; meat fabrication; menu and facilities design; nutrition; nutrition and food service; restaurant opportunities; sanitation; saucier; seafood processing; soup, stock, sauce, and starch production; wines and spirits.

FACILITIES

Catering service; 10 classrooms; computer laboratory; food production kitchen; garden; gourmet dining room; laboratory; learning resource center; library; student lounge; teaching kitchen.

TYPICAL STUDENT PROFILE

99 total: 74 full-time; 25 part-time.

FINANCIAL AID

Program-specific awards include 5 Gertrude Marshall Scholarships, 1 National Restaurant Association Scholarship ($500–$2000). Employment placement assistance is available.

APPLICATION INFORMATION

Students may begin participation in January and August. Applications are accepted continuously. Applicants must submit a formal application.

CONTACT

Director of Admissions, Apprenticeship Division, PO Box 30808, Salt Lake City, UT 84130-0808. Telephone: 801-957-4066. Fax: 801-957-4895.

UTAH VALLEY STATE COLLEGE

Culinary Arts Institute

Orem, Utah

GENERAL INFORMATION

Public, coeducational, four-year college. Suburban campus. Founded in 1941. Accredited by Northwest Association of Schools and Colleges.

PROGRAM INFORMATION

Offered since 1990. Accredited by Council on Hotel, Restaurant and Institutional Education. Program calendar is divided into semesters. 24-month associate degree in culinary arts.

PROGRAM AFFILIATION

American Culinary Federation; National Restaurant Association; National Restaurant Association Educational Foundation.

AREAS OF STUDY

Baking; beverage management; buffet catering; controlling costs in food service; culinary French; culinary skill development; food preparation; food purchasing; food service communication; food service math; garde-manger; ice carving; international cuisine; introduction to food service; kitchen management; management and human resources; meal planning; meat cutting; menu and facilities design; nutrition; nutrition and food service; patisserie; restaurant opportunities; sanitation; saucier; seafood processing; soup, stock, sauce, and starch production; wines and spirits.

FACILITIES

Bake shop; catering service; 3 classrooms; computer laboratory; food production kitchen; gourmet dining room; learning resource center; lecture room; library; public restaurant; teaching kitchen.

STUDENT PROFILE

36 full-time. 31 are under 25 years old; 3 are between 25 and 44 years old; 2 are over 44 years old.

Utah Valley State College (*continued*)

FACULTY

5 total: 3 full-time; 2 part-time. 2 are industry professionals; 2 are master chefs; 1 is a master baker; 1 is a culinary-certified teacher. Prominent faculty: Greg Forte, CEC, CCE, AAC; R. Troy Wilson, CEC; Diana Fallis, CCC, CEPC. Faculty-student ratio: 1:10.

SPECIAL PROGRAMS

ACF Conference and competitions, field trips to food service operations in Las Vegas, internship experience in Europe, Alaska, and other locations.

TYPICAL EXPENSES

Application fee: $30. In-state tuition: $1290 per and fees $221 semester. Out-of-state tuition: $4515 per and fees $221 semester. Program-related fees include $150 for uniforms; $515 for knives; $500 for kitchen fees (per semester).

FINANCIAL AID

In 2004, 12 scholarships were awarded (average award was $500). Program-specific awards include work-study program in college banquet halls. Employment placement assistance is available. Employment opportunities within the program are available.

HOUSING

Average off-campus housing cost per month: $300.

APPLICATION INFORMATION

Students may begin participation in January and August. Applications are accepted continuously. Applicants must submit a formal application and complete prerequisite courses.

CONTACT

Julie Slocum, Advisor, Culinary Arts Institute, 800 West University Parkway, Orem, UT 84058. Telephone: 801-863-8914. Fax: 801-863-6103. E-mail: slocumju@uvsc.edu. World Wide Web: http://www.uvsc.edu.

VERMONT

CHAMPLAIN COLLEGE

Hospitality Industry Management

Burlington, Vermont

GENERAL INFORMATION

Private, coeducational, four-year college. Urban campus. Founded in 1878. Accredited by New England Association of Schools and Colleges.

PROGRAM INFORMATION

Offered since 1979. Program calendar is divided into semesters. 1-year certificate in tourism and event management. 1-year certificate in hotel/restaurant management. 2-year associate degree in tourism and event management. 2-year associate degree in hotel/restaurant management. 4-year bachelor's degree in tourism and event management. 4-year bachelor's degree in hotel/restaurant management.

PROGRAM AFFILIATION

American Culinary Federation; Council on Hotel, Restaurant, and Institutional Education; National Restaurant Association; Vermont Lodging and Restaurant Association.

AREAS OF STUDY

Controlling costs in food service; culinary skill development; food preparation; food purchasing; food service math; introduction to food service; kitchen management; management and human resources; nutrition; nutrition and food service; restaurant opportunities; sanitation; soup, stock, sauce, and starch production.

FACILITIES

5 classrooms; 2 computer laboratories; 2 demonstration laboratories; food production kitchen; gourmet dining room; 2 laboratories; learning resource center; lecture room; library; public restaurant; snack shop; student lounge; teaching kitchen; bistro.

TYPICAL STUDENT PROFILE

85 total: 70 full-time; 15 part-time. 80 are under 25 years old; 5 are between 25 and 44 years old.

SPECIAL PROGRAMS

10-day spring break European tour, paid internship, resort management apprenticeship (during senior year).

FINANCIAL AID

Employment placement assistance is available. Employment opportunities within the program are available.

HOUSING

Coed, apartment-style, and single-sex housing available.

APPLICATION INFORMATION

Students may begin participation in January and August. Applications are accepted continuously. Applicants must submit a formal application, letters of reference, an essay, SAT or ACT scores; TOEFL score for international applicants.

CONTACT

Director of Admissions, Hospitality Industry Management, 163 South Willard Street, Burlington, VT 05401. Telephone: 802-860-2727. Fax: 802-860-2767. World Wide Web: http://www.champlain.edu.

JOHNSON STATE COLLEGE

Hospitality and Tourism Management

Johnson, Vermont

GENERAL INFORMATION
Public, coeducational, four-year college. Rural campus. Founded in 1828. Accredited by New England Association of Schools and Colleges.

PROGRAM INFORMATION
Offered since 1986. Program calendar is divided into semesters. 4-year bachelor's degree in tourism management. 4-year bachelor's degree in food service management. 4-year bachelor's degree in lodging management.

PROGRAM AFFILIATION
American Hotel and Lodging Association; Council on Hotel, Restaurant, and Institutional Education; National Restaurant Association; National Restaurant Association Educational Foundation; Vermont Lodging and Restaurant Association.

AREAS OF STUDY
Beverage management; controlling costs in food service; dining room management; food preparation; food purchasing; introduction to food service; kitchen management; management and human resources; menu and facilities design; menu explosion analysis; restaurant opportunities; sanitation; wines and spirits.

FACILITIES
Cafeteria; catering service; 6 classrooms; coffee shop; 3 computer laboratories; food production kitchen; learning resource center; 2 lecture rooms; library; snack shop; student lounge.

STUDENT PROFILE
71 full-time. 58 are under 25 years old; 13 are between 25 and 44 years old.

FACULTY
8 total: 4 full-time; 4 part-time. 1 is a culinary-certified teacher; 1 is a certified hospitality educator. Prominent faculty: Reed A. Fisher; Todd Comen; Norm Mcelvany; James Black. Faculty-student ratio: 1:16.

SPECIAL PROGRAMS
Paid internships and General Manager Mentorship Program, trip to the New York Hotel Show, 4-day tour of hotel and restaurant facilities in Canada.

TYPICAL EXPENSES
Application fee: $30. In-state tuition: $3156 per semester full-time (in district), $263 per per credit hour part-time. Out-of-state tuition: $6816 per semester full-time, $568 per per credit hour part-time. Tuition for international students: $6816 per semester full-time, $568 per per credit hour part-time. Program-related fees include $150 for food production course; $40 for foodservice management course; $40 for beverage management course.

FINANCIAL AID
In 2004, 25 scholarships were awarded (average award was $1000). Employment placement assistance is available.

HOUSING
Coed, apartment-style, and single-sex housing available. Average on-campus housing cost per month: $375. Average off-campus housing cost per month: $400.

APPLICATION INFORMATION
Students may begin participation in January and August. Applications are accepted continuously. In 2004, 78 applied; 51 were accepted. Applicants must submit a formal application, letters of reference, an essay, interview (recommended).

CONTACT
Penny Howrigan, Associate Dean for Enrollment Services, Hospitality and Tourism Management, 337 College Hill, Johnson, VT 05656. Telephone: 802-635-1219. Fax: 802-635-1230. E-mail: jscapply@jsc.vsc.edu. World Wide Web: http://www.jsc.vsc.edu.

NEW ENGLAND CULINARY INSTITUTE

Occupational Studies in Culinary Arts

Montpelier, Vermont

GENERAL INFORMATION
Private, coeducational, culinary institute. Small-town setting. Founded in 1980. Accredited by Accrediting Commission of Career Schools and Colleges of Technology.

PROGRAM INFORMATION
Offered since 1980. Accredited by Accrediting Commission of Career Schools and Colleges of Technology. Program calendar is divided into quarters. 10-month certificate in pastry arts. 10-month certificate in baking. 10-month certificate in basic cooking. 15-month associate degree in hospitality and restaurant management. 18-month bachelor's degree in hospitality and restaurant management (must have 60 prior credits). 2-year associate degree in baking and pastry arts. 2-year associate degree in culinary arts.

PROGRAM AFFILIATION
American Culinary Federation; American Institute of Wine & Food; Council on Hotel, Restaurant, and Institutional Education; International Association of Culinary Professionals; James Beard Foundation, Inc.; National Restaurant Association; National Restaurant Association Educational Foundation; Women Chefs and Restaurateurs.

AREAS OF STUDY
Baking; beverage management; buffet catering; controlling costs in food service; culinary French; culinary skill development; food preparation; food purchasing; food

Passion = Profession

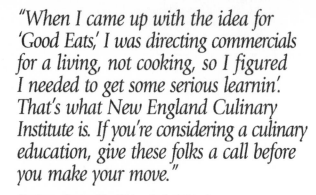

"When I came up with the idea for 'Good Eats,' I was directing commercials for a living, not cooking, so I figured I needed to get some serious learnin'. That's what New England Culinary Institute is. If you're considering a culinary education, give these folks a call before you make your move."

Alton Brown, Creator of *Good Eats* on the Food Network
James Beard Award Winner
Graduate — New England Culinary Institute

- **Hands-on**
- **Small class sizes - average 7:1 student/ teacher ratio with maximum of 10 in production classes**
- **Paid internships**
- **Enrollments in March, June, September, and December**
- **Scholarships available**
- **Named IACP "2005 Cooking School of the Year" finalist**
- **Degrees available in Culinary Arts, Baking & Pastry Arts and Hospitality & Restaurant Management**
- **Accredited Member, ACCSCT**

Transform your passion into a rewarding profession at NECI. Call us today at **877.223.6324** or visit us us at **www.neci.edu** to start your journey.

Where you learn it by living it
www.neci.edu

NEW ENGLAND CULINARY INSTITUTE®

service communication; food service math; garde-manger; introduction to food service; kitchen management; management and human resources; meal planning; meat cutting; meat fabrication; menu and facilities design; non-commercial preparation; nutrition; nutrition and food service; patisserie; restaurant opportunities; sanitation; saucier; seafood processing; soup, stock, sauce, and starch production; wines and spirits.

FACILITIES
2 bake shops; bakery; 3 cafeterias; 2 catering services; 20 classrooms; coffee shop; 2 computer laboratories; 12 food production kitchens; 2 gardens; 2 gourmet dining rooms; 2 laboratories; 2 learning resource centers; 2 libraries; 7 public restaurants; student lounge; non-commercial food kitchen.

STUDENT PROFILE
823 full-time. 544 are under 25 years old; 268 are between 25 and 44 years old; 11 are over 44 years old.

FACULTY
84 total: 84 full-time. Faculty-student ratio: 1:7 culinary arts; 1:8 basic cooking; 1:15 in food and beverage management.

SPECIAL PROGRAMS
6-month paid internship following 6-month residency in culinary arts or baking and pastry arts, 6-month paid internship following calendar year in residency in hospitality and restaurant management, 6-month paid internship following 15-week residency in basic cooking or baking and pastry arts.

TYPICAL EXPENSES
Tuition: $18,650-$20,995 per year for associate and bachelor degree programs; $8875 per year for certificate programs. Program-related fees include $400 for books (culinary arts); $250 for knives (culinary arts and basic cooking); $1000 for books (hospitality and restaurant management); $10 for books (basic cooking); $300 for knives (hospitality and restaurant management).

FINANCIAL AID
Employment placement assistance is available. Employment opportunities within the program are available.

HOUSING
Coed, apartment-style, and single-sex housing available. Average on-campus housing cost per month: $470.

APPLICATION INFORMATION
Students may begin participation in January, March, June, September, and December. Applications are accepted continuously. In 2004, 1102 applied; 750 were accepted. Applicants must interview; submit a formal application, letters of reference, an essay, high school transcripts or GED.

CONTACT
Dawn Hayward, Director of Admissions, Occupational Studies in Culinary Arts, 250 Main Street, Montpelier, VT

05602-9720. Telephone: 802-223-6324. Fax: 802-225-3280. E-mail: admissions@neci.edu. World Wide Web: http://www.neci.edu.

See display on page 340.

VIRGINIA

THE ART INSTITUTE OF WASHINGTON

Arlington, Virginia

GENERAL INFORMATION
Private, coeducational, four-year college. Suburban campus. Founded in 2000. Accredited by Southern Association of Colleges and Schools.

PROGRAM INFORMATION
Offered since 2001. Program calendar is divided into quarters. 2-year associate degree in culinary arts.

PROGRAM AFFILIATION
National Restaurant Association.

AREAS OF STUDY
Baking; beverage management; controlling costs in food service; culinary skill development; food preparation; food purchasing; food service math; garde-manger; international cuisine; introduction to food service; kitchen management; management and human resources; meal planning; meat cutting; menu and facilities design; nutrition; sanitation; soup, stock, sauce, and starch production.

FACILITIES
Bake shop; classroom; 3 food production kitchens; library.

FINANCIAL AID
Employment placement assistance is available.

HOUSING
Apartment-style housing available.

APPLICATION INFORMATION
Students may begin participation in January, April, July, and October. Applications are accepted continuously. Applicants must interview; submit a formal application, an essay, high school diploma or GED.

CONTACT
Director of Admissions, 1820 North Fort Myer Drive, Arlington, VA 22209. Telephone: 703-358-9550. Fax: 703-358-9759. World Wide Web: http://www.aiw.artinstitutes.edu/.

See color display following page 380.

JAMES MADISON UNIVERSITY

Hospitality and Tourism Management

Harrisonburg, Virginia

GENERAL INFORMATION
Public, coeducational, comprehensive institution. Small-town setting. Founded in 1908. Accredited by Southern Association of Colleges and Schools.

PROGRAM INFORMATION
Offered since 1974. Accredited by Council on Hotel, Restaurant and Institutional Education. Program calendar is divided into semesters. 4-year bachelor's degree in entertainment. 4-year bachelor's degree in meeting planning. 4-year bachelor's degree in food and beverage management. 4-year bachelor's degree in club and resort management. 4-year bachelor's degree in hospitality and tourism management.

PROGRAM AFFILIATION
Club Managers Association of America; Council on Hotel, Restaurant, and Institutional Education; National Restaurant Association; National Restaurant Association Educational Foundation.

AREAS OF STUDY
Beverage management; buffet catering; culinary skill development; food preparation; food purchasing; gastronomy; introduction to food service; management and human resources; restaurant opportunities.

FACILITIES
Classroom; computer laboratory; demonstration laboratory; lecture room; snack shop.

STUDENT PROFILE
245 total: 240 full-time; 5 part-time. 240 are under 25 years old; 5 are between 25 and 44 years old.

FACULTY
9 total: 6 full-time; 3 part-time. 7 are industry professionals; 1 is a master chef; 1 is a master baker; 1 is a culinary-certified teacher. Prominent faculty: Brett Horton; Reg Foucar-Szocki; Steve Welpott; Ronald Cereola, MBA, JD. Faculty-student ratio: 1:16.

SPECIAL PROGRAMS
Six day tour of California wineries, culinary project with The Greenbrier, paid internships.

TYPICAL EXPENSES
Application fee: $50. In-state tuition: $16,090 per year full-time (in district), $246 per per credit hour part-time. Out-of-state tuition: $25,526 per year full-time, $701 per per credit hour part-time.

FINANCIAL AID
In 2004, 7 scholarships were awarded (average award was $1000). Employment placement assistance is available. Employment opportunities within the program are available.

HOUSING
Coed and single-sex housing available. Average off-campus housing cost per month: $400.

APPLICATION INFORMATION
Students may begin participation in January, May, and August. Application deadline for fall is March 1. Application deadline for spring is October 15. In 2004, 150 applied; 35 were accepted. Applicants must submit a formal application, an essay, SAT/ACT scores.

CONTACT
Brett Horton, CMAA Virginias Chapter, Faculty Fellow, Hospitality and Tourism Management, College of Business, MSC 0205, Harrisonburg, VA 22807. Telephone: 540-568-3037. Fax: 540-568-2754. E-mail: hortonbw@jmu.edu. World Wide Web: http://www.jmu.edu/hospitality.

J. SARGEANT REYNOLDS COMMUNITY COLLEGE

School of Culinary Arts, Tourism, and Hospitality

Richmond, Virginia

GENERAL INFORMATION
Public, coeducational, two-year college. Urban campus. Founded in 1972. Accredited by Southern Association of Colleges and Schools.

PROGRAM INFORMATION
Offered since 1973. Program calendar is divided into semesters. 2-year associate degree in hospitality management. 2-year associate degree in culinary arts.

PROGRAM AFFILIATION
American Culinary Federation; Confrerie de la Chaine des Rotisseurs; Council on Hotel, Restaurant, and Institutional Education; Foodservice Educators Network International; International Association of Culinary Professionals; National Restaurant Association; National Restaurant Association Educational Foundation; Society of Wine Educators.

AREAS OF STUDY
Baking; beverage management; buffet catering; community nutrition; controlling costs in food service; culinary skill development; food and beverage service management; food preparation; food purchasing; garde-manger; international cuisine; introduction to food service; kitchen management; management and human resources; meat cutting; meat fabrication; menu and facilities design; nutrition; nutrition and food service; patisserie; restaurant opportunities; sanitation; saucier; seafood processing; soup, stock, sauce, and starch production; total quality management for hospitality; wines and spirits.

FACILITIES

Bake shop; bakery; cafeteria; catering service; 5 classrooms; 4 computer laboratories; demonstration laboratory; food production kitchen; laboratory; 3 learning resource centers; 3 lecture rooms; 3 libraries; snack shop; student lounge; 2 teaching kitchens.

STUDENT PROFILE

114 total: 44 full-time; 70 part-time. 53 are under 25 years old; 52 are between 25 and 44 years old; 9 are over 44 years old.

FACULTY

12 total: 2 full-time; 10 part-time. 9 are industry professionals; 1 is a culinary-certified teacher; 2 are registered dietitians; 1 is a certified hotel administrator. Prominent faculty: David J. Barrish, CHA; Eric Breckoff; Joseph Formica, PhD. Faculty-student ratio: 1:18.

SPECIAL PROGRAMS

Semi-annual "President's Dinner" (multi-course, white glove gastronomic event), mentorship with Virginia Chefs Association professional chefs, advanced placement for previous experience.

TYPICAL EXPENSES

In-state tuition: $76.05 per credit hour full-time (in district), $76.05 per credit hour part-time. Out-of-state tuition: $224.25 per credit hour full-time, $224.25 per credit hour part-time. Program-related fee includes $1000 for textbooks.

FINANCIAL AID

In 2004, 6 scholarships were awarded (average award was $500); 60 loans were granted (average loan was $2000). Program-specific awards include Virginia Hospitality and Travel Association Scholarship, American Hotel Foundation Scholarship. Employment placement assistance is available.

HOUSING

Average off-campus housing cost per month: $600.

APPLICATION INFORMATION

Students may begin participation in January, May, and August. Applications are accepted continuously. In 2004, 40 applied; 40 were accepted. Applicants must submit a formal application and submit a formal application and academic transcripts.

CONTACT

David J. Barrish, Director, School of Culinary Arts, Tourism, and Hospitality, 701 East Jackson Street, Richmond, VA 23219. Telephone: 804-523-5069. Fax: 804-786-5465. E-mail: dbarrish@jsr.vcc.edu. World Wide Web: http://jsr.vccs.edu/hospitality.

NORFOLK STATE UNIVERSITY

Tourism and Hospitality Management

Norfolk, Virginia

GENERAL INFORMATION

Public, coeducational, comprehensive institution. Urban campus. Founded in 1935. Accredited by Southern Association of Colleges and Schools.

PROGRAM INFORMATION

Offered since 1988. Program calendar is divided into semesters. 4-year bachelor's degree in tourism and hospitality management.

PROGRAM AFFILIATION

Council on Hotel, Restaurant, and Institutional Education; National Restaurant Association; National Restaurant Association Educational Foundation.

AREAS OF STUDY

Controlling costs in food service; food preparation; food purchasing; management and human resources; menu and facilities design.

FACILITIES

4 classrooms; 2 computer laboratories; demonstration laboratory; 2 lecture rooms; library.

STUDENT PROFILE

55 total: 51 full-time; 4 part-time.

FACULTY

3 total: 2 full-time; 1 part-time. 3 are industry professionals. Prominent faculty: Lawrence E. Epplein, CHE. Faculty-student ratio: 1:18.

SPECIAL PROGRAMS

Bachelor degree available on-line.

TYPICAL EXPENSES

Application fee: $25. In-state tuition: $204 per credit hour part-time, $3060 per per semester (15 hours) (out-of-district). Out-of-state tuition: $7965 per per semester (15 hours) full-time, $531 per credit hour part-time. Program-related fee includes $35 for matriculation fee.

FINANCIAL AID

In 2004, 9 scholarships were awarded (average award was $400). Employment placement assistance is available. Employment opportunities within the program are available.

HOUSING

Apartment-style and single-sex housing available. Average on-campus housing cost per month: $400.

APPLICATION INFORMATION

Students may begin participation in January and August. Applications are accepted continuously. Applicants must submit a formal application and SAT or ACT scores.

Norfolk State University *(continued)*

CONTACT
Lawrence E. Epplein, Interim Department Chair, Tourism and Hospitality Management, Tourism and Hospitality Management, 700 Park Avenue, Norfolk, VA 23504. Telephone: 757-823-2490. Fax: 757-823-8058. E-mail: leepplein@nsu.edu. World Wide Web: http://www.nsu.edu.

NORTHERN VIRGINIA COMMUNITY COLLEGE

Hospitality Management/Culinary Arts

Annandale, Virginia

GENERAL INFORMATION
Public, coeducational, two-year college. Suburban campus. Founded in 1965. Accredited by Southern Association of Colleges and Schools.

PROGRAM INFORMATION
Offered since 1965. Program calendar is divided into semesters. 1-year certificate in hotel management. 1-year certificate in culinary arts. 1-year certificate in food service management. 2-year associate degree in hotel management. 2-year associate degree in hospitality management. 2-year associate degree in nutrition management. 2-year associate degree in food service management.

PROGRAM AFFILIATION
American Dietetic Association; Council on Hotel, Restaurant, and Institutional Education; National Restaurant Association.

AREAS OF STUDY
Baking; buffet catering; controlling costs in food service; food preparation; food purchasing; food service communication; food service math; garde-manger; introduction to food service; management and human resources; meal planning; menu and facilities design; nutrition; nutrition and food service; patisserie; restaurant opportunities; sanitation.

FACILITIES
Cafeteria; 3 classrooms; 2 computer laboratories; demonstration laboratory; food production kitchen; garden; gourmet dining room; learning resource center; 3 lecture rooms; library; student lounge; teaching kitchen.

STUDENT PROFILE
350 total: 100 full-time; 250 part-time. 50 are under 25 years old; 250 are between 25 and 44 years old; 50 are over 44 years old.

FACULTY
10 total: 3 full-time; 7 part-time. 3 are industry professionals; 1 is a master chef; 1 is a culinary-certified teacher; 3 are registered dietitians. Prominent faculty:

Bonita Wong, CCC, CCE; Janet Sass, MS, RD; Howard Reichbart, MS; Ben Hiatt, MS. Faculty-student ratio: 1:20.

SPECIAL PROGRAMS
ACF apprenticeship program, ACF regional student hot food competitions, New York international hotel/restaurant show and tour.

TYPICAL EXPENSES
In-state tuition: $1200 per semester full-time (in district), $80 per credit hour part-time. Out-of-state tuition: $3000 per semester full-time, $225 per credit hour part-time. Program-related fees include $50–$75 for uniform; $50–$100 for knives and equipment case; $100–$300 for books.

FINANCIAL AID
In 2004, 4 scholarships were awarded (average award was $500). Program-specific awards include industry internships (paid). Employment opportunities within the program are available.

HOUSING
Average off-campus housing cost per month: $900.

APPLICATION INFORMATION
Students may begin participation in January, May, and August. Application deadline for spring is January 10. Application deadline for fall is August 23. Application deadline for summer is May 16. In 2004, 75 applied; 75 were accepted. Applicants must submit a formal application.

CONTACT
Janet M. Sass, Program Head, Hospitality Management, Hospitality Management/Culinary Arts, 8333 Little River Turnpike, Annandale, VA 22003. Telephone: 703-323-3458. Fax: 703-323-3509. E-mail: jsass@nvcc.edu. World Wide Web: http://www.nvcc.edu.

STRATFORD UNIVERSITY

School of Culinary Arts and Hospitality Management

Falls Church, Virginia

GENERAL INFORMATION
Private, coeducational, university. Suburban campus. Founded in 1976. Accredited by Accrediting Council for Independent Colleges and Schools.

PROGRAM INFORMATION
Offered since 1990. Accredited by American Culinary Federation Accrediting Commission. Program calendar is continuous. 12-month diploma in culinary arts. 15-month associate degree in baking and pastry arts. 15-month associate degree in hotel and restaurant management. 15-month associate degree in culinary arts. 30-month bachelor's degree in hospitality management.

PROGRAM AFFILIATION

American Culinary Federation; American Institute of Baking; American Institute of Wine & Food; Council on Hotel, Restaurant, and Institutional Education; Institute of Food Technologists; International Association of Culinary Professionals; National Restaurant Association; Women Chefs and Restaurateurs.

AREAS OF STUDY

Baking; controlling costs in food service; culinary skill development; food preparation; food purchasing; food service math; garde-manger; international cuisine; introduction to food service; kitchen management; management and human resources; meat fabrication; menu and facilities design; nutrition; nutrition and food service; patisserie; sanitation; saucier; seafood processing; soup, stock, sauce, and starch production; wines and spirits.

FACILITIES

Bake shop; 10 classrooms; coffee shop; computer laboratory; 3 food production kitchens; 2 gourmet dining rooms; library; public restaurant; snack shop; 2 student lounges; 4 teaching kitchens.

STUDENT PROFILE

266 total: 173 full-time; 93 part-time.

FACULTY

15 total: 12 full-time; 3 part-time. 15 are industry professionals; 5 are culinary-certified teachers. Prominent faculty: Glenn Walden, CEC, CCE; Richard King, CEC, CCE; Paul Hutchinson, CEC, CCE; Mitchell Watford, CEC. Faculty-student ratio: 1:17.

SPECIAL PROGRAMS

Guest chef demonstrations, paid internships, field trips.

TYPICAL EXPENSES

Application fee: $100. Tuition: $295 per credit hour full-time, $295 per credit hour part-time. Program-related fees include $2560 for food, uniforms, knives; $100 for activity fee.

FINANCIAL AID

In 2005, 25 scholarships were awarded (average award was $1000). Program-specific awards include American Academy of Chefs Scholarship, Nation's Capital Chefs Association Scholarship, AIWF Scholarship. Employment placement assistance is available. Employment opportunities within the program are available.

HOUSING

Apartment-style housing available. Average on-campus housing cost per month: $550. Average off-campus housing cost per month: $800.

Stratford University *(continued)*

APPLICATION INFORMATION
Students may begin participation year-round. Applications are accepted continuously. In 2005, 300 applied; 300 were accepted. Applicants must interview; submit a formal application.

CONTACT
Saibatu Kamarah, Admissions Department, School of Culinary Arts and Hospitality Management, 7777 Leesburg Pike, Suite 100, Falls Church, VA 22043. Telephone: 703-821-8570. Fax: 703-734-5336. E-mail: admissions@ stratford.edu. World Wide Web: http://www.stratford.edu.

TIDEWATER COMMUNITY COLLEGE

Culinary Arts

Norfolk, Virginia

GENERAL INFORMATION
Public, coeducational, two-year college. Urban campus. Founded in 1968. Accredited by Southern Association of Colleges and Schools.

PROGRAM INFORMATION
Offered since 1997. Accredited by ACF. Program calendar is divided into semesters. 1-year certificate in catering. 1-year certificate in classical cooking. 1-year certificate in kitchen management. 2-year associate degree in lodging management. 2-year associate degree in food and beverage management. 2-year associate degree in hospitality management culinary arts specialization.

PROGRAM AFFILIATION
American Culinary Federation; National Restaurant Association; National Restaurant Association Educational Foundation.

AREAS OF STUDY
Baking; buffet catering; controlling costs in food service; culinary French; culinary skill development; food purchasing; garde-manger; international cuisine; meat cutting; meat fabrication; nutrition; sanitation; seafood processing; soup, stock, sauce, and starch production; wines and spirits.

FACILITIES
2 classrooms; demonstration laboratory; 2 food production kitchens; gourmet dining room; library.

STUDENT PROFILE
307 total: 162 full-time; 145 part-time. 32 are under 25 years old; 68 are between 25 and 44 years old; 13 are over 44 years old.

FACULTY
10 total: 2 full-time; 8 part-time. 6 are industry professionals; 2 are culinary-certified teachers. Faculty-student ratio: 1:12.

SPECIAL PROGRAMS
Culinary competitions, cooperative education (apprenticeship).

TYPICAL EXPENSES
Application fee: $10. In-state tuition: $68.10 per credit hour full-time (in district), $68.10 per credit hour part-time. Out-of-state tuition: $215.55 per credit hour full-time, $215.55 per credit hour part-time.

FINANCIAL AID
In 2004, 2 scholarships were awarded (average award was $1500). Employment placement assistance is available. Employment opportunities within the program are available.

APPLICATION INFORMATION
Students may begin participation in January, May, and August. Applications are accepted continuously. Applicants must submit a formal application.

CONTACT
Information Center, Culinary Arts, 300 Granby Street, Norfolk, VA 23510-9956. Telephone: 757-822-1122. Fax: 757-822-1060. World Wide Web: http://www.tc.cc.va.us.

VIRGINIA INTERMONT COLLEGE

Culinary Arts Department

Bristol, Virginia

GENERAL INFORMATION
Private, coeducational, four-year college. Small-town setting. Founded in 1884. Accredited by Southern Association of Colleges and Schools.

PROGRAM INFORMATION
Offered since 2002. Program calendar is divided into semesters. 2-year associate degree in baking and pastry arts. 2-year associate degree in culinary arts. 4-year bachelor's degree in culinary management. 4-year bachelor's degree in pastry arts.

PROGRAM AFFILIATION
American Culinary Federation; Council on Hotel, Restaurant, and Institutional Education; National Restaurant Association; National Restaurant Association Educational Foundation.

AREAS OF STUDY
Baking; beverage management; breakfast; buffet catering; cake decorating; chocolate; commercial baking; confectionery show pieces; controlling costs in food service; culinary skill development; food preparation; food purchasing; food service communication; food service math; garde-manger; hospitality law; international cuisine; introduction to food service; kitchen management; management and human resources; meal planning; meat fabrication; menu and facilities design; nutrition; nutrition and food service; patisserie; restaurant opportunities;

sanitation; saucier; seafood processing; soup, stock, sauce, and starch production; wines and spirits.

FACILITIES
Bakery; catering service; 10 classrooms; 3 food production kitchens; learning resource center; 15 lecture rooms; 2 libraries; 2 public restaurants; snack shop.

STUDENT PROFILE
43 total: 40 full-time; 3 part-time.

FACULTY
6 total: 3 full-time; 3 part-time. 3 are industry professionals; 2 are culinary-certified teachers. Prominent faculty: Rick Barger; Dadang Djajadireja; William Rawstrom. Faculty-student ratio: 1:12.

SPECIAL PROGRAMS
Junior Competition Team.

TYPICAL EXPENSES
Application fee: $25. Tuition: $16,895 per year full-time, $220–$420 per credit hour part-time. Program-related fees include $395 for complete knife set and 3 sets of uniforms; $200–$500 for textbooks (per semester); $1100 for culinary program fee.

FINANCIAL AID
Program-specific awards include 200-hours practical experience (paid). Employment placement assistance is available. Employment opportunities within the program are available.

HOUSING
Coed, apartment-style, and single-sex housing available.

APPLICATION INFORMATION
Students may begin participation in January and September. Applications are accepted continuously. In 2005, 75 applied; 55 were accepted. Applicants must submit a formal application and ACT or SAT scores, high school diploma.

CONTACT
Roger Lowe, Dean of Admissions, Culinary Arts Department, 1013 Moore Street, Bristol, VA 24201. Telephone: 276-466-7856. Fax: 276-466-7855. E-mail: rogerlowe@vic.edu. World Wide Web: http://www.vic.edu.

VIRGINIA STATE UNIVERSITY

Hospitality Management

Petersburg, Virginia

GENERAL INFORMATION
Public, coeducational, university. Small-town setting. Founded in 1882. Accredited by Southern Association of Colleges and Schools.

PROGRAM INFORMATION
Offered since 1981. Accredited by Council on Hotel, Restaurant and Institutional Education, Accreditation Commission for Programs in Hospitality Administration (ACPHA). Program calendar is divided into semesters. 4-year bachelor's degree in hospitality management.

PROGRAM AFFILIATION
American Culinary Federation; American Dietetic Association; American Hotel and Lodging Association; Council on Hotel, Restaurant, and Institutional Education; International Food Service Executives Association; Multicultural Hospitality and Foodservice Alliance; National Coalition of Black Meeting Planners; National Restaurant Association; National Restaurant Association Educational Foundation; National Society for Minorities in Hospitality.

AREAS OF STUDY
Beverage management; food and beverage management; food preparation; food purchasing; lodging; meal planning; meeting and event planning; nutrition and food service; restaurant management.

FACILITIES
2 classrooms; computer laboratory; food production kitchen; gourmet dining room; lecture room; public restaurant; snack shop; teaching kitchen; lodging labs; automated front desk.

STUDENT PROFILE
85 total: 80 full-time; 5 part-time. 77 are under 25 years old; 2 are between 25 and 44 years old; 1 is over 44 years old.

FACULTY
4 total: 3 full-time; 1 part-time. 3 are industry professionals; 1 is a culinary-certified teacher. Prominent faculty: Deanne Williams, EdD, CHE; Yan Zhong, PhD; Cary Snow, CEC. Faculty-student ratio: 1:20.

SPECIAL PROGRAMS
Paid internships, conferences relating to the hospitality industry, professional development seminars, international study tour, annual food show and exhibition.

TYPICAL EXPENSES
Application fee: $25. In-state tuition: $1503 per semester. Out-of-state tuition: $5150 per semester.

FINANCIAL AID
In 2005, 8 scholarships were awarded (average award was $2000). Program-specific awards include assistance with trip costs, industry sponsorships. Employment placement assistance is available. Employment opportunities within the program are available.

HOUSING
Coed and apartment-style housing available. Average off-campus housing cost per month: $400.

Virginia State University (*continued*)

APPLICATION INFORMATION
Students may begin participation in January and August. Applications are accepted continuously. Applicants must submit an essay and submit a formal application and letters of reference.

CONTACT
Dr. Deanne Williams, Program Director, Hospitality Management, PO Box 9211, Petersburg, VA 23806. Telephone: 804-524-6753. Fax: 804-524-6843. E-mail: dwilliam@vsu.edu. World Wide Web: http://www. hospitality/hospitalitymanagement.htm.

WASHINGTON

THE ART INSTITUTE OF SEATTLE

Culinary Arts Program

Seattle, Washington

GENERAL INFORMATION
Private, coeducational, two-year college. Urban campus. Founded in 1982. Accredited by Northwest Association of Schools and Colleges.

PROGRAM INFORMATION
Offered since 1996. Accredited by American Culinary Federation Accrediting Commission. Program calendar is divided into quarters. 1-year diploma in the art of cooking. 1-year diploma in baking and pastry. 2-year associate degree in culinary arts.

PROGRAM AFFILIATION
American Culinary Federation; Confrerie de la Chaine des Rotisseurs; National Restaurant Association; National Restaurant Association Educational Foundation.

AREAS OF STUDY
Baking; beverage management; buffet catering; confectionery show pieces; controlling costs in food service; food preparation; food purchasing; food service communication; food service math; garde-manger; international cuisine; introduction to food service; kitchen management; management and human resources; meal planning; meat cutting; meat fabrication; menu and facilities design; nutrition; patisserie; sanitation; saucier; seafood processing; soup, stock, sauce, and starch production; wines and spirits.

FACILITIES
Bake shop; 3 food production kitchens; garden; gourmet dining room; learning resource center; 2 lecture rooms; library; public restaurant; 2 student lounges; 4 teaching kitchens.

TYPICAL STUDENT PROFILE
313 full-time.

SPECIAL PROGRAMS
Day tours to Pike Place Market, culinary competitions, student-run school herb and vegetable garden.

FINANCIAL AID
Employment placement assistance is available. Employment opportunities within the program are available.

HOUSING
Apartment-style housing available.

APPLICATION INFORMATION
Students may begin participation in January, April, July, and October. Applications are accepted continuously. Applicants must interview; submit a formal application and an essay.

CONTACT
Director of Admissions, Culinary Arts Program, 2323 Elliott Avenue, Seattle, WA 98121-1642. Telephone: 206-448-6600. Fax: 206-269-0275. World Wide Web: http://www.ais.edu.
See color display following page 380.

BATES TECHNICAL COLLEGE

Culinary Arts Program

Tacoma, Washington

GENERAL INFORMATION
Public, coeducational, two-year college. Urban campus. Founded in 1940. Accredited by Accrediting Commission of Career Schools and Colleges of Technology.

PROGRAM INFORMATION
Offered since 1950. Program calendar is divided into quarters. 22-month associate degree in culinary arts.

PROGRAM AFFILIATION
American Culinary Federation; Washington State Chefs Association.

AREAS OF STUDY
Baking; buffet catering; controlling costs in food service; convenience cookery; culinary French; culinary skill development; food preparation; food purchasing; food service communication; food service math; garde-manger; health and safety; international cuisine; introduction to food service; kitchen management; management and human resources; meal planning; meat cutting; meat fabrication; menu and facilities design; nutrition; nutrition and food service; patisserie; restaurant opportunities; sanitation; saucier; seafood processing; soup, stock, sauce, and starch production; wines and spirits.

FACILITIES
2 bake shops; 2 cafeterias; 2 catering services; 2 classrooms; 2 coffee shops; 2 computer laboratories; 2 demonstration laboratories; 2 food production kitchens; 2 learning resource centers; 2 lecture rooms; 2 libraries; 2 teaching kitchens.

FINANCIAL AID
Employment placement assistance is available.

APPLICATION INFORMATION
Students may begin participation year-round. Applications are accepted continuously. Applicants must interview; submit a formal application, and take COMPASS placement test.

CONTACT
Director of Admissions, Culinary Arts Program, 1101 South Yakima Avenue, Tacoma, WA 98405. Telephone: 253-680-7247. Fax: 253-680-7211. World Wide Web: http://www.bates.ctc.edu/.

BELLINGHAM TECHNICAL COLLEGE

Culinary Arts

Bellingham, Washington

GENERAL INFORMATION
Public, coeducational, two-year college. Small-town setting. Founded in 1957. Accredited by Northwest Association of Schools and Colleges.

PROGRAM INFORMATION
Offered since 1957. Accredited by American Culinary Federation Accrediting Commission. Program calendar is divided into quarters. 1-quarter certificate in pastry. 1-year certificate in culinary arts. 2-year associate degree in culinary arts.

PROGRAM AFFILIATION
American Culinary Federation; National Restaurant Association Educational Foundation.

AREAS OF STUDY
Baking; management and human resources; nutrition; sanitation.

FACILITIES
Bake shop; bakery; cafeteria; catering service; classroom; coffee shop; computer laboratory; demonstration laboratory; food production kitchen; garden; gourmet dining room; learning resource center; lecture room; library; public restaurant; snack shop; student lounge.

STUDENT PROFILE
50 full-time.

FACULTY
8 total: 3 full-time; 5 part-time. 5 are industry professionals; 2 are culinary-certified teachers. Prominent

Bellingham Technical College *(continued)*

faculty: Michael S. Baldwin, CEC, CCE; Heidi Sattenee; Brian McDonald, CCE, CEC. Faculty-student ratio: 1:24.

SPECIAL PROGRAMS
ACF culinary competitions, 6 week internship.

TYPICAL EXPENSES
Application fee: $35. Tuition: $3000 per year. Program-related fees include $1000 for books; $250 for cutlery; $100 for supplies; $350 for uniforms.

FINANCIAL AID
In 2004, 8 scholarships were awarded (average award was $750); 11 loans were granted (average loan was $4500). Program-specific awards include work study. Employment placement assistance is available. Employment opportunities within the program are available.

HOUSING
Average off-campus housing cost per month: $350–$800.

APPLICATION INFORMATION
Students may begin participation in January, April, and September. Application deadline for fall is September 17. Application deadline for winter is December 29. Application deadline for spring is April 1. In 2004, 50 applied; 50 were accepted. Applicants must submit a formal application, be at least 16 years of age, and complete an entrance exam.

CONTACT
Michael Baldwin, Chef Instructor/Department, Culinary Arts, 3028 Lindbergh Avenue, Bellingham, WA 98225. Telephone: 360-752-8400. Fax: 360-752-7400. E-mail: mbaldwin@btc.ctc.edu.

CLARK COLLEGE

Culinary Arts

Vancouver, Washington

GENERAL INFORMATION
Public, coeducational, two-year college. Urban campus. Founded in 1933. Accredited by Northwest Association of Schools and Colleges.

PROGRAM INFORMATION
Offered since 1958. Program calendar is divided into quarters. 18-month certificate in restaurant management. 18-month certificate in baking management. 21-month associate degree in baking. 21-month associate degree in restaurant management. 9-month certificate of completion in baking. 9-month certificate of completion in cooking.

PROGRAM AFFILIATION
American Culinary Federation; National Restaurant Association; National Restaurant Association Educational Foundation; Retailer's Bakery Association; The Bread Bakers Guild of America.

AREAS OF STUDY
Baking; beverage management; buffet catering; candy making; confectionery show pieces; controlling costs in food service; convenience cookery; culinary French; culinary skill development; food preparation; food purchasing; food service communication; food service math; garde-manger; introduction to food service; kitchen management; management and human resources; meal planning; meat cutting; meat fabrication; menu and facilities design; nutrition and food service; patisserie; restaurant opportunities; sanitation; saucier; seafood processing; soup, stock, sauce, and starch production; specialty cake decorating; wines and spirits.

FACILITIES
2 bake shops; bakery; cafeteria; catering service; 6 classrooms; 4 computer laboratories; 2 demonstration laboratories; 2 food production kitchens; garden; gourmet dining room; 2 learning resource centers; 3 lecture rooms; 2 libraries; 2 public restaurants; 2 snack shops; student lounge; 5 teaching kitchens; bakery retail store.

TYPICAL STUDENT PROFILE
75 full-time. 25 are under 25 years old; 40 are between 25 and 44 years old; 10 are over 44 years old.

SPECIAL PROGRAMS
Winery and restaurant tours in Portland-Seattle area, culinary arts and baking competitions.

FINANCIAL AID
Program-specific awards include lab-fee reduction and department scholarships for summer quarter students. Employment placement assistance is available. Employment opportunities within the program are available.

APPLICATION INFORMATION
Students may begin participation in January, April, June, and September. Application deadline for fall is September 20. Application deadline for winter is January 4. Application deadline for spring is April 3. Application deadline for summer is June 20. Applicants must submit a formal application.

CONTACT
Director of Admissions, Culinary Arts, 1800 East McLoughlin Boulevard, MS 19, Vancouver, WA 98663-3598. Telephone: 360-992-2143. Fax: 360-992-2839. World Wide Web: http://www.clark.edu/.

HIGHLINE COMMUNITY COLLEGE

Hotel and Tourism Management

Des Moines, Washington

GENERAL INFORMATION
Public, coeducational, two-year college. Urban campus. Founded in 1961. Accredited by Northwest Association of Schools and Colleges.

PROGRAM INFORMATION
Offered since 1986. Program calendar is divided into quarters. 1-year certificate in hotel and tourism management. 2-year associate degree in hotel and tourism management.

PROGRAM AFFILIATION
Council on Hotel, Restaurant, and Institutional Education; International Association of Culinary Professionals; Washington State Hotel & Lodging Association.

AREAS OF STUDY
Beverage management; food and beverage management; management and human resources.

FACILITIES
Classroom; library.

TYPICAL STUDENT PROFILE
60 total: 50 full-time; 10 part-time. 6 are under 25 years old; 48 are between 25 and 44 years old; 6 are over 44 years old.

SPECIAL PROGRAMS
660-hour internship, articulated transfer to four-year programs in U.S. and Switzerland, Event, Meeting and Conference Planning Certificate.

FINANCIAL AID
Program-specific awards include CHRIE scholarships, Lodging Management Program and ProStart scholarships. Employment opportunities within the program are available.

APPLICATION INFORMATION
Students may begin participation in January, April, and September. Applications are accepted continuously. Applicants must submit a formal application.

CONTACT
Director of Admissions, Hotel and Tourism Management, 2400 South 240th Street, Des Moines, WA 98198-9800. Telephone: 206-878-3710 Ext. 3855. Fax: 206-870-4850. World Wide Web: http://flightline.highline.edu/hoteltourism.

LAKE WASHINGTON TECHNICAL COLLEGE

Culinary Arts

Kirkland, Washington

GENERAL INFORMATION
Public, coeducational, two-year college. Suburban campus. Founded in 1949.

PROGRAM INFORMATION
Offered since 1983. Accredited by American Culinary Federation Accrediting Commission. Program calendar is divided into quarters. 4-quarter certificate in bakery arts. 4-quarter certificate in culinary arts. 6-quarter associate degree in bakery arts. 6-quarter associate degree in culinary arts.

PROGRAM AFFILIATION
American Culinary Federation; National Restaurant Association.

AREAS OF STUDY
Baking; buffet catering; controlling costs in food service; convenience cookery; culinary French; culinary skill development; food preparation; food purchasing; food service communication; food service math; garde-manger; international cuisine; introduction to food service; kitchen management; management and human resources; meal planning; meat cutting; meat fabrication; menu and facilities design; nutrition; nutrition and food service; restaurant opportunities; sanitation; saucier; seafood processing; soup, stock, sauce, and starch production.

FACILITIES
Bake shop; cafeteria; classroom; computer laboratory; demonstration laboratory; food production kitchen; garden; gourmet dining room; learning resource center; lecture room; library; public restaurant; teaching kitchen.

TYPICAL STUDENT PROFILE
65 full-time.

SPECIAL PROGRAMS
Culinary competitions, ProStart Program for high school students.

FINANCIAL AID
Program-specific awards include Washington Restaurant Association scholarships. Employment placement assistance is available. Employment opportunities within the program are available.

APPLICATION INFORMATION
Students may begin participation in January, April, June, and September. Applications are accepted continuously. Applicants must interview; submit a formal application.

Lake Washington Technical College *(continued)*

CONTACT

Director of Admissions, Culinary Arts, 11605 132nd Avenue, NE, Kirkland, WA 98034-8506. Telephone: 425-739-8349. Fax: 425-739-8298. World Wide Web: http://www.lwtc.ctc.edu/culinaryarts.

NORTH SEATTLE COMMUNITY COLLEGE

Culinary Arts and Hospitality

Seattle, Washington

GENERAL INFORMATION

Public, coeducational, two-year college. Urban campus. Founded in 1970. Accredited by Northwest Association of Schools and Colleges.

PROGRAM INFORMATION

Offered since 1970. Accredited by American Culinary Federation Accrediting Commission. Program calendar is divided into quarters. 18-month certificate in restaurant cooking. 2-year associate degree in culinary arts and hospitality. 6-month certificate in dining room service. 6-month certificate in commercial cooking. 9-month certificate in restaurant management.

PROGRAM AFFILIATION

American Culinary Federation.

AREAS OF STUDY

Baking; convenience cookery; food preparation; food purchasing; kitchen management; management and human resources; meal planning; sanitation; saucier; soup, stock, sauce, and starch production.

FACILITIES

Bake shop; cafeteria; catering service; 4 classrooms; computer laboratory; 2 food production kitchens; gourmet dining room; laboratory; learning resource center; lecture room; library; public restaurant; teaching kitchen.

TYPICAL STUDENT PROFILE

65 total: 60 full-time; 5 part-time. 20 are under 25 years old; 35 are between 25 and 44 years old; 10 are over 44 years old.

FINANCIAL AID

Program-specific awards include professional catering association scholarships, North Seattle Rotary scholarship. Employment placement assistance is available. Employment opportunities within the program are available.

APPLICATION INFORMATION

Students may begin participation in January, April, and September. Applications are accepted continuously. Applicants must interview.

CONTACT

Director of Admissions, Culinary Arts and Hospitality, 9600 College Way North, Seattle, WA 98103-3599. Telephone: 206-528-4402. Fax: 206-527-3714. World Wide Web: http://www.northseattle.edu/culinary.

OLYMPIC COLLEGE

Culinary Arts and Hospitality Management

Bremerton, Washington

GENERAL INFORMATION

Public, coeducational, two-year college. Suburban campus. Founded in 1946. Accredited by Northwest Association of Schools and Colleges.

PROGRAM INFORMATION

Offered since 1978. Accredited by American Culinary Federation (ACF). Program calendar is divided into quarters. 18-month associate degree in culinary arts. 3-month certificate in prep cook. 6-month certificate in line cook. 9-month certificate in sous-chef. 9-month certificate in culinary arts/dining room service.

PROGRAM AFFILIATION

American Culinary Federation; Council on Hotel, Restaurant, and Institutional Education; National Association of College Services; National Restaurant Association; National Restaurant Association Educational Foundation; United States Personal Chef Association; Washington State Chefs Association.

AREAS OF STUDY

Baking; beverage management; buffet catering; controlling costs in food service; convenience cookery; culinary French; culinary skill development; food preparation; food purchasing; food service communication; food service math; garde-manger; international cuisine; introduction to food service; kitchen management; management and human resources; meal planning; meat cutting; meat fabrication; menu and facilities design; nutrition; nutrition and food service; sanitation; saucier; seafood processing; soup, stock, sauce, and starch production.

FACILITIES

Cafeteria; catering service; classroom; food production kitchen; gourmet dining room; learning resource center; lecture room; library; public restaurant; snack shop; student lounge; teaching kitchen; banquet hall.

STUDENT PROFILE

54 total: 37 full-time; 17 part-time.

FACULTY

3 total: 2 full-time; 1 part-time. 2 are industry professionals; 2 are culinary-certified teachers. Prominent faculty: Nick Giovanni; Steve Lammers, CCE; Dan Puniesto; Christopher Plemmons, CEC. Faculty-student ratio: 1:13.

SPECIAL PROGRAMS

5-day gourmet cooking class, specialty training in specific cuisine areas, 6 week internships.

TYPICAL EXPENSES

In-state tuition: $817.50 per quarter full-time (in district), $69.30 per credit part-time. Out-of-state tuition: $1333.90 per quarter full-time, $114.75 per credit part-time. Program-related fees include $50 for lab fees (includes lunch); $300 for uniforms and tools; $165 for textbooks.

FINANCIAL AID

In 2004, 2 scholarships were awarded (average award was $500); 33 loans were granted (average loan was $5000). Program-specific awards include afternoon employment opportunities in food service. Employment placement assistance is available. Employment opportunities within the program are available.

HOUSING

Average off-campus housing cost per month: $600.

APPLICATION INFORMATION

Students may begin participation in January, April, and September. Application deadline for fall is September 20. Application deadline for winter is December 30. Application deadline for spring is March 28. In 2004, 75 applied; 60 were accepted. Applicants must interview, and take pre-admission test.

CONTACT

Steve T. Lammers, Chef Instructor, Culinary Arts and Hospitality Management, 1600 Chester Avenue, Bremerton, WA 98337-1699. Telephone: 360-475-7571. Fax: 360-475-7575. E-mail: slammers@oc.ctc.edu. World Wide Web: http://www.oc.ctc.edu/~oc/.

SEATTLE CENTRAL COMMUNITY COLLEGE

Seattle Culinary Academy

Seattle, Washington

GENERAL INFORMATION

Public, coeducational, two-year college. Urban campus. Founded in 1941. Accredited by Northwest Association of Schools and Colleges.

PROGRAM INFORMATION

Offered since 1941. Accredited by American Culinary Federation Accrediting Commission, American Culinary Federation. Program calendar is divided into quarters. 5-quarter certificate of completion in specialty desserts and breads. 6-quarter associate degree in specialty desserts and breads. 6-quarter certificate of completion in culinary arts. 7-quarter associate degree in culinary arts.

PROGRAM AFFILIATION

American Culinary Federation; Council on Hotel, Restaurant, and Institutional Education; National Restaurant Association Educational Foundation; Slow Food International; The Bread Bakers Guild of America; Washington Restaurant Association; Women Chefs and Restaurateurs.

AREAS OF STUDY

Baking; buffet catering; confectionery show pieces; controlling costs in food service; culinary skill development; food preparation; food service math; garde-manger; international cuisine; introduction to food service; management and human resources; menu design; nutrition; patisserie; restaurant opportunities; sanitation; saucier; soup, stock, sauce, and starch production.

FACILITIES

Bake shop; bakery; cafeteria; catering service; 5 classrooms; computer laboratory; demonstration laboratory; 5 food production kitchens; garden; gourmet dining room; 3 lecture rooms; library; 2 public restaurants; snack shop; student lounge; student activity center.

STUDENT PROFILE

150 full-time. 40 are under 25 years old; 90 are between 25 and 44 years old; 20 are over 44 years old.

FACULTY

14 total: 9 full-time; 5 part-time. 2 are industry professionals; 6 are culinary-certified teachers; 1 is a registered dietitian. Prominent faculty: Diana Dillard; Keijiro Miyata, CCE, CEC, AAC; Scott Samuel; Linda Chauncey. Faculty-student ratio: 1:18.

SPECIAL PROGRAMS

Chef-of-the-Day (students create a menu and oversee its production for the restaurant), newly developed sustainable course, 20 hour externship and culinary competitions.

TYPICAL EXPENSES

In-state tuition: $710.25 per quarter. Out-of-state tuition: $2446.25 per quarter. Program-related fees include $100 for food lab fees; $10 for food handler's permit; $30 for technology fee (per quarter); $300 for hand tools; $200 for uniform.

FINANCIAL AID

In 2004, 9 scholarships were awarded. Program-specific awards include Les Dames D'Escoffier scholarship (full-tuition), 2-3 food-related scholarships ($700), Quillisasau Farm School Scholarships. Employment placement assistance is available.

APPLICATION INFORMATION

Students may begin participation in January, April, and September. Applications are accepted continuously. In 2004, 250 applied; 150 were accepted. Applicants must submit a formal application and COMPASS scores or college transcripts that reflect the students level of math and English.

Seattle Central Community College *(continued)*

CONTACT

Joy Gulmon-Huri, Program Manager, Seattle Culinary Academy, Mailstop 2BE2120, 1701 Broadway, Seattle, WA 98122. Telephone: 206-587-5424. Fax: 206-344-4323. E-mail: cularts@sccd.ctc.edu. World Wide Web: http://seattleculinary.com.

SOUTH PUGET SOUND COMMUNITY COLLEGE

Food and Hospitality Services

Olympia, Washington

GENERAL INFORMATION

Public, coeducational, two-year college. Suburban campus. Founded in 1970. Accredited by Northwest Association of Schools and Colleges.

PROGRAM INFORMATION

Offered since 1990. Program calendar is divided into quarters. 18-month associate degree in food service management. 18-month associate degree in food service technology. 9-month certificate in food service technology. 9-month certificate in commercial baking.

PROGRAM AFFILIATION

American Culinary Federation.

AREAS OF STUDY

Baking; buffet catering; controlling costs in food service; convenience cookery; culinary French; culinary skill development; food preparation; food purchasing; food service communication; food service math; garde-manger; international cuisine; introduction to food service; kitchen management; management and human resources; meal planning; meat cutting; meat fabrication; menu and facilities design; nutrition; nutrition and food service; patisserie; restaurant opportunities; sanitation; saucier; seafood processing; soup, stock, sauce, and starch production; wines and spirits.

FACILITIES

Bake shop; bakery; cafeteria; catering service; classroom; computer laboratory; food production kitchen; garden; gourmet dining room; laboratory; learning resource center; lecture room; library; public restaurant; student lounge; teaching kitchen.

TYPICAL STUDENT PROFILE

50 total: 40 full-time; 10 part-time.

SPECIAL PROGRAMS

Gourmet Club.

FINANCIAL AID

Program-specific awards include scholarships from endowment. Employment placement assistance is available. Employment opportunities within the program are available.

APPLICATION INFORMATION

Students may begin participation in January, April, and September. Applications are accepted continuously. Applicants must submit a formal application.

CONTACT

Director of Admissions, Food and Hospitality Services, 2011 Mottman Road, SW, Olympia, WA 98512-6292. Telephone: 360-754-7711 Ext. 5347.

SOUTH SEATTLE COMMUNITY COLLEGE

Culinary Arts Program

Seattle, Washington

GENERAL INFORMATION

Public, coeducational, two-year college. Suburban campus. Founded in 1970. Accredited by Northwest Association of Schools and Colleges.

PROGRAM INFORMATION

Offered since 1975. Accredited by American Culinary Federation Accrediting Commission. Program calendar is divided into quarters. 15-month certificate in restaurant and food service production. 15-month certificate in catering and banquet operations. 18-month certificate in pastry and specialty baking. 2-year associate degree in restaurant and food service production. 2-year associate degree in catering and banquet operations. 2-year associate degree in pastry and specialty baking.

PROGRAM AFFILIATION

American Culinary Federation; American Institute of Baking; Council on Hotel, Restaurant, and Institutional Education; National Restaurant Association; National Restaurant Association Educational Foundation.

AREAS OF STUDY

Baking; beverage management; buffet catering; confectionery show pieces; controlling costs in food service; convenience cookery; culinary skill development; food preparation; food purchasing; food service communication; food service math; garde-manger; international cuisine; introduction to food service; kitchen management; meal planning; meat cutting; nutrition; nutrition and food service; patisserie; sanitation; saucier; seafood processing; soup, stock, sauce, and starch production.

FACILITIES

Bake shop; 2 bakeries; cafeteria; 2 catering services; 8 classrooms; coffee shop; 3 computer laboratories;

demonstration laboratory; 3 food production kitchens; garden; gourmet dining room; laboratory; learning resource center; 8 lecture rooms; library; 2 public restaurants; snack shop; student lounge; 3 teaching kitchens.

TYPICAL STUDENT PROFILE
150 full-time. 60 are under 25 years old; 60 are between 25 and 44 years old; 30 are over 44 years old.

FINANCIAL AID
Employment placement assistance is available. Employment opportunities within the program are available.

APPLICATION INFORMATION
Students may begin participation in January, March, June, and September. Applications are accepted continuously. Applicants must take ASSET or COMPASS test and submit official college transcript.

CONTACT
Director of Admissions, Culinary Arts Program, 6000 16th Avenue, SW, Seattle, WA 98106-1499. Telephone: 206-764-5344. Fax: 206-768-6728. World Wide Web: http://www.chefschool.com.

SPOKANE COMMUNITY COLLEGE

Culinary Arts Department

Spokane, Washington

GENERAL INFORMATION
Public, coeducational, two-year college. Suburban campus. Founded in 1963. Accredited by Northwest Association of Schools and Colleges.

PROGRAM INFORMATION
Offered since 1963. Accredited by American Culinary Federation Accrediting Commission. Program calendar is divided into quarters. 1-year certificate in commercial baking. 2-year associate degree in commercial baking. 2-year associate degree in culinary arts. 2-year associate degree in hotel and restaurant management.

PROGRAM AFFILIATION
American Culinary Federation; National Restaurant Association; National Restaurant Association Educational Foundation; Washington State Restaurant Association.

AREAS OF STUDY
Baking; beverage management; buffet catering; controlling costs in food service; culinary skill development; food preparation; food purchasing; food service communication; food service math; garde-manger; international cuisine; introduction to food service; kitchen management; management and human resources; meal planning; meat cutting; meat fabrication; menu and facilities design; nutrition; nutrition and food service; patisserie; restaurant opportunities; sanitation; saucier; seafood processing; soup, stock, sauce, and starch production; wines and spirits.

FACILITIES
Bake shop; bakery; cafeteria; 4 classrooms; computer laboratory; 2 food production kitchens; gourmet dining room; learning resource center; 4 lecture rooms; library; public restaurant; student lounge; 2 teaching kitchens; pastry shop.

TYPICAL STUDENT PROFILE
80 full-time.

FINANCIAL AID
Program-specific awards include 6–8 Chef Boy-Ar-Dee awards ($1500). Employment placement assistance is available. Employment opportunities within the program are available.

APPLICATION INFORMATION
Students may begin participation in January, April, and September. Applications are accepted continuously. Applicants must submit a formal application and letters of reference.

CONTACT
Director of Admissions, Culinary Arts Department, North 1810 Greene Street, Spokane, WA 99207-5399. Telephone: 509-533-7284. Fax: 509-533-8108. World Wide Web: http://www.scc.spokane.edu.

WASHINGTON STATE UNIVERSITY

School of Hospitality and Business Management

Pullman, Washington

GENERAL INFORMATION
Public, coeducational, university. Rural campus. Founded in 1890. Accredited by Northwest Association of Schools and Colleges.

PROGRAM INFORMATION
Offered since 1932. Program calendar is divided into semesters. 4-year bachelor's degree in hospitality business management.

PROGRAM AFFILIATION
American Culinary Federation; Council on Hotel, Restaurant, and Institutional Education; International Food Service Executives Association; National Restaurant Association; National Restaurant Association Educational Foundation; Society for Foodservice Management; Society of Wine Educators.

AREAS OF STUDY
Baking; beverage management; buffet catering; controlling costs in food service; culinary skill development; food preparation; food purchasing; introduction to food service; kitchen management; management and human resources; menu and facilities design; nutrition; nutrition and food service; restaurant opportunities; sanitation; soup, stock, sauce, and starch production; wines and spirits.

Washington State University (*continued*)

FACILITIES

2 catering services; classroom; computer laboratory; demonstration laboratory; food production kitchen; laboratory; lecture room; library; public restaurant; teaching kitchen; expresso shop.

TYPICAL STUDENT PROFILE

187 total: 173 full-time; 14 part-time. 178 are under 25 years old; 9 are between 25 and 44 years old.

SPECIAL PROGRAMS

Food shows, paid culinary and foodservice internships, semester abroad in Switzerland.

FINANCIAL AID

Program-specific awards include special program activity scholarships. Employment opportunities within the program are available.

HOUSING

Coed, apartment-style, and single-sex housing available.

APPLICATION INFORMATION

Students may begin participation in January and August. Applications are accepted continuously. Applicants must submit a formal application.

CONTACT

Director of Admissions, School of Hospitality and Business Management, 470 Todd Hall, Pullman, WA 99164-4742. Telephone: 509-335-5766. Fax: 509-335-3857. World Wide Web: http://www.cbe.wsu.edu.

WEST VIRGINIA

MOUNTAIN STATE UNIVERSITY

Beckley, West Virginia

GENERAL INFORMATION

Private, coeducational, comprehensive institution. Small-town setting. Founded in 1933. Accredited by North Central Association of Colleges and Schools.

PROGRAM INFORMATION

Offered since 2001. Program calendar is divided into semesters. 2-year associate degree in culinary arts. 4-year bachelor's degree in culinary arts.

PROGRAM AFFILIATION

American Culinary Federation.

FACILITIES

Cafeteria; classroom; 4 computer laboratories; library; 3 teaching kitchens.

TYPICAL STUDENT PROFILE

75 total: 71 full-time; 4 part-time.

SPECIAL PROGRAMS

Culinary competitions, internship and practicum experiences, mentoring relationships.

FINANCIAL AID

Employment placement assistance is available.

HOUSING

Coed housing available.

APPLICATION INFORMATION

Students may begin participation in January and August. Applications are accepted continuously. Applicants must submit a formal application.

CONTACT

Director of Admissions, PO Box 9003, Beckley, WV 25802-9003. Telephone: 304-929-INFO. Fax: 304-253-3463. World Wide Web: http://www.mountainstate.edu.

SHEPHERD UNIVERSITY

Culinary Arts Program

Martinsburg, West Virginia

GENERAL INFORMATION

Public, coeducational, four-year college. Rural campus. Founded in 1871. Accredited by North Central Association of Colleges and Schools.

PROGRAM INFORMATION

Offered since 1993. Program calendar is divided into semesters. 1-year certificate in culinary arts. 2-year associate degree in culinary arts.

PROGRAM AFFILIATION

American Culinary Federation; National Restaurant Association.

AREAS OF STUDY

Baking; beverage management; buffet catering; confectionery show pieces; controlling costs in food service; convenience cookery; culinary French; culinary skill development; dining room service; food preparation; food purchasing; food service communication; food service math; garde-manger; introduction to food service; introduction to hospitality; kitchen management; management and human resources; meal planning; meat cutting; meat fabrication; menu and facilities design; nutrition; nutrition and food service; patisserie; restaurant opportunities; sanitation; saucier; seafood processing; soup, stock, sauce, and starch production; wines and spirits.

FACILITIES

Bake shop; bakery; cafeteria; 2 catering services; 2 classrooms; computer laboratory; demonstration laboratory; food production kitchen; laboratory; learning resource center; 21 lecture rooms; library; student lounge; 2 teaching kitchens; greenhouse.

TYPICAL STUDENT PROFILE
30 total: 20 full-time; 10 part-time. 10 are under 25 years old; 10 are between 25 and 44 years old.

SPECIAL PROGRAMS
Internship placements (paid), community projects.

FINANCIAL AID
Employment placement assistance is available. Employment opportunities within the program are available.

HOUSING
Coed, apartment-style, and single-sex housing available.

APPLICATION INFORMATION
Students may begin participation in January, May, and August. Applications are accepted continuously. Applicants must submit a formal application and academic transcripts.

CONTACT
Director of Admissions, Culinary Arts Program, 3274 Hedgesville Road, Martinsburg, WV 25401. Telephone: 304-754-7925. Fax: 304-754-7933. World Wide Web: http://www.shepherd.wvnet.edu/.

WEST VIRGINIA NORTHERN COMMUNITY COLLEGE

Culinary Arts Department

Wheeling, West Virginia

GENERAL INFORMATION
Public, coeducational, two-year college. Small-town setting. Founded in 1972. Accredited by North Central Association of Colleges and Schools.

PROGRAM INFORMATION
Offered since 1974. Accredited by American Culinary Federation Accrediting Commission. Program calendar is divided into semesters. 1-year certificate in culinary arts. 2-year associate degree in culinary arts.

PROGRAM AFFILIATION
American Culinary Federation; National Restaurant Association; National Restaurant Association Educational Foundation.

AREAS OF STUDY
Baking; confectionery show pieces; controlling costs in food service; culinary skill development; food preparation; food purchasing; garde-manger; international cuisine; management and human resources; meal planning; menu and facilities design; nutrition; patisserie; sanitation; saucier; seafood processing; soup, stock, sauce, and starch production; wines and spirits.

FACILITIES
Bake shop; 3 classrooms; 4 computer laboratories; demonstration laboratory; food production kitchen;

gourmet dining room; laboratory; 3 learning resource centers; 3 lecture rooms; 3 libraries; 3 student lounges; teaching kitchen.

TYPICAL STUDENT PROFILE
57 total: 45 full-time; 12 part-time.

FINANCIAL AID
Employment placement assistance is available. Employment opportunities within the program are available.

APPLICATION INFORMATION
Students may begin participation in January and August. Applications are accepted continuously. Applicants must submit a formal application.

CONTACT
Director of Admissions, Culinary Arts Department, 1704 Market Street, Wheeling, WV 26003. Telephone: 304-233-5900 Ext. 4273. World Wide Web: http://www.northern.wvnet.edu/.

WISCONSIN

BLACKHAWK TECHNICAL COLLEGE

Culinary Arts Program

Janesville, Wisconsin

GENERAL INFORMATION
Public, coeducational, two-year college. Rural campus. Founded in 1968. Accredited by North Central Association of Colleges and Schools.

PROGRAM INFORMATION
Offered since 1980. Accredited by American Culinary Federation Accrediting Commission, American Culinary Federation. Program calendar is divided into semesters. 2-year associate degree in culinary arts. 4-month certificate in quantity production. 4-month certificate in baking.

PROGRAM AFFILIATION
American Culinary Federation; National Restaurant Association.

AREAS OF STUDY
Baking; beverage management; buffet catering; confectionery show pieces; controlling costs in food service; culinary French; culinary skill development; food preparation; food purchasing; food service math; garde-manger; international cuisine; introduction to food service; kitchen management; management and human resources; meal planning; meat cutting; menu and facilities design; nutrition; restaurant opportunities; sanitation; saucier; seafood processing; soup, stock, sauce, and starch production; wines and spirits.

Blackhawk Technical College *(continued)*

FACILITIES

Bake shop; bakery; cafeteria; 2 classrooms; computer laboratory; demonstration laboratory; food production kitchen; gourmet dining room; laboratory; learning resource center; lecture room; library; public restaurant; teaching kitchen.

STUDENT PROFILE

83 total: 62 full-time; 21 part-time. 60 are under 25 years old; 15 are between 25 and 44 years old; 8 are over 44 years old.

FACULTY

6 total: 2 full-time; 4 part-time. 3 are industry professionals; 4 are culinary-certified teachers. Prominent faculty: Joseph Wollinger, CEC, CCE; Mark Olsen, CEC; Rob Gamble; Kate Thomas, CEPC. Faculty-student ratio: 1:8.

SPECIAL PROGRAMS

Culinary competitions, externships, National Restaurant Association show in Chicago.

TYPICAL EXPENSES

Application fee: $25. In-state tuition: $1295 per semester full-time (in district), $80 per credit part-time. Out-of-state tuition: $8493 per semester full-time, $499.60 per credit part-time. Program-related fees include $125 for uniform; $50–$250 for cutlery.

FINANCIAL AID

In 2004, 4 scholarships were awarded (average award was $750); 32 loans were granted (average loan was $1250). Employment placement assistance is available.

HOUSING

Average off-campus housing cost per month: $600.

APPLICATION INFORMATION

Students may begin participation in January and August. Application deadline for fall is August 25. Application deadline for spring is January 6. In 2004, 41 applied; 41 were accepted. Applicants must submit a formal application.

CONTACT

Joseph Wollinger, Coordinator, Culinary Arts Program, 6004 Prairie Road, Jamesville, WI 53547. Telephone: 608-757-7696. Fax: 608-743-4407. E-mail: jwollinger@blackhawk.edu. World Wide Web: http://www.blackhawk.edu/eo/associate/culinary.htm.

FOX VALLEY TECHNICAL COLLEGE

Culinary Arts and Hospitality Department

Appleton, Wisconsin

GENERAL INFORMATION

Public, coeducational, two-year college. Urban campus. Founded in 1967. Accredited by North Central Association of Colleges and Schools.

PROGRAM INFORMATION

Offered since 1973. Accredited by American Culinary Federation Accrediting Commission. Program calendar is divided into semesters. 1-year certificate in hospitality supervisor. 1-year certificate in advanced baking. 2-year associate degree in hotel and restaurant management. 2-year associate degree in culinary arts.

PROGRAM AFFILIATION

American Culinary Federation; Fox Cities Lodging and Hospitality Association; International Food Service Executives Association; National Restaurant Association; National Restaurant Association Educational Foundation; Wisconsin Restaurant Association.

AREAS OF STUDY

Baking; beverage management; buffet catering; confectionery show pieces; controlling costs in food service; convenience cookery; culinary French; culinary skill development; food preparation; food purchasing; food service communication; food service math; garde-manger; international cuisine; introduction to food service; kitchen management; management and human resources; meal planning; meat cutting; meat fabrication; menu and facilities design; nutrition; nutrition and food service; patisserie; restaurant opportunities; sanitation; saucier; seafood processing; soup, stock, sauce, and starch production; wines and spirits.

FACILITIES

Bake shop; bakery; cafeteria; catering service; 2 classrooms; computer laboratory; demonstration laboratory; 4 food production kitchens; garden; gourmet dining room; learning resource center; lecture room; library; public restaurant; snack shop; student lounge; teaching kitchen.

STUDENT PROFILE

240 total: 120 full-time; 120 part-time. 140 are under 25 years old; 50 are between 25 and 44 years old; 50 are over 44 years old.

FACULTY

8 total: 6 full-time; 2 part-time. 8 are industry professionals; 3 are culinary-certified teachers. Prominent faculty: Albert Exenberger, CEC, CCE, AAC; Jeff Igel, CEC, CCE, FMP, CFE, CDM; Scott Finley, CEC. Faculty-student ratio: 1:50 lecture; 1:12 lab.

SPECIAL PROGRAMS
Culinary and ice carving competitions, annual 7-day culinary tour (locations alternate), 4-day trip to National Restaurant Association show in Chicago.

TYPICAL EXPENSES
Application fee: $30. In-state tuition: $1800 per semester full-time (in district), $100 per credit part-time. Out-of-state tuition: $600 per credit part-time. Program-related fees include $225 for knives (beginning set); $500 for books (per semester); $100 for uniforms (per semester).

FINANCIAL AID
In 2004, 60 scholarships were awarded (average award was $250). Employment placement assistance is available. Employment opportunities within the program are available.

HOUSING
Average off-campus housing cost per month: $300.

APPLICATION INFORMATION
Students may begin participation in January, June, and August. Applications are accepted continuously. In 2004, 120 applied; 120 were accepted. Applicants must submit a formal application.

CONTACT
Jeffrey S. Igel, Chair, Culinary Arts and Hospitality Department, 1825 North Bluemound, PO Box 2277, Appleton, WI 54912-2277. Telephone: 920-735-5643. Fax: 920-735-5655. E-mail: chefjeff@fvtc.edu. World Wide Web: http://www.fvtc.edu.

GATEWAY TECHNICAL COLLEGE

Culinary Arts

Racine, Wisconsin

GENERAL INFORMATION
Public, coeducational, two-year college. Urban campus. Founded in 1911. Accredited by North Central Association of Colleges and Schools.

PROGRAM INFORMATION
Offered since 1970. Program calendar is divided into semesters. 2-semester certificate in management skills. 2-semester certificate in line cooking. 2-semester certificate in health-care services. 2-semester certificate in food and beverage. 2-semester certificate in design and service. 2-semester certificate in basic cooking skills. 2-year associate degree in culinary arts.

PROGRAM AFFILIATION
National Restaurant Association; National Restaurant Association Educational Foundation.

AREAS OF STUDY
Baking; buffet catering; controlling costs in food service; food preparation; food purchasing; garde-manger;

international cuisine; kitchen management; meal planning; nutrition; sanitation; soup, stock, sauce, and starch production.

FACILITIES
Bakery; cafeteria; catering service; 2 classrooms; computer laboratory; food production kitchen; gourmet dining room; laboratory; lecture room; library; public restaurant; student lounge; teaching kitchen.

TYPICAL STUDENT PROFILE
40 total: 30 full-time; 10 part-time. 24 are under 25 years old; 14 are between 25 and 44 years old; 2 are over 44 years old.

SPECIAL PROGRAMS
Culinary competitions.

FINANCIAL AID
Program-specific awards include Wisconsin Restaurant Association scholarships, National Restaurant Association scholarships ($800), Wisconsin School Foodservice Worker scholarships ($250). Employment placement assistance is available. Employment opportunities within the program are available.

APPLICATION INFORMATION
Students may begin participation in January and August. Applications are accepted continuously. Applicants must submit a formal application and take placement test.

CONTACT
Director of Admissions, Culinary Arts, 1001 South Main Street, Racine, WI 53403-1582. Telephone: 262-619-6406. Fax: 262-619-6301. World Wide Web: http://www.gtc.edu.

MADISON AREA TECHNICAL COLLEGE

Culinary Trades Department

Madison, Wisconsin

GENERAL INFORMATION
Public, coeducational, two-year college. Urban campus. Founded in 1911. Accredited by North Central Association of Colleges and Schools.

PROGRAM INFORMATION
Offered since 1960. Accredited by American Culinary Federation Accrediting Commission. Program calendar is divided into semesters. 1-year diploma in food service production. 1-year diploma in baking/pastry arts. 2-year associate degree in culinary arts.

PROGRAM AFFILIATION
American Culinary Federation; International Food Service Executives Association; National Restaurant Association;

Madison Area Technical College *(continued)*

National Restaurant Association Educational Foundation; Retailer's Bakery Association; The Bread Bakers Guild of America.

Areas of Study

Baking; buffet catering; controlling costs in food service; culinary French; culinary skill development; food preparation; food purchasing; food service communication; food service math; garde-manger; international cuisine; introduction to food service; management and human resources; meal planning; meat cutting; menu and facilities design; nutrition; sanitation; soup, stock, sauce, and starch production; wines and spirits.

Facilities

Bake shop; bakery; 2 cafeterias; catering service; computer laboratory; demonstration laboratory; 2 food production kitchens; gourmet dining room; learning resource center; lecture room; library; snack shop; student lounge; 2 teaching kitchens.

Student Profile

105 total: 80 full-time; 25 part-time. 63 are under 25 years old; 21 are between 25 and 44 years old; 21 are over 44 years old.

Faculty

8 total: 4 full-time; 4 part-time. 3 are industry professionals; 1 is a master baker; 4 are culinary-certified teachers. Faculty-student ratio: 1:18.

Special Programs

2-credit internship, field experiences (domestic and international), culinary competitions.

Typical Expenses

Application fee: $30. In-state tuition: $1575 per semester full-time (in district), $80.50 per credit part-time. Out-of-state tuition: $9000 per semester full-time, $510.30 per credit part-time. Program-related fees include $200 for knives; $120 for uniforms; $200–$300 for books (per semester).

Financial Aid

In 2004, 8 scholarships were awarded (average award was $350); 35 loans were granted (average loan was $2500). Employment placement assistance is available. Employment opportunities within the program are available.

Housing

Average off-campus housing cost per month: $600.

Application Information

Students may begin participation in August. Application deadline for fall is July 1. In 2004, 90 applied; 90 were accepted. Applicants must submit a formal application and academic transcripts.

Contact

Linda Williams, Administrative Assistant, Culinary Trades Department, 3550 Anderson Street, Madison, WI 53704-2599. Telephone: 608-246-6368. Fax: 608-246-6316. E-mail: lwilliams@matcmadison.edu. World Wide Web: http://matcmadison.edu.

MILWAUKEE AREA TECHNICAL COLLEGE

Culinary Arts

Milwaukee, Wisconsin

General Information

Public, coeducational, two-year college. Urban campus. Founded in 1912. Accredited by North Central Association of Colleges and Schools.

Program Information

Offered since 1954. Accredited by American Culinary Federation. Program calendar is divided into semesters. 1-year technical diploma in baking production technical diploma. 1-year technical diploma in food service technical diploma. 2-year associate degree in culinary arts.

Program Affiliation

American Culinary Federation; Council on Hotel, Restaurant, and Institutional Education; National Restaurant Association Educational Foundation; Wisconsin Restaurant Association.

Areas of Study

Baking; beverage management; buffet catering; confectionery show pieces; controlling costs in food service; culinary skill development; food preparation; food purchasing; food service math; garde-manger; international cuisine; introduction to food service; management and human resources; meal planning; menu and facilities design; nutrition; patisserie; restaurant opportunities; sanitation; soup, stock, sauce, and starch production.

Facilities

Bake shop; bakery; cafeteria; 3 classrooms; computer laboratory; demonstration laboratory; 2 food production kitchens; gourmet dining room; library; 2 teaching kitchens.

Student Profile

100 total: 65 full-time; 35 part-time. 25 are under 25 years old; 60 are between 25 and 44 years old; 15 are over 44 years old.

Faculty

15 total: 11 full-time; 4 part-time. 11 are industry professionals; 1 is a master baker; 11 are culinary-certified teachers; 2 are certified hospitality educators. Prominent faculty: John Reiss, CEC, CCE; Tom Surwillo, CEC, CCE; Paul Carrier, CCC, CFBE. Faculty-student ratio: 1:10.

Special Programs

Culinary competition.

TYPICAL EXPENSES
In-state tuition: $6100 per associate degree; $3000 for diploma. Out-of-state tuition: $34,000 per associate degree; $16,500 for diploma. Program-related fee includes $110 for cutlery knife kit.

FINANCIAL AID
In 2004, 12 scholarships were awarded (average award was $500). Program-specific awards include Five Star Culinary Endowment Grant. Employment placement assistance is available. Employment opportunities within the program are available.

HOUSING
Average off-campus housing cost per month: $400.

APPLICATION INFORMATION
Students may begin participation in January and August. Application deadline for first day of class each semester. Applicants must submit a formal application and math and reading placement tests.

CONTACT
Patricia Whalen, Instructional Chair, Culinary Arts, Culinary Arts, 700 West State Street, Milwaukee, WI 53233. Telephone: 414-297-7897. Fax: 414-297-7990. E-mail: whalenp@matc.edu. World Wide Web: http://www.matc.edu/utility/clas/prog/food/culi.htm.

MORAINE PARK TECHNICAL COLLEGE

Culinary Arts/Food Service Production

Fond du Lac, Wisconsin

GENERAL INFORMATION
Public, coeducational, two-year college. Small-town setting. Founded in 1967. Accredited by North Central Association of Colleges and Schools.

PROGRAM INFORMATION
Offered since 1976. Accredited by American Culinary Federation Accrediting Commission. Program calendar is divided into semesters. 1-semester certificate in food production. 1-semester certificate in bakery/deli. 1-year certificate in specialty baking. 1-year certificate in school food service. 1-year certificate in culinary basics. 1-year technical diploma in food service production. 2-year associate degree in culinary arts.

PROGRAM AFFILIATION
American Culinary Federation; National Restaurant Association; Wisconsin Restaurant Association.

AREAS OF STUDY
Baking; beverage management; buffet catering; controlling costs in food service; convenience cookery; culinary skill development; food preparation; food purchasing; food service communication; food service math; garde-manger;

international cuisine; introduction to food service; kitchen management; meal planning; menu and facilities design; nutrition; nutrition and food service; restaurant opportunities; sales and service; sanitation; saucier; seafood processing; soup, stock, sauce, and starch production.

FACILITIES
Bake shop; bakery; cafeteria; catering service; 2 classrooms; 3 computer laboratories; demonstration laboratory; 2 food production kitchens; gourmet dining room; learning resource center; 2 lecture rooms; library; public restaurant; snack shop; student lounge; teaching kitchen.

STUDENT PROFILE
78 total: 60 full-time; 18 part-time.

FACULTY
5 total: 3 full-time; 2 part-time. 1 is a culinary-certified teacher; 1 is a certified baker, 3 certified chefs. Prominent faculty: David Weber; James Simmers; Ron Spiech; Tom Endejan. Faculty-student ratio: 1:12.

SPECIAL PROGRAMS
Culinary competitions, National Restaurant Association Convention, attendance at Wisconsin Restaurant Association and Inn Keepers Convention.

TYPICAL EXPENSES
Application fee: $30. In-state tuition: $80.50 per credit full-time (in district), $80.50 per credit part-time. Out-of-state tuition: $510.30 per credit full-time, $510.30 per credit part-time. Program-related fees include $110 for uniforms; $105 for cutlery; $96 for material fees.

FINANCIAL AID
In 2004, 4 scholarships were awarded (average award was $500). Program-specific awards include paid internships. Employment placement assistance is available.

HOUSING
Average off-campus housing cost per month: $400.

APPLICATION INFORMATION
Students may begin participation in January, March, August, and October. Applications are accepted continuously. In 2004, 45 applied; 41 were accepted. Applicants must interview; submit a formal application.

CONTACT
Pat Olson, Dean, Business and Culinary Arts, Culinary Arts/Food Service Production, 235 North National Avenue, PO Box 1940, Fond du Lac, WI 54936-1940. Telephone: 920-924-3333. Fax: 920-924-1356. E-mail: polson@morainepark.edu. World Wide Web: http://www.morainepark.edu.

NICOLET AREA TECHNICAL COLLEGE

Culinary Arts

Rhinelander, Wisconsin

GENERAL INFORMATION
Public, coeducational, two-year college. Rural campus. Founded in 1968. Accredited by North Central Association of Colleges and Schools.

PROGRAM INFORMATION
Program calendar is divided into semesters. 1-year technical diploma in food service production. 13-credit certificate in catering. 14-credit certificate in baking. 2-year associate degree in culinary arts. 8-course certificate in food service management.

PROGRAM AFFILIATION
American Culinary Federation; National Restaurant Association; National Restaurant Association Educational Foundation; Wisconsin Restaurant Association.

AREAS OF STUDY
Baking; beverage management; buffet catering; controlling costs in food service; culinary skill development; food practicum; food preparation; food purchasing; food service math; garde-manger; international cuisine; introduction to food service; management and human resources; meal planning; menu and facilities design; nutrition; nutrition and food service; restaurant opportunities; restaurant practicum; sanitation; saucier; soup, stock, sauce, and starch production; wines and spirits.

FACILITIES
Cafeteria; classroom; demonstration laboratory; food production kitchen; gourmet dining room; learning resource center; lecture room; library; student lounge; teaching kitchen.

TYPICAL STUDENT PROFILE
40 total: 20 full-time; 20 part-time. 16 are under 25 years old; 20 are between 25 and 44 years old; 4 are over 44 years old.

SPECIAL PROGRAMS
Internship in culinary arts (2 credits), attendance at the Central Regional ACF conference, culinary competition at the Wisconsin Restaurant Association Show.

FINANCIAL AID
Program-specific awards include Wisconsin Restaurant Association scholarships, NRA Education Foundation scholarships, Professional Management Program scholarships. Employment placement assistance is available. Employment opportunities within the program are available.

APPLICATION INFORMATION
Students may begin participation in January and August. Application deadline for fall is August 15. Application deadline for spring is January 15. Applicants must submit a formal application, academic transcripts, and complete an Accuplacer test.

CONTACT
Director of Admissions, Culinary Arts, Box 518, Rhinelander, WI 54501-0518. Telephone: 715-365-4451. Fax: 715-365-4411. World Wide Web: http://www.nicoletcollege.edu.

UNIVERSITY OF WISCONSIN-STOUT

Department of Hospitality and Tourism

Menomonie, Wisconsin

GENERAL INFORMATION
Public, coeducational, comprehensive institution. Small-town setting. Founded in 1891. Accredited by North Central Association of Colleges and Schools.

PROGRAM INFORMATION
Offered since 1969. Program calendar is divided into semesters. 2-year master's degree in hospitality and tourism. 4-year bachelor's degree in hotel, restaurant, and tourism management.

PROGRAM AFFILIATION
Council on Hotel, Restaurant, and Institutional Education; National Restaurant Association; National Restaurant Association Educational Foundation.

AREAS OF STUDY
Beverage management; buffet catering; controlling costs in food service; food preparation; food purchasing; introduction to food service; kitchen management; management and human resources; meal planning; menu and facilities design; nutrition; nutrition and food service; restaurant opportunities; sanitation; soup, stock, sauce, and starch production; wines and spirits.

FACILITIES
Bake shop; cafeteria; catering service; 10 classrooms; computer laboratory; 2 food production kitchens; gourmet dining room; 5 lecture rooms; 2 public restaurants; 2 teaching kitchens.

STUDENT PROFILE
552 total: 500 full-time; 52 part-time.

FACULTY
16 total: 13 full-time; 3 part-time. 14 are industry professionals; 2 are master chefs. Prominent faculty: Jafar Jafari, PhD; Phil McGuirk; Joe Holland; Peter D'Souza. Faculty-student ratio: 1:31.

SPECIAL PROGRAMS
2-week wine and food pairing course in Palmade Mallorca (Spain) and Australia, catering opportunities.

TYPICAL EXPENSES

Application fee: $35. In-state tuition: $6591 per year. Out-of-state tuition: $16,924 per year.

FINANCIAL AID

In 2004, 40 scholarships were awarded (average award was $500). Employment placement assistance is available. Employment opportunities within the program are available.

HOUSING

Coed housing available. Average on-campus housing cost per month: $150. Average off-campus housing cost per month: $225.

APPLICATION INFORMATION

Students may begin participation in January and August. Applications are accepted continuously. In 2004, 226 applied; 170 were accepted. Applicants must submit a formal application.

CONTACT

Doug Kennedy, Program Director, Department of Hospitality and Tourism, 405 Home Economics Building, Menomonie, WI 54751. Telephone: 715-232-2543. Fax: 715-232-2588. E-mail: kennedyd@uwstout.edu. World Wide Web: http://www.uwstout.edu.

WAUKESHA COUNTY TECHNICAL COLLEGE

Hospitality and Culinary Arts Department

Pewaukee, Wisconsin

GENERAL INFORMATION

Public, coeducational, two-year college. Suburban campus. Founded in 1923. Accredited by North Central Association of Colleges and Schools.

PROGRAM INFORMATION

Offered since 1971. Accredited by American Culinary Federation Accrediting Commission. Program calendar is divided into semesters. 1-year certificate in meeting and event management. 1-year certificate in baking/pastry. 1-year diploma in culinary arts. 2-year associate degree in culinary management. 2-year associate degree in hospitality and tourism management.

PROGRAM AFFILIATION

American Culinary Federation; Council on Hotel, Restaurant, and Institutional Education; International Food Service Executives Association; National Restaurant Association; National Restaurant Association Educational Foundation; Tasters Guild International.

AREAS OF STUDY

Baking; beverage management; controlling costs in food service; culinary skill development; food preparation; food purchasing; food service math; garde-manger; international cuisine; introduction to food service; kitchen management; management and human resources; menu and facilities design; nutrition; restaurant opportunities; sanitation; soup, stock, sauce, and starch production; wines and spirits.

FACILITIES

Cafeteria; 3 computer laboratories; demonstration laboratory; food production kitchen; gourmet dining room; learning resource center; 2 lecture rooms; library; student lounge; 2 teaching kitchens.

TYPICAL STUDENT PROFILE

215 total: 75 full-time; 140 part-time.

SPECIAL PROGRAMS

2-week culinary and hospitality study tour of Europe, 1-week educational cruise with Norwegian Cruise Lines, culinary competitions.

FINANCIAL AID

Program-specific awards include funds available from WCTC foundation for international study opportunities. Employment placement assistance is available. Employment opportunities within the program are available.

APPLICATION INFORMATION

Students may begin participation in January and August. Applications are accepted continuously. Applicants must submit a formal application.

CONTACT

Director of Admissions, Hospitality and Culinary Arts Department, 800 Main Street, C-012, Pewaukee, WI 53072. Telephone: 414-691-5303. Fax: 414-691-5155. World Wide Web: http://www.wctc.edu.

WYOMING

SHERIDAN COLLEGE

Hospitality Management/Culinary Arts

Sheridan, Wyoming

GENERAL INFORMATION

Public, coeducational, two-year college. Small-town setting. Founded in 1948. Accredited by North Central Association of Colleges and Schools.

PROGRAM INFORMATION

Offered since 1994. Program calendar is divided into semesters. 1-year certificate in culinary arts. 1-year certificate in hospitality management. 2-year associate degree in hospitality management.

PROGRAM AFFILIATION

American Hotel and Lodging Association; National Restaurant Association; National Restaurant Association Educational Foundation; Wyoming Lodging and Restaurant

Sheridan College *(continued)*

Association; Wyoming State-Wide Consortium for Hospitality Management; Wyoming Travel Industry Coalition.

AREAS OF STUDY

Baking; beverage management; confectionery show pieces; controlling costs in food service; culinary skill development; food preparation; food purchasing; front office operations; garde-manger; international cuisine; introduction to food service; kitchen management; law; management and human resources; marketing; meal planning; meat cutting; meat fabrication; menu and facilities design; nutrition; nutrition and food service; restaurant opportunities; sanitation; security and loss; soup, stock, sauce, and starch production; wines and spirits.

FACILITIES

3 classrooms; 2 computer laboratories; demonstration laboratory; food production kitchen; garden; learning resource center; lecture room; library; 3 student lounges; teaching kitchen; compress video classroom.

STUDENT PROFILE

22 total: 20 full-time; 2 part-time. 14 are under 25 years old; 8 are between 25 and 44 years old.

FACULTY

2 total: 1 full-time; 1 part-time. 1 is an industry professional; 1 is a culinary-certified teacher; 1 is a certified hospitality manager. Prominent faculty: Monty Blare; Kim Eckerman. Faculty-student ratio: 1:10.

SPECIAL PROGRAMS

Attendance at Wyoming Governor's Conference on Travel and Tourism, internships (paid and unpaid), Tours of hotels, restaurants, guest ranches, ski resorts.

TYPICAL EXPENSES

In-state tuition: $670 per semester full-time (in district), $58 per credit part-time. Out-of-state tuition: $1722 per semester full-time, $150 per credit part-time. Program-related fees include $45 for online fee; $25 for shirt and name tag; $250 for cutlery/garmetsts.

FINANCIAL AID

In 2004, 6 scholarships were awarded (average award was $500). Program-specific awards include Sheridan County Liquor Dealers Association Scholarship ($750), ProMgmt. Scholarship ($850), National Tourism Foundation Scholarship-Wyoming ($500). Employment placement assistance is available. Employment opportunities within the program are available.

HOUSING

Coed and single-sex housing available. Average off-campus housing cost per month: $400.

APPLICATION INFORMATION

Students may begin participation in January and August. Applications are accepted continuously. In 2004, 5 applied; 5 were accepted. Applicants must interview; submit a formal application.

CONTACT

Monty D. Blare, Director, Hospitality Management/ Culinary Arts, Box 1500, Sheridan, WY 82801. Telephone: 307-674-6446 Ext. 3508. Fax: 307-672-2103. E-mail: mblare@sheridan.edu. World Wide Web: http://www. sheridan.edu.

CANADA

THE ART INSTITUTE OF VANCOUVER

Dubrulle Culinary Arts

Vancouver, British Columbia, Canada

GENERAL INFORMATION

Private, coeducational, culinary institute. Urban campus.

PROGRAM INFORMATION

Program calendar is divided into quarters. four eleven-week-quarter diploma in Culinary Arts. four eleven-week-quarter diploma in Baking and Pastry Arts. four eleven-week-quarter diploma in Hospitality and Restaurant Management. six eleven-week-quarter advanced diploma in Culinary Arts and Restaurant Ownership. two eleven-week- quarter certificate in Baking and Pastry Arts (Level 1 and 2). two eleven-week-quarter diploma in Entrepreneurship and Restaurant Ownership.

AREAS OF STUDY

Baking; beverage management; buffet catering; controlling costs in food service; culinary skill development; food purchasing; garde-manger; kitchen management; management and human resources; menu and facilities design; patisserie; restaurant opportunities; sanitation.

FACULTY

Prominent faculty: Chef Soren Fakstorp.

TYPICAL EXPENSES

Application fee: $50. Program-related fees include $75 for student fees (per quarter); $475 for lab fees (per quarter).

WE'RE *Tasteful* ARE YOU?

You see food as more than simple sustenance. Cooking is your art form.
We'll help you to transform your abilities into a creative career with a hands-on,
real-world education and personalized attention from our experienced faculty.

Culinary Arts
The Art Institutes℠

Administrative Office: 210 Sixth Avenue, 33rd Floor, Pittsburgh, PA 15222-2603

1.800.542.4860 • artinstitutes.edu/ptc

Degree and non-degree programs available in Culinary Arts

WE'RE OUT THERE℠
GETTING CREATIVE CAREERS STARTED.

FINANCIAL AID
Employment placement assistance is available. Employment opportunities within the program are available.

APPLICATION INFORMATION
Students may begin participation in January, April, July, and October. Applications are accepted continuously. Applicants must interview; submit a formal application, an essay, TOEFL for students whose first language is not English.

CONTACT
Admissions Director, Dubrulle Culinary Arts, 700 West Georgia Street, Vancouver, BC V6E3V7. Telephone: 866-717-8080. Fax: 604-684-8839. E-mail: aivinfo@aii.edu. World Wide Web: http://www.aiv.artinstitutes.edu/.
See color display following page 380.

CANADORE COLLEGE OF APPLIED ARTS & TECHNOLOGY

School of Hospitality and Tourism

North Bay, Ontario, Canada

GENERAL INFORMATION
Public, coeducational, technical college. Rural campus. Founded in 1967.

PROGRAM INFORMATION
Offered since 1967. Program calendar is divided into semesters. 1-year certificate in chef training. 2-year diploma in culinary management. 3-year diploma in culinary administration.

PROGRAM AFFILIATION
American Culinary Federation; Canadian Federation of Chefs and Cooks; Canadian Restaurant Association; Council on Hotel, Restaurant, and Institutional Education.

AREAS OF STUDY
Baking; beverage management; buffet catering; confectionery show pieces; controlling costs in food service; convenience cookery; culinary French; culinary skill development; food preparation; food purchasing; food service communication; food service math; garde-manger; international cuisine; introduction to food service; kitchen management; management and human resources; meal planning; meat fabrication; menu and facilities design; nutrition; nutrition and food service; patisserie; restaurant opportunities; sanitation; saucier; seafood processing; soup, stock, sauce, and starch production; wines and spirits.

FACILITIES
Bake shop; bakery; cafeteria; 4 classrooms; 2 computer laboratories; demonstration laboratory; food production kitchen; gourmet dining room; learning resource center; lecture room; library; public restaurant; student lounge; teaching kitchen; experimental food lab.

TYPICAL STUDENT PROFILE
95 total: 90 full-time; 5 part-time. 76 are under 25 years old; 16 are between 25 and 44 years old; 3 are over 44 years old.

SPECIAL PROGRAMS
Tour of culinary sites in the Caribbean region, provincial and international student competitions.

FINANCIAL AID
Employment placement assistance is available. Employment opportunities within the program are available.

HOUSING
Single-sex housing available.

APPLICATION INFORMATION
Students may begin participation in September. Application deadline for fall is May 15. Applicants must submit a formal application.

CONTACT
Director of Admissions, School of Hospitality and Tourism, 100 College Drive, North Bay, ON P1B 8K9, Canada. Telephone: 705-474-7600 Ext. 5218. Fax: 705-474-2384. World Wide Web: http://www.canadorec.on.ca.

CULINARY INSTITUTE OF CANADA

Charlottetown, Prince Edward Island, Canada

GENERAL INFORMATION
Public, coeducational, culinary institute. Urban campus. Founded in 1983.

PROGRAM INFORMATION
Offered since 1983. Program calendar is divided into trimesters. 1-year certificate in pastry arts. 2-year diploma in culinary arts.

PROGRAM AFFILIATION
Canadian Federation of Chefs and Cooks; Confrerie de la Chaine des Rotisseurs; Council on Hotel, Restaurant, and Institutional Education; International Association of Culinary Professionals.

AREAS OF STUDY
Baking; beverage management; buffet catering; confectionery show pieces; controlling costs in food service; convenience cookery; culinary French; culinary skill development; food preparation; food purchasing; food service communication; food service math; garde-manger; international cuisine; introduction to food service; kitchen management; management and human resources; meal planning; meat cutting; meat fabrication; menu and facilities design; nutrition; nutrition and food service; patisserie; restaurant opportunities; sanitation; saucier; seafood processing; soup, stock, sauce, and starch production; wines and spirits.

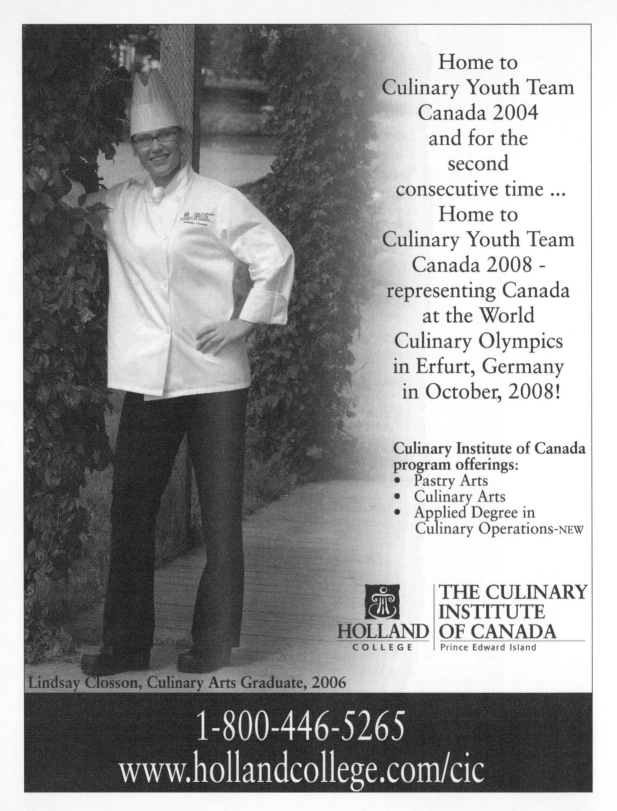

Home to
Culinary Youth Team
Canada 2004
and for the
second
consecutive time ...
Home to
Culinary Youth Team
Canada 2008 -
representing Canada
at the World
Culinary Olympics
in Erfurt, Germany
in October, 2008!

**Culinary Institute of Canada
program offerings:**
- Pastry Arts
- Culinary Arts
- Applied Degree in
  Culinary Operations-NEW

HOLLAND
COLLEGE

THE CULINARY
INSTITUTE
OF CANADA
Prince Edward Island

Lindsay Closson, Culinary Arts Graduate, 2006

1-800-446-5265
www.hollandcollege.com/cic

FACILITIES
Bake shop; bakery; cafeteria; 5 catering services; 14 classrooms; 3 computer laboratories; demonstration laboratory; 7 food production kitchens; gourmet dining room; learning resource center; lecture room; 2 public restaurants; snack shop; 2 student lounges; 6 teaching kitchens.

STUDENT PROFILE
215 full-time.

FACULTY
21 total: 15 full-time; 6 part-time. 8 are industry professionals; 10 are culinary-certified teachers. Faculty-student ratio: 1:18.

SPECIAL PROGRAMS
5-month paid internship, 1-week educational study tour, culinary competitions.

TYPICAL EXPENSES
Application fee: Can$40. Tuition: Can$6450 per year. Program-related fees include Can$400 for books; Can$300 for knives; Can$750 for lab fees; Can$1035 for uniforms and laundry; Can$90 for student union fee.

FINANCIAL AID
In 2004, 20 scholarships were awarded (average award was Can$1000). Employment placement assistance is available.

HOUSING
On-campus housing available. Average on-campus housing cost per month: Can$500.

APPLICATION INFORMATION
Students may begin participation in March and September. Application deadline for spring is January 5. Application deadline for fall is February 25. Applicants must submit a formal application and resume.

CONTACT
David Harding, Culinary Programs Manager, 4 Sydney Street, Charlottetown, PE C1A 1E9, Canada. Telephone: 902-894-6805. Fax: 902-894-6801. E-mail: dharding@hollandc.pe.ca. World Wide Web: http://www.hollandcollege.com.

See display on page 366.

DUBRULLE INTERNATIONAL CULINARY & HOTEL INSTITUTE OF CANADA

Vancouver, British Columbia, Canada

GENERAL INFORMATION
Private, coeducational, culinary institute. Urban campus. Founded in 1982.

PROGRAM INFORMATION
Offered since 1982. Accredited by Canadian Education Training Accreditation Commission, Private Post-Secondary Education Commission of British Columbia. Program calendar is divided into trimesters. Certificate in three levels of Wine and Spirit Education Trust of London. Diploma in Sommelier Guild. Diploma in food and beverage server apprenticeship. 1-year diploma in part-time culinary. 1-year diploma in hotel and resort administration. 13-week diploma in professional bread making. 17-week diploma in supervisory development and applied culinary. 2-year diploma in business management and advanced culinary operations. 4-month diploma in Asian techniques and Asian classics. 4-month diploma in hospitality business management. 4-month diploma in advanced and culinary and supervision. 4-month diploma in pastry and desserts. 4-month diploma in culinary. 6-semester associate degree in international hospitality management.

PROGRAM AFFILIATION
British Columbia Restaurant and Foodservices Association; Canadian Federation of Chefs and Cooks; Canadian Sommelier Guild; Council on Hotel, Restaurant, and Institutional Education; International Association of Culinary Professionals; Les Dames d'Escoffier; Society of Wine Educators.

AREAS OF STUDY
Baking; beverage management; buffet catering; confectionery show pieces; controlling costs in food service; convenience cookery; culinary French; culinary skill development; food preparation; food purchasing; food service communication; food service math; garde-manger; international cuisine; introduction to food service; kitchen management; management and human resources; meal planning; meat cutting; meat fabrication; menu and facilities design; nutrition; nutrition and food service; patisserie; restaurant opportunities; sanitation; saucier; seafood processing; soup, stock, sauce, and starch production; wines and spirits.

FACILITIES
Bake shop; bakery; catering service; 2 classrooms; computer laboratory; 4 demonstration laboratories; 6 food production kitchens; gourmet dining room; 3 lecture rooms; 5 teaching kitchens; herb garden.

TYPICAL STUDENT PROFILE
650 total: 300 full-time; 350 part-time. 20 are under 25 years old; 618 are between 25 and 44 years old; 12 are over 44 years old.

SPECIAL PROGRAMS
17-week international practicum placement (France, England, Hong Kong, the Philippines, or U.S.), caterers to Vancouver Symphony and U.S. Consulate, numerous demonstrations at culinary events.

FINANCIAL AID
Program-specific awards include tuition reduction for students enrolling within 12 months of high school graduation (Can$500), tuition reduction for students taking

Dubrulle International Culinary & Hotel Institute of Canada *(continued)*

a second training program (Can$500), 4 months as chef's assistant in exchange for partial tuition. Employment placement assistance is available. Employment opportunities within the program are available.

APPLICATION INFORMATION
Students may begin participation in January, May, and September. Applications are accepted continuously. Applicants must interview; submit a formal application and letters of reference.

CONTACT
Director of Admissions, 300-609 Granville Street, PO Box 10366, Vancouver, BC V7Y 1G5, Canada. Telephone: 604-738-3155. Fax: 604-738-3205. World Wide Web: http://www.dubrulle.com.

HUMBER COLLEGE OF APPLIED ARTS & TECHNOLOGY

School of Hospitality, Recreation, and Tourism

Toronto, Ontario, Canada

GENERAL INFORMATION
Public, coeducational, comprehensive institution. Urban campus. Founded in 1967.

PROGRAM INFORMATION
Offered since 1982. Program calendar is divided into semesters. 1-year certificate in culinary arts. 2-year diploma in culinary arts.

PROGRAM AFFILIATION
American Vegan Society.

AREAS OF STUDY
Baking; confectionery show pieces; controlling costs in food service; culinary French; culinary skill development; food preparation; food purchasing; food service communication; food service math; garde-manger; international cuisine; introduction to food service; kitchen management; meal planning; meat cutting; meat fabrication; menu and facilities design; nutrition; patisserie; sanitation; saucier; seafood processing; soup, stock, sauce, and starch production; wines and spirits.

FACILITIES
Bake shop; bakery; 3 cafeterias; 2 catering services; 12 classrooms; 2 coffee shops; 6 computer laboratories; demonstration laboratory; 4 food production kitchens; 4 gardens; gourmet dining room; learning resource center; lecture room; library; 2 public restaurants; 2 snack shops; 3 student lounges; teaching kitchen.

STUDENT PROFILE
365 total: 280 full-time; 85 part-time. 243 are under 25 years old; 27 are between 25 and 44 years old.

FACULTY
21 total: 6 full-time; 15 part-time. 13 are industry professionals; 12 are master chefs; 2 are master bakers; 5 are culinary-certified teachers. Prominent faculty: Klaus Theyer, CCC; Frank Formiella, CCC; Robert McCann, CCC; Anthony Bevan, CCC. Faculty-student ratio: 1:20.

SPECIAL PROGRAMS
European exchange program, BA articulation with Thames Valley University, London, culinary competition England and Penn State College USA, field practicum.

TYPICAL EXPENSES
Application fee: Can$65. Tuition: Can$2200 per year. Tuition for international students: Can$11,000 per year. Program-related fees include Can$250 for chef uniforms; Can$390 for tool kit (knives); Can$200 for textbooks; Can$70 for manuals.

FINANCIAL AID
In 2004, individual loans were awarded at Can$750. Employment placement assistance is available.

HOUSING
Coed and single-sex housing available. Average on-campus housing cost per month: Can$460. Average off-campus housing cost per month: Can$600.

APPLICATION INFORMATION
Students may begin participation in January and September. Application deadline for fall is August 1. Application deadline for winter/spring is December 1. In 2004, 890 applied; 120 were accepted. Applicants must submit a formal application.

CONTACT
Rudi Fischbacher, Culinary Programs Coordinator, School of Hospitality, Recreation, and Tourism, 205 Humber College Boulevard, Toronto, ON M9W 5L7, Canada. Telephone: 416-675-6622 Ext. 5530. Fax: 416-675-3062. E-mail: rudi.fischbacher@humber.ca. World Wide Web: http://www.humber.ca.

LE CORDON BLEU PARIS, OTTAWA CULINARY ARTS INSTITUTE

Ottawa, Ontario, Canada

GENERAL INFORMATION
Private, coeducational, culinary institute. Urban campus. Founded in 1988.

PROGRAM INFORMATION
Offered since 1988. Program calendar is divided into quarters. 10- to 12-week certificate in superior pastry. 10- to 12-week certificate in superior cuisine. 10- to 12-week

certificate in intermediate pastry. 10- to 12-week certificate in basic pastry. 10- to 12-week certificate in intermediate cuisine. 10- to 12-week certificate in basic cuisine. 4-week certificate in introduction to catering. 8-month diploma in culinary arts.

PROGRAM AFFILIATION
American Institute of Wine & Food; Canadian Federation of Chefs and Cooks; Canadian Restaurant and Food Services Association; Confrerie de la Chaine des Rotisseurs; International Association of Culinary Professionals; James Beard Foundation, Inc.; Women Chefs and Restaurateurs.

AREAS OF STUDY
Baking; buffet catering; confectionery show pieces; culinary French; culinary skill development; garde-manger; meat cutting; patisserie; saucier; soup, stock, sauce, and starch production; wines and spirits.

FACILITIES
Demonstration laboratory; food production kitchen; gourmet dining room; learning resource center; lecture room; library; public restaurant; student lounge; 2 teaching kitchens.

TYPICAL STUDENT PROFILE
270 full-time. 54 are under 25 years old; 189 are between 25 and 44 years old; 27 are over 44 years old.

SPECIAL PROGRAMS
One-week programs in cuisine and pastry topics of general interest, short workshops in boulangerie, chocolate, sugar work, and creative cakes, introduction to catering.

FINANCIAL AID
Program-specific awards include Canadian Federation of Chefs and Cooks Awards Can$5500), International Association of Culinary Professionals awards (Can$5500). Employment placement assistance is available.

APPLICATION INFORMATION
Students may begin participation in January, March, June, September, and October. Applications are accepted continuously. Applicants must submit a formal application, an essay, secondary school transcript.

CONTACT
Director of Admissions, 453 Laurier Avenue East, Ottawa, ON K1N 6R4, Canada. Telephone: 613-236-2433. Fax: 613-236-2460. World Wide Web: http://www.cordonbleu.edu.
See color display following page 380.

LIAISON COLLEGE

Culinary Arts

Hamilton, Ontario, Canada

GENERAL INFORMATION
Private, coeducational, culinary institute. Urban campus. Founded in 1996.

PROGRAM INFORMATION
Offered since 1996. Accredited by Ontario Apprenticeship Board, Ministry of Colleges and Universities. Program calendar is continuous. 300-hour diploma in cook (advanced). 300-hour diploma in cook (basic). 400-hour diploma in hospitality administration. 80-hour diploma in personal chef.

PROGRAM AFFILIATION
Canadian Federation of Chefs and Cooks; Canadian Restaurant and Food Services Association; Cuisine Canada; Women in Food Industry Management.

AREAS OF STUDY
Baking; buffet catering; controlling costs in food service; convenience cookery; culinary French; culinary skill development; food preparation; food purchasing; food service communication; food service math; garde-manger; international cuisine; introduction to food service; kitchen management; management and human resources; meal planning; menu and facilities design; nutrition; nutrition and food service; patisserie; restaurant opportunities; sanitation; saucier; seafood processing; soup, stock, sauce, and starch production.

FACILITIES
Bake shop; classroom; gourmet dining room; lecture room; teaching kitchen.

STUDENT PROFILE
800 total: 600 full-time; 200 part-time. 300 are under 25 years old; 375 are between 25 and 44 years old; 125 are over 44 years old.

FACULTY
22 total: 15 full-time; 7 part-time. 22 are culinary-certified teachers. Prominent faculty: Michael Elliott, CCC; Tom Hummel; Oleg Popov, CCC; Wanda MacDonald. Faculty-student ratio: 1:15.

SPECIAL PROGRAMS
Culinary competitions, day trips to culinary interest spots, Co-op (optional).

TYPICAL EXPENSES
Application fee: Can$100. Tuition: Can$6495 per 300 hours-4 months full-time, Can$6495 per 300 hours-10 months part-time. Program-related fees include Can$400 for utensil/tool kit; Can$200 for uniform; Can$125 for text; Can$70 for fees/dues.

Liaison College *(continued)*

FINANCIAL AID
In 2004, 4 scholarships were awarded (average award was Can$800). Program-specific awards include full-payment discounts. Employment placement assistance is available. Employment opportunities within the program are available.

HOUSING
Average off-campus housing cost per month: Can$500.

APPLICATION INFORMATION
Students may begin participation year-round. Applications are accepted continuously. In 2004, 1400 applied; 600 were accepted. Applicants must interview; submit a formal application, letters of reference, mature student testing.

CONTACT
Susanne Mikler, Director of Admissions, Culinary Arts, 1047 Main St E, Hamilton, ON L8M IN5, Canada. Telephone: 800-854-0621. Fax: 905-554-1010. E-mail: liaisonhq@liaisoncollege.com. World Wide Web: http://www.liaisoncollege.com.

MALASPINA UNIVERSITY–COLLEGE

Culinary Arts

Nanaimo, British Columbia, Canada

GENERAL INFORMATION
Public, coeducational institution. Small-town setting. Founded in 1968.

PROGRAM INFORMATION
Offered since 1968. Program calendar is continuous. 1-year certificate in culinary arts.

PROGRAM AFFILIATION
British Columbia Restaurant and Foodservices Association; Canadian Federation of Chefs and Cooks; Canadian Restaurant Association; Confrerie de la Chaine des Rotisseurs.

AREAS OF STUDY
Baking; buffet catering; confectionery show pieces; controlling costs in food service; convenience cookery; culinary French; culinary skill development; food preparation; food purchasing; food service communication; food service math; garde-manger; international cuisine; kitchen management; meal planning; meat cutting; meat fabrication; menu and facilities design; nutrition; nutrition and food service; patisserie; restaurant opportunities; sanitation; saucier; seafood processing; soup, stock, sauce, and starch production.

FACILITIES
Bake shop; 2 bakeries; 2 cafeterias; catering service; 4 classrooms; computer laboratory; demonstration laboratory; 2 food production kitchens; gourmet dining room; laboratory; learning resource center; 2 lecture rooms; library; 2 public restaurants; student lounge; 2 teaching kitchens; herb garden.

TYPICAL STUDENT PROFILE
144 full-time.

SPECIAL PROGRAMS
On-the-job training at 4 and 5 diamond hotels and restaurants, BC Hot Competition, Salon Culinaire Vancouver and Victoria.

FINANCIAL AID
Employment placement assistance is available. Employment opportunities within the program are available.

HOUSING
Coed and apartment-style housing available.

APPLICATION INFORMATION
Students may begin participation in February, March, May, August, October, and December. Applications are accepted continuously. Applicants must interview; submit a formal application, an essay, complete grade 12 or provincial equivalent, and take entrance examination.

CONTACT
Director of Admissions, Culinary Arts, 900 Fifth Street, Nanaimo, BC V9R 5S5, Canada. Telephone: 250-740-6137. Fax: 250-740-6455. World Wide Web: http://www.mala.ca.

MOUNT SAINT VINCENT UNIVERSITY

Business Administration and Tourism and Hospitality Management

Halifax, Nova Scotia, Canada

GENERAL INFORMATION
Public, coeducational, comprehensive institution. Suburban campus. Founded in 1873.

PROGRAM INFORMATION
Offered since 1986. Accredited by Canadian Association for Cooperative Education. Program calendar is divided into semesters. 2-year certificate in tourism and hospitality management. 3-year diploma in tourism and hospitality management. 4-year bachelor's degree in tourism and hospitality management.

PROGRAM AFFILIATION
Canadian Food Service Executives Association; Council on Hotel, Restaurant, and Institutional Education; Nova Scotia Restaurant and Food Service Association; Sommelier Guild of Canada; Tourism Industry Association of Canada; Tourism Industry Association of Nova Scotia; Travel and Tourism Research Association.

AREAS OF STUDY
Beverage management; controlling costs in food service; culinary skill development; food preparation; food

purchasing; food service communication; food service math; international cuisine; introduction to food service; kitchen management; management and human resources; meal planning; menu and facilities design; nutrition and food service; sanitation; wines and spirits.

FACILITIES

Classroom; computer laboratory; demonstration laboratory; food production kitchen; gourmet dining room; laboratory; learning resource center; lecture room; library; student lounge; teaching kitchen.

STUDENT PROFILE

126 total: 100 full-time; 26 part-time. 98 are under 25 years old; 25 are between 25 and 44 years old; 3 are over 44 years old.

FACULTY

4 total: 3 full-time; 1 part-time. Prominent faculty: Nancy Chesoworth, BA, BEd, MAEHD, PhD; James Macaulay, BSc, MBA, MPS; Candace Blayney, BA, BEd, MBA. Faculty-student ratio: 1:31.

SPECIAL PROGRAMS

3 work terms of cooperative education, study tour.

TYPICAL EXPENSES

Application fee: Can$30. Tuition: Can$1068 per unit of credit full-time (in district), Can$1068 per per unit of credit part-time. Tuition for international students: Can$2053 per unit of credit full-time, Can$2053 per per unit of credit part-time. Program-related fee includes Can$1068 for work term administration (per term work).

FINANCIAL AID

In 2004, 2 scholarships were awarded (average award was Can$1275). Program-specific awards include mandatory work terms. Employment placement assistance is available. Employment opportunities within the program are available.

HOUSING

Coed, apartment-style, and single-sex housing available. Average on-campus housing cost per month: Can$650. Average off-campus housing cost per month: Can$700.

APPLICATION INFORMATION

Students may begin participation in January and September. Applications are accepted continuously. In 2004, 140 applied; 86 were accepted. Applicants must submit a formal application.

CONTACT

Karl Turner, Assistant Registrar, Business Administration and Tourism and Hospitality Management, 166 Bedford Highway, Halifax, NS B3M 2J6, Canada. Telephone: 902-457-6117. Fax: 902-457-6498. E-mail: admissions@msvu.ca. World Wide Web: http://www.msvu.ca.

NIAGARA COLLEGE CANADA

Niagara Culinary Institute

Niagara on-the-Lake, Ontario, Canada

GENERAL INFORMATION

Public, coeducational, two-year college. Suburban campus. Founded in 1967.

PROGRAM INFORMATION

Offered since 1980. Accredited by Ontario Ministry of Training Colleges and Universities. Program calendar is divided into semesters. 1-year certificate in chef training. 2-year diploma in tourism marketing operations. 2-year diploma in hotel and restaurant management. 2-year diploma in culinary management (co-op). 3-month certificate in baker apprentice (advanced). 3-month certificate in baker apprentice (basic). 3-month certificate in cook apprentice (advanced). 3-month certificate in cook apprentice (basic). 4-year bachelor's degree in hospitality operations management.

PROGRAM AFFILIATION

American Culinary Federation; Canadian Federation of Chefs and Cooks; Council on Hotel, Restaurant, and Institutional Education; International Wine & Food Society; National Restaurant Association.

AREAS OF STUDY

Baking; beverage management; buffet catering; controlling costs in food service; convenience cookery; culinary French; culinary skill development; food preparation; food purchasing; food service communication; food service math; garde-manger; international cuisine; introduction to food service; kitchen management; management and human resources; meal planning; menu and facilities design; nutrition; nutrition and food service; patisserie; sanitation; saucier; seafood processing; soup, stock, sauce, and starch production; wines and spirits.

FACILITIES

Bake shop; cafeteria; catering service; 7 classrooms; 2 computer laboratories; demonstration laboratory; food production kitchen; gourmet dining room; learning resource center; lecture room; library; student lounge; 3 teaching kitchens; vineyard; pub; winery.

TYPICAL STUDENT PROFILE

256 total: 250 full-time; 6 part-time.

SPECIAL PROGRAMS

Participation in community and industry special events, cooperative work placements providing practical experience both domestically and internationally, post-graduate certificate program.

FINANCIAL AID

Program-specific awards include need-based culinary industry assistance. Employment placement assistance is available. Employment opportunities within the program are available.

Niagara College Canada *(continued)*

HOUSING
Coed housing available.

APPLICATION INFORMATION
Students may begin participation in January and September. Applications are accepted continuously. Applicants must submit a formal application.

CONTACT
Director of Admissions, Niagara Culinary Institute, 135 Taylor Road, RR #4, Niagara on-the-Lake, ON L0S 1J0, Canada. Telephone: 905-641-2252 Ext. 4636. Fax: 905-988-4317. World Wide Web: http://www.niagarac.on.ca.

NORTHERN ALBERTA INSTITUTE OF TECHNOLOGY

School of Hospitality

Edmonton, Alberta, Canada

GENERAL INFORMATION
Public, coeducational, two-year college. Urban campus. Founded in 1963.

PROGRAM INFORMATION
Offered since 1965. Program calendar is divided into semesters. 1-semester certificate in retail meat cutting. 1-year certificate in hospitality management. 1-year certificate in baking. 1-year certificate in culinary arts. 2-year diploma in hospitality management. 2-year diploma in culinary arts. 3-year journeyman's certificate in cooking or baking.

PROGRAM AFFILIATION
American Institute of Baking; Canadian Culinary Federation; Confrerie de la Chaine des Rotisseurs; Council on Hotel, Restaurant, and Institutional Education; Cuisine Canada; International Association of Culinary Professionals; International Sommelier Guild; International Wine & Food Society; The Bread Bakers Guild of America.

AREAS OF STUDY
Baking; beverage management; buffet catering; confectionery show pieces; controlling costs in food service; convenience cookery; culinary French; culinary skill development; food preparation; food purchasing; food service communication; food service math; garde-manger; gastronomy; international cuisine; introduction to food service; kitchen management; management and human resources; meat cutting; meat fabrication; menu and facilities design; nutrition; patisserie; sanitation; saucier; seafood processing; soup, stock, sauce, and starch production; wines and spirits.

FACILITIES
Bake shop; bakery; 2 cafeterias; catering service; 3 classrooms; 2 computer laboratories; demonstration laboratory; food production kitchen; gourmet dining room; 2 learning resource centers; lecture room; library; public restaurant; snack shop; 3 student lounges; 10 teaching kitchens; mixology laboratory.

STUDENT PROFILE
600 total: 380 full-time; 220 part-time. 460 are under 25 years old; 110 are between 25 and 44 years old; 30 are over 44 years old.

FACULTY
33 total: 30 full-time; 3 part-time. 3 are industry professionals; 5 are master chefs; 5 are master bakers; 20 are culinary-certified teachers. Prominent faculty: Perry Michetti, CCC; Mike Gobin, CCC; Mike Maione, CCC; Alan Domonceaux, CBS. Faculty-student ratio: 1:14.

SPECIAL PROGRAMS
Culinary Team for competitions, study tours, international student exchange.

TYPICAL EXPENSES
Application fee: Can$40. Tuition: Can$3300 per 2 semesters full-time (in district), Can$8 per instructional hour (tuition differs for night and weekend courses) part-time. Tuition for international students: Can$10,000 per 2 semesters. Program-related fees include Can$250–Can$500 for student supplies; Can$350 for knives; Can$100 for lab fee (per semester).

FINANCIAL AID
In 2004, 20–25 scholarships were awarded (average award was Can$750). Employment placement assistance is available. Employment opportunities within the program are available.

HOUSING
Average off-campus housing cost per month: Can$600.

APPLICATION INFORMATION
Students may begin participation in January and September. Applications are accepted continuously. In 2004, 600 applied; 360 were accepted. Applicants must submit a formal application, an essay, transcripts from secondary-level school.

CONTACT
Perry Michetti, Manager, School of Hospitality, 11762-106 Street, Edmonton, AB T5G 2R1, Canada. Telephone: 780-471-8679. Fax: 780-471-8914. E-mail: perrym@nait.ca. World Wide Web: http://www.nait.ca/schoolofhospitality.

NORTHWEST CULINARY ACADEMY
OF VANCOUVER

Vancouver, British Columbia, Canada

GENERAL INFORMATION
Private, coeducational, culinary institute. Urban campus. Founded in 2003.

PROGRAM INFORMATION
Offered since 2003. Accredited by Private Career Training Institutions Agency of BC "PCTIA". Program calendar is continuous. 12—15 week certificate in practicum (work experience). 15-week diploma in professional restaurant patisserie. 15-week diploma in professional pastry and bread. 15-week diploma in professional culinary.

PROGRAM AFFILIATION
British Columbia Chefs' Association; British Columbia Restaurant and Foodservices Association.

AREAS OF STUDY
Baking; buffet catering; confectionery show pieces; controlling costs in food service; culinary French; culinary skill development; food preparation; food service math; garde-manger; international cuisine; kitchen management; meal planning; meat cutting; menu and facilities design; nutrition; nutrition and food service; patisserie; sanitation; saucier; seafood processing; soup, stock, sauce, and starch production; wines and spirits.

FACILITIES
Bake shop; classroom; demonstration laboratory; food production kitchen; learning resource center; library; teaching kitchen; chef's demo station; kitchen lab; chef's table and pastry shop.

STUDENT PROFILE
140 full-time. 63 are under 25 years old; 73 are between 25 and 44 years old; 4 are over 44 years old.

FACULTY
5 total: 4 full-time; 1 part-time. 3 are industry professionals; 3 are culinary-certified teachers; 1 is a pastry chef instructor. Prominent faculty: Tony Minichiello; Christophe Kwiatkowsky; Ian Lai; Marco Ropke. Faculty-student ratio: 1:12.

SPECIAL PROGRAMS
Culinary competitions, work experience in catering setting, edible schoolyard project.

TYPICAL EXPENSES
Application fee: Can$50–$100. Program-related fees include Can$400–$495 for knife kit; Can$400 for chef's uniform; Can$110 for text book culinary; Can$135 for pastry toolkit (supplement); Can$132 for text book-pastry.

Northwest Culinary Academy of Vancouver *(continued)*

FINANCIAL AID
In 2005, 1 scholarship was awarded (award was Can$2500). Program-specific awards include see our Web site for details. Employment placement assistance is available.

HOUSING
Average off-campus housing cost per month: Can$700.

APPLICATION INFORMATION
Students may begin participation in January, April, and September. Applications are accepted continuously. Applicants must interview; submit a formal application, letters of reference, an essay, English fluency, good health (confirmed by doctor).

CONTACT
Tony Minichiello or Christophe Kwiatkowsky, Chef Instructors, Owners, 2725 Main Street, Vancouver, BC V5T 3E9, Canada. Telephone: 866-876-2433. Fax: 604-876-7023. E-mail: chefs@nwcav.com. World Wide Web: http://www.nwcav.com/.

OKANAGAN UNIVERSITY COLLEGE

Culinary Arts

Kelowna, British Columbia, Canada

GENERAL INFORMATION
Public, coeducational, comprehensive institution. Urban campus. Founded in 1964.

PROGRAM INFORMATION
Offered since 1964. Program calendar is continuous. 10-month certificate in culinary arts. 24-month diploma in advanced culinary arts. 3-year certificate in culinary arts apprenticeship. 6-month certificate in culinary arts/ESL.

AREAS OF STUDY
Baking; beverage management; buffet catering; confectionery show pieces; controlling costs in food service; convenience cookery; culinary French; culinary skill development; food preparation; food purchasing; food service communication; food service math; garde-manger; international cuisine; introduction to food service; kitchen management; management and human resources; meal planning; meat cutting; meat fabrication; menu and facilities design; nutrition; nutrition and food service; patisserie; restaurant opportunities; sanitation; saucier; seafood processing; soup, stock, sauce, and starch production; vegetarian cooking; wines and spirits.

FACILITIES
Bakery; cafeteria; catering service; 2 classrooms; coffee shop; computer laboratory; demonstration laboratory; 3 food production kitchens; garden; gourmet dining room; library; public restaurant; snack shop; teaching kitchen.

STUDENT PROFILE
260 total: 90 full-time; 170 part-time. 195 are under 25 years old; 52 are between 25 and 44 years old; 13 are over 44 years old.

FACULTY
8 total: 6 full-time; 2 part-time. 8 are industry professionals; 6 are master chefs; 1 is a master baker; 7 are culinary-certified teachers; 4 are certified chefs de cuisine. Faculty-student ratio: 1:18.

SPECIAL PROGRAMS
Culinary competitions, work placements, working/training with internationally renowned chefs.

TYPICAL EXPENSES
Application fee: Can$30. Tuition: Can$3200 per 40 weeks. Tuition for international students: Can$14,500 per 40 weeks. Program-related fee includes Can$850 for supplies (books, knives and uniform).

FINANCIAL AID
In 2004, 5 scholarships were awarded (average award was Can$250). Program-specific awards include 2 Canadian Hospitality Foundation Awards (Can$500-Can$1500). Employment opportunities within the program are available.

HOUSING
Coed housing available. Average on-campus housing cost per month: Can$400. Average off-campus housing cost per month: Can$600.

APPLICATION INFORMATION
Students may begin participation in January, March, May, September, and November. Applications are accepted continuously. In 2004, 150 applied; 90 were accepted. Applicants must submit a formal application.

CONTACT
Michelle Sinclair-McCarron, Admissions Department, Culinary Arts, 1000 K.L.O. Road, Kelowna, BC V1Y 4X8, Canada. Telephone: 250-762-5445. Fax: 250-862-5466. E-mail: msinclair@okanagan.bc.ca. World Wide Web: http://www.ouc.bc.ca.

PACIFIC INSTITUTE OF CULINARY ARTS

Vancouver, British Columbia, Canada

GENERAL INFORMATION
Private, coeducational, culinary institute. Urban campus. Founded in 1996.

PROGRAM INFORMATION
Offered since 1996. Accredited by Private Career Training Institutions Agency of British Columbia. Program calendar is divided into quarters. 6-month diploma in baking and pastry arts. 6-month diploma in culinary arts.

PROGRAM AFFILIATION
British Columbia Restaurant and Foodservices Association; International Association of Culinary Professionals.

AREAS OF STUDY
Baking; buffet catering; confectionery show pieces; culinary French; food preparation; garde-manger; international cuisine; introduction to food service; meal planning; nutrition; patisserie; restaurant opportunities; sanitation; saucier; soup, stock, sauce, and starch production; wines and spirits.

FACILITIES
Bake shop; catering service; coffee shop; 4 food production kitchens; gourmet dining room; 4 lecture rooms; public restaurant; 4 teaching kitchens; chocolate studio; cake-decorating studio.

STUDENT PROFILE
175 full-time. 81 are under 25 years old; 77 are between 25 and 44 years old; 17 are over 44 years old.

FACULTY
14 total: 14 full-time. 3 are industry professionals; 1 is a master chef; 1 is a master baker; 9 are culinary-certified teachers. Faculty-student ratio: 1:12 –15.

SPECIAL PROGRAMS
Industry field days at local farms, fisheries, etc., Guest Chef speakers, culinary competitions.

TYPICAL EXPENSES
Application fee: Can$100. Tuition: Can$12,575 per diploma. Program-related fees include Can$500 for uniforms and shoes; Can$150 for textbooks; Can$500–$900 for knives.

FINANCIAL AID
In 2005, 3 scholarships were awarded (average award was Can$500). Employment placement assistance is available. Employment opportunities within the program are available.

HOUSING
Average off-campus housing cost per month: Can$600–$1000.

APPLICATION INFORMATION
Students may begin participation in January, April, June, and September. Applications are accepted continuously. In 2005, 225 applied; 200 were accepted. Applicants must interview; submit a formal application and letters of reference.

CONTACT
Kim Gotzke, Director of Admissions, 1505 West 2nd Avenue, Vancouver, BC V6H 3Y4, Canada. Telephone: 800-416-4040. Fax: 604-734-4408. E-mail: info@picachef.com. World Wide Web: http://www.picachef.com.

St. Clair College of Applied Arts and Technology

Hospitality

Windsor, Ontario, Canada

GENERAL INFORMATION
Public, coeducational, two-year college. Urban campus. Founded in 1967.

PROGRAM INFORMATION
Offered since 1994. Program calendar is divided into semesters. 1-year certificate in chef training. 2-year diploma in hotel and restaurant management. 2-year diploma in culinary management.

PROGRAM AFFILIATION
Council on Hotel, Restaurant, and Institutional Education; Ontario Restaurant, Hotel & Motel Association; Ontario Tourism Education Corporation; Windsor/Essex County Tourism and Convention Bureau.

AREAS OF STUDY
Baking; beverage management; buffet catering; confectionery show pieces; controlling costs in food service; culinary French; culinary skill development; customer service; food preparation; food purchasing; food service communication; food service math; garde-manger; hospitality marketing; international cuisine; introduction to food service; kitchen management; management and human resources; meal planning; menu and facilities design; nutrition; nutrition and food service; patisserie; restaurant opportunities; sanitation; saucier; soup, stock, sauce, and starch production; wines and spirits.

FACILITIES
Cafeteria; catering service; 2 classrooms; coffee shop; 4 computer laboratories; 2 demonstration laboratories; 2 food production kitchens; 2 gardens; gourmet dining room; learning resource center; 2 lecture rooms; library; public restaurant; 2 snack shops; student lounge; 2 teaching kitchens.

STUDENT PROFILE
265 total: 220 full-time; 45 part-time. 172 are under 25 years old; 53 are between 25 and 44 years old; 40 are over 44 years old.

FACULTY
10 total: 4 full-time; 6 part-time. 4 are industry professionals; 4 are master chefs; 2 are culinary-certified teachers. Prominent faculty: Eva Cross; Marc Johnston, CCC; Kerstin Schneider; Ken Reynolds. Faculty-student ratio: 1:20.

SPECIAL PROGRAMS
Guest lecture and tours of local casinos, banquet facilities, and wineries, domestic internship opportunity, regional culinary competition (annual).

TYPICAL EXPENSES
Application fee: Can$75. In-state tuition: Can$2103 per year full-time (in district), Can$4.26 per credit hour part-time. Out-of-state tuition: Can$11,520 per year. Program-related fees include Can$400–Can$500 for kitchen tools and uniforms; Can$250 for certification fees; Can$400 for textbooks.

FINANCIAL AID
In 2004, 7 scholarships were awarded (average award was Can$500–$1500). Program-specific awards include South Western Ontario Vintners Association bursary. Employment placement assistance is available. Employment opportunities within the program are available.

HOUSING
Apartment-style housing available.

APPLICATION INFORMATION
Students may begin participation in September. Application deadline for fall is March 1. In 2004, 480 applied; 410 were accepted. Applicants must submit a formal application.

CONTACT
Kerstin Schneider, Program Coordinator, Hospitality, 2000 Talbot Road West, Windsor, ON N9A 6S4, Canada. Telephone: 519-972-2727 Ext. 4140. Fax: 519-972-2748. E-mail: ksneider@stclaircollege.ca. World Wide Web: http://www.stclaircollege.ca.

Southern Alberta Institute of Technology

Professional Cooking

Calgary, Alberta, Canada

GENERAL INFORMATION
Public, coeducational, two-year college. Urban campus. Founded in 1916.

PROGRAM INFORMATION
Offered since 1948. Accredited by Alberta Learning. Program calendar is divided into semesters. 1-year certificate in baking. 12-month diploma in professional cooking. 2-year diploma in professional baking. 6-month certificate in retail meat cutting. 8-month certificate in pastry chef.

PROGRAM AFFILIATION
Canadian Federation of Chefs and Cooks; Canadian Restaurant Association; Confrerie de la Chaine des Rotisseurs; Council on Hotel, Restaurant, and Institutional Education; World Association of Chefs and Cooks.

AREAS OF STUDY
Baking; beverage management; confectionery show pieces; controlling costs in food service; culinary French; culinary skill development; food preparation; food purchasing; food service communication; food service math; garde-manger;

ice carving/fat sculpture; international cuisine; introduction to food service; kitchen management; management and human resources; meal planning; meat cutting; meat fabrication; menu and facilities design; nutrition; nutrition and food service; patisserie; restaurant opportunities; sanitation; saucier; seafood processing; soup, stock, sauce, and starch production; wines and spirits.

FACILITIES

2 bakeries; 3 cafeterias; catering service; 5 classrooms; 2 coffee shops; computer laboratory; 3 demonstration laboratories; 3 food production kitchens; gourmet dining room; 2 laboratories; learning resource center; lecture room; library; 2 public restaurants; 6 snack shops; student lounge; 2 teaching kitchens; test kitchen; bakery merchandizing classroom; retail shop.

TYPICAL STUDENT PROFILE

205 full-time. 123 are under 25 years old; 62 are between 25 and 44 years old; 20 are over 44 years old.

SPECIAL PROGRAMS

5-day study tours to food processing and manufacturing sites, 1-month exchange programs in France and Austria, 5-day study tour to selected wine areas and 14-day study tour to Thailand, Australia, and Napa Valley.

FINANCIAL AID

Employment placement assistance is available. Employment opportunities within the program are available.

HOUSING

Apartment-style housing available.

APPLICATION INFORMATION

Students may begin participation in January, May, and September. Application deadline for September term is February 28. Application deadline for January term is October 31. Applicants must submit a formal application and academic transcripts.

CONTACT

Director of Admissions, Professional Cooking, 1301 16th Avenue, NW, Calgary, AB T2M 0L4, Canada. Telephone: 403-284-8943. Fax: 403-284-7034. World Wide Web: http://www.sait.ab.ca/academic/applied/programs/pgm8.htm.

STRATFORD CHEFS SCHOOL

Stratford, Ontario, Canada

GENERAL INFORMATION

Private, coeducational, culinary institute. Small-town setting. Founded in 1983.

PROGRAM INFORMATION

Offered since 1983. Accredited by Ontario Ministry of Training Colleges and Universities-Apprenticeship Branch. Program calendar is divided into semesters. 2-year diploma in professional cookery.

AREAS OF STUDY

Baking; controlling costs in food service; culinary French; culinary skill development; food preparation; food purchasing; food service communication; food service math; garde-manger; international cuisine; introduction to food service; kitchen management; management and human resources; meal planning; meat cutting; menu and facilities design; nutrition; nutrition and food service; patisserie; restaurant opportunities; sanitation; saucier; seafood processing; soup, stock, sauce, and starch production; wines and spirits.

FACILITIES

2 classrooms; 2 demonstration laboratories; 3 food production kitchens; gourmet dining room; 2 teaching kitchens.

TYPICAL STUDENT PROFILE

70 full-time. 20 are under 25 years old; 48 are between 25 and 44 years old; 2 are over 44 years old.

SPECIAL PROGRAMS

Apprenticeship program, international guest chefs.

FINANCIAL AID

Employment placement assistance is available.

APPLICATION INFORMATION

Students may begin participation in November. Applications are accepted continuously. Applicants must submit a formal application, an essay, kitchen interview, personal interview.

CONTACT

Director of Admissions, 68 Nile Street, Stratford, ON N5A 4C5, Canada. Telephone: 519-271-1414. Fax: 519-271-5679. World Wide Web: http://www.stratfordchef.on.ca.

UNIVERSITY OF GUELPH

School of Hospitality and Tourism Management

Guelph, Ontario, Canada

GENERAL INFORMATION

Public, coeducational, university. Suburban campus. Founded in 1964. Accredited by Association of Universities and Colleges of Canada.

PROGRAM INFORMATION

Offered since 1969. Program calendar is divided into trimesters. 1-year master of business administration in hospitality and tourism. 4-year bachelor of commerce in hotel and food administration.

PROGRAM AFFILIATION

American Dietetic Association; Council on Hotel, Restaurant, and Institutional Education.

University of Guelph *(continued)*

AREAS OF STUDY

Foodservice management; hotel management; tourism management.

FACILITIES

6 cafeterias; catering service; coffee shop; 4 computer laboratories; 2 demonstration laboratories; food production kitchen; gourmet dining room; 2 laboratories; learning resource center; library; public restaurant; snack shop; student lounge; teaching kitchen.

TYPICAL STUDENT PROFILE

700 total: 650 full-time; 50 part-time. 550 are under 25 years old; 100 are between 25 and 44 years old.

SPECIAL PROGRAMS

Fall study abroad semester in France, semester exchange programs in Mexico, England, and Australia, co-operative education program in Hotel and Food Administration.

FINANCIAL AID

Employment placement assistance is available. Employment opportunities within the program are available.

HOUSING

Coed, apartment-style, and single-sex housing available.

APPLICATION INFORMATION

Students may begin participation in September. Application deadline for fall is April 1. Application deadline for winter (for transfers only) is November 1. Application deadline for spring (for transfers only) is March 1. Applicants must submit a formal application and background information sheet describing previous hospitality-related work experience and reasons for applying.

CONTACT

Director of Admissions, School of Hospitality and Tourism Management, ON, Canada. Telephone: 519-824-4120. Fax: 519-823-5512. World Wide Web: http://www.uoguelph.ca/liaison/majors/hofo.shtml.

INTERNATIONAL

AUSTRALIA

CANBERRA INSTITUTE OF TECHNOLOGY

Faculty of Tourism and Hotel Management

Canberra, Australia

GENERAL INFORMATION

Public, coeducational, culinary institute. Suburban campus. Founded in 1976.

PROGRAM INFORMATION

Offered since 1976. Accredited by ACT Accreditation and Registration Council. Program calendar is divided into semesters. 1-year certificate in culinary skills. 1-year diploma in food and beverage service. 24-month advanced diploma in hospitality. 3-year degree in hotel management. 6-month certificate in food production. 6-month graduate certificate in hotel management.

PROGRAM AFFILIATION

Restaurant and Catering Association.

AREAS OF STUDY

Baking; beverage management; buffet catering; confectionery show pieces; controlling costs in food service; convenience cookery; culinary French; culinary skill development; food preparation; food purchasing; food service communication; food service math; garde-manger; international cuisine; introduction to food service; kitchen management; management and human resources; meal planning; meat cutting; meat fabrication; menu and facilities design; nutrition; nutrition and food service; patisserie; restaurant opportunities; sanitation; saucier; seafood processing; soup, stock, sauce, and starch production; wines and spirits.

FACILITIES

Bakery; cafeteria; 4 catering services; 8 classrooms; coffee shop; 2 computer laboratories; 6 demonstration laboratories; 2 food production kitchens; garden; 4 gourmet dining rooms; laboratory; 3 learning resource centers; 2 lecture rooms; library; 4 public restaurants; snack shop; student lounge; 6 teaching kitchens.

TYPICAL STUDENT PROFILE

2,000 total: 1000 full-time; 1000 part-time. 1500 are under 25 years old; 300 are between 25 and 44 years old; 200 are over 44 years old.

SPECIAL PROGRAMS

Annual internship (degree program) within Australia or at international venue, culinary competitions and industry internships (culinary skills diploma), industry site visits during duration of programs.

FINANCIAL AID

Employment placement assistance is available. Employment opportunities within the program are available.

HOUSING

Coed, apartment-style, and single-sex housing available.

APPLICATION INFORMATION

Students may begin participation in February and July. Application deadline for summer is January 20. Application deadline for winter is June 20. Applicants must submit a formal application.

CONTACT

Director of Admissions, Faculty of Tourism and Hotel Management, GPO Box 826, Canberra, Australia. Telephone: 61-2-62073542. Fax: 61-2-62073209. World Wide Web: http://www.cit.act.edu.au.

LE CORDON BLEU AUSTRALIA

Regency Park, SA, Australia

GENERAL INFORMATION

Private, coeducational, four-year college. Suburban campus. Founded in 1998.

PROGRAM INFORMATION

Offered since 1998. Program calendar is divided into semesters. 18-month master's degree in gastronomy. 2-year advanced diploma in restaurant and catering management. 2-year diploma in professional culinary management. 2-year master's degree in International hospitality and restaurant management. 2.5-year bachelor's degree in restaurant and catering management. 9-month certificate in commercial cooking. 9-month certificate in pastry.

PROGRAM AFFILIATION

American Culinary Federation; American Institute of Wine & Food; Confrerie de la Chaine des Rotisseurs; Council on Hotel, Restaurant, and Institutional Education; International Association of Culinary Professionals; James Beard Foundation, Inc.

AREAS OF STUDY

Accounting; beverage management; business plan development; controlling costs in food service; culinary skill development; finance; food and wine philosophy; food preparation; food purchasing; human resources; information technology; international cuisine; kitchen management; legal aspects of food service management; management and human resources; marketing; menu and facilities design; nutrition; restaurant opportunities; sanitation; soup, stock, sauce, and starch production; wines and spirits.

FACILITIES

Bakery; cafeteria; classroom; coffee shop; computer laboratory; demonstration laboratory; garden; gourmet dining room; learning resource center; lecture room; library; public restaurant; student lounge; auditorium; butchery; winery; food science laboratory.

STUDENT PROFILE

520 total: 500 full-time; 20 part-time.

FACULTY

40 total: 40 full-time. 40 are industry professionals. Prominent faculty: Paul Reynolds; Stan Szczypiorski; Brian Lawes. Faculty-student ratio: 1:15.

SPECIAL PROGRAMS

1-year paid internship for bachelor and advanced diploma programs, 6 month paid internship for diploma program.

TYPICAL EXPENSES

Application fee: A$500. Tuition: A$59,400 per 2-5 years-bachelor. Tuition: A$39,600 per 2 years-advanced diploma, A$55,000 for bachelor; A$37,000 for advanced diploma; A$20,000 for masters degree; A$24,000 for MBA. Program-related fee includes A$1980 for professional culinary tool kit.

FINANCIAL AID

In 2005, 25 scholarships were awarded (average award was A$10,000). Program-specific awards include required paid internship within Australia (up to 1 year). Employment opportunities within the program are available.

HOUSING

Apartment-style housing available. Average on-campus housing cost per month: A$950. Average off-campus housing cost per month: A$800.

APPLICATION INFORMATION

Students may begin participation in January and July. Application deadline for January/February intake is November 30. Application deadline for July intake is May 31. Applicants must submit a formal application, letters of reference, 2 passport photos, evidence of English fluency (if English not first language), evidence of satisfactory completion of year 12 or equivalent.

CONTACT

Nina Lucas, Manager, Client Services, Days Road, Regency Park, SA, Australia. Telephone: 61-8-83463700. Fax: 61-8-83463755. E-mail: australia@cordonbleu.edu. World Wide Web: http://www.lecordonbleu.com.au.

See color display following page 380.

LE CORDON BLEU SYDNEY CULINARY ARTS INSTITUTE

Sydney, Australia

GENERAL INFORMATION

Private, coeducational, culinary institute. Suburban campus. Founded in 1996.

PROGRAM INFORMATION

Offered since 1996. Accredited by Training and Skills Commission South Australia. Program calendar is divided into quarters. 10-week certificate 1 in basic cuisine. 10-week certificate 1 in basic patisserie. 2-year diploma in professional culinary management. 22-week certificate II in

Le Cordon Bleu Sydney Culinary Arts Institute *(continued)*

intermediate cuisine. 22-week certificate II in intermediate patisserie. 36-week certificate lll in superior patisserie. 36-week certificate lll in superior cuisine.

PROGRAM AFFILIATION
Council on Hotel, Restaurant, and Institutional Education; International Association of Culinary Professionals; James Beard Foundation, Inc.

AREAS OF STUDY
Australian cuisine; baking; buffet catering; confectionery show pieces; controlling costs in food service; culinary French; culinary skill development; food preparation; food purchasing; food service math; French cuisine; garde-manger; international cuisine; kitchen management; management and human resources; meal planning; meat cutting; menu and facilities design; nutrition and food service; patisserie; sanitation; saucier; seafood processing; soup, stock, sauce, and starch production.

FACILITIES
Cafeteria; classroom; demonstration laboratory; garden; gourmet dining room; learning resource center; lecture room; library; public restaurant; snack shop; student lounge; teaching kitchen.

STUDENT PROFILE
600 full-time. 350 are under 25 years old; 200 are between 25 and 44 years old; 50 are over 44 years old.

FACULTY
15 total: 15 full-time. 8 are industry professionals; 10 are master chefs; 6 are master bakers; 12 are culinary-certified teachers. Prominent faculty: Lynley Houghton; Patrick Harris; Herve Boutin. Faculty-student ratio: 1:12.

SPECIAL PROGRAMS
Post graduate opportunities through Le Cordon Bleu in Adelaide, opportunity to mix and match course components in different world-wide locations.

TYPICAL EXPENSES
Application fee: A$500. Tuition: A$7500–A$9500 per 10 weeks per certificates level course. Program-related fee includes A$1980 for uniforms and equipment tool kit.

APPLICATION INFORMATION
Students may begin participation in January, April, July, and October. Applications are accepted continuously. In 2005, 1000 applied; 600 were accepted. Applicants must submit a formal application and proof of English language proficiency (if English not first language), evidence of completion of year 11 in high school.

CONTACT
Admissions Manager, Culinary Arts Program, Days Road, Regency Park, Australia. Telephone: 61-8-83463700. Fax: 61-8- 883463755. E-mail: australia@cordonbleu.edu. World Wide Web: http://www.lecordonbleu.com.au.

See color display following page 380.

FINLAND

HAAGA INSTITUTE POLYTECHNIC

Hotel, Restaurant, and Tourism Management

Helsinki, Finland

GENERAL INFORMATION
Private, coeducational institution. Suburban campus. Founded in 1969.

PROGRAM INFORMATION
Offered since 1993. Accredited by Council on Hotel, Restaurant and Institutional Education, European Foundation for the Accreditation of Hotel School Programs. Program calendar is divided into terms, terms. 3.5-year bachelor's degree in hotel, restaurant, and tourism management.

PROGRAM AFFILIATION
Council on Hotel, Restaurant, and Institutional Education; European Hotel and Tourism Schools Association; Hotel and Catering International Management Association.

AREAS OF STUDY
Beverage management; controlling costs in food service; culinary French; food preparation; food purchasing; food service communication; food service math; international cuisine; introduction to food service; kitchen management; management and human resources; meal planning; menu and facilities design; nutrition; nutrition and food service; restaurant opportunities; sanitation; wines and spirits.

FACILITIES
Cafeteria; 12 classrooms; 3 computer laboratories; food production kitchen; gourmet dining room; learning resource center; 2 lecture rooms; library; public restaurant; student lounge; teaching kitchen; wine cellar.

TYPICAL STUDENT PROFILE
600 full-time. 550 are under 25 years old; 50 are between 25 and 44 years old.

SPECIAL PROGRAMS
Managerial projects, paid internships in Finland and abroad, exchange semester abroad.

FINANCIAL AID
Employment placement assistance is available. Employment opportunities within the program are available.

HOUSING
Single-sex housing available.

APPLICATION INFORMATION
Students may begin participation in August. Application deadline for spring is January 7. Applicants must interview; submit a formal application, an essay, written exam, and TOEFL scores.

CONTACT

Director of Admissions, Hotel, Restaurant, and Tourism Management, Pajuniityntie 11, PO Box 8, Helsinki, Finland. Telephone: 358-9-58078326. Fax: 358-9-58078 387. World Wide Web: http://www.haaga.fi.

FRANCE

ECOLE DES ARTS CULINAIRES ET DE L'HÔTELLERIE DE LYON

Hotel, Restaurant and Culinary Arts

Lyon-Ecully, Cedex, France

GENERAL INFORMATION

Private, coeducational, culinary institute. Small-town setting. Founded in 1990.

PROGRAM INFORMATION

Offered since 1990. Program calendar is divided into semesters. 2 to 5-year diploma in management and culinary arts. 3-year bachelor's degree in culinary arts. 3-year bachelor's degree in hotel and restaurant management. 3-year diploma in hotel management. 4-month certificate in cuisine and culture. 5-year master's degree in administration in hotel and foodservice.

PROGRAM AFFILIATION

Council on Hotel, Restaurant, and Institutional Education.

AREAS OF STUDY

Baking; beverage management; buffet catering; confectionery show pieces; controlling costs in food service; culinary French; culinary skill development; food preparation; food purchasing; food service math; garde-manger; introduction to food service; kitchen management; management and human resources; meal planning; meat cutting; meat fabrication; menu and facilities design; nutrition and food service; patisserie; soup, stock, sauce, and starch production; wines and spirits.

FACILITIES

Bakery; cafeteria; catering service; 11 classrooms; computer laboratory; 6 demonstration laboratories; 2 food production kitchens; garden; gourmet dining room; library; public restaurant; student lounge; teaching kitchen; vineyard.

STUDENT PROFILE

240 full-time. 210 are under 25 years old; 30 are between 25 and 44 years old.

FACULTY

45 total: 20 full-time; 25 part-time. 5 are industry professionals; 4 are master chefs; 1 is a master baker; 10 are culinary-certified teachers. Prominent faculty: Alain Le Cossec, MOF; Franck Petagna, MOF; Elaine Boissy, MOF. Faculty-student ratio: 1:3.

SPECIAL PROGRAMS

Visits to area surrounding Lyons, 5-month internship each year France or abroad.

TYPICAL EXPENSES

Application fee: 950 euros. Tuition: 9600 euros per per year. Program-related fee includes 1100 euros for uniforms and set of knives 1st year only.

FINANCIAL AID

Employment placement assistance is available. Employment opportunities within the program are available.

HOUSING

Coed housing available. Average on-campus housing cost per month: 360 euros. Average off-campus housing cost per month: 500 euros.

APPLICATION INFORMATION

Students may begin participation in April, May, and October. Applications are accepted continuously. In 2004, 300 applied; 100 were accepted. Applicants must interview; submit an essay and submit a formal application.

CONTACT

Suzanne Weber, Director of Admissions, Hotel, Restaurant and Culinary Arts, Château du Vivier, B.P. 25, Lyon-Ecully, Cedex, France. Telephone: 33-4 72 18 02 20. Fax: 33-478-43-33-51. E-mail: suzanne.weber@institutpaulboux.com. World Wide Web: http://www.each-lyon.com.

ECOLE SUPÉRIEURE DE CUISINE FRANÇAISE GROUPE FERRANDI

Professional Bilingual Culinary, Pastry, and Bread Baking Programs

Paris, France

GENERAL INFORMATION

Coeducational, culinary institute. Urban campus. Founded in 1932.

PROGRAM INFORMATION

Offered since 1986. Accredited by United States Department of Education. Program calendar is divided into trimesters. 7-month certificate in classic French pastry and bread baking. 9-month C.A.P. certificate in French cuisine. 9-month certificate in culinary arts.

AREAS OF STUDY

Baking; buffet catering; confectionery show pieces; controlling costs in food service; culinary French; culinary skill development; food preparation; French cuisine; garde-manger; meat cutting; patisserie; sanitation; saucier; soup, stock, sauce, and starch production; wines and spirits.

Ecole Supérieure de Cuisine Française Groupe Ferrandi
(continued)

FACILITIES

Bakery; cafeteria; catering service; 10 classrooms; 3 computer laboratories; demonstration laboratory; 4 food production kitchens; gourmet dining room; laboratory; learning resource center; 4 lecture rooms; library; public restaurant; 10 teaching kitchens.

STUDENT PROFILE

24 full-time. 8 are under 25 years old; 16 are between 25 and 44 years old.

FACULTY

20 total: 20 full-time. 20 are industry professionals; 4 are master chefs; 3 are master bakers; 20 are culinary-certified teachers. Prominent faculty: Eric Robert, MOF, MCF; Christian Foucher, MCF; Alain Courtois, MOF, MCF. Faculty-student ratio: 1:10.

SPECIAL PROGRAMS

Excursions to French wine regions, 1 end-of-year gastronomic excursion, 3-month apprenticeship program after completion of 9-month program.

TYPICAL EXPENSES

Application fee: 300 euros. Tuition: 16,700 euros for 9 months (includes knives); 14,300 euros for 7 months (includes knives).

FINANCIAL AID

Employment opportunities within the program are available.

HOUSING

Average off-campus housing cost per month: 400–$700 euros.

APPLICATION INFORMATION

Students may begin participation in September. Application deadline for fall is May 1. In 2004, 80 applied; 25 were accepted. Applicants must interview; submit a formal application, letters of reference, and an essay.

CONTACT

Stephanie Curtis, Coordinator, Professional Bilingual Culinary, Pastry, and Bread Baking Programs, 10 rue Poussin, Paris, France. Telephone: 33-1-45270909. Fax: 33-1-45252137. E-mail: stecurtis@aol.com. World Wide Web: http://www.escf.ccip.fr.

LE CORDON BLEU

The Grand Diplôme, The Diploma and Certificate Program

Paris, France

GENERAL INFORMATION

Private, coeducational, culinary institute. Urban campus. Founded in 1895.

PROGRAM INFORMATION

Offered since 1895. Program calendar is divided into trimesters, terms. 1-trimester certificate in basic, intermediate, superior pastry. 1-trimester certificate in basic, intermediate, superior cuisine. 1-year diploma in basic, intermediate, and superior cuisine. 1-year diploma in basic, intermediate, and superior pastry. 1-year diploma in Le Grande Diplôme-cuisine and pastry. 4-day certificate in French culinary technique (regional). 4-day certificate in French pastry technique (bread baking). 4-week certificate in professional in pastry. 5-week certificate in professional in cuisine.

PROGRAM AFFILIATION

American Institute of Wine & Food; Confrerie de la Chaine des Rotisseurs; Council on Hotel, Restaurant, and Institutional Education; International Association of Culinary Professionals; James Beard Foundation, Inc.; National Association for the Specialty Food Trade, Inc.; National Restaurant Association.

AREAS OF STUDY

Baking; cheese; confectionery show pieces; culinary French; culinary skill development; food preparation; garde-manger; meal planning; meat cutting; patisserie; saucier; soup, stock, sauce, and starch production; wines and spirits.

FACILITIES

2 demonstration laboratories; food production kitchen; student lounge; 4 teaching kitchens; boutique; showroom.

STUDENT PROFILE

380 full-time. 300 are under 25 years old; 80 are between 25 and 44 years old.

FACULTY

12 total: 12 full-time. 10 are master chefs. Prominent faculty: Didier Chantefort; Nicolas Bernardé. Faculty-student ratio: 1:12.

SPECIAL PROGRAMS

4-day program in French culinary technique, Mediterranean flavors, French regional cuisine and bread baking; 1-2 day vineyard and cultural excursions, professional internships, guest chefs.

TYPICAL EXPENSES

Application fee: 500-1500 euros. Tuition: 30,950 euros per Grand Diplôme; 18,550 euros per cuisine diploma; 13,950 euros per pastry diploma full-time, 5170–7290 euros for 1 trimester part-time. Program-related fees include uniform package (included in tuition); equipment package (included in tuition).

FINANCIAL AID
In 2005, 15 scholarships were awarded (average award was 10,000 euros). Program-specific awards include work-study program. Employment placement assistance is available.

HOUSING
Average off-campus housing cost per month: 800 euros.

APPLICATION INFORMATION
Students may begin participation in January, March, June, September, and November. Applications are accepted continuously. In 2005, 420 applied. Applicants must submit a formal application, an essay, application fee.

CONTACT
Christel Hernandez, Admissions Director, The Grand Diplôme, The Diploma and Certificate Program, 8, rue Léon Delhomme, Paris, France. Telephone: 33-1-53682250. Fax: 33-1-48560396. E-mail: paris@cordonbleu.edu. World Wide Web: http://www.cordonbleu.edu.

See color display following page 380.

GREECE

ALPINE CENTER FOR HOTEL & TOURISM MANAGEMENT

Glyfada, Greece

GENERAL INFORMATION
Private, coeducational, four-year college. Suburban campus. Founded in 1987.

PROGRAM INFORMATION
Offered since 1987. Accredited by European Foundation for the Accreditation of Hotel School Programs. Program calendar is divided into semesters. 1-year certificate in food and beverage operations. 1-year certificate in catering management. 2-year certificate in culinary arts.

PROGRAM AFFILIATION
Council on Hotel, Restaurant, and Institutional Education; Hotel and Catering International Management Association; International Hotel and Restaurant Association.

AREAS OF STUDY
Beverage management; buffet catering; confectionery show pieces; culinary skill development; food preparation; food purchasing; food service communication; garde-manger; international cuisine; introduction to food service; kitchen management; management and human resources; meal planning; meat cutting; menu and facilities design; nutrition; nutrition and food service; patisserie; restaurant

opportunities; sanitation; saucier; seafood processing; soup, stock, sauce, and starch production; wines and spirits.

FACILITIES
Bake shop; bakery; cafeteria; catering service; 9 classrooms; computer laboratory; demonstration laboratory; food production kitchen; garden; gourmet dining room; learning resource center; 10 lecture rooms; library; snack shop; student lounge; teaching kitchen.

TYPICAL STUDENT PROFILE
30 full-time.

SPECIAL PROGRAMS
Professional excursions to wineries and catering facilities, culinary competitions, two 5-month internships; distance learning programs; 6-month foundation program.

FINANCIAL AID
Employment placement assistance is available. Employment opportunities within the program are available.

HOUSING
Single-sex housing available.

APPLICATION INFORMATION
Students may begin participation in October. Application deadline for fall is September 30. Applicants must interview; submit a formal application, letters of reference, an essay, take placement test.

CONTACT
Director of Admissions, PO Box 70235, 70 Possidonos Avenue, Glyfada, Greece. Telephone: 30-2108983210. Fax: 30-2108981189. World Wide Web: http://www.alpine.edu.gr.

IRELAND

BALLYMALOE COOKERY SCHOOL

Midleton, County Cork, Ireland

GENERAL INFORMATION
Private, coeducational, culinary institute. Rural campus. Founded in 1983.

PROGRAM INFORMATION
Offered since 1983. Program calendar is continuous, year-round. 3-month certificate in culinary training.

PROGRAM AFFILIATION
Euro-Toque; International Association of Culinary Professionals; Slow Food International; The Bread Bakers Guild of America.

AREAS OF STUDY
Baking; buffet catering; controlling costs in food service; convenience cookery; food preparation; food purchasing; garde-manger; international cuisine; meal planning; nutrition; patisserie; sanitation; seafood processing; soup, stock, sauce, and starch production; wines and spirits.

Ballymaloe Cookery School (*continued*)

FACILITIES
Gourmet dining room; library; teaching kitchen; demonstration kitchen; organic garden.

TYPICAL STUDENT PROFILE
56 full-time.

SPECIAL PROGRAMS
Range of short courses on various topics.

FINANCIAL AID
Employment placement assistance is available.

HOUSING
Apartment-style housing available.

APPLICATION INFORMATION
Students may begin participation in January and September. Applications are accepted continuously. Applicants must submit a formal application and letters of reference.

CONTACT
Director of Admissions, Shanagarry, Midleton, County Cork, Ireland. Telephone: 353-21-4-646785. Fax: 353-21-4-646909. World Wide Web: http://www.cookingisfun.ie.

ITALY

APICIUS–THE CULINARY INSTITUTE OF FLORENCE

Florence, Italy

GENERAL INFORMATION
Private, coeducational, culinary institute. Urban campus. Founded in 1996.

PROGRAM INFORMATION
Offered since 1996. Program calendar is divided into semesters. 2- to 3-semester certificate in master in Italian cuisine. 2- to 3-semester certificate in food communications. 2- to 3-semester certificate in Italian bakery and pastry. 2- to 3-semester certificate in wine expertise. 2- to 3-semester certificate in food packaging and design. 2- to 3-semester certificate in hospitality management. 2- to 3-semester certificate in culinary arts.

PROGRAM AFFILIATION
Association of Professional Italian Chefs; International Association of Culinary Professionals.

Apicius The Culinary Institute of Florence programs are designed both for those approaching "the art of Italian cooking" for the first time, or for experts in the field wishing to refresh and deepen their cultural and practical experience. We consider cooking to be an art, a complete experience involving all of the senses in its appreciation.

Located in the historic center of Florence, the new state-of-the-art facility is just moments away from such treasures as the Duomo, the Ponte Vecchio, the San Lorenzo Church, the Uffizi, etc. The Florence central, indoor food market is nearby, allowing students to learn about and use the freshest, most enticing ingredients available in the city.

Apicius Professional Semester and One-Year Certificate Programs are offered in Culinary Arts, Wine Expertise, Food Communications and Hospitality Management. Professional programs include internships at one of many fine Florentine restaurants, hotels or wineries. Private customized classes and Non-Professional courses at Apicius may be taken for one day, a week, a month or for a semester. Special group courses can be arranged by request.

Apicius • The Culinary Institute of Florence (US Office) • 7151 Wilton Avenue, Suite 202 • Sebastopol, CA. 95472 USA
Tel: (707) 824 - 8965 • Toll Free: (800) 655 - 8965 • Fax: (707) 824 - 0198 • www.culinaryinstituteofflorence.com

AREAS OF STUDY

Baking; culinary skill development; food preparation; international cuisine; meal planning; meat cutting; patisserie; restaurant opportunities; soup, stock, sauce, and starch production; wines and spirits.

FACILITIES

4 classrooms; computer laboratory; 3 demonstration laboratories; 2 food production kitchens; garden; 2 lecture rooms; library; public restaurant; 3 student lounges; 3 teaching kitchens; state of the art wine appreciation room.

STUDENT PROFILE

100 full-time. 70 are under 25 years old; 15 are between 25 and 44 years old; 15 are over 44 years old.

FACULTY

13 total: 10 full-time; 3 part-time. 5 are master chefs; 1 is a master baker; 7 are culinary-certified teachers. Prominent faculty: Marcella Ansaldo; Duccio Bagnoli; Andrea Trapani; Diletta Frescobaldi. Faculty-student ratio: 1:8.

SPECIAL PROGRAMS

Internships in local restaurants/hotels/wineries, 10-day tours of Tuscany, private customized cooking classes.

TYPICAL EXPENSES

Application fee: $75. Tuition: $5500 per semester full-time, $2800 per monthly part-time. Program-related fee includes $250 for student service fee.

FINANCIAL AID

In 2005, 3 scholarships were awarded (average award was $1000). Employment placement assistance is available.

HOUSING

Apartment-style housing available. Average on-campus housing cost per month: $950.

APPLICATION INFORMATION

Students may begin participation in January, June, July, and September. Application deadline for spring is November 1. Application deadline for fall is July 1. In 2005, 80 applied; 80 were accepted. Applicants must submit a formal application.

CONTACT

Marilyn Etchell, Admissions Officer, 7151 Wilton Avenue, Suite 202, Sebastopol, CA 95472. Telephone: 707-824-8965. Fax: 707-824-0198. E-mail: mae@studyabroaditaly.com. World Wide Web: http://www.culinaryinstituteofflorence. com/.

THE INTERNATIONAL COOKING SCHOOL OF ITALIAN FOOD AND WINE

Bologna, Italy

GENERAL INFORMATION

Private, coeducational, culinary institute. Urban campus. Founded in 1987.

PROGRAM INFORMATION

Offered since 1987. Program calendar is divided into weeks, weeks. 1-week certificate in foundation of Italian cooking.

PROGRAM AFFILIATION

International Association of Culinary Professionals; James Beard Foundation, Inc.; New York Association of Cooking Teachers; Women Chefs and Restaurateurs.

AREAS OF STUDY

Italian cuisine.

FACILITIES

Food production kitchen; 3 gourmet dining rooms; 3 public restaurants; teaching kitchen; 2 vineyards; pasta production kitchen; pizza production kitchen.

TYPICAL STUDENT PROFILE

10 full-time.

SPECIAL PROGRAMS

Private tours and tastings in Emilia-Romagna and Piedmont regions.

APPLICATION INFORMATION

Students may begin participation in May, June, September, and October. Applications are accepted continuously. Applicants must submit a formal application.

CONTACT

Director of Admissions, 201 East 28th Street, Suite 15B, New York, NY 10016-8538. Telephone: 212-779-1921. Fax: 212-779-3248. World Wide Web: http://www.marybethclark. com.

ITALIAN CULINARY INSTITUTE FOR FOREIGNERS–USA

Costigliole d'Asti (AT), Italy

GENERAL INFORMATION

Private, coeducational, culinary institute. Small-town setting. Founded in 1991.

PROGRAM INFORMATION

Offered since 1991. Program calendar is continuous. 3-month certificate in master-culinary arts-Italian. 6-month diploma in master-culinary arts-Italian.

Italian Culinary Institute for Foreigners–USA *(continued)*

AREAS OF STUDY
Baking; buffet catering; food preparation; garde-manger; Italian cuisine; meat cutting; seafood processing; soup, stock, sauce, and starch production; wines and spirits.

FACILITIES
Bakery; classroom; computer laboratory; demonstration laboratory; food production kitchen; gourmet dining room; laboratory; lecture room; library; teaching kitchen; vineyard.

TYPICAL STUDENT PROFILE
100 full-time. 50 are under 25 years old; 40 are between 25 and 44 years old; 10 are over 44 years old.

SPECIAL PROGRAMS
Visits to wineries and food producers.

HOUSING
Coed and apartment-style housing available.

APPLICATION INFORMATION
Students may begin participation in March, April, June, September, and October. Applications are accepted continuously. Applicants must submit a formal application, letters of reference, and an essay.

CONTACT
Director of Admissions, 126 Second Place, Brooklyn, NY 11231. Telephone: 718-875-0547. Fax: 718-875-5856. World Wide Web: http://www.icif.com.

ITALIAN FOOD ARTISANS

Torino/Alba, Italy

GENERAL INFORMATION
Private, coeducational institution. Small-town setting. Founded in 1993.

PROGRAM INFORMATION
Offered since 1993. Program calendar is divided into weeks. 1-week certificate of completion in Italian regional cuisine.

PROGRAM AFFILIATION
American Institute of Wine & Food; International Association of Culinary Professionals; Oldways Preservation and Exchange Trust; Roundtable for Women in Foodservice; Slow Food International.

AREAS OF STUDY
Baking; culinary skill development; food preparation; food purchasing; international cuisine; Italian cuisine; Italian regional cuisine (truffles, risotto); wines and spirits.

FACILITIES
Garden; gourmet dining room; teaching kitchen; vineyard; farmhouse kitchen.

STUDENT PROFILE
150 part-time. 30 are under 25 years old; 50 are between 25 and 44 years old; 70 are over 44 years old.

FACULTY
9 total: 1 full-time; 8 part-time. 3 are industry professionals; 4 are master chefs; 1 is a master baker; 1 is a culinary-certified teacher. Prominent faculty: Pamela Sheldon Johns, Cookbook Author; Burton Anderson; Massimiliano Mariotti. Faculty-student ratio: 1:4.

SPECIAL PROGRAMS
1 week: olive harvest and olive oil production in Tuscany, 1 week: cheese-making workshop)pecorino, mozzarella, ricotta), 1 week: grape harvest and wine-making workshop in Tuscany.

TYPICAL EXPENSES
Tuition: $2650–$2950 per week (includes housing) and all meals and ground transportation part-time.

HOUSING
Coed and apartment-style housing available.

APPLICATION INFORMATION
Students may begin participation in March, April, May, June, July, August, September, October, and November. Applications are accepted continuously.

CONTACT
Pamela Sheldon Johns, Program Director, 27 West Anapamu Street #427, Santa Barbara, CA 93101. Telephone: 805-963-7289. Fax: 805-456-0653. E-mail: pamela@foodartisans.com. World Wide Web: http://www.foodartisans.com.

ITALIAN INSTITUTE FOR ADVANCED CULINARY AND PASTRY ARTS

Satriano, Italy

GENERAL INFORMATION
Private, coeducational, culinary institute. Suburban campus. Founded in 1997. Accredited by Accrediting Commission of Career Schools and Colleges of Technology.

PROGRAM INFORMATION
Accredited by Selected Chef and Culinary Federations. 3-month certificate in Regional Italian Cuisine.

PROGRAM AFFILIATION
American Culinary Federation; Confrerie de la Chaine des Rotisseurs; International Association of Culinary Professionals; National Restaurant Association.

AREAS OF STUDY
Baking; buffet catering; confectionery show pieces; controlling costs in food service; convenience cookery; culinary skill development; food preparation; food purchasing; food service math; garde-manger; international cuisine; introduction to food service; kitchen management;

meal planning; meat cutting; menu and facilities design; patisserie; sanitation; saucier; soup, stock, sauce, and starch production; wines and spirits.

FACILITIES
Bake shop; cafeteria; 2 classrooms; coffee shop; demonstration laboratory; food production kitchen; 3 gardens; 2 laboratories; 2 lecture rooms; public restaurant; student lounge; teaching kitchen; 2 vineyards.

STUDENT PROFILE
1,100 total: 550 full-time; 550 part-time. 150 are under 25 years old; 350 are between 25 and 44 years old; 50 are over 44 years old.

FACULTY
25 total: 5 full-time; 20 part-time. 25 are industry professionals; 14 are master chefs; 2 are master bakers; 7 are culinary-certified teachers; Sommelier, Maestro Oleano (Olive Oil Master). Prominent faculty: Fabio Bertuni (Master Baker); Fabio Momolo (Master Chef, Italia Natural Culiary Team); John Nocita (Sommelier, Maestro Oleano); Walter Zasoni (Master Patissier). Faculty-student ratio: 1:7.

SPECIAL PROGRAMS
Tour of Artisan Food Makers in Italy, Participation in International Culinary Competitions, 3-6 months internships in Italy.

TYPICAL EXPENSES
Tuition: 8500 euros per 3 months full-time, 2500 euros per 1 week full immersions part-time.

FINANCIAL AID
In 2004, 4 scholarships were awarded (average award was 16,000 euros). Program-specific awards include Sponsorship for selected participants to compete in international events. Employment placement assistance is available. Employment opportunities within the program are available.

APPLICATION INFORMATION
Students may begin participation in January, February, April, May, June, September, and October. Applications are accepted continuously. In 2004, 2000 applied; 550 were accepted. Applicants must submit a formal application and an essay.

CONTACT
Prof. John Nocita, Director, Via T. Campanella, 37, Satriano, CZ, Italy. Telephone: 39-334 333 2554. Fax: 39-0967 21189. E-mail: johnn@italianculinary.it. World Wide Web: http://www.italianculinary.it.

SCOULA DI ARTE CULINARIA "CORDON BLEU"

Florence, Italy

GENERAL INFORMATION
Private, coeducational, culinary institute. Urban campus. Founded in 1985.

PROGRAM INFORMATION
Offered since 1985. Accredited by Italian Association of Culinary Teachers. Program calendar is continuous. 1-week certificate in Tuscan cooking. 1-week certificate in new Italian cooking. 1-week certificate in advanced Italian cooking. 1-week certificate in basic Italian cooking. 2-month certificate in advanced international cooking. 2-month certificate in pastry (international). 2-month certificate in basic cooking (international). 8-month certificate in professional study in Italian cooking.

PROGRAM AFFILIATION
Commanderie des Cordons Bleus de France; International Association of Culinary Professionals.

AREAS OF STUDY
Baking; chocolate; food preparation; international cuisine; Italian regional and traditional cooking; meal planning; patisserie; saucier; seafood processing; soup, stock, sauce, and starch production; wines and spirits.

FACILITIES
Classroom; gourmet dining room; library; teaching kitchen.

TYPICAL STUDENT PROFILE
310 total: 10 full-time; 300 part-time.

FINANCIAL AID
Employment placement assistance is available.

APPLICATION INFORMATION
Students may begin participation in January and September. Application deadline for fall is July 30. Application deadline for spring is November 30.

CONTACT
Director of Admissions, Via Di Mezzo, Florence, Italy. Telephone: 39-55-2345468. Fax: 39-55-2345468. World Wide Web: http://www.cordonbleu-it.com.

JAPAN

LE CORDON BLEU JAPAN

Classic Cycle Program

Tokyo, Japan

GENERAL INFORMATION
Private, coeducational, culinary institute. Urban campus. Founded in 1991.

PROGRAM INFORMATION
Offered since 1991. Program calendar is divided into trimesters. 3-month certificate in advanced bakery. 3-month certificate in basic bakery. 3-month certificate in advanced pastry. 3-month certificate in superior cuisine. 3-month certificate in advanced cuisine. 3-month certificate in intermediate cuisine. 3-month certificate in basic cuisine. 3-month certificate in basic pastry. 3-month certificate in superior pastry.

PROGRAM AFFILIATION
Confrerie de la Chaine des Rotisseurs; James Beard Foundation, Inc.

AREAS OF STUDY
Baking; buffet catering; culinary French; patisserie; wines and spirits.

FACILITIES
2 demonstration laboratories; lecture room; student lounge; 4 teaching kitchens.

STUDENT PROFILE
1382 full-time.

FACULTY
14 total: 14 full-time. 14 are master chefs. Prominent faculty: Patrick Lemesle; Cédric Maton; Eric Lepage; Dominique Gros.

SPECIAL PROGRAMS
Introduction to cuisine, pâtisserie, and boulangerie, French cuisine and dietetics, cheese courses.

TYPICAL EXPENSES
Application fee: 52,500 yen. Tuition: 555,000 yens –707,000 yens for 3 months. Program-related fee includes 36500–90500 yen for uniforms, knives set, pastry/cuisine tools.

FINANCIAL AID
In 2005, 1 scholarship was awarded (award was 581,000 yen).

APPLICATION INFORMATION
Students may begin participation in January, April, July, and October. Application deadline for winter is December 15. Application deadline for spring is March 15. Application deadline for summer is June 15. Application deadline for fall is September 15. In 2005, 1382 applied; 1382 were accepted. Applicants must submit a formal application.

CONTACT
Taeko Okabe, Student Service and Sales Manager, Classic Cycle Program, ROOB-1, 28-13 Sarugaku-cho, Shibuya-ku, Tokyo, Japan. Telephone: 81-3-54890141. Fax: 81-3-54890145. E-mail: tokyo@cordonbleu.edu. World Wide Web: http://www.cordonbleu.co.jp.

See color display following page 380.

NEW ZEALAND

THE NEW ZEALAND SCHOOL OF FOOD AND WINE

Foundation Cookery Skills

Christchurch, New Zealand

GENERAL INFORMATION
Private, coeducational, culinary institute. Urban campus. Founded in 1994.

PROGRAM INFORMATION
Offered since 1995. Accredited by New Zealand Qualifications Authority. Program calendar is divided into trimesters. 15-week certificate in introduction to cookery and hospitality. 16-week certificate in foundation in cookery skills. 22-week certificate in restaurant and cafe management.

PROGRAM AFFILIATION
Restaurant Association of New Zealand.

AREAS OF STUDY
Baking; beverage management; controlling costs in food service; culinary French; culinary skill development; food preparation; food service math; garde-manger; international cuisine; management and human resources; meal planning; meat cutting; menu and facilities design; nutrition; patisserie; sanitation; saucier; seafood processing; soup, stock, sauce, and starch production; wines and spirits.

FACILITIES
2 classrooms; computer laboratory; demonstration laboratory; food production kitchen; library; public restaurant; teaching kitchen.

STUDENT PROFILE
80 full-time. 20 are under 25 years old; 50 are between 25 and 44 years old; 10 are over 44 years old.

FACULTY
4 total: 4 full-time. 2 are industry professionals; 1 is a master chef; 1 is a culinary-certified teacher. Prominent

faculty: Celia Hay, MBA; Philippe Meyer; Gabrielle Lewis; Lois Blackie. Faculty-student ratio: 1:12.

SPECIAL PROGRAMS

Local vineyard tours, trips to relevant conferences, certification in wine.

TYPICAL EXPENSES

Application fee: $56.25. Tuition: $3500 per certificate programs in cookery and management; $3000 per certificate program in introductory cookery and hospitality. Program-related fees include $1000 for cooking equipment; $245 for textbooks.

FINANCIAL AID

Employment placement assistance is available. Employment opportunities within the program are available.

HOUSING

Average off-campus housing cost per month: $320.

APPLICATION INFORMATION

Students may begin participation in January, February, May, July, September, and October. Applications are accepted continuously. In 2004, 100 applied; 100 were accepted. Applicants must interview; submit a formal application and letters of reference.

CONTACT

Celia Hay, Director, Foundation Cookery Skills, Box 25217, Christchurch, New Zealand. Telephone: 64-3-3797501. Fax: 64-3-3662302. E-mail: chay@foodandwine.co.nz. World Wide Web: http://www.foodandwine.co.nz.

PERU

LE CORDON BLEU PERU

Le Cordon Bleu Peru

Lima, Peru

GENERAL INFORMATION

Private, coeducational, culinary institute. Urban campus. Founded in 1994. Accredited by Accrediting Commission of Career Schools and Colleges of Technology.

PROGRAM INFORMATION

Offered since 1994. Accredited by Council on Hotel, Restaurant and Institutional Education. Program calendar is divided into semesters. 18-month diploma in administration of hotels and restaurants. 2-year diploma in bar and cocktails. 2-year diploma in pastry. 2-year diploma in cuisine. 3-year diploma in alimentary industries. 3-year diploma in gastronomy and culinary arts. 4-year diploma in hotel and restaurant administration.

AREAS OF STUDY

Beverage management; culinary French; culinary skill development; international cuisine; kitchen management; nutrition; patisserie; sanitation; wines and spirits.

FACILITIES

12 classrooms; coffee shop; computer laboratory; 2 demonstration laboratories; 9 laboratories; lecture room; library; public restaurant; 6 teaching kitchens.

STUDENT PROFILE

910 total: 710 full-time; 200 part-time. 570 are under 25 years old; 134 are between 25 and 44 years old; 6 are over 44 years old.

FACULTY

92 total: 12 full-time; 80 part-time. Prominent faculty: Dr. Sixtilio Dalmau Castañon, Director; Sra. Patricia Dalmau de Galfré, Administrative Assistant; Chef Jaques Benoit, Culinary Director.

SPECIAL PROGRAMS

Practical opportunities.

TYPICAL EXPENSES

Tuition: $18,700 per 3 years full-time, $2200 per 18 months part-time. Program-related fee includes $950 for uniforms, cutlery, books, and insurance (accidental).

HOUSING

Average off-campus housing cost per month: $200.

APPLICATION INFORMATION

Students may begin participation in March and August. Application deadline for fall is February 1. Application deadline for winter is June 1. In 2005, 460 applied; 260 were accepted. Applicants must submit a formal application.

CONTACT

Fabiola Chac, Secretary, Gastronomy Direction, Le Cordon Bleu Peru, Av. Nunez de Balboa 530, Miraflores, Lima, Peru. Telephone: 51-1-2428222 Ext. 210. Fax: 51-1-2429209. E-mail: fchac@cordonbleuperu.edu.pe. World Wide Web: http://www.cordonbleuperu.edu.pe.

See color display following page 380.

PHILIPPINES

CENTER FOR CULINARY ARTS, MANILA

Quezon City, Philippines

GENERAL INFORMATION

Private, coeducational, culinary institute. Urban campus. Founded in 1996.

Center for Culinary Arts, Manila (*continued*)

PROGRAM INFORMATION
Offered since 1996. Accredited by Technical Education and Skills Development Authority (Philippines). Program calendar is divided into terms. 1-year certificate in baking and pastry arts. 2-year diploma in culinary arts and technology management.

PROGRAM AFFILIATION
Council of Hotel and Restaurant Educators of the Philippines; International Association of Culinary Professionals; National Restaurant Association; National Restaurant Association Educational Foundation.

AREAS OF STUDY
Asian cuisine; baking; beverage management; breads; breakfast; buffet catering; culinary French; culinary skill development; Filipino cuisine; food preparation; food service communication; food service math; French cuisine; garde-manger; international cuisine; management and human resources; meal planning; meat cutting; meat fabrication; nutrition; patisserie; quantity foods; sales/marketing; sanitation; saucier; seafood processing; soup, stock, sauce, and starch production; specialty desserts; wines and spirits.

FACILITIES
3 classrooms; computer laboratory; 11 food production kitchens; learning resource center; 4 lecture rooms; library; public restaurant; student lounge; pastry shop; 2 beverage service laboratories.

TYPICAL STUDENT PROFILE
200 full-time. 175 are under 25 years old; 25 are between 25 and 44 years old.

SPECIAL PROGRAMS
Continuing Education Program.

FINANCIAL AID
Program-specific awards include partial- and full-scholarships available. Employment placement assistance is available. Employment opportunities within the program are available.

APPLICATION INFORMATION
Students may begin participation in January, June, August, and October. Application deadline for June intake is June 1. Application deadline for August intake is August 1. Application deadline for October intake is October 1. Application deadline for January intake is December 15. Applicants must interview; submit a formal application, letters of reference, an essay, academic transcripts, and results of medical examination.

CONTACT
Director of Admissions, 287 Katipunan Avenue, Loyola Heights, Quezon City, Philippines. Telephone: 63-2-4264825. Fax: 63-2-4264836. World Wide Web: http://cca-manila.com.

REPUBLIC OF KOREA

LE CORDON BLEU KOREA

Seoul, Republic of Korea

GENERAL INFORMATION
Private, coeducational, culinary institute. Urban campus. Founded in 2002.

PROGRAM INFORMATION
Program calendar is divided into quarters. 1-year diploma in culinary arts. 10- to 20-week certificate in culinary arts.

AREAS OF STUDY
Baking; culinary French; patisserie.

FACILITIES
Demonstration laboratory; food production kitchen; library; student lounge; 5 teaching kitchens.

TYPICAL STUDENT PROFILE
500 full-time. 300 are under 25 years old; 200 are between 25 and 44 years old.

SPECIAL PROGRAMS
Workshops for gourmet enthusiasts.

APPLICATION INFORMATION
Students may begin participation in February, May, September, and November. Applicants must submit a formal application and an essay.

CONTACT
Director of Admissions, 53-12 Chungpa-dong 2 Ka, Yongsan-Ku, Seoul, Republic of Korea. Telephone: 82-2-719-6961. Fax: 82-2-719-7569. World Wide Web: http://www.cordonbleu.co.kr.

See color display following page 380.

SOUTH AFRICA

CHRISTINA MARTIN SCHOOL OF FOOD AND WINE

Durban, South Africa

GENERAL INFORMATION
Private, coeducational, culinary institute. Urban campus. Founded in 1973. Accredited by Accrediting Council for Independent Colleges and Schools.

PROGRAM INFORMATION
Offered since 1973. Accredited by American Culinary Federation Accrediting Commission. Program calendar is continuous. 1-year diploma in patisseurier. 1-year diploma

in food preparation and culinary art. 6-month certificate in patisseurier. 6-month certificate in food preparation and culinary arts.

PROGRAM AFFILIATION

Confrerie de la Chaine des Rotisseurs; Council on Hotel, Restaurant, and Institutional Education; International Association of Culinary Professionals; International Wine & Food Society; Women Chefs and Restaurateurs.

AREAS OF STUDY

Baking; beverage management; buffet catering; confectionery show pieces; controlling costs in food service; convenience cookery; culinary French; culinary skill development; food preparation; food purchasing; food service communication; food service math; garde-manger; international cuisine; introduction to food service; kitchen management; management and human resources; meal planning; meat cutting; menu and facilities design; nutrition; nutrition and food service; patisserie; restaurant opportunities; sanitation; saucier; seafood processing; soup, stock, sauce, and starch production; wines and spirits.

FACILITIES

Bake shop; 2 bakeries; cafeteria; 3 catering services; 3 classrooms; coffee shop; computer laboratory; 2 demonstration laboratories; 3 food production kitchens; garden; gourmet dining room; learning resource center; lecture room; library; public restaurant; snack shop; student lounge; 5 teaching kitchens.

STUDENT PROFILE

100 total: 60 full-time; 40 part-time.

FACULTY

100 total: 60 full-time; 40 part-time. 10 are master chefs; 20 are master bakers; 10 are culinary-certified teachers. Prominent faculty: M Barry, Chef Cuisine; E. Bewilliec, Master Patissier; D. Carl, Chef Cuisine; W. Whittaure, Chef Cuisine. Faculty-student ratio: 1:10 student; 1:1 teacher.

SPECIAL PROGRAMS

Lindt Chocolate and Sugar Course, culinary competitions.

TYPICAL EXPENSES

Tuition: $13,230 per one year full-time, $30 per 1day part-time.

FINANCIAL AID

Employment placement assistance is available. Employment opportunities within the program are available.

APPLICATION INFORMATION

Students may begin participation in January. Application deadline for spring is October 1. Application deadline for summer is November 1. Application deadline for winter is July 1. Application deadline for autumn is September 1. In 2004, 60 applied. Applicants must interview; submit a formal application and letters of reference.

CONTACT

M. Barry, Director, PO Box 4601, Durban, South Africa. Telephone: 031-3032111. Fax: 031-3123342. E-mail: chrisma@iafrica.com.

SWITZERLAND

DCT HOTEL AND CULINARY ARTS SCHOOL, SWITZERLAND

European Culinary Center

Vitznau, Switzerland

GENERAL INFORMATION

Private, coeducational, two-year college. Small-town setting. Founded in 1992. Accredited by New England Association of Schools and Colleges.

PROGRAM INFORMATION

Offered since 1997. Accredited by Council on Hotel, Restaurant and Institutional Education, Swiss Hotel Schools Association, American Culinary Federation's Accrediting Commission. Program calendar is divided into quarters. 11-week certificate in European food and beverage service. 11-week certificate in foundation in European cuisine. 11-week certificate in European pastry and chocolate. 11-week certificate in European gourmet cuisine. 12—18 month advanced diploma in European culinary management.

PROGRAM AFFILIATION

American Culinary Federation; Council on Hotel, Restaurant, and Institutional Education; International Hotel and Restaurant Association; National Restaurant Association; Swiss Chef Association; World Association of Cooks Societies.

AREAS OF STUDY

Baking; beverage management; chocolate; confectionery show pieces; controlling costs in food service; culinary skill development; European pastries; food preparation; food purchasing; food service communication; garde-manger; international cuisine; introduction to food service; kitchen management; management and human resources; menu and facilities design; nutrition; nutrition and food service; patisserie; sanitation; saucier; soup, stock, sauce, and starch production; wines and spirits.

FACILITIES

Bakery; 7 classrooms; computer laboratory; food production kitchen; laboratory; learning resource center; library; student lounge; 2 teaching kitchens.

STUDENT PROFILE

45 full-time. 40 are under 25 years old; 4 are between 25 and 44 years old; 1 is over 44 years old.

FACULTY

9 total: 3 full-time; 6 part-time. 4 are industry professionals; 2 are master chefs; 1 is a master baker; 2 are culinary-certified teachers. Prominent faculty: Dr. Birgit Black, Dean; Swiss Master Chef Patrick Diethelm; Swiss Master Chef Urs Meichtry; Chef Stacy Black, CEC. Faculty-student ratio: 1:8.

DCT Hotel and Culinary Arts School, Switzerland
(continued)

SPECIAL PROGRAMS
6-9 month paid internship in Switzerland, tours of wineries and chocolate factories, study European cuisine-In Europe.

TYPICAL EXPENSES
Application fee: 80 Sw Fr. Tuition: 9500 Sw Fr per 3-month term (includes room and board). Program-related fee includes 1000 Sw Fr for required medical and liability insurance, uniforms, texts and classroom supplies, field trips.

FINANCIAL AID
Program-specific awards include paid Swiss internships in top-ranked restaurants. Employment placement assistance is available. Employment opportunities within the program are available.

HOUSING
Coed housing available. Average off-campus housing cost per month: 500–$700 Sw Fr.

APPLICATION INFORMATION
Students may begin participation in January, April, July, and October. Applications are accepted continuously. In 2005, 75 applied; 50 were accepted. Applicants must submit

a formal application and transcripts, prior diplomas, TOEFL or equivalent, proof of high school graduation or professional experience.

CONTACT
Mrs. Sharon Spaltenstein, Director of Marketing and Admission, European Culinary Center, Seestrasse, Vitznau, Switzerland. Telephone: 41-413990000. Fax: 41-413990101. E-mail: culinary@dct.ch. World Wide Web: http://www. culinary.ch.

UNITED KINGDOM

COOKERY AT THE GRANGE

The Essential Cookery Course

Near Frome, Somerset, United Kingdom

GENERAL INFORMATION
Private, coeducational, culinary institute. Rural campus. Founded in 1981.

PROGRAM INFORMATION

Offered since 1981. Program calendar is divided into four-week cycles, four-week cycles. 1-month certificate in cookery.

AREAS OF STUDY

Baking; culinary skill development; food preparation; general cookery; meal planning; meat cutting; menu and facilities design; soup, stock, sauce, and starch production; wines and spirits.

FACILITIES

Garden; student lounge; teaching kitchen.

STUDENT PROFILE

24 full-time.

FACULTY

8 total: 3 full-time; 5 part-time. Faculty-student ratio: 1:7.

TYPICAL EXPENSES

Tuition: £2750–£3090 per certificate (includes housing).

HOUSING

Coed housing available.

APPLICATION INFORMATION

Students may begin participation in January, February, May, June, July, August, September, October, and November. In 2004, 202 applied; 208 were accepted. Applicants must submit a formal application.

CONTACT

William and Jane Averill, The Essential Cookery Course, The Grange, Whatley, Near Frome, Somerset, United Kingdom. Telephone: 44-1373836579. Fax: 44-1373836579. E-mail: info@cookeryatthegrange.co.uk. World Wide Web: http://www.cookeryatthegrange.co.uk.

LE CORDON BLEU–LONDON CULINARY INSTITUTE

Le Cordon Bleu Classic Cycle Programme

London, United Kingdom

GENERAL INFORMATION

Private, coeducational, culinary institute. Urban campus. Founded in 1895.

PROGRAM INFORMATION

Offered since 1933. Accredited by American Culinary Federation Accrediting Commission. Program calendar is divided into quarters. 10-week certificate in basic cuisine. 10-week certificate in superior patisserie. 10-week certificate in superior cuisine. 10-week certificate in basic patisserie. 10-week certificate in intermediate cuisine. 10-week certificate in intermediate patisserie. 30-week diploma in cuisine. 30-week diploma in patisserie. 30-week diploma in grand diplome.

PROGRAM AFFILIATION

American Institute of Wine & Food; Confrerie de la Chaine des Rotisseurs; Council on Hotel, Restaurant, and Institutional Education; International Association of Culinary Professionals; James Beard Foundation, Inc.

AREAS OF STUDY

Baking; buffet catering; cheese; confectionery show pieces; controlling costs in food service; culinary French; culinary skill development; food preparation; food purchasing; international cuisine; introduction to food service; kitchen management; meal planning; nutrition; nutrition and food service; patisserie; sanitation; table service; wines and spirits.

FACILITIES

2 bakeries; 2 demonstration laboratories; food production kitchen; student lounge; 4 teaching kitchens.

FACULTY

8 total: 8 full-time. 8 are master chefs; 2 are specialists in cheese, nutrition, and wine. Prominent faculty: Chef Yann Barraud; Chef John Power. Faculty-student ratio: 1:10.

SPECIAL PROGRAMS

Restaurant market tours and hotel visits, exchanges between Le Cordon Bleu Schools worldwide, culinary competitions.

TYPICAL EXPENSES

Tuition: £3250-£18,945 for 5 weeks-9 months.

FINANCIAL AID

In 2005, 10 scholarships were awarded (average award was £2230). Program-specific awards include International Association of Culinary Professionals scholarship, James Beard Foundation scholarship. Employment placement assistance is available. Employment opportunities within the program are available.

HOUSING

Average off-campus housing cost per month: £1400.

APPLICATION INFORMATION

Students may begin participation in January, March, April, June, July, August, September, and October. Applicants must submit a formal application, curriculum vitae, and letter of motivation.

CONTACT

Admissions Officer, Le Cordon Bleu Classic Cycle Programme, 114 Marylebone Lane, London, United Kingdom. Telephone: 44-20-79353503. Fax: 44-20-79357621. E-mail: london@cordonbleu.edu. World Wide Web: http://www.cordonbleu.net.

See color display following page 380.

LEITH'S SCHOOL OF FOOD AND WINE

London, United Kingdom

GENERAL INFORMATION
Private, coeducational, culinary institute. Urban campus. Founded in 1975.

PROGRAM INFORMATION
Offered since 1975. Program calendar is divided into trimesters. 1-month certificate of completion in cookery (beginners/advanced). 1-month certificate in practical cookery. 1-term certificate in food and wine (advanced). 1-term certificate in food and wine (intermediate). 1-term certificate in food and wine (beginners). 1-week certificate of completion in advanced skills. 1-week certificate of completion in beginners' skills. 1-week certificate of completion in easy dinner parties. 1-year diploma in food and wine. 10-class (evenings) certificate of completion in intermediate skills. 10-class (evenings) certificate of completion in beginners' skills. 2-term diploma in food and wine. 5-class certificate in wine.

AREAS OF STUDY
Baking; buffet catering; chocolate; confectionery show pieces; controlling costs in food service; culinary French; culinary skill development; easy dinner party; fish cookery; food preparation; food purchasing; game; healthy eating; international cuisine; introduction to food service; Italian; kitchen management; meal planning; meat cutting; menu and facilities design; nutrition; nutrition and food service; patisserie; restaurant opportunities; sanitation; saucier; seafood processing; soup, stock, sauce, and starch production; wines and spirits.

FACILITIES
Demonstration laboratory; food production kitchen; lecture room; library; student lounge; 3 teaching kitchens.

STUDENT PROFILE
546 total: 96 full-time; 450 part-time.

FACULTY
27 total: 17 full-time; 10 part-time. 5 are industry professionals; 12 are master chefs; 10 are culinary-certified teachers. Prominent faculty: Caroline Waldegrave; Alison Cavaliero; Jenny Stringer. Faculty-student ratio: 1:8.

SPECIAL PROGRAMS
Excursions to Billingsgate and Smithfield markets, recipe writing competition, restaurant work placements.

TYPICAL EXPENSES
Tuition: £13,965 per 9 months full-time, £570 per week part-time. Program-related fees include £94 for knives; £30 for supplementary equipment to knife set; £60 for course literature; £90 for basic food handlers course; £20 for aprons.

FINANCIAL AID
Employment placement assistance is available. Employment opportunities within the program are available.

HOUSING
Average off-campus housing cost per month: £400.

APPLICATION INFORMATION
Students may begin participation in January, March, April, July, August, September, and December. Applications are accepted continuously. In 2004, 120 applied; 96 were accepted. Applicants must interview (if possible); submit a formal application and letters of reference.

CONTACT
Claire Macdonald, Registrar, 21 St Alban's Grove, London, United Kingdom. Telephone: 44-20-72290177. Fax: 44-20-79375257. E-mail: info@leiths.com. World Wide Web: http://www.leiths.com.

ROSIE DAVIES

Courses for Cooks

Frome, United Kingdom

GENERAL INFORMATION
Private, coeducational institution. Rural campus. Founded in 1996.

PROGRAM INFORMATION
Offered since 1996. Program calendar is divided into months, months. 1-month certificate in basic cooking in chalets. 1-month certificate in basic cooking on yachts. 1-month certificate in basic cooking.

AREAS OF STUDY
Baking; beverage management; buffet catering; controlling costs in food service; convenience cookery; culinary French; culinary skill development; food preparation; food purchasing; food service communication; food service math; international cuisine; introduction to food service; kitchen management; meal planning; meat cutting; menu and facilities design; nutrition; nutrition and food service; patisserie; sanitation; saucier; seafood processing; soup, stock, sauce, and starch production; wines and spirits.

FACILITIES
Food production kitchen; garden; library; student lounge; teaching kitchen.

TYPICAL STUDENT PROFILE
35 full-time. 15 are under 25 years old; 14 are between 25 and 44 years old; 6 are over 44 years old.

HOUSING
Coed housing available.

APPLICATION INFORMATION
Students may begin participation in January, February, April, June, September, October, and November. Applications are accepted continuously. Applicants must submit a formal application.

CONTACT
Director of Admissions, Courses for Cooks, Penny's Mill, Nunney, Frome, United Kingdom. Telephone: 44-1373836210. Fax: 44-1373836018. World Wide Web: http://www.rosiedavies.co.uk.

TANTE MARIE SCHOOL OF COOKERY

Woking, Surrey, United Kingdom

GENERAL INFORMATION
Private, coeducational, culinary institute. Urban campus. Founded in 1954. Accredited by Accrediting Council for Independent Colleges and Schools.

PROGRAM INFORMATION
Offered since 1954. Accredited by British Accreditation Council for Independent Further and Higher Education. Program calendar is divided into trimesters. 3-month certificate in Cordon Bleu cookery. 6-month intensive diploma in Cordon Bleu cookery. 9-month diploma in Cordon Bleu cookery.

AREAS OF STUDY
Baking; buffet catering; confectionery show pieces; controlling costs in food service; convenience cookery; culinary French; culinary skill development; food preparation; food purchasing; garde-manger; international cuisine; introduction to food service; kitchen management; meal planning; meat cutting; meat fabrication; menu and facilities design; nutrition; nutrition and food service; patisserie; restaurant opportunities; sanitation; saucier; seafood processing; soup, stock, sauce, and starch production; wines and spirits.

FACILITIES
Classroom; coffee shop; demonstration laboratory; garden; lecture room; library; student lounge; 5 teaching kitchens; demonstration theatre.

STUDENT PROFILE
158 total: 98 full-time; 60 part-time.

FACULTY
10 total: 7 full-time; 3 part-time. 2 are industry professionals; 8 are culinary-certified teachers. Prominent faculty: Miss Claire Alexander; Mrs. Susan B. Alexander; Mrs. Marcella O'Donovan. Faculty-student ratio: 1:10.

SPECIAL PROGRAMS
4-day course on wines and spirits, 1-day course on food safety and hygiene, 1-4 week Cordon Bleu Cookery courses available.

TYPICAL EXPENSES
Application fee: £400. Tuition: £4000 per term (11 weeks). Tuition: £1800 per 1 month course. Program-related fee includes all inclusive of extras.

FINANCIAL AID
In 2004, 5 scholarships were awarded (average award was £2000). Program-specific awards include United Kingdom students may apply for a United Kingdom student loan. Employment placement assistance is available. Employment opportunities within the program are available.

HOUSING
Average off-campus housing cost per month: £365.

APPLICATION INFORMATION
Students may begin participation in January, April, July, September, October, and November. Applications are accepted continuously. Applicants must submit a formal application.

CONTACT
Mrs. Marcella O'Donovan, Principal, Woodham House, Carlton Road, Woking, United Kingdom. Telephone: 44-1483726957. Fax: 44-1483724173. E-mail: info@ tantemarie.co.uk. World Wide Web: http://www.tantemarie. co.uk.

VIRGIN ISLANDS (BRITISH)

NEW ENGLAND CULINARY INSTITUTE AT H. LAVITY STOUTT COMMUNITY COLLEGE

Tortola, Virgin Islands (British)

GENERAL INFORMATION
Public, coeducational, culinary institute. Small-town setting. Founded in 2000. Accredited by Accrediting Commission of Career Schools and Colleges of Technology.

PROGRAM INFORMATION
Program calendar is divided into semesters. 2-year associate degree in culinary arts.

AREAS OF STUDY
Baking; beverage management; buffet catering; controlling costs in food service; convenience cookery; food preparation; food purchasing; food service communication; food service math; garde-manger; international cuisine; introduction to food service; kitchen management; management and human resources; meal planning; meat cutting; meat fabrication; menu and facilities design; nutrition; nutrition and food service; sanitation; soup, stock, sauce, and starch production; wines and spirits.

New England Culinary Institute at H. Lavity Stoutt Community College *(continued)*

FACILITIES
Bakery; cafeteria; 2 classrooms; coffee shop; 2 computer laboratories; demonstration laboratory; food production kitchen; gourmet dining room; learning resource center; 2 lecture rooms; library; student lounge; 2 teaching kitchens.

SPECIAL PROGRAMS
One-year paid internship.

FINANCIAL AID
Employment placement assistance is available. Employment opportunities within the program are available.

HOUSING
Single-sex housing available.

APPLICATION INFORMATION
Students may begin participation in February and August. Applications are accepted continuously. Applicants must interview; submit a formal application, letters of reference, an essay, high school diploma or transcript.

CONTACT
Director of Admissions, PO Box 3097, Road Town, Tortola, Virgin Islands (British). Telephone: 284-494-4994. Fax: 284-494-4996. World Wide Web: http://www.necibvi.com.

VIRGIN ISLANDS (U.S.)

UNIVERSITY OF THE VIRGIN ISLANDS

Hotel and Restaurant Management Program

St. Thomas, Virgin Islands (U.S.)

GENERAL INFORMATION
Public, coeducational, comprehensive institution. Small-town setting. Accredited by Middle States Association of Colleges and Schools.

PROGRAM INFORMATION
Offered since 1962. Program calendar is divided into semesters. 2-year associate degree in hotel and restaurant management.

PROGRAM AFFILIATION
Educational Institute American Hotel and Motel Association.

STUDENT PROFILE
19 total: 10 full-time; 9 part-time. 16 are under 25 years old; 3 are between 25 and 44 years old.

FACULTY
2 total: 2 part-time. 1 is a certified hospitality educator. Prominent faculty: Samuel A. Rey, CHE. Faculty-student ratio: 1:10.

TYPICAL EXPENSES
Application fee: $20. In-state tuition: $1365 per semester full-time (in district), $91 per credit part-time. Out-of-state tuition: $4095 per semester full-time, $273 per credit part-time.

FINANCIAL AID
Employment placement assistance is available.

HOUSING
Single-sex housing available. Average on-campus housing cost per month: $270. Average off-campus housing cost per month: $600.

APPLICATION INFORMATION
Students may begin participation in January and August. Application deadline for fall is April 30. Application deadline for spring is October 30. In 2004, 6 applied; 5 were accepted. Applicants must submit a formal application and an essay.

CONTACT
Carolyn Cook, Director of Enrollment Management, Hotel and Restaurant Management Program, 2 John Brewers Bay, St. Thomas, VI 00802. Telephone: 340-693-1224. Fax: 340-693-1155. E-mail: ccook@uvi.edu. World Wide Web: http://www.uvi.edu.

PROFILES OF APPRENTICESHIP PROGRAMS

ALABAMA

ACF GREATER MONTGOMERY CHAPTER

Montgomery, Alabama

PROGRAM INFORMATION
Approved by the American Culinary Federation. Academic requirements are met through a chef-taught curriculum and at Trenholm State Technical College (degree available). Special apprenticeships available in baking and pastries and catering; hospitality management.

PLACEMENT INFORMATION
Participants are placed in 1 of 32 locations, including full-service restaurants, hotels, private clubs, fine dining restaurants, and catering businesses. Most popular placement locations are Wyn Lakes Country Club, City Grill, and Embassy Suites.

APPRENTICE PROFILE
Number of participants in 2004: 102. Applicants must interview; submit a formal application, an essay, and letters of reference (recommended).

TYPICAL EXPENSES
Basic cost of participation is $68 per semester hour for state residents, $136 per semester hour for nonresidents. Program-related fees include $200 for uniforms; $145 for knife set; $55 for ACF Junior Chapter membership.

ENTRY-LEVEL COMPENSATION
$7–$8 per hour.

CONTACT
Mary Ann Campbell, Director of Culinary Arts and Hospitality Management, 1225 Airbase Boulevard, Montgomery, AL 36108. Telephone: 334-420-4495. Fax: 334-420-4491. E-mail: mcampbell@trenholmtech.cc.al.us.

ARIZONA

CHEFS ASSOCIATION OF SOUTHERN ARIZONA, TUCSON

Tucson, Arizona

PROGRAM INFORMATION
Approved by the American Culinary Federation. Academic requirements are met at Pima Community College (degree available). Special apprenticeships available in pastry.

PLACEMENT INFORMATION
Participants are placed in 1 of 9 locations, including hotels, country clubs, restaurants, and casinos. Most popular placement locations are Hilton El Conquistador, Desert Diamond Casino, and Accacia Restaurant.

APPRENTICE PROFILE
Number of participants in 2004: 20. 5 apprentices were under 25 years old; 15 were between 25 and 44 years old. Applicants must submit a formal application.

TYPICAL EXPENSES
Application fee: $100. Program-related fees include $300 for uniforms and equipment; $60 for ACF dues (junior chapter).

CONTACT
Barry Infuso, Culinary Director, 5901 South Calle Santa Cruz, Tucson, AZ 85709-6000. Telephone: 520-206-5164. Fax: 520-206-5143. E-mail: barry.infuso@pima.edu.

CALIFORNIA

ORANGE EMPIRE CHEFS ASSOCIATION

Costa Mesa, California

PROGRAM INFORMATION
Approved by the American Culinary Federation. Academic requirements are met at Orange Coast College (degree available). Special apprenticeships available in pastry.

PLACEMENT INFORMATION
Participants are placed in 1 of 25 locations, including hotels, clubs, and restaurants. Most popular placement locations are the Ritz Carlton Hotel, Waterfront Hilton, and Anaheim Hilton.

Orange Empire Chefs Association *(continued)*

TYPICAL APPRENTICE PROFILE
Applicants must interview; submit a formal application and an essay.

CONTACT
Director of Apprenticeship Program, 2701 Fairview Road, Costa Mesa, CA 92628. Telephone: 714-432-5835 Ext. 2. Fax: 714-432-5609.

SAN FRANCISCO CULINARY/PASTRY PROGRAM

San Francisco, California

PROGRAM INFORMATION
Academic requirements are met through a chef-taught curriculum and at City College of San Francisco. Special apprenticeships available in pastry (4000 hours).

PLACEMENT INFORMATION
Participants are placed in hotels/clubs/restaurants. Most popular placement locations are the Palace Hotel, the Hilton Hotel, and Michael Mina Restaurant.

APPRENTICE PROFILE
Number of participants in 2004: 13. 13 apprentices were between 25 and 44 years old. Applicants must interview; submit a formal application and letters of reference; have a high school diploma or GED.

TYPICAL EXPENSES
Program-related fees include $100 for uniforms; $150 for equipment (knives).

ENTRY-LEVEL COMPENSATION
$79.87 per 8-hour shift.

CONTACT
Joan Ortega, Director, 760 Market Street, Suite 1066, San Francisco, CA 94102. Telephone: 415-989-8726. Fax: 415-989-2920. E-mail: joanlortega@aol.com.

COLORADO

ACF COLORADO CHEFS ASSOCIATION

Denver, Colorado

PROGRAM INFORMATION
Approved by the American Culinary Federation. Academic requirements are met through a chef-taught curriculum.

PLACEMENT INFORMATION
Participants are placed in 1 of 30 locations, including hotels, restaurants, and country clubs. Most popular placement locations are the Brown Palace Hotel, the Hyatt Regency Hotel Downtown, and Broadmoor Hotel.

TYPICAL APPRENTICE PROFILE
Applicants must submit a formal application, letters of reference, and an essay; have a high school diploma or GED; must be 17 years of age.

CONTACT
Director of Apprenticeship Program, Johnson&Wales University, 7150 Montview Bouevard, Denver, CO 80220. Telephone: 303-264-3005. Fax: 303-264-3007. World Wide Web: http://www.acfcoloradochefs.org.

FLORIDA

ACF CENTRAL FLORIDA CHAPTER

Orlando, Florida

PROGRAM INFORMATION
Approved by the American Culinary Federation. Academic requirements are met through a chef-taught curriculum and at Mid Florida Tech.

PLACEMENT INFORMATION
Participants are placed in 1 of 20 locations, including hotels, theme parks, independent restaurants, convention/banquet centers, and hospitals. Most popular placement locations are Marriott Hotels, Disney, Swan, and Dolphin Hotel, and Hyatt Regency Grand Cypress Hotel.

TYPICAL APPRENTICE PROFILE
Applicants must interview; submit a formal application and letters of reference.

CONTACT
Director of Apprenticeship Program, c/o Mid Florida Tech, 2900 West Oakridge Road, Orlando, FL 32809. Telephone: 407-855-5880 Ext. 2286. Fax: 407-251-6197. World Wide Web: http://www.mft.ocps.k12.fl.us.

ACF GREATER FT. LAUDERDALE CHAPTER

Coconut Creek, Florida

PROGRAM INFORMATION
Approved by the American Culinary Federation. Academic requirements are met through a chef-taught curriculum and at Atlantic Technical Center.

PLACEMENT INFORMATION

Participants are placed in 1 of 20 locations, including hotel and resorts, restaurants, hospitals and retirement homes, retail bakeries, and country clubs. Most popular placement locations are Westin Diplomat Hotel and Resort, Radisson Bridge Resort Hotel (Carmens), and Marriott Hotel and Resort.

TYPICAL APPRENTICE PROFILE

Applicants must interview; submit a formal application.

CONTACT

Director of Apprenticeship Program, 9731 North West 1st Place, Coral Springs, FL 33071. Telephone: 954-344-0817. Fax: 954-344-3584.

ACF PALM BEACH COUNTY CHEFS ASSOCIATION

Boca Raton, Florida

PROGRAM INFORMATION

Approved by the American Culinary Federation. Academic requirements are met through a chef-taught curriculum and at Palm Beach Community College (degree available).

PLACEMENT INFORMATION

Participants are placed in 1 of 4 locations, including country clubs, restaurants, and hotel/resort. Most popular placement locations are the Breakers Hotel and Boca Raton Resort.

TYPICAL APPRENTICE PROFILE

Applicants must interview; submit a formal application and an essay; have 460 hours of culinary-related work experience.

CONTACT

Director of Apprenticeship Program, 4275 Wood Ride #C, Boynton Beach, FL 33436. Telephone: 561-967-2487 Ext. 135. World Wide Web: http://www.acfpalmbeach.com.

ACF TREASURE COAST CHAPTER

Fort Pierce, Florida

PROGRAM INFORMATION

Approved by the American Culinary Federation. Academic requirements are met at Indian River Community College (degree available). Special apprenticeships available in pastry and cook's apprentice.

PLACEMENT INFORMATION

Participants are placed in 1 of 90 locations, including restaurants, hotels, country clubs, and institutional settings. Most popular placement locations are Bent Pines Golf Club, Ian's Tropical Grill, and Indian River Plantation-Marriott.

APPRENTICE PROFILE

Number of participants in 2004: 100. 70 apprentices were under 25 years old; 20 were between 25 and 44 years old; 10 were over 44 years old. Applicants must interview; submit a formal application; have a high school diploma or GED; must be 18 years of age.

CONTACT

John Fredericks, Instructor, 3209 Virginia Avenue, Ft. Pierce, FL 34981-5596. Telephone: 772-462-7641. Fax: 772-462-4796. E-mail: jfrederi@ircc.edu. World Wide Web: http://www.acfchefs.org/chapter/fl121.html.

TAMPA BAY CULINARY ASSOCIATION

Tampa, Florida

PROGRAM INFORMATION

Approved by the American Culinary Federation. Academic requirements are met through a chef-taught curriculum.

PLACEMENT INFORMATION

Participants are placed in 1 of 5 locations.

TYPICAL APPRENTICE PROFILE

Applicants must submit a formal application.

CONTACT

Director of Apprenticeship Program, Manatee Technical Institute, 5603 34th Street West, Bradenton, FL 34210. Telephone: 941-751-7960 Ext. 2113. Fax: 941-751-7927.

TECHNICAL EDUCATION CENTER-OSCEOLA

Kissimmee, Florida

PROGRAM INFORMATION

Approved by the American Culinary Federation. Academic requirements are met through a chef-taught curriculum.

PLACEMENT INFORMATION

Participants are placed in 1 of 12 locations, including hotels, restaurants, and institutions. Most popular placement locations are Universal Studios, Disney World, and the Radisson Hotel.

TYPICAL APPRENTICE PROFILE

Applicants must interview; submit a formal application, an essay, and letters of reference; have a high school diploma or GED.

CONTACT

Director of Apprenticeship Program, 501 Simpson Road, Kissimmee, FL 34744. Telephone: 407-344-5080. Fax: 407-344-5089.

GEORGIA

ACF GOLDEN ISLES OF GEORGIA, CULINARY ASSOCIATION

Sea Island, Georgia

PROGRAM INFORMATION
Approved by the American Culinary Federation. Academic requirements are met through a chef-taught curriculum and at Coastal Georgia Community College (degree available). Special apprenticeships available in pastry.

PLACEMENT INFORMATION
Participants are placed in 1 of 5 locations, including restaurants, dining rooms, banquet halls, and cafeterias.

TYPICAL APPRENTICE PROFILE
Applicants must interview; submit a formal application and an essay; take math and English tests.

CONTACT
Director of Apprenticeship Program, The Cloister Hotel, Sea Island, GA 31561. Telephone: 912-638-3611 Ext. 5725. Fax: 912-634-3908.

KANSAS

JOHNSON COUNTY COMMUNITY COLLEGE

Overland Park, Kansas

PROGRAM INFORMATION
Approved by the American Culinary Federation. Academic requirements are met at Johnson County Community College (degree available).

PLACEMENT INFORMATION
Participants are placed in 1 of 60 locations, including hotels, restaurants, country clubs, casinos, and health-care facilities. Most popular placement locations are the Westin Crown Center Hotel, Hyatt Regency Hotel, and Mission Hills Country Club.

APPRENTICE PROFILE
Number of participants in 2004: 145. Applicants must interview; submit a formal application.

TYPICAL EXPENSES
Basic cost of participation is $64 per credit hour for state residents, $145 per credit hour for nonresidents, $145 per credit hour for international residents. Program-related fee includes $180 for apprenticeship fee/registration of DOC and ACF.

ENTRY-LEVEL COMPENSATION
$7.50 per hour.

CONTACT
Lindy Robinson, Assistant Dean, Johnson County Community College, 12345 College Boulevard, Overland Park, KS 66210. Telephone: 913-469-8500 Ext. 3250. Fax: 913-469-2560. E-mail: lrobinsn@jccc.edu.

LOUISIANA

DELGADO COMMUNITY COLLEGE

New Orleans, Louisiana

PROGRAM INFORMATION
Approved by the American Culinary Federation. Academic requirements are met through a chef-taught curriculum and at Delgado Community College (degree available).

PLACEMENT INFORMATION
Participants are placed in 1 of 80 locations, including restaurants, hotels, hospitals, and convention centers. Most popular placement locations are Ritz-Carlton Hotel, Hilton Hotel, and Brennan's Family Restaurants.

TYPICAL APPRENTICE PROFILE
Applicants must submit a formal application, letters of reference, ACT scores, and a high school diploma or GED.

CONTACT
Director of Apprenticeship Program, 615 City Park Avenue, New Orleans, LA 70119. Telephone: 504-483-4208. Fax: 504-483-4893. World Wide Web: http://www.dcc.edu/.

MARYLAND

ANNE ARUNDEL COMMUNITY COLLEGE

Arnold, Maryland

PROGRAM INFORMATION
Approved by the American Culinary Federation. Academic requirements are met at Anne Arundel Community College (degree available).

PLACEMENT INFORMATION
Participants are placed in country clubs, hotels, fine dining restaurants, bakeries, and catering operations. Most popular placement locations are The Maryland Club, Baltimore Country Club, and Renaissance Hotel.

TYPICAL APPRENTICE PROFILE

Applicants must interview; submit a formal application, an essay, and letters of reference; have a high school diploma or GED.

CONTACT

Director of Apprenticeship Program, 101 College Parkway, Arnold, MD 21012-1895. Telephone: 410-777-2065. Fax: 410-777-1143. World Wide Web: http://www.aacc.edu.

MASSACHUSETTS

MASSACHUSETTS CULINARY ASSOCIATION

Leicester, Massachusetts

PROGRAM INFORMATION

Approved by the American Culinary Federation. Academic requirements are met through a chef-taught curriculum.

PLACEMENT INFORMATION

Participants are placed in restaurants and hotels.

TYPICAL APPRENTICE PROFILE

Applicants must interview; submit letters of reference and an essay.

CONTACT

Director of Apprenticeship Program, 1230 Main Street, Leicester, MA 01524. Telephone: 508-892-9090. Fax: 508-892-3620. World Wide Web: http://www.castlerestaurant.com.

MICHIGAN

ACF BLUE WATER CHEFS ASSOCIATION

Clinton Township, Michigan

PROGRAM INFORMATION

Approved by the American Culinary Federation. Academic requirements are met through a chef-taught curriculum and at Macomb Community College (degree available).

PLACEMENT INFORMATION

Participants are placed in restaurants and hotels.

APPRENTICE PROFILE

Applicants must interview; submit a formal application, letters of reference, and an essay.

TYPICAL EXPENSES

Application fee: $110. Basic cost of participation is $68 per credit hour for state residents (in-district), $104 per credit hour for state residents (out-of-district), $135 per credit hour for nonresidents. Program-related fees include $60 for initial uniform; $75 for annual ACF junior membership; $150 for cutlery.

ENTRY-LEVEL COMPENSATION

$9 per hour.

CONTACT

David F. Schneider, Chef/Educator, Department Coordinator, 44575 Garfield Road, Room K-124-1, Clinton Township, MI 48038. Telephone: 586-286-2088. Fax: 586-226-4725. World Wide Web: http://www.macomb.edu.

ACF MICHIGAN CHEFS DE CUISINE ASSOCIATION

Farmington Hills, Michigan

PROGRAM INFORMATION

Approved by the American Culinary Federation. Academic requirements are met through a chef-taught curriculum and at Oakland Community College (degree available).

PLACEMENT INFORMATION

Participants are placed in 1 of 60 locations, including restaurants, clubs, and hotels. Most popular placement locations are the Detroit Athletic Club, the Palace of Auburn Hills, and the Bloomfield Hills Country Club.

APPRENTICE PROFILE

Number of participants in 2004: 45. Applicants must interview; submit a formal application, letters of reference, and an essay.

TYPICAL EXPENSES

Application fee: $110. Basic cost of participation is $55.15 per credit hour for state residents, $93.35 per credit hour for nonresidents, $130.90 per credit hour for international residents. Program-related fees include $125 for books; $150 for lab fees (per semester); $100 for ACF dues.

ENTRY-LEVEL COMPENSATION

$8–$12 per hour.

CONTACT

Chef Kevin Enright, Apprentice Coordinator, 27055 Orchard Lake Road, Farmington Hills, MI 48334. Telephone: 248-522-3710. Fax: 248-522-3706. E-mail: kmenrigh@oakland.cc.edu.

MISSOURI

CHEFS DE CUISINE OF ST. LOUIS ASSOCIATION

St. Louis, Missouri

PROGRAM INFORMATION
Approved by the American Culinary Federation. Academic requirements are met at St. Louis Community College at Forest Park (degree available). Special apprenticeships available in baking and pastry.

PLACEMENT INFORMATION
Participants are placed in 1 of 42 locations, including country clubs, hotels, fine dining restaurants, and casinos. Most popular placement locations are Old Warson Country Club, Westwood Country Club, and Bellerive Country Club.

APPRENTICE PROFILE
Number of participants in 2004: 4. Applicants must interview; submit a formal application, an essay, and letters of reference; complete one semester of studies.

TYPICAL EXPENSES
Basic cost of participation is $78 per credit for state residents (in-district), $103 per credit for state residents (out-of-district), $138 per credit for nonresidents, $148 per credit for international residents. Program-related fee includes $125 for ACF application.

CONTACT
Brian Hardy, Executive Chef, Gatesworth 1 McKnight Place, St. Louis, MO 63124. Telephone: 314-993-0111. World Wide Web: http://www.stlcc.edu.

COLUMBIA MISSOURI CHAPTER ACF

Columbia, Missouri

PROGRAM INFORMATION
Approved by the American Culinary Federation. Academic requirements are met through a chef-taught curriculum and at Johnson County Community College (degree available).

PLACEMENT INFORMATION
Participants are placed in 1 of 2 locations, including private clubs, hotels, and restaurants. Most popular placement locations are University Club and Capital Plaza Hotel.

APPRENTICE PROFILE
Number of participants in 2004: 3. Applicants must interview; submit a formal application and letters of reference.

TYPICAL EXPENSES
Basic cost of participation is $700–$900 per semester. Program-related fee includes $50 for memberships dues for junior chapter of ACF.

ENTRY-LEVEL COMPENSATION
$6.50–$7.75 per hour.

CONTACT
Daniel Pliska, Executive Chef, University Club of Missouri, 107 Donald W. Reynolds Alumni Center, Columbia, MO 65211. Telephone: 573-882-2433. Fax: 573-884-2063. E-mail: pliskad@missouri.edu. World Wide Web: http://acfchefs.missouri.org.

NEBRASKA

ACF PROFESSIONAL CHEFS AND CULINARIANS OF THE HEARTLAND

Omaha, Nebraska

PROGRAM INFORMATION
Approved by the American Culinary Federation. Academic requirements are met at Metropolitan Community College (degree available).

PLACEMENT INFORMATION
Participants are placed in 1 of 21 locations, including country clubs, hotels, restaurants, and casinos. Most popular placement locations are The Happy Hollow Country Club, Doubletree Hotel, and Ameristar.

APPRENTICE PROFILE
Number of participants in 2004: 25. Applicants must submit a formal application.

TYPICAL EXPENSES
Basic cost of participation is $35 per credit hour for state residents, $65 per credit hour for nonresidents.

ENTRY-LEVEL COMPENSATION
$7.50–$10 per hour.

CONTACT
James E. Trebbien, Academic Director, PO Box 3777, Omaha, NE 68103. Telephone: 402-457-2510. Fax: 402-457-2833. E-mail: jtrebbien@mccneb.edu. World Wide Web: http://www.acfchefs.org/chapter/ne032.html.

NEVADA

THE FRATERNITY OF EXECUTIVE CHEFS OF LAS VEGAS

North Las Vegas, Nevada

PROGRAM INFORMATION
Approved by the American Culinary Federation. Academic requirements are met through a chef-taught curriculum and at Community College of Southern Nevada (degree available).

PLACEMENT INFORMATION
Participants are placed in hotels.

CONTACT
Director of Apprenticeship Program, 3200 East Cheyenne Avenue, Z1A, North Las Vegas, NV 89030. Telephone: 702-651-4818. Fax: 702-651-4743. World Wide Web: http://www.acfchefs.org/chapter/nv013.html.

HIGH SIERRA CHEFS ASSOCIATION

Carson City, Nevada

PROGRAM INFORMATION
Approved by the American Culinary Federation. Academic requirements are met at Truckee Meadows Community College (degree available), Lake Tahoe Community College (degree available). Special apprenticeships available in pastry.

PLACEMENT INFORMATION
Participants are placed in hotels, casinos, restaurants, commissaries, and resorts. Most popular placement locations are Harrah's Lake Tahoe Casino, Harrah's Reno Hotel and Casino, and Peppermill Casino.

TYPICAL APPRENTICE PROFILE
Applicants must interview; submit an essay and letter of reference; have previous employment experience; take culinary math aptitude test.

CONTACT
Director of Apprenticeship Program, One College Drive, South Lake Tahoe, CA 96150. Telephone: 530-541-4660 Ext. 334. Fax: 530-541-7852.

NEW HAMPSHIRE

ACF GREATER NORTH NEW HAMPSHIRE CHAPTER

Dixville Notch, New Hampshire

PROGRAM INFORMATION
Approved by the American Culinary Federation. Academic requirements are met through a chef-taught curriculum and at New Hampshire Community Technical College (degree available).

PLACEMENT INFORMATION
Participants are placed in 1 of 20 locations, including resorts, hotels, table cloth restaurants, cafeterias, and country clubs. Most popular placement locations are the American Club (WI), Williamsburg Inn (VA), and John's Island Club (FL).

TYPICAL APPRENTICE PROFILE
Applicants must interview; submit a formal application, letters of reference, and an essay.

CONTACT
Director of Apprenticeship Program, Balsams Grand Resort Hotel, Dixville Notch, NH 03576. Telephone: 603-255-3861. Fax: 603-255-4670.

NEW YORK

MID-HUDSON CULINARY ASSOCIATION

New Paltz, New York

PROGRAM INFORMATION
Approved by the American Culinary Federation. Academic requirements are met at Culinary Institute of America (degree available).

PLACEMENT INFORMATION
Participants are placed in hotel/resort.

TYPICAL APPRENTICE PROFILE
Applicants must interview; submit a formal application, letters of reference, and an essay.

CONTACT
Director of Apprenticeship Program, 1000 Mountain Rest Road, New Paltz, NY 12561. Telephone: 845-256-2070. Fax: 845-256-2107. World Wide Web: http://www.mohonk.com.

North Carolina

ACF Sandhills/Cross Creek Chefs Association

Pinehurst, North Carolina

Program Information
Approved by the American Culinary Federation. Academic requirements are met at Sandhills Community College (degree available). Special apprenticeships available in pastry.

Placement Information
Participants are placed in 1 of 6 locations, including clubs and hotels.

Typical Apprentice Profile
Applicants must interview; submit a formal application and a 500-word essay; have a high school diploma or GED; 2 years of related work experience (preferable).

Contact
Director of Apprenticeship Program, c/o Pinehurst Resort and Country Club, PO Box 4000, Carolina Vista, Pinehurst, NC 28374. Telephone: 910-235-8439. Fax: 910-295-8402. World Wide Web: http://www.pinehurst.com.

ACF Triad Chapter NC

Jamestown, North Carolina

Program Information
Approved by the American Culinary Federation. Academic requirements are met at Guilford Technical Community College (degree available).

Placement Information
Participants are placed in 1 of 8 locations, including restaurants, hotels, country clubs, retirement communities, and catering services.

Typical Apprentice Profile
Applicants must submit a formal application and North Carolina Department of Labor Apprenticeship Agreement.

Contact
Director of Apprenticeship Program, 601 High Point Road, PO Box 309, Jamestown, NC 27282. Telephone: 336-454-1126 Ext. 2302. Fax: 336-819-2032.

Ohio

ACF Cleveland Chapter

Cleveland, Ohio

Program Information
Approved by the American Culinary Federation. Academic requirements are met through a chef-taught curriculum and at Cuyahoga Community College (degree available).

Placement Information
Participants are placed in 1 of 30 locations, including country clubs, hotels, hospitals/schools, restaurants, and retirement communities.

Typical Apprentice Profile
Applicants must interview; submit a formal application, letters of reference, and an essay.

Contact
Director of Apprenticeship Program, Cuyahoga Community College, 2900 Community College Avenue, Cleveland, OH 44115-3196. Telephone: 216-987-4087. Fax: 216-987-4086.

ACF Columbus Chapter

Columbus, Ohio

Program Information
Approved by the American Culinary Federation. Academic requirements are met at Columbus State Community College (degree available).

Placement Information
Participants are placed in 1 of 55 locations, including hotels, catering firms, clubs, and restaurants. Most popular placement locations are Cameron Mitchell Restaurants, all Country Clubs in the Central Ohio area, and Hyatt Regency-Hyatt on Capital Square.

Apprentice Profile
Number of participants in 2004: 100. 80 apprentices were under 25 years old; 25 were between 25 and 44 years old; 10 were over 44 years old. Applicants must interview; submit a formal application, an essay, letters of reference, and academic transcripts.

Typical Expenses
Application fee: $10. Basic cost of participation is $69 per quarter credit hour for state residents, $152 per quarter credit hour for nonresidents, $183 per quarter credit hour for international residents. Program-related fees include $125 for lab fees; $65 for ACF apprentice registration.

Entry-Level Compensation
$8 per hour.

CONTACT

James Taylor, Apprenticeship Coordinator, Columbus State Community College, 550 East Spring Street, Columbus, OH 43215. Telephone: 614-287-5061. Fax: 614-287-5973. E-mail: jtaylor@cscc.edu. World Wide Web: http://www. acfcolumbus.org.

PENNSYLVANIA

ACF LAUREL HIGHLANDS CHAPTER

Youngwood, Pennsylvania

PROGRAM INFORMATION

Approved by the American Culinary Federation. Academic requirements are met through a chef-taught curriculum and at Westmoreland County Community College (degree available). Special apprenticeships available in culinary arts and baking and pastry.

PLACEMENT INFORMATION

Participants are placed in 1 of 100 locations, including clubs, resorts, hotels, fine dining facilities, and institutional feeding sites.

APPRENTICE PROFILE

Number of participants in 2004: 71. 51 apprentices were under 25 years old; 14 were between 25 and 44 years old; 6 were over 44 years old. Applicants must submit a formal application and take a physical exam.

TYPICAL EXPENSES

Application fee: $10. Basic cost of participation is $780–$1170 per 12–18 credits (1 semester) for state residents (in-district), $1560–$2340 per 12–18 credits (1 semester) for state residents (out-of-district), $2340–$3510 per 12–18 credits (1 semester) for nonresidents. Program-related fees include $150 for uniforms; $125 for knives; $200 for lab fees.

ENTRY-LEVEL COMPENSATION

$5.15 per hour.

CONTACT

Janice Grabowski, Director of Admissions, Westmoreland County Community College, Youngwood, PA 15697-1898. Telephone: 724-925-4123. Fax: 724-925-5802. E-mail: grabowskij@wccc-pa.edu. World Wide Web: http://www. wccc-pa.edu.

BUCKS COUNTY COMMUNITY COLLEGE

Newtown, Pennsylvania

PROGRAM INFORMATION

Academic requirements are met through a chef-taught curriculum and at Bucks County Community College (degree available).

PLACEMENT INFORMATION

Participants are placed in 1 of 120 locations, including hotels, restaurants and country clubs, contract food services, extended-care facilities, and supermarkets.

APPRENTICE PROFILE

Number of participants in 2004: 65. Applicants must interview; submit a formal application and an essay.

TYPICAL EXPENSES

Application fee: $30. Basic cost of participation is $89 per credit hour for state residents (in-district), $178 per credit hour for state residents (out-of-district), $267 per credit hour for nonresidents. Program-related fees include $160 for knives and pastry kits; $100 for uniform.

ENTRY-LEVEL COMPENSATION

$6.76–$10.41 per hour.

CONTACT

Earl R. Arrowood, Chef Apprenticeship Program Coordinator, 275 Swamp Road, Newtown, PA 18940. Telephone: 215-968-8241. Fax: 215-504-8509. E-mail: arrowood@bucks.edu. World Wide Web: http://www.bucks. edu.

TENNESSEE

GAYLORD OPRYLAND CULINARY INSTITUTE

Nashville, Tennessee

PROGRAM INFORMATION

Approved by the American Culinary Federation. Academic requirements are met at Nashville State Community College (degree available). Special apprenticeships available in baking and pastry.

PLACEMENT INFORMATION

Participants are placed in food services within Gaylord Opryland Resort.

TYPICAL APPRENTICE PROFILE

Applicants must interview; submit a formal application, letters of reference, an essay, and official high school/ college transcripts.

Gaylord Opryland Culinary Institute *(continued)*

CONTACT
Director of Apprenticeship Program, 2800 Opryland Drive, Nashville, TN 37214. Telephone: 615-902-8039. Fax: 615-871-6546. World Wide Web: http://www. gaylordopryland.com.

WISCONSIN

ACF CHEFS OF MILWAUKEE, INC.

Germantown, Wisconsin

PROGRAM INFORMATION
Approved by the American Culinary Federation. Academic requirements are met through a chef-taught curriculum and at Milwaukee Area Technical College (degree available). Special apprenticeships available in programs to meet student needs and abilities.

PLACEMENT INFORMATION
Participants are placed in 1 of 25-30 locations, including restaurants, hotels, private clubs, and catering operations. Most popular placement locations are Barttolotta's Restaurant, North Shore Country Club, and The Hilton Milwaukee.

APPRENTICE PROFILE
Number of participants in 2004: 43. 16 apprentices were under 25 years old; 5 were between 25 and 44 years old; 5 were over 44 years old. Applicants must interview; submit a formal application; must have state-registered apprentice contract.

TYPICAL EXPENSES
Application fee: $30. Program-related fees include $350 for uniforms, cutlery set, books; $110 for ACF logbook; $75 for ACF junior membership for ACF local chapter.

ENTRY-LEVEL COMPENSATION
$10–$12 per hour.

CONTACT
Paul J. Carrier, Culinary Apprentice Coordinator, 700 West State Street, Milwaukee, WI 53233. Telephone: 414-297-7862. Fax: 414-297-7990. E-mail: carrierp@matc.edu. World Wide Web: http://www.acfchefsofmilwaukee.com.

■ CANADA ■

SOUTHERN ALBERTA INSTITUTE OF TECHNOLOGY

Calgary, Alberta, Canada

PROGRAM INFORMATION
Approved by the American Culinary Federation. Academic requirements are met through a chef-taught curriculum and at Southern Alberta Institute of Technology.

PLACEMENT INFORMATION
Participants are placed in 1 of 150 locations, including hotels, restaurants, golf clubs, hospitals and long-term care facilities, and catering establishments. Most popular placement locations are Fairmont Banff Springs Hotel, Catch Restaurant, and Marriot and Hyatt Hotels.

TYPICAL APPRENTICE PROFILE
Applicants must interview; submit a formal application.

CONTACT
Director of Apprenticeship Program, 1301 16th Avenue, NW, Calgary, AB T2M 0L4, Canada. Telephone: 403-284-8943. Fax: 403-284-7034. World Wide Web: http://www.sait. ab.ca/academic/applied/features/feat1.htm.

INDEXES

Certificate and Diploma Programs

U.S.

Associate Degree Programs

Bachelor's Degree Programs

Master's Degree Programs

Doctoral Degree Programs

■ ALPHABETICAL LISTING OF SCHOOLS AND PROGRAMS ■

(A) = Apprenticeship Programs   *(P) = Professional Programs*

(A) = Apprenticeship Programs　　*(P) = Professional Programs*

(A) = Apprenticeship Programs   (P) = Professional Programs

(A) = Apprenticeship Programs   (P) = Professional Programs